Blacks in the New World
Edited by August Meier and John H. Bracey

*A list of books in the series appears at the end of this volume.*

AFRICA IN AMERICA

MICHAEL MULLIN

# Africa in America

Slave Acculturation and
Resistance in the
American South and the
British Caribbean,
1736–1831

UNIVERSITY OF ILLINOIS PRESS
Urbana and Chicago

Illini Books edition, 1994
© 1992 by the Board of Trustees of the University of Illinois
Manufactured in the United States of America
1  2  3  4  5  C  P  5  4  3  2  1

This book is printed on acid-free paper.

Library of Congress Cataloging-in-Publication Data
Mullin, Michael, 1938–
    Africa in America : slave acculturation and resistance in the
American South and the British Caribbean, 1736–1831 / Michael
Mullin.
       p.   cm. — (Blacks in the New World)
    Includes bibliographical references and index.
    ISBN 0-252-01889-3 (cl. : alk. paper). — ISBN 0-252-06446-1
(pbk. : alk. paper).
       1. Slaves—Southern States—Social conditions.   2. Slaves—
Caribbean, English-speaking—Social conditions.   3. Slavery—
Southern States—Insurrections, etc.   4. Slavery—Caribbean,
English-speaking—Insurrections, etc.   I. Title.   II. Series.
E443.M85   1992
973'.0496—dc20                                            91-852
                                                            CIP

*To the memory of my parents, Mary Ellen DeVe (della Védova)
and Gerald Wallace Mullin*

The further we get, the more clearly we see the extent of our ignorance. Our principal contribution is not a body of knowledge, but a method of study.

— Nino Tenbergen

# Contents

# Illustrations in Text

## Maps in Text

# Acknowledgments

Linda Mather of Mather Graphics, Davis, California, made the maps in this text. The background for the section on Matthew Gregory "Monk" Lewis is as much the work of Miriam Taylor, my colleague at Hull, as it is mine. My appreciation as well to David Hosford and Norman Samuels for making possible a most productive year as visiting professor at Rutgers, Newark, and to Paul Goldstene, Joseph Holloway, Robert Middlekauff and John Ward who read drafts. Released time from California State University, Sacramento, helped, as did funds from a National Endowment of the Humanities Younger Humanist Fellowship and a summer stipend from the Colonial Williamsburg Research Center. At different stages, three people who read the entire manuscript made useful suggestions and encouraged me to keep the faith: Daniel Crowley, Elaine Connolly, and August Meier. To them I am especially grateful.

# Introduction

Antigua, the British West Indies, October 1736. At a Sunday gathering, an African named Court who was organizing a conspiracy danced in the center of a ring, raised a shield, and from his followers demanded in his own language an oath that promised death to whites and destruction to any black who revealed their plans. Struck by a dangerous twist to what began as an ordinary pastime, slaves on the side, who as Coramantee (of the Gold Coast of West Africa) understood the gravity of Court's language and gestures, moved to break up the performance. Their decision helped unravel the largest rebellion in the history of Antiguan slavery.

Virginia and Jamaica, 1831. Nearly a century later in Southampton County, Virginia, Nat Turner led the only sizeable slave uprising in the antebellum era. After a bloody revolt, and while waiting trial and execution, Turner portrayed himself in a long confession as a conjurer experienced in numerology, dream interpretation, and prophetic visions of black and white angels fighting in the sky.

A few months later, Baptist slaves in Jamaica left a chapel service in Montego Bay and began a major revolt of slaves who had sworn oaths, some on the Bible, others on a concoction of blood and gunpowder, to fight for "The Free." This was the rebels' word for an imaginary emancipation proclamation that slaves believed had been sent out by the king, only to be hidden away and ignored by their owners. The Jamaica rebellion, the largest ever in Anglo-America, lasted about ten days. In its course more than five hundred blacks and a few whites were killed, and parts of most of the estates in the western third of the island were burnt down.

Major Anglo-American slave rebellions occurred in clusters at roughly thirty-year intervals in the century from the 1730s to the 1830s. Their leadership was of two kinds: native African through the 1760s, and Creole (American-born) thereafter. While Africans usually organized to reject whites and slavery completely, either, as they put it, "by finding a way back home [to Africa]" or by killing indiscriminately, the objectives of Creole rebels were more political—and ambiguous. In a long history of persistent but often ineffectual slave resistance, Africans as if instinctively cooperated when attempting to free themselves. By contrast, Creoles usually favored individual strategies of liberation. But in the last years of slavery, Creoles overcame the difficulties they had encountered in working together and organized the largest rebellions ever.

The purpose here is to examine the relationship between slave acculturation and the changing nature of slave resistance. To make this problem somewhat manageable is to ask a familiar question, and a few others that follow from it. Why were slave rebellions in the South fewer and smaller than those in the Caribbean? Why did most slaves never rebel? What were the ideas, objectives, and leadership of those who did? And why, in the last years of slavery, was a segment of the Creole elite (artisans and drivers) in some instances able to lead conservative field hands into major revolts when such alliances had previously failed?[1]

The focus on resistance is not to make heroes and heroines, or to catalog as many revolts and plots as possible. This has been done often and well. Instead it is to use slave resistance to describe differences in the values and ways of Africans and Creoles. This comparison also opens new perspectives on slave economic, family, and religious strategies that became the basis of two variants of African America: Southern and Caribbean.[2]

The interpretations of those who write about these issues may be divided between arguments that emphasize slaves as victims, or as often rebellious creators of remarkably resilient and independent communities.[3] Scholars who pursue the latter point of view, known as the resistance or culture-and-community approach, call attention to the African roots of such expressive forms of slave life as religion, music, and folklore.[4] This approach amplifies the insight of the Brazilianist Roger Bastide that slave resistance was often cultural as well as political: the resistance of a people to being swallowed up by a foreign way of life. In this case resistance may be understood as a refusal to abandon one's values and traditions as well as— at another, more familiar level—singular acts ranging from quiet sabotage to organizing and fighting back.[5]

Skepticism regarding the resistance perspective, however, is widespread and caught neatly in Willie Lee Rose's caustic remark that it would seem that slavery was "a totally dehumanizing institution that dehumanized nobody."[6] By refusing to be distracted by expressive forms of slave culture and the African wellsprings that nourished them, scholars of the victim, or "damage," viewpoint rivet attention on immediate structural conditions as ultimately decisive — and tragic — with regard to the formation of slave personalities, leadership, and communities.

Resistance, or a lack of it, is an important feature of the debate about slavery and its legacies. To argue that rebellion was endemic and a matter of revolts rather than malingering and tool breaking is to encourage views of slaves as having a life of their own that was sometimes beyond their master's control or even understanding. By contrast, to see slaves as typically acquiescent and dependent is to enhance damaging interpretations of a slavery that incapacitated.

In taking the measure of these possibilities, contemporaries and most scholars observed that generally Africans were more likely than Creoles to resist dangerously. Paralleling this insight are contrasting regional approaches to the problem. In the Caribbean, the dominating presence of Africans as essentially a tribal and nonliterate people has encouraged anthropological approaches, long views, and cultural explanations of their transformation as slaves. Southern slavery, on the other hand, has been dominated by perspectives that collapse time by concentrating on the antebellum period, when the institution was more than two hundred years old. This chronological strategy compromises the African contribution and resistance views generally. The antebellum era opens with the abolition of the slave trade that before 1808 had steadily renewed from original sources the African dimension of a slave population that was already the most assimilated in the Americas. By providing little sense of how slavery changed through time, the vantage point makes it easy to talk about the Creoles, who in the last years of slavery had become more dominant than the once-dangerous Africans.

This book centers on an earlier period, the late 1700s and early 1800s, when the slave trade was at its peak, most slaves were still Africans in parts of the South and much of the Caribbean, and many were also "new Negroes" (the recently enslaved who did not speak English well and were called "new" until they did so). Discussion builds on a series of premises that have guided my earlier work: that slavery ought to be construed essentially as a clash between two ways of life, European settler and African (becoming African American); that in the context of the dialectical process this encounter set in motion the ensuing patterns of resistance were part of an acculturation process whose pace and content was governed by a slave's origin (African or Creole), task assignment (field, household, or artisanal), and work environment (as the degree of a slave's mobility on and off the plantation); and that the study of cultural change and patterns of resistance provides a useful measure of slavery's impact through time on blacks as individuals and as a people.[7]

For some there is a more direct route to problems of this kind. Demography, it is argued, not imprecise and subjective cultural categories, provides better explanations for regional differences in the size and frequency of slave resistance; a key to the problem is proportions of Africans to Creoles. Where the more dangerous Africans outnumbered Creoles, as in the Caribbean, rebellion was rife. Where they did not, as in the South, major resistance was negligible because it stemmed from a uniquely self-reproducing slave population that much earlier than elsewhere was mostly Creole. On any account, although blacks were a majority on each of the islands, they were so in only a few Southern states; overall, whites outnumbered them by two to one.

Population figures among other arithmetic calculations, although leaving impressions of scientific rigor and precision, do not take us very far in resolving such matters as the nature of conflict between ways of life and the compromises or blends that result, variously referred to as acculturation or Creolization. More rewarding, if the evidence is available, is to begin phases of the argument with geographical explanations and the actual words and understandings that contemporaries used when confronting the problem at hand. This useful path is revealed by a remark of a major figure, a Jamaican royal governor (the Earl of Balcarres).[8] In the revolutionary 1790s, Balcarres sized up the ten-to-one ratio of blacks to whites in his colony (the highest in the British West Indies) and said that it made no difference whether Jamaica had three hundred thousand slaves or five hundred thousand. Instead, what counted was a matter of geopolitics: which people, white or black, settled the huge mountain interior. Balcarres was mindful of the blacks' determination to use the nurturing slopes either as maroon settlements (armed and organized groups of runaways), or as market gardens to feed themselves while expanding the unsupervised activities (such as Court's conspiratorial dance in Antigua) that accompanied the slaves' weekend provisioning industry. The governor's remark points to links between patterns of terrain and adaptation — so important on a frontier such as plantation America whose settlers did not enjoy our "secondary environment" of technological comforts — that must be examined if regional versions of Creolization are to be understood properly.

Hence, although plantation slavery is usually assumed to be the whole of the slaves' experience, three situations, as I suggested in *Flight and Rebellion: Slave Resistance in Eighteenth-Century Virginia*, are used here to examine patterns of resistance and cultural change both on and off the plantation. Maroons and incoming Africans, who were not a part of the plantation settings that everywhere stifled rebellion, represent an initial stage of acculturation and resistance. The second stage may be described by the more seasoned or Creole plantation slaves, who typically kept their anger and frustration under wraps; and the third stage by assimilated artisans who, developing their skills both on and off the plantation, led the large pre-emancipation rebellions.

Accordingly, this book is divided into thirds, with each part describing a stage of acculturation and style of resistance. Part 1, "The Unseasoned," opens with a sketch of Britain's South Atlantic empire and of the four plantation regions that form the basis of the study: the Chesapeake Bay (Maryland and Virginia), the Carolina lowcountry (coastal South Carolina and Georgia), and, in the Caribbean, Jamaica, a large and mountainous island, and Barbados, one of the small and flat Windward Islands. Against this background, I discuss why new Negro resistance was so persistent and dangerous in Jamaica and so negligible in Virginia. How did incoming Africans, of whom we know very little, provoke whites in some societies to talk about them as representative of actual African societies — "Ibo" or "Congo" for instance — and somewhat later as "shipmates" and "country-men," while elsewhere they were individualized as their new groups were ignored? Given regional variations that ranged from careless to informed in identifying new Negroes, it is important to ask as well how this nomen-clature may be used to trace, more precisely than we have before, the development of the Creole norms that accompanied basic changes in the character of resistance. Part 2, "Plantation Slaves," is divided between white and slave perceptions of resistance and acculturation. In the first half, case studies of plantations — their crops, routines, and management styles — are used to raise the question of the extent to which relations between slave and master were paternalistic in a way that may have stifled resistance. In the second half the focus shifts to the slaves' economic, family, and religious practices which, it is argued, must be seen as a unit. Here I ask how the "internal economy" of slave provision grounds and markets (if any) shaped gender relations, domesticity, and outlook. Or, to put it differently, when slave families in the Caribbean — but rarely in the South — were often polygynous in conception (and sometimes in practice), how did domestic arrangements shape patterns of acculturation and resistance — or acquies-cence — in the two regions?

Part 3, "The Assimilateds," concerns the efforts of Creoles during the age of democratic revolutions (1775–1815) to lead rural blacks into rebellion. In the first of a two-stage development, assimilateds formed associations, usually urban, whose real intent from their day to ours has been controversial to observers and scholars. Were the societies insurrectionary or for self-improvement? Should emphasis be placed on such external influences as the abolitionist movement and revolutionary examples in France, North America, and Haiti, or on developments within the slaves' own communities, when accounting for the surge in resistance at the end of the eighteenth century? And, more generally, why did revolutionary leadership pass to Creoles at a time, around 1800, when more Africans were imported than ever before? As for the second and more successful stage of revolt that accompanied the mass Christianization of slaves, the main question posed is, What role did religions, including Christianity, play in slave resistance?

Case studies are referred to throughout to infuse the whole with a sense of specific places, times, and people and to facilitate the revisions that my arguments should encourage. In the case of the Africans of Part 1, the primary purpose is not to breathe a kind of rationality into their actions,[9] but rather to describe their outlook as closely as possible. When the sources allow, discussions begin with the ordinary contemporary perceptions of observable behavior, which is part of an inductive approach most suitable given the characteristically thin and fragmented nature of much of the available evidence.

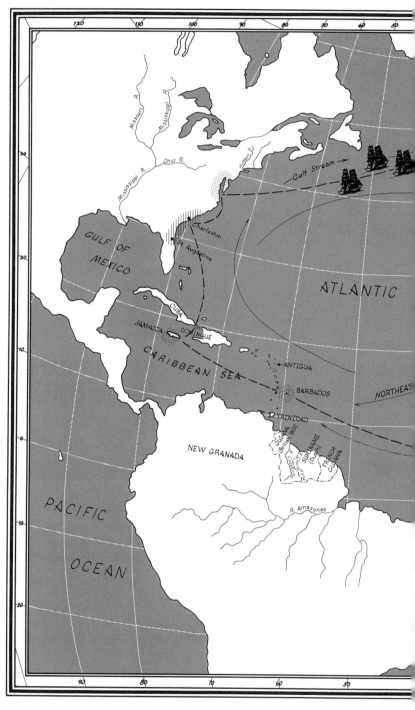

A Lambert azimuthal projection centered at 20 degrees north, 40 degrees west;

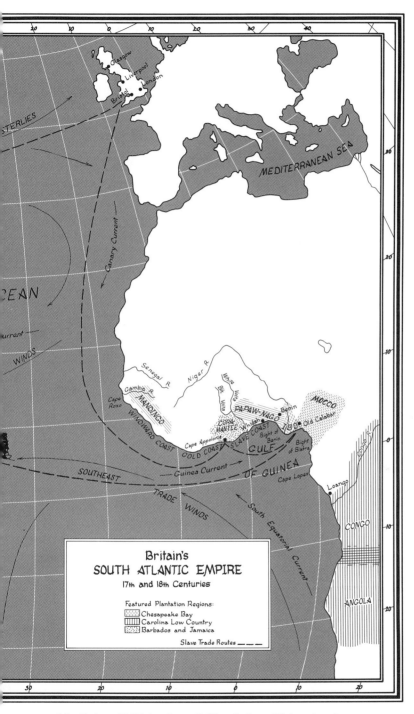

Glasgow
Liverpool
London
Bristol

STERLIES

Canary Current

CEAN

urrent

WINDS

MEDITERRANEAN SEA

Senegal R.

Niger R.

Cape
Roxo

Gambia R.

MANDINGO

WINDWARD COAST

Wind Vara

Blk Vara

Cape Appolonia

CORO
MANTEE

PAPAW-NAGO

Whydah

Benin

MOCOO

IBOE

Old Calabar

GOLD COAST

SLAVE COAST

GULF

Bight of
Benin

Bight
of Biafra

Congo R.

Guinea Current

OF GUINEA

Cape Lopaz

Loango

SOUTHEAST

TRADE

WINDS

South Equatorial Current

CONGO

ANGOLA

**Britain's**
## SOUTH ATLANTIC EMPIRE
### 17th and 18th Centuries

Featured Plantation Regions:
▦ Chesapeake Bay
▥ Carolina Low Country
▧ Barbados and Jamaica

Slave Trade Routes _ _ _

generated by Robert T. Richardson, California State University, Sacramento.

PART I

# The Unseasoned

# 1

# Naming Africans

She is a Chamba [but] speaks Mungola well.
— Jamaica, 1795[1]

Not much attention has been paid to the actual language ordinary people used to distinguish new Negroes. However, a West Indian vocabulary that described those who had just been unloaded from the slaver is waiting to be recovered and measured against the received wisdom about what the first slaves were like: what the Middle Passage did to them and, on coming ashore, their initial efforts to make sense of what had happened, and, occasionally, to do something about it immediately. For their part, whites had to invent words to describe new Negroes as one people or another; when the Africans first fought back, which they did in a limited number of ways, whites had to find terms to describe these patterns as well. But I refer here to only the Caribbean; for those of us trained to view slavery from the perspective of North America, the period between when the gangplank lowered and when new Negroes arrived at the plantation is uncharted territory. To turn from meager Southern sources to their West Indian equivalent to study this problem is to enter another world of discourse — She "looks more like an Eboe than a Coramantee"[2] — that must be confronted if contemporary understandings of resistance and acculturation are to be examined carefully and usefully.

In some societies, incoming Africans were identified ethnically, as Ibo or Coramantee for instance; whereas in others, whites simply lumped them together as "Guiney Negroes," or more vaguely as "outlandish." Naming of this kind varied from careless to deliberate, depending on how menacing the Africans were considered to be.[3] Where whites saw them as dangerous, they described them as members of actual societies and cultures, but where they were not, ethnicity was ignored.* When the problem is examined by region, whites in the Caribbean usually singled out Gold Coast Coramantee as threatening, while for a time South Carolinians thought similarly about Angolans. However in the Chesapeake Bay region, Africans as Africans were rarely troublesome. Soon put out of sight and out of mind, their ethnicity never became a conventional way of talking about them.

Traces of what was essentially a process of communication are all that remain in the surviving evidence of two complex and interrelated problems: regional versions of the names whites invented to describe rebellious Africans, and the Africans' determination — the results of which varied enormously from one region to another — to recreate a usable past in slavery. Comprising an array of west and central African peoples, new Negroes manifested original identities by tribal names, languages, ritual scars, and habits of mind. Some made even more emphatic statements about who they were when as runaways, insurrectionists, or maroons they attempted to return home or to make an Africa in the American wilderness. These choices confounded whites, who, in attempting to police and sell the newcomers, exposed their own attitudes about Africa and Africans in the sparse and prosaic notes, in newspapers and plantation records, principally, that trace the first encounters between the two peoples.

An African's self-definition through resistance, and the care or indifference with which it was recorded, began as soon as some were brought ashore. While aboard the slaver these new Negroes made a plan to escape at the first opportunity and to return to the point of disembarkation in order to find a way "back home" to Africa: four Fante (Coramantee), for instance, were described in an 1801 Jamaican newspaper advertisement as fugitives who "told some of their shipmates, whom they solicited to go with them, they would proceed to the sea-side by night, and remain in the bush through the night, and the first Canoe they found by the seaside they would Set sail for their Country, which they conceived was no great distance."[4]

The Fante may have been tragically ignorant of the great distance they had been carried. However, their design to return to where they were first unloaded, among other choices they would make, and the whites' attempts to understand these decisions, provide a straightforward way of talking about the combinations of African carryovers and local circumstances that chan-

---

* "Ethnicity" is a euphemism for tribal, as in "to what tribe do you belong?" which is no longer good form. "Nationality" is preferred but only used occasionally because it may be confused anachronistically with "nationalism," as in black nationalism.

neled the choices and learning we label variously as acculturation, assimilation, or Creolization.

If incoming Africans were brought to such colonies as Jamaica, help was available from those who spoke their own language and had been slaves for awhile. This network, subsequently, forced whites to speak more precisely about the newcomers—not as commodities but as the social beings they were—in order to make their societies more secure. Whites began to refine the generic "new Negro" and instead spoke of "countrymen" and "shipmate"—respectively, Africans of the same langauge group and of the same slaver cargo—in order to recapture fugitives readily. These terms also point to the embryonic institutions that were spun off as Africans began the process of becoming African Americans.

To see the process of institution-building on the ground is to put the new Negro's first escape into action. As an idea, the Africans' goal was the same regardless of where in plantation America they were first brought ashore. How it was executed, however, depended upon a combination of two conditions. The first was whether they were carried to a compact Caribbean island, or to the vast expanses of mainland North America. The other was the character of a colony's slave trade market, because a buyer's objectives, relative wealth, and location could literally fill the historical record with shipmates and countrymen—or wipe them from it as if these people and new beginnings never existed.

A purpose of this chapter, then, is to lay the foundation for an argument that a correlation existed between the degree to which ethnicity was asserted by Africans and recognized by whites, and a mitigation of the worst ravages of the racism inherent in slavery. Where ethnicity was sustained, slaves retained a more collective identity and were more likely to be treated as a people and to resist by organizing with others. Where ethnicity was not maintained, slaves displayed an assimilation and seemed to give up more than they got. In this situation, blacks were regarded as they were legally—as objects—and they usually resisted individually.

An outline of the major features of Britain's South Atlantic empire and its more prominent plantation societies refines the inquiry into the connections between resistance by the new arrivals and the whites' recognition or denial of their African heritage, of which ethnicity was a vital part. The following sketches also underline the role of geography in shaping the slave trade and the initial choices that new Negroes made. The four societies featured in this study are described in the order of their founding; and, where the available evidence allows, as in the case of the Chesapeake Bay region, brief mention is made of the relationship between the slave trade and patterns of new Negro resistance.

Among the last of the new and aggressive European nation states to acquire overseas colonies in the early modern period, Britain became the most successful imperial power of them all. In the beginning, the island nation's New World settlements were most unpromising, however. By the 1630s they included a handful of fisheries in Newfoundland, a few villages on the rocky New England coast, the tidewater of the Chesapeake Bay, and a scattering of the smaller Caribbean islands that had been largely ignored by the Iberians. But in an era of sail-driven ships (basically launching platforms for the huge guns monopolized by the new dynastic states), the British navy proved to be the biggest, the best, and the basis of a South Atlantic empire of plantations and slaves.[5]

The empire, on one level, was a creation of prevailing currents of wind and ocean. Moving outward in a vast clockwise manner from Western Europe to Africa, the currents swept west across the South Atlantic to the Caribbean, and north and east to North America before bending back, eastward across the North Atlantic to Europe. The empire, on another level, was also defined by strategic sites and the commodities they commanded: slaves from West Africa, sugar from the Caribbean islands — Barbados, St. Kitts, Antigua, and Jamaica, principally; and, from mainland America, rice and indigo from the Carolina lowcountry (coastal South Carolina and Georgia), and tobacco and wheat from Maryland and Virginia, the Chesapeake Bay region.

While settlers in the middle and New England colonies came out with families (and often with ministers) determined to sink roots and make the colonies their home, whites who arrived in plantation America were often "wild young bachelors" who hoped to survive deadly tropical diseases and make a fortune to spend at home in England. Their get-rich-quick-and-get-out attitude contributed to a transitory and unstable mood in societies where early settlers, like miners during a gold rush, lived hard and died readily in what demographers have aptly termed "the fast life."[6]

Nonetheless, in time a local aristocracy clawed its way into a place in the sun. Possessing preponderant amounts of wealth, the rich planters are often characterized as exercising power and influence far out of proportion to their number. Yet they were also colonists whose authority was shared and continually threatened by imperial laws and officials. The ensuing conflict between the metropolitan center and the colonial periphery was eventually resolved for a time — for Southerners, but not West Indians — by the successful conclusion of the American Revolution. This war left Caribbean planters dangerously isolated and vulnerable to the liberalizing reforms of a mother country undergoing a transformation of its own. In early-nineteenth-century Britain, both the Industrial Revolution and the middle class grew considerably while an abolitionist movement was nurtured that the Southern aristocracy was not forced to confront until much later, and only after it had achieved both political power nationally and a territorial base.

The great planters were also constricted economically. The monoculture they unwittingly created withered urban growth and with it a middle class and home market. The classic instance of the development was Barbados, where a "Sugar Revolution," which erupted suddenly in the mid-seventeenth century, transformed a society of small farmers to one dominated by large estates that pumped out the cash crop and little else. This left the island overpopulated and intensively planted as early as 1700, making the entire society, from beach to beach, one vast sugar plantation. Unable to compete in a game with such high stakes — acquiring expensive processing factories and gangs of slaves — the middle class emigrated. The process was repeated to a degree in the American South, where farmers, confronted by big and expanding plantations, either retreated into the margins—pine barren, marsh, and inland slope — or moved west of the Appalachians.

Monoculture intensified the colonial dilemma of great planters, masterful at home but passive before the caprices of the international cycles of supply, demand, and price. In the tropics planters big and small regarded these cycles as they did the weather, anxiously and just as unpredictable and beyond control. The four societies that figure in this study may be reduced to three by combining Maryland and Virginia as the Chesapeake Bay society, Georgia and South Carolina as the Carolina lowcountry, and Barbados and Jamaica as the Caribbean.

Barbados, as Richard Sheridan observes, was a colony of firsts: first to attract English settlers in considerable numbers; the first British colony to introduce sugarcane and successfully sell it internationally; and the first to be transformed from a society of semisubsistence farms to a slave-based plantation regime.[7]

At about fourteen by twenty miles, about the size of one county in a Southern mainland colony, Barbados, founded in 1628, was densely populated by 1700. A moderate climate and trade winds of eighteen to twenty knots powered mills and contributed to the health and well-being of the inhabitants of "Little England," one of the most secure of the plantation colonies. In an era of sail-driven ships Barbados stood in the open Atlantic and apart and windward from the chain of islands. This position made it most difficult for Caribbean-based fleets to invade at a time when other small islands were readily passed back and forth between the competing European states.

Intensively developed by the early eighteenth century, when tobacco planters in the Chespeake region were still a generation away from their short "Golden Age" and South Carolina was a raw frontier, Barbados by the late 1700s was satiated. The slave trade had dwindled to a trickle, and

incoming Africans who were not transshipped to the new frontiers of nearby
St. Vincent, Trinidad, or Guiana on the South American continent were
mixed into an assimilated slave population — equal numbers of men and
women, naturally growing and mostly Creole — and so were usually not
identified ethnically.

The island is described in the early 1800s by Michael Craton as the most
firmly established of all British sugar possessions, and as having a planter
class of "unparalleled social arrogance." Given a high proportion of resident
landowners, a deeply entrenched middle class of merchants, managers, and
professionals, and "the fervent support" of a relatively large number of
poorer whites, "the dominant culture," Michael Craton concludes, "was the
nearest equivalent in the Caribbean to the racist civilization of the southern
United States."[8]

In the colonial South, a rural order characterized by the anti-urban outlook
of planters who chose to reside on their own estates (which one called
appropriately "fortresses of independency") is the key to understanding
Chesapeake Bay society, which constituted a unique corner of Britain's
Atlantic empire.[9] The prominence of the Virginians as revolutionaries and
early presidents encourages incautious views that this plantation society was
somehow typical. It was not. Rice made far greater fortunes than tobacco,
and, as plantation life in Carolina was built around absenteeism and a
flourishing slave trade, it was far more representative of plantation America
than were the Chesapeake societies of Virginia and Maryland.

While a goal of great planters was often to establish a lineage on broad
acres graced by a fine Georgian mansion, the tidewater tobacco lords pursued
that vision more rigorously than their counterparts elsewhere. In sharp
contrast to West Indian absentees ensconced in England, tobacco planters
were not adventurers but settlers who lived on estates that they made their
only homes. Giving their rural retreats Roman names like Sabine Hall, they
saw themselves as patriarchs of families that by the Golden Age of the
1730s and 1740s were considered to include the slaves — "the black members
of my family" — as well. Here the convenient rationalization of slavery as
essentially paternalistic had some basis in fact.[10]

One of North America's primary geographical features, the Chesapeake
Bay and its tributaries, comprising more than 1,100 miles of navigable
coastline, shaped the rural isolation of tidewater plantation life. On pen-
insulas carved out by large estuarian rivers, the rich built homes that
represented their ideal of the rural and arcadian existence of the English
squirearchy. In time the estates, which became modestly self-sufficient by
means of the many skills provided by the rapidly assimilating slaves, were
seen as self-contained manors, veritable autarchies. Few wished to live cooped
up in towns, so the Assembly tried to create urban life by legislative fiat

(the Cohabitation Acts), testimony to the peculiar potency of the visions that guided this, the most rural, self-contained, and xenophobic planter class in British America.

In this region sales of new Negroes often took place aboard the slaver, or if ashore, at a planter's wharf.[11] Either way, incoming Africans were widely scattered, and so rarely seen in the records as cooperating with each other as fugitives. Market features also contributed to a new Negro disorganization that has been used incorrectly to characterize incoming Africans everywhere. Commanding the only self-reproducing slave population in the hemisphere, large tobacco planters by about 1740 were no longer as active in the market as they once had been. Instead, they relied on their slaves' natural increase. Therefore, principal buyers were small or beginning planters who, purchasing a few at a time and often in pairs, expected the Africans to settle quickly and make the monogamous families that would add slave children to modest wealth.

Not only was the average slaveholding much smaller in the Chesapeake Bay region than in the Caribbean and along the rice coast (and so new Negroes were less likely to encounter other countrymen), but tobacco cultivation also extended far inland. Small buyers carried new Negroes to farms located well off the major river highways, either between them or more remotely to the west or into the hilly piedmont. Even if they were purchased by wealthy slaveholders whose home plantations were conveniently located on deep water and far down the major estuarian rivers, the effect was still the same: new Negroes were isolated. The rich sprinkled them among people — usually Creoles, well entrenched and protective of the same — who lived on small and remote satellite plantations, called *quarters*. These circumstances, which channelled their social life in ways unknown to slaves in the other regions, made Africans in the Chesapeake Bay region more susceptible to rapid and thorough deculturation than they were elsewhere.

In the Chesapeake, new Negroes were forced into the most menial tasks and seldom seen off the plantation. Hence whites ordinarily concerned themselves with other whites, or with relatively assimilated artisans and domestics. The isolation of the Africans shaped encounters between the two peoples in which the slaves' past was generally ignored and forgotten. By contrast, as a matter of course in the Caribbean whites dealt with great numbers of Africans, at all stages of acculturation; off the plantation. Although most new Negroes worked in the field, a portion were market slaves, washerwomen, domestics, artisans, and, at the end of the century, soliders as well.

Situated about ninety miles south of Cuba and a thousand miles to the leeward of such small islands of the Lesser Antilles as Barbados, Jamaica was generally not a secure place. Snatched from Spain in 1655, and so developed much later than England's other Caribbean possessions, the island had the highest ratio, ten to one, of blacks to whites in British America.[12] The proximity of Spanish Cuba, and the presence of formidable maroon bands in the mountainous interior, sustained frontier conditions long after Barbados and the Leewards had matured.

At fifty by a hundred and fifty miles the island is four times as large as the combined area of the other British islands, but much of it was too mountainous for tropical agriculture. Only half of the land is arable. Heavily indented with bays and harbors formed in part by rivers and streams rarely navigable more than a few miles into the interior, the island's topography is remarkably diverse. Jamaica rises from the coastal plain, where nearly all the big sugar estates were located, to the Blue Mountains, which are more than seven thousand feet high.

Economic "take off" and the transition to large estates—chiefly through improvements in credit and marketing machinery and the supply of African slaves—did not take place until about 1730. Yet, by the second half of the eighteenth century, Jamaica was not only "the jewel" and wealthiest possession of British America, but also more thoroughly developed than any other plantation colony. By the early 1800s, a sizeable portion of slaves worked crops and trades other than sugar for owners who were often absentees.

In Jamaica (as in South Carolina) large planters, profiting from dynamic economies, dominated slave marts until the end of the trade. Forced to contend with expanding opportunities and 'African' slave populations characterized by skewed sex ratios (considerably more men than women) and by deaths exceeding births, planters bought all the new Negroes they could afford, and sometimes more. They did not think of their new possessions as couples who would raise children, however. Instead, adopting the economically rational decision to "buy rather than breed," they sustained slave numbers by buying imported Africans in lots that were roughly 70 percent male rather than by encouraging slave women to bear and raise children who would be unproductive for several years. Ironically, this strategy sustained the unbalanced sex ratios and depressed the birthrates that fueled the slave trade and the steady renewal of the African cultures that made white Jamaicans so insecure.

Within twenty-five years of the founding of Carolina in 1662 about one person in four was black. By 1708 numbers of whites and blacks were roughly even, or three thousand of each; thirty years later there were twenty thousand whites and nearly twice as many blacks, or about thirty-nine thousand. No other mainland colony experienced the "black majority" so common in the islands throughout the slavery era.[13] Rice planters, who one day would have the largest concentration of slaves per unit in the

South, had achieved by mid-century the manpower and technology sufficient to dam and dike the tidal rivers; they then moved down to the coast from the inland cypress swamps. Thereafter major staple production developed quickly, and the economy surged.

The large land reclamation projects that transformed the coast into rice plantations added to fierce malarial conditions. Consequently, during "the season" from May to November, when the mosquitoes swarmed that were the vectors of the dreaded wasting disease, whites abandoned the coastal parishes that were already preponderantly peopled by blacks. Under their own drivers, another West Indian feature, slaves worked in tasks, not in gangs, as their owners lived elsewhere or traveled about during much of the year. Although not as famous as the Lees and Jeffersons of Virginia, the Carolina aristocracy of Middletons, Pinckneys, and such French Huguenots as Hugers, Laurens, and Manigaults were among the wealthiest in the thirteen mainland colonies. They were also "amphibious," as Sir Lewis Namier said of the English squirearchy, for they often owned more than one estate and spent much of their time, out of the season, traveling between their properties. Such absenteeism was another West Indian feature of society, as was the decision to fill up their malarial holdings with Africans, to buy rather than breed.

As in Jamaica, the population of South Carolina for a while remained immigrant and pioneer in character: unhealthy, mostly male, and afflicted by high death rates until natural immunities to deadly local diseases built up through successive generations. A low birth rate compounded this condition. For much of the eighteenth century (as in the islands) most of the minority of slave women were native Africans and notoriously infertile compared to the more fecund local-born women. In plantation societies of this type — undergoing rapid development and so requiring sizeable annual importations of Africans — deaths exceeded births by about 5 percent a year. Hence, as importations of Africans surged in the 1720s (for there was now sufficient demand and money available for planters to absorb entire slaver cargoes rather than providing only a subsidiary market to the main one in the Caribbean) natural increase among blacks declined.

A long view of the slave trade and black mortality rates reveals that the various nineteenth-century emancipations in America liberated about six million slaves, roughly two-thirds of whom — four million — were from the Southern states. Yet when compared to the numbers of Africans imported into the British West Indies (and to Brazil, which alone absorbed about 70 percent of all slaves taken from Africa), Southern importations were minuscule. This, and "other peculiarities" of Southern slavery as summarized by C. Vann Woodward, included the high ratio of whites to blacks, the largest slave population of all but derived from the smallest number of slaves imported, who underwent the longest period of acculturation and were the farthest removed from their African origins when freed.[14]

Thus, in the four societies proportions of Africans to Creoles and of slaves to whites in the last quarter of the eighteenth century may be summarized as follows: In the Caribbean, blacks outnumbered whites from four to five to one in Barbados and ten to one in Jamaica. In Jamaica, a majority of the slaves were African into the early 1800s, but in Barbados, where the slave trade dropped off precipitously late in the century, Creoles predominated numerically about seven to one over Africans. In the Chesapeake Bay region, two people in five were blacks, of whom no more than one in ten were African following the last surge of importations in the 1760s. And in the Carolina lowcountry, three in five were slaves, about half of whom were African into the 1770s (from a high of about three to four in five in the 1740s).

Given the population, settlement, and slave trade patterns of the Chesapeake Bay region, which scattered and isolated new Negroes, it is not surprising that settlers there employed only a few words to describe incoming Africans. By contrast, the same patterns in the Caribbean and the Carolina lowcountry concentrated new Negroes and made it easier for them to co-operate. Consequently, whites in the two regions had to develop a more supple and extensive vocabulary to describe and control the growing and diverse number of Africans in their midst.

With this sketch of the four plantation societies in hand, the problem of the regional meanings of ethnicity and its expression, or repression, by whites and blacks can be addressed. In the following discussion the obvious comparisons are contrasting; Caribbean versus Southern habits provide extreme contrasts represented here by Virginia and Jamaica. There are important exceptions to this scheme, however. Of the four societies, Barbados, even though it is usually compared to South Carolina, is actually often comparable to Virginia and Maryland, the Chesapeake Bay colonies. The slave trade was negligible in both societies by the late eighteenth century when slaves in their own way had come to be assimilated, especially in the obvious sense of no longer being regarded as a real threat to white security. In Jamaica and South Carolina, on the other hand, the African slave trade prevailed until its abolition in 1807. Maroons in Jamaica and the Cherokee in South Carolina also contributed significantly to the tense and unsettled character of both societies for much of the eighteenth century.

Whites everywhere referred to unacculturated Africans as "new Negroes." In the Chesapeake Bay region, incoming Africans were also called "outlandish," and Creoles were known as "country-born." "Outlandish" was unheard of elsewhere, and "country" designated origin in Africa not America, for example, the person "is of the Coramantee country." In Jamaica, and for awhile in South Carolina, whites occasionally used "nation" in place of country. Local-born slaves were called "Creoles" in the Caribbean and "Carolina-born" in the lowcountry. Concerning designations that placed slaves in actual African societies — she is a "Chamba" for instance — historians have assumed conveniently that such terms were used without much consistency or knowledge of whether reference was to a port, region, language group, or to an actual society in Africa. That this harmful assumption will no longer do is indicated by confident and conventional West Indian characterizations: he has "a look of a Congo," "Chamba but may be taken as a Coramantee," and "I advise you to have nothing to do with them [the 'Negroes you mention']" for they are "Angola and Mundingo" (Appendix 1).[15]

These observations, made by businessmen, are conventional and typical. As sources they also represent, as Marc Bloch put it so well, "witnesses in spite of themselves." That is, they were not written for wide public consumption to explain or justify slavery, nor for future readers, as were the more familiar warlike Coramantee and docile Angolans that litter contemporary accounts. Consequently, the following does not concern ideology as explicit discourse, for instance the familiar intellectual debate of this era, "The Negro's Place in Nature." This issue is about the array of assumptions — that blacks were heathen, dirty, and libidinal — which, it is argued, the English brought with them to America. Instead, the issue here is ethnicity as lived experience seen in the conversation of those slave traders, estate managers, and overseers whose massive and intimate dealings with Africans can still be traced in such routine and practical documents as newspapers, legal records, and plantation accounts.

In the Southern colonies, whites identified Africans ethnically when they arrived and seldom later. However, an unusual attention to ethnicity beyond a slaver sale took place at a particular moment in South Carolina history — the development of a frontier with new Negroes. In the 1760s, as lowcountry entrepreneurs organized the settlement of coastal Georgia and East Florida, which for a time became a cultural enclave of South Carolina, they referred to new Negroes by their African tribal names, languages, and provenance. Buying a few Africans at a time for the new royal governor of East Florida, a Savannah merchant, for example, wrote that to date he had sent twenty-four and advised adding more "young Gambians or Gold Coast [as] they are fit to work immediately & the next year will be as good hands as any & less inclined to wander." He also had to find a slave interpreter, he continued, one who spoke the language of a Negro woman whose "country [tribal] name" was Sulundie.[16]

When Carolina businessmen talked about Africans, two peoples drew more than passing interest. Ibo were considered unsuitable for rice production, and Angolans were seen as inclined to run away to Spanish Florida.

To the undercurrent of mildly ambivalent views everywhere that Ibo in some situations became suicidally despondent, Carolinians added the charge of physical fraility as well. "Our people are very delicate in what they buy," and although "mad" for Africans, wrote Henry Laurens, the mainland's biggest slave trader, "Callabars [Ibo] won't go down."[17] Iboes came from the Bight of Biafra, a region that supplied 40 percent of all new Negroes imported to the Chesapeake, a much larger proportion than any other nationality. In South Carolina, however, Iboes comprised only about 5 percent of new Negroes brought in, whereas 40 percent were Congo-Angolans.

Carolinians were as concerned about the array of peoples of central and southwestern Africa (whom they called "Congo" and "Angolas") as Jamaicans were about the societies that comprised Coramantee. Throughout the 1730s sizeable groups of Angolans fled from the lowcountry to the Spanish presidio at East Florida; at the end of the decade, they led a mass escape in that direction, the largest mainland rebellion during the colonial period. (Even larger was the rising in 1811 at Point Coupée, Louisiana, then a part of New France.) Angolans shipped to the lowcountry were attracted by the Spanish king's proclamation to free all runaways of foreign rivals who arrived and converted nominally to Catholicism. At this time, a fugitive slave notice reserved for this people a potent word, "nation," a word rarely heard in the South but more often in Jamaica: "As there is an abundance of Negroes in this Province and as there is [an] abundance of that Nation, [my runaway] may chance to be harboured among some of them."[18]

In comparable documents from the Chesapeake Bay region an African presence is minimal. The few instances in which a people stand out, such as Mandingoes, are accountable more to the Africans' own efforts (when as runaways who had been recaptured they were asked to identify themselves) than to a white's curiosity or need to establish origin. Beyond the newspapers there are only scattered traces of an African presence in letters and legal records. "Ebo Natt" and "Ebo Sue" are, respectively, from a 1748 Essex County will and a 1722 letter of Robert "King" Carter, the richest tobacco planter, who once noted a purchase of Gambians as "preferable to any country by 40 shillings per head." Carter's kinsman, John Carter of Shirley Plantation, reacted in the 1730s to an unsuccessful sale of Angolans by offering to be the middleman for Gambian "or Gold Coast Negroes," but said he would not accept on consignment those from "any [other] port," a comment that suggests that Virginians designated ethnicity by reference to an African's point of exportation, whereas West Indians did the same more precisely by identifying a new Negro's language.[19]

Africans do appear momentarily in a local legal record, when they were presented to have their ages estimated for tax assessments. From Caroline County, Virginia, the largest in territory and slaves: "Amy [adjudged to be]

9 years . . . Sam & Harry, 9 years, Venus, 12 years, Lilly, 7 years." And from Fairfax County in the Northern Neck, more of the same. Nondescript Anglo-Saxon names—George, Amos, Kate and Dick—are scattered among the usual biblical and place names—Hannah, Rebecca, Solomon, Bethsheba, London, Glasgow and York. This sudden effacement of tribal names makes a sharp impression when compared to the Sulundies, Ma Vaunges, Quaws, Phibbahs, and Coombahs who poke through comparable sources from Jamaica and South Carolina.[20]

Jamaicans—who alone referred to slaves by their country of origin long after they were first unloaded and sold—sprinkled tribal designations throughout their plantation records. An estate attorney's report in 1771 that no more slavers were due from the Gold Coast brought an absentee's rejoinder to "buy Eboes [then] from Calabar."[21] Reporting the arrival in Antigua of a few cargoes "from the Gold Coast which are the best esteemed Slaves here," another attorney mentioned that some "Gambia Slaves" he had sold previously had "gained good Reputation."[22] In similar circumstances the representative of another buyer advised that those offered for sale "are what we call Windward Negroes, Chambas, Dunkerers &c, the worst kind of negros imported here for labour except Angolas." To use Angolans "for Sugar Works," he continued, "is throwing away money."[23] The same Jamaican proprietor was later informed in the 1790s that "Gold Coast Negroes," the males about eighteen, "& the females about 16 years of age [are] the best calculated for sugar Estates."[24] Even when absentees had lived some years in England after once personally making a stake in the islands, their managers continued to identify slaves ethnically as if they were making routine reports in the evening to a resident owner: "All are healthy except Isaac, the thick little Moco fellow who has of late been a little blo[a]ted, we suspect him of eating dirt."[25]

While much of this is opaque, more of it points to understandings that were common and assumed. While surveying the slaves of empire loyalists who came into his island at the end of the Revolutionary War, a Jamaican attorney initially identified them as "American" before he looked beyond that level of assimilation to their real origins, then he referred to them as "a set of soft Angola and Mundingo Negroes." Another group of new arrivals was dismissed abruptly by a manager as "many Mandingoes . . . I bought none." Earlier, the same buyer characterized Chamba by their distinctive ritual scars—"those with Cutt Faces"—and as a people who did not do well at his own plantation.[26] Some understanding of the assumptions that supported remarks of this kind occasionally surface. An advocate general for Jamaica made the following stereotypical allusion to suicidal Ibo: Hope, who took his own life following a quarrel with friends, was "a very good Negroe generally, but an Eboe." When Ibo were not available to establish a settlement (a new plantation), a manager explained that he did not buy because Ibo constituted "the country that will answer best there." (Settlements were usually in upland wilderness areas and thus close to enticing villages of maroons. In this case, however, the choice of nationality made sense because Ibo in Jamaica were hardly ever reported as maroons).[27]

These purchasing strategies should not be dismissed as idiosyncratic or of a context that is irretrievably lost. On two occasions, as revealed in separate plantation records, Ibo women were paired with Coramantee men, evidently as a way of domesticating a people who were notorious as warriors. Moreover, in a different kind of source (akin to a planter's how-to manual), William Beckford noted that often new Negro women, among whom he singled out Ibo, considered themselves as bound to "the spot" of their first born.[28] In other words, in each instance, it was assumed that as Ibo stuck and stayed, their new mates, the dangerous Coramantee, would be inclined to do the same.

Thus a few patterns, as the following section indicates, do emerge once kinds or classes of sources are laid back to back. Plantation registers that list slaves by ethnicity, for instance, are usually Jamaican, kept by large estates, and chiefly from the western parishes of Cornwall County, the center of significant slave rebellion throughout the slavery era. A 1778 ledger for one such estate of 488 slaves (York in Trelawny Parish, belonging to the Tharp family, who with ten plantations and more than two thousand slaves were among the wealthiest planters in Anglo-America) listed men and women from the major supply sources of western and central Africa.[29] The degree of refinement within an entity, as indicated in the ledger, was the same as that used by advertisers for slaver cargoes in the gazettes: for Gold Coast people (Coramantee, Fante, and Asante); for Biafran (Ibo and Moco); and for Congo-Angola (Congolese Angolans, Mungola, and "Portuguese Congo"). Newspaper descriptions of fugitives from this vast region included a new Negro woman with a crucifix necklace; another as bearing a "Spanish" mark, presumably a cross shape (probably Chokwe); and a third as speaking "Portuguese."[30] Mandingoes and Papaw-Nagoes are also prominent on the register. Jamaicans sometimes saw the latter as one, and sometimes separately; they were, respectively, Manding of Senegambia, Yoruban, and Fon of Dahomey from the Bight of Benin.

Ethnicity was also used to distinguish slaves of the same name in plantation registers. In an 1807 list from Westmoreland Parish, Jamaica, slaves numbered 44 and 45, both named Peter, were then distinguished as Banda and Ibo; three Fannys were Creole, Ibo, and Congo. Also from the western parishes, an official in the 1790s reported matter-of-factly that a driver had "harangued his countrymen and others—Coramantee and Mandingo—to join him [as maroons] in the woods."[31]

If a people were singled out in evidence of this type, they were usually Coramantee, the most conspicuous and important nationality in Anglo-America. Written on the border of a slave register was a special count of Africans imported from the Gold Coast, followed by a note that in 1765 and 1766 the number halved because of "the War between the Ashantees & Fantees." West Indians, officials particularly, kept close watch on Coramantee, who were also singled out in a 1772 census for Tobago, where their importation was soon prohibited. Like Jamaica, Tobago was volatile, and it, too, contained large interior communities of maroons.[32] Meanwhile, in stable and secure Barbados, where ethnic labels were uncommon, Coramantee were so popular that one planter accused unscruplous slave traders of altering the ritual scars of "other Negros to make them pass for this Country."[33]

In many ways for white Jamaicans, Ibo and Coramantee were opposites. Ibo were despondant and suicidal; Coramantee were physically and mentally tough, enterprising, and uncommonly stoic when tortured and executed. Bryan Edwards, who spiced his ethnic stereotypes with more insightful anecdotes, mentions the branding of a group of new Negroes, young Coramantee and Ibo men (brands, according to John Stedman, were small, silver, bore the owner's initials, and were applied over a dab of olive or palm oil to the face or chest). Led forward at the branding, an Ibo boy who happened to be first in line "screamed dreadfully." His countrymen immediately took up his cries. Meanwhile the Coramantee youths, laughing aloud, came forward, thrust out their chests and took the brand without flinching "in the least," and then "snapt their fingers in exultation over the poor Iboes."[34]

But the most careful and systematic use of ethnic distinctions are found in thousands of newspaper advertisements for runaways. The advertisements are also highly comparable in format and content from one region to another and make the debate about the importance of ethnicity more precise by providing the largest number of slaves whose distinctively African features—ritual scarring, languages, and dialects—were attributed to members of specific west and central African societies. They are also the best indication of the increasing objectification of black people in the South, rather than to their continual reputation as the carriers of African traditions into New World slavery in the Caribbean.

The gist of an effective advertisement, in a form like contemporary classifieds, was to save money and time by using a minimum of words to make a picture to readily identify and lead to the recapture of valuable property. From long experience, Jamaicans knew a great deal about shipmates, countrymen, and the new Negroes' first reactions. They said as much in notices that, being succinct and informative, were the most effective that appeared anywhere.* Advertisers wrote for a public able to depict Africans by reference to norms or stereotypes of national characters: "Looks more like an Eboe than a Coramantee"; and "Chamba but may be taken as a Coramantee."[35] Whites identified ethnicity in three ways: by general appearance, usually referred to as "looks," patterns of ritual scarification, and, most commonly, by an African's language or dialect. Like many references to ethnicity in the plantation correspondence, designations such as "looks Ibo" defy ready explanation and serve as a reminder of a lore that has been lost. "Looks Coramantee" or "Congo" were common in Jamaica throughout the slavery era, especially before 1800, but figured only twice in the South: in 1773 in South Carolina for an Ibo and in 1734 in Virginia in reference to Madagascars, a people whose physical features were conspicuous (neither very African nor white) to settlers who became increasingly obsessed with their slaves' physical rather than cultural characteristics.[36] This was a basic sign of a society in which blacks were relatively assimilated and so assumed to be under control.

Scarring patterns, the second way of establishing ethnicity, vary considerably among a people, even from village to village. The purpose of ritual scarification ranges from the cosmetic to the cosmological, and its use has declined sharply in the twentieth century. Eighteenth-century West Indians used the patterns confidently — "Eboe with marks of Moco" — and expressed surprise when noting adults did not have them: "no Country marks whatever."[37]

These comments are by Jamaicans who distinguished slaves by ritual scars long after they were assimilated. An urban slave and a baker, for instance, who in other societies would have been depicted solely on the basis of his skill, was also characterized by ritual markings (of which there are a few instances here and nowhere else of their use into the second generation by Creoles). Jamaicans were most adept at identifying Chamba by scars, which comprised three or four angled and paralleled slashes on

---

* Nearly a thousand new Negroes were described in the approximately 9,550 runaway notices in the newspapers examined. The papers (most of them *Royal Gazettes*) were published between 1732 and 1806 in six plantation societies: Annapolis, Maryland, Williamsburg, Virginia, Charleston, South Carolina, Savannah, Georgia, and Kingston, Spanish Town, and Montego Bay, Jamaica, as well as Bridgetown, Barbados. The advertisements identified fugitives personally by name, age, height, skin color, and conspicuous scars. Depending on time and place, they also depicted runaways culturally or psychologically: by ethnicity, patterns of ritual scarification, language or dialect, grooming, and by such mannerisms as tics, aphasia, and "addiction" to alcohol (Appendix 2).

each cheek or a temple: "Supposed to be a Chamba (4 or 5 cuts on each cheek)"; Mungola Country but "country marks somewhat like Chamba"; or simply, "some small cuts on her temples . . . or rather, as called, cambas."[38]

While Southerners usually described marks literally and said little more, Caribbean whites sometimes pushed further. Unsure of a fugitive's nationality, one owner nonetheless wrote appreciatively: "countrymarks on his Face, chest & belly which have been finely carved in his Country." When at the end of the eighteenth century new Negroes were incorporated as soldiers in the new black West Indian regiments, they were identified more thoroughly than usual. A recruit's village or district as well as nationality was included in the regimental succession registers; in at least one instance, a sketch of an elaborate ritual mark was put into "John Rock's" file.[39]

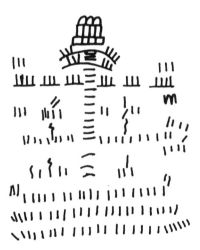

Country marks were handled differently in the South, where whites, not sure of what or whom they were describing, used more words with less care and precision than the West Indians did. "Three Gashes on each Temple, agreeable to the African custom," "A Negro mark between his Eye-Brows," and from George Washington, "He has a Mark on one of his shoulders (his Left I think) that goes down his Arm about 6 Inches long, and 3 broad pitts in the Skin, or the Skin raised up in little Holes as thick as they can stand." Carolinians also used typography in a few instances to represent such patterns as )))) or 1111. The exception to these concerned the people who throughout the empire were better known than any: "marked in the face as the Gold Coast slaves usually are." Otherwise, diamonds, stars, and clusters of dots fill the notices from this region and make each description seem unique instead of what it actually was—tribal.[40]

The third way of depicting ethnicity, and for Jamaicans the primary means, was by reference to a language or dialect. Two new Negroes said to be "marked like Chamba Negroes" were, nonetheless, identified as Nagoes (Yorubans); another, without scars, was said to "speak . . . Chamba"; or, more specifically, "Country can't be discovered as his language can't be understood by any Negro on said Property"; or, "none of [my] Negroes . . . can understand her [but] supposed to be Chamba, Nago or Papaw."[41]

These depictions are important because they contradict the common assumption that for reasons of security incoming Africans of the same language group were scattered so that those who were kept together could not readily understand one another.[42] Instead, in certain times and places, new Negroes not only formed their own diverse language communities but also sustained them. Some did so as they learned another African language while acquring their captors' English. From Jamaica, an Ibo was identified as "speaks Moco may pass as Moco"; a Chamba woman, who had only been in the country twelve months, already spoke Mungola "well" and English "very well." A Mandingo woman in five months already spoke sufficient Coramantee and English "to be understood." A man fourteen years in the country spoke "French and other Negro languages besides his country language," which may have denoted simply a patois, but the word "language" suggests otherwise.[43] Whites sometimes spoke through interpreters; at other times it seems they were able to recognize different African languages on their own, which may account for the new Negro fugitives who were advertised as selling goods in town, even though they spoke English "indifferently" or not at all. For instance, typically Jamaican is the comment that she "speaks not altogether plain English; but from her talk she may easily be discovered to be a Coramantee."[44]

In distinguishing Africans by their languages and dialects, Jamaicans were most discriminating about Coramantee. On occasion they took care in pinning down their origin within the Gold Coast: He is "from Crefree, on the Gold Coast, he speaks little or no English, and very bad Coramantee." A remark that implied knowledge of a Coramantee's home district within the larger cultural area included "[he is a] New Negro of Sucko, part of the Coramantee Country [but] understands little or no Coramantee."[45] Chamba — who on the basis of the advertisements may be seen as a people brought down from the far northern interior of the Gold Coast forests and savannahs — were most often linked with Coramantee in designations based on speech: Quashy, a Chamba who "speaks Coramantee well"; Primus, also a Chamba who was further described as "understands Coramantee"; or more abstractly, Simon, a Chamba, who "may be taken as a Coramantee."[46]

Characterizations of this kind from Chesapeake Bay sources indicate that whites of the region attempted to describe a people from another world.

Discrete, disconnected, and quaint pictures fill their descriptions of new Negroes and include a kind of talkee-talkee that one would expect from settlers who acted as if new Negroes babbled, and that the only language spoken in the society was English. In depictions of runaways who lived by the great bay, or who attempted to escape across it, the Chesapeake was "grandywater." The word is unheard of in Jamaican descriptions of slaves— probably at a much earlier level of second language acquisition—who continually attempted to cross the open sea to Cuba from northside parishes. Virginians would say "by his tongue he is outlandish," or "talks in her own language very fast," or "African-born retains much of his country dialect, can not speak so as to be understood in English." Jamaicans, however, would simply write: "Moco, but speaks Ebo."[47] South Carolinians did both— denied and recognized—languages in their midst other than English: "speaks no other tongue but English," or both "speak the Bombra language."[48]

As for Barbados, comparable sources are meagre. There are no runs of newspapers before the 1780s, a time when the local sale of new Negroes was negligible. Fragments from the late eighteenth century display, in the first instance, an awkwardness and, in the second, a chauvinism character-istic of Virginian usage: "[She is] an African which is discovered by her speech although she has been here from her youth," and—for a new Negro—"knows nothing of the English language."[49]

Although Southern whites were uncertain about Africans as represen-tatives of particular societies, they did leave informative traces of African identities in advertisements of another kind, those for new Negro fugitives who were recaptured. The "taken up," as they were called, were so common in Jamaica that they were simply listed in the newspapers. In the South, however, jailers described them more fully, and sometimes recorded as best they could what they heard as they tried to coax or threaten fugitives to tell where they had run from and how long they had been away. In each region the Africans' distinctive way of indicating time and place was recorded similarly. In two societies, Jamaica and to a degree in South Carolina, the whites' notations indicate that regardless of how long an African had lived in a plantation colony, he or she remained distinctively African about location conceptually in time and place: "Says . . . that he has made two crops for his master, and has been absent from his service two moons"; or "They say they have been ten Moons from home," wrote a jailer, who reckoned the fugitives so described were from somewhere in the Carolinas. "Says he came away from Virginia when they put corn in the ground to plant," "belongs to a man who makes tar and saws lumber," and from the land of "long leaf pine" (a specific up-country Georgia locale) all appeared. Even Africans who were no longer "new" (as well as some Creoles) continued old habits of mind by communicating when and where, as "he came away when he was done cutting rice," and "that her master was a single man settling a new Estate."[50]

In the same situation West Indian owners recognized explicitly that time telling pointed to different philosophical outlooks — theirs and the Africans': "They're not acquainted with our ways of computing it [time]" is from Antigua (1736); from the same era in Jamaica — "for Negroes don't know how to express themselves by number," and even more explicitly, "Though a clever fellow, Cudjoe had not yet adopted our modes of calculating time or distance." A century later a Jamaican official said of blacks simply, "They don't use figures."[51]

Use of the term *shipmate* — an embryonic institution that appeared in some advertisements — also highlights sharp regional contrasts in perceptions of Africa and Africans by ordinary people.[52] The comparisons between South Carolina and Jamaica versus the Chesapeake Bay region (and often, Barbados) break down, and the South becomes a unit in contrast to the Caribbean. Unheard of in conventional Southern discourse, the concept *shipmate* recurs repeatedly in the Caribbean, especially in Jamaica. Recall the new Negroes' first escape plan, to return to where they first came ashore, a design Jamaicans understood clearly: a runaway was "purchased in the recent sales of the *Vulture,*" or "purchased out of the last ship."[53] Compare the explicit reference to the near miss in the following two notices, the first from South Carolina (1759) was framed by the slave herself; the second is from the Caribbean: She says "that their master has a negro wench named *Betty,* and that she came out of the same ship with th[e]m." The West Indian version is that "He can be identified by mentioning names of his countrymen and shipmates."[54] Recognition that shipmates would gather as runaways could indicate direction of flight as well: gone "to Kingston having been purchased there," or "probably lost in the Liguanea Mountains trying to find his way back to the ship" — a startling view of the new Negroes' regard for the slaver as a rallying point.[55]

Even years after the slave trade ended in 1807, Jamaicans continued to talk about Africans as they always had. In 1819 a Coramantee runaway was described as probably harbored in Kingston, "as he has both shipmates and countrymen in that City." A few years earlier, a Chamba was identified as African in three ways, by the slaver out of which she came ("Capt. Crosbie's *Trusty*"), by her shipmates, and by her tribal name. She was "seen going windward and with several shipmates. She was very partial to her shipmates and no doubt has attached herself to some of them; she is generally addressed by her country name, JAPPA."[56]

From the Chesapeake Bay region, a somewhat comparable remark identified a slaver and the date and location of the sale of its cargo: "I bought him last August, at Mr. *John Blackwell's,* on board of Capt. *William Davis* of *Hampton* and 'tis supposed he may be gone that way."[57] But within a generation, as far as whites were concerned, flight by incoming Africans was random: "As he was only landed in the country three days before his elopement, he could therefore have no particular route to prosecute, nor can he speak English sufficient to give any account of himself."[58]

The thousands of new Negroes who were imported yearly into British America to work the whites' plantations were regarded generally as strange and threatening. In a variety of documents—newspapers, legal, and plantation records—their white captors named the newcomers' most conspicuous and customary features in order to control the blacks while making white society more secure. New Negroes were identified ethnically because prospective buyers, desiring value for money, considered some groups to be hardier, more docile, or more intelligent than others. But as will be seen, the more careful and persistent depictions of ethnicity were to ensure the safety of whites in those societies where Africans as countrymen and shipmates were recognized as dangerously able and willing to organize armed resistance.

Fugitive slave notices are an especially effective source because they conveniently compress a society's conventional understandings about how Africans acted when they first arrived. Where Africans were described knowledgably with regard to their ethnic origins, ritual scars, and languages, they operated longer—and were so identified—as members of particular societies within west and southwestern Africa. Although Jamaicans (and South Carolinians for a time) used ethnic designations regularly, Virginians and Barbadians did not. Jamaicans alone commonly called attention to the new Negroes' ability to suddenly construct and employ such networks, or "fictive kin," as shipmates and countrymen.

Regional differences in the ordinary perceptions of Africans who had just come from the slaver also signaled the kind of desperate possibilities— nil in some societies, surprisingly varied in others—that new Negroes discovered when they disembarked, put the Middle Passage behind them, and sought to make the first attempt to get clear of the whites whom so many regarded as voracious devourers. Africans did so by resisting variously as fugitives, insurrectionists, or maroons. Each act and the outlook from which it stemmed may also be regarded as a self-definition that further shaped the whites' view of Africans, and as another indication of what the societies were like in which the first acculturative choices were made by or forced upon the new arrivals.

# 2

## Africans Name
## Themselves

I speak chiefly of imported Africans,
who are the most to be feared.
— Edward Long, 1774[1]

The literature on slavery is rich with suggestions about what the Middle
Passage did to black people.[2] Most of these views are based on the understanding that accidents from painful bodily injuries to searing emotional
defeats, or combinations of both, throw people back on their internal cir-
cuitry: 'tuck in, take no chances,' says the battered psyche. Whether this
is what happened generally to Africans is impossible to say given the paucity
of the sources. Evidence does show, however, that for a year or two as
Africans changed from captives to seasoned plantation slaves, great numbers
of them made conscious choices as they fought back as fugitives, insurrectionists, and maroons. Although it is easy to demonstrate that enslavement
did not immobilize personalities or native languages, the real need is to
build into our interpretations some idea of what the first African Americans
were like who never experienced plantation slavery. To do so is to infer
from the rebellious actions of the unseasoned certain attitudes and practices
that became features of slave life and as such were displayed in resistance
from its beginnings to the final preemancipation rebellions.

Africans are rarely heard in the voluminous documentation of the international slave trade. When they are, the fear that pervaded all other fears
was of the whites as malevolent spirits who ate their victims. After a forced

march from the interior, Olaudah Equiano, an Ibo, saw for the first time
the white cannibals' slaver

> riding at anchor, and waiting for its cargo. [The sight] filled me with
> astonishment, which was soon converted into terror. . . . When I was
> carried on board. . . . I was now persuaded that I had got into a world
> of bad spirits. . . . I fell motionless on the deck and fainted. When I
> recovered a little, I found some black people about me. . . . I asked
> them if we were not to be eaten by those white men with horrible
> looks, red faces, and long hair. . . . We soon anchored . . . off Bridgetown
> [Barbados] . . . They pointed to the land, signifying we were to go
> there. We thought by this, we should be eaten . . . at last the white
> people got some old slaves from the land to pacify us. They told us
> we were not to be eaten.[3]

Both peoples contributed to the associations of enslavement with can-
nibalism and violent death. When Edward Long, the Jamaican planter and
historian, questioned Africans he discovered that they "believe they are
bought in order to be fattened, roasted, and eaten," that their bones would
be ground into gunpowder, and that Frenchmen, who were known to love
red wine, were in fact drinking human blood. Countrymen of the new
arrivals, Long implied, should be sent among them in order to calm their
fears. Otherwise new Negroes are likely to either hang or drown themselves.
They will throw themselves overboard or try to starve to death, wrote a
slaver captain in the 1690s, "For they believed when they died that they
returned home to their own country and to their friends."[4] Haunted by
fears of his white captors as cannibals, a young Mandingo said (after he
was recaptured in Jamaica as a fugitive) that "he came to this Island in a
Guineaman & belonged to a Captain who called him *Boatswain*. All the
other negroes in the Cargo were sold but he & one other, who were going
to go to England but their shipmates told them if they went again on Salt
Water they would be eaten & so they escaped."[5]

This man was among the more than nine hundred and eighty new
Negroes described between 1732 and 1805 in newspapers published in the
three regions. There are all sorts of ways of counting runaways, only a few
of which add up to much: proportions both of women to men and of
individual to group attempts within particular ethnic groups, and of differences in ratios of women to men runaways regionally. The latter varied
significantly, from only 5 percent in Virginia to twice that proportion in
Jamaica. Overall, flight by new Negroes was usually desperate, unsuccessful,
and mostly by men.

Those who were unloaded in Jamaica and who ran away there made
choices and confronted possibilities — of staying at large for a time and

receiving help to do so—that exceeded by a considerable degree the grim situations that faced new Negroes brought to the mainland South. The Jamaican sources are the best available regarding the immediate reactions of incoming Africans, whose experiences ranged from those who once at large barely managed to stay alive, to others who in a surprisingly short time somehow acquired the means of remaining free indefinitely. Accordingly, advertisers, who normally used an initial word or two to signal to readers a conventional type of action by new Negroes, called attention to five situations: first, "STRAYED" announced an African who had walked away from or was lost somewhere between the sale and the new plantation home and thus should be readily apprehended locally. Second, "ENTICED" or "DECOY'D" described new Negroes who seemed to be more strongly motivated and perhaps aided by either an experienced slave or a white or free person of color. The third, and most typical, situation concerned small groups of two or three runaways, who were usually countrymen and occasionally shipmates. The fourth described enterprising Africans who had forged new kinship groups. The fifth publicized small groups of runaways who, although comprised of those who spoke different languages, were somehow able to organize.

New Negroes advertised as STRAY'D, who threw themselves or wandered confusedly into desperate situations, included a starving Fante who could not speak English—"the account he gives of himself is, that he jumped overboard from the ship about six weeks ago & has ever since been living in the woods"—and a Bambara country man who left in the road others who were purchased with him and "after living from time to time in the canes, hunger compelled him to come out." A Congolese woman, who was probably pregnant when enslaved, was found beneath a bush, weak with hunger and holding a four-week-old infant. With a newborn infant in his arms, another Congolese walked into Cabbage Valley Estate and directed the overseer to a little camp back in the woods. His "wife" lay here, sick from giving birth and with her back burned because she lay too near their fire.[6]

Other new Negroes instantly took hold. However they did so not in the countryside, to which one might think they were more accustomed, but in town, where they received help. To make connections so quickly after being unloaded in a strange and hostile land implies a type of communication among the very new of new Negroes that is now difficult to explain. "Violet," a Papaw Nago, was representative; she was called "new" but described too as "probably around Kingston." Two Mocoes, who had been imported, respectively, five weeks and five months previously, were both described as "well known." One of them was well known in Port Royal, a parish that attracted runaways including new Negroes because its terrain provided convenient cover and ranged from a densely settled urban area around the king's shipyard to the abrupt, dense wilds of Long Mountain. A new Negro who used a similar area (next door in St. Andrew Parish) was described as "He is probably lost in the Liguanea Mountains trying to find his way back to the ship" [the slaver], and a Nago boy who sold wood about Kingston (even though he spoke little or no English) was well known in the mountains above Liguanea Plain.[7]

New Negroes who used the stratagem of looking busy while actually in flight evidently hit the ground running, and were sometimes encouraged to do so by Africans who were long-time residents. Another new arrival was described as "a good negro till he got connected with PRUDENCE, his wife." This woman, an Ibo who had worked in Kingston for twenty-nine years, was clearly in charge. The couple took a change of clothing, new blankets, two wood bowls, knives, forks, spoons, and an iron cooking pot. Two Congolese men said they had once lived on a mountain (an under-developed provision plantation) and when their master died, they went into the woods "and continued there for several years." Bringing with them good clothing, pots, bills, axes, and bows and arrows, they came in voluntarily and asked "to make their home here."[8]

The exploits of small groups of countrymen, by far the most common tactic pursued by new Negro fugitives, are best illustrated by those who arrived in the 1790s. In this decade more Africans were imported than ever before, and from sources that had shifted south and east (from Mandingo, Chamba, and Coramantee of Senegambia and the Windward and Gold coasts) to the Bight of Biafra (Ibo and Moco) and Congo-Angola. In the first months of the new decade several groups of Ibo and Moco were described in versions of "bought from the recent sale of the *Vulture* cargoes," or simply, "purchased out of the last ship." Among groups of this kind were a man and three women discovered in a small canoe several leagues at sea, suggesting that the Africans were serious about attempting a return home or perhaps sailing north to Cuba.[9]

Groups larger than three were unusual; these occasionally comprised new Negroes who were listed as ENTIC'D or DECOY'D away, and countrymen who were probably bilingual. Three of four Mandingo who ran off in 1792 spoke English poorly or not at all; the fourth, Tom, called "Autaum" by his countrymen, spoke very good English and had been "a trader in his country." Another buyer's anxiety about black African slave dealers was explicit: He may sell them "as that was his trade in his own Country." How common was this? Thomas Thistlewood, the manager of a small leeward plantation who left a marvelous plantation diary, mentioned a similar situation with this difference: the instant dealer, who enticed away a few Africans, was himself a new Negro. This kind of activity, which could not have taken place in a vacuum, is another sign of the intricate networks that new Negroes contracted or constructed themselves shortly after they disembarked.[10]

Another tactic by the unseasoned that invites rethinking of the resiliency of their tribal ways and upbringings and of the psychological consequences of enslavement concerns groups of fugitives who spoke different languages. Sometimes these groups comprised people who lived adjacent to one another in West Africa and spoke languages that according to contemporaries were closely related — Ibo and Moco, on the one hand, and Chamba and Coramantee on the other — or, those who during enslavement may have acquired a pigeon, an emergency language, that allowed them to cooperate with others who normally spoke a language other than their own. An Ibo boy, fourteen, and a Moco girl, sixteen, who were shipmates became unusually young runaways. Having run away twice before, the girl, "looking rather thin," was returned from one escape by the maroons of Scots Hall. Usually, however, members of the larger and ethnically mixed groups were quite dissimilar culturally. Two Ibo, a Coramantee, and a Congolese attempted to leave Jamaica in a canoe, and five Bonny Country men and a Congolese went to sea in a twenty-four-foot canoe. When a Mundingo was recaptured, he said that three Coramantee who had joined him had "hung themselves in the woods."[11]

These examples are important. As tribal people, new Negroes would consider as fundamental to their survival the forming of alliances in whatever direction they could. If the ethnically mixed groups of fugitives signaled a readiness and capacity of some to form bonds beyond the initial and more familiar groupings of countrymen and shipmate, this would be an important initial step toward the construction of a Creole norm.

In Barbados the exploits of new Negro fugitives were channelled by the island's compactness and absence of rugged terrain. Yet although only a few new Negro runaways were a matter of record, they accounted for most of those who ran off with others. As in Jamaica, Africans in this flat, treeless island established networks, and then used the teeming port of Bridgetown as a sheltering 'wilderness.' These included two men with filed teeth, "who say they are brothers"; two others who spoke "very little English" were harbored by "several countrymen" in town; and another who probably avoided towns. When recaptured, he handed over a three-foot spear.[12]

On the mainland, in the great reaches of Southern plantation societies, the new Negroes' plan to rejoin shipmates at the landing point was usually risky and self-defeating. Flight by new Negroes brought to South Carolina reveals two geographies. Some returned to Charleston, whereas others headed up country, where many eventually bent their way southward toward the unsettled English frontier of Georgia (recently founded in 1733), and on into Spanish Florida. Of the first objective, one owner wrote that " 'Tis supposed

[they] have gone an East[ward] course as long as they could, thinking to return to their own country that way." These men left the Welsh Track, far inland, on the northwestern frontier. Their journey to the coast, if they ever reached it, was at least three times as long as it would be for a new Negro fugitive making his way to a beach in Jamaica, the largest English island.[13]

In the Carolina lowcountry fugitives often prepared for a trek by burdening themselves with cooking pots, axes, and hoes. Given the watery character of the rice coast, they were more likely than elsewhere to take small boats, especially cypress canoes.[14] Older residents occasionally rode horses, and one took a pack of hunting dogs. The following journeys by new Negroes were without parallel in the Caribbean. An African purchased in Charleston and transported a thousand miles to Pensacola, West Florida, was three months and three hundred miles on his way back to Charleston by way of "the Indian Nation" when his escape was publicized. A Calabar (Bight of Biafra) was described in part as already well acquainted at Cheehaw, Ponpon, Horse Savannah, Beech Hill, "and from thence to the Cherokee Nation." Mary was described as well known in Charleston, Beaufort (seventy miles southward), Savannah, and Augusta (also on the Savannah River but eighty miles upstream from the coast), a range in which all of the English Caribbean islands would fit comfortably.[15]

In the Chesapeake Bay colonies, where whites were studiously vague about how Africans thought and acted, new Negro fugitives were assumed to be either incapable or unable to command the resources, mental or social, on which to fall back. "Landed in the country only three days ago," reported a mercantile firm (probably the importers), "he could therefore have no particular route to prosecute . . . [but] as he said to get to his country."[16] Given the reticence of whites about African ways in this region, one is never sure exactly what the record obscures. The largest reported group of new Negro runaways anywhere was from Virginia. "Persuaded [that] they could find the Way back to their own Country," fourteen Africans (including a twelve-year-old girl) ran from the headwaters of the James River into the frontier.[17]

In sum, the overwhelming impression of mainland new Negroes, whether unloaded in the Chesapeake or Carolina lowcountry, is of men and women who were often stymied by the weather and vast and unfriendly distances. The comparatively few who did run off, did so after they were brought to the plantation, where as "outlying" (not actually fugitives) they sat in lonely camps before smouldering fires and in the evening came in for food from slave cabins and kitchens. Those who did manage to break out of the plantation orbit, or who left before they arrived, became stragglers about swamps or on the sea coast, trying forlornly to find a way back home "over grandywater." Following long and fruitless sojourns in a vast Southern frontier, they were recaptured exhausted, cold, poorly clothed, and sometimes frost-bit or naked.[18]

Flight, however, does not convey well the anger and willingness of some Africans to fight back violently and effectively, nor the extent to which magic and ritual pervaded their existences. Others, especially those brought to the Caribbean, rose up, killed, pillaged, and torched buildings before singing and marching with their loot, beneath magic banners, into mountain interiors. Seemingly unafraid of whites or death, driven by martial drumming, dancing, and ritual oaths, these Africans drank their foe's blood, ate their hearts, and sometimes when cornered took their own lives; or, when captured and executed by a slow fire or starvation in a gibbet, joked and unflinchingly died, thereby further enhancing daunting Coramantee reputations. This type of resistance, whose alien and primitive nature is difficult to convey, is referred to by Monica Schuler as "rebellions of the spear."[19]

In Jamaica in 1760, Coramantee organized a large and terrifying revolt that resulted in the deaths of ninety whites, four hundred blacks, and the "transporation" (exile) of another six hundred. The uprising began in St. Mary's Parish, where it was soon spent and broken. But the potent ritual that fueled it was carried across the great central spine of the island and used to reignite rebellion in Thistlewood's southside Westmoreland Parish. There, near midnight May 26, 1760, half-dressed whites came riding in bare-backed and wild with fear, and, as Thistlewood wrote, "told me I should probably be murdered in a Short time."[20]

Before midday Thistlewood had hurried to the estate of the local big planter, returned to his own, mustered in nearby Savannah la Mar, and come home again — to chaos and paranoia. "Strange Various Reports, with Tumults & Confusion," and a clerk who "growles like a Madman shot at several Negro boys [and] wounded Oliver" were the first of a string of entries in his diary. He also noted rebels at a neighboring estate who "came with a Shout . . . & began to tear the Great House to Pieces"; later in the day, while "under the most dreadful apprehensions," he armed his own slaves as neighbors passed and pleaded "for God's Sake take Care of [your] Self." Sitting one evening with a friend, they saw a black woman run along the road "Crying the Bush was full of Negroes."[21]

Confusion and anxiety continued throughout a hot, dry summer and into the fall. Armed planters, militia, sailors, and parties of Treaty Maroons (runaways who had signed treaties with the settlers) came and went, and with them rumors that Crawford's Negroes would rise — "a great fear." Jacobsfield Negroes had risen, "& People almost frightened out of their Witts!"; "Saw Mr James' House Burnt to Night." News came of the capture of a rebel "town" — "pallisade[d] & dry wall[ed]" — that was taken with its plunder of gunpowder, ruffled shirts, hats, shoes, cravats "& [a] fine ma-goghany chest full of clothes."[22]

After months of tension and uncertainty, the whites, apparently mentally exhausted and letting-down, became strangely apathetic about the need to maintain even minimal security. "Several . . . get little done," Thistlewood noted, "indeed as Dr. Wedderburn observes here seems to be a total relaxation of government civil & Military . . . more than 500 Negroes on the road to Leeward every Sunday [for the markets]," but "few" had passes, and "no person questioning them!" Thistlewood continually used his journal to try and sort out exactly what had overtaken them. "At the beginning of the Rebellion a Shaved head amongst the Negroes was the Signal of War," he wrote in October, and then named five locally, including two women and "our Jackie," who "This very day . . . [had] their heads remarkably shaved." (As in West Africa, a sign perhaps, not as Thistlewood assumed, of preparing to fight, but rather of mourning those who had fought and died.)[23]

The first Saturday following the local outbreak of Jamaica's largest eigh-teenth-century rebellion, soldiers brought from the bush Mr. Foot's Coffee, who had once worked at Thistlewood's. As one of "their grandies," Coffee had "his hair shaved in the form of a Crop. . . . It is said he cut the heart and Tongue out of a white." A slaver captain, who reported more ritual acts, said he saw "The Signal of War—the Wooden Sword adorn'd with Parrotts Feathers—Carried in Procession at spring Path." Thistlewood iden-tified another leader as Wager, "the King of the Rebels," who was brought out with a guard of three, and "I asked Wager if he knew any of our Negroes, he said he knew Lewie & wish'd him good bye."[24]

The prisoners were swept into town and quickly condemned to the dramatic executions that momentarily relieved months of tension and grim fear. "Last Tues. Davie—who is Jibett'd alive—Seeing David Lopez & an-other White person fighting Said: 'Tha' good, me love for See So.'" Another rebel, who had offered his guard, a plantation bookkeeper, money and the appointment as overseer at Midegham Estate if he would let him escape, was executed by a strong fire set at a distance. The fire "crept up" slowly, but the African "never flinch'd, moved a foot, nor groan'd, or Cried oh!" Captain Forrest's Goliah, who was also hung up in a gibbet, had "cutt off Mr. Rutherford's thigh, & pick'd out his eyes whilst Alive." As for Forbe's "Mercury [he] Sucks the Blood of Negroes Executed." And Cardiff while being burnt alive warned the crowd about the Coramantee oath: that "mul-titudes . . . took Swear, who now lay Still, that if they failed of Success in this Rebellion to rise again the same day two years."[25] A month later, Thistlewood also wrote, "an old Saying, or Proverb, which fright[en]s many People!

One thousand Seven hundred and Sixty three
Jamaica, no more an Island shall be+
+(not for the Whites)"[26]

True to an oath, which whites called "the Swear," Coramantee rose twice
again in the most troubled decade in Jamaica's long history as a slave society.
In the mid-1760s they struck at Cornwall Estate which belonged to an
ancestor of the gothic novelist Gregory "Monk" Lewis. About thirty-one
blacks, most of whom were shipmates, entered the great house, "hacked
everything they found in it to pieces," and in an hour killed nineteen.[27]

Gold Coast slaves also dominated revolts in other Caribbean societies.
The slave Court, who danced with an *ikem* shield during the Antigua
conspiracy of 1736, was imported as a child. He was brought from the Gold
Coast, where, the royal governor's tribunal explained, the dance was used
to declare war publicly. The Coromantee king during this ceremony "appears
at the place appointed under a canopy with his officers of state, guards and
music, the people forming a semi-circle about him. Bearing an ikem, or
shield of wicker and a lance, the king dances until he tires, when he delivers
the ikem to the next dancer. Eventually, the king returns, dances with his
general and then commands an oath from his followers."[28]

If the concept of a Gold Coast warrior prince as slave and cultural hero —
the carrier into New World settings of African concepts of royalty and
warfare — seems improbable, it should be emphasized that the Antiguan
episode was not unique. Late-seventeenth-century Barbados provides a gaudy
contemporary explanation of the slaves' "grand design" to choose a king,
an old Gold Coast Negro, who would be crowned while arms were paraded
and trumpets of elephant tusk were sounded to "give Notice of their general
Rising."[29]

For Thistlewood and his Cornwall neighbors the links between Gold
Coast royal warrior traditions and local slaves were vivid and personal. Of
Wager, a leader of the 1760 rebellion, the manager wrote that before he
was enslaved, Wager had conducted business on the Gold Coast with his
employer's father, an official for the Royal African Company. For Wager
"alias Aponza"

> was a prince in guinea, tributary to the King of dorme, the King of
> dorme [Dahomey] has Conquer'd all the Country for 100 Miles round
> him. Aponzo came to Visit the late Mr. John Cope, my employer's
> Father, when Governour of Cape Coast Castle, attended by a Guard
> of 100 Men, well arm'd. He was surpriz'd and took Prisoner when
> hunting, and Sold for a Slave, brought to Jamaica, & Sold to Capt.
> Forest. In Jamaica Mr. Cope knew him again, and Wager used when
> a Slave sometimes to go to Strathbogie [Estate] to see Mr. Cope who

had a Table set out, a Cloth Laid, & for him; and would have purchased him & Set him home, had Capt. Forest Come to the Island—Wager Came to this Country 6 or 7 years ago.[30]

Comparable rebellions in the American South were rare, smaller, and, if Coromantee were involved, they were unnamed. In the mainland South whites were too numerous, and too well armed and organized on the frontiers as well as on the seaboard. They also controlled Indian allies, such as the Catawba of South Carolina, who were most effective trackers, as were the Moskito Indians in Jamaica in the 1730s. Hence Africans who chose to rebel had little choice but to try and fight their way beyond provincial boundaries. For a generation, the 1730s to 1763, this was a feasible tactic because it was the official policy of the Spanish in St. Augustine to attempt to weaken the colonies of their European rivals by welcoming fugitives from those colonies. The ancient New World city of St. Augustine, where recent archaeological excavations have revealed an extensive neighborhood of black refugees dating from the early 1700s, was also the objective of the largest rebellion in the colonial South, in 1731 at Stono River, South Carolina.[31]

The Stono revolt was unusual because it was provoked by the English-Spanish rivalry along the southern flank of the lowcountry. The Stono rebels were Angolans, part of a poorly supervised road crew that rose up and, after ransacking a warehouse for arms, began a violent march that ended with a dance in a clearing. Determined to fight their way south to the Spanish presidio, the slaves burnt several plantations and killed more than forty whites. A contemporary account captures the energy of this extraordinary affair, which resembled a Caribbean rebellion of the spear:

> they passed Mr. Wallace's Tavern towards day break, and said they would not hurt him, for he was a good Man and kind to his Slaves. . . . They marched on towards Mr. Rose's resolving to kill him; but he was saved by a Negroe, who having hid him went out and pacified the others. Several Negroes joyned them, they calling out Liberty, marched on with Colours displayed, and two Drums beating, pursuing all the white people they met with. . . . They halted in a field, and set to dancing . . . thinking they were now victorious over the whole Province, having marched ten miles & burnt all before them.[32]

Officials called the rebels "deserters," which is instructive. Governors' reports to the assembly and runaway notices in the early 1730s indicate that the rebellion was one of a series of group flights by Angolans to St. Augustine.[33] A few months before Stono, for instance, three Angolans were advertised as missing by a small planter who shortly thereafter lost his house in the rebellion. The new Negroes had been branded with a "B just above the nipple" and carried with them an issue of clothing and blankets.[34]

Angolans brought to the Carolina lowcountry were able to take advantage of a communication network established by their countrymen who lived in Spanish Florida. While attempting to educate his readers to the fact that the Angolans' patois was not Spanish but Portuguese, which is "as Scotch is to English," one contemporary described the network this way: "Amongst the Negroes Slaves, there are a People brought from the Kingdom of *Angola* in *Africa,* many of these speak *Portugueze* (which Language is as near *Spanish* as *Scotch* is to *English*) by reason that the Portugueza have considerable settlements, and the Jesuits have a Mission and School in that Kingdom, and many thousands of the Negroes there profess *the Roman Catholick* Religion."[35]

In South Carolina as well as the Caribbean, the 1730s saw major slave conflict. By contrast, comparable insurrectionary activity in the Chesapeake Bay region included little more than eight months of inconsequential plotting in a southern Maryland tobacco county. The Prince George conspiracy surfaced in a colony where new Negroes were readily absorbed, and assimilated Creoles early on moved to the fore of what little resistance there was. Hence, although the Maryland plot seems to have involved principally Africans who spoke their own language or a patois, its leader, Jack Ranson, was a Creole. The conspirators' objectives—for a plot rumored to have concerned two hundred slaves (only one was executed and four acquitted)— were similar to that which broke out much later at the end of the century when Creoles assumed leadership of major slave resistance: the rebels would kill all white men, make wives of their women, and unite the two Maryland shores. Within a generation of the Prince George disturbance, the only traces of organized slave resistance in this assimilated society were annual payments to constables for suppressing tumultuous meetings and, in 1752, a more specific reference to the slaves' potentially "riotous" annual festival.[36]

A far more serious form of resistance, however, was the development of maroonage—communities of runaway slaves. Hence it is important to note a sharp difference between the Caribbean and the South: although evidence of this kind of resistance abounds for the former (and for Latin America generally), it is sparse for mainland Anglo-America. The one instance of reported maroonage in eighteenth-century Virginia, for example, concerned slaves of a new plantation at the head of the James River. In 1729 this group "formed a Design to withdraw and to fix themselves in the fastnesses of the neighbouring Mountains: They had found means to get into their possession some Arms & Ammunition, and they took along with them some Provisions—their cloaths, bedding and working Tools [to] . . . a very obscure place."[37] In this report the governor also explained that the maroons were pursued "diligent[ly]," because their "design . . . might have proved as dangerous to this Country, as is that of the Negroes in the Mountains of Jamaica."[38]

In South Carolina, the Stono Rebellion may also be seen as aiming toward a maroon settlement. Generally, however, throughout this region maroons made only a brief and insignificant appearance when during the American Revolution they set up small camps on the margins of the lower Savannah River. Maroons of this type—male raiders—are hardly comparable to the large and formidable villages of armed new Negro fugitives that took root in the Caribbean.[39]

The almost complete absence of a maroon dimension and tradition to slave culture in the South is on first view a puzzle. In each region maroonage depended on a terrain of relatively inaccessible wilderness, and the Southern frontier was vast and rugged. It was also filled with formidable Indians and well-armed, land-hungry pioneers. In the Caribbean, on the other hand, geography was decisive. In Antigua—flat, treeless, and drying out—maroonage never established itself; and in Barbados, intensively developed by 1700, armed and organized runaways had to seek bases outside—across a strait—in the lush and protective wilds of St. Vincent. But in the extensive mountains of Jamaica, maroons flourished, which led more than one royal governor to lecture English officials about why troops could not simply wade in and defeat the runaways. "[Military] service here is not like that in Flanders or any part of Europe," explained Royal Governor Edward Trelawny in 1738. "Here the great difficulty is not to beat, but to see the enemy. The men are forct to march up the currents of rivers, or over steep mountains & precipices without a track, thro such thick woods that they are obliged to cut their way almost every step; . . . in short, nothing can be done in strict conformity to usual military preparations."[40]

As another group of New World blacks who were not of the plantation, maroons sought to achieve the new Negro objective of finding a way back home by building fortified settlements in the mountain interiors of such volcanic islands as Dominica and Jamaica. Once in place on consecrated ground, and as a means of easing the pain of displacement and the unintelligibility of capture, maroons struggled to reconstitute the traditional families to which all but the most assimilated of African Americans aspired. By including spirits of the dead as family, they managed to sustain old sanctions that in African fashion they put into 'play': for three centuries maroons have drummed, chorused, and danced in order to call down the shades of maroons past who protect, guide, and punish. This was a source of their prestige in the slave quarters, especially among those who continued to think that the ability to stay white power flowed from supernatural sources.

In a rich and extensive literature, the first maroons in the Americas generally are characterized as vagabonds and bush fighters, whose tactics — the false retreat, ambush, and night attack — complemented their small numbers and a formidable habitat. Incessant fighting, marching, and incorporating newcomers kept maroon societies martial, unstable, and ethnically mixed. Nor were they independent and self-sufficient; instead, they returned continually to raid the plantations from which they came originally, seeking food, more fighters, and women. Raiding was dangerous but necessary; because they were male, maroon populations did not increase naturally.[41]

Maroons in the British Caribbean, however, do not fit the general view very well. In Jamaica, as new Negroes learned to be maroons, such features as ethnicity, the incorporation of newcomers, and the maintenance of family life created societies that were more stable and self-contained than elsewhere in the Americas. Maroons soon realized that long-term survival precluded raiding. Some made the change by keeping themselves small, family-based, and hidden. Others — larger bands that were the most militarily formidable maroons in British plantation America — pursued similar strategies while alternately fighting effectively to maintain their independence. This group achieved legal status with the signing of peace treaties in the late 1730s and have come down to the present as separate communities, although they now are losing some of their distinctiveness.*

The treaty Maroons have been studied since the mid-eighteenth century in a literature that is polemical, repetitious of basic themes, and marked by controversies that have changed little in two centuries of interpretation. The historiographical stakes are high because what begins as a problem of what maroons were actually like readily spills over into larger questions of slave resistance, and of the nature of slavery itself. By employing a rich trove of underused primary sources, the proposal here is to build up pictures of Maroon leadership, women, and settlement strategies, the controversial issues in a long historiographic tradition in which scholars — and maroons themselves — have divided over the question of what constituted being a maroon. Did maroonage mean essentially periodic contact with whites through trade, raids, and war; that is, maroons primarily as former slaves and bandits? Or did being a maroon mean creating an alternative to slavery by abandoning the plantation ambience in order to live domestic, self-contained, and remote existences?[42] To see Maroons from the latter point

---

\* The treaty Maroons, hereafter distinguished from maroons generally by a capital *M*, are the basis of discussion.

To his captors and tormentors, the maroon headman Balla said, "Cut off my head, I can't be killed." He also "expressed much anxiety" about his tie-tie, the obeah or charm around his ankle, the governor wrote. He wanted it buried with him. Then, turning to his five-year-old son, Balla "bid [him] to remember [that] the Beckeys or White Men had killed his Father." (Governor Orde to Sydney, Roseau [Dominica], April 16, 1786). Engraving from John Gabriel Stedman, *Narrative of a Five Years' Expedition. . . .* (London, 1806).

of view is to pull them toward the center of African-American studies where they belong, because Maroon societies were close to what Africans initially would have done in the New World if they could have developed independently. The cultural perspective complements the way maroons were looked at by their white contemporaries; it also clarifies the maroon contribution to the old debate among African Americans between strategies of assimilation and separatism. That is, to describe maroons as isolated, sedentary, and relatively self-sufficient villagers is to see them in the families that ensured an antiassimilationist way of life. While acculturation and resistance by other blacks was often reactive, Maroons were usually careful and selective borrowers of those items of white society that seemed to represent a useful power—medicine, baptism, literacy, and firearms. Yet one group came to rely too heavily on informal arrangements and alliances with local whites, the Leeward Maroons of Trelawny Town. They lost it all; defeated in a bitter war in the 1790s, they were exiled to Canada.

As in the case of the new Negroes, the discussion, which centers on the Trelawny Town Maroons, should begin with the views of the Maroons' contemporaries. Many whites knew the Maroons well, some as their neighbors, others because they had studied them firsthand including at least one who learned the Leeward Maroons' "kromanti"—Coramantee—language. As visitors, whites witnessed Maroon dances and other ceremonies, enjoyed their hospitality, slept with and married some of their women, and, like modern anthropologists, tried to see Maroons as possessing a culture. In the western parishes slaves called Maroons "Cudjoe Negroes"; whites, who also assumed that basic features of Leeward society were Coramantee, called them "the wild Negroes."[43] Thistlewood, who met the Jamaican hero Cudjoe and visited Accompong Town, once jotted in his diary: "Coramantee is the Wild Negroes Court Language"; and another contemporary and expert on Maroons called their funerals "Coramantie ceremonies."[44] The Jamaican proclivity for identifying slaves by the African languages they spoke also surfaced in an expedition against Maroons in 1730, when a militia commander complained about a black guide who could speak neither Papaw (Dahomean) nor Coramantee.[45]

Assuming that Maroon society had a culture, contemporaries took exception to the rare instances when frustrated officials sought to demean them as bandits. Edward Long, no friend of Maroons, asked how they could be designated rebellious when they had lived in Jamaica since Spanish times and never submitted to the English.[46] Later, a hostile royal governor (Balcarres) called them "A Nation [and] a People," to which Bryan Edwards added that official policies had helped keep Maroons "A DIFFERENT PEOPLE . . . a community of sentiments and interests."[47]

Whites voiced these opinions because they understood that the policy of using the treaties to incorporate Maroons as allies was a distinct failure. Hence, during every major slave plot or actual rebellion, while slaves hacked and burned, the government's real concern was which way the Maroons might go.[48] Treaty or no, Maroon support was not taken for granted. As one royal governor put it explicitly in the early 1770s: "As to the people called Maroons, or wild Negroes we are sorry to observe that from some defect in the System of their establishment . . . in 1739, they have never become properly incorporated with the rest of the Inhabitants, nor are they interested in the defence of the Country; and their conduct in the late Insurrection of the Slaves [Tackey's in 1760] sufficiently proved that they are not to be depended upon."[49] A few years, later a conspiracy in the western parishes unnerved whites as never before because for the first time Creoles, not Africans, were its leaders. Nonetheless, officials as usual soon focused their anxiety on the Maroons. The country was "naked," the slaves were "insolent," and if implicated the Maroons might do "the greatest Mischief."[50] The governor offered three explanations for why Maroons were so dangerous years after they had signed the treaties that were to make them otherwise: the Maroons' "manner of Life," their strategic location "in the very heart of the Country," and the "very high Idea the Slaves Entertain of them."[51]

What is lacking in much of the present-day writing about Maroons (and slaves) is an idea of how they lived, that is of what their "manner of Life" was actually like. Tracings of this subjective issue are buried in the diaries of soldiers and the depositions of slaves who either fought against Maroons or for a time traveled with them. During the 1776 Creole conspiracy, three Maroons entered a slave's house at Gilcrist Plantation; two of them were "coalblack." The third — "yellow," tall, and with beads on his wrists — said, "Negroe Man fool for thinking white man better than Cudjoe [Negro]."[52] Or from the heat of battle:

> We marched on the 2nd [September 1732] through steep terrain rested in a heavy downpour during which we heard the Rebellious Negroes playing on the top of a High Hill over us. . . . [They] Hallow'd to us to come up, for they was ready for us and told us three times we come for to fight 'em, and [then] runaway like a Parcell of White liver'd sons of Bitches, I told the men to keep talking to them and with [the] best shots quietly [went] up the hill.[53]

Later, a rebel called down and said "in his Country Language" that if he was not killed he would come in. So, "we promised him very fair by one of our Negroes that Spoke to him." The Maroon approached, "till he had a fair sight of the Negro [interpreter] that spoke to him," whom he then shot. With this, the slave porters (the "baggage Negroes") fled the ambush and streamed back through the woods to a site later identified as the Maroons'

"Dancing place." Or: the sentinels call out "all's well" wrote another soldier, and the Maroons replied, "Ki! Ki! Becara [white man] call all's well, while we teeve [thieve] your corn" [take it right out from under your nose, in other words]. And, "[They] blowed their horns, then called to us to Come up . . . they told us they would dine with us very soon, they would Barbecue us."[54]

When in the late 1730s the Leeward Maroons were finally quelled, whites made a last effort to contact them peaceably and negotiate. During these sessions Cudjoe fell at Colonel Guthrie's feet and embraced his legs. This legendary gesture, it is argued, represented an obsequious sublimation of Cudjoe's hatred and contempt for whites and demonstrates that Stanley Elkins's Sambo, the stereotypical docile and childish slave, existed in all plantation societies including Jamaica, where the type was known as "Cuffee" (or Kofi, a Coramantee day-name).[55] In contrast to this interpretation, another soldier's diary puts an entirely different meaning on the Maroon's notorious performance. Kept by the whites' second in command, Lieutenant Francis Sadler, the diary indicates that Cudjoe's puzzling act was part of a dance. The diary further restores the cultural dimension by placing the negotiations in a proper context of time and the exchange of women and music:

> Saturday 17th [February 1738/39]. At day-break beat to arms and ordered 80 shot to stay and guard our baggage . . . we marched on towards the town. . . . Having got possession. . . . The Negroes got at some distance between the cockpits, sounded their horn and sang; and at last, began to talk to us, and we to them. . . .
>
> Sunday, 18th . . . we heard them in three . . . bodies, some blowing their horns, and some singing. . . . In some little time, they began to talk to us and we to them. . . . Captain Cudjoe and Captain Cuffee came down. . . . Colonel Guthrie and Captain Sadler met them there, and had a long conference with them. . . . They were very much pleased with our music, and several of them danced.
>
> Monday 19th . . . [we] told them that if they would deliver up a little negro girl, they took from Mr Welch . . . we would deliver to them the wench we took from them, which they readily agreed with. . . . we marched . . . several of them followed us with presents of quocos, plantains, &c. So ended the day. . . .
>
> Wednesday 21st. Two negroes came up to us, and told us that Capt. Cudjoe was in the open ground with some of his people, and desired that we would come to him; for he would not come to us, on account he had no room in the woods to dance . . . Col. Guthrie, Captain Sadler and 10 other gentlemen, went down. . . . We carried our drum, French

horn and bagpipes, They received us seemingly with a great deal of joy; they sounded their horn, we beat the drum and sounded our French horn; gave them some tunes with the bagpipe, which they seemed mightily pleased with . . . Capt. Cudjoe danced and showed a great many antic tricks, fell at col. Guthrie's feet several times; hugged him; and had a long conference with him, and so parted.[56]

These scenes from the First Maroon War (in the 1730s) signaled the end of an era (1650s–1730s) during which Maroons grew from scattered bands of new Negro rebels to complex societies that were intermittently nomadic or sedentary. In writing about them, white soldiers, whether part of an expedition or later visiting peaceably, usually recorded without judgment what they saw—villages with gardens, dancing places, a statue "of their own staining," and sizable household inventories of roots, gourds, and cloth-ing.

Monday, the 24th [1732] . . . took a Strick View of the Town reck-on'd all the Houses. At the top . . . there was a Guard House of 35 foot long each the flat that the Houses was built on did not contain One Acre, there was 35 Houses divided into several Appartments. In the Houses we got between 40 and 50 bags of corn, Planting flower, corn flower, dry'd Plantains, Jerk'd Hog, dryed hogs Feet, several Bags of Peas, Cocos, Casada, all which they brought from Montego Bay town, besides Wild Yams, China roots, thatch Cabbage, Mountain Cabbage which they got about the Mountain.[57]

In settings of this kind, Maroon women lived more stable existences than did those who found themselves among raiders who incessantly plun-dered and skirmished. However, even in the beginning, when maroons had to live hard and dangerously, women and children were members of bands. Dropping out of a major trek in the 1730s, an Ibo boy, for example, said that in the morning his group crossed the river at Wag Water and fell upon a plantation in a desperate search for food, ammunition, and clothing. For weeks they had lived on wild fruit as many "died very fast in the Manchas [hammocks]." Four men were killed who could not keep up, and when Pompey deserted them, they put to death a woman and her two children, whom Pompey had supported.[58]

Women and children are actually heard at one point in the evidence—stifling their cries as they crouched in limestone caves while artillery shells burst above them during the devastating Second Maroon War (1795–96). Toward the end of this debacle, the children, hungry and ill, ate *yapi* (green yams) and suffered stomach disorders. A Maroon man who had lost two infants from "fluxes" said that his grown daughter, Lattice, had a baby "thrown away" on the ninth day of life.[59]

As athletic and accomplished bush fighters, maroon men excelled at the deadly game of skirmishing, an extension of the long and arduous treks, "walks," for which they were so well known. For maroons who lived by hit-and-run, families were a dangerous burden; for women, skirmishing turned their world inside out. It threatened the gardens and children that helped make march camps villages and, at least temporarily, ended the hand-to-mouth existences that were the fate of so many. War also disrupted and diminished the contribution of women to the survival of fragile societies. How many infants, after all, could be carried on forced marches? And what were the effects of incessant marching, and of diets insufficiently nourishing, on conception rates, or on wanting to conceive in the first place?[60]

Yet some women were forced to live like this, as part of outlaw camps that eked out an existence from limited resources; others, in the big treaty towns, contributed importantly to Maroon economic and family life. Given the reactions of women to hard and bitter wartime experiences, it is assumed they made choices about one settlement policy or another. These preferences may be used to characterize three types of settlement strategies—forager camps, remote and self-contained villages, and treaty towns.

Using the term *town* indiscriminately, contemporaries described settlements that ranged in complexity from a few thatch huts and scratch root crops to large villages that commanded livestock, cash crops, communal buildings, and trade networks. Settlements may also be characterized by legal status (treaty or outlaw); location (remote or accessible—"parasitic"—to plantations);[61] size (camp or village); population growth (naturally or by recruitment); and structural complexity (measurable by the extent and kind of a town's trade, marriage, and political exchanges with neighbors, slave and free). Towns ought to be seen as a process as well as place; that is, as a series of adaptive strategies whereby maroons grew crops and generally kept self-contained or raided, ignored whites or sought revenge on them. Although intrinsic sources of maroon institutions and values warrant attention, in order to balance recent emphasis on the external forces that shaped maroonage, the latter cannot be ignored. Persistent military pressure could turn maroons of all types into desperate foragers. The catagories overlap, one kind of settlement could and did develop into another; during their long history, the treaty Maroons moved through all three stages.

Raider camps complement interpretations of Maroons as former slaves and male outlaws. Raiders lived in temporary towns placed against cliffs, with ropes nearby for a quick escape, or beside ravines, with rocks at hand that could be rolled down upon pursuers. Raiders placed their camps close to the plantations from which they came and never were able to leave completely because they produced hardly any of the food and small stock that in other towns supported stability, peace, and families. Forced to raid, or chosing to live that way, maroons of this type foraged in the lowlands, where they often challenged blacks as well as whites, for in Jamaica and the Ceded Islands slaves usually grew their own food.

Remote and self-contained settlements were more suitable for women and families. They were placed remotely in order to discourage the contacts of war, trade, and visiting that invited discovery and destruction. Living hidden if not forgotten lives, these people kept to an original meaning of the term — as in marooned, abandoned — and fit best the people whom the West Indian poet John Hearne had in mind when he said maroons were not so much abandoned by history as opted out of it.[62]

Treaty town Maroons lived in large and extended families in sizeable and permanent villages. In the late eighteenth century, treaty Maroons made an array of informal alliances with both black and white neighbors. They also married out, chased some runaways, and traded in tobacco and livestock as well as for guns, ammunition, and such amenities as salt, rum, and sugar.

The treaty Maroons' origins are unclear. What is known is that the Windward Maroons were from Spanish times (before 1655) and comprised Africans of different ethnic groups; the Leeward people were descendants of several large late-seventeenth-century Coramantee rebellions of the spear. On any account, by the 1730s both bands had fought the English to a standstill, nearly collapsed themselves, and concluded the treaties that are the source of their ambiguous reputation and legacy.

At this point their population surged.[63] Within ten years, a census of 660 Maroons revealed that about 40 percent were women and between a quarter and a third were children. Within a generation, the population doubled to more than 1,300; between 1749 to 1796, the ratio of women to men jumped from about two to three in every five adults, or from 44 to 56 percent of the adult population. An even more emphatic sign (in a larger society where slaves — infants particularly — had a very high death rate) that Maroons had become a naturally growing population was the increase of children from about one in four, 27 percent of the whole, to a point in the 1790s when nearly every other Maroon was under fifteen. Thus when Robert C. Dallas investigated them in the late 1700s (in what remains in many ways the best study), nearly all of the Leeward Maroons were not only "born in the woods" but also at least three generations removed from remote plantation origins. Because their founding ancestors were new Negroes, neither slave nor plantation culture and identities were ever a part of their makeup and way of life. The concern here is with those (types two and three) who followed policies of unobtrusive self-sufficiency. This stance, practiced early on and enshrined by Cudjoe, offered families the best chance to survive and to ensure the continuity of African values and ways in New World plantation societies.

From their obscure beginnings Maroons understood the importance of keeping to themselves. A contemporary (one of many) who understood this policy wrote that early English Jamaica was actually two societies, one white and "maritime" (coastal), the other maroon and "mountain."[64] Shortly after the conquest of Spanish Jamaica in 1655, Maroons set up in the mountains, where they lived "in[n]ocently" and presumably well. They ate wild hogs, fish, and "multipl[ied] fast." Slaves fled to their towns but were treated "severely" so that others, and inevitably soldiers, would not follow. This idyll vanished, however, in the early 1700s when white settlers encroached. The Maroons broke into small groups, pushed deeper into the interior, and disappeared. As the whites' slave guides aged and died, haunts, paths, and eventually the Maroons themselves were forgotten.

In the early eighteenth century runaway bands in Jamaica were con-solidated in the east by Nanny and in the west by Cudjoe. In the west, a frontier until the 1750s, the Leeward bands lived at the edge of the Cockpits, a desolate region of limestone karst—outcroppings that form a labyrinth of steep ravines, sinks, overhangs and caves. At the opposite end of the island, the Windward Maroons lived on ridges near the juncture of the John Crow and Blue mountains, which rise to more than seven thousand feet between Kingston and Port Antonio in a northside parish (Portland) that was long a notoriously rainy and unhealthy frontier. Political consol-idation accompanied a more basic adaptational change whereby the Maroons who had achieved a critical size and internal coherence crossed over from one way of life to another as they abandoned nomadic existences for sizeable fortified villages of provision grounds and livestock linked to small satellite settlements or encampments.[65]

A humpback who was in other ways perceived as a leader in African fashion—as power and force personified—Cudjoe led the Leeward Maroons during the middle decades of the eighteenth century. His leadership, which is best understood in light of the traditional strategy of living inconspicuously in family-based villages, reinstituted the Spanish maroons' venerable policy of keeping out of the way of whites. As born in the woods and raised in a band formed by his father (probably a warrior in one of the large late-seventeenth-century revolts by Coramantee new Negroes), he was charac-terized accurately by the 1743 writer as a "very sensible and Prudent Man." When a large group of Windward people in the mid-1730s arrived in his territory, he refused to accommodate them. Food resources were limited, and their aggressiveness against lowland settlers was "indiscret[e]"; for "it was a rule with him always, never to provoke whites."[66]

This attitude became Leeward policy after 1740 and was refined in time as the Maroons accepted gifts of cattle from the legislature, and occasionally invited in physicians and Anglican clerics. They also formed informal

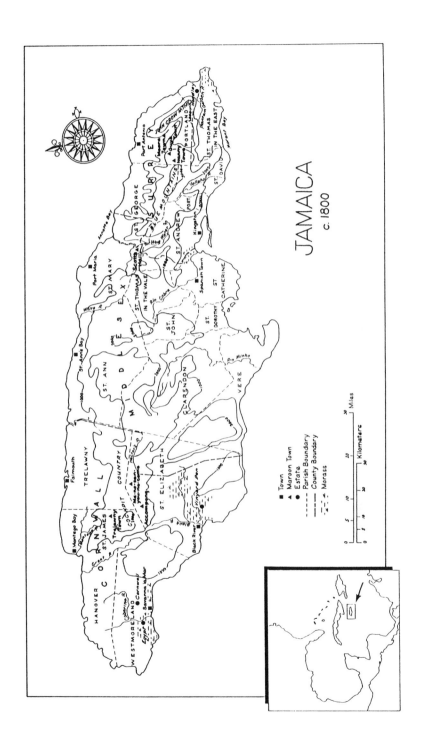

JAMAICA
c. 1800

■ Town
▲ Maroon Town
● Estate
‑ ‑ ‑ Parish Boundary
—·—· County Boundary
≈≈≈ Morass

Miles
50
Kilometres
50
10
10
20
5
10

CORNWALL

MIDDLESEX

SURREY

HANOVER
Montego Bay
ST. JAMES
TRELAWNY
Falmouth
COCKPIT COUNTRY
Maroon Town
Trelawny Town
WESTMORELAND
Savanna la Mar
Cornwall
Egypt
Black River
ST. ELIZABETH
Accompong
Great R.
Cabarita R.
Black River
ST. ANN
St. Ann's Bay
Rio Bueno
St. Anne's Bay
CLARENDON
Rio Minho
VERE
Milk R.
Dry Harbour
ST. MARY
Port Maria
White R.
ST. GEORGE
Annotto Bay
ST. THOMAS IN THE VALE
ST. JOHN
ST. DOROTHY
Spanish Town
ST. CATHERINE
Rio Cobre
Scott's Hall
FIVE MOUNTAINS
JOHN CROW MTNS
Moore Town
Nanny Town
PORTLAND
Port Antonio
Hope Bay
Buff Bay R.
ST. ANDREW
Kingston
PORT ROYAL
ST. DAVID
ST. THOMAS IN THE EAST
Morant Bay
Morant R.
Plantain Garden R.
Yallahs R.

alliances with powerful local planters, whose names they gave to their own sons, as they policed the planters' slaves selectively. In return they took slave women as wives and thereby gained access to the women's upland grounds, which during the 1795 War blunted the effects of the whites' scorched-earth tactics. During this war the royal governor characterized arrangements between Trelawny and the most powerful western families (the Vaughans, Palmers, and Jameses) as an "Imperium in Imperio."[67]

Additional views of the African culture and institutions that were the basis of Maroon identity and resistance in this era surfaced during two major disturbances in the 1790s. The sources for the Second Maroon War (1795-96) are particularly extensive because the decision to exile the defeated Trelawny Town Maroons divided Jamaican political society and eventually spilled over into British politics as well. *The History of the Maroons* by Robert C. Dallas (1803) was part of the conflict. His sections on Maroon women, for instance, were meant to reply, explicitly, to Bryan Edwards and other eastern politicians of Balcarres' faction who would portray Maroons as godless savages in order to rationalize any measure that would erase them from Jamaica.[68] To Edwards's propaganda that the Maroons made beasts of burden of their women, Dallas replied that women's status was representative of societies at the Maroons' stage of development. He then described women not as the products of plantation raids but of a culture's sanctions and ceremonies marking traditional rites of passage.

A Maroon daughter's coming of age was announced by a feast where hogs were offered, young people danced, and families came forward to place bits of money (and the parents pieces of gold) into the young woman's mouth. After this feast and rite the young women, who impressed the sources as winsome, outspoken, and strong, remained single for a time. As the men followed their traditional walks, women were not idle or burdened by a double standard. Could it be otherwise, given the sexual division of so many activities — which was probably mythically sanctioned — whereby men and women spent much time among their own?[69]

Maroons married without religious or court ceremonies. When a woman consented to live with a man, kinsmen exchanged gifts: clothing and trinkets were made for the bride; hogs and poultry passed from the bride's family to the groom. A man could have as many wives as he could afford, but few had more than two, and most had only one. Polygyny was costly, a present to one wife required a gift of equal value to the others, and while each wife had her own property, husbands shared theirs with all their wives. Fathers visited wives in turn and had to notice only the children of the wife with whom they lived at the time. A breach of the "decorum," concerning the exclusive attention to a woman's children, could make a mother exceptionally jealous. Otherwise, Dallas wrote, she was indifferent to her husband's "extra-gallantry."[70]

Near the end of the 1795 War, white officials assumed that in defeat women would be deserted and children killed.[71] However when families surrendered intact, they had to be included in postwar imperial schemes. In Nova Scotia where the Maroons were exiled, missionaries pushed them to adapt monogamy and tried to convince the men that it was in their best interest to leave their families several months a year to be trail-blazers on the Canadian frontier. Asked to foreswear the polygynous relations upon which his society was based, one Maroon replied increduously: "You say me mus forsake my wife. 'Only one of them.'–'which dat one? Jesus Christ say so? Gar a'mighty say so? No, No, massa; Gar-a'mighty good; he no tell somebody he must forsake him wife and children. . . . No, massa, dis here talk no do for we.' "[72]

Dallas also appreciated how easily and well the Maroons supported themselves simply and efficiently among abundant natural and manufactured resources. Reflecting the Enlightenment's interest in natural man unfettered by institutions, he characterized Maroons as a village society unburdened by an army, taxes, written laws, or police, for "right and wrong were supposed to be understood without being defined."[73]

Yet by the time Dallas gathered his material, late in the century, the snake had entered the garden. Economic developments including cash sales from tobacco and stock breeding, soil exhaustion, and land hunger had wrought fundamental changes that Dallas interpreted in terms of values. "Among a people for whom ambition" was unknown, "a provident disposition" had recently intruded: "Strangers to the passions which stimulate superfulous industry," Maroons were now "feel[ing] the advantages [of] money."[74] A rare surviving statement about why they went to war (disastrously) in 1795 complements Dallas's insight, as it strikes a nostalgic note: "Buckra [whites] had spoiled the Country and when they had got the better of them, they would live very easy."[75]

Nonetheless, defeat in war should not obscure Maroon achievements relative to white society in terms of two basic indices of civilization in the eighteenth-century islands: self-sufficiency in food resources and a naturally growing population. What is known about Trelawny population and economy speaks eloquently about Maroon progressiveness and plantation backwardness. As opposed to plantation monoculture, the Maroons developed a diversified, progressive economy that balanced enterprises ranging from stone age gathering of wild game and fruits to modern blacksmithing and livestock management. Their population growth and famous health and vigor, which intermittently spurred white plans to ghettoize and dehabilitate them through contact with alcohol and lowland diseases, also demonstrated an ability to make up shortages in one area with food resources from another.[76] In the 1780s, while the Maroons continued to grow naturally, plantation mono-culture — which did produce superior weapons and fortunes — could not feed itself sufficiently to offset the impact of the wartime embargoes, storms, and droughts that resulted in the starvation and death of more than ten thousand slaves.

A disturbance in 1798 provides another view of African-oriented resis-tance, in this instance of maroons who lived more remotely and indepen-dently than those in the big treaty towns. The evidence is based on dep-ositions of two women who lived in a settlement that had recently been taken over by raiders who were only a step ahead of the militia. This group, carefully distinguished as "hav[ing] no wives or children to attach them to one place like the maroons," was led by Cuffee. Motivated by revenge, this maroon leader would burn Peru, Fontibelle, and all back settlements in order "to get room," he said, "to kill James McGhie . . . [and] once they got him they will be done." McGhie was one of the wealthiest planters in the northside area of conflict.[77]

Patty's deposition, the governor explained, provided a "tolerable correct Idea of th[e] disturbance" that commanders in the field (while applauding Cuffee's military prowess) referred to as a "war." A head driver's wife, Patty was taken from her provision ground by Cuffee's party, which took two days, as she reckoned distance, to walk to a town where authority was ethnic and vascillated in form between headman leadership and an informal equality. In the settlement some spoke Coramantee, "tribes" lived in their own districts, and Cuffee was "stiled Headman, but on occasion all were headmen, as they all talk one word." Patty also insisted that other women for whom she apparently tried to provide alibis were also carried off by men: Jissamina after the maroons burnt her house, and Blanche by her husband, the second driver of Peru Estate. Catalina, Sally, and Statira were "always inclined" to return to their owners, and, as for Tomas, she was the mother of a born-in-the-woods child who was named after Old Quaco, an elderly obeah figure around whom the 1798 group had formed.[78]

These women were caught in a dangerously ambivalent situation created when Cuffee's party joined or muscled its way into a town that was not an ordinary Cockpit retreat for marauding maroons. Instead, the settlement, bearing various names, surfaced over a fifty-year period during major dis-turbances. By the Second Maroon War it was already more than twenty years old and known as Congo Town to the Trelawny Maroons. Dismantled during that war it was quickly reoccupied by the 1798 generation and renamed Highwindward, "the place of greatest safety." Destroyed again, it was soon reoccupied a third time and completely rebuilt more extensively than ever until its rediscovery in 1823.[79]

The women's 1798 depositions, then, catch Congo Town/ Highwindward midpoint in a long recorded history that stretched from the 1770s to the 1820s. Used by Cuffee as one of a string of march camps, it was a home capable of holding more than a hundred people, according to the field commander, who said it was also a "little town of Huts [with]... well beaten paths in various directions." Maroons had local food resources, gathered wild fruit, and used two provision grounds at some distance but "never" any others.[80]

Juba's testimony was also enclosed by the governor as "not differ[ing] in any material aspect" from Patty's. A McGhie slave who had lived for three years at Highwindward, Juba was more caustic than Patty about Cuffee's skirmishing that threatened them all. She spoke about the town's last days and Cuffee's decision to forage for wild yams (*himba*), which, she implied, was a pretext to desert the town when trouble started. (Apprehensive about pursuit parties drawing in, he had consulted Old Quaco, who said his "tie-tie (magic anklet) ga[ve] him notice" that the militia was "not coming that day nor the next but very soon.") When Cuffee left, he took the best weapons.[81] The militia officer who eventually traced the raiders to their base in his own way agreed with Juba. Perhaps a local man and aware of more than he reported, the officer said the McGhie maroons had "lived quietly there" and "grievously complained" about Cuffee's risky intrusion.[82]

Surprisingly, maroons persisted in returning to the site, which after its rediscovery in 1823 was described as sizeable. It had fourteen buildings, some with shingle roofs and wood floors, none less than twenty-five feet in length; one, probably communal, was seventy feet long, rectangular and open in the middle. The maroons, who in the 1820s raised poultry, hogs, and two hundred acres of "very fine" provisions (among the most extensive on record including those at the treaty towns), this time bestowed a name denoting their self-contained stance: Me No Sen You No Com.[83]

The Maroons' successful adaptations in a formidable wilderness environment must not be seen as mindless. As westerners, Robin Horton explains, we insist on comparing our science to what we take to be its equivalent — religion — among tribal people.[84] To do so implies that Africans were not scientific in their own way. More profitably, Horton proposes, African technology ought to be compared to ours. That said, Maroon technology consisted of ideas as well as hardware such as hoes, bills, and traps.

Maroon learning, however, is also not very accessible. What is to be made of such traces of beliefs and knowledge as maroon and new Negro blood oaths and deadly play in war — chorusing at militia, fascination with music, including the enemy's, and the dances by Cudjoe and the Stono rebels at what for the whites must have seemed to have been the most inappropriate of times? A twentieth-century Maroon colonel described Nanny,

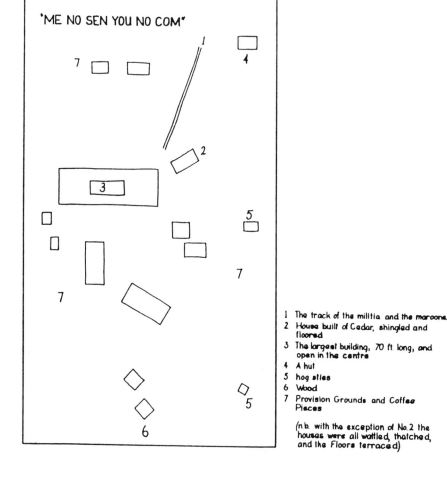

'ME NO SEN YOU NO COM'

1 The track of the militia and the maroons.
2 House built of Cedar, shingled and floored
3 The largest building, 70 ft. long, and open in the centre
4 A hut
5 hog sties
6 Wood
7 Provision Grounds and Coffee Pieces

(n.b. with the exception of No. 2 the houses were all wattled, thatched, and the Floors terraced)

the famous Windward leader and obeah woman, to a field researcher as having "so much science about her." In fact, she possessed more science than Cudjoe, as demonstrated by her well-known feat *Nantu-compong,* catching soldiers' bullets between her thighs.[85] At this point in our understanding of Maroon knowledge, Moses I. Finley's characterization of the ancient Greeks is apt. They are — like the Maroons — "desperately foreign" to modern sensibilities.[86]

A clue of what being a maroon perhaps meant, however, lies in the record of Me No Sen You No Com. When the militia fell upon the 1823 generation, they surprised a group of women and children cooking around a fire. "Hey! dem buckra hab em pruance to come back!" a woman challenged.[87] More profitably, one should ask why maroons repeatedly did "come back" to a place known to whites. In the monotonous labyrinthine Cockpit formations there were innumerable alternate locations that were naturally fortified and known only to maroons. A persuasive answer is that maroons returned periodically for more than fifty years because the site was deemed sacred: inhabited by dead maroons, all of whom — in an African sense of time-reckoning — would be, as the recently deceased, hardly dead at all. As shades the dead watched until living kin returned (in each of the three phases caught in the records) to renew the rites that linked the two worlds at this particular spot: Congo Town/Highwindward/Me No Sen.

In contrast to maroons who chose to live by raiding, women of the remote settlements conceived, raised, and buried their people in potent territory as far removed as possible from the sources of ritual contamination emanating from the coastal estates. And Maroons who employed the self-contained strategy fulfilled a primary aim of the first resistance by new Negroes regardless of where they were brought ashore in Anglo-America — to find a way home. Once at the water's edge, however, they were forced to turn inward, where in a few plantation societies some developed a sane and remote space to recreate families that, in the African manner, included the dead as well as the living.

The absence of a maroon dimension in the South, a serious loss for Southern slaves, is symbolized by the emphasis in studies of resistance on such individuals as Harriet Tubman. Tubman is celebrated as one who used the Underground Railway to conduct numerous nameless runaways to freedom in the North and Canada. Although one can only surmise what would have happened had these rebels had decided to remain in the South (Nat Turner was a runaway who returned voluntarily), it is possible to consider the cultural and ideological consequences of the presence, or absence, of an African — and maroon — dimension to slave acculturation and resistance.

# 3

# The Blood Oath, Play,
# and Ancestors

I observed their Notions of these Matters ["the Immortality of
the Soul"] were extremely obscure, yet from the Customs they
[the slaves] use at their Burials, I can gather some faint Remains
of their knowledge.
— Charles Leslie, 1740[1]

Slave resistance in the Caribbean was for a time African in character, an
orientation that exposed an acculturation that was slower and more voluntary than that experienced by Southern slaves. When slaves were Christianized, a process that accelerated cultural change in each region, the
progress of acculturation in the South was comparatively rapid and thorough
because the blacks' traditional cosmologies were already in disarray. In the
last years of slavery conversion usually discouraged serious rebellion. In the
Caribbean, on the other hand, Christianization, which inspired major resistance, was held up until the slaves themselves judged the traditional and
dynamic sources of their rites and knowledge to be ineffectual. In Jamaica,
slaves experimented with a variety of cults, including Christianity, as they
struggled to find an antidote to the whites' power and magic. Consequently,
religion, as contemporaries understood, was a far more important element
in resistance to slavery in the Caribbean than it ever was in the South.

New Negroes were dangerous because of a knowledge they brought with
them overseas that white Jamaicans attributed not to Africans indiscriminately but to Coramantee. Raised in village societies that were part of new
and expanding military states on the Gold Coast, most Coramantee under-

stood combat. They were also unique because their version of the ancestralism that pervaded Africa had developed during the struggles of state-
making, from its most representative form as a family cult to a national
religion and the basis of their formidable political unity. As an intregal part
of incessant warfare and political consolidation on the Gold Coast, Coramantee ancestralism in Jamaica became a potent ritual that into the 1760s
propelled resistance and for a time threatened to become the common
property of all slave rebels. Temperamentally, Coramantee lived at a high
pitch according to their most informative outsider, who typifies the historic
Asante as taunt and "geared-up."[2]

Proud, physically and mentally tough, and esteemed as hard workers,
Coramantee could also be unusually loyal. However, they were not to be
trusted warned Edward Long, who worked to prohibit their importation by
reminding his countrymen of the way Coramantee organized resistance.

> When assembled for the purposes of conspiracy, the obeiah-man, after
> various ceremonies, draws a little blood from everyone present; this
> is mixed in a bowl with gunpowder and grave dirt; the fetishe or
> oath is administered, by which they solemnly pledge themselves to
> inviolable secrecy, fidelity to their chiefs, and to wage perpetual war
> against their enemies; . . . Few or none of them have ever been known
> to violate this oath, or to desist from the full execution of it, although
> several years may intervene.[3]

To this Long added cryptically that *"plays"* were "always" Coramantee
"rendezvous for hatching plots." Plays, of which Long had nothing more
to say, were dramatic funeral celebrations of dance, drumming, and song
that astute whites realized often preceded major forms of resistance.[4]

Funeral practices, as scholars have long argued, are the clearest signs of
African contributions to the slave's worldview.[5] Celebrations associated with
memories of the dead provided slaves with mooring posts. In taking the
performers among them who had learned intricate and athletic dance steps
and routines to times and places more of their own choosing, the rites
represented an alternative reality to the tragic predicament in which they
found themselves. The problem of the meanings of slave funerals and their
African content deserves attention in order to correct notions that, until
Christianization gave blacks something to think about, a distinctively non-
Western philosophical orientation was at most only a small part of the
slaves' adaptive strategies. The purpose of this chapter is to offer a version
of that outlook based on three elements that contemporaries such as Long
associated with funerals and resistance: veneration of the elderly and recently
deceased kin, the blood oath rite, and play. For convenience, each is discussed

in turn, after looking first at contemporary accounts of the burial practices that stood at the center of new Negro ritual and intellectual speculation.

Slave funerals were rarely a matter of record for the mid-eighteenth-century Jamaican manager Thomas Thistlewood, whose own slaves and those in his charge were mostly African, and many at any one time were new Negroes as well. Random and unreflective as they are, the comments encourage a view that what Thistlewood described was ordinary practice. That is, he usually noted only the burials of slaves who counted socially. For those who did not—"died a Negroe Man at Salt River named Ned, a Mule died at Paradise [Estate]"—his account is representative of the absence of attention to their burial and its commemoration. The manager's notes also indicate that the timing of interments varied, and did so in intriguing ways. Of Hector, once a troublesome and harassed new Negro who never developed much of a social network, Thistlewood mentioned that the African died "about 2 A.M . . . and had him buried." Will's remains were also readily shunted away: "Moria came home from Dr. Wedderburn's, said Will had died. Breakfast time Sent Cudjoe & Solon to bury him." Of such expeditious and unceremonial burials as these, Yoruba ("Nago") say proverbially that corpses without kin are unburied corpses.[6] Concerning whether slaves were cremated or buried, I have found only one contemporary account that mentions the former (Edward Long). Maroons by the late eighteenth century used coffins that were put in the enclosures surrounding their houses and yards. Slaves, too, kept family remains nearby; according to Long, ashes were buried in the earthern floors of their huts.[7]

At other times, however, actual funerals were arranged for those of a solid social niche that, as in the cases of runaways, some new Negroes were able to establish shortly after they arrived. When the new Negro Daphne died, she was buried at the same time as "the Boy," of whom Mountain Lucy, a prominent slave woman, had "miscarried of last Saturday Night," five days before the joint burial. At these times large crowds gathered: "Last Night & today; a vast company, with Singing, & at the Negroe houses, with Franke, for the loss of her husband Quashie. She killed a heifer and several hogs," Thistlewood wrote, in order "to entertain her Company with."[8]

There were important differences in the burial practices and beliefs of whites and blacks. When Thistlewood's mulatto son died, the corpse was put in the ground with the trappings of a respectable Anglican rite. A subdued graveside service followed a genteel wake during which for a time the corpse remained in the house. Friends visited, including slaves, to whom Thistlewood made small presents of his son's possessions. As a Christian funeral, the expectation was that the soul, seen as a detached, spiritual essence, was on its way to a timeless realm. For the slaves, however, the soul of the deceased, having gone just "around the corner," remained dangerously disruptive until it was properly disconnected from the family it had recently left (and would in time rejoin ritually). This process of rearrangement, based on a belief that the existences of the living and dead were intimately linked, was the primary objective of funerals conducted by all but the most acculturated of slaves.[9]

Into the second generation African ways of dying and death remained largely unassimilated and forceful sanctions, not only in Jamaica but also throughout the Caribbean. In 1758 Thistlewood noted that when Mulatto Will died he wanted to "be buried at . . . his Mother (Dionah's) right hand, and that no Negroes Should Sing &c."[10] Slaves "sing all the way" to the burial site, wrote Charles Leslie in the first (1740) and best contemporary account of a slave funeral. Like many writers fascinated by slave funerals, Leslie said blacks were buried in savannahs. There, mourners sacrificed a hog, which was quartered and a portion made into "a kind of soup," put in a calabash, and waved three times. All then sat down. Musicians returned to their drums, women shook gourd rattles — "a hideous Noise" — others placed the soup at the head and the rum at the feet of the corpse and then filled the grave with earth. Afterward the celebrants ate and drank and than sang on the way home.[11]

Singing and dancing were part of a large and noisy late-eighteenth-century burial in Barbados described by the physician George Pinckard. At the cemetery, where ancestors were customarily approached by the obligatory gifts ("sacrifices") and rites that served to encourage them to act predictably, grave diggers told Pinckard that Jenny, the deceased, was an African and a washerwoman. Jenny's fellow workers had "full faith" in her transmigration "to meet her friends, at their place of nativity: and their persuasion that death was only a removal from their present to their former home; a mere change from a state of slavery to a state of freedom."[12] At the burial ground, Pinckard also witnessed an elderly black woman who chanted "an African air" while a chorus sang "not a solemn requiem" but loud and lively. Others danced with five "antick" fishermen who were a conspicuous presence in the large procession that had wound through Bridgetown before entering the cemetery. Once the corpse was lowered, the earth around was smoothed about, and several women who each threw a handful of soil onto their friend's grave cried out, "God bless you, Jenny, good-by! Remember me to all friends t' other side of the sea, Jenny! Tell 'em me come soon! Good-by, Jenny, good-by! See for send me good — to-night, Jenny! good-by, good-night, Jenny, good-by!" The celebrants also expected to hear from Jenny "before [the] morning" concerning the requests they asked her to convey beyond the grave.[13]

Jenny's burial was public when most were not, especially those known as "plays," which were performed at night. When prominent blacks died, kin and close friends mobilized neighborhood slaves to conduct a play shortly after the burial. Thistlewood writes, "Gave Phibbah leave to go to Salt River to Night, to a Play, for old Oliver, who was buried a few Nights ago."[14] Where plays were held—in slave quarters, or more remotely in savannahs and other clearings—is unknown. An Anglican missionary, who in 1729 mentioned a play in a burial ground, described "Sacrifices of food & strong liquors to the dead, who may hurt them" and an event of "various instruments of horrid music [and] howling & dancing above the graves of the Dead."[15] Slave funeral dances were a "warlike . . . strongly agitated . . . running, leaping and jumping with many violent and frantic gestures and contortions," wrote Long's contemporary Bryan Edwards, who also observed that the dancing was performed for those of the deceased who had been elderly or respected.[16] The dances were often a feature of the larger ceremony of play, when spirits of the dead, after being summoned by the rhythms of drum and song, descended, entered, and possessed entranced performers, whose feats represented the spirit's presence and guidance.[17]

A sense of the drama and energy of the rite is difficult to convey. But two African Americans who visited Guyana Maroons in the 1970s did capture the charged atmosphere at the moment of the ancestors' arrival:

> The excitment of the crowd grew more intense. . . . Many of the women stood together to one side of the drums. . . . They seemed to be encouraging spiritual stimulation for the men pounding the drums in short intervals. In the center, between the drummers and the crowd, a mammoth fire was built with logs and boards. . . .
>
> As the fire blazed large, the drums beat louder and more frantically, and the people grew more excited. Many were chanting songs, some were dancing, and the children stood spellbound by the entrancing events. . . . The smoke grew stronger, the wood on the fire turned to burning coal, and the crowd moved back to form a big circle.
>
> Emerging from the smoke a few figures could be distinguished moving in and out of the smoke like phantoms. . . . Their bodies were covered with the sacred white clay. . . . As the dance intensified, the spirits of ancestral warriors were said to enter their bodies. Many in the audience went into trances, gyrating in imitation of the dancing medicine men. . . . [who] leapt into the burning fire for so long they had to be pulled out by others, yet no one seemed even slightly burned or injured.[18]

Slaves played throughout the era of slavery, sometimes secretly, other times with the leave of whites, who were never too sure what plays were. (As apparently another form of dancing, play seemed to be only a pastime.) Depositions concerning a 1791 plot in Jamaica expose the interpenetration of dinners, dances, and plays, as in slaves who "made a Ball," "made a Supper," or were accused of being "at the play of the Conga Country." The only Jamaican runaway explicitly advertised as "dangerous" was also "remarkable for attending Negro plays . . . [as] a famous Banjaw Man." "Brinjah," to a student of Jamaican Creole, is a comical person; to "banja" is to play the fool — recall the "antick" fishermen at Jenny's Bridgetown funeral.[19]

On the other hand, whites readily and clearly understood the menacing intent of the blood oath, a rite that like play revealed the new Negroes' determination to use the dead to reestablish family as it was understood in Africa. Whenever they uncovered evidence of the potent oath ceremony — a weapon forged on the Gold Coast during the Coramantee rise to nationhood and empire — whites immediately prepared for serious trouble.

Conceived by Africans as a spirit, oaths were sealed with a drink of blood from a slashed finger or wrist, caught in a calabash, and mixed usually with rum, gunpowder, and "grave dirt." "Taking the Swear," as it was called, was also the most powerful ritual sanction in the worlds of slave and maroon. They saw blood and soil from a grave as representing the dead, whom, Leslie wrote, were ingested this way: "They range themselves in that Spot of Ground which is appropriate for the Negroes' Burying-place, and one of them opens a Grave. He who acts the Priest takes a little of the Earth, and puts [it] into every one of their Mouths; they tell, that if any has been guilty [of breaking the oath], the Belly swells and occasions their Death."[20] In the late eighteenth century the possibility that slaves would be allowed to testify in court created a sharp public debate about the kind of oath to which they would swear. As a letter-writer to the *Barbados Gazette* explained, blacks "will swear by anything of which they appear to have a solemn and awful Idea: *By the Sun! By the Moon! . . . or By Grave Dirt . . . ;* as it is certain, the Solemnity of this Oath, appears to be connected with *their Ideas* of the *Survivance of departed Souls,* and *of future Rewards and Punishments under the Decrees of Divine Power."*[21] To this, a Jamaican added that a slave's "oath in court . . . will avail nothing against a compact entered into over the graves of their shipmates and relations, and solemnised with grave dirt and blood." Drinking "grave water," Thistlewood noted, constituted the "most solemn oath amongst Negroes."[22]

The taking of oaths by slave rebels was ubiquitous thoroughout the slavery era. Maroons and new Negroes used the blood oath to recruit fighters; once they settled down, the Leeward Maroons used the ceremony periodically to pledge their towns' support to the peace treaty that meant so much to them.[23] Among the Akan-speaking people of West Africa (the linguistic classification that includes the historic Gold Coast Coramantee) to swear an oath is to do so on one's lineage. For Asante, the major Gold Coast military state in slave times, a "Who are you?" question is understood socially as

"To what totemic clan do you belong?" It is asked as "What oath do you swear?" The matrilineal Akan also practice dual descent—reckoning one's being and legal existence from both male and female sides of a family. In this scheme, semen is male, blood is female. In Akan societies, in which women are accorded unusually prominent status and some real authority, blood is exclusively female. Blood also signifies nationality: it is public, it fixes one's legal and political existence, and it is used in oath rites to bind groups. No matter how widely scattered, rite participants remained brothers —"all of one blood."[24]

While Maroons and slaves lived differently, they shared certain philo-sophical premises that centered on veneration of the elderly and the recently deceased. Maroon leaders—older and often seers—and other heads of fam-ilies were the ancestors to whom Maroon families sacrificed annually. Slaves did the same: "They scatter provisions at graves, the object of which, as I understood, was of holding communion with the dead," replied a planter to a Parliamentary Committee's question, "What is the Negro's chief en-tertainment?"[25]

Elaborate funerals, plays, annual graveside sacrifices, and the blood oath stemmed from a basic feature of the first slaves' non-Western and unas-similated way of thinking—companionship with the recently deceased. This was not a remote and abstract ancestor worship, but a fellowship with the dead, who in important ways become the living dead. As a Ghanaian mayor explained recently, "you see, the afterlife is all-important. A person isn't really dead and gone, he has merely moved around the corner. He still wields power, so good relations must be maintained." Blood and dancing, as some white Jamaicans realized, were vehicles by which slaves brought the dead into their deliberations. While watching a dance performance in Dahomey, an African turned to Robert Farris Thompson and said, "It is our blood that is dancing." In Kinshasa, Zaire, a Kongo taxi driver told Thompson that "our ancestors gave us these dances, we cannot forget them."[26]

Complementing slave ideas that the living dead helped sustain com-munity and traditions through time was a profound respect for the elderly, who, it was understood, had one foot in the grave, as we might say. Once older people had died and were poised strategically in the nearby world of spirits, they could do good or harm depending in part on the quality of the memories they left behind. Memories in turn would texture the attitudes and ritual observances of surviving kin, who could never be too certain that a spirit called down in play would help or harm. Africanists confirm that even in the bosom of one's own family security was never a certainty. The family was "a primordial source" of security and well-being, but its members were also the persons most able and likely—as witches—to harm. "The ambiguity of the region between good and evil," Jan Vansina explains, "lies in the rapidity with which good may turn to evil" for "behind the smiling face may lurk the hating heart."[27] While in Western culture good and evil "have long been viewed as distinct, unchanging absolutes that war with one another," argues Douglas Fraser, "belief in many African societies centers largely on powers regarded as neither eternally good nor bad but potentially either and often complementary to one another."[28] What these commentators have described is the emotional and ideological basis of witchcraft which, T. C. McCaskie explains, "run[s] like a fever" through Asante history — and through West Indian history as well.[29]

More likely to commit suicide than any other group of slaves, new Negroes also understood, as whites realized, that at death their souls transmigrated home to Africa. In turn, spirit migration was closely linked to reincarnation. This facet of their outlook uncovers notions of the self. For an African, the concept of an existence in another person by way of transmigration and reincarnation, Alan Merriam explains, is "precisely" the Christian idea of immortality. Where we see a contrast between life and death and, by our way of thinking, each reincarnation is a separate entity with a beginning and an end, Africans see death as only a temporary displacement of the spirit to another vehicle for its continued existence. For them, life encompasses several existences combined into a single consciousness and extending over such a long period that an ending becomes too vague to be considered with much care.[30]

African ideas of the self, then, are different and more complex than our Western ideas. While we see ourselves as relatively autonomous, "encapsulated in a skin," Africans view personality not as a closed and private entity, John Beattie explains, but as an open force field, "an arena" in a world that is "charged with meanings and laden with messages." In this view physical forces are thought of as interwoven with one's own life in a world that "speaks."[31]

Wope *se* woka a*se*m kyer*e* Nyame a, ka kyer*e* mframa: If you want to talk to God, tell it to the Wind.[32] In a universe presumed to be "totally inspirited," Africans and slaves did not make the Western distinction between physical and spiritual existences. In their view, each object, living and inanimate, has its own spirit or power that guides it "as a steersman controls his canoe."[33] This is one way of putting what is often termed "animism," the familiar shorthand reference to African understandings that humankind, animals, plants, and even inanimate objects are cut from the same cloth and so often react to similar forces or powers.

That signs of this knowledge surfaced repeatedly in the sources until the end of slavery reinforces the argument that "the head is the last to go." Cultural anthropologists use this insight as a reminder that although a people's consumption patterns and even much of their expressive culture may be assimilated, their minds as fundamental conceptual categories are not so readily changed. Under torture and execution by slow fires, Cora-mantee were capable of enduring pain by mental feats reminiscent of the holy men in India who walk on beds of white-hot embers. Similarly, toward the end of an all-night dance given by a new Negro for some of her shipmates and friends, Thistlewood noted that a Coramantee, Maputu/Charles, ap-parently in a trance, struck his arm several times with the blade of a machete without harming himself.[34]

Play of another kind entered the slaves' celebrations at Christmas, a season that always heightened the nagging insecurity of Caribbean, and especially Jamaican, whites. For the holidays, slaves made elaborate head-pieces and masks, the oldest and most prestigious of which was called the "Joncanoe" or "John Canoe." At Axim, a major slaving station on the Gold Coast, Canoe (John Curante) was a powerful middleman in the eighteenth-century trade. "Canue" or "Jananeen" was the name given by John Barbot, a traveler to the coast, to the masks that made the people who wore them be considered as spirits of the dead.[35]

African and slave understandings regarding twinning and reincarnation marked the Jamaican career of the Baptist missionary William Knibb. Ar-riving on the eve of emancipation and the island's largest slave revolt, Knibb replaced his brother (who died shortly after his arrival) with whom he shared a remarkable family resemblance. This duplication made slaves at once wary and wonderfully curious, "Ah him got him Broder mouth, him Broder face, and him Broder beak" and, more directly, "Escuse me massa, me must look," "How de, Sweet Massa, me glad to see Massa," and "me know Massa by him Broder. Ah, him just like him Broder, he him Broder come again."[36] When explaining a slave child's death Knibb set his science against theirs: "His poor mother will have it that when he came to fetch his ticket, he thought I was my Brother's Patre or ghost, and that it frightened him to death; but the real cause was drinking water when heated."[37]

Signs of the traditions of Africans without slave identities, the unseasoned new Negroes and Maroons, are sufficiently clear in the Caribbean but opaque in the American South. New Negro institutions of shipmate and country-men were rudimentary, but their mere presence in Caribbean records en-courages efforts to see them as part of a whole rather than as some aberrant "survival." A recent study of slave burials in the Deep South concluded that they were of two kinds, either directed by the owner and Christian in character, or "a quick process of placing the corpse between two boards, or merely wrapping it in a blanket, in a shallow, unmarked, grave."[38] However, archaelogical investigations of black graveyards from the Carolina lowcountry to east Texas display burials marked as Africans would do. Charles Ball, a runaway whose autobiography was published, wrote about the placing of a bow, arrow, and minature canoe in the grave of a slave child whose parent was African.[39]

Important expressions of African traditions do surface in the South, although at first view they seem to be only the idiosyncratic creations of isolated individuals and defy efforts to retrieve context. But field research including archaeological studies have turned up intriguing findings of mortars that may have been used as drums, and a sixteen-inch iron statue of what is arguably an ancestral spirit was found beneath an eighteenth-century blacksmith forge in Virginia.[40] Moreover, in an 1800 rebellion in Virginia, a recruiter proposed the enlistment of "Outlandish people," those who "deal with Witches and Wizards, and thus useful in Armies to tell when any calamity was about to befall them."[41] Nothing more was heard of this plea, which recalls Coramantee war practices in both Jamaica and West Africa. As such, it is out of context in a Chesapeake Bay society in which among all nationalities the Ibo — rarely mentioned in rebellions of the spear — were numerically preponderant.

More commonly, however, the earliest surviving sources reveal a comparatively acculturated people, especially in the Upper South. If new Negroes had not run away, an inescapable conclusion would be that African values had been readily and irretrievably lost. Still, the designs of new Negroes, from ritual markings to reckoning place and time to inquisitive jailers, demonstrate West African upbringings and indicate that for a while they thought as new Negroes did in the Caribbean.

Consider time reckoning, which is about predispositions, the deep-set cognitive processes conditioned by the oral cultures in which new Negroes were raised.[42] Listen to South Carolina slaves telling time in a 1749 investigation of a conspiracy. Among the accused, assimilated boatmen and artisans counted time as we do, abstractly in standard units of days, weeks, and months: "about four or five months ago," or "Two or three months before Christmas." The Africans, however, reckoned time as "before the Potatoes were all taken," or "the time of digging potatoes," "when the corn was about three feet high," and "in the time of the last great Snow."[43] In making distinctions between oral and literate societies, it is customary at this point to call attention to the Africans' items of expressive culture — myths, tales, proverbs, and the habits of improvisation — that such learning and memory transfer entailed. More is at stake than that, however.

To define a culture as either oral or literate, respectively African and white in this instance, is to recognize that each constitutes a different way of structuring the world.[44] To cross over as slaves did from an oral culture — in which education is done through storytelling, music, and especially dancing — to a written culture is to do nothing less than free brains for tasks of a different nature. In oral societies, remembrancers (as record keepers and historians are called) in particular must commit great feats of memory as they cram and clutter storage cells with lists of an unusually practical and pedestrian nature, such as lineages of rulers and fiscal accounts. In order to facilitate this kind of record keeping and thinking, individuals make associations between what is to be committed to memory and the natural objects that often spoke to them: "We ran away from the land of long leaf pine," or "the attack would be when the corn was three feet high."

Marking time is also part of a people's sense of history. Reckoned as it was by the lowcountry Gullah, time is two-dimensional and foreshortened (in verb tenses), with a long past and present and virtually no future explains the Kenyan scholar John Mbiti. For traditional Africans, Mbiti writes, "time is simply a composition of events which have occurred, those which are taking place now and those which are immediately to occur. What has not taken place or what has no likelihood of an immediate occurrence falls in the category of 'No-time.' What is certain to occur, or what falls within the rhythm of natural phenomena, is in the category of inevitable or *potential time.*" Therefore, "The linear concept of time in western thought, with an indefinite past, present and infinite future, is practically foreign to African thinking."[45]

Time reckoning notwithstanding, the meager African presence in Southern records forces different explanatory strategies than those used for the Caribbean. My recourse in *Flight and Rebellion* was to a general "orientation" or "values" rather than to Herskovits's concrete and tangible "carryovers." Lawrence Levine's study of "black culture, black consciousness" pivots on the recognition that the Southern variant of slavery eroded any semblance of an institutional life akin to West African practices and values.[46] For Levine, such items of expressive culture as work songs and spirituals enable him to work backward to the basic features of what he also regards as the Southern slaves' essentially non-Western cultural base, an argument that ends evocatively with a passage from Mary Kingsley, an intrepid English traveler who described Africans—for whom there was "very little gap between things"—before the hunt. "They rub substances into their weapon to strengthen the spirit within it, talking to it, reminding it of the care they have given it. Bending over a river, they talk to its spirit with proper incantations, asking it to upset the canoes of their enemies, to carry down with it the malignant souls of unburied human beings or the ravages of the plague." Kingsley mentions that an individual at a bush fire or in the village palaver house would suddenly turn around and say, "You remember that, mother?" to a being she could not see but who to the individual was there. To the African, she concluded, "everything is real, very real, horribly real."[47]

Because New Negroes did not make the world intelligible as we do—

empirically, rationally, and progressively — does it make good sense to see their "beliefs" and "religion" (as we would say) as simply another part of an ideological superstructure? We regard ancestor spirits as a matter of belief, Igor Kopytoff explains, but Africans see them as a matter of knowledge: They do not believe the spirits of dead are active in their affairs. They know they are.[48]

The first African Americans knew they had ancestors, or at the very least real (although deceased) parents. Such knowledge is at the root of social organization. After all, can any society hold together without a set of assumptions, hardened into beliefs and institutionalized practices and sanctions, that must be asserted ritually from time to time? Ancestralism was transfered to the New World in play, the sine qua non of a slave community building on a traditional African base. The heart of ancestralism was the trance of a possessed dancer whose intricate and demanding steps were learned. This is an African retention at the psychological level argues Erika Bourguignon, and as such is a more fundamental carryover than the continuity of cultural content.[49] To know one has ancestry, however, is a core element of identity. With enslavement, ancestry was suspended until slaves in some societies were able through play to reinstitute their deceased parents. Thus possession dancing was commemorative, the new Negroes' statement that they had a useable past.[50]

This past was recreated differently in the Americas, however. West Indian slaves were able to put the pieces of ancestralism into place more readily and thoroughly than did their Southern counterparts. The Caribbean slave's accomplishment was tangible; it was accountable to land they acquired to grow their own food. In many African societies land is understood to belong to the ancestors. For Asante, Asase Yaa, an earth spirit and the Old Mother, gave land to the ancestors, its real owners. When a corpse is buried their permission is sought: "We have come to beg you for this spot, so that we may dig a hole."[51]

What can be made then of such elements of African cosmology as play for purposes of making a useable African past for American Negro slavery and as a vehicle slaves used to recover their useable past? Wyatt MacGaffey, whose work is informed by the clear recognition of the difficulties encountered in shuttling mentally between African and Western information systems, argues that rituals that call the dead down initiate resolutions, or even become "programs of reform."[52] Given that forms of play were a feature of the resistance of slaves at all stages of acculturation until the end of slavery, is it helpful to mark off the cosmology of the unseasoned as other-worldly, in line with our customary positioning of idealist (or mentalist) explanations on one side and materialist ones on the other? On one level, Maroons and new Negroes did not make such distinctions. On another level, their spirituality, as will be seen, flowed from materialistic motivations and from a context of clearly perceived political and ideological consider-ations.[53] Consequently, to dub these choices archaic or prepolitical is to indulge in a particularly demeaning form of ethnocentrism. Whether the structure of new Negro thought provided the clearest views of their dilemma and how to resolve it is another matter.

Africans arrived in the New World after a Middle Passage that is so often seen as traumatic and soul-destroying, even by those scholars who use an acculturation approach. An influential and sympathetic argument for an African dimension in slave life begins with the view that Africans did not "compose, at the outset, *groups* . . . [but rather] *crowds,* and very hetero-geneous crowds at that."[54] The fact, however, that incoming Africans arrived with a plan in mind that required a quick invention of countrymen and shipmates demonstrates that they were actively involved from the beginning in their own liberation. New Negroes readily formed contacts with Africans who had been slaves for a time, and then organized a resistance that even included cross-cultural enterprises.

Resistance by the unseasoned ought to be seen in light of both the activity itself and the mental designs that infused it. New Negro burials, representing an intellectual system with its own logic, indicate that new Negroes dealt with their dilemma symbolically, and that their symbols were made in their ancestral home. This resiliency of spirit in the face of enslavement, which was more than a matter of ideology, and later while seasoning underlines the importance of Peter Berger's remark that the "human craving for meaning . . . appears to have the force of instinct."[55]

PART II

# Plantation Slaves

# 4

# Plantations:
# Case Studies

This section will examine three facets of plantation slavery from the perspectives of both blacks and whites. From the vantage point of whites, chapter 4 comprises case studies of routines, management styles, and relations among slaves, their supervisors, and their owners. Chapter 5 considers the "scientific" reformers who in the South would make plantations more profitable by regimenting routines and rationalizing accounting techniques and in the Caribbean would encourage population growth by promoting the fertility of slave women and the survival of their infant children. Then, from the vantage point of slaves, chapters 6–8 consider their economic, family, and religious strategies that stemmed from the hitherto neglected problem of the ways slaves were fed—or fed themselves. How, it is asked, did distinctive regional systems of slave maintenance, now called the "internal economy," shape such primary institutions as the family and religion? And, in turn, how did slave kinship and religious patterns both reflect and shape acculturation and resistance? Finally, discussion of these problems clears the way for a consideration of the circumstances in which some plantation slaves did organize and fight back.

That resistance by plantation slaves was customarily negligible in most times and places, however, was not a matter of slaves lying down and giving in. In fact, just the opposite was more often the case. A fair proportion of slaves on most plantations resisted. However, they did so in a quiet, day-to-day way that did not add up to much. Theirs was a rebelliousness that seldom challenged slavery, nor much less curtailed appreciably productivity and profit. What it certainly brought slaves in return, however, was beatings, imprisonment in stocks, jails, or a hole in the ground, or, less violently, demotion or a withdrawal of some privilege such as leave to visit or work off the plantation.

What was the nature of plantation authority, and who or what kept the lid on? Were slaves terrorized or bought off? Did they internalize a master's view of them and of the way they ought to behave? Did slaves police themselves and, if so, to what extent and why? One of the best ways to consider these issues is to examine individual situations. The case studies offered here go only part way in resolving these questions, but, when coupled with a focus on slaves among themselves, some answers are possible. The case studies are also paradoxical. On the one hand, the relations among slaves, overseers, and owners are often obscure and defy characterization. On the other hand, at special moments—when voices and emotions poke through what to our modern sensibilities seem to be the grossly improbable and sometimes extreme situations that were endemic on plantations—the studies may inspire a recognition that surely in this instance slavery must have been something like this.

The case studies range in time from the 1750s to the 1860s and in place from Virginia and South Carolina to Jamaica and Barbados. The documents upon which they are based, primarily published and principally diaries and letterbooks, were selected for their un-self-conscious, episodic, and self-contained character. Replete with conversations overheard and quirky scenes, they are like snapshots, a condition I have tried to retain because it exposes some of the difficulties of typifying relations between owners and slaves. The studies also indicate that any model of those relations that assumes a close and familiar relationship between the two does not work well in areas of considerable absenteeism, such as the Caribbean throughout the slavery era and the Carolina lowcountry before 1815.[1] Nonetheless, as those who write from a paternalistic view of master–slave relations have insisted, the studies do underline the importance of keeping both whites and blacks constantly in view.

Colonists who sailed into Britain's South Atlantic empire found the Chesapeake Bay region to be the best place to realize an immigrant's age-old dream (and soon the "American Dream") of a second chance, a new beginning. By the second quarter of the eighteenth century, a few settlers and their descendants had achieved in Maryland and Virginia a semblance of the Southern version of that dream. Largely by the efforts of their servants and slaves, a wilderness was transformed into tobacco plantations and small farms. The planters who lorded over this domain viewed their holdings as manors and themselves as fathers of a flock of dependents free and slave—the latter customarily referred to as "the black members of my family."

One of them, who made a highly self-conscious return from the convivial atmosphere of London to a Virginia frontier in order to claim a handsome inheritance, described his life of "contentment" in the "silent country" as akin to that of a patriarch in arcadia. "Like one of the patriarchs, I have my flocks and my herds, my bond-men and bond-women, and every soart of trade amongst my own servants, so that I live in a kind of independence on every one, but Providence. . . . We are very happy in our Canaans if we could but forget the . . . flesh-pots of Egypt."[2]

The pastoral ideal, however, did not take hold among the rice and sugar planters who settled the Carolina lowcountry and the Caribbean. Here deadly tropical diseases, too many blacks to whites, too few white women, and a bureaucratic organization geared to absenteeism produced a style of plantation management that was not as personal and familial as that employed farther north in the region of tobacco, wheat, and general farming. Thus, in tidewater Virginia and Maryland, there were no slave drivers, and planters did much of their own overseeing.

Nor did the rich among rice and sugar planters establish themselves with the same degree of tenacity as did their counterparts in the Chesapeake region. They were itinerants who spent much of their time traveling about between their several plantations and to fancy town houses in Charleston, Montego Bay, Kingston, Bridgetown, or to sea island and mountain resorts. Or, if they could afford to do so, they lived as absentees in England. Consequently, the most visible and permanent residents were the slaves, whose supervisors (the absentees' representatives) were often themselves adventurers, not settlers, who died readily or soon moved on to acquire their own land and slaves, or to drop out to Mobile or the Spanish Main.

The case studies provide a convenient and graphic way of assessing these conditions. The first concerns most directly the acculturation perspective for American Negro slavery, in this instance a new planter's acculturation as well as that of the Africans in his charge.

## Jamaica (1750s–80s): The Diary of Thomas Thistlewood

> + Jenny's face and belly very much mark'd [i.e., by ritual scars]. She says she was a grande man's Pickinniny: that he had a horse, Cattle, & Slaves of his own, that she was Stole when he was not at home.
>
> Hear Mr. Cope has got the Clap, and Supposed from the new Negroe girl Charity, who lives with Damsel.
> — Thistlewood, 1752, 1768[3]

Having sailed once, to the east, in search of fortune overseas, Thomas

A Surinam planter in
his morning dress by
the poet and engraver
William Blake, from
John Gabriel Stedman,
*Narrative of a Five
Years' Expedition . . . .*
(London, 1806)

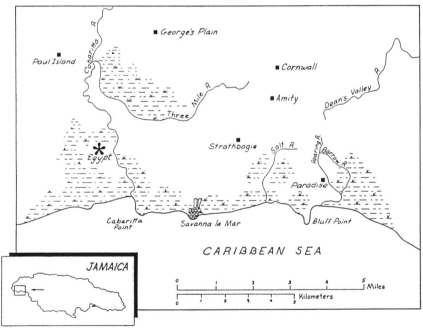

Location of Egypt Estate

Thistlewood (ca. 1721–86) left again in spring 1750 for the West Indies, where in April he arrived at Kingston, Jamaica. For Thistlewood, an Englishman raised on the bleak Lincolnshire fen, the tropics were a wonderland. The mountains were "grotesque," prices dear, and a Negro market was filled with yams, limes, Guinea corn, plantains—and women: "Some Black girls laid hold of us, and gladly would have had us gone in with them."[4]

Riding west to find work as a surveyor, a plan that fell through, Thistlewood in time changed his mind about ways of succeeding on a plantation frontier. He agreed to oversee. In Jamaica, as a friend put it, even "a Rat Catcher might . . . get an Estate." So in early July—"without a farthing," on a borrowed mule, and accompanied by a slave guide—he rode into Vineyard Pen (St. Elizabeth Parish), a satellite provision farm for a complex of three sugar estates in neighboring Westmoreland Parish. The pen included sixty-three slaves, eighty-six sheep, eighty goats, and several hundred head of cattle that grazed on a thousand acres of scratch savannah and rich marsh shaped by a meandering river, rock outcroppings, and sinks.[5]

Little is known about the first reactions of new Negroes to plantation slavery. But three features of Thistlewood's long and remarkable diary throw light on their seasoning and the setting in which it took place: Thistlewood's own acculturation, his love affairs with the African slave women who shaped that acculturation, and a slave resistance that was seasonal, not very threatening, and put down hard.

While acclimatizing, Thistlewood often fell back upon his traditional English reference points. Bedding down in a shed when he first came onto Vineyard (for the overseer's house was in disrepair), he spent one evening "Much disturb'd by Negro Musick" and the next peering into a looking glass, watching the play of his shadow against a wall lit by "a single firefly Cupped in [his] hand," while trying to read notes to Pope's *Essay on Man.*[6] A stay-at-home and an avid reader, Thistlewood shared a polite Enlightenment literary culture that was the birthright of English planters from the Chesapeake to Guyana. Into the late eighteenth century this tradition also continued to mix the miraculous and the scientific. An entry for one of his frequent exchanges of books with friends referred to Glanville on Witches and Close on Fluids. Thistlewood read Latin and the popular and major intellectual figures Hume, Locke, Franklin, and Voltaire, whose skepticism he mixed with alchemic and other folk observations. On the tropical edge of empire, however, the new imponderables of landscape and slaves intruded continually and bent minds away from literate culture. A set of reading notes ends pungently, "we have Black [land] Crabbs daily now vastly full of eggs."[7]

More comfortable and adept in the wilderness than people are now, Thistlewood was also a keen outdoorsman whose curiosity and understanding about local plants and animals served as a meeting ground for him and the Africans: it was his door to their languages and lore, and theirs to his English. As he seasoned, his notes progressed from a learning that attributed bits of knowledge not simply to Africans indiscriminately, but to particular peoples. Language intrigued him: The Negro ground corn begins "to Ear, or Babe as they Call it." "Threw stones today at a black owl or at a patton as the Negroes Call it." Guinea corn is "Call'd by the Coramantee Negroes, Cocotee," "She is a Bumbarah Negroe, or what the Coramantees Call Crappah or Tennedanes, being brought into this Country young."[8]

Notes on slave lore followed a similar pattern. At first nondescript, they came to be infused with smatterings of African learning and often touched on the supernatural. "Negroes, Say if you hurt a Carrion Crow or her Eggs (or a yellow Snake) that you will never be Well, till they be Well, Spoil'd or dead." "Catts, scratch against cashew trees to know the true reason Why." "Squeeze the Juice of pigeon pear leaves in the Eye, and it will make you See Clear." A local slave woman cured "Dorwood of the belly ache with a boiled herb on the point of a knife."[9] Or, consider this bit of sympathetic magic: "To Cure the Jaundice, Contrive to Steal Some of the affected Person's Urine, In which boil an Egg hard, which pill and put it on an Ant's Nest, and as the Ants consume [the] egg, the Person will gradually recover."[10]

In January of his first year Thistlewood rode to the tiny port of Lacovia, at the mouth of Black River, to report his employer's holdings. "At this great Meeting," people acted as if they were returning to civilization from some primeval setting, "rubbing & Wiping their eyes, many times, others complaining of Aches and Pains, People look as if they were risen from their graves." Gossip flew — Mr. Banton's story of the Barbados woman "that was Kist by three of them (at Kingston) in a Short space, he, the Middle one; Yet She laid the Bastard Child to him." Accompong, leader of a major Leeward Maroon town, made a showy appearance. Resplendent in ruffled shirt, a blue broadcloth coat — with scarlet cuffs, gold buttons, and white leather buckles — and barefoot, the Maroon was accompanied by a son and "many" of his wives. That evening Thistlewood summed up the socializing by recalling that before the gathering he had not seen a white person for nearly three weeks.[11]

As Thistlewood opened to the new land, to its lush scenery, stirring music, and available women, his seasoning ended. This was marked by two incidents, one on his first Christmas in the Torrid Zone, and the other at a "housewarming" for his new Negro girlfriend. The setting for Christmas was extraordinary — logwood plants in full bloom, trees and ground cover a rich verdue, "and I think better than ever in England in the middle of Summer" — but its celebration was traditionally English: "Plenty of guns firing on every Side [this] morning, all drinking Egg punch." As for the slaves' holiday music and dance that on arrival seemed to be only "diversions" and "Odd Motion," they were now described more appreciatively: "At Night had Creolian, Congo, and Coramantee &c Musick & Dancing Enough."[12]

In the ensuing months Thistlewood courted the Congolese woman Worree or Morina (her new slave name), and in the spring made a deal with the slave headman to build "the little lady" a house, which he sketched in his diary:[13]

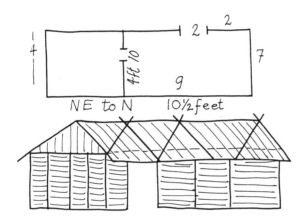

For Morina's "house warming" several months later, he provided sugar, four bottles of rum, beef and a pepper pot. Morina added ten pints of corn to make fonje — "to treat the Negroes, and Especially her Ship Mates." Later, a night of dancing highlighted by special performances gave way to an early morning possession: "They were very Merry all Night, Mr. Markman's Caser Sang and Drum'd, Guy and Charles, Phibbah & Wonicher danced Congo, &c. Some tip top Performances we had. Morina herself got very drunk as well as Many others. I Satt up a good Part of the Night Serving their Friends, Charles at five Struck his Naked Arm Many Times with the Edge of a Bill, Very hard, yet received no harm."[14]

In a society in which men in the mid 1700s outnumbered women at least three to one, African women readily became intermediaries between whites and blacks. In the dense faint lines of Thistlewood's small, neat hand are recorded the new human landscapes being etched in Jamaica by English and African. Food, sex, man, and beast follow hard upon one another or interpenetrate in a diary sprinkled with the concerns of men about their virility and satisfying women: "Negroes say rat turd powder dried & sprinkled upon anything & given to a woman You want forces her to desire you." Or, " 'Tis Said Eating much Cane, or Drinking much Beverige, makes a Woman so loose and open, as Altho' she had just been Concerned with [a] man, and getts many a Negroe Woman a Beating from their husbands." And, "Negro youths in this Country take unclariffy'd Hoggs lard, and Chasse into their yard by a fire Side to make their Member large."[15]

Thistlewood began slowly. When he slept with a woman he scrupulously identified her by nationality and tribal name as well as by her new one. He also noted the tryst's time and place, sprinkling his tallies with Latin, as if he were a gentleman cruising Drury Lane instead of an overseer coupling in a frontier still house or savannah: About "12 att Night, Cum Cynthia, alias Nacumma . . . Sup: Lect: Mett in Scipio['s] Domo. She is a Bumbarah Negroe. . . . At night Cum Phib[bah]: equalls 87 times this last year."[16] Emotionally self-sufficient and brave in many ways, Thistlewood hurt when he was without the steady companionship of a slave woman. At times so "pox'd" he could not rise, he still craved their company and was grateful when he got it. The women sensed his needs, and as best they could manipulate them: "Last Night Morina kept away," and "Jenny not come, began her Tricks again." Phibbah—who became his lifelong companion and makes an impression as a strong, likeable, and competent woman desired by many—several times dallied conspicuously in the "Great House" after Thistlewood had been more callous than usual. Or, she left his bed and went to her house in the slave quarter "and would not come Near me."[17]

Competition for the women was keen, and Thistlewood's proprietary regard for those in his charge was simply ignored by his employer (who lived elsewhere), other friends and acquaintances, and by at least one outside slave. When a former overseer visited him, dined, shot duck, and ended up in Phibbah's house, he wrote jealously, "Found him hid up on Phibbah's bed in a pretended Sleep. Dischar'd him" and whipped Phibbah for "harbouring." Parting with Jenny, a steady girlfriend between Morina and Phibbah, he wrote, "She is too Impudent & troublesome impertuning for Sugar, rum, &c for [the] Negroe Fellows." A few nights later, however, they were again sleeping together. Still later: "hear Jackie keeps her now."[18]

Thistlewood nearly always paid for his liasons in small coin (a bitt or two), food, beads, old clothing, or such broken utensils and tools as a pocketknife. Some women, particularly on Sunday mornings, made themselves available to him. Others he cornered. With three—Morina, Jenny, and Phibbah—he had longer affairs during which he always had trysts with other slaves. The women in turn gave him varieties of ambivalent messages, including some based clearly on African upbringings. Some would not sleep with a strange man when they were breast feeding, he wrote, "for Say they (for a woman to do so, is almost Murder) because the different Nature or Seed, shall probably alter the woman's milk so, as to make the Child Sick." This African custom may have been behind Phibbah's decision, which she obviously did not like making, to provide a "Sweet-heart" for Thistlewood while she lay-in and then prepared herself to breast feed for more than two years.[19]

Resistance, and a commonplace sordid cruelty used against it, were also part of the setting into which new Negroes were incorporated. A vigilant opponent who whipped slaves frequently, usually for taking food or running away, Thistlewood faced a series of run-ins in 1754. In this year of more than average food shortages, he watched one evening as "nearly every Negro on the estate" took cane out of the mill, and Teresa actually "march[ed]" off with her four bundles — "Must be for their hogs." Later, when Toney broke away from a whipping and jumped into the river, Thistlewood stripped, followed, and "was forced to knock him down when I came at him, for he threatened me with his stick . . . with much to do I tied his hands behind him, and brought him home." In the same month the head man, Mason Quashee, who had been riding Thistlewood about his girlfriend's privileges — ducking out of night work — was "extreemly impudent, and Saucy [and] threatened my life," Thistlewood wrote. Then five days later when he passed Toney's hut, he was attacked by Congo Sam, a runaway for three weeks. "Murder, murder," Thistlewood cried as he grabbed at the hoe that Sam was trying to use on him as a hatchet. His pleas were ignored by several slaves crossing a nearby bridge and by two women, both of whom had slept with him. The women, however, spoke to Congo Sam in his "country language," and "I was much afraid of them." Unusually disturbed, Thistlewood made several entries in his diary as a way of figuring what the string of incidents meant. At least three other slaves, including Mason Quashee and Phibbah, "knew that Congo Sam meant to murder me by Toney's hut."[20] To this he added a few days later, "Note: Last Friday in the field, Quashee told me (before all the Negroes) that I should not cutt much more Meat here!" When asked, "what are you going to do Poison or Murder me?" the driver seemed to back down. He would invent a story for the owner, he replied, and get the manager turned out (fired).[21] In time Thistlewood left for his own place, and wrote that the slaves of Egypt Plantation had named him "privately" in their African language "Abbaume Appēa i.e. no for play" (that is, he has a short fuse; he doesn't fool around).[22]

In this setting, the new Negroes seasoned by Thistlewood and the slaves in his charge reacted in one of two ways. Most kept their heads down and scraped through by avoiding serious conflict with older residents black and white. Others, virtually all young men, stole food and clothing and ran off. They were not advertised as true runaways, however, they were only "outlying" locally. Later most of this group either returned on their own or were brought in by another slave. Finally, a few of the women, perhaps as potential "girlfriends" and "Sweet-hearts," were put into the kitchen or the house.

When new Negroes first came onto the plantation, food dominated Thistlewood's notes about them. During seasoning the manager often recorded daily notes about "hand-feeding" the new arrivals with corn flour and salted meat, contending with spoiled supplies—only a "Bitt of bad Salt Butter"—or worse, with no food at all. In this case, the owner sometimes rode in and left a few odd coins for each new Negro, who was then expected to buy food from slaves who had established provision grounds.[23]

At Vineyard Pen two new Negro adolescent boys ("man-boys") were often hungry and runaway. George left with baskets of breakfast he was to carry to the field workers. Robin ran off to sit before a fire in the morass, where at times he was joined by Old Titus, crab-catcher and basket-weaver. After Robin threatened a slave girl with a knife and broke into Phibbah's house, two slave head men, as if to say enough is enough, set their hunting dogs on his track. Discovering the boy's "store"—an old watering pot, flour, butter, and Coffee's new shirt—and then Robin himself, they dragged the new Negro back, naked and wounded, at the end of a rope. At first Thistlewood assumed Robin had been stabbed to keep him from implicating others—"a Nest of Thieves and Villains"—but later decided that the wound was probably self-inflicted.[24]

In May 1754, the owner sent up an Ibo new Negro, whom the slaves named Hector, Thistlewood noted; when more arrived, he wrote that "we," meaning he and the slaves, named them Adam, Nero, Morris, and Moll. The manager also distributed a few tools, put the Africans in the houses of the older residents as a way of getting them started, and fed them boiled rice thrice daily. At night, they received a shad, caught readily in the morass. The next day the Africans worked with the older slaves, and a week later were assigned plots in the provision ground.[25]

In mid-January 1756, a group of ten new Negroes husked corn, a light task, the day after they were first brought on. A few days later some who weeded about the sugar works were led by Chrishea. How she communicated is unknown, but Thistlewood at the time mentioned, "If you Can learn a new Negro to Count to twenty, he will learn to pronounce most English Words very Well."[26] Then on Friday of their first week as slaves, the Africans were given their first tool, a basket, which was used to carry manure to holes that had been dug to receive cane roots. So, within a week and a day, the 1756 group was introduced to dunging, an important but not nearly as arduous a task as holing.

By the middle of the second week, this group of Africans began to display the diverse reactions to enslavement that are momentarily caught in the newspaper notices for runaway new Negroes. Recall that these reactions ranged from a desperate and often hungry bolt into nearby woods on the one hand, to resiliant and resourceful ploys on the other. Achilles, as an example of the latter, took Doll—who was not new—sold her and while on his way "home" was himself robbed of clothing, tobacco, a dram, and a gun, all of which he had somehow acquired while as a new Negro escaping and selling a long-time resident. "It's remarkable," Thistlewood wrote.[27]

A week later another new Negro, Derby, who resisted for the next several months even though he was punished brutally for it, was whipped and put overnight in the stocks for breaking and eating young cane. Thistlewood also "made Egypt shit in his mouth." For about a month after this, Derby "Continue[ed] Sullen, Won't Eat or drink, or Care for Whipping." Taken up as a runaway at another time, Derby, who "Pretended to be wonderous Ill" until his slave captors dropped their guard, "threw himself" off Cabaritta Bridge, swam forty yards, and hid in the crab thatch bordering the marsh. Two weeks later he was caught eating canes by Port Royal, himself not too long ago a rebellious new Negro, and again Hector was "made [to] Shit in his Mouth," a type of punishment now called "Derby's dose."[28]

Mid-summer was the cruel season. On Egypt Plantation, Thistlewood's irritability and random one-bitt sex, and the slaves' cane breaking and three-to-four day absenteeism, increased mishaps and resistance dramatically (about fourfold). Slaves who normally kept out of the manager's way (and diary) stole food and in at least one instance ate what they should have known better to leave alone. New Negro Zachery, found "speechless" by the road one day, was dead the next. People "reason" he ate raw cassava. After six months in the island, for a new Negro not to know how to prepare a basic root food properly by first leaching its juices, or being so hungry and otherwise desperate as not to care, is suggestive.[29] When another new Negro actually threatened suicide Thistlewood acted characteristically—immediately and brutally: "To day Nero Would not Work, but threaten'd to Cutt his own throat. Had him Whipp'd, gagg'd, & his hands tied behind him, that the Mosskitoes and Sand flies might Torment him to some Purpose."[30] Two weeks after this, Nero was caught in the hot house [hospital] with a woman, before a fire and roasting a large Muscovia duck, "feathers, gutts & all."[31]

The available record provides traces of the fate of some new Negroes over time. As another African who was bound, gagged, and left to the insects for running off, Hazat was eventually made a driver. He remained in and out of trouble as well, being flogged, for instance, in July 1758, after leaving for two days without permission. This reaction was common among plantation slaves, new Negroes particularly, who regardless of the consequences disappeared for a few days in order to take stock and cool off, if only, it seems, so they did not jeopardize themselves by resisting more seriously. Another new Negro, the Ibo boy Lincoln, was named after the manager's home town and was the first African Thistlewood bought for himself. Lincoln eventually contracted crab yaws and for selling stolen goods (in the lean, hungry month of August when most trouble occurred) was branded on both cheeks. As a good shot, his accomplished foraging may have saved some during the starving time following the great hurricane of October 1780. Several years after Thistlewood died, Lincoln was described in a runaway notice as an Ibo who came "to the Island quite young." Now grown stout and elderly, he was well known in the small port town of Savannah la Mar as a fisherman and proger. He sold fish and land turtles while claiming the right to "hire his own time."[32]

While reflecting on the lives and chances of Africans during his era, Thistlewood once noted a planter who in fourteen years had purchased 190 new Negroes and had lost 141 of them. "For keeping new Negroes alive during seasoning," he mused, "prudence & Industry [were] highly necessary," but "nothing succeeds like Luck."[33]

Throughout plantation America a death rate for Africans that far exceeded the same for Creoles primed the slave trade, which helped sustain slave populations that did not reproduce themselves. Yet in one corner of Britain's plantation empire, Africans and their Creole descendants did become by the 1720s a unique, naturally growing slave population. This corner was the Chesapeake Bay region where wealthy planters like Thistlewood's contemporary Landon Carter, also an avid diarist, no longer relied on importations of new Negroes to replenish the ranks of the enslaved. Here African ways had all but disappeared, consequently, Carter's diary conveys sharply different pictures than Thistlewood's of slaves and their relations with whites.[34]

### Virginia (1760s–70s): The Diary of Colonel Landon Carter of Sabine Hall

> I record only the extraordinary manouvres to let those who may be curious in my life, or after my death who shall Peruse these little books, see how surprizingly they have treated a Parent ever fond of them and indeed kind to them.
> — Sept. 1775[35]

The diaries of Thomas Thistlewood and Landon Carter are the best of their kind that have survived from the old British Empire. Dowries and a princely inheritance of about thirty thousand acres, several plantations, and about two hundred slaves made Carter exceptionally wealthy. He was also one of the most prolific writers of his day on local politics. A self-made man who lived anonymously on an unsettled frontier, Thistlewood held only a few minor offices during his life. At scratch militia musters on dusty Savannah la Mar training grounds, he traded bits of political gossip that he later recorded minimally: "hear Knowles is made Governor." This unobtrusive apathy was fitting, for Thistlewood's generation lived in a part of the empire that was slowly and inelegantly winding down. In his neighborhood the great event—Cudjoe's treaty with Colonel Guthrie—had come and gone by the time he began his journal. Carter, on the other hand, was a colonel of militia and a representative in the provincial assembly. He also lived in momentous times. As the diary opens, the elite to which Carter belonged was entering the great event of its existence, the contest between the rights of Parliament and local assemblies that led to the American Revolution and the founding of a new nation.

In a region where wealthy planters commanded large and scattered holdings, Carter surveyed his diverse operations on horseback and dispensed food, as manor lords do, out of great larders. He made his rounds alone or accompanied by his waitingman Nassau. His few close friends were men in a Cheapeake Bay society where the rich lived among their white families and usually kept their hands off the slave women.

For Carter and his class, who considered Virginia to be their only home, plantations came to be a way of life. Unique among English planters in this regard, they participated exhaustively in the overseeing of the intricate routines of tobacco planting instead of delegating some responsibility as they should have done. The center of this operation was the great mansion house; Carter built his Sabine Hall—"a perfect fortress of Independency"—for the ages. With good brick and stone, he made a neat, square, self-contained Georgian town house flanked by an office, kitchen, and craft shops.[36]

Dominated by the great Georgian brick mansion house with lawns sweeping down to a deep-water wharf, the large tobacco plantation embodied the master's desire "to live independent of every one but Providence." Autarchy—to create self-contained manors replete with the amenities and services one normally expects to find exclusively in a town—was a core value of this archaic elite.[37] Robert Carter, a nephew of Landon's, built Nomini Hall, comprised of thirty-three outbuildings including a cooperage, carpentry, a tannery, a blacksmith forge and a spinning and weaving center.[38]

This setting complemented the great planter's patriarchal concept of authority and the slave resistance it shaped. Carter and his class were nurtured on Sir Robert Filmer's *Patriarcha,* the political tract of the Restoration Era. Filmer, who argued that duty and submissiveness to father/

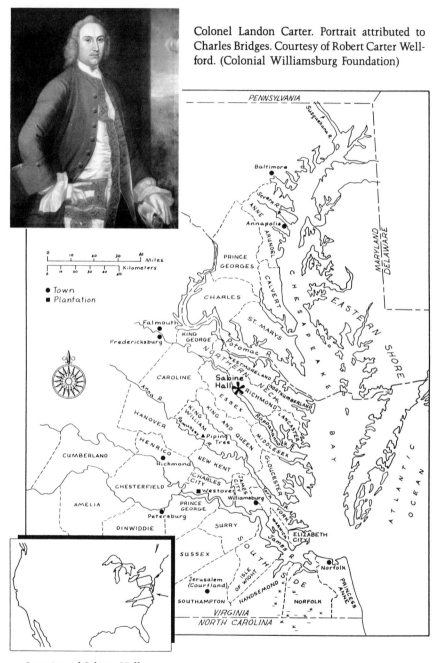

Colonel Landon Carter. Portrait attributed to Charles Bridges. Courtesy of Robert Carter Wellford. (Colonial Williamsburg Foundation)

Location of Sabine Hall

king/God were part of the natural order, appear in Carter's diary in this fashion: "to be sure when Principles of order and society decline, other duties must . . . How can you love God whom you have not seen, and dispise Parents who you have seen"; and "Obedience to Parents is much a duty to God and nature." Disappointed in a son considered to be a wastrel and an inveterate gambler, Carter left his diary open to a warning that he would disinherit the young man if he did not remain and help mind the shop, and to an accusation that the son was responsible for Carter's runaway slaves.[39]

In this region, where slave resistance was often regarded as a transgression of the Fifth Commandment—Honor thy father and thy mother—both slave and free acted as if each understood they had certain rights, duties, and responsibilities toward one another.[40] As the masters put it, "I must again desire you will keep Tommy strictly to his Duty & obedience," or "Cruelty to the poor slaves is a thing I always Abhored. I would think myself happy could I keep them to there [*sic*] duty without being Obliged to correct them." "Began this morning," Carter noted, "to enforce my resolution of correcting the drunkenes[s] in my family by an example on Nassau." When two runaways sent word to their master, Carter's neighbor John Tayloe, that they would not return unless he either hired them out or sold them, Tayloe replied, "I will do neither until they return to a sense of duty."[41]

Planters, who refused to give their intermediaries real power, personally and persistently intervened in all major aspects of the slaves' work and time off. "Set[ting] all the springs in motion," is the way Byrd put it.[42] To be successful in the declining world tobacco market, eighteenth-century planters had to be diligent estate managers. As they constantly rode over their plantations and out-quarters, they assigned tasks, doctored slaves, chose mates, and generally overlooked few opportunities to shove their Judeo-Christian values into the slaves' developing communities and worldviews. An assiduous attention to routine was typical of the tobacco aristocrats, whose exploits as managers demonstrate that the essence of truly paternalistic relations with slaves was the master's continual presence on the plantation and willingness to know each slave by name. Representative of Carter's notes of this kind are, "Made a Visit to my Plantation this day, that is, into every hole and corner of them," and "every toe has been as active as it could possibly be."[43]

Chesapeake Bay planters grew an array of crops, but at Sabine Hall tobacco was the staple, and one that required careful supervision.[44] More susceptible than either rice or sugar to injury or destruction through casual carelessness, tobacco in its early life-cycle was delicate. Grown to tender shoots in the warm and sheltered lees of south exposed slope, the seedlings were eventually pulled and rapidly transplanted to permanent beds at the optimum moment during a "season," a gentle spring rain. When the warm rain came, a gang of slaves with wheelbarrows rushed off to Carter's and neighboring planting beds, usually John Tayloe's at Mount Airy, to gather, transplant, and shape little hills around thousands of seedlings in receiving beds that had been carefully banked and manured. Great care was taken in "drawing" the fragile shoots, which were to be one size and "topwide with good roots below." During this operation, planters remained on the spot, commanding allegiance. If Carter disliked the receiving beds, fine-tuning and a last-minute drama was enacted: "Ordered Lawson to make his people with little small sticks break every clod to pieces" and cover down the beds with uprooted bushes. Still, about a third of the time a round of transplanting night and day was lost because the seasons quit unexpectedly, so the soil baked, hardened, and choked the shoots, and the entire process had to be repeated.[45]

Slaves also worked in corn and other crops during the late spring and through the summer. Then in the fall, with the harvest and the need to prepare the weed for shipment overseas, they had to contend again with an intensification of the planter's fussy and knowledgable surveillance. Riding by a tobacco house, Carter "smelt a very strong and putrid smell" and immediately ordered stalks for inspection (stalks of cut tobacco are hung upside down in drying sheds to allow the flavorsome resin to run down into the leaves). He did not want leaves from anywhere in the shed, rather those from "some sticks in the 3 tier . . . above the jo[y]ce and that below it [in] the 2d room from the gable end." The examination followed; the leaves were black and wet; stems swelled, wet, and rooted where they joined the stalk; and here too the weed smelt "strong and putrid." His instructions had been disobeyed concerning thinning and drying. The fat end of the stalk was to be put in the scaffolding, not the other way around.[46]

One of Carter's interminable counts included the note that a hand with a hoe may hill three thousand plants per day, in hard ground half that, or 1,500.[47] Such calculations dot the personal records of the planter-managers of the Chesapeake Bay region. Jefferson made them and so did Washington. At one level the Virginians' obsession with measures of productivity attests to fears that the slaves were taking advantage of them. At another level, however, the records indicate how hard and diligently these rich men worked for their money and the lengths to which they went in order to perfect systems to offset the slaves' quietly persistent acts of sabotage: "But as to all work I lay down this rule: My overseers tend their foreman close for one day in every Job; and deducting 1/5 of that day's work, he ought every other day to keep up to that. Therefore, by dividing every gang into good, Middling, and indifferent hands, one person out of each is to be watched for 1 day's work, and all of the same division must be kept to his proportion."[48]

The diary makes a dreary story of the field slaves' quiet but persistent attacks on productivity. Slaves, Carter complained, report ill every day but Sunday, which they considered a "holy day." Men who were supposed to be treading wheat slept while the boys who were left to do the job neglected it. Whether malingering or working, the planter was rarely satisfied with either the slaves or their "hare brained," "impudent" supervisors. Even though Carter would note "wenches running with baskets of Corn on their heads for more than a mile," he would record the slaves' "lazy sweat." Or, "I find it is almost impossible to make a negro do his work well."[49] "Every day," he sighed, "I discover, the sordidness of a Slave and the prodigeous thoughtlessness of Overseers,"[50] and "I believe my people [are] all out of their senses for I cannot get one of them to do a thing as I would have it and as they do it even in their own time they have it to do again immediately."[51]

The paternalistic role, which rich tobacco planters assumed more skillfully than planters did in the other regions, was a difficult one. While some, such as Robert Carter, played it with consummate skill, Landon Carter did not.[52] An embittered man, Jack Greene argues, Carter realized he had failed to impress his illustrious generation of the Revolutionary Era even though he was one of its most prolific political writers.[53] In the smaller world of his own plantation, Carter knew that "disciplining" slaves and instilling a sense of "duty" required discretion. However he was too mistrustful and too aggravated by the slightest threat to his person to carry off effectively and gracefully the role of patriarch in a large family, which extended outward from the home plantation to include the small up-country tobacco quarters, its hands, and its overseers.[54]

Still, Carter relaxed some and his voice changed before children, the elderly, and the ill. "Killed a fine mutton this day; ordered some broth for the sick. Nassau tells me they are all mending. I hope in God they are; . . . they are human creatures and my soul I hope delighteth in releiving them." This from a planter who said slaves were devils and should never be free. Indeed, moments of calm and security were few. The contests seldom ended. Carter kept coming back to the slaves — at work, or ill, or when they asked him to intervene in a spate — expecting gratitude or even a modicum of enthusiasm about their slavish existences. "My people seem to be quite dead hearted, and either cannot or will not work," and "I must declare I saw no care on my whole plantation, but everybody did what they pleased, Came, Went, Slept or worked as they would." After many years of this he felt like Ecclesiastes and wrote "corn fields tire as overseers do." After another run-in with a slave gardener, "too impudent and sawcy to follow orders," he noted "How to mend myself I cannot tell, as I am so old."[55]

The remaining case studies are of the period after the late-eighteenth-century revolutions in North America, France, and Haiti that ushered in the modern world, and with it abolitionism. The antislavery movement frightened Caribbean planters, who as colonists could not hide as easily as their mainland American counterparts from the philanthropic and evangelical movements that transformed English political culture. This is underlined by the remark of a Barbadian plantation manager who was unusually concerned about the welfare of the slaves under his supervision. Samson Wood, after ameliorating working conditions by erecting rain shelters for his field workers and proudly noting an increase of thirteen slave children, on writing the absentees John and Thomas Lane exalted righteously, "Let my Humanity... for a moment triumph. Go tell it to the Wilberforces."[56] His allusion was to William Wilberforce of Hull, a member of Parliament and an abolitionist, who had a reputation in West Indian slave quarters akin to that of Lincoln's among Southern blacks.

### Barbados (1790s): Samson Wood, Manager of Newton and Seawell Estates, St. Philips Parish

> Activity & exercise keep . . . me alive, 'tis the property of my constitution.
>                                                   — Samson Wood, 1801[57]

In 1803 three prominent planters appraised Newton and Seawell estates in Christ Church Parish, Barbados. They estimated the value of the adjoining estates' 441 slaves, sugar works, and crops on 802 acres to be £58,300 and added an unusual note for proceedings of this kind: that Samson Wood — the manager whose recent death was the occasion for the viewing — ought to be commended to the absentee proprietors John and Thomas Lane for his "humanity and Judgement."[58]

In his climb to the top at the two estates, Wood struggled first against an experienced and indulgent manager and next against a slave family of house servants and artisans dominated by Old Doll. Of his new wife, who aided Wood's rise, the proprietor was assured that the marriage had "injured no one," and that "nothing on Earth" would be done detrimental to his interest; she is *"your housekeeper"* and "a valuable acquisition to Us." Wood, who made an issue of living frugally and obsequiously reminding the proprietor of the same, wrote later that "Not an ounce of any thing have I touched, without charging myself for it, even to the very oats for my own horse." "The grass does not grow under my feet, all the country see

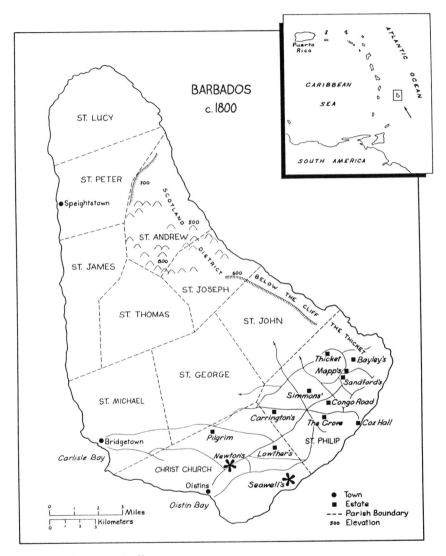

BARBADOS
c. 1800

ATLANTIC OCEAN

CARIBBEAN
SEA

Puerto
Rico

SOUTH AMERICA

ST. LUCY

ST. PETER

• Speightstown

SCOTLAND DISTRICT

ST. ANDREW

ST. JAMES

ST. JOSEPH

BELOW THE CLIFF

ST. JOHN

THE THICKET

ST. THOMAS

Thicket ■  ■ Bayley's
Mapp's ■
            ■ Sandford's
Simmons' ■
         ■ Congo Road
ST. GEORGE

Carrington's ■
         The Grove ■  ■ Cox Hall
ST. MICHAEL
                      ST. PHILIP
• Bridgetown
                Pilgrim ■
Carlisle Bay          Newton's ✳  Lowther's ■
        CHRIST CHURCH
                              Seawell's ✳
        Oistins •
Oistin Bay

| | Town |
| ■ | Estate |
| --- | Parish Boundary |
| 500 | Elevation |

0  1  2  3  Miles
0  1  2  3  Kilometers

Location of Newton Hall

that." While in route to the naval station in Jamaica, the absentees' younger brother visited and "look[ed] into everything." His report anticipated by a few years the appraisors': The slaves were "rapidly increasing, a certain sign of Happiness & good treatment," and Wood was "diligent and conscientious." In a house nearly bare of furniture, the brother concluded, Wood kept time with an hourglass and should be sent a proper clock in order to further bind him "to your Interest."[59]

Newton Estate was situated along the ridge that overlooks the south coast; Seawell lay at the foot of the ridge and had soil that was easier to work. Newton, however, enjoyed more reliable rainfall.[60] By the 1790s Seawell contained 344 acres, thirty-six of which were in sugarcane and ninety-four in cotton, which for a time in the 1790s was a popular crop along the south coast because it was considered to be less labor intensive than sugar. At Newton, half of its 458 acres were used for growing cane, and food crops dominated the remainder of the tillable land.

As part of an encyclopedic report he wrote in order to introduce the proprietors to Barbadian plantation life, Wood referred repeatedly to the estate plan. "Plans," as estate surveys or maps were called, were commissioned by proprietors who wished to sit at home yet still be in the picture while making decisions, as they did for their other estates in England or Ireland.[61] Both estates, Wood began, were divided into relatively small fields or "pieces" of five to ten acres and labeled *A* to *Z*. The fields of sugar estates, especially in compact Barbados, were kept small, squared, and laced with roads for easy access to the mill—the factory or "works." Cane that is cut and on the ground more than half an hour quickly looses its sweetness. From this fact, important features of an estate's layout and production routines followed as a matter of course.

Grouped in a huge square in the center of the estate, the sugar works included a mill, boiling house, curing houses, and distillery where the cane was crushed to make sugar and its by-products, rum and molasses. Of a size and complexity without equal on mainland tobacco and rice plantations, the factory required huge grinding stones driven by windmills or animals, extensive masonry for foundations and walls, highly specialized utensils, and the plumbing for the great and small vats. Mountains of dry, pulped cane refuse (*bagasse*) were needed to stoke around-the-clock fires that clarified and distilled. Wood also pointed out the hospitals, the stocks for locking up troublesome slaves, and the windmills that added to the factory character of the yard. Beyond the yard stood Wood's plain house, situated so a manager could "enjoy the sight of all the doors [of the factory] at one view."

There were other smaller, far less imposing buildings—some of stone, but most of Guinea grass and cane trash—"scattered about the hill looking picturesque and pretty amongst a few shrubs." The slaves who lived in these huts were important for the capital investment they represented as well as for their labor. They constituted a third of the appraised value of both estates, a fair increase from earlier appraisals. Because the estate was an old one, Africans were virtually unknown at Newton. Of 121 adults (fifty men and seventy-one women) only three were native Africans and the rest Creoles in a 1796 inventory. The few who were born outside the estate were very old, more than fifty, and longtime residents. Infants and children numbered 132.[62]

In this society of limited means, the old and the young were squeezed in order to increase productivity. As part of the "hogmeat" gang, young children collected fodder under the direction of an aged and decrepit governess. Several old men, living as watchmen in isolated huts on the wastes and margins of the fields, trapped rats and challenged trespasses by man and beast. Others were carpenters, coopers, and masons or boilers and firemen during crop time. But with the harvest nearly everyone at Newton (and in every sugar plantation account I have encountered), including artisans, were sent to the fields to cut and haul cane. Typically, proportionately more women than men served in the fields; other than working as housekeepers, cooks, or governesses in the hospitals or for the children, few women could ever expect to use a skill such as craftsmanship of one kind or another as a vehicle to escape regular field routine.[63]

Wood habitually pictured himself as the beleaguered but quick-stepping helmsman who overcame all in order to deliver cargo to his employers: "a moment at my pen, a moment at the coppers." By 1796 he had assumed sole control of both estates in what was not considered to be a good year: Newton produced fifty hogsheads of sugar, and Seawell, twelve thousand pounds of cotton. Wood felt compelled to explain himself more than he usually did. "I have not set a foot off of Newton for 10 weeks, not for an hour" except to cross over to Seawell.[64]

As for the proprietor's specific questions — "Now to answer yours para-graphically" — the manager next considered the slaves. They were "now & then" a little refractory because a previous supervisor had "relaxed Disci-pline" and because a decision of overseers at Seawell to cut allowances had "taught them to Steal." Thus Wood ordered "a little correction" which, he said, he had never done before; in time, with the help of such older slaves as George Saur, "order" was restored. That is, "by feeding them well . . . I have destroy'd some of the propensity to thieving & its consequence run[n]ing away."[65]

George Saur was an elderly artisan and member of the estate's most influential family. Headed by Old Doll, the family was described in the 1796 report as "those who have a kind of right to be idle," and who "remain at their ease and leisure" while receiving food and clothing allowances equal to the others. The source of the family's hold on the owners is not clear. Some were mulattoes; the family had leverage and at least one of the women journeyed to England, where she successfully petitioned the proprietors for her freedom. As for Saur, who was eventually rewarded with a handsome funeral at plantation expense, he did all he could to keep his kin "in some order." This was a task, for while he was successful with the boys and men and the matriarch kept to herself, the younger women, Mary Ann and Jenny, were "outrageous." Determined to reform them morally, Wood took the young women into his household as seamstresses. However, the women were soon turned out as "saucy & insolent." Shortly thereafter, one became a bookkeeper's lover and bore his child. Wood hired a white midwife, only to discover that Old Doll had "stood Granny," and that the baby soon died a few days after Wood was told she was "fine." I have a "confession," he reported, that the infant was "overlaid [smothered]."[66]

When another of Doll's family became the mistress of Wood's lenient predecessor, the move transformed the dull and mildly repressive social life at Newton. Dancing, cock fights, and gaming tables "were plentiful [and] ... every relaxation and debauchery was allowed." At this juncture, a young man of Doll's family, at the attorney's insistence, was convicted and executed on a second offense. This loss, which seemed to catch all off-guard, outraged the family, who may have helped ease the previous manager out of his job.[67]

Wood's accounts of the conflict with Doll's group are similar in tone to those of Landon Carter concerning his household people and favored artisans. Both Newton and Carter's Sabine Hall were self-contained; their slaves continually scrutinized; and Wood, like Carter, occasionally talked about slaves paternalistically: "I treat them as their father, yet preserve the strictest discipline" and "The grown-up ones are my friends, the young my children." Of course both planters seemed to command considerable power and authority, yet in practice they were often playing catch-up. For his part, Wood mixed harsh and indulgent strategies, and in the end decided that slaves were "the most extraordinary animals to deal with ... and there is no such thing as knowing their passions, propensities, or humours" from one day to the next.[68]

The manager's ambiguous rhetoric about managing slaves is as revealing as what Wood chose to report. He once explained that elderly slaves who had died were those who "really ... did nothing." This came in a request for heavy coats, "what the sailors call Dread-noughts," which he promised not to distribute unless it was damp or wet; "I cannot but have the most exquisite Sensibility of these Objects, who are administering to our support by their daily labour. They *should* have every comfort & every encouragement we could give them, that leads not to imprudence or indulgence too injurious to ourselves."[69] Slaves indeed require "strict Government," particularly those who are "never [to] be pleased." Sometimes he had to be outwardly "stern & firm," but while doing so, "my heart is melting" and "nature obliges me to run from the scene to my Chamber all dissolved in tears of bitter Grief."[70]

But to the old paternalistic rigmarole, another, novel, note was struck: how to link "humane" working conditions with efficient and profitable management strategies. Wood made "every modern improvement" in the sugar factory in order to "ease . . . the Negroes' convenience & utility." And where he once ordered a little correction with the whip, he now locked people up. Increasingly, the slaves were "under due order," gauged in part by how many reported sick. For Wood, order also meant that the slaves worked with "ease and with knowledge," which strikes another innovative note. If a Negro did not know his work or would not do it, "what good is fine weather and careful preparations." Finally, Wood even extended his ideas of "The management of the Negroes [which] is one of [the] great principle[s] of estate management" into the realm of slave leisure. He turned "Harvest Home," the traditional end-of-season celebration in Barbados, into a "sober dance."[71]

Wood's methods represent an early example of the rationalization of plantation routine, including new methods for punishing slaves, that characterized large nineteenth-century estates in both the antebellum South and in the Caribbean. In both regions, record keeping, more detailed and comprehensive than previous (and often on printed forms), was a feature of the push to maximize efficiency. This reform made it possible to pinpoint each slave's daily routine and, in the cotton South, each hand's productivity. Wood's records were a step in this direction:[72]

| | |
|---|---|
| 5 May. | |
| Negroes in the lst Gang holeing for Indian Corn | 54 |
| watching | 3 |
| tying up Trash | 12 |
| Sick: Mingo, Toney, Lilly, Judy, Hester | |
| Bellah, Toubah, & Peggy | 7 |
| Lineing Land to hole for Canes | 3 |
| in the Distilling House | 3 |
| Takeing care of two Cows | 1 |
| " of Betty Hannah | 1 |
| With the Carters | 5 |
| total | 89 |
| Negroes 2nd Gang heaping up Cane tops | 18 |
| Carrying Trash for Distillery House | 1 |

| With the Cart | | 1 |
| Sick, Baram and Phillis | | 2 |
| | total | 22 |

| Negroes in the third Gang picking meat for the Stock | 46 |

It is difficult to see the slaves in this estate's record. The manager, however, did let slip once that they considered him "an oddity" and had "prophicied . . . long before" he caught the fever that eventually killed him. Troubled as well by an unspecified financial embarrassment, Wood sailed to England to put his case to the proprietors. This lot, currishly insensitive to how well he had served them, kept the sick man at arm's length as the Barbadian, suffering in an English winter—"the cold punishes me most vilely"—took the waters at Tunbridge Wells before dying discreetly at a cabinetmaker's near Goodge Street off Tottenham Court Road.[73]

## Jamaica (1816): Gregory 'Monk' Lewis: The Absentee as Outsider

> I care nothing about rank in life, nothing about what other people may think or may say; and have always, both in my public writings and private life, shown (what Mr. Pitt was pleased to call) pleasure in spitting in the face of public opinion. I live as much with actors, and musicians, and painters, as with princes and politicians. . . . But I absolutely require that people should possess some quality or other to amuse me or interest me, or I had rather be by myself. . . . being bored is to me positive torture.
>
> And so much for negro gratitude![74]

Coming ashore in the West Indies for the first time, Thistlewood had found the scenery "grotesque," the blacks' music "odd" and a nuisance, and the town women inviting. Arriving a half-century later, on the other side of 1789 and in the Romantic Era, Matthew Gregory "Monk" Lewis, of the literary and theater groups of London, found the new scenery "picturesque." Confronted by the slaves' John Canoe pageant, he plunged into the crowd before commenting appreciatively on the parade's "Set Girls," who were costumed in rival colors, the red and the blue, of the British admirals of the Jamaica naval station.[75]

The plantations of Lewis and Thistlewood were a few miles outside of the Savannah la Mar. On them society was in part shaped by contrasting terrains and their degree of development. Thistlewood had come to a raw frontier and settled on the swampy borders of the lower Cabaritta River,

Matthew Gregory "Monk" Lewis (National Portrait Gallery, London)

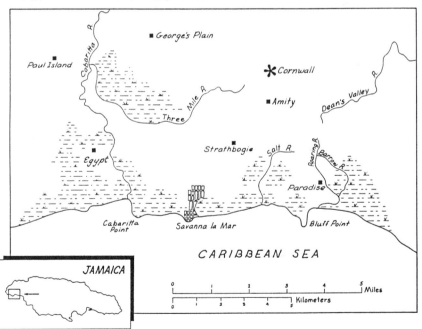

Location of Cornwall Estate

whereas Lewis's Cornwall Estate was higher and drier in a neighborhood that in a half century had become quiet and settled. For Lewis, "maroon" meant a way of cooking pig and turtle by barbeque, with coals, hot stones, and smoke rather than fire.[76]

Lewis viewed flogging as the intolerable root evil. Remove it, and the plantation system may be completely reformed. Disliking beatings intensely, as if to say 'how may one whip someone you know personally,' he severely chastized a house slave for boxing the slave's niece about the ears. After all, it was "base," Lewis said, for a man to strike a woman. Thistlewood had whipped women as well as men. For him, flogging slaves was only of passing interest, after which he sometimes readied himself for a tramp or fishing expedition with those he had recently beaten. He and the clerks coupled promiscuously with the slave women; Lewis ordered that any employee who meddled with a woman was to be discharged instantly. The two planters do stand on either side of a divide — the French Revolution and abolitionism. None of the sacred fundamentals of the modern liberal creed — the inviolability of the individual, the enormity of violence — are present in Thistlewood's writing.[77]

"Blacks are wiser now, massa," than they were. Slaves had also changed in the interval of sixty years. Their dances, which Thistlewood habitually attributed to particular ethnic groups and could not completely separate from the throbbing drums of Coramantee risings, had by Lewis's time become a rich multicultural melange of African and European modes. Now the cutting edge of cultural innovation, of music and dancing at the least, was urban. Black town women constructed ornate costumes for entertainments in which groups or bands displayed elements of the British navy or Brittania with scepter rode on a car. Jumping up for Carnival (before Peter Minshall) as Plains Indians, U.S. sailors, or Humphrey Bogart seemed only a short step away.

Nonetheless, Lewis discovered that off the streets and in the more private areas of slave existence old meanings persisted:

> I asked one of my Negro servants this morning whether old Luke was a relation of his.
> "yes," he said.
> — "Is he your uncle, or your cousin?"
> — "No, massa."
> — "What then?"
> — "He and my father were shipmates, massa."[78]

In the early-nineteenth-century Jamaican towns of Lewis's journal, slave music and dance were Creole, that is, mixed. However, plantation politics in many ways remained ethnic. Concerning slaves who came to him with complaints, it was "the whole body of Eboes" who also lived in their own district at Cornwall; the drums that beat incessantly on weekends were Ibo gombays; and the leader of an 1816 plot was an "Eboe King."[79]

Lewis's slaves used him, enjoyed him, laughed at him. As an artist and outsider in his native England, he was able to enter into their lives to a surprising degree. They called him, variously, "tatta" and "husband." We should not be put off by Lewis's mannered posturing, however. He was a keen and sympathetic observer, and, like Thistlewood, he recorded information that others ignored.[80]

Byron described Lewis as "a jewel of a man" but "pestilently prolix and paradoxial and personal." A temperament so self-consciously idiosyncratic — yet conventional too in other ways of which Lewis himself was unaware — makes his useful journal a personal testimony whose biases may be misconstrued unless something is known of its author. Lewis was a friend of Scott, Lord Byron, and Tom Moore when they were at the height of their fame. Friendships with "actors" grew out of his experience of staging his own melodramas. Getting ghosts on stage and corpses off were problems more real to him than the economies of monoculture. Lewis mentioned that his grandfather was buried on Cornwall Estate in "a family mausoleum, which looks for all the world like the theatrical representation of the 'tomb of all the Capulets.' " His own wealth, however, seems actually to have been derived from his father's career as deputy secretary of war. Lewis had a political life as well, but it was brief and uneventful. From 1796 to 1802 he was a silent and seldom present M.P. for Hindon, Wiltshire. Lewis's predecessor in the post was another Jamaica heir, William Beckford, the author of *Vathek.* There is no evidence of their personal acquaintance, but Lewis was already, like Beckford, a novelist of garish and tainted celebrity.[81]

In 1794, as a nineteen-year-old attaché to the British embassy at The Hague and "horribly bit by the rage for writing," Lewis exorcised "the devil *ennui*" by dashing off, in ten weeks, his one novel, *The Monk.* A brisk montage of every gothic cliche — cloisters, dungeons, the Inquisition, a Faustain pact, the Bleeding Nun, the Wandering Jew, rape, incest, and blasphemy — it still gets a line in histories of English literature. More of a novelty in 1795, "the Monk is a romance, which if a parent saw in the hands of a son or a daughter, he might reasonably turn pale" wrote Coleridge in 1797. In 1800, however, *The Monk* [Le moine] was rated the best of the English gothic novels by the Marquis de Sade. Alarmed at the prospect of a prosecution for blasphemy, Lewis revised and expurgated the novel's second edition, but for the rest of his life he was "Monk" Lewis, committed to permanent unconventionality.[82]

Lewis's motive for visiting the two Jamaica estates he had inherited on the death of his father — an absentee — was pure "humanity." He expected by his mere presence to redress not merely the slaves' grievances but also the evils of the system itself. There is an airy bohemeian irresponsibility about his humanitarianism. Forbidding the use of the "execrable cart-whip," he reflects: "and if the estate must go to rack and ruin without its use, to rack and ruin the estate must go."[83]

Every contemporary who knew Lewis comments on his generosity, attentiveness, and benevolence. He believed in paternalism and practiced it. In 1816, between his first and second visit to Jamaica, he revised his will, stipulating that his heir must spend three months there every three years. In 1818, during the return voyage after his second visit, he died of yellow fever. He did, thereby, achieve a sort of martyrdom to his love for humanity. His journal, covering the years from 1815 to 1817, reads at times like the synopsis of an opera: the drama of a planter's relations with his slaves. It is a drama motivated by his longing for affection and by the slaves' quick perception of his need.

Coming on to Cornwall Estate (of 3,600 acres and about three hundred slaves), Lewis was touched by his welcome. As he wrote his mother, "Nothing could equal the rapture of the poor people—the shouts . . . the wild laughter, their strange and sudden bursts of singing and dancing." And "twenty voices at once enquired after uncles, and aunts, and grandfathers, and great-grandmothers of mine, who had been buried long before I was in existence. . . . [One] complained,—'So long since none come see we, Massa; good Massa, come at last.' As for the old people, they were all in one and the same story: now they had lived once to see Massa, they were ready for dying to-morrow, 'them no care.' "[84]

This demonstrative welcome is familiar. Fanny Kemble, a London actress of the same ambient as Lewis, described a similar scene a few years later at her absentee husband's Georgia sea island plantation.[85] And, like Lewis, Kemble sensed that the slaves would soon expect "benefits" for warm greetings. Lewis doubted the slaves' sincerity but without bitterness, because this theatrical stylization of feeling is precisely what he understood and enjoyed—underlining the importance of expectations and values owners brought with them and, as slaves noted repeatedly, the importance of an owner's temperament:

> All this may be palaver; but certainly they at least play their parts with such an air of truth, and warmth, and enthusiasm, that, after the cold hearts and repulsive manners of England, the contrast is infinitely agreeable. . . . I find it quite impossible to resist the fascination of the conscious pleasure of pleasing; and my own heart, which I have so long been obliged to keep closed, seems to expand itself again in the sunshine of the kind looks and words which meet me at every turn. . . .[86]

Lewis believed that the slaves did not have to work hard except for the one month when cane holes were dug and manured, when, in any case, a jobbing gang was hired. "I am assured that many of my slaves are very rich and their property is 'inviolable.'" As far as he could see, the only evils of slavery were physical cruelty, the petty tyranny of drivers and bookkeepers, the negligence of attorneys, and the ignorance of absentee proprietors like his father.[87]

Insofar as Lewis's objectives were purely humanitarian, he was successful. At the end of his first three months' stay, he promulgated a new code of laws that regulated and restricted the white managers' power to punish and substituted incarceration for the whip as the normal punishment for skiving and malingering. He received "profuse . . . expressions of gratitude" and, returning two years later, was pleased to find that his slaves had not a single complaint to make. Of the baffling duplicity inherent in the slaves' desire to please, he wrote, "now when I see a mouth grinning from ear to ear with a more than ordinary expansion of jaw, I never fail to find, on enquiry, that its proprietor is one of those who have been punished during my absense." Before leaving Jamaica for the last time, Lewis played the part of his peoples' law-giver, fixing punishments for all future time and settling the slaves' property disputes. They treated him like a king: "I must acknowledge, however, that the negro principle that 'massa can do no wrong,' was of some little assistance to me on this occasion." He went home happy. His slaves had given him what he wanted: "gratitude, affection, and goodwill."[88]

Lewis was soon in considerable trouble, however, on another front. The local assize court cited him for being overindulgent, interceding on behalf of slaves with his neighbors, and, worst, for putting abroad "dangerous doctrines." The locals also realized that Lewis held that Negro evidence should be heard in court. Much of this was pardonable by the early 1800s, but what the slaves did with Lewis's reputation in the quarters was far more threatening and precisely what they made of news of the abolition debate in England a generation later on the eve of the 1831 insurrection in the same western parishes. A story circulated that Good King George III and Wilberforce had given Lewis a paper that set slaves free, but that once in Jamaica, Lewis was prevented from showing the document, which slaves thereafter called "The Free." The whites' action was an error because it was also believed that at home in England Lewis was a big man who occupied a great chair that was filled temporarily in his absence by the prince regent.[89]

A gaudy flower grew out of this luxuriant growth. Conspirators elected an Ibo king, and slaves developed songs some considered subversive. As was his habit when he struck a serious pose, Lewis went out into the neighborhood and listened to what the slaves were actually singing. He concluded, "as far as I can make out," the songs deal only with the slaves' private situation and not at all with slavery in general. Or so they seemed to be at least when he was around. The little children screamed about the estate, "We varry well off." What the grown people sang was somewhat different. Phillis, "the family minstrel," interpreted for him, and Lewis decided he preferred the music of the Iboes of Black River to that of his "Cornwall bards" because the former attempted rhyme and meter.

NEGRO SONG AT CORNWALL

Hey-ho-day! me no care a dammee!. . .
Me acquire a house. . .
Since massa come see we — oh!

Hey-ho-day! neger now quite eerie, . . .
For once we see massa — hey-ho-day!
When massa go, me no care a dammee,
For how them usy we — hey-ho-day![90]

Lewis interlined his translations: "dammee" as "a damn"; "having a house" as "I have a solid foundation to build on"; and "eerie" as "hearty," which earlier on he called "buckish."

Lewis distributed money, clothes, favors, and attention, increased holidays, and dismissed unpopular bookkeepers. He promulgated "a new code of laws," introduced plows, oxen, and stud bulls, and built a new hospital. However, the "awkwardness" and the "obstinacy" of the slaves frustrated the project to substitute oxen for manpower, "They broke plough after plough, and ruined beast after beast, till the attempt was abandoned in despair." All the stud bulls were dead within a fortnight of their arrival.[91] The women workers then struck unanimously, and production fell.

> The negroes certainly are perverse beings. They had been praying for a sight of their master year after year; they were in raptures at my arrival; I have suffered no one to be punished, and shown them every possible indulgence during my residence amongst them; and one and all they declare themselves perfectly happy and well treated. Yet, previous to my arrival, they made thirty-three hogsheads a week; in a fortnight after my landing, their product dwindled to twenty-three; during this last week they have managed to make but thirteen. Still they are not ungrateful; they are only selfish: they love me very well, but they love themselves a great deal better. . . .[92]

Lewis was an experienced reformer by the time he swooped down on Hordley, his estate in St. Thomas in the East Parish. He first distributed a little money, a few "play-days," and then settled in and listened to the slaves' grievances. Next came major personnel changes: he removed the attorney, physician, four bookkeepers, and four drivers; and, to constrain the overseers' brutalities, he published a list of punishments per offense.[93] On the return voyage, which Lewis did not survive, he recorded the Coramantees' Anancy/Spider stories.[94] Shortly thereafter he died and was buried at sea.

## A Georgia Rice Plantation (1833–67): Charles and Louis Manigault's Gowrie

> We have lived to witness Strange times.
> — Louis Manigault,
> November 1861[95]

In 1833 Charles Manigault, the heir of an old and wealthy South Carolina Huguenot family, purchased a Georgia rice plantation. Located on a small island in the lower Savannah River a few miles upstream from the port of that name, Gowrie comprised 220 acres of improved rice land, eighty acres of woodland, and fifty slaves. To buy the site Manigault, an absentee who lived in South Carolina, paid $20,000 cash (from the sale of bank stock) and "made use of all my mercantile knowledge to make the place pay the other half" of the $40,000 purchase price. Later he wrote proudly that in fourteen years the plantation had paid for itself at least twice. In the meantime his slaves doubled the original size of the rice fields to more than five hundred acres, to which in 1848 he added East Hermitage, an adjoining tract. Initially progress was slow, however, and for some slaves deadly. In the first year they made about two hundred barrels of rice — eventually they often produced twice that amount — the next year cholera killed eight. "But I stuck to it," Manigault said, "& did not despair."[96]

After 1852 Charles Manigault's son, Louis, lived on Gowrie for six months when malarial mosquitoes were not in season. The father, who seems never to have set foot on the place, worried about appearances. He wished to show the neighborhood that he was knowledgeable and attentive to detail. Order the best cloth available for the slaves' clothing is a theme in several directives to various local managers. He also fussed about the garden and fence around the dwelling house and about a new tidal-powered mechanical thresher: "My anxiety on the subject arose from the strong desire I always feel of carrying on every branch of my planting interest on Savannah River in the most triumphant & successful manner."[97]

Land reclamation and pounding machinery made rice plantations costly enterprises that soaked up quantities of labor and money. Capitalization took at least $50,000, and could go as high as $500,000, for outlays that included the largest slave settlements in the antebellum South. In the 1860 census twenty of the seventy-four plantations across the South with three hundred

Charles Manigault

Louis Manigault

SOUTH CAROLINA

Charleston

Port Royal
Beaufort

Ogeechee R.

Savannah R.

Argyle Island

*Gowrie
Plantation*

Savannah

ATLANTIC OCEAN

Altamaha R.

GEORGIA

Sunbury

Satilla R.

**GEORGIA
c. 1850**

Okefenokee
Swamp

St. Mary's R.

Suwanee R.

FLORIDA

St. John's River

St. Augustine

| 0 | 10 | 20 | 30 | 40 | 50 |
Miles
| 0 | 10 | 20 | 30 | 40 | 50 |
Kilometers

Location of Gowrie Plantation

to five hundred slaves, eight of the thirteen with five hundred to a thousand slaves, and the only plantation with more than a thousand slaves were rice plantations situated on a strip of coastal plain that extended from Georgetown on the north, seventy miles south to Charleston, and southward beyond the Savannah River and through the Georgia sea islands.[98]

Channeled by an elaborate system of levees, canals, and drainage ditches, the tides pushed fresh water onto the rice fields and through the mills that were geared to the harvesting "engines." Rice plantations, like sugar estates, had "works," rudimentary factories, which also made it easy for slaves to be difficult. "Our machine," Manigualt said, has "to contend against all kinds of contrariété," and, more drastically, "I presume like many other things where Negroes are concerned, that manual labor is better than any out of the way attempt at machinery." As for the slave overseer stationed at the feeder rollers, he "will never call out to them to feed up unless he thinks that he is watched by any one." Manigault concluded with a sigh heard from Sabine Hall to Cornwall Estate, "and so it goes!"[99]

Nonetheless, rice harvesting at Gowrie was mechanized, and slaves worked the machines. The thresher, the best on the river, was Manigault's pride. "Its motion is so powerful & irresistable — so regular, & yet working with ease, & apparently requiring so little motive impulse." When the tides were right, and the thrasher's primitive rollers and belts worked because they were fed properly, the machine was far more productive than the ancient rice coast method of beating grain from the stalk with flails.[100]

Machinery encouraged rationalization in other areas, including the most important one, work rates and their accountability: "Amount threshed is 13,680 [lbs.] (1846) against 13,390 (1845) exclusive of seed. So the difference in favour of the crop of 1846 is 370 [290] bushels, and the time saved is just 28 days."[101] And, "while 10 Bushels per hand on the threshing floor is a day's task still that one day with another throughout the season the average is not more than 7 Bushels of threshed Rice to the hand so that my force say 35 flail sticks at 7 Bush[els] each is 245 per day. So that if you beat out with the thresher 490 per day (& only by the day's tide) this will be double, while all the men are out at important field work — this is a triumph!"[102]

The "labor-saving" machines, on the other hand, made it easier to push slaves into the most difficult task of any in the three regions, constructing and repairing a hundred acres of embankments and seventy-five miles of ditches, sluice, and trunk canals that defined the fields or "pieces." Absentees and managers wrote continually about individual pieces: "we have the Nos. 9, 10, 11, 12, & 13 ditched out. . . . and we are now at work on the No. 10 cutting down some of those high hills & throwing the earth in the creek." Weak spots in a section's levee were especially noteworthy, and in time acquired a character of their own. Shaped by a sharp bow of the river, number 12 would someday cut through; the break would come during a flood, or "freshet," which "are really awful." The first flood Manigault experienced "really scared [him] pretty well."[103] Freshets caused "blow outs"; as a flood coursed through a plantation with awesome and uncontrollable power, it often blew out huge levees, sluice gates, and great wooden trunks the size of automobiles. One break was described as forty feet wide, twenty-four feet deep, and at its bottom only sand "& that kind of boiling."[104]

Floods came in the spring, when planters repeatedly checked the river off their docks for the size of debris. If "No trash at all," they knew that upstream the river was not boiling over its banks and gathering the flotsom that downstream would root and tear. But when the natural reservoirs (the inland swamps) brimmed and high water threatened upstream off Augusta, the sound of the river at Gowrie became a deep sucking rumble as it tossed huge, cruising logs as if they were sticks. The slaves then collected drinking water and put the Great House "in freshet order." One Sunday evening, expecting trouble, Manigault was relieved to find only "a few Chips" in the river. But the next day his island was hit hard. "The Plantation looks like some old ship that has just weathered a Gale, & all battered & bruised about."[105]

The river nourished as well, however. Incoming ocean tides pushed onto fields the fresh water that was channeled by the canal system that controlled the successive floodings and drainings that drowned weeds and fed the tender shoots of rice. Kept erect by the flow and barely above it, the shoots were open to the sun while protected from the voracious rice birds and rats that swarmed at this time. The river also teemed with fish and shellfish that slaves added to a diet of corn, molasses, and—during the harvest—bacon sides. For warmth and cooking fires, slaves crossed the river to cut firewood on an adjoining island reserved for that purpose. Wood was precious and used to cook and heat rooms in drafty cabins in numbing midwinter. Wood fires helped prevent "Peunomonia—that dreadful disease, from which we all suffer so much on Sav[anna]h River."[106]

But cholera, a water-born disease, not pneumonia, was the principal killer. Claiming at least thirty-eight victims in twenty years from 1834 to 1854, it thrived at Gowrie, where reclamation projects made the plantation a latticework of drainage ditches. One ditch ran as an open sewer through the slaves' settlement, another was for drinking water. Returning with his people from an upland retreat following an epidemic, Louis asked his father for a supply of soap and noted that ducks no longer lived about the slaves' houses nor swam in ditches that had not been cleaned in years—nor could they be, as he reckoned, lest they release a noxious vapor. The causes of cholera were unknown, but the plantation people sensed that filth, water, and disease were somehow linked and realized that the place was dangerously unhealthy. At one point when Lewis completed a ledger that included slave deaths, he wrote: "c. stands for Cholera," and "this List fills me with melancholy as I recall some sad scenes."[107]

Like other big antebellum plantation operations, Gowrie was organized by a comprehensive set of regulations as a substitute for Manigault's presence.[108] The island setting contributed to confining rules. No slaves were to work outside. The plantation boat was to be used only to carry supplies and seek medical help, others were to be locked up, not at the landing but beneath the house. As for "Negro boats" or canoes found on the place, they were to be "Cut" (set adrift) or locked in the mill. Overseers were also enclosed. None were to be hired who were from "the Carolina, or Georgia shore, or whose family resides anywhere on or near the Savannah River," Manigault wrote, otherwise they would continually visit elsewhere.[109] Following an old lowcountry tradition of rich planters who usually had more than one estate, Manigault preferred managers who lived off the premises and on the plantations of their chief employment. A nonresident manager was suitable, he reasoned, because Gowrie was small, compact, and could be overlooked by a walk-through twice a day concluded by an evening session with the driver to set up the next day's work.

The regime of a rice slave was unique in Anglo-America. Lowcountry slaves worked in tasks, not in gangs, and so worked more at their own pace under black supervisors and were free to leave the field when a day's task was finished. However, this routine did not loosen the whites' authority which, before the Civil War, was never seriously challenged. Runaways "without cause" were usually sold, and other rebellious slaves were punished on the plantation, either by example and ridicule, or more drastically, they were sent off to solitary confinement in the public jail at Savannah. "Now see how easy it is to fix 'a bad disposed nigger' " sets the proper tone for the Manigaults' casually confident manner when confronted by troublesome slaves.[110]

"You a[l]luded to one or two fractious negroes," Charles Manigault advised his son. "The way to fix them" is to tie their hands in front and have them waiting in the provision room when the others file in and assemble. "Preach them a short sermon on the propriety of Conduct, & make the Driver proceed with them." Concerning Jacob, the old man lectured, bear in mind that old plantation maxim "never to threaten a Negro." If you do, he will run, and if "a Negro succeeds in dodging & running from you, the annoyance is great." Wait for a chance to tie him up, when he is with the driver. Then jail him in Savannah for three weeks, "when he will be glad to get home again." Before he is released, have the jailers "jog his memory [whip him] again." Give Jacob "my Compliments . . . & tell him that you wrote to me of his conduct, & I say if he don't change for the better, I'll sell him to a slave trader who will send him to New Orleans."[111]

The Manigaults "fixed" slaves without a paternalistic regard for whether they were women or men. "I found Betty & Margaret apparently in a state of true repentance," a manager wrote after picking them up from the Savannah jail. He noted that they were allowed "to go to the fire, as it was very cold"; otherwise, they had been in solitary confinement, without a fire and whipped periodically. Returned to Gowrie after this ordeal, the women were considered to be well "cooled." A sense of what the cold was like (to say nothing of the beatings) is conveyed in an overseer's note written a few days later with hands so numbed he could barely hold the pen while reporting that the slaves were "coughing, blowing, sneezeing and shivering."[112]

Although most recaptured runaways were sold, two others were imprisoned in a hole in the ground for three months on Silk Hope, the Manigault's home plantation in South Carolina. Occasionally, Charles Manigault strolled out after dinner so he could hear the men plead to get out. Once he took with him a few Gowrie Negroes who were visiting Silk Hope and asked the prisoners if they had any "commands" that could be taken back to Gowrie.[113]

In this oppressed community with few of the paternalistic bonds that allegedly characterized antebellum slavery elsewhere, the coming of the Civil War gave slaves an opportunity to express another side of their "well disposed" natures. Ten men, three forceably, were removed from Gowrie shortly after Union gunboats invaded the sea islands. It was feared they would probably run away — or organize.

With the coming of the war, resistance increased significantly. Its nature changed, and the Manigaults' comments about the problem assumed a Jamaican character during major maroon disturbances. One day the whites seemed carefree and confident, the next they were profoundly depressed and expected to be murdered in their beds. "Every thing on the plantation, and as far as the eye Can reach, is going on in our usual quiet manner, and the News Paper . . . alone indicates that we are having troubles in our midst." Then two paragraphs further on is a note that the Christmas holidays are "always a very bad time for Negroes, and it is always a God-Send . . . when that Holyday is over," especially this year.[114]

In summer 1861, relations at Gowrie began to come apart. Betsey, the nurse, poisoned several children at the cholera camp. Running away increased considerably, and professional slave catchers searched the slaves' cabins, where at a former driver's they uncovered weapons and gunpowder. From this point, both Manigaults talked incessantly about Hector and Jack Savage. The latter, who had spent time in the hole, was eventually sold (and when the war ended returned to his family). Louis was afraid of Savage, and believed that he was capable of murder and might burn the house down. Charles wrote that after the war planters would have to find a new method of governing Negroes, to which his son replied in so many words, Was it all worth it? At war's end he noted in his journal, "We are all resolved never to have a Negro in our house again."[115]

Yet Gowrie carried on, even though by February 1862 the sea islands were occupied by the Union army, called locally "the Abolitionists." The crop that year made $16,030.88, and near the end, March 1864, the slaves were still inclined to plant three hundred acres in rice.

Two and a half years later during Reconstruction, Louis Manigault made a painful and nostalgic return. He brought along his young son and name-sake, "that hereafter in life he might remember it." A freak tide prevented the usual water passage up river, so the little party traveled overland from Savannah and stopped first at the old Potter mansion, the grandest on the river. Its new tenant was recently a Union general, and his foremen those who had once been leaders at Gowrie, Driver John, Big Hector, George, and Charles, the trunk-minder. Manigualt talked to neighborhood blacks, heard "River News," and sent word he would like to visit his former slaves and Gowrie. The party moved on.[116]

"The cruel hand of War was now clearly to be seen . . . a few remaining brick of the foundations." Some fields were flooded ("Negro negligence")— he blamed Savage, who was asleep in his house. The current was unusually swift. Manigault asked to be carried over, George called him Massa and did so. George's wife, Betty—"she always bore a good character"—took charge of his young son. She built a fire, dried clothing, and boiled eggs, all to the youngster's delight. The men black and white pushed on. Ancient plantation trees lay devastated, Manigault listed them and when they were planted. As for the large double houses for Negroes, they were "wilderness." From out of them, however, came a few, not sure how to act. Some shook the planter's hand and called him by name: "Wha mek you no come back? . . . a Massy! You tink I can lib in de Chimney."[117]

Manigault led the way. "I imagined myself for the moment a Planter once more as if followed by Overseer and Driver." And the women? They were not as forthcoming. "Why not! after all I did for them"—shoes, ear rings, calicoes, and kerchiefs. "They were once pleased to greet me, but now not even lifting the head as I passed."[118]

As examples of styles of plantation authority, of ways of getting slaves to work as efficiently as possible, the case studies may be divided between those of Samson Wood and Monk Lewis, on the one hand, and Carter, Thistlewood, and the Manigaults on the other. Although there is some overlapping, in practice the former can be said to have used rewards and incentives to motivate, whereas the latter used the threat or actuality of physical violence—sale, beatings, the stocks, and solitary confinement in a public jail or a hole in the ground—in order to keep slaves in line. In the first instance, where power and authority were more disguised and diffused than in the second, there was an element of persuasion and consent in the acquiescence of slaves, who presumably made choices and imposed sanctions on themselves as features of their incorporation.

Expressing process as either-or is to put difficult matters too simply, however. Nor is discussion of why most plantation slaves did not rebel satisfactory until the slaves' own institutions and values are considered. The development of these features shifted abruptly in the early nineteenth century as agricultural reformers perfected new ways of regimenting slave lives.

# 5

# "Scientific" Planters: The Ideology of Industrial Regimentation in Mature Slave Societies

> Unfortunately, power and its concomitant, efficiency, were qualities which the Old European Order [1660–1800] could not provide, or could not provide consistently. Thus the Revolution, when it came, liberated Governments and rulers as well as peoples.
> — John Kenyon, 1979

> When the planters became more "accurate," they subordinated every human concern to the single goal of production.
> — David Brion Davis, 1974[1]

Were planters capitalists or medieval seigneurs, that is, forward or backward looking? This useful question is part of a larger controversy, the nature of antebellum society and the coming of the Civil War.[2] If war came as an irreconcilable clash between two qualitatively different leadership classes, a Northern bourgeoise whose relations with its factory workers were capitalist versus a Southern seigneurial aristocracy that ruled paternalistically, then the South may be seen as having made by 1860 a unique way of life. But, if as Barrington Moore, Jr., among others argue, North and South were essentially varieties of capitalism, one commercial and industrial, the other agricultural, then the argument that the Civil War was an encounter between rival civilizations is meaningless.[3]

Patterns of resistance and accommodation by plantation slaves are part of the problem in this fashion: To regard the Southern planter's authority as impersonal and bureaucratic, as it was in Northern factories, is to reinforce the view of both regions and their leaders as modern and capitalist, and so as highly comparable. But to argue that paternalism effectively stifled resistance complements views that planters were outmoded. This chapter pursues the argument that planters were indeed modern and capitalist and does so by looking at a neglected aspect of planter ideology — concepts of agricultural reform that sought to organize slave life totally. This goal, which ought to be viewed comparatively, in the South was embodied in "Management of Negroes" articles in antebellum agricultural journals and new printed ledger books meant to rationalize comprehensively plantation accounts and operations.[4]

New World planters were caught up in the pervasive middle-class reform movement that swept through Western nations following 1815. In commercial and industrial areas, reformers sought disciplined self-control through safer, cleaner cities (with lights, channelled sewage, and a professional constabulary) and God-fearing, sober, and punctual factory workers. In plantation areas reform followed basic regional differences in slave life and the degree to which it was controlled by the routines and supervision styles that had been worked out through time between whites and blacks. In the South, where whites had matters well in hand, reformers could contend with the basic issue of how to increase production, whereas West Indians were forced to reform reproduction. With the abolition of the slave trade, what were the best methods, they asked, for maintaining slave numbers by enhancing the fertility of slave women and the care of their infants?

The issue, in both regions, is not the extent to which concepts and practice were one (although slave life on big antebellum plantations probably was increasingly regimented), but what the techniques themselves say about the modern, as opposed to the precapitalist, character of master–slave relations.

While a concern of reformers everywhere was the control of slave time off, the perceptions and practice of slave "leisure" differed significantly from one region to the other. Slave mobility, meaning movement on and off the plantation, was massive, ordinary and unchallenged in the Caribbean, where there never was a pass and patrol system comparable to its more rigorous equivalent in the South. Thistlewood, for instance, lived in a dangerous time and neighborhood, yet his and surrounding plantations were remarkably porous to a measureable degree. "No for play" Thistlewood numbered passes and totaled them yearly on the inside covers of his journals (while complaining that his neighbors with scores more slaves simply ignored the pass system altogether). Year to year, scores made hundreds of trips off the various plantations in Thistlewood's charge, and they did so in a leeward neighborhood that was wide-open on weekends when few slaves remained on estates if they desired to be elsewhere. Unsupervised slave gatherings occurred to such an extent that on one occasion a newspaper item mentioned a rural market of more than a thousand slaves. No record comparable to Thistlewood's has come to light for a Southern plantation, but the experiences of the slaves in the case studies for the South were probably not exceptional. Other than favorites and the odd slave allowed to have and visit a mate nearby, large groups of slaves did not travel regularly on their own business as well as pleasure as in the Caribbean.[5]

Contrasting regional traditions concerning slave leisure and mobility were ultimately based upon how well owners knew each of their slaves and what that familiarity meant to them. To make the plantation one's only home, as most Southern planters did, was to care about perceptions that one was in control of orderly slaves. By contrast, in the Caribbean, where absenteeism was rampant, especially among the largest slave holdings, planters did not carry on as if they identified with each slave's behavior or the collective reputation of a gang. Absenteeism, however, in the South increased during the antebellum era. Owners of the largest concentrations of slaves per unit (where increasingly most of the eventually four million antebellum slaves came to live) were absent much of the time, especially in areas of sizeable holdings of slaves (more than three hundred): the rice coast and the sugar region south of Baton Rouge, where more than 60 percent of the plantations by the 1850s were partnerships. Consequently, as in the Caribbean, Southern labor relations became increasingly impersonal and bureaucratic.

Schemes to organize slave lives to a degree unknown in the colonial era were now attractive to owners, who regarded them as substitutes for their constant presence on the plantation and were no longer as reluctant to delegate real authority as their colonial counterparts had been. For their part, "scientific" reformers, understanding that large planters were no longer paternalistic fathers of families black and white but managers of businesses that happened to be agricultural, offered programs to regiment and motivate slaves in order to maximize profitability.[6]

That large plantations were incompatible with the old familial and paternal character of slavery during the colonial era was the argument of "Farmer," who wrote a "Management of Negroes" article from Virginia, the archetypal paternalistic society. "True paternalism," according to Farmer, could only work on small units where owners resided and participated in management. Frederick Law Olmsted, the most prescient of antebellum travelers, picked up the theme of size and treatment.

> As a general rule, the larger the body of negroes on a plantation or estate, the more completely are they treated as mere property, and

in accordance with a policy calculated to insure the largest pecuniary returns. . . . It may be true, that among the wealthier slaveowners, there is oftener a humane disposition, a better judgement, and a greater ability to deal with their dependents indulgently and bountifully, but the effects of this disposition are chiefly felt, even on those plantations where the proprietor resides permanently, among the slaves employed about the house or stables, and perhaps a few old favorites in the quarters. It is more than balanced by the difficulty of acquiring a personal interest in the units of a large body of slaves, and an acquaintance with the individual characteristics of each.[7]

As to the familiar argument that large planters were more likely to operate paternalistically because they alone could afford to provide a more stable and less impoverished maintenance, Olmsted asked his readers not to be misled by amounts of slave food and clothing. "The chief difficulty is to overcome [the slaves'] great aversion to labor. If a man owns many slaves, therefore, the faculty which he values highest, and pays most for, in an overseer, is that of making them work. Any fool could see that they were properly supplied with food, clothing, rest and religious instruction."[8]

Convinced of the industrial character of antebellum slavery, Olmsted referred to its depersonalized laborers as "the mass," which planters realized "must be reduced to a system."[9] At this point, typically, the "Management of Negroes" articles picked up the refrain, for instance, "have . . . all matters as far as possible reduced to a system," one of them read, because a plantation could be "considered a piece of machinery; to operate successfully, all of its parts should be uniform and exact, and the impelling force regular and steady." For "no more beautiful picture of human society can be drawn than a well organized plantation."[10] The field hands' stultifying routines made them cogs. "The stupid, plodding, machine-like manner in which they labor, is painful to witness," Olmsted reported.

> This was especially the case with the hoe-gangs. One of them numbered nearly two hundred hands (for the force of two plantations was working together), moving across the field in parallel lines, with a considerable degree of precision. I repeatedly rode through the lines at a canter, with other horsemen, often coming upon them suddenly, without producing the smallest change or interruption in the dogged action of the laborers, or causing one of them to lift an eye from the ground.[11]

Olmsted's industrial images are complemented by Sidney Mintz's insistence on the modernity of slavery: "Slaves were not *primarily* a source of . . . sexual gratification, of the satisfaction of sadistic impulses, or of anything else but profit—and of profit—within a frankly capitalistic system.... These were no serfs toiling on isolated manors, no captives of war endowing their masters with prestige, but industrial workers whose work was principally agricultural."[12]

Accordingly, in the late eighteenth century Southern agricultural reform moved beyond such pedestrian concerns as the more effective use of marl fertilizers and crop rotation to the matter of increasing efficiency and profitability by rationalizing plantation organization and management. To do so, reformers reasoned, was to curb the quietly persistent sabotage of slaves by systematically shaping their behavior. The new proposals and their public discussion were surprisingly modern in tone and reach. In order to make the plantation "the Negroes only home," "reduce everything to a system," that is, "introduce a daily accountability in every department." Or, as Frederick Douglass put it in a word, make the plantation a "circle," a total experience for slaves.[13]

To implement the "system" was to organize dimensions of the slave existence that were previously untouched in colonial plantation records of any kind. Bedding, diet, housing, tempo of field songs, and details of the slaves' religious, associational, and family lives were objects of efforts to orchestrate major aspects of slave life and leisure as planters built dance places and chapels with licensed preachers and conducted big-brother Sunday inspections. As one management of Negroes expert put it, "My mode of making such reviews is the following: I appoint a certain hour for attending to this matter on each Sabbath.... Every Negro distinctly understands, that at this hour he will be reviewed.... My business here is to call their respective names, and to see that everyone has had his head well combed and cleaned, and their faces, hands, and feet well washed."[14] The entire program was unfolded in agricultural journals.

## Management of Slaves

I have ever maintained the doctrine that my negroes have no time whatever; that they are always liable to my call without questioning for a moment the propriety of it; and I adhere to this on the grounds of expediency and right. The very security of the plantation requires that a general and uniform control over the people of it should be exercised.... To render this part of the rule justly applicable, however, it would be necessary that such a settled arrangement should exist on the plantation as to make it unnecessary for a negro to leave it, or to have a good plea for so doing. You must, therefore, make him as comfortable at home as possible, affording him what is essentially necessary for his happiness—you must provide for him yourself, and by that means create in him a habit of perfect dependence on you.[15]

Indispensable to schemes "to keep slaves at home" inculcated with "a habit of perfect dependence" was the study of behavior: "the temper and disposition of each negro should be particularly consulted. . . . When an overseer first goes upon a plantation to live, he should study their dispositions well."[16]

A quiet but significant advance in the technology of record keeping accompanied the call for a comprehensive plantation organization. Control and organization would be enhanced by keeping track of such statistical notes as slave births and deaths, physicians' visits, allowances of clothing and supplies, and quarterly inventories of stock, tools, crops, and—most importantly—productivity.

Compared to colonial crop books and daybooks, entries for antebellum slaves were more abstract and uniform:[17]

| NAMES | MON | TUES | WED | THUR | FRI | SAT | TOTAL/ SUN SICK |
|---|---|---|---|---|---|---|---|
| Richard | Roll logs | Ploughed | Hauled | Hauled | Ploughed | Chopped | |
| Emma | Cleaning up trash | Clear new ground | Clean up ground | Clean up ground | Scraped ditches | Shrubbed | |
| Big Henry | Pile and Burn | Shrubbing over Bayou | Burned | Burn | Cleaned new ground | Cleaned new ground | |

and,

> 1840. When a negro gets to be 50 years old his task must be reduced from 50 rows to 40. When a woman has children, her task must be 40 rows instead of 50. All the negroes under 20 years must have less than a full task, say from 17 to 20 years of age about 45 rows. All of the age of 11, 12, and 13 years to work two to a task. They all go at 10 years old and the first year must with their mothers and both together make one task.[18]

In place of cramped notes taken on the margins or blank sheets of hand-sized almanacs, reformers such as Thomas Affleck of Mississippi designed and published detailed printed ledger pages that brought together in one place several of the miscellaneous records that planters customarily noted. The colonial almanacs were "comic absurdities" when compared to the new comprehensive ledgers, which the historian Robert Williams, argues were "essentially consistent with the intent and purpose of modern cost-accounting, and followed the best and most advanced principles of efficient administrative management."[19] The account books, for example, considered the often neglected factors of capital depreciation, labor costs, and social welfare. One of the new ledgers, which allowed the planter to lay out a coherent plan for his operations while providing a quick summary of his property and its workings, was advertised in *De Bow's Review* in 1850.

### 3. PLANTATION ACCOUNTS

Thomas Affleck, of Mississippi, published, several years ago, a Plantation Record and Account Book, of which Weld & Co., of New Orleans, are now the agents and part proprietors. . . . there are heads of inventories of stock, implements and tools; for daily records of events on the plantation; for quarterly abstracts; of cotton picked each day, names of negroes picking, averages, &c.; of articles furnished to the negroes during the year; of overseers' supplies; of birth and deaths on the place; of physicians' visits and names etc., of patients; of bales [of] cotton made; average weight and sales; with full and ample directions to the planter in enabling him to keep the accounts with greatest ease.

Price. — No. 1, for a plantation of forty hands, or under, $2.50. No. 2, for a plantation of eighty hands, or under $3.00. . . .

The planting community and the press have fully recognized the simplicity and completeness of this work, and its perfect adaptation to the end in view — that of affording to planters and their overseers a plain and uniform book of blanks, embracing every record and account necessary to be kept upon a plantation.[20]

In sum, in the half-century of war and revolution from 1763 to 1815, Anglo-American plantations diverged from a common norm. In the South, big slaveholders sought to make their plantations efficient and smooth-running factories in the field, all-encompassing experiences for slaves. However in the Caribbean, where ironically the big sugar estate actually looked and functioned more like a modern factory, it was impossible for agricultural reformers to propose an industrial style of plantation organization and discipline because of the way slaves lived.

When William Fitzherbert, a Caribbean absentee, visited his Barbados plantation in the 1770s he saluted in his diary its experienced overseer. As "an exceedingly Sensible Man," the manager had assured Fitzherbert that the slaves "have as good [an] understanding as any white People; that talking to some for their offences, was infinately more Serviceable than whipping [them]" and that "he made it his chief love to . . . study their dispositions."[21] At precisely this point — the problem of slave behavior — Southern scientific reformers began their "Management" articles. However, as a West Indian, Fitzherbert did not continue in this vein because he could not.

Instead, he shifted his remarks to a question that preoccupied his generation and focused reforms, and whose complex domestic nature defied efforts to regiment slave lives: What could be done about low fertility and high death rates, particularly among infants? Fitzherbert noted, "Negroes increase [reproduce themselves] if proper management & Care is taken of them." His manager's tenure may have been long and the greatest part of the estate's three hundred Negroes had been born during his administration; nonetheless, slave "children Dyed for want of Care of their mothers & themselves."[22]

The movement to promote natural increase was often put in moral and religious terms, and some influential reformers were clerics. The Reverend James Ramsay, an old St. Kitts hand and author of one of the best antislavery tracts, couched his ideas as many did, in the big view—a frontal attack on the heathen character of slaves and a determination to bring to them finally an English civilization whose benefits were private property and a Christian morality defined as monogamy.

Of two planter reformers Ramsay describes, one represented a standard of "good treatment" that was unique in the Caribbean—an increase in the fertility of slave women.[23] This planter left off buying new Negroes when his force numbered 160, which then grew naturally to 180. This unusual feat was accountable to the slaves' food, land allotments, and property generally. The planter provided twice as much food as usual, larger and more conveniently situated provision grounds in which it was grown, and "all had some little property": a hog, goat sty, and money from the sale of garden crops. With this start, slaves bought decent clothing, more food, and set up comfortable huts. Resistance also figured in the equation. It was negligible, a runaway, out two days only, was accountable to an overseer who had "debauched" one of the slave's wives. In concluding, Ramsay noted that the planter "seemed to have hit the medium between governing too much and too little. His people were always ready at command, but *they had the full power of themselves and their time, when the plantation work did not employ them.*"[24]

The other reformer, "a slave to method," used rewards and some rudimentary psychological techniques. Hard-working and careful, he took over a weak and puny gang on a plantation known for its difficult soil. Yet the slaves were soon healthier, and there were fewer deaths and greater crops than before. "The secret of his management"? The planter disciplined by a "presentation of punishment": a "public explanation" and an exhortation to avoid the fault was made before the entire gang. "Often the contempt & reproach of the culprit's fellows make the severest part of the correction." The owner also used a reward system. If the gang worked well for a week, they were given Saturday afternoon off; when one was troublesome, the entire gang went unrewarded. "This makes them become guardians of each other's conduct."[25]

In the 1780s one of the most interesting reformers, Joshua Steele of Dublin, London, and Bridgetown, Barbados, used an elaborate bookkeeping scheme to make his approximately three hundred Negroes salaried tenants ("Copyhold Bond-slaves").[26] As an absentee for thirty years who had status as well as wealth, Steele arrived in Barbados late in life. He became a chief justice, a member of the Governor's Council, and an avid reformer, who in 1790 told William Dickson, an abolitionist, that he was going to "experiment" with extracting labor by "voluntary means, instead of the old method of *violence.*"[27]

In the first year Steele paid holers (whose task was commonly recognized as the most difficult), and the next put entire gangs on wages while establishing half-acre tenants, on about a hundred acres, at an annual rent of 6 percent of their value (£50 per acre). Abolishing the whip, he also instituted a system of indirect rule based on two traditional leadership groups. Elders would comprise a court or jury, and the seven drivers, as "constitution *rulers,*" were "magistrates over all the gang, and were charged to see, at all times, that nothing should go wrong in the plantations; but that, on all necessary occasions, they should assemble and consult together, how any such wrong should be immediately rectified." The seven also made "daily or occasional reports of all occurrences, to the proprietor or his delegate."[28]

Accountability by means of comprehensive records was the centerpiece of Steele's company store as well. Here slaves had the option of taking their wages in goods. Minor crops of corn, grain of all sorts, yams, eddoes, potatoes, rum, and molasses "are brought into a regular cash account by weight and measure, charged to the copyhold store-keeper at market prices" before they are sold to slave buyers. Further accounts were of "what is paid for daily subsistence, and of what stand in their arrears." As for the land rents, "the fines and forfeitures for delinquencies, their head-levy and all other casual demands, is accurately kept in columns with great simplicity, in books which check one another."[29]

Ultimately, agricultural reform took different paths in the two regions because Southern slaves were a naturally growing population and Caribbean slaves were not. Reform in the Caribbean pivoted on what was so often referred to as "the causes of depopulation." The northern Wales absentee Lord Penrhyn was told by his agent that the "true principal" of a planter is to take care of "the breeding women," for they are certainly "the Nerves . . . the cream of his Estate." To this end, reforms the manager instituted included taking women out of the field as soon as they were noticeably pregnant and putting them into such "light" work as hoeing fences, planting, picking, and boiling oil nuts. Rewards were given to both new mothers and the midwife "to perform her duty with attention and ability." For "every child she brings to me a month old," the manager explained, "I give her 6/8 [6 shillings, 8 pence] and to the Mother of the infant 3/4 to buy the little Stranger a Fowl to commence its little Stock in life. These are small triffles, they operate strongly [on the] minds of these people and feel confident that they have the regard and affection of their master."[30]

Against a background of that peculiarly effective mix of bourgeois morality and evangelism that fueled abolitionism and then the disciplining of industrial workers in the early nineteenth century, progressive slaveholders of the generation of Monk Lewis and Samson Wood placed their ameliorative reforms in the context of saving the blacks for the benefits of a Western civilization construed as resting on the twin pillars of property rights and monogamy. They saw the two as intimately linked and argued that reform should begin by whetting further the Negro's appetite for possessions. Missionaries helped shape the attack: "in short, the grand point at present to be aimed at is the civilization of them, and making them industrious, thereby rendering them first human beings before you attempt to make them Christians."[31] William Young, who left the best late-eighteenth-century traveler's account, framed the argument this way: "Before a Negro places such a value on money as is here supposed, he must have acquired many of the refinements and artifical necessities of civilized life. He must have found uses for money."[32] As to the reformers' fundamental concern, that slaves acquire a sense of personal property rights that would promise better things, none put the matter better than the West Indian historian Robert Renny, who wrote in 1807:

> In every country, and, in every age, the first step towards the civilization of man, has been to inspire him, with an idea, and a desire to property. When he has something which appertains to himself, and which separates his interest from that of his neighbours . . . he is . . . less disposed to turbulence, acquires an interest in the welfare of the community, and becomes a peaceable subject, . . . Let the planter then even from motives of policy, endeavour to inspire the Negro with just ideas of property. Let a small portion of it be alloted to him by law; and let the produce, whatever it may be, either in nature or quantity, be solely his own.[33]

Reformers such as Joshua Steele faced a different set of problems than their antebellum counterparts. High death rates, hungry slaves, and legendary feats of white sadism should not obscure the extent to which strong and resilient slave institutions in the Caribbean channelled second-generation agricultural reform. While Southerners could think about slaves bureaucratically, that is as "hands" or more abstractly as cyphers in their cotton picking weight ledgers, slaves in the Caribbean as "proto-peasants" — and as potential mothers—could not be so depersonalized and regimented. Faced with high slave death rates and the end of the steady infusions of new Negroes because of the abolition of the slave trade by 1808, reformers had to concentrate almost exclusively on how fertility and infant survival could be encouraged in order to save the institution itself.

Steele could also spin schemes about slaves as wage-earning tenants because by the late eighteenth century blacks had acquired the material base of grounds and markets that made such reforms conceivable. They had become what scholars now refer to as proto-peasants, and so, by definition, linked to the market economy. In achieving economic leverage, slaves were able to check the kinds of totalitarian sentiments expressed both in the Southern reformers' drive to rationalize plantation slavery and in the actual operation of such big plantations as the Manigaults' Gowrie.

Explanations of resistance or acquiescence in each region ought to be twofold, social and psychological. In asking in the first instance, What were the social pre-conditions for resistance? attention should be focused on the ways reformers would reorganize plantations. In the South, the goal was to maximize slave cooperation and productivity; in the Caribbean, to encourage slave fertility and infant care. In the case of the latter, the important question is, What psychological factors predisposed slaves to resist, or to go along, according to individual or group estimation of acceptable strategies in a situation like slavery? The balance of this section, which centers on the infrastructure of grounds and markets and the family and religious practices that stemmed from this base, seeks to provide some answers to these questions.

# 6

## The Slaves' Economic Strategies:
## Food, Markets, and Property

> The emergence of peasant communities upon the Caribbean
> landscape represented from the first — and to some extent, still
> represents — resistance to the will of the plantation system to
> turn every citizen into a faceless, interchangeable atom in 'the
> labor pool,' and to harness every local resource for its own
> needs.
>
> — Sidney Mintz, 1974[1]

As businessmen, planters continually searched for ways to reduce expenses.
One means was to have slaves grow their own food at the cost of giving
them land and the time off to do so. This method of slave maintenance
became the slave institution in the Caribbean, especially in such mountainous and volcanic islands as Jamaica and the Ceded Islands where only
a portion of land was suitable for sugarcane; the remainder — the slope, the
ridges of the interior spine — was given over to the slaves as their "mountain,"
where they could grow their own food.

Through hard work, luck, and holding on grimly to the advantage of
providing for themselves (other than allowances of salt fish and imported
grain) the mass of West Indian blacks in time accumulated amounts and
kinds of property that are startling if one begins (as I did) with a perspective
of slave maintenance that was Southern and antebellum. Slaves on all islands
owned flocks of fowl and such small stock as pigs and goats, which, along
with other marketable products such as fodder (Guinea and Scotch grasses),
firewood, fruit, vegetables, and fish, generated the Caribbean's justly famous

large and flourishing slave-dominated markets. This enterprise, as Sidney Mintz and Douglas Hall argue in a seminal essay,[2] was important for the future as well. It provided the base for the modern internal marketing system in the West Indian islands. No equivalent development occurred in the American South, where generally slaveholders, not their slaves, controlled surpluses including livestock and did not allot provision grounds anywhere close to the size and distance from the home plantation that were the case in the Caribbean.[3] The argument is not that there was not a modicum of slave-controlled food production in the South, or even some scratch marketing, but rather that it was negligible when compared to the cluster of social developments that stemmed from the internal economies of Caribbean plantation societies.\* Rather, the argument here is that plantation authority was a function not so much of paternalism or plantations as prisons, but rather more directly of the slave's experience of the organization of maintenance. Through time Southerners came to realize that the cultivation and distribution of food as "allowances" conveniently and effectively controlled slaves. West Indians agreed but were often unable to use food in this manner because slaves provisioned themselves.

Slaves who grew much of their own food and marketed surpluses constantly and readily traveled beyond plantation boundaries. Those who did not, namely the mass of Southern slaves, were susceptible to stifling organizational schemes (as described in the "Management of Negroes" articles) that made plantations "their only home." In the South, slaves were fed allowances, a practice that enhanced views of them as chattel, while enforcing a slave's sense of being confined and dependent. By contrast, where blacks fed themselves, as in the Caribbean, the process diluted white power, and slaves acted as if planters owned only their labor, not their lives or personalities.

---

\* Others are more optimistic than I am about the extent of antebellum slave grounds and selling. Barbara J. Fields, for instance, argues that most slaves in sugar and rice areas "and perhaps more than we now realize in cotton-producing areas — had possession if not ownership of garden plots and livestock." Her conclusion, however, does point in the right direction. Slaves engaged in local provision markets and sold produce to their owners," but they "*stood outside the realm of market relations*" (my emphasis).[4]

Here and throughout the remainder of this section my concern is that historians of Southern slavery do not react to the argument by simply pointing to slave gardens and perhaps a bit of poultry and small stock as the equivalent to West Indian practices. As we shall see, they were not. Instead, it is the way that Caribbean slave property and commerce intersected with the larger social and cultural context that counted most.

To examine the problem of slave maintenance is to uncover the institutional origins of what appears to be variants of Creolization, one Southern, the other Caribbean. What began in some societies as a simple expedient of allowing slaves to grow and gather their own food and dispense with surpluses became a formidable strategy: advancing a family's interests through time by using property for inheritances and to venerate the dead. Africanists call this combination the "family estate," which when refashioned in the Caribbean shaped plantation authority, control, and resistance decisively. The family estate enforced a cultural conservatism on the slaves' part that until the last years of slavery served as a brake on significant forms of resistance. It is important to note that separating the economic strategies of slaves from other modalities of their ways of life may facilitate discussion, but to do so is to obscure the slaves' view of property acquisition as part of domestic and religious outlooks and practices. Thus when women, who dominated marketing in the islands, "divorced" they tore in half the *cotta* [headcloth] used to support the market basket.[5]

Hence, it is the social dimensions of food production and distribution that make the regional contrast so important. The exclusively Caribbean features of slave maintenance deserve emphasis in three respects. The first was the mobility of the ordinary slave (of women particularly) from plantation to mountain to market, creating sizeable and usually expanding hinterlands that (by the time artisans moved to the fore) were to an extent beyond the routine control of whites. The second, the rise of the family estate, gave slaves a stake in the plantation, the promise of a future, and in time the means and determination to defend that future. Third, the Caribbean food system provided opportunities for slaves to accumulate the surpluses and property that sustained families and religions that were African in character. Consequently, an indispensable task that is long overdue in slavery studies is to uncover the linkage, if any, between the domestic economy and religion throughout plantation America. Of this difficult problem, a noted specialist on West Indian slavery, Barry Higman, perceives Africans brought to the New World as isolated individuals who had lost their social cohesion, including family norms. Nonetheless, Higman locates a central issue when he describes, as a source of the Africans' isolation, a process that "dislocated their linking of genealogy and locality, and the veneration of specific pieces of land."[6]

Recently, there has been great interest among scholars in studying what has been called the "peasant breach" or the "internal economy of slavery," that is, in slaves as proto-peasants. Here the thrust of the argument is that one should examine New World slave quarters for the possible linkage of a genealogy, locality, and religion based on "the veneration of specific pieces of land." How Caribbean slaves accomplished this, as we shall see, was to build on the achievements of the unseasoned, who, regardless of the pain and tragedy of enslavement, were socially cohesive. New Negroes retained their native languages as they organized with countrymen and shipmates in attempts to "find a way back home." Once on the plantation, the Africans' profound desire to return home was redirected and reshaped symbolically in the blood oath and play, among other manifestations of an ancestralism sustained by the "linking" of family to a particular spot of plantation ground.

The primary consideration in this connection, then, is the regional character of slave maintenance and its social consequences. In order to demonstrate the ingenuity and pervasiveness of slave property accumulation in the Caribbean, recourse is made to the case studies. They provide the most satisfactory comparisons of seasoning, and they also dramatize the extent to which West Indian slaves, while acquiring property and marketing, gained leverage as well. By contrast, the absence of these activities and values among Southern slaves kept them impoverished and with little with which to bargain. In short, what follows concerns what slaves did in the face of regional differences in the emerging internal economies evident from the beginning when new Negroes were seasoned. This seasoning in the Caribbean, but not in the South, meant that Africans were first incorporated as "inmates" through blacks helping blacks, including making newcomers somewhat self-sufficient in food. Soon thereafter they were given a plot of ground.

The South was one vast allowance area, increasingly so in the antebellum period. However, this situation was not always the case. In the dim origins of mainland slavery, from the mid to late 1600s, Africans were brought into an extensive frontier where presumably they were expected to help provide for themselves. Nonetheless, a black's pioneer resourcefulness as a fundamental way of abetting the ignominy of enslavement did not last. As the great families emerged in the Chesapeake Bay society by the 1730s, and in the Carolina lowcountry a generation later, food production on the big estates (where most slaves lived) came to be a part of a gang's—not an individual's or a family's—normal routine. Thus a significant feature of slave life was dominated by whites, more thoroughly even than in the flat, dry Caribbean allowance environments of Antigua and Barbados, and in the niches of such large and topographically diverse islands as Jamaica, where parts of the southern coastal plain, the parishes of Vere and southern Clarendon, jut into the sea as a peninsula. This plain, dotted with estates without "mountains," was notoriously dependent upon imported food and so a major site of slave deaths by starvation during the droughts, storms, and wartime embargoes of the 1780s. The Carolina lowcountry was a partial and unimportant exception to the allowance character of the South. Tasking gave slaves time off to develop a food system that until about the mid-

eighteenth century was marginally comparable to that won and fiercely
protected by West Indian slaves. Carolina's frontier provisioning system was
truncated, however. It never generated slave marketing in any manner
comparable to the volume and intensity of the Caribbean's.

Basic regional differences in systems of slave maintenance were set in
motion the moment Africans arrived on the plantation and seasoning began.
In both Southern and Caribbean usage "seasoning" comprised the familiar
idea of acclimating incoming Africans to new and often dangerous weather
and disease environments. However, in the Caribbean, an additional and
paramount meaning was to establish a new Negro's maintenance, which
was principally a matter of housing, food, and training. "When a new Negro
has been two or three years in the country," explained a plantation physician,
"and acquainted with the language and manners of it, and has got his
provision ground in such a state as to supply himself with food, we consider
him then as a seasoned Negro." Another doctor, appointed to inspect new
Negroes brought to Trinidad, also connected seasoning with provision grounds.
This official observed shrewdly that generous allotments of grounds would
alleviate high mortality rates by helping the new arrivals overcome the
"chagrin" of enslavement.[7]

New Negroes in the Caribbean were introduced to plantation slavery not
by whites, but by other Africans who were often the new arrivals' countrymen. These seasoned Africans either boarded slavers or went into the
merchant yards, where they tried to quiet fears and tell new Negroes in
their own language what to expect. Once on the plantation, the Africans
were put as inmates for several months in the households of established
slaves. For instance, Thistlewood once noted that when his employer sent
up a new Negro, "our Negroes have Nam'd him Hector, I put him to live
with London."[8]

One of the best descriptions of seasoning in the islands is by William
Young, a wealthy absentee and author of a late-eighteenth-century travel
account. Young said inmates were "the practice" and a trade-off between
white supervisors and slaves who took the Africans in. In turn, the new
Negroes were shown how to survive and get by as they worked in their
mentors' provision ground and were fed by the owner or supervisor until
their own plots were bearing.[9]

Inmates also focused the resentment that was seldom far below the surface
of any plantation. To the rich and experienced Jamaican attorney Simon
Taylor, care was to be taken that established slaves did not make "slaves"
of inmates. Complementing this view is Young's observation that "com-
petiton" for an inmate's labor was "violent, and troublesome in the extreme"
because "every negro in his garden, and at his leisure hours [is] earning
much more than what is necessary to feed him."[10] An inmate's labor would

make larger "surplus for sale, market, and for feeding his stock." To these warnings, however, Thistlewood added another side—the bonds that the shadowy institution engendered could be deep and long-lasting. "Old Phibbah, an Invalid, died, had her grave dug, and buried, gave old Sharper Some dram as She took him a New Negro, and he got her a Coffin made."[11]

By contrast, the rare Southern account of seasoning concerns the new Negro individually, not socially. That is, buyers worried about the age, sex, and size of their purchase and its timeliness: Could the new Negro be put in the field before late autumn frosts? On inmates, the sources are silent.

Seasoning also set in motion the practices we now call the "internal economy" of slavery. Important regional differences in that feature of slave life may be examined more thoroughly in the case studies that further expose variations in the way new Negroes and their descendants obtained food, property, and the ability to market. Thistlewood's diary, for instance, provides rare glimpses of the reception of incoming Africans and their incorporation into an ongoing plantation economy.

The diary describes three types of slave economic activity—provisioning, marketing, and gift-giving. First, provisioning included the "hand-feeding" of Africans who had just arrived from the slaver, the gardens of older residents, and the extensive use of local markets during annual late-summer droughts when food was scarce. Second, Thistlewood wrote of two kinds of marketing, his and the slaves'. The former was carried out by itinerant slave peddlers, usually favored women who sold such household products as beeswax candles, seeds, and vegetables from the manager's large garden. The latter was by slaves who bartered or sold their own commodities. Third, a continual circulation of goods by way of both gift exchanges and loot taken from slave poachers reinforced plantation communities that were mean, harassed, and fragile. Most important, Thistlewood's jottings provide contexts: the physical setting of an economic activity and its place in a sequence of events. These demonstrate a relationship between food and a resistance (typical of plantation slaves) that was monotonously periodic. In dry summer months trouble increased precipitously, particularly in such drought years as 1760 (the eve of Tackey's Rebellion) and produced such evocative jottings as "many Negroes from the Country Estates, Arm'd with Knives, Bills, Cutlasses, Maschets, clubs, fought our Negroe Men and got away."[12] Conversely, unusually wet and bountiful years yielded very few entries regarding hunger, resistance, and whippings.

In 1754—a particularly dry and troublesome year—the search for food was hard and relentless. On March 20, Thistlewood, another white man, Ambo the driver, and two field slaves took a boat to the mouth of Cabaritta River, a major collecting area and site of Tophill, the slaves' provision grounds. The little party walked about, assayed goat dung and hog tracks, but found

no game. When the foragers returned empty-handed, small gifts of food—
shrimp, eggs, and yams—began to make the rounds.[13] By early June the
plantation had to contend with a severe drought: "Gave" the Negroes
Saturday off and "made them" work in their grounds, Thistlewood wrote
for several weeks running. Meanwhile, he was also helping with the seasoning of eight new Negroes. The new arrivals were put in the houses of
older residents and fed from three sources: imported (rice), cultivated (corn),
and collected (fish). In mid-July the manager cut the new Negroes' daily
allowance to six fish each, to which he added two bitts apiece, expecting
them to buy sustenance, a quick lesson for a new Negro in both the value
of ready cash and of establishing one's own food supply.[14]

As the drought wore on, depredations increased. One June Saturday
afternoon Thistlewood and a few slaves, at the river's mouth, confiscated
a gun and powder from a Negro cutting timber, and from another, a canoe,
thirty bunches of Scotch grass (fodder), crabs, crabbing baskets, a calabash,
ropes, four knives, a shirt and frock, flints and punk for lighting tobacco
pipes, and six bitts. Later the loot was distributed in this fashion: to Mulatto
Sam, a shirt, crab baskets, a knife, one of the punks, and two bitts "in
money." To Crookshanks the clerk, his choice of the knife "he liked best,"
and a knife each to two other slaves.[15] Later when Thistlewood had a run-
in with the de Costas's "huxtering" women, from whom he took a porringer
containing buns and butter and two small rolls of tobacco, he noted: "shar'd
all amongst our Negroes."[16]

Drought and hunger for locals, both black and white, set in play "you
scratch my back I'll scratch yours." At one point in the dry, hard summer,
Thistlewood sent two men and two mules over "for anything Mrs. Anderson
Could send."[17] Edging into a bleak summer,[18] the manager continued to
plant corn in the prime cane land in which young shoots scorched and
died under a relentless sun. A few weeks later Thistlewood and another
overseer shot and bled in their stys more than thirty hogs identified as
belonging to the slaves, an impressive number for a modest-sized plantation
that was only marginally profitable. Friday of the same week he completed
the exchanges of provision grounds: "Morris's & Quacco's to Melia, Bellas'
to Moll . . . Adam & Nero must make themselves ground in Ruinate."[19]

Thistlewood liked to form little parties of Sunday guests to hunt duck,
fish, dine, and sometimes chase slave poachers. Egypt Plantation's bountiful
margins of morass and river teemed with food and fuel. Beginning Saturday
afternoon and into Sunday, neighboring slaves tested Thistlewood's vigilance
as they pursued a productive leisure of their own by fishing and gathering
on Egypt's fringes the grasses and reeds that fed stock and cooking fires and
mended their houses. In the feast-or-famine situation that prevailed mid-
summer in this niche of Cornwall, the "strange" slaves' foraging was per-

sistent and brave as well as sustaining.[20] If challenged, they sometimes pulled a knife or stabbed at Thistlewood with a fish gig.

Not all poachers were treated the same by Thistlewood, whose reactions may have reflected the local pecking order. If a poacher's owner was unknown, he could be handled roughly, stripped of his possessions and clothing, whipped, and put in the stocks overnight before he was sent away. If owned by a Rickett or Barclay, however, the slave was usually treated more circumspectly. Of a Crawford Estate slave (Big Owner), who killed a local slave's guinea cock, Thistlewood noted that he confiscated the slave's frock and knife as a kind of collateral until the slave made restitution. Of two slaves who belonged to the Barclays' Kirkpatrick Estate, "pretending to look for runaways" and "very Impudent Fellows," he simply "reprimanded" them and "let them goe again." Of another trespasser he wrote: "rode to Captain Forests' Maismore Estate and had a discourse with Mr. Smith about Yaw taking Quacco's 7 bitts worth of fish. They agreed to make satisfaction."[21] Seven bitts in spring 1759 was not inconsiderable; it would buy 135 plantains, two or three of which constitute a meal. Meticulous by nature, Thistlewood sometimes made shopping lists before he interceded on behalf of his slaves. When some of his men and women were robbed by Retrieve Plantation slaves, he noted carefully:

Big Doll had 5 Bitts worth of Plantanes took from her . . . by Akoi
Mountain Lucy 2 bitts worth of plantains & 1 bitt of Fish, by one of
    the White People
Cubba 4 Bitts worth of fish, by Quasheba Betty 5 Bitts worth of fish,
    by white people, in Billey's house
Casar 2 bitts worth of Fish & Plantanes by Cork, in the Road[22]

The manager of Retrieve's promise—to make inquiries "and get redress if possible"—was accomplished a few days later.[23]

Thus one type of circulation of goods (about twice a month in dry, bad years) concerned Thistlewood's efforts to "recompense" his slaves who had been robbed by Negroes from other plantations. Traps, nets, baskets, knives, and bills passed among the Egypt women and men who accompanied the whites on their Sunday forays. Catching trespassers and "making prize" was sport of sorts. It was also an important way of convincing slaves, new Negroes especially, of such notions and practices as the merits of individual possessions and the plantation as their territory to be defended against interlopers. This may have reinforced some sanctions from their upbringings, but on balance promises a more direct way of talking about cultural change as in part the substitution of communal for individualistic strategies and outlooks.[24]

The second kind of enterprise concerned trading, by the slaves for themselves as well as by Thistlewood. Damsel in Savannah la Mar "Sold for me . . . 14 eggs, 2 bitts, Indian Kale 2, Cab[b]age 7 Savoys 3 = 7 = 89 [bitts] in all,"[25] is a representative entry of the sizeable business that was carried on by slaves selling products from the manager's household and impressive garden. From these sales Thistlewood made year-end accounts by tallying entries like the following: "2 Oct [1780] sold: honey, asperagus, ochre, forbidden fruit, shallon tips, total: 1174 bitts (of sales to date)."[26]

Slaves mentioned in the diaries acquired property by selling an owner's produce or portions of a forager's loot, and they came by more money and goods in a variety of circumstances. Before dining at a friend's shortly after arriving in Jamaica, Thistlewood gave necklaces to two women, a bitt to a washerwoman, and two bitts and a snuff box to a stable keeper. Arriving at Egypt Plantation, he gave the former overseer's fishing boat to an old driver (a newcomer trying to play politics, Thistlewood was not so generous later on).[27]

On this frontier blacks and whites acted in exchanges as if small coin was rare and barter the rule. Small coin was available, yet gifts of kind circulated continually. Thistlewood gave away food, rum, old clothing, such tools as pen and pocketknives, as well as ducks and fish and even alligator teeth. Bottles of rum went to slaves who delivered messages; the same to Plato for "detecting" London; and to Ambo, a driver, a secondhand greatcoat made in London in 1744. Several times he paid Phibbah and other slave women for making or mending his clothing. Many little gifts, but most often a bitt or two, went to slave women for a Sunday lay.[28]

Transactions among slaves that were recorded usually concerned only those who were close to Thistlewood's household. However one senses that they represent the proverbial tip of the iceberg. By midcentury entrepreneurial activity among those who were situated strategically was extensive among slaves of every rank: new and longtime residents, African and Creole, men and women, penniless and propertied. Nor were all transactions minor. In May 1758 Thistlewood noted that the driver of Paul Island Estate was to receive every third foal for caring for a mare belonging to Phibbah, who sold other foals to a slave for £4.10 and Colonel Barclay's Ansebez for £7 at terms of £5.10 "down" and the remainder in three months.[29]

A third type of economic activity uncovered in the diaries describes the continual circulation of gifts. Some, as the term is used commonly, were "presents." When Phibbah sent crabs to Mrs. Mould, Thistlewood noted that this was "a present," with the implication that no return was expected. Nonetheless, Mrs. Mould did send "back" a new handkerchief. At other times, a slave would give Thistlewood a choice piece of fruit, a coconut, land crabs, or a cut of meat from his or her own foraging. But what was expected in return usually cannot be traced in later entries. From Phibbah he received a "Packey, Curiously Marked" calabash sent to her by a driver, Sam, "Nanny's husband," neither of whom are featured in the journals.[30]

At other times a gift was conventional, and its intent explicit. When holers on hire came onto Egypt, gifts were usually exchanged between the manager, the gang's driver, and sometimes the woman water carrier — a bottle of rum or a coconut, as if to say "let us put our best foot forward and ease through the difficult first days." (There are numerous instances of holers returning home abruptly in the early afternoon because they were put off by some unmentioned breach of the ground rules.) Many such exchanges were to keep gears greased and routines running as smoothly as possible in what was a highly exploitive, and occasionally violent, setting.

Networks etched by "gifts" are especially intriguing. In early September 1767, after nearly twenty years in Jamaica, Thistlewood left Egypt Plantation and established nearby his own place, Breadnut Pen. Immediately a flow of gifts began, mostly in Thistlewood's direction, from his own and neighborhood slaves and from local slaves to his (as an extension perhaps of the "housewarming" ethic for the new Negro Morina described in chapter 4). Phibbah and Egypt Lucy sent butter, bread, goat peppers, potatoes, and a pineapple; Harry at Egypt sent two cats, presumably as mousers. When slaves delivered their little statements personally, Thistlewood was uncommonly social: "Kirkpatrick [Pen] Old Quashie, brought me 2 alligator Pears [avocadoes], gave him dinner, punch &c." Phibbah also loaned him coin for supplies, hardware, and work that required hard cash (which Thistlewood used to buy a firkin of butter, window hinges, and window framing by Cumberland). A gift of land turtles for the newly dammed duck pond — to help the little settlement get off the ground — may be construed as a sign of the kind of sentiments, interests, and forces that held so many West Indian plantations together.[31]

In October 1780 western Jamaica was devastated by a great hurricane. The storm's impact was enormous: "2 October 1780, This Evening, gloomy, dark & dismal in the south, & East very Wild, the Sea roars . . . prodigiously." The next day, the storm uprooted trees and drove them through buildings, a tied-down stable "went like a cobweb," and in a terrifying moment, a tidal wave swept away most of Savannah la Mar. Rarely outwardly emotional, in the aftermath of the gale Thistlewood said he had bad dreams, that his neighbors had aged ten years, and "our nerves [are] so affected." Gifts flowed more conspicuously than at any other time, as such humble vegetables as turnips, as well as ducks, a horn of gunpowder, cashew nuts, and a quarter of mutton went around among whites and blacks. Thistlewood sent linen, coconuts, kegs of salt, and two teal to Phibbah. Lincoln gave Thistlewood a jug of rum. Thus sharing food was one way in which this small plantation community picked itself off the floor. In general, gift giving demonstrated slaves' determination to make a potentially soul-destroying situation manageable by reminding their supervisors that tribal ways of maintaining allegiances, obligations, and duties could work in America as well as in Africa.[32]

Although not as full as Thistlewood's, the relatively sparse comments of Monk Lewis and Samson Wood touch similar concerns: the links between slave hunger and resistance, the role of property in incorporating Africans into plantation settings, and the importance of individual possessions to slaves.

When a local cleric reminded Lewis that Sunday was the Lord's Day and that he ought to order his slaves to attend church, the minister was reminded flatly that Sundays were "the absolute property of the negroes for their relaxation, as Saturday is for the cultivation of their grounds. . . . I will not suffer a single hour of it to be taken from them for any purpose whatever."[33] As for his slaves' property, Lewis noted that their livestock was pastured with his own, a practice he estimated cost the estate about £12 a year per animal. The slaves, expecting Lewis to be the "general purchaser" of their marketable cattle, set a price of £15 regardless of quality for every three-year-old horned creature.[34]

In time, livestock and land holdings were the objectives of basic reforms on Lewis's two estates. At Hordley Estate he decreed that each slave should own only one large stock animal and an unspecified portion of provision ground. Some individuals, and presumably families as well through "the practice [of] beques[ts]," had accumulated "several" houses and "numerous" garden plots.[35] Newton Estate was a different matter, however, because it was situated on the allowance island of Barbados, which meant that slaves accumulated property far more slowly and never to the extent that slaves did in provision societies. Wood's scavenging was as assiduous as Thistlewood's, but there was so little to go around. Lacking the extensive reserve of lagoon, morass, and savannah that marked Egypt and Breadnut Pen, Wood and the slaves made do with subsistence strategies that were literally marginal: potatoes and pumpkins "run . . . Luxuriantly, squash, bonair, peas of various kinds grow here," he wrote, and "no spot whatever even an apparent heap of Stones is left without its vine growing over bare rock from some happy fissure of earth."[36]

In writing about the slaves' diet, Wood described potatoes as "a sweet root" that tasted like a chestnut and usually weighed ten pounds![37] The slaves, who also liked beans, which were rare on the estate, used salt fish to garnish such staple dishes as cookoo, "a kind of bread or rather pudding" of boiled corn flour. They also mixed "vegetables & esculents . . . with their dumplins [to] make a luxurious broth" and cooked with pigeon peas and such ground roots as sweet potatoes, yams, and eddoes, all typical in the

Caribbean but especially important in allowance areas.[38] During the harvest Wood provided full allowances, which he claimed was "not customary," because it was assumed that the slaves would eat as much raw cane as possible. During holing, he doubled allowances.[39] Implying an understanding of a diet's effect on fertility, he noted that the policy during his first years of larger allotments of more nutritious food curtailed exhausting and illegal nighttime foraging and increased the number of surviving infants to the extent that the estate would soon be "overstocked."[40]

But one group, Doll's family, was not subject to the spartan existences of the others. While Newton slaves subsisted principally on roots, bits of offal, and salt fish, Doll's enterprising brood thrived on a variety of delicacies. "Their houses," Wood reported, "were perfect shops for dry goods, rum, sugar, and other commodities." Betsey, at the time a runaway in England attempting to obtain her freedom from the proprietor, was married to a huxter, whom Wood implied had fenced the family's stolen goods.[41] Overall, feeding slaves — "our parental care" — was, according to Wood, "the most difficult part of management & gives more trouble to a man's mind & body than any thing else."[42]

An archaeological investigation of the slave burial ground at Newton complements Wood's comments on the slaves' socioeconomic activities. Ninety-two graves dating from the late 1600s to the early 1800s yielded goods that were extremely sparse. Chiefly tobacco pipes and jewelry of teeth, beads, and shells, none could be accounted as exclusively slave in origin — let alone African — without recourse to supporting site and literary evidence. Presumably, the commodities were the products of a circulation by barter, gift, and theft from the big house to the slaves' quarters. The results of this archaeological investigation are fitting symbols of the material impoverishment of plantation slaves in allowance areas. Conversely, when the project directors sought to link a slave pottery style to its Jamaican equivalent, they were able to cite in that provision society a relatively extensive find and a specific design provenance: Coramantee.[43]

Views of slave participation in provisioning, marketing, and property accumulation in Southern records are incomparably meagre when set against the same for the Caribbean. In this regard, the case studies for the South bear a single message: "Keep slaves at home, and what little if any subsistence they raise must be sold to the master and not beyond plantation boundaries." In his plantation manual *Arator,* John Taylor of Virginia put the matter this way: "The best source for securing their happiness, their honesty and their usefulness, is their food. . . . One great value of establishing a comfortable diet for slaves, is its conveniency as an instrument of reward and punishment."[44] Archaeological research in Southern slave quarters complements the stark historical record of slave entrepreneurial activities. From a

Georgia sea island site, archaeologists uncovered only very modest remains: buttons, pipe stems, and cheap crockery so common that it was sold from Carolina to Wyoming.[45]

While food production incessantly pushed Caribbean slaves outside estate boundaries, the opposite was the case in the South, where the "privilege" of providing a portion of their food—chiefly vegetables, chickens, and eggs— was seen by owners as a way, one of many, of binding slaves to the plantation. The peculiarly enervative character of black poverty in this country began with this policy in which whites assiduously monopolized economic resources and outlets.

In their diaries and letters colonial planters seldom mentioned slave economic activity of any kind because there was so little of it. Maryland and Virginia slaveholders gave slaves allowances as stinting as those provided for slaves on Antigua and Barbados: a peck of corn a week per hand. As George Washington put it, "The old ration was a heaping and squeezed peck of unsifted meal per worker, and 1/2 peck to non-workers except suckling children . . . [the] new ration of a struck peck came about because people complained and hurt my feelings." For reasons that are not entirely clear, the great planters found it difficult to be generous and to separate food allowances from their obsession with being taken advantage of by slave thieves. They were also stung to the quick by any charge that they were stingy—which they often were. Washington continued, "I will not have my feelings hurt with complaints of this sort, nor lye under the imputation of starving my negroes, and thereby driving them to the necessity of thieving to supply the deficiency. To prevent waste or embezzlement is the only inducement to allowancing them at all."[46]

Reacting to an overseer's criticism, Landon Carter noted that it was "always" his policy for slaves to raise little items for sale. However, he determined what they purchased. He distributed only one shirt, for instance, so his people would earn and buy linen for a second one "instead of buying liquor." And his nephew, the equally wealthy Robert Carter, provided the minimum of clothing, which, he reasoned, would motivate his slaves to use Sundays for working for themselves in their little gardens and chicken pens in order to buy what he did not give them.[47] Landon Carter described his slaves' chickens in this manner: "My Poor Slaves raise fowls, and eggs in order to exchange with their Master now and then; and, [al]though I don't value the worth of what they bring, Yet I enjoy the humanity of refreshing such poor creatures in what they (though perhaps mistakenly) call a blessing. Indeed, I hope this is a good way of selling what I may have to spare out of my own sumptuous fare; and not to injure the small profits which I am content with."[48]

Fragments of this kind reveal an extensive use of positive incentives in this, the quintessential paternalistic society. A 1720 ledger notes payment to slave sawyers "to Encourage them to Work"; in 1760 a planter ordered the overseer to give the Negroes rugs (probably sleeping mats) "when they have sufficiently earned them." A Virginia Harrison, desiring delivery of two letters, offered black boatmen a half dollar initially and a full dollar on delivery in order "to do their business expeditiously & faithfully."[49] The manager for the Lloyds, a rich Maryland Eastern Shore family that owned more than three hundred slaves, described such slave-controlled food resources as dunghill fowls, milk cows, and fish from seining. The slaves were allowed, however, to trade only with the owner, who gave them in return such goods — not cash — as lard, meat, and linen.[50]

On Gowrie, the Manigaults' regulations that connected slave economic activities and plantation organization were facilitated by the compact setting. Gowrie was small and every "Inch" of its arable land was put into rice. With the exception of fish, the Manigaults were the source of the slaves' food.[51] Charles Manigault's aim was to tie slaves securely to his diseased little money-maker. Allowing them a monopoly in chickens was part of this policy. "I had for years past to deny Overseers keeping poultry — because this is the only thing my people can raise for themselves (they having no spot to plant) except the trifle near their houses & near my dwelling, which enable[s] them to procure some little extra Comforts for themselves, & which tends to attach them to their homes."[52]

The Manigaults' confident control of slaves' time off surfaces repeatedly and contrasts sharply with West Indian practice.

> You mentioned . . . that you would mix the allowance & give out part Fish & part Bacon the same day — this is bad. Allowance is at best a troublesome job, & should be got over as quick as possible. The Negroes should have no picking & chusing. The fish ought to be got through first & you perhaps had best open a Barrell & count how many fish are in it — then count noses & see if one B[arrel] won't give 2 fish to each grown Negro for it is only the grown ones that draw meat you know.[53]

Manigault regulated the dole to the day and hour, and, typical of the antebellum era, his regimentation of slave leisure and domesticity began with the mechanics of distribution. Make allowances on Sunday, he ordered, "in preferance to any other day [because] this has much influence in keeping them at home that day."[54] If allowances are given out Saturday instead, "some of them would be off with it that same evening to the shops to trade & perhaps would not be back until Monday morning." This was followed by a directive, "I allow no strange Negro to take a wife on my place, & none of mine to keep a boat."[55]

Traces of what slaves did with their allowances rarely occur in this voluminous record, or elsewhere. Perhaps this was accountable to the fact that they were allowed so little space in which to express preferences. A leading notion was to give the slaves as little choice as possible in order to dampen their well-known desire to socialize by way of barter. When Manigault sent cloth for the clothing of "new comers," he insisted that the slaves be given a second issue only after they had presented the first made up. "Negroes are too fond of putting things aside, or swapping them away." Manigault's example, that some were "so apt to swap & sell"—a discovery that truly "provoked" him—was that some large thick jackets "which cost me so much trouble & money to get made up in Charleston have been seen on the backs of my neighbor's Negroes."[56]

The whole of the American South, and such flat or dry islands as Barbados and Antigua, were allowance societies and as such are highly comparable on the basis of the extensive domination of slave maintenance by whites, and the negligible amounts of food resources that slaves controlled. The two regions are not comparable, however, with regard to the other dimension of provisioning—slave property and marketing. Both developments, which were incidental in the South but institutions by the mid-eighteenth century throughout the Caribbean, point to basic differences between plantation slavery and its legacies in the two regions.

In the Caribbean, slave property accumulation began with the acquisition of a provision ground. As Governor Balcarres described allotments,

> This Country [Jamaica] differs from all European Settlements. *There* the Vallies are fertile, & produce the necessaries for the sustenance of Man. *Here* it is exactly the reverse; the Vallies produce nothing but Sugar Canes, the sustenance of Man is received from the Mountains. . . . Every Settlement on the Low Grounds has a Mountain as its appendage, that is parcelled out to the Slaves, and every Negro has his particular Lot apportioned to him for raising his Provisions, which is absolutely his Property, and his whole dependence. . . .[57]

Allotments were an acre or more in some Caribbean societies, merely "bits" and "pieces" in others. Their origins are obscure, but snippets indicate a haphazard development from local and practical deals worked out between slaves and supervisors in a distinctively West Indian system of plantation authority that was diffuse and shared. A witness at the Parliamentary slave trade hearings in the late 1780s mentioned that his Grenadan estate incurred heavy expenses from feeding slaves imported grain until "after some years," when estate grounds were full and bearing, the slaves proposed feeding themselves—salt provisions such as beef, pork, and fish excepted—if in return they were given Saturday afternoons off.[58] The practice caught on, and in both St. Vincents and Grenada (mountainous Ceded Islands) planters came to rely on slave-grown produce and only imported quantities of food during droughts. Occasionally, when his slaves asked for fresh land, he directed the gang as part of their regular routine to clear a new section, thus suggesting that the task was too difficult for slaves in small number and on their own time.

There are indications in plantation records from early-eighteenth-century Barbados of a transition to allowances as part of a larger shift from one economic stage to another. During the first, or pioneer, stage, it is assumed that in the South as well as the Caribbean most slaves fed themselves wherever frontier conditions prevailed. This was true of such places as the Georgia piedmont in the late-eighteenth-century, Arkansas, and parts of the up-country black belt in the antebellum era. In 1721 a manager for the Society of the Propagation of the Gospel in South Carolina, for instance, alluded to the slaves' self-sufficiency in this manner: "[Slaves] formerly... had Considerable quantity of provision of their own produce, whereas now for some years past they have had nothing but what has been given them by their owners which makes it hard for the Slave and Chargeable to their Masters." At about the same early period, S.P.G. missionaries also complained at a general meeting that slaves could not attend Sunday worship because they were expected to work in their grounds.[59]

A few of the actual layouts of allotments, which overseers or owners in the Caribbean sketched on the spot, have come to light. One plan from 1777 for a small pen in St. Ann's Parish (northside, Jamaica) indicates that corn was grown throughout, and potatoes next to Quashy's allotment, which was one of twenty-six. Most were made to individuals including women, only one of whom is paired, Eve with Good Luck; the other five or six were on their own.[60]

Over the ridge in Westmoreland Parish, Thistlewood made a drawing while tramping and trying to estimate proportions of cornfield and provision grounds:[61]

A more elaborate estate plan, also from Cornwall (Lord Penrhyn's estates), displays grounds in Clarendon Parish that were divided between the two systems. The low, flat southward peninsular projection of the parish (such as the neighboring parish of Vere) provided no slope for grounds, and so slaves were fed by allowances and died by the hundreds during the famines of the early 1780s, those in the mountainous northern section, the location of Penrhyn's grounds, grew their own food. These near-in grounds were fairly recent; none are indicated on an 1750 map, either because they were as yet undeveloped or else located at some distant and unmarked mountain. By the 1760s, however, Penrhyn's people had developed Bullard's Pen of 1,200 acres, 230 of which were in pasture and Negro houses, and two of

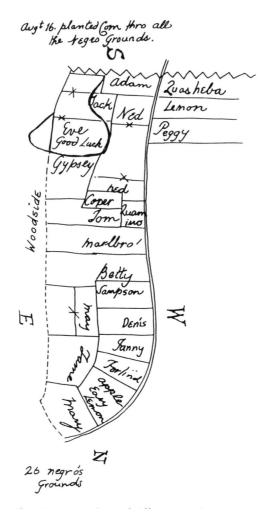

Slave Provision Ground Allotments, Jamaica

the three possible food crops were close to the houses: cornfields ("pieces") of respectively twenty-three, twenty-five, and twelve acres. Then, in a late 1760s' plan, a reference table indicates thirty-nine cane pieces divided between two sugar works, and ranging in size from one to nineteen acres each (most between fifteen and twenty-three) whose names seemed to follow in many cases habitations or haunts of slaves—Cooper Tamer's or Copper Sam's, Quaw's, Murphey John's, Congo Tom's, and Pompey's. Another plan, for Denbigh New Works, features 650 acres in cane, five in pasture sur-

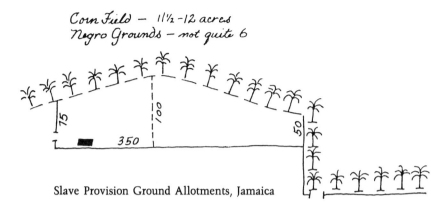

Slave Provision Ground Allotments, Jamaica

rounding the works, a hundred acres in pasture and Negro houses. One is marked ♡ for 139 acres, and one marked ◇ for 214 acres for the "Old Negro Grounds now in Pasturage."[62]

Assigning grounds individually, and to women as well as to men, were radical departures for Africans who came from societies where land was owned collectively and usually by patrilineal groups but sometimes by matrilineal ones as well. The slaves' swidden methods, which could engross large sweeps of plantation upland, were also African. Reminding an absentee that new fuel sources of logwood and bamboo might not be available to stoke the sugar boilers, William Sutherland, a manager, wrote:

> the Negroes on the Estate have occupied all the Mountain land with their Provision grounds. You may observe that surely they have too much land for the provision grounds. But the case is this. Their ground provisions such a Yames, cocos, Potatoes &c will not bear except in new land [cut] out of the woods, or in such land as has been allowed to lye over for several years & grow up with Bushes. The way that the Negroes do is—After they take one or two crops of Cocos or Yames from their grounds they then allow that ground to grow up for several years in bushes & in the mean time they clear & plant some other land, by which means they occupy a much larger quantity of land than one would think was necessary for them.[63]

While admitting that such methods at first view seemed wasteful and left little upland for general use, Sutherland advised against restricting grounds and making do with plantain walks (groves). Planters agree, he continued, that every encouragement must be given to slaves to plant ground provisions and depend less on plantain walks; consequently, slaves are to be given as much land as possible and, once it was cleared, "never" be deprived of it.

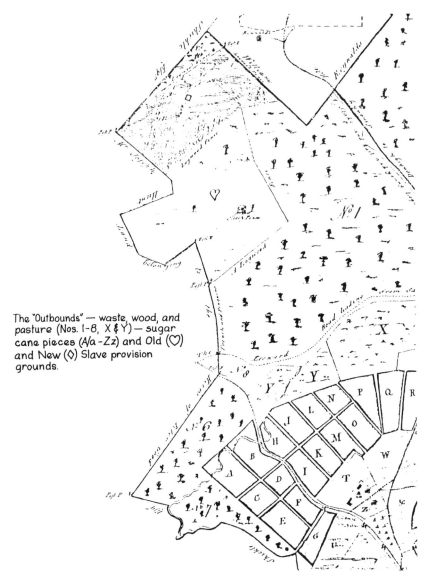

The "Outbounds" — waste, wood, and pasture (Nos. 1-8, X & Y) — sugar cane pieces (A/a -Zz) and Old (♡) and New (◊) Slave provision grounds.

Old and New Provision Grounds, Lord Penrhyn's Denbigh New Works, Jamaica

This attitude was general and reinforced by the terrible hurricanes of the 1780s that set planters against the cultivation of plantains (hitherto a major food source) because the tall and graceful trees shattered in high winds.[64]

Provisions grounds in Jamaica were often some miles distant from the home plantation. For slaves who lived on a pen or settlement, grounds may have been only a walk of less than an hour, but if the "mountain" served an estate on the coastal plain, it may have been several hours away — and many were. Monk Lewis's for Cornwall Estate and Perrin's for Blue Mountain were about eight miles off. Slaves may not have regarded distances of this kind as a hardship, however. Food-collecting meant leave to travel, often for a good portion of the weekend, and along the way slaves cultivated the "connexions" that crop up in so many advertisements as those who "harboured" fugitives. Grounds were also settings for such unsupervised activity as trading and other dealings with maroons, runaways and slaves from other estates (Appendix 4).

Further south on such flat Caribbean islands as Antigua and Barbados, slaves were fed allowances that they mixed with yams, eddoes, cassava, various leafy vegetables, cocos, plantains, and herbs grown in small plots about their huts. Asked by the governor to answer an important set of Parliamentary questions on all major aspects of slave life in 1788, a very rich owner with estates of more than a thousand acres in three parishes (probably Joshua Steele) reported that allowances in Barbados were customary only and not sanctioned by law. "Nor [were they] enforced by general custom so it happens . . . many Proprietors, some with land, some without an acre, neither feed nor clothe" their slaves. Instead, they gave them time off to help themselves as best they could "by Plunder, or by working on Sundays and holidays for any one that will pay them." Provision grounds, ranging in size from a few square yards (measured as "perches") to a quarter of an acre, were "rare" because they were located only on very large estates.[65]

In an allowance society such as his own, explained John Braithwaite, Parliamentary agent for the Barbados Assembly, food was grown for the owner's "account . . . but not for the Negro for himself," nor did planters set aside pens for cattle, pasture, and corn. Instead, they "annexed" to the estate small plots for food crops, which were worked by "some" slaves as part of their normal routine. Putting a slave's livelihood in the hands of whites could jeopardize lives. Because the Barbadian slave "[eats] from his master's purse, and every mouthful was measured in cash," Braithwaite explained, to a planter in debt there "may be a fatal difference to his Negroes whether Corn is at 5, 10 or 15 shillings per bushel." When the weather worsened in Caribbean allowance societies, slaves were nearly helpless. As an Antiguan white explained in the 1780s, "from this Drought [the slaves] had nothing in the World to keep them alive, but what they got from their owners." Thus in allowance societies slaves owned grounds around their little huts and rarely elsewhere.[66]

There were all sorts of ways, hidden in the records, that Caribbean slaves acquired property to add to their allotments, and artisans in all regions earned money by working on their own time. The attorney for a lieutenant governor's Jamaican estate in 1783 charged the estate for paying from his own pocket, 7/6 [7 shillings, 6 pence] to slave masons "working on their own time."[67] From accounts for John Tharp's York Estate at the other end of the island are payments in the 1780s to mule men, to a carpenter for Sunday work on a Negro's house, to a slave who brought home a runaway from the Spanish Town workhouse, and an entry with the name of eighteen slaves paid 2/6 each for Sunday work during crop time.[68] A wealthy stone mason and slaveowner testified (during the trials of slave conspirators in Jamaica in 1791) that when he sold his Windsor Estate, the provision grounds were appraised at £280. However, when he decided to allow the slaves to put a value on their grounds and some stock, he paid three times that sum, or £1000.[69]

Records of another kind describe the sale to whites of commodities controlled by slaves. Payment was sometimes substantial. In 1790 a York Estate manager paid a slave £10 for a young Spanish horse and £18 to Robert for a mule.[70] Goats and pigs are one matter, cows and horses quite another. How many of the following remain to be uncovered? From one of Hampden Estate's yearly accounts, the common "Increase and Decrease of Stock" for 1779, a note appeared at the foot of the page: "Bought of the Estate's Negroes": two mule colts, ten mares, two horses, one colt, and six fillies (mules are sterile and so take considerable finesse in breeding from a male donkey and a mare horse).[71] In a 1798 slave list for the Perrin family's Vere Estate (an allowance subregion in a provision society), Jamaica Cury, an old man of fifty-seven, is listed as responsible for "Minding the Head Driver's Stock."[72]

Amounts and types of slave property accumulation from the more impoverished slave communities of allowance islands are also impressive. References to slave livestock in Barbados, which has been pictured herein as a threadbare allowance society hardly conducive to the acquisition of substantial property by slaves, include a 1816 note about a free woman of color who, when she abandoned a relationship with her slave mate, sold his cattle. The estate then sued in the master's name for the recovery of the slave's property.[73] In reporting that "in general" the slaves were "happy," Samson Wood of Newton Estate noted that it would delight the proprietor to see their little possessions, their stock, fowl, goats, hogs, milk cows, and horses.[74] A slave is named in the records for Turner's Hall as having deposited £25 for safe-keeping with the attorney.[75] And from three estates of a truly princely absentee, Lord Harewood (whose extensive business records were destroyed in World War II), is a note listing the property of apprentices (former slaves not yet legally freed) in the 1830s, that included five horses, fifty-five heads of cattle, 263 sheep, and 138 swine. But this inventory is incomplete, "[I have included only] what ha[s] come under the eye," the manager Thomas Marshall added, because the workers "conceal" property. Their poultry, for example, "is innumerable." On Mount Eagle alone, blacks had to use wagons to carry £350 worth of their sugar and ginger to markets. As for the other two estates, although the crop accounts were not enclosed, Marshall knew that the people on them produced "considerable" sugar, alloes, and cotton as well as "an incredible quantity of Stock."[76]

Not surprisingly, the more impoverished allowance islands of Barbados and Antigua also had sizeable populations of white poor whose distress was eased by slave philanthropy. John Luffman, author of one of the best eighteenth-century travel accounts, wrote from Antigua that slaves chiefly supplied the Sunday markets, which, when the ships did not come in, kept whites from starving. Writing a generation later, another Antiguan mentioned indigent whites, especially out-of-work sailors, whom slaves fed, clothed, and often sheltered "without the slightest wish or prospect of receiving remuneration." They do this "with the kindness and affection of a parent," wrote Mrs. Flannigan, who concluded that although Barbadian slaves were even more philanthropic, those of Antigua were "not [far] behind" if at all.[77]

Another perspective of the slaves' slow but significant accumulation of property is provided by such "unconscious evidence" as newspaper advertisements and missionaries' accounts of fee collections. Of the latter, in Antigua in 1806 a primarily slave congregation paid £900 in collection money. In Barbados in the same year a slave woman was described as at one time a seller of dry goods and the owner of a house in Lightfoot's ground, where she lived with Jimmy Black, her free husband. Another, incomparable, notice mentions a slave cooper who, failing to appear after being sold to a new owner, was threatened with the sale of his three houses.[78]

Also intriguing are allusions to the beginnings of status consciousness among slaves. An Anglican missionary in Jamaica reported home that blacks, who called a mule a "horse-Negro," accordingly referred to Moravian missionaries (notorious for leading spartan existences) as "Parson Negroes & are generally contemptuous of [their] poverty."[79]

Housing also began to be a source of status among slaves. In contrast to the typical antebellum barrack-row housing, Caribbean slaves often built their own dwellings. James Tobin, a slave-trade witness, mentioned houses of two rooms as customary except for "the better kind of Negroes," whose houses were timbered, boarded and shingled.[80] Sir Phillip Gibbes, a Barbadian absentee and author of *Instructions for the Treatment of Negroes,* wrote about "Negroes of the first distinction" who had longer houses of "two very good chambers & a good sized room for a kitchen." As for framed houses, they should be "at least 18 feet long" and given only to the principal Negroes as "the inferior Negroes Will not take care of them." Principal Negroes, Gibbes explained, required the extra "apartment," which could be used to lodge an "inmate whom the master of the house receives to do the drudgery of the Family" or be further divided into a storeroom or kitchen. From Jamaica, Barry Higman calls attention to an 1818 account in which head slaves, people "entrusted with duties of responsiblity or skill," owned houses that were, in some instances, situated in the center of an actual compound or enclosure, and "in general very superior to the others."[81]

In time, entire neighborhoods, if not villages, reflected the beginnings of distinctions of class as well as color. In an evening's ride a Barbadian traveler saw one settlement of what seemed to be half-built, filthy slave houses set on an exposed "scorching worn-out hill[side]"; another settlement was comprised of "comfortable" well-thatched huts of two to three rooms, most of which were enclosed by gardens with varieties of orange, avocado, and plantain trees.[82]

Relations between the propertied and "poorer sort" of slaves are occasionally alluded to in managers' reports about the endemic food problems in the islands. In one, slaves who "never work grounds for themselves" were discussed.

> it is a custom for the better [s]ort of Negroes to get as many of the poor, worthless n[egroes] [torn] possible to work their grounds for them on Sundays [and in return] generally give them as much Provisions as they can eat. But when a time of Scarcity comes and when Provisions are selling high they wont give them a morsell, the consequences of which are that the better sort of Negroes in times of scarcity are not only wallowing in Provisions but are selling them while the poorer sort are absolutely starving.[83]

As in African villages, "Principal Negroes" on Caribbean plantations were in the center of the action. They were objects of intense scrutiny when insurrections threatened, as in Jamaica in 1791 when they suddenly stopped taking care of their precious grounds. In this instance, a royal governor's discussion of "rich" and "poor" slaves proceeded as follows:

> had the observation [about grounds which abruptly were left untended] respected only the poorer kind of Negroes, it might have been attributed to that indolence and neglect that had occasioned them to be

poor, but when those who by superior skill in culture, and habitual industry have become comparatively rich and acquired a superiority of consequence with the other Negroes all at once cease their industry and neglect their only source of wealth and consequence, there must be some cause. . . .[84]

The governor also included in his report intelligence provided by the manager of a large gang of 167 slave masons. The manager's concern was the state of provisions. He had to know in advance how, once on the job, his sizeable group would be fed; and in this regard his "dependence therefore," especially in an impending crisis, was "chiefly on the head & Rich Negroes."[85]

"Head" or "principal Negroes" had a meaning in the Caribbean without equivalent in the South. At first view they seem to be somewhat comparable to favored house people, artisans, or drivers, but they were not. Head Negroes in the islands comprised those who were especially hard-working and fortunate enough to have accumulated considerable property and the extra help, family members, or inmates to expand production, although they were not co-opted by their success. As for the "poor" slaves in the embryonic hierarchy emerging in the late-eighteenth-century Caribbean — the weak, unlucky, indigent, and some new Negroes — they were part of "the pot gang" fed by a general dole from the estate's reserve.

There is no Southern equivalent to a reform that the British government promoted in 1826 for "The Establishment of Savings banks for the better protection" of slave property, defined in a note as including the right to dispose of land, money, cattle, tools, and furniture of any value but not weaponry and ammunition. Finally, another clause — calling attention to an important political feature of slave property and enterprise (or its absence) — stipulated that slaves could declare heirs whose names were to be recorded.[86] The most important long-term affect of this development is readily summarized by Douglas Hall. Emancipation, he explains, "did not create any group of landless agricultural labourers [in Jamaica] who were entirely dependent on wage labour for a living."[87] By contrast, sharecropping and peonage, which stemmed from landlessness, were the lot of Southern freedmen.

Against the Caribbean record, then, the economic strategies of slaves in the South appear to be a world apart. Comparability of evidence is the first problem, for Southern sources concerning slave property and marketing in the colonial era are more fragmented, sporadic and meagre than their West Indian counterparts. Only bits and pieces exist in Chesapeake Bay planters' records from a 1767 account book:

Memorandum of Money to be paid Mr. Ambler's Negroes
    To Rose for 3 1/2 hhds. of Cotton at 1/3 £         0.4.4 1/2
    To Nero for 2 3/4 hhds. of Cotton at   *           3.5 1/2
    To Daniel                               .... 2.6
    To Maximus                        ...0.7.1
    The Ballance due to the sd. Seaton for his wage
    is £4.8.8 1/4[88]

From Maryland guardian accounts, Talbot County, in the 1790s comes "1 Decayed pine tree sold Negro Dick." A Randolph Farm account notes that the wages of Negro wheat cutters were paid in such produce as starch and sugar.[89] One of the most complete of its kind is Thomas Jefferson's ledger of payments to slaves of a shilling or two for "going up a chimney," bringing home stray horses, or to ferrymen for delivering letters; in other words, gratuities for errands and the like. Jefferson also paid for such produce as eggs, chickens, half a bushel of potatoes, for a wooden bowl, and at least twice borrowed a few coins from Jupiter and Jamey, his personal servants. About a third of the total paid for chickens, however, was paid to local whites who supplied them.[90]

South Carolina records are more promising, as are those for the antebellum era generally.[91] In contrast to the Chesapeake Bay region, few available plantation accounts exist from the colonial lowcountry. However entries of payments made to slaves for produce and services are more numerous, as would be expected in a tasking system of labor where slaves had time off to work their own garden plots and chicken coops. Carolina slaves acquired property, but in small doses usually as incentives and so largely beyond any planning on their part. Henry Ravenel's daybook, like Jefferson's, includes entries in which slaves were paid for a basket, trees, rails, corn, myrtlewax, poultry, beef, rice, and a hog; there are as many entries for women as men.[92] Small indigo and sea island plantations around Savannah (Christ Church Parish) provide entries from the 1780s and 1790s, some of which were quite handsome. For example, Quaw, a boatman, received $18 for boat hire and going to Charleston with Mrs. Gibbons; there is also a long account with Carpenter Isaac, to whom at one point in 1796 the Gibbons family owed $80. His owner was a Mrs. Fox, who once was paid directly. In other ledgers from this region slaves also provided hogs, potato slips, twelve bushels of corn, and, from another Gibbons family account book, were compensated £2.18.4 for hauling up boards of the wharf and £1.9.8 for bringing up a raft from Coston's Wharf "& securing it in Musgrove's Creek."[93]

Much of this is concentrated in the old rice coast, even into the antebellum era. From the plantation book for Society Hill in the sandhills of the Great Pee Dee River comes:

1 Dec[ember] 1859    The hands picked together 830 lbs cotton
2 Dec[ember]         The hands picking in their own cotton today

This was soon followed by another account:

Negros, cotton 1861:

| Hampton | 132. | 145 | 35 | = | 312 |
|---|---|---|---|---|---|
| Bob | 47 | 60 | 22 | = | 129 |
| Prince | 72 | 60 | 20 | = | 152 |
| Ranter | 123 | 145 | 28 | = | 296 |
| Tom | 55 | 70 | 16 | = | 141 |
| Mundy | 124 | 165 | 30 | = | 319 |

Hampton also made 3 3/4 bushels corn
Mark            "  1 1/4   "

1860   14 slaves had their own cotton patches which yielded from 81 to 387 lbs: 2,401[94]

As for the Manigaults, Charles allowed slaves to market where he lived, but not those on Gowrie. A few Silk Hope slaves did exchange chickens with the master for cloth, as the following account and shopping list indicates:

I have not yet bought the following as well cotton goods are so dear at present [July 30, 1861]

8 chickens from Nelly        75 cents
7    "     "  Dinah          62 1/2 cents
5    "     "  Mary           50 cents

They say blue twill.

9 chickens for [from] Peter at 23 cents [scratched out]
18 3/4 cents per pair: Blue Twill . . .
7 chickens from Stephney, He wants nothing
3 chickens from Cenaphy, White homespun[95]

In the records of the Heyward family's huge estate, one of South Carolina's wealthiest, is evidence from the early nineteenth century of a West Indian arrangement. Slaves had two hours off each day to do as they pleased, and, to all full field hands who would use the privilege, the supervisors alloted high lands for provision crops. However there is no evidence of slaves openly marketing surpluses and so creating the social differentiation that marked the larger Caribbean plantation slave settlements. The most recent and comprehensive study of a lowcountry planter summarizes the slaves' penurious existences. "Chaplin's rewards and punishments," writes Theodore Rosegarten, "were meant to remind his slaves that everything they had, they had through his benevolence." The master cloaked himself in this role because he "thought of himself as a great provider." As the scientific agricultural reformers put it, "Slaves should not be allowed to do anything for themselves in order to cultivate attitudes of absolute dependence."[96]

Nonetheless, some slaves were able to express themselves economically on the rare occasions when they were able to buy outside. Consumption patterns from the slaves' bits of wherewithall are exposed in a rare account of slave purchases at a back-country Scots factor's store in the Virginia piedmont. In this region where whites owned only a few slaves or none at all, blacks and whites lived close together, and attitudes toward slave marketing may have been more relaxed. Still, the factor and his slave customers seemed to have been on a short leash. Accounts are qualified with notes, for example, "John Martin, Security" or Thomas Holland's Dublin "by the consent of his Master."[97] The slaves bought mostly cloth, an item cited more than any other as stolen goods in slave trials. Because a few paid in kind, the ledger indicates what they brought in (and presumably produced) as well: "January 17, 1801. By Isham for h[al]f his Crop [of] Corn & fodder: £1.10.6." In exchange, slaves took items of apparel, food, utensils and small tools, spectacles, a dozen buttons, a great deal of cloth, hankerchiefs, a pair of shoes (made on credit for Jack), molasses, sugar, whiskey, brandy, a chamber pot, a screw auger, pewter plates, a pocketknife, and a dozen knives and forks. The store served as a bank as well. Adam's account notes credit for odd-jobbing and deposits of produce, for burning a coal kiln (6/), for two horse collars made for John Radford, for seven barrels and two bushels of corn (£2.19.6), and for a parcel of tobacco. In return, in about a year's time (1802) this slave bought mostly cloth — linen, oznabrugs, and homespun — and black ribbon, sugar, a wool hat, and a quart of whiskey, paper, pins, molasses, a dozen needles, and a tin pan.[98]

In all, thirty-one slaves belonging to fifteen owners were part of the store accounts (other blacks may have been free because no owners were indicated). Wood's Nan, who made the largest single purchase, had an account dated 1800–1804 that included such purchases as two tin cups, plums, a woman's cloak for £1.18 (the largest single item in the ledger), 4 1/2 yards of red durant cloth, a quart of brandy, sugar, paper pens, a tumbler, and a skillet. For all of this she made intermittant small cash payments of between 1/6 and 16/, for a total of £2.18.9.[99]

Selling marked the most significant differences in slave society in the two regions. In the Caribbean, slave marketing was conspicuous, pervasive, and dominated by women.[100] In the South, it was customarily furtive, underground, and conducted mostly by men who were often house servants. Although Southern slaves did obtain goods and found a way to trade them, their participation in the commercial activity of Southern towns displayed little of the mass, energy, and property accumulation that propelled slave marketing in the Caribbean. From the late eighteenth century, when the records first reveal a modicum of selling by slaves, it is immediately apparent that most whites, who habitually sought to blur distinctions between theft and marketing, begrudged slaves' economic opportunities. For their part, what slaves offered for sale, as reported in a variety of records, was often small, readily transportable, and often sold at night in the countryside, especially in the Chesapeake Bay region.

However, in the third quarter of the eighteenth century, an illicit trade was so extensive in Virginia that one writer to the *Gazette* noted that robberies took place "in every part of the country"; another complained that "hen-houses, dairies, barns, graneries, gardens and even patches and fields may be and are robbed in every convenient moonshiny night." Slaves fenced stolen goods or items their masters did not want to sell themselves. They were accused of trading with "proprietors of numerous little stores erected about" in remote "pretty towns" and to others, the "night sellers of liquors," the "common proprietors of orchards," and to small farmers who made cider and brandy. Slave sellers were generally paid in kind rather than in cash for their work as middlemen.[101]

Landon Carter wrote a series of letters to the press complaining of "night-time robberies" for purposes of sale to "these night shops . . . amongst us." He opposed "Suffering a Slave or servant on any pretense or with license from a master to sell to anybody whatever; for at best they must steal what they sell."[102] Washington put the issue more directly: "If [slaves are] . . . presume[d] to sell *one thing* they may and will be suspected of selling *every thing* they can do with impunity." Consequently, the president ordered his slaves' dogs killed because they aided in robberies and the timothy seed mixed with sand so it would not be sold in nearby Alexandria.[103]

Legal efforts to curtail slave marketing throw light on what blacks sold and how they went about it. Early in the eighteenth century, in the turbulent 1730s, a Charleston, South Carolina, grand jury presentment mentioned "the very great Grievance and . . . intolerable hardship" accountable to the black "Hucksters of Corn, Peases, Fowls &c." who "watch Night and Day on the Several Wharfs" and in effect forestalled while selling to locals at "an exorbitant price."[104] Later, in 1773 a Cape Fear, North Carolina, advertiser cited "several" persons who made "a practice of buying from my Negroes whatever they pillage from my House in town or Plantation below."[105]

Such activity went on up and down the Atlantic seaboard and was often conducted by slaves, not for themselves but, as Carter's public tirade implied, on a master's behalf — an important contrast to Caribbean practice. Not surprisingly, legal efforts to stem surrogate selling by slaves did not get very far. In 1752 the legislature refused to make a law prohibiting slaves from selling poultry, and ten years earlier when a Surry County petition asked the Virginia House of Burgesses to prohibit both slave crops and marketing licensed by owners, the petition was rejected.[106]

Glimpses of the Southern slaves' feeble marketing practices must be laboriously squeezed from a variety of records. In a Virginia circuit court in Kent County in the 1790s, a John Sugar was fined two thousand pounds of tobacco for "negro dealing." Later sessions presented slaves for stealing eighteen shoulders of bacon, Negro Betty for theft of fifteen yards of Irish linen, and Negro York for selling cider without a license.[107] Runaway notices from the Chesapeake Bay region show a few slaves scratching out a meagre existence selling such marginal products as shellfish or eggs. One man "dealt very freely in Williamsburg in the oyster and fish way — in their seasons"; another made his living in the new capital of Richmond, "trading with a small cart."[108] According to records of Virginia Baptist denominations, Crawla, excommunicated in 1790 for selling on Sundays, was singular; usually black Baptists were expelled for cardplaying and adultery rather than for breaking the Sabbath.[109] A wealthy Virginia slaveholder wrote his steward about the desirability of trading bacon for chickens from the "country people or rather Negroes who are the general Chicken merchants."[110]

A somewhat broader view of slaves who marketed is provided by runaway notices from the Carolina lowcountry. Of the seventeen South Carolina fugitives listed as market Negroes, only three were women (in contrast to the Caribbean, where market garden selling was almost exclusively by women). What they did is described minimally: "sells cakes other things" and "used to go about town to sell things." Of the men who marketed, four, as butchers, were specialized; one traded from a mule cart; and others sold greens, fruit, and veal, the only commodities specified. Together these descriptions contribute to the impression that selling was not routine and open as it was in the islands. Instead, the common appellation "attends market" actually distinguished favored servants only — those attached to a gentleman's town house — and few others (Appendix 4). When his slave gardener took ill, the Revolutionary War general Thomas Pinckney, for instance, wrote diffidently that "I have offered to let him stay in the gardener's Room next to the Coach house in King Street & to tend the Market for his own profit with what vegetables he may raise in the Garden over & above what may be wanted for your family use. He is very civil."[111]

A sign that in uncontested nooks and crannies the restrained character of slave marketing prevailed into the antebellum era is evident in a 1824 complaint from a Washington, Georgia, newspaper concerning wary crowds of blacks around tippling houses: "they slip in and out. . . . I often and almost every Sabbath see load after load of wood, hay, fodder and other articles for market hauled through the streets in waggons, carts, etc., and stop in the square until the owner can go and find a purchaser."[112]

"The whole Negro population of the island seems in motion," and "Negroes are the only market people. No body else dreams of selling provisions" are the startled and typical reactions of travelers to a Caribbean market.[113] In the islands, markets were on Sunday—an impossibility in the evangelized South—and those in Jamaica were an old institution dating back at least to 1724. In that year a missionary reported that in the three towns, Kingston, Port Royal, and Spanish Town, slaves traveled from thirty miles around to provision "all ranks especially tradesmen, their families and horses" and sold their own and their masters' produce.[114] The market in Roseau, Dominica, sprawled across a large open and paved square in the center of a town of five hundred houses. A fish, vegetable, and fruit market, it was attended by Negroes who traveled from as much as eight miles distant. Slaves often earned $3 to $4 and, according to the island's contemporary historian Thomas Atwood, seldom returned home without at least 50 to 60 shillings.[115]

In the Caribbean, laws to check marketing illuminate what slaves had to sell and what whites tried to keep out of their reach. St. Kitts slaves by 1752 could not sell salted beef, fish, and other imported merchandise for reasons that appeared often throughout the islands—because the blacks' shops and stalls hurt poor whites trying to eke out a subsistence in the same manner as the slaves. An act specified that slaves could continue to sell greens, roots, grass, green beans, cassava, milk, eggs, fresh fish, small stock, fresh butter, fruits of every kind, firewood, and cotton.[116] A Spanish Town fire and rubbish ordinance stipulated that slaves who were either the property of townsmen or hired to them could not sell poultry, eggs, fruit, vegetables, grass, or corn. These goods could, however, be taken to market by a slave if the slave carried an annual permit and the commodities were from the plantation of origin. A similar law in Trinidad proclaimed that provisions and poultry were "always exempted" from any controls while prohibiting such "stolen goods" as lumber and cut wood prepared for joiners and carpenters, cut and squared plank, staves, shingles, any clothing or jewelry, and horses, mules, cattle, dogs, sheep, and goats. The penalties for owners of slave hucksters were high, a $100 fine and up to six months in jail; the slave received a public whipping. Slaves licensed as sellers by the Board of Cabildo (i.e., the city council), however, were exempted from all provisions of the act.[117]

Slave markets were also a centerpiece of life in allowance islands. John Luffman has left a vivid picture of the St. John's, Antigua, market and of the social activities that swirled at its edges. On Sunday mornings before the Negroes' afternoon dances and plays, the market was set up in the south end of St. John's, on land of an "Esquire" between three roads leading out of town. It was larger than London's Royal Exchange and filled with "many"

hundreds of Negroes and mulattoes who sold poultry, pigs, kid goats, vegetables, and fruit. The sellers assembled at dawn, and by mid-morning were
joined by crowds of customers who added to the noises and the smells from
sweating bodies, ripe fish, meat, and greens that carried more than a quarter
of a mile. By 3 P.M. business was nearly completed, and people overflowed
into huxters' clapboard and shingle shops, swilled new rum grog, danced,
and diced for dogs they had worked all day to buy. Meanwhile some turned
out to stroll — or to fight — in Otto's pasture, where "the law seldom interfere[d]."[118]

Town slaves were more openly self-confident and aggressive than those
in the countryside. Black town people understood the anxieties of whites,
especially those who were new arrivals, whom they plied with "a variety
of inuendoes" about the perils of seasoning: "Ki massa, we sorry for that
poor Buckra him to go to the parson's pen [graveyard]."[119] At St. Vincents,
Kingston (which does not have a natural harbor), when slaves waded out
to carry ashore passengers who arrived drenched, the blacks assured them
that "Salt water very good indeed, Massa, for white man's skin: buckra
nebber, nebber catch a death of cold in salt water, 'less, Massa, buckra
happened to be drowned in it."[120] Off Port Royal, Jamaica, ship passengers
were met by women higgling fruit from a canoe. Pushing off to return, a
woman sang as the others clapped and chorused:

> New-com buckra
> He get sick,
> He tak fever
> He be die;
> He be die.[121]

By the end of the century most European travelers were unprepared for
the expanding suburban areas that seemed to them and local whites to be
noisy, rude, chaotic, and slipping from control. In 1784 the captain of the
James Street Fire Company in Bridgetown, Barbados, requested parish representatives to "suppress & abate such sheds & low houses erected & now
erecting by negro & mulatto slaves & free negroes, which are not only
public nuisances but afford fuel to spreading flames."[122] Or, as others put
it, Bridgetown was a continued scene of filth, dirt, riot and disorder, a place
of "Balls, routs, [and] Assemblies" by those who "have assumed an insolent
& provoking deportment towards the legitimate inhabitants of the Island."[123]

For the mass of plantation slaves in the South — increasingly so in the
nineteenth century as towns were generally closed off to them — the impression is one of lives that were rude and impoverished. The following complementary views represent the comparatively feeble character of slave economic activities, which should not be confused with their general material

conditions. Beneath a slave living area at the Bray Plantation, the King's Mill site, the archaeologist William Kelso has noted that numerous little pits were uncovered. They were what we would call cubbyholes, lockers in which slaves stored their provisions, roots, potatoes, and cooper coins, virtually worthless by the late 1770s.[124] When a Polish poet visited Mount Vernon in 1798, home of one of the wealthier planters in North America, he was startled by the poor quarters and food provided for President George Washington's slaves.

> We entered some Negroes huts — for their habitations cannot be called houses. They are far more miserable than the poorest of the cottages of our peasants. The husband and his wife sleep on a miserable bed, the children on the floor. A very poor chimney, a little kitchen furniture amid this misery — a tea-kettle and cups. . . . A small orchard with vegetables situated close to the hut. Five or six hens, each with ten or fifteen chickens, walked there. That is the only pleasure allowed to the negroes: there are not permitted to keep either ducks or geese or pigs.[125]

The impact of the contrasting systems of slave maintenance was felt long after the end of slavery. West Indian planters were forced to attend a preview of that epochal event, as the rising tide of abolition finally closed the African slave trade in 1807. Beset by dwindling numbers of laborers, who unlike Southern blacks were seldom part of populations that grew naturally, reformers such as Joshua Steele well before 1807 began to imagine slaves as even more on their own resources, as wage-earning tenants. That Steele and others could think about the problem of slave population, and of slavery itself, from a free-market perspective was in part accountable to the material base of grounds and markets that Caribbean slaves had struggled to create and defend over time.

In England, in a House of Commons speech in 1803 John Foster Barham referred to his slaves' "political state" in terms now used to call attention to slaves as proto-peasants. In order to explain the slaves' infertility, Barham compared their domesticity on two plantations. As a large sugar estate situated in a salubrious climate near the coast, Mesopotamia possessed a good water supply, soil that was easy to work, and slaves who owned considerable property because they sold surpluses in nearby Savannah la Mar. By contrast, Island Estate was wet and damp, with stiff soil and slaves who, with no market at hand, were poor. Yet the island people were more healthful because they were relatively sequestered, immobile, and conse-quently lived in stable and monogamous families. Meanwhile, to their loss, the slaves of low-land Mesopotamia pursued markets and lovers in Savannah la Mar to the impairment of their health and fertility. One could not say that their customs were African, Barham reasoned, because his slaves, originally from an array of African societies, had assimilated, he implied, to a common norm. It was impossible, moreover, on any account to change either the slaves' "habits and manners" or the "peculiarities" of the estates on which they lived. "To interfere in their domestic lives," he concluded, would be "dangerous and ineffectual" and could only be done by altering their "political state."[126]

The features of the slaves' "political state" center on family and religion (chapters 7 and 8). These features are, first, the profound attachment of slaves to the plantation as home; second, slave courtship and domestic arrangements; and third, the many permutations of obeah — witchcraft — that infused plantation slave resistance before field hands were Christianized by evangelicals.

# 7

## Family

The problem of the black family may stand for the larger problem of the evolution of black culture in slavery.

— Elizabeth Fox-Genovese and
Eugene D. Genovese, 1983

They were tribal. To know this is to know a great deal about them [slaves in families].
— Orlando Patterson, 1977[1]

In making new families Africans had to negotiate continually between their own traditions and the demands of slavery. The compromises inherent in this process are exposed in a remarkable will by a Jamaican slave whose bequests stemmed from his plantation existence (including the disposition of the kind of slave property that was customary and widespread in a provisioning system such as Jamaica's) while his funeral instructions, about chorusing and shipmates, point forcefully to the African past. In March 1758 Thistlewood wrote a "Memorandum, how mulatto Will's goods are to be disposed of at his Death: his Wives Shipmate Silvia to have his Cow, her daughter Hester, the heifer; Damsel, his Wife [Jimmey Hay's Wife (underlined)], the Fillie and [the] rest of what he has; he desires to be buried at Salt River at his Mother (Dionah's) right hand, and that no Negroe Should Sing."[2]

Slave family and religion did blend African traditions and plantation routines. How the two combined and what the ensuing patterns or syncretisms were like form the nub of controversies regarding the origins of the modern matrifocal black family and the character and legacies of slave religion. Although quantification has been the rage in the new social history, and demography the darling of studies of slave family—birth and death rates, child spacing, and completed family size—the purpose here is to continue to pursue the main argument. Slavery should be construed essentially as an encounter between the values and ways of two quite different people, Africans and European settlers.

The mulatto's will is at once an economic, religious, and cultural statement. As such, it is an invitation to see family, property, and acculturation as a piece in an argument that slave families were culturally conservative in the Caribbean yet assimilative in the South because of the systems of maintenance there. As either provision or allowance, these systems steered slaves toward domestic arrangements that in orientation were either African and polygynous or Christian and monogamous. Because black families in the Caribbean were based on provision grounds, they were imbued with African notions of property as corporate; that is, as owned by the dead, used by the living, and thus a focal point for ritual. In the South, however, slave families were landless, customarily monogamous, and rarely if ever focused by property strategies meant to perpetuate a family conceived as comprising both the living and the dead. Within these parameters, gender relations in the two regions indicate that the stereotypical black family—mother-centered, with anomalous father-husband—was in a formative stage. However these familiar institutional forms were rather different in meaning and function from one region to the other because the Caribbean family was more conspicuously African in character than its Southern equivalent.

Probably more than we realize, attitudes about the beginnings of the black family have been shaped by our own cultural biases. These biases are fortified by an uncritical acceptance of a view of Africans as victims who barely scraped by, and of antebellum slavery as representative of slavery generally. Undeniably, by the early 1800s Africans, always hard-pressed in North America, were no longer culturally influential. In the South, most couples with children were, or wanted to be, part of two-parent, monogamous unions. A comparative view complicates this conventional picture while opening a different line of inquiry. Living in the midst of Africans, Caribbean whites talked about black families as organized around shipmates, the born ground, polygamy, and inheritances. As for the slaves, it is suggested that the sexual predation of white men (as seen in Thistlewood's diary) and the commanding participation of black women in grounds and marketing unexpectedly provided women with a bit of freedom and leverage, which thereby may have further strained slave gender relations. In any case, it does seem that account should be taken of both the skewed sex ratios on many eighteenth-century estates (of so many more men than women) and of the possibility that having children was no longer as important as it had been in Africa.

The new Negroes' struggles in the Caribbean to create networks and instant kin based on countrymen, shipmates, and inmates constituted the beginnings of the African-American family. It was understood that as shipmates, men and women of the same slaver cargo regarded one another as brothers and sisters and would not mate, even though they were not related biologically.[3] This effort by new Negroes to sort out and anchor ideas of who should have intercourse with whom was important. In effect, it established an incest sanction which, anthropologists argue, is the basis of family formation.

Once slave households were underway, they varied considerably from one parent to two, father or mother centered, with children belonging to both, either, or to neither head of household.[4] Historians who make reconstitutions usually base them on plantation registers of slaves listed by household. This convenient method raises problems, however. How the registers were made is usually unclear. Was the census taken on the spot by a driver or clerk? Reported individually by the head of household? Or (more likely) was it drawn up in the manager's house in a reasonable and tidy fashion to show an absentee that all was in order despite the incessant movement of slaves on and off the plantation? The registers also make an impression that households were stable and static when in effect, they were remarkably fluid, porous, and extended and in other ways inaccessible to the whites' surveillance and record keeping. Plantations were confining, so slaves often courted and mated elsewhere if they could. As one owner, unhappy with this tendency, put it for so many:

> it is better that the Ladies should see company at Rooms's [Estate], than that the Gentlemen of Rooms's should be obliged to seek the company of the Ladies elsewhere: the child becoming the property of the Proprietor of the female. With respect to the preference to be given between the purchase of raw Slaves and that of seasoned Negroes, it is to be consider'd, that, the former will be more likely to remain at home than the latter, as they will of course attach themselves to those with whom they get first acquainted or at least in the Neighbourhood; but, Negroes who have lived in any other parts of the Island, having formed attachments elsewhere, will ramble, let the distance be what it may, to their old Quarters, and thereby become of little use to their owners from undergoing more fatique than they are able to bear.[5]

Given the practice by Caribbean slaves of making hidden households on and off the plantation, Sidney Mintz's warning about what did and did not constitute a slave household is apt. One should not postulate that a household occupied by "what is called a 'family' necessarily includes a co-residing sociological 'father'." Nor should we equate household with family or "marriage" with a sacramental or civil service. "We cannot suppose that serial unions are the equivalent of 'promiscuity', or that the *irrelevance* of societal norms means the *absence* of societal norms." In short, Mintz concludes, terms like *family* and *marriage* raise the same problem as do *monarchy* and *theocracy*, even though "for many purposes we are inclined to suppose that such terminology has a genuine cross-cultural validity."[6]

Plantation registers as informal censuses will continue to mislead until they are correlated with other sources. A facet of family life highlighted in the fugitive slave advertisements, for example, is geographical mobility to the degree that was self-imposed; Caribbean slave families were extended to a remarkable extent. Members lived separately and perhaps often by choice, occasionally on different properties where women as well as men customarily kept their own households and grounds.[7]

The fugitive slave advertisements expose ordinary usages of kin nomenclature. As in the case of ethnic designations in the same source, the identification of sisters, aunts, grandparents, and the like was minimal in the South and far richer in the Caribbean. This is odd. Given that the advertisements' purpose was to recover valuable property expeditiously and that the majority of plantation slaves everywhere ran off to visit kin, it made good sense to be as explicit as possible about a fugitive's "connections" and their whereabouts. One would expect, then, to find the most refined use of kinship terms in societies such as Virginia and Barbados, where the slave trade was no longer important. In such places slaves had the time — and thus the Creole, not African, survival rates — to establish extensive networks of two or three generations' duration and depth. However in South Carolina and Jamaica, where the trade thrived throughout the eighteenth century and kept many plantation communities in flux, families presumably would develop more slowly. One would expect that the use of kin terms would be more modest because less family existed for the fugitive to work with. The corresponding views incapsulated in the notices indicate that these assumptions are only partially valid. The most refined use of kin terms to specify a fugitive's whereabouts were Caribbean, the most rudimentary were from the Chesapeake Bay region, and South Carolinian usage ranged between the two, that is, between an expansive or a minimal recognition of slave kin. Caribbean advertisers referred to aunts, uncles, grandparents, and a godmother while alluding to polygamous, monogamous, extended, or nuclear families. Southerners, however, acted typically as if slave families were always and exclusively nuclear.[8]

Planters in the Chesapeake Bay region used only the most obvious and unavoidable designations—fathers, mothers, and occasionally a brother or sister—to focus attention on where a fugitive might be found. In this region where absenteeism was rare, paternalism was something more than an ideological sleight of hand to blunt abolitionist attacks. A planter's reticence to see family as much more than women and children stemmed from a truly patriarchical and proprietary view of blacks as members of the master's family. By contrast, planters in the Carolina lowcountry and in the Caribbean seldom implied that their own—itinerant—families included blacks as well.

Probate records also reveal important regional differences in common understandings of how slave families were constituted. While Chesapeake Bay region planters spoke of black families as being comprised almost exclusively of women and children,[9] in the Carolina lowcountry (the records of which focus Herbert Gutman's argument for slave domestic stability in two-parent, monogamous households) men were commonly included by whites' unique habit of designating slave parents. The reference would be to Ben, his wife Linda, and her child, or to "their" or "his" children.[10]

More is at issue here than simply a matter of the conventions concerning the most informative and effective means of securing the return or disposition of valuable property. Rather, the question is the willingness—in regions other than the Chesapeake—to try and describe the whole of a slave's world, of which a most important feature was the born ground. This exclusively West Indian concept was mentioned by an Antiguan planter who, on the eve of emancipation, argued that most of his former slaves would remain on the estate and "attach themselves strictly to the Soil" because "it is one of the properties of a creole negro to be fond of the place of his birth; he calls it (I have heard them call it so myself) his born ground; in fact, the associations of his childhood are all laid there."[11]

The born ground warrants a closer look, for at times it was a serious obstacle to economic planning. In the 1790s Balcarres wrote that while slaves in the Windward Islands were "mere Chattel, here [in Jamaica] that kind of Property savours more of the Soil," by which he meant that, paradoxically, West Indian planters often found themselves tied to their estates in ways the more migratory Southern planters never were.[12] While Southerners pushed their slaves without much difficulty into the greatest internal migration in U.S. history, the filling up of the Deep South in the early 1800s, Jamaicans, equally compelled to move, encountered serious problems from slaves who resisted displacement.

Beset by sizeable slave mortalities accountable to very high infant mortality rates[13] and by a reasonable fear that the abolition of the slave trade would therefore mean the end of slavery itself, many West Indian planters gave up. As their estates slid into bankruptcy, turned to ruinate, or both, some considered a move upland, where the climate was healthier, crops such as coffee were not as arduous as sugar, and slave women would be denied ready access to the towns where markets and lovers dampened their willingness to have children and to care well for the ones they had. However, the whites' schemes often ran against the slaves' determination to remain close to their precious homes, grounds, market networks, and burial places.

Faced with the conflicting interests of proprietor and slave, some supervisors even resisted the first step of a move—taking an informal census. Posting home to England the obligatory annual inventory of "stock," an attorney apologized for including the cattle but not the slaves. To "examine" them "minutely" would make them anxious that they are to be sold and "produces discontents."[14] A manager who spent two years putting slave houses on a healthier site explained: "These things must be done by degrees as it makes the old Negroes uneasy to remove from their old habitations where their little planting & fruit trees are, but all the new people are removed from it."[15] When moves did get underway, they could seem to be endless. Balcarres, whose impetuous flair as governor left a permanent mark on Jamaica, purred cautiously when as an absentee he wished to move entrenched slave families: "If you can do it with Secrecy, I should Say with profound Secrecy. . . . do it slowly take you[r] Time. . . . Get your ground ready at Martin Hill to receive them with every possible Comfort. . . . Let no Negro go . . . until every Comfort is provided, give them on their arrival easy work & then let some of them make a visit to Balcarres Plantation to report their Happiness."[16]

Confronted by moves they did not want, some slaves reacted creatively, others sickened and died. One solution was for slave leaders to ask a wealthy neighbor to buy them all. A group for sale that lived near Blue Mountain Estate was bought after its "head people" approached the estate attorneys, who then justified the purchase to the absentee by pointing out that the new slaves had grounds within ten miles, "connections" at Blue Mountain, and actually already had houses on the estate even though they were owned elsewhere. Given West Indian domestic patterns, one wonders if this was all that unusual; some Leeward Maroons kept houses on neighboring plantations as well as in their own village.[17]

Others resisted relocation more passively, however. The owner of a worn-out northside ginger plantation was told that to move the slaves, "all born on the Place," was to risk the slaves "pining away."[18] This allusion to dirt eating, a common and deadly affliction in the islands, is complemented by a terse entry by Thistlewood, who in 1782 mentioned a Maurray slave, who after being sold, ate dirt, drank grave water, and died. When it came his turn, Thistlewood noted simply, "a Visible Grief in all our Negroes . . . on Acc[oun]t of Moving."[19] His contemporary, William Beckford, also connected moves, which he said could be more destructive than a plague, to mysterious and wasting illnesses.[20]

Slaves struggled against plans to move them because leaving threatened the perpetuation of a family through time. Slaves would sicken mysteriously when faced by the loss of property, which they regarded not simply as a commodity but as heritable. As one planter explained, grounds are distributed among the nearest relatives if no provision is made before hand.[21] According to another planter, "the Negroe Ground as it is called is never changed so that a Slave being in possession of a Valuable tract of Land, may at his Death bequeath it to his son or Friends (provided such Son or Friend is a Slave of his Master) & no other Slave, nor can any other person whatever molest him in the Possession, unless his Master chuses to dispossess him of it."[22]

This remarkable effort by slaves to make a heritable estate is displayed in evidence from Jamaica and the Ceded Islands—societies distinguished by formidable mountains, abundant maroonage, and largely undeveloped interiors even as late as 1800. Determined to redistribute more equitably property accumulated by his slaves, Monk Lewis "made it public" that no one was to own more than "one house, with [a] sufficient portion of ground for his family." After all, some had "inherit[ed]...several" houses and "numerous" gardens while others had little.[23] Needing heavy draft animals on one of his estates, Joseph Barham proposed buying them from the slaves (among whom the "rich" were identified as those who owned more than a hundred head). In reply, his manager warned that they should not "compell those to sell *who have no Children* [my emphasis]."[24] Evidently, it was understood that they would lean first on those propertied slaves who were childless, because those who did have children would not be inclined to sell cattle destined to be a legacy. From Grenada, a planter who claimed that he had slaves who owned property worth "40, 50, 100" and "even a few" worth £200 sterling testified that this "property [was] regularly conveyed from one generation to another without any interference whatever."[25] Beckford said the same; slaves "absolutely respect primogeniture," and "the eldest son takes an indisputed possession of his father's property immediately after his decease."[26] Edward Long explained how the custom worked: the grandfather, called "father" by the slaves, "nominates a sort of trustees, or executors, from the nearest kin, who distribute them among the legatees, according to the will of the testator, without any molestation or interruption, most often without the enquire of their master."[27]

Heritable property was a source of conflict as well, however. In 1826 an anonymous writer attributed the low birthrate in Jamaica to "a peculiar custom" of slave parents, who "do all they can" to keep their children at home (even to age forty) and "subject to & dependent upon them." Parents accomplished their own form of control and authority by holding on to family grounds into old age, thus delaying division among adult children eager to establish their own households. Therefore, to reverse declining birthrates, the writer recommended giving fresh land to young adults, or making their parents do so, as Monk Lewis did. Once "independent in food," slaves would make permanent unions, become "attached to a spot," have children, and begin to approach North American population growth rates.[28]

Given the heavy spiritual burdens that West Indian slaves (and maroons) placed on family members living and dead, and their tenacious hold on particular "spots" — born grounds and gravesites — a case can be made that what the more established black families tried to do in the Caribbean was based on the way land was thought of and used in Africa. There, Africanists refer to the "family estate," a concept that calls attention to the sacred and corporate nature of a family's land, which is not seen as a marketable commodity but rather traditionally as tilled collectively and controlled by the eldest male, but corporate in the sense of belonging to the ancestors and being the focal point of commemorative ritual.[29] Thus the presence or absence of slave property and markets does not fully explain the diverging paths of acculturation and resistance in the Caribbean and the South. Rather, it is what slaves did domestically with their economic leverage that made for the significant differences, and the concept of "the family estate" may sharpen regional comparisons of slave domesticity.

Distinctive courtship and marriage practices flowed from and reinforced the slaves' diverse meanings and uses for property. In the Caribbean, slave domestic relations were polygynous, African in origin, and the most difficult to change. Alone among missionaries, who usually regarded the practice of "plural mates" (the common term) as "licentiousness," one cleric argued that slaves' domestic bonds were "by no means to be regarded in the light of promiscuous concubinage" but rather as "Polygamy."[30] The anonymous author of the 1826 birthrate study noted that although slaves would accept baptism, to interfere in their domestic concerns led to "acts of poisoning & obeah." Among them "polygamy" was an "innate Custom" and African, whereas attachment to one woman was "entirely an adoption from the European [and] . . . daily increasing as Africans die off."[31]

"Unconscious evidence" in plantation records and newspapers also in-dicates that polygamous households may have been more common than previously realized. Barham's manager "generally attributed" the low birth-rate on Island Estate "to [the slave women's] uncontinency & their being so much addicted to polygamy which is scarcely possible to prevent."[32] Polygynous households also poke through the runaway notices of the face-to-face society of Barbados, where owners were able to include names and addresses of a fugitive's mates. Ned Boy was one of two carpenters described in the same notice as having three wives; they lived respectively at Mr. Charles Padmore's Estate, Mr. Spellow's, and Captain Thomas Phillip's in Bridgetown. Phil, who had three wives, was also characterized as handsome, young, and black, with long hair; he had once been a porter. His owner, who as usual learned the whereabouts of his slave's mates, mentioned women at Mrs. Penny's at the lower end of Swan Street, at Mr. Leach's in the Roebuck, and a third near the Barracks. A comment that begins to uncover the complexities one would expect if remnants of African polygyny marked slave domesticity — relations of wives to each other, for instance — concerned a young woman whose owner suspected that she was harbored either by her husband or by his second wife, Peggy.[33] In Barbados, eleven fugitives in 283, not quite 4 percent, were advertised as having two or three wives, the majority the latter, or thirty wives total.

For Jamaica, only six runaways were listed as polygamous. One, Fanny, had a "Plurality of husbands," and a waitingman was described as having "several wives." Polygyny must have been as extensive as elsewhere, and probably more so, but several factors obscured its survival. Jamaica was large, its plantations more open than those elsewhere, and because owners did not know their slaves as well, they lacked information about the mates of a fugitive that whites in compact Barbados had at their fingertips.[34]

It is also noteworthy that in the advertisements of each of the four plantation societies women were listed as mates, that is, as "wives." From Maryland, a fugitive said to "keep . . . three wives" was also described as "pretends to be religious." Another man was characterized in part as "supported and concealed . . . by several Negro Women whom he calls his Wives." And Cambridge, a waterman was "so well known as to need no other description . . . [he] has a Wife at almost every landing on *Rappahannock, Mattapony,* and *Pamunkey* Rivers."[35]

Among the 1,280 fugitive men in Virginia a negligible number, two, were listed as polygamous, a fraction compared to Barbados. And in South Carolina, only a few among the 2,582 fugitive men were listed as having more than one mate. An impressionistic source suggests otherwise, however. An English traveler noted that on the great antebellum Heyward family rice estate, the master did not interfere in any way that did not concern his own interest. "[The slaves] may have two or three wives apiece so long as they do not quarrell."[36] These examples nothwithstanding, for the whole of the American South, where evangelical Christianity mounted a largely successful assault on plural mates, a more convincing overview of slave domesticity is that of *Time on the Cross* and the Gutman study. After initial sexual trysts young black people usually settled into monogamous unions.

When the alien Judeo-Christian ethic did begin to reorient slave gender relations and family strategies, the results contrasted sharply from one region to the other. Remember that agricultural reformers pursued different objectives regionally, in part because Southern slaves comprised a naturally growing population and Caribbean slaves did not. Caribbean reform centered, therefore, not on behavioral modification, but on "the causes of depopulation," about which planters and managers, by the 1790s, were surprisingly knowledgeable.[37] They recognized the importance of sex ratios and the connections between infertility on the one hand, and yaws and other venereal diseases on the other. They were also aware (without the germ theory of disease) that cutting the umbilical cord could lead to tetanus ("lockjaw") and that breast feeding inhibited conception.

Thistlewood's diary indicates that before the 1780s whites were not too concerned about slave "promiscuity" and its effects on rates of conception. This attitude changed, however, when monogamy came to be seen as indispensable to schemes of reform that would reverse population losses. If slaves made lifelong unions, reformers reasoned, they would no longer exhaust themselves by nighttime traveling and socializing in towns. Once encouraged to settle in at home, women would want to have children and take better care of those they had.

Characteristically, Monk Lewis offered the most prescient insight to "the causes of depopulation." He directed his reforms at the women and their African custom, in typically sparse environments, of spacing births around long periods of breast feeding. Convinced that this practice was harmful, he sent for the women and informed them that on the first day of the fifteenth month following a birth all infants would go to the weaning house; mothers of recently born would have a grace period of two months.[38] In reaction, his slave mothers insisted that they should not do field work during the two years that they breast fed. "Of course their demands were rejected, and they went home in high discontent; one of them, indeed, not scrupling to declare aloud, and with a peculiar emphasis and manner, that if the child should be put into the weaning-house against her will, the attorney would see it dead in less than a week. . . . This is the sixth death in the course of the first three months of the year, and we have not as yet a single birth for a set-off. Say what one will to the negroes, and treat them as well as one can, obstinate devils, they will die!" Most importantly, Lewis realized that a low birthrate was in part a conscious decision: "they do not like their situation," he wrote, and so "they are barren."[39]

Thistlewood and Landon Carter are representative of regional differences in perceptions of slave women and child rearing. Put simply, in the Caribbean before about the 1790s women were neither expected to have children nor to care well for those they did have. In the South it was assumed they did both normally. Before the 1770s (and the advent of abolitionism), the issue only surfaces in the Caribbean in the schemes of agricultural reformers, whereas in the South, pregnant women, mothers, and children fill plantation sources of all kinds.

Carter's diary is full of slave women who used their fecundity to slow plantation routines in ways unheard of in the Caribbean. The slave mothers who were breast feeding told the overseers that it was master's order they were to feed their infants "five times [daily]." Carter had the women whipped and reduced nursing "to half an hour before they went to work, half an hour before their breakfast; and half an hour before they go in at night." But the women persisted. The overseers were "simpletons"; "Our Wenches have all taken it into their head[s] to cry out at this busy time." Carter also accused the "Bellyed [pregnant] women of [having been] idle" for five months.[40]

By contrast, Thistlewood rarely mentioned expectant mothers or a slave child by name, let alone referred to children generally. Once, however, when switching gangs from one place to another and after naming the individuals involved, he added as an afterthought, "and enough of the picaninnies about" as if to toss in enough black children to complete the setting. As for expectant or nursing mothers, like his contemporaries Thistlewood regarded them as a nuisance: "Sent Little Lucy (Moria's pickinniny) to Egypt, to Hagar to Wean from the Breast." In order to hire out Coobah he first "made [her] leave her child with Nanny & g[a]ve a bitt, 4 herrings, to each."[41]

In time, the West Indian whites' callous regard for children may have rubbed off as it coupled with unusual opportunities for some black women who chose to play the field, particularly those who lived close to a town. At this point a remarkable change in outlook occurred as the women abandoned African values that emphasized that above all else these adults were to live in families and women were to make the children who perpetuated a family through time. Thistlewood recorded graphically a sign of the new ethic.[42]

Sat. 1 Oct. 1768
x Phibbah's Coobah, marked on Silvia's Smock bosom D T S E H for dago her husband, Mr Meylor's Tom her Sweetheart, and J[oh]n Hart . . e whom she is supposed to love best, and other Ornaments:

```
*******   D T S E H   ******
*   *   *              *   *   *
*******                ******
```

```
##########
#  A flour-  # (all that/the/heart
#    ish     # Love/s/ best)
##########
```
here's Meat for Money
If you're fit, I'm ready
But take Care you don't fish in the pon

This statement by Coobah and Silvia was echoed by another young woman whose family was implicated in a dangerous conspiracy. After discussing rebellion with "strange" Negroes who had come on and off the estate, the driver was questioned by his godmother, who apparently reminded him that he might be jeopardizing them all. To this the godmother's daughter added as the driver walked by, "Pho! I'm headman of my own house. . . . & I dont want to hear of any other Head Man."[43]

Given the potent combination of a polygynous heritage and skewed sex ratios West Indian slaves had to create some kind of orderly domestic ground rules beyond the original shipmate incest taboo. Their solution may have been in part to have men circulate among households as they shared women/ wives. That some polyandry (as well as polygamy) did occur is suggested by John Shipman, a scholarly Methodist preacher, who wrote in 1820 that there were "rather few" women who did not keep more husbands than one, "& frequently many husbands, all cohabit with her with the knowledge of each other."[44]

Plunged into a situation where it was understood that women were both shared and had considerably more say in the arrangement than in Africa, some men were concerned about obtaining wives and then holding on to them. From the bottom of an early eighteenth-century Virginia inventory, a note that Roger hung himself in the old tobacco shed ended with "not any reason, he being hindred from keeping other negroes men's wifes besides his owne." From the same is a note that George, who was sick in the stomach and eventually died, "Said his Country men had poysened him for his wife."[45] The eighteenth-century novelist Edward Kimber portrays a Coramantee revolt in Maryland that was motivated in part by the absence of available women.[46] More than a century later in Jamaica during the trials following the 1831 rebellion, a slave testified that he had been married to Sarah Atkinson for three months but did not live with her. Asked why he married, he replied that "Mr Whitehouse [a missionary] told us if we marry nobody can take away our wives."[47]

If polygyny was part of the outlook of slaves early on, it is useful to ask what effects that practice had on the self-views of men. "Resistance" scholars notwithstanding, slavery was often profoundly demoralizing, although demoralization may have been blunted in the Caribbean, where expectations about gender roles were conditioned by the more widely accepted polyga- mous strategies. If this was so, it may be assumed that there was considerable coming and going between households, particularly of men between the households of women, rather like the contemporary Haitian custom of *placage*. The most important older male in the mother's household was her brother, the childrens' uncle, and not the actual father. The mother- child bond, while of the special quality it has always had in the African- American community, was perhaps in the Caribbean not the same kind of beleaguered outpost or last resort that it has been in North America. Nor was the bond considered as a sign, at least in the white world, that a black man was not doing his job.[48]

To rethink the problem of regional differences in slave family and gender relations in light of such traditional practices as the family estate and polygamy is to reassert the absolute necessity of viewing slave economy, family, and religion as a unity. To do so contrasts sharply with the thrust of studies of antebellum slave culture and community in which it is assumed that black family life tended to become involved with the values of the dominant white culture. What whites did have to offer is what one Af- ricanist has termed "the sentence of monogamy."[49]

Once African values and ways are allowed to penetrate understandings of slave life, in this case the unity of the slaves' domestic economy and outlook, issues bob to the surface that are much richer, comparable, and aware of black cultural resiliency than those generated by the white cultural hegemony approach. Consider, first, the new Negroes' inception of family, using the shipmate incest sanctions, fed by the archaic and deeply rooted idea of woman as pawn. After observing that Kpelle (Manding/Sierra Leone) stratification is based primarily on the production of economic surpluses to attract dependents, Carol Bledsoe argues "that the control of women is central to the Kpelle system of stratification, as well as that of many other African societies."[50] To this another Africanist has added that the acquisition of women and the values placed on cattle and on personal security within some type of client relationship were "perhaps the most widespread values in traditional Africa." Accordingly, "women are valued for child-producing properties, for their economic contribution to the household, and for the affinal relationship they represent to a husband and his kin."[51] More gen- erally, any human group forming a self-sufficient social system in due course, explains Dominique Zahan, does so to control the entrances and exits of women for purposes of marriage. After all, "this should not come as a surprise to any one who is aware of the fundamental role played by women (often unbeknownst to them) in African society. In fact, even though religion in Africa is principally a man's affair, its reason for being is woman, guardian of life and link between the living and the dead, between the past and the future."[52]

In turn, to recognize the religious dimension of African family economy is to dramatize the West Indian women's radical departure from traditional norms concerning bearing and raising children. This departure, ironically, was set in motion by a traditional institution — women's marketing in West Africa. From an African perspective, to want to have many children and to cherish them is customary and makes good sense. Children who survive and prosper increase the chances of one fulfilling the annual graveside sacrifices that keep a deceased parent's spirit in mind, and so intact.[53]

Africa provides additional ways of understanding the domestic arrangements of early slaves. In West Africa, husbands and wives are commonly polite and formal toward one another, which is appropriate for societies where much time is spent among members of one's own gender. A familiar example is the practice of women serving meals to the men first and then eating with the children. In both West Africa and much of slave Jamaica, women either had houses where they could sleep on their own, as they had their own grounds, or lived for much of the time with a parent or parents. It is too easy to assume that a young slave couple would wish to establish their own home before all else. This was not the case in West Africa, where married couples (among the Akan) did not do so, if at all, until they were in their thirties. Matrilineality, then, unusual throughout the world except in Africa before the slave trade, became a prominent feature in those New World regions dominated by Africans. A description of the Akan may stand for many: "One of the strongest motives is the desire, among both men and women, for domestic independence of the effective minimal lineage consisting of the children and daughters' children of one woman."[54]

Perhaps slavery — in particular niches — provided some African women and many of their daughters with ways to break out of archaic traditions (as proclaimed by the embroidery on Silvia's frock) whereby they were prized by men as pawns in exchanges. In the pain and degradation of enslavement, some, especially if they lived and marketed in a suburban area like Barham's Mesopotamia — and in Jamaica thousands did so — found themselves usually among other women and so more in a space of their own making. For them, monogamy and bearing and raising children as slaves for massa or busha (overseer) may not have been as important as it later became during the missionary period on the eve of emancipation (and much earlier throughout the South). By that time many may have seen respectability, not freedom of movement and choice, as more desirable. At the very least, relatively few slave women were any longer the "clients" or pawns of black men. And before it is assumed that such clientage was transferred to white men, it is necessary to investigate further the differences between monogamous and polygamous practices in the two plantation regions. The effort to push back into the eighteenth century a model of stable, two-parent, monogamous slave families with little "divorce" will not do in the Caribbean and may be unsuitable for the colonial South as well.[55] If this approach to what both whites and blacks at the end of the century were saying incessantly in their own ways about slave infertility and infant care is feasible, then it would not be the first or last time that women, during those periods of rapid change that promised outlets from male domination, have set economic opportunity and self-liberation before domesticity. These proposals, however, should be seen in light of the spiritual views that pervaded the West Indians' "political state" and were so often in both regions a conspicuous feature of resistance as well.

# 8

## Plantation Religion and Resistance

> The economic reason, as usual, explains nothing; slavery, even
> more than an economic fact, is a human fact, that is, psycho-
> logical and in a wide sense religious and cultural.
> — Alberto Moravia, 1972[1]

Interpretations of slave religion often begin with developments in the late
eighteenth century when the sources open up and there is a good story to
tell: the formation of separate Negro churches in Philadelphia, Williamsburg,
and in Georgia on the Savannah; and, in the Caribbean, the arrival of black
Baptist preachers from the South who accompanied the British evacuation
of émigrés following the American Revolution.[2]

To begin this way, so late in the game, makes sense. We know little
about the religious outlook of the mass of field slaves before the early 1800s,
and will never know much more because the surviving sources are too
thin. Still, the problem warrants close attention given the controversy about
the relationship between slave conversion and socialization and the larger
problem of the role of religion in popular revolutionary movements. An
important argument depicts conversion as another form of the planter's
hegemonic control of slave life. Christianity may have imbued blacks with
dignity and self-respect, such teachings as "servants obey your masters" and
"prepare for the next life which will be better than this one" obscured the
real sources of their oppression and thereby stifled efforts to organize effectively against slavery. A resistance reply to this damage argument is that
such slave innovations as spirituals, the shout, and counterclockwise shuffle

dance demonstrate an Africanized Christianity — the "invisible religion" — that formed the base for the considerable cultural autonomy blacks achieved in antebellum slave quarters. As for the Caribbean, in the early nineteenth century Christian converts led the largest rebellions ever, and it has been argued that religion played an important role in the major antebellum conspiracy of Denmark Vesey (1822) and the rebellion of Nat Turner (1831).[3]

Given the conspicuously dramatic regional contrasts that appear — even with relatively meagre sources — in what slaves made of Christianity and what it did to them, it is best to proceed plainly. The following case studies are intended to open profitable lines for future inquiry into the complex problem of religion and resistance. The first case study concerns obeah, a shorthand for the new Negroes' African knowledge (chapter 3) and seen here as on a decline as the outlook of plantation slaves. The second study, set in South Carolina, concerns a crucial episode in the early 1730s when the Gullah, the most African of mainland black people, first encountered evangelical preachers. The third views conversion in Virignia at a later stage and as another avenue of advancement for slaves who embraced an assimilation that promoted self-interest, mobility, and literacy. The fourth case study opens discussion of missionary Christianity in the Caribbean, a development that may be divided into urban and rural styles, accommodating slaves in the first instance and readily getting out of control in the second. While the main focus throughout is on religion as, in part, another way of talking about slave acculturation, attention is also paid to the role of religion in the limited forms of resistance by plantation slaves. Until the last years of slavery, rural people generally did not organize resistance as did the new Negroes before them and the assimilated artisans who moved to the fore of the struggle in the last quarter of the eighteenth century.

## Obeah

Witch beliefs flourish in political ambiguity
— Mary Douglas, 1980[4]

Obeah was a "science" brought from Africa and practiced by those who were older, crafty, formidable in appearance, and "always" African, wrote the Jamaican historian Bryan Edwards. Intentionally mysterious, obeah figures were respected and revered by the slaves, who took every precaution to keep their identities hidden. Obeahmen were "consulted upon all occasions," Edwards explained, "in order to revenge injuries and insults, discover and punish thieves and adulterers; to predict the future, and for the conciliation of favour."[5]

More commonly, obeahmen and women were doctors in the Western sense of those who cured ostensibly by putting medicines on or in the body.

Thistlewood's Coramantee girlfriend Phibbah early in their relationship sought out Quashiba to cure her chronic headaches. The obeahwoman "sett" Phibbah's head in what Thistlewood called a "performance" in which Phibbah's temples were rubbed with a herb solution, her head bound tightly with a band, then she was told (sensibly, assuming she had migraines from Thistlewood's persistent bird-dogging and bullying) not to speak to anyone for several hours.[6] Thistlewood also mentioned an African "who used to gather a few leaves of a plant, and Squeeze Some of the Juice in the Eye" of a fevered person, who would sweat in five minutes, presumably as the fever broke. His informant had "Seen this leaf, but does not know it," but the obeahman was "a Coramantee [who] Said he used it in his Country."[7]

Slave as opposed to modern doctors also healed psychically, so they were experts in the prevention, diagnosis, and cure of misfortune. This popular responsibility, for feelings of victimization were common among plantation people, is a central issue in African cosmology but only peripheral in mainstream Christian thought and ritual.[8] African villagers often see disease and misfortune as spiritual matters. A "medicine-man," explains the Kenyan scholar and Anglican John Mbiti, is in effect both doctor and pastor to the sick, and his medicines in modern Africa are much the same as those used two hundred years ago in Jamaica. They are made from plants, herbs, powders, bones, seeds, roots, juices, leaves, liquids, minerals, charcoal, and the like and may be part of more general applications in which the healer may bleed or apply massages, needles, or thorns.[9] Equipment of this kind was proscribed in a 1760 anti-witchcraft law in Jamaica that was directed at women as well as men and renewed in 1938: "Any Negro or other Slave who shall pretend to any Supernatural Power, and be detected in making use of any Blood, Feathers, Parrots' Beaks, Dogs' Teeth, Alligators' Teeth, broken Bottles, Grave Dirt, Rum, Egg-shells, or any other materials relative to the Practice of Obeah or Witchcraft . . . upon Conviction . . . [shall] suffer Death or Transportation."[10]

Curing and counseling by slaves went on all around whites, who sometimes like Thistlewood were a part of these enterprises. Still, white people could not realize that obeah worked as a religion, not even Monk Lewis. According to books, blacks have no religion, Lewis exclaimed, but this is "quite incompatible" with their ideas concerning spirits and the existence of an afterlife. No one has "God bless you" on their lips more than a Negro, nor means "so sincerely damnation when he utters such to an enemy." As far as Lewis could see, however, as he described obeah page after page, slaves did not have "external forms of worship."[11] From the evidence of the complaints and stories brought to him, he sensed that obeah and poisoning were closely linked; that an obeahman's psychological dominance was based on his unofficial power over life and death. It was obviously disruptive of white authority. Exasperated, Lewis eventually declared, "I should make it a crime even so much as to mention the word Obeah on the estate."[12]

A few years later (in 1820) John Shipman, a Methodist missionary, summarized the whites' understandings in "Thoughts on the Present State of Religion among the Negroes of Jamaica."[13] Individuals long in the habit of watching Negroes, Shipman declared, described their styles of witchcraft as ranging from "harmless" to a major threat to security. Harmless obeah, for instance, was sought to protect property, uncover secrets, predict the future, charm overseers in order to prevent punishment, and—penciled in and interlined—was used by women to attract men. Its "regular ceremonies" incorporated such small and common items as cats' teeth, feathers tied in the corner of frocks, and bottles of rainwater, with five-penny pieces on their cork stoppers set in provision grounds. The bottles, or more representationally small doll images, were placed as warnings to potential thieves (and are mentioned in Thistlewood). On the other hand, a more "alarming" manifestation of obeah often began with the ceremonies of the first type but killed with poisons clients obtained for use against enemies black and white. Although "the medicinal effects of [plants] are well known to Negroes" generally, Shipman wrote, "Obeah people know best how to make up a poison properly." As for the third type of witchcraft, it was commanded by the "very dreadful" Myal men who knew how to apply a powerful and esoteric poison that immobilized victims before they were mysteriously brought back to life during a dance.[14]

Going beyond Shipman's focus on the techniques of obeah, it should be emphasized that slaves often regarded matters of health and fortune in a social rather than a personal context, that is, as problems of a family's welfare. Recall the anonymous writer cited in chapter 7, who in 1826 attributed the negative birthrate in Jamaica to the control of property by the elderly. He argued that by delaying the age when young slave adults were able to form their own households, this practice provoked generational strife—and witchcraft.[15] Or, as the east African Azande say, "jealousy comes first and witchcraft follows."[16] To excel in communities of severely limited means, where the source of everyone's wherewithal is the same, is to invite accusations of witchcraft that served, among other aims, to cut down to size the selfish who enjoyed "unnatural" success.

Envy was never far below the surface on many Caribbean plantations, where some victims of obeah gave up, ate dirt, and wasted away. This malady, endemic on certain estates, was a popular entry in contemporary medical manuals:

> The Slightest painful Sansaton [*sic*] in the Head, the Bowels, or any other part; any casual hurt, or less, confirms his [the slave's] appre-

hensions, and he believes himself the devoted victim of an invisible and irresistable agency; sleep, appetite, and Chearfulness forsake him, his Strength decays, his disturbed imagination is haunted without respite. Dirt or any other unwholesome Substance becomes his only Food; he contracts a morbid Habit of body, and gradually Sinks into the grave.[17]

For the Jamaican physician, Thomas Dancer, dirt eating could be explained rationally—a sudden change in routine, a new supervisor, or a move from lowland homes to the mountains—that is, to a point where there was no apparent cause, in which case the "terror" of witchcraft must be strongly suspected. When a Negro "conceives himself to be under Obeah" every accident and indisposition is attributed to "the effect of magic, and his existence becomes a misery."[18]

No source conveys very well a sense of the sudden power of a deadly sanction which, working invisibly, convinced healthy people that no matter what they did they would soon die. There are a few instances in plantation records, however, of attornies trying to explain inexplicable losses to an absentee. These include mention of an African woman on an Antiguan estate who consulted a "fortune teller" after losing her goat. The obeahman identified the thief by his distinctive ritual scars. Seeking redress through the estate manager, the woman was told (through an interpreter) that she needed "better proof." Next morning in the field, she had only a few words — "nothing like a Quarrel"—with Walker, an African who bore scars similar to those described in the obeah ceremony. Subsequently, "Walker turn'd in as usual with the other slaves at noon," and while the others ate "he hang'd himself in his House."[19] In another instance, a wainman on a Jamaican estate paid the usual fee (2/6) and consulted an obeahman about a lost steer. "Other wainmen" he said, traveled "the same road, on the same day, had lost none of their Cattle."[20]

Why me? in other words. The epistimological underpinnings of this orientation to misfortune are outlined in E. E. Evans-Pritchard's classic account of the Azande granary that suddenly collapsed and killed a man sleeping in its shade. In asking "why?" Azande recognize the empirical data, as we would have it, that wood structures rot and in time may endanger. However, they consider the more engaging and relevant questions to be, Why did the granary fall when it did? Why on that particular person— victim—and not someone else, or on no one at all? In short, Africans (and slaves) considered misfortune, including illness, as social in origin, as products of relationships that have gone badly awry; many, especially Coramantee, hold that witches can attack only within a family. Hence, a conspicuous African practice in the Caribbean was to use the coffin at a funeral to detect the witch responsible for the death. Slaves understood that the spirit of the corpse moved the coffin bearers, as if they were on automatic pilot, through the slave quarters until it directed them to stop in front of the witch's house.[21]

The following discussion provides more satisfactory pictures of three obeahmen at work in the early 1800s in Jamaica and Berbice, British Guiana. My purpose is to indicate in another way the complex and ambiguous nature of plantation authority and the degree to which resistance was both focused and limited by the more unassimilated styles of traditional religion.

"Long the terror" of Monk Lewis's Cornwall Estate, Adam was in his mid-thirties, solidly built, and of great strength and intelligence. Demoted from "principal to governor" and accused of poisoning twelve men and women, he made a flamboyant record before the proprietor's first visit. Spared on this occasion, after his sister, a house servant and lover of a Cornwall trustee, intervened for him, Adam was "living in a state of utter excommunication" when Lewis arrived.[22]

The persistent rumors that the obeahman commanded evil arose from a combination of events: a manager's complaints that Lewis's policies encouraged "insubordination," a strike by the slave women, and inexplicable illnesses and deaths, particularly of newborn. A mother who had lost nine of ten, and her most recent infant to lockjaw, came to Lewis and cried, "Oh, massa, till nine days over we no hope of them." (Tetanus infection killed approximately a third to a half of all infants within the first two weeks.) When they overheard Adam cautioning his daughter not to drink from a spring that their own children used, more women came forward to accuse the obeahman of poisoning the source.[23]

In reaction, Lewis decided to check black obeah with the "white obeah" of Christian conversion. Adam remained proud and confident in his own esoteric knowledge and abilities, however; after all, did he not control Lewis? When the proprietor was away visiting Hordley, his Windward estate, the slave boasted he would have the driver Sully replaced and sent Lewis a letter "with the grossest lies," while taking care to sign it with his new baptismal name (as opposed to the nickname "Bonaparte" in which he exulted). The head blacksmith's son died suddenly, and the plantation cook reported that the obeahman gave her a white powder to put into Sully's food. "The terror this produced" led several principal slaves to ask to be removed to Hordley. For beating Rachel with a whip and throwing a man into the river, Adam was finally charged with assault to kill.

Determined to gather the best evidence possible, otherwise the slave simply would be flogged and returned to the estate, Lewis searched Adam's house and found a musket, ammunition, and a string of beads. In court, the obeahman said he had learned to read "for the sole purpose" of reciting the Lord's Prayer. When sentenced, he replied cooly, "Well! I can't help it!" The judgment was guilty, and the penalty was exile. But before Adam was shipped to Cuba, Lewis noted, "it was no easy matter to prevent his hanging himself."[24]

The "most damning" piece of evidence against the slave was the bead string — proof, it was assumed, that Adam practiced Myal. This major form of obeah "always" began, Lewis wrote, with a dance.[25] In discussing slave religion in the Caribbean, it would be difficult to exaggerate the importance of dancing, which in the following instance propelled the ritual killing of the Myal victim, who was later "brought back to life." The victim is first danced by assistants, Lewis writes:

> till the man loses his senses, and falls on the ground to all appearances and the belief of the spectators a perfect corpse. The chief Myal-man then utters loud shrieks, rushes out of the house with wild and frantic gestures, and conceals himself in some [nearby] wood[s]. At the end of two or three hours he returns with a large bundle of herbs, from some of which he squeezes the juice into the mouth of the dead person; with others he anoints his eyes and stains the tips of his fingers, . . . chanting all the while something between a song and a howl. . . . A considerable time elapses . . . but at length the corpse gradually recovers . . . .[26]

Dancing, dreams, and visions were vehicles whereby West Indian slaves received revelation and experimented with and publicized new knowledge. Turning one's body into a receptor could make for powerful displays even when the precise nature of the lore or advice "received" could not be documented. In early-nineteenth-century Guiana, a plantation society marked by a surging slave trade and a weak Creole culture, an outbreak of possession dancing became a matter of record wherein performers were said to dance "like maniacs" as they bit clumps of grass and tore out chunks of earth with their hands. As one woman's testimony was recorded, "I was in hysterics, constantly laughing."[27]

This woman had performed a proscribed dance, the "water-mama," which erupted later on an estate in Berbice, British Guiana. The episode, taken from trial transcripts, also provides a grim and sordid view of plantation politics when an obeahman, Willem, was brought to Op Hoop van Beter Estate "to put [the estate] in order." He did so by transforming himself into a spirit, the "Minje Mama," who ordered the ritual flogging of Madalon, an old Congolese woman. This encounter, which may have included Myal rites, went on for two or three days and ended violently: "[I] saw Willem strike [her] . . . with a shovel," a slave testified, "she fell down, and cried out, 'You are killing me' "; Willem said "No, we are not killing you, but

I will drive the bad story out of your head." As the suspected witch fell at his feet, the obeahman told his audience that "he was god Almighty's Toboco, or child, and should make her get up again." "Toboco," "Attatta Sara," "Monkesi Sava," and "Alite Sara" were some of the names the slaves gave to Willem, to the dances he performed, and, presumably, to the spirits he became while dancing.[28]

Madalon's deadly ordeal began before the driver's door. Here she was whipped (or purged?) with a calabash and fire sticks, had pepper rubbed into her genitals, and was run back and forth by an assistant. Too weak to finish her row the next day, others helped and in the evening were threatened by Willem for doing so. Again Madalon was beaten (with switches from a babba tree) and suspended from a mango tree.

To a local officer's accusation that slaves were flogged at the obeahman's orders even though he was from another estate, Willem replied that he had been born on Op Hoop van Beter and that his parents still lived there. Madalon's husband Munro also questioned Willem's authority when he came to the estate to find out more about how his wife died. Willem, who by now seemed to be clearly in charge, assembled the men and ordered some to whip Munro because as an outsider he had first gone to the manager's for permission to come on the estate. Fortuyn then spoke up for Munro, reminding the obeahman that it was he who had brought him to the estate in the first place, and that he "could not beat Munro for nothing." Backing down a bit, Willem asked "How [he] dare[d] to go first to the manager's house?" to which Munro replied sarcastically that he did so only to show his pass. He would have brought it to Willem if he thought "he could read it."[29]

Eventually the court got around to the drivers, who as part of the official authority on the estate seemed to have conveniently disappeared during the episode. The head driver's 'I don't know anything' replies to eight questions in part were: "the Minje Mama dance was not danced on the estate"; "No; Willem did not order any of the negroes to be flogged"; "I have not seen anything of it"; "I was not there [at Madalon's death]; I was sick"; and "I know nothing about the business." "I am only under-driver, and all reports are made to the head driver." Another, Kees, said, "I am but a boy, recently put in charge of the plantation boat; it was the responsibility of the head drivers to stop the dance, but I had not the authority... I do not go to the field with the people, and I have no authority over them." Kees was convicted, whipped at the base of the mango tree, and put into chains for seven years. The first driver and Willem/Attatta Sara were executed.[30]

A year later in Jamaica, an obeahman was tried for his role in a conspiracy, the second that had been organized by a former governor's slaves.[31] That governor, the Earl of Balcarres, who had defeated and exiled the Trelawny

Town Maroons in 1796, had continued his astute, tough, and controversial policies in other areas. In the tumultuous era of democratic revolutions, he promoted the use of black and free colored soldiers while resettling in Jamaica white émigrés and their slaves fleeing the nearby Haitian Revolution. It was the émigrés' slaves that Balcarres wanted. They knew how to grow coffee, a highland crop whose successful propagation, he reasoned, would encourage whites rather than maroons to settle the interior mountains.

Balcarres's geopolitics had unexpected results, however. Twice on his own upland, northside coffee estate, French-speaking slaves organized revolts. The second one, in 1823, was an unusually mature conspiracy; the slaves conducted military drills for more than a year. Their leaders tried hard to infuse the plot with a ritual that would encourage followers to actually fight. The munitions they had secured by purchase (not theft) from Kingston shopkeepers were carried by mules over the mountains.

The conspirators, as rebels did at other times, tried one kind of obeah before switching to another. The first was Haitian and delivered by Baptiste, a French émigré slave whose power eventually was viewed as "not sharp enough," as one slave put it. Hence, on the eve of the annual Christmas holiday, when the conspirators held their final military exercises and rites, Jack, a local obeahman, moved to the fore.

When asked to hide the weapons and to administer an oath, this man consulted four little wood "dolls" in a plate of rum, and later figures or "jacks" in a miniature coffin. From a reading of the latter, it was determined that whites would not be around during the conspirators' final preparation. At this meeting, Jack also administered a "great swear" of rum, blood, and gunpowder. Another cut his hand, poured blood into the mixture, and vowed "By God! Every one must all stand to the battle." All swore "Yes" to this, as well as to the pledge that "all were to have one heart, one tongue and one desire" and to death in three days to any one who broke the oaths. They then marched into a cowpen and formed rings wherein the obeahman stripped and rubbed each rebel's skin with a plant, ground to a powder and described variously as that which would make them invisible, "give spirit," and "mash the skins of whites if they touch you."[32]

An African in an age of Creoles and missionaries, Jack turned himself in when the conspiracy fell apart. He implied in his confession that his world had begun to come apart when he was sold from a place and job that he liked at Gordon Hall Estate. Since then he "never kn[ew] what it was to have a fowl, a pig, a door mouth, a cocoa head!" He ended up on another estate as a runaway being harbored in return for his supernatural skill. Seeking ritual action against his wife's lover Charles, the slave who provided a cover for Jack gave him a piece of Charles's clothing, presumably as an avenue to direct malevolent magic at the lover's spirit. Jack was also to let Charles "know he was not to trouble big somebody's wife." When sentenced, Jack "invoked the Bible and the Almighty" and said, "He knew that his doctoring was what buckra called obeah. [But] Buckra had their own fashion; in Guinea [West Africa], a negro could doctor." He was sorry and hoped God would forgive him. His owner (to whom he turned himself in) had taken away his job as carpenter, a task that he liked and did well.[33]

These brief descriptions indicate that obeah cannot be seen in isolation. The power and knowledge summoned by its esoteric rites concerned the fundamental well-being of slaves, their health, loves, property, and families. As such, obeah both fed and contributed to the same passions and allegiances that fueled the other major features of the plantation's political culture — ethnic rivalry and contests over turf. Together these features frustrated organized resistance in the countryside by keeping slaves divided, local in outlook, and often demoralized. The available documents concerning the resistance that this ambience produced often mention a grim and divisive bitterness between African and Creole. For example, accounts in 1788 of the notorious Jamaican maroon raider Three-finger Jack describe his band of runaways as chiefly Congolese and committed to killing "every Mulatto & Creole Negro they [could] catch."[34] Ethnic animosity is also overheard at about the same time in various accounts of slave rebels "determine[d] to kill the Boy on Account of his being a Creole," or yelling "Shoot the Mulatto rascal," or screaming at a slave putting out a fire the raiders had set, "You d——d Chamba cut-fac'd Son-of-a-B——h" (an allusion to the distinctive ritual scars of the Chamba).[35]

Violence between insurgents and conservative plantation slaves who typically stuck-and-stayed could be awesome. Each group was cohesive in its own way and convinced that its means of dealing with slavery was appropriate. In Tobago in 1770 a band that was mostly Coramantee ambushed a driver, and on another estate killed or wounded three other slaves including a woman and child before shooting a few whites and tossing them alive into a fire.[36] In Grenada in 1795 slaves rose up in a major war (which Michael Craton mentions as the closest equivalent in the English Caribbean to the Haitian Revolution). Again, however, divisions among plantation people ruined promising beginnings. Rather than join the rising, an observer reported, "field Negroes & particularly the Africans" hid in burnt-out houses, the skirts of woods, or in their own adjacent gardens before coming in and going back to work when troops reoccupied the plantations.[37]

The field slave's regard for the plantation as turf complemented the characteristically local and personal uses of obeah. Thistlewood's diary exposes the vicious intricacies of the poaching industry that stemmed from a territoriality that was part of the determination of hard-pressed rural people to make estates, their only homes, to be defended against outside blacks who were known everywhere by the potent term *strangers*. Whites understood this desire and exploited it. In explaining his controversial scorched-earth tactics that in the 1795 War were to set hungry Maroons against slaves, Balcarres said that slaves consider as an "Enemy" anyone who depredates provision grounds.[38]

Plantation politics were complex, and conflict among plantation people is only part of the story. For another part, attention should be continually focused on two arenas, plays and grounds, which by the late 1700s had become off-limits to whites. Here slave and maroon met amicably as well as competitively as they bargained, shared, and fought over women, food, intelligence, trade arrangements, and efficacious magic. At the beginning of the 1795 War, for instance, Balcarres sought to secure his flank by invoking the treaty and summoning a settlement of Windward Maroons to wait on him in Kingston. Sensing a trap, the Mooretown Maroons refused to move until they had consulted a nearby plantation obeahman.[39] A few years earlier in the mountainous hinterland of Montego Bay, runaways "of different [African] countries" united under the command of two obeahmen, one of whom, Brutus, had recently escaped from life imprisonment. This man set up a town that was soon growing sugarcane and provisions, which were traded to plantation slaves for rum, salt, and "other necessaries." The maroons' plantation contact was Harry, an artisan and a "party Negro" (that is, one entrusted with leading slave trackers and rangers in parties sent out to bring in fugitives like Brutus and his followers). Instead, Harry used the excess gunpowder and hunting dogs at his disposal to trade to the maroons for the jerked meat of the wild hogs that had roamed since Spanish days.[40]

Toward the end of the century, obeah lost a degree of influence among slaves. How this came about is not well documented, although it was widely accepted that slaves regarded baptism as protection against malevolent forms of witchcraft. There are indications of the blendings and overlappings that the process entailed in the following three incidences. Sarah Gilbert, a Methodist from a leading Antiguan family, wrote about obeahmen "as once the terrors of estates," who by 1803 had become innocuously specialized. At race courses, planters used them to hex black jockeys who rode competing mounts. In Jamaica in the 1770s, the white supervisor of the Trelawny Maroons asked that an Anglican priest be sent in to help officiate at the annual swearing of allegiance to the treaty. While the Maroons customarily used blood when making oaths, some—especially the younger adults—now preferred baptismal water as a way of symbolically binding themselves to an agreement. Somewhat later, an Anglican missionary criticized Jamaican statutes as only "partial[ly]" successful in suppressing the slaves' religious meetings, their instruments, dancing, and singing on the grounds that the laws simply prevented "that amusement which was the chief reasons why the young attended" in the first place. After all, it was well known that the older slaves often used such gatherings not for entertainment, but to plot rebellion. Evidently, young Creole adults (Maroon or slave), who while on their way to more individualized city existences would one day convert hymns and spirituals to black blues, had begun by the late 1700s to turn away from such basic expressions of their parents' communal outlook as blood oaths and other worshipful forms based on dance and music.[41]

The South as an allowance region like Antigua (and so without records of extensive African kinds of resistance and the obeah that drove it) provides little comparable evidence of traditional slave knowledge. When the sources do open up, witchcraft was no longer a system of thought, if it ever was, but survived as random tracings of fears and ambitions. An investigation that complements the West Indian material nicely is Alli Alho's *The Religion of Slaves,* which is based on the major sources for the study of antebellum slave religion: spirituals, fugitive slave narratives, and Federal Works Progress interviews with former slaves during the 1930s.[42]

The interviews indicate that as in the Caribbean, Southern blacks hung metaphysical understandings on the problem of ancestral spirits. They also sought charms to cure illnesses and to offset misfortune generally, but usually to find success in love or gardening (which, we may surmise, was a greater problem for Caribbean slaves given their complex and unsupervised domestic and economic enterprises).[43]

Two features of Southern witchcraft, however, are reminiscent of major dimensions of Caribbean obeah: possession and the transmigration of the spirit home to Africa. Drawing exclusively from rice coast informants (descendants of Gullah), Alho cites Bruurs Butler, who remembered the "Golla," the original Africans, even though they had all died. They were bearers of tales about Africans so spiritually potent that on occasion they could fly. Carrie Himilton mentioned two new Negroes, a man and a woman, who declared before a gathering (perhaps before they took their own lives), "We gwine back home, goodie by, goodie by . . . and jis like a bud they flew out uh sight." Another sea islander told of an 1844 whipping by a particularly cruel overseer, after which the slaves like migrating birds, "say 'quack, quack, quack' and dey riz up in duh sky . . . and fly right back tuh Africa." For slaves everywhere a more fearsome ride was that of a witch or malevolent spirit. Ed Thorpe mentioned an African grandmother who talked about the witches who rode people unceremoniously: "Dey could take off deah skins an hang un up an go out as cats."[44]

Comparing African and African-American sorcery as "essentially different," Olho concludes that the Southern type "manifests itself as limited social techniques concerned with social relations on an individual level."[45] Unlike the Caribbean versions, obeah in the South had lost its public and ceremonial context. Thus the most promising comparison of all, malicious sorcery and its antidotes, was a problem in the South for the solitary and secretive conjurer or "root doctor" such as Nat Turner. However, in Jamaica, the same person was confronted collectively and ceremonially by Myal, a cult energized by a drumming and dancing that was readily wiped out in the South by the inhibited and morally self-righteous Christian evangelicals, who by the mid-eighteenth century were attracting great numbers of blacks.

## Cultures on the Defensive:
## Evangelism and Resistance in South Carolina

> There ain't supposed to be any such thing as nachel death
> here. . . . Everything that happens is caused by conjure. They
> just don't leave anything to God.
> — Lizzie Jenkins, 1971[46]

A terrain — vast, watery, and isolated — shaped the encounter between Christianity and the Gullah people of coastal South Carolina and Georgia. Cultural isolation contributed to the Gullah's retention of African philosophical underpinnings; they reacted to evangelism with trances sometimes followed by oracular announcements. However, white evangelicals effectively suppressed the dancing that generated major resistance in the West Indies.

A local historian characterizes the mid-twentieth-century Georgia sea islands by way of its fishermen, and thereby catches the seemingly timeless quality of a region and its people, for whom the waterways are a way of life. Eking out a meager existence, fishermen spit on their bait for luck, throw away the thirteenth shrimp or fiddler crab, and always start out with the same rig they used for the last big catch. A flight of pelicans or gulls is a good omen, but only if there is an uneven number across the sky. Small, odd-shaped pieces of driftwood may be kept as good luck charms by islanders for whom a personal enemy, not fate — "bad mouth" not bad luck — causes misfortune. Coastal whites seldom question these customs explains Betsy Fancher, "they have learned that the Gullah are in some ways much closer to reality than they are."[47]

Two centuries ago missionaries made the first attempts to impose their Christian reality on that of the Gullah. Fresh from England, the Anglicans portrayed the region (in lengthy reports to the Bishop of London) as a bleak frontier caught in threatening and fundamental change as large rice plantations pushed aside extractive pioneer industries such as saw milling, naval stores, cattle herding, and tanning. Recently devastated by Indians in the Yamassee War, the colony was divided into North and South Carolina in 1719, which helped end periods of uneven government and not much government at all. Still, for more than a decade deadly epidemics, pirate attacks, and rumors of invasion by the Spanish from their base in Florida continued to unsettle.

While local churches may help instill community and in other ways mitigate frontier conditions of this nature, the established church was ineffectual because it did not appeal to common people. A parish census taken by an Anglican missionary in 1730, for St. Paul's in the heart of the sea islands, revealed that only a fourth (452) of a population of 1,818 whites were professing Anglicans, a handful of whom, forty, were communicants. Of the 3,042 blacks who lived in the parish, one was a convert and twenty-five were listed as runaways who had "deserted" four months before the Stono Rebellion to the Spanish garrison at St. Augustine, Florida.[48] As for those who remained behind, they were isolated, as another missionary said, like "a Nation within a Nation. In all country settlements, they live in Contiguous houses, and often 2, 3 or 4 families of them in one House. . . . They labour together and converse almost wholly among themselves."[49]

In the long-term, conversion to Christianity lessened the cultural isolation of the Gullah. In the short run, however, when confronted by Anglicans and evangelicals as representatives of distinctively different modes of worship, lowcountry blacks exhibited a strong preference for evangelicals who were also socially marginal. The revivalists' new style of preaching was attractive because by inspiring shouting, swaying, and sometimes ecstatic attention it promised to reinforce slaves' traditional patterns of spirituality.

To appreciate the choices the Gullah made, the competing religions should be compared in broad and elementary terms. As slaves, the Gullah had been forced into a culture whose official religion had lost much of its power and persuasiveness as it devolved into demystified, sanitized reenactments by professionals before passive audiences. Anglicans worshipped indoors; evangelicals often did so out of doors where worship began. Their wilderness camps were often instant settlements of a special ambience created by the powerfully extravagant sermons and their backdrop: the seekers' wagons, campfires, lanterns in the evening strung from trees, and, on the edges, crowds of blacks appraising white religious ceremonies that for the first time were somewhat intelligible. Meanwhile, Anglicans put congregants in seats, with their hands in laps, eyes fixed on a minister who in a thronelike pulpit read dry homilies on obedience. As products of nonliterate ways of making the world sensible, blacks could not readily fathom the missionaries' insistence that memorizing the Apostles' Creed and Lord's Prayer had much to do with worship as they once knew it, that is, infused with song and dance. Every culture dances, although ours no longer does so very well; and dance, especially in the Africans' oral cultures, was once a form of prayer. In the early 1700s, the African slave trade was running full tide, and slaves

everywhere south of the Chesapeake Bay region were relatively unassimilated. Consequently, they were not enthusiastic about the first missionaries.
"Too much talky, talky, not enough to eat" is the way a Barbadian slave
described Anglicanism.[50]

Slave perceptions of Christianity changed dramatically in the Carolina
lowcountry when a major religious revival swept through the sea islands
in the 1730s. The "Awakening" was set in motion by George Whitefield,
a Methodist and one of the most influential preachers ever. Originally
Anglican reformers who eventually became a separate denomination, Methodists believed in equality, for all were created in the image of God; they
were also driven by a desire to engage ordinary people, whose problems,
the revivalists decided, could be mitigated by rigorous programs of moral
reform. To stimulate this reformation and the glorious salvation it would
ensure, Methodists created a warm and inspiring service of communal song
and prayer. Whitefield brought this message to the lowcountry people who
were ready for a new way, or at least a respite from recent turmoil and
afflictions.[51]

For their part, a few great planters were immediately caught up in the
evangelists' potent revivals. And, in time, more of them could be heard
throughout the old colonial South addressing slave co-worshippers as "black
brother" Will or "black sister" Suckey (these novel sentiments are Robert
Carter's). As a wealthy Virginia convert, Carter manumitted more than four
hundred slaves, who represented a good portion of his fortune. Meanwhile,
other great planters changed direction as well and occasionally did so spec-
tacularly.[52]

In March 1741, the talented daughter of a prominent lowcountry family,
Eliza Pinckney, wrote her father in Antigua about a prominent planter,
Hugh Bryan, who "has been very much deluded by his owne fancys and
imagined he was assisted by the divine spirit to prophecy C[ha]r[le]s town
and the Country as farr as Pon-pon bridge should be destroyed by fire and
sword, to be executed by the Negroes before the first day of next month."[53]

Captivated by Whitefield and determined in his own way to continue
the revivalist's work, Bryan and his vision came out of an unusual upbring-
ing. Captured by Indians as a boy and taken hostage to St. Augustine, Bryan
kept himself going by absorbing a Bible he had acquired during his long
forced march south. After his return, the planter became a fervent reborn
Christian, who like many evangelicals then was an abolitionist at heart.
When he camped for several days in the woods in 1741 with large numbers
of people, "especially Negroes," his imagination, the authorities stated gin-
gerly, "became greatly excited and diseased." What actually took place at
the gathering is unclear. However, the record suggests that Bryan tried to
recreate Moses's parting of the Red Sea. Seized by "an invisible spirit," he

took up a stick as if he would "divide the waters before him" and, guided "by a direct course and without looking at the ground," he thrust into the water "till he was up to his chin," at which point his brother saved him from drowning.[54]

The real nature of Bryan's "disease," as the authorities put it, was that he talked about servile insurrection. Under the pretext of religion, this scion of one of the sea islands' leading families denounced slavery while mentioning procuring guns and blacks marching on Charleston. "People in gen[era]l were very uneasy," Eliza Pinckney continued, "they dreaded the consequences of such a thing being put in the head of the slaves, and the advantage they might take of us."[55]

The government thought Bryan insane, yet reports of people acting as if they were possessed were common during this strange period.[56] Our slaves, complained Anglican missionaries, are being taught "Enthusiasms" rather than religion. They "pretend to see visions, and receive Revelations."[57] The dangers of teaching slaves to read, so they had access to the Bible, was the issue of another report about a gifted and "very sober" slave, "the best scholar of all the Negroes in my Parish." Having read in a religious pamphlet about "the several judgem[en]ts" that afflicted sinful people," this slave convert left "abruptly" after warning his master that "there would be a dismal time and the moon would be turned into Blood and there wou'd be [a] dearth of darkness."[58]

In time a prophet emerged whose preparation, visions, and mission were remarkably similar to Nat Turner's seventy years later in Southampton County, Virginia. Philip John, a free mulatto, the governor reported, attempted "to stir up Sedition among the Negroes, by telling them that he had seen a vision, in which it was reveal'd to him, that in the Month of September the White People shou'd be all underground, that the Sword shou'd go thro' the Land, and it shou'd Shine with their blood, that there should be no more White King's Governor or great men, but the Negro[e]s shou'd live happily & have Laws of their Own."[59] After telling various slaves to "work where you please, god Almighty has given me other work to do," Philip John went into the woods, returned in a week, and told his wife "that God Almighty had been with him. . . . [and soon] all the white Buckrass" would be killed.[60]

The Gullah's distinctive spirituality carried into the 1800s and beyond. In the second year of the Civil War when Northern abolitionist school teachers arrived, the spiritual quests of the sea island blacks again became a part of the historical record. When considering their new teachers' approaches to religion, the Gullah preferred the New Yorkers because they were evangelicals, rather than the New Englanders who were Unitarian. For their part, the teachers complained that the blacks' religion seemed to take too much time and got in the way of their work. "I am at my wit's end," one wrote, because of the young people's "seeking"—up at all hour's of the night "wandering, as they said, 'out in the wilderness.'" Of the Gullah's shout-and-response another said simply, "I never saw any thing so savage," it is "certainly the remains of some old idol worship."[61]

In the early 1930s Lydia Parrish, a compiler of sea island songs, helped organize a large musical festival (Bessie Smith and the Sea Island Singers came out of this society). On a memorable night, Parrish writes, a black man from Broadfield made the "sign of Judgment" with uplifted arms and led sixty swaying singers in the shout "Can't Hide." The musicians began to move quietly, as in a trance, and it was soon evident from a peculiar heart-clutching quality in the rhythm that they were "possessed" by it. Song followed song, and the spell was not broken. Some in the audience wept, others applauded, but the Negroes appeared unaware of their surroundings. Several middle-aged Southerners said it was the first time they had seen the Negroes "get happy."[62]

It is difficult to characterize the real nature of the first contact between evangelicals and lowcountry slaves. Culturally, the Gullah had moved beyond West Indian slaves; there was no evidence here of a ritual attributed to a particular African people, or much less of some syncretic obeah rite. But the few accounts of the reactions of Gullah to revivalism point consistently to the vision and trance states that encourage efforts to put the problem in a framework of "crisis cults."[63]

Until the evangelicals' descent on a receptive population of blacks and whites, the Gullah may be said to have been caught between very different religious orientations—African and Anglican. Their reaction was like that of rural folk around the world in similar circumstances facing a colonizer's way of life (and vastly superior technology) with traditions that were diverse, enervated, and on the verge of being overwhelmed. In their search for "a more satisfying culture,"[64] as the anthropologists of revitalization movements would argue, blacks initially fell back on prophetic dreams, trances, and visions that the revivalists' potent sermon style seemed to sanction. Conversion for them (unlike the same process among black converts in the Chesapeake Bay region) at this stage did not narrow the cultural gulf between slave and free. Instead, conversion among the Gullah was a form of retrenchment; in the few instances of the resistance it inspired, it seemed to be unusually private as well. Chapter 9 considers more progressive and public efforts by slaves to mitigate an acculturation that could produce in particular regions such as the Chesapeake Bay, as a scholar of "primitive messianisms" argues, "socially disentegrating and individually neuroticizing effects."[65]

## Christian Conversion and Self-Improvement:
## Slaves and the Great Awakening in Virginia, 1750–90s

There was something peculiar about the way African slaves
were evangelized in America.
— Albert J. Raboteau, 1978[66]

The Great Awakening in the Chesapeake Bay region did not produce
wilderness prophets, millennial visions, or possession states. Nor did slave
groups display such signs of the initial contact between Africans and English
colonists as plays and obeah. If these forms occurred at all, they did so years
before the Great Awakening peaked in Virginia about the time of the
American Revolution. Instead, first accounts catch slaves at a relatively late
stage of cultural change, and as imbued with beliefs and values that seldom
wrinkled the social fabric.[67] When the long revival struck, most slaves were
Creole rather than African, and many were attracted to the essentially
nonrevivalistic—literate—features of Christianization.

Historically, Chesapeake Bay planters were more willing than those elsewhere to proselytize blacks and to allow them the bit of learning that Bible
study required. To do so satisfied both idealistic and practical considerations.
Bringing the Christian God to benighted pagans was a major objective for
founding colonies, and conversions complemented the planters' unique vision to be resident masters of autarchic plantations.[68]

By midcentury the established religion of Anglicanism was poorly served
by its clerical representatives and had devolved into a code of behavior.
These developments blunted the energy and appeal of a revivalism, which
was not able to change its appearance as a means to an end—so often
defined as self-discipline, self-improvement, and other internalizations of a
work ethic that whites defined as necessary to do a job well.

The first stages of revivals did not disturb slavery.[69] In contrast to the
Baptist phase of the Great Awakening that came later, these gatherings were
subdued, a characteristic that complemented the demeanor of the Presbyterian itinerant who led them. Tall and decorous, an essayist and poet as
well as a preacher, Samuel Davies discouraged such emotional reactions as
crying and fainting during his services. Still, as a revivalist, the preacher
believed in a religion of the heart as well as of the mind, and that overtly
emotional responses to sermons were a sign both of an efficacious service
and of the power of grace loosened among a people searching for personal
regeneration.[70] Davies's evangelism was primarily eschatological; sinners
must diligently prepare their souls immediately in order to enter the spiritual
realm. Life, a bittersweet pilgrimage, is filled with illusions; death, which
is imminent, is the threshold to a more real existence. There is also little
suggestion in Davies's sermons (as opposed to the great nineteenth-century

revivals of Charles G. Finney and others) of societies of reborn creating a "heaven on earth" by eliminating sins defined socially as drinking—or slavery.

Planters opened their quarters to evangelicals because they saw among their slaves, Davies said, "the visible Reform"—"Sobriety & deligence." As one slave told the preacher, " 'I knew nothing of that Jesus I heard you speak about. I lived quite careless [concerning] what will become of me when I die; but I now see such a life will never do, and I come to you, Sir, that you may tell me some good things concerning Jesus, and my duty to God, for I am resolved not to live any more as I have done.' Such a simple address is very striking to me," Davies added, "and would my time allow, I could give you many [more] specimens." This pliant slave also asked, "What is my Duty to God?"[71]

The first Presbyterian revivals broke out in the 1750s in Hanover, an extensive piedmont county of small farms and plantations with a population evenly divided between whites and blacks. Up-country people were ready. Feeling themselves in the midst of "an undone situation," hungry and seeking deliverance, they had already begun to turn away from a wayward and inept Anglican clergy; a large lay group was reading George Whitefield's sermons.

Addressing planters, Davies stressed the necessity of humane treatment toward those whom he "constantly" referred to as family members, a concept that fit neatly the domestic character of slavery in the region. He also mentioned children and slaves "in the same breadth," according to George Pilcher, and referred to all family members—children, slaves, and parents—as having the same religious duties and privileges. Expressing surprise at the absence of planter opposition, the preacher was a conscientious teacher who relied heavily on books and generally promoted slave literacy as a door to salvation. He distributed numerous spellers and the popular hymnals of Isaac Watts to his black converts, whom he addressed as if they were lower-class Englishmen. The slaves regarded books as "*a Reward* of their Industry," he wrote. "They expect *Books* as soon as they are capable of using them"; and "I am told, that in Almost every house in my congregation, and in Sundry other places [the slaves] spend every leisure hour in trying to learn."[72] Converts desired to "learn to read . . . from a pious Thirst after Christian Knowledge, some from Curiosity & some from Ambition," Davies reported. For slaves, the actual textual content of revivalism made more difference in this region than elsewhere. As the most acculturated in Anglo-America, Chesapeake Bay slaves were more accustomed to white English, whereas in the lowcountry and Caribbean, missionary reports continually cited as a major obstacle to the conversion the fact that whites and blacks spoke different languages. Some slaves also thought that baptism would put them "upon an Equality with their Masters." As Davies realized, they also grasped the essential individualistic character of a conversion experience in which the repentant sinner awash in guilt steps forward—alone—to make the decision for Christ.[73]

The assumptions that revivalists made about the real ambitions of slaves and the extent of their assimilation is conveyed in a 1755 sermon on the occasion of the disastrous defeat of the British General Edward Braddock in the first year of the French and Indian War.[74] The sermon assumes an audience of slaves who as Protestant converts and adept in English would realize how much they had to lose if the French won. If slaves fell into French hands, Davies warned, they would have to pray in Latin, give up the Bible, "and instead of worshipping God through Jesus Christ, you must worship images and pictures made of stone, wood, or canvas."[75]

The initial phase of the prolonged Awakening in Virginia may be seen as another dimension of society that encouraged slaves to behave properly while adjusting to whites' peculiarly virulent nativism and distinctive need for plantation diversification by means of slave artisanship. Compared to the other regions, more openings existed in this society for slaves who chose to put themselves forward as religious leaders, especially following the arrival of the Separate Baptists in the 1760s. Based on congregational autonomy, this group's polity provided opportunities for talented and ambitious blacks to become exhorters and occasionally even preachers. As the Great Awakening peaked in the last quarter of the century, the number of blacks who preached before racially mixed audiences increased perceptively.[76] Closer views of the new group of assimilated exhorters are provided by newspaper notices for seventeen who were advertised as converts of one kind or another between 1768 and 1793. The notices mention "a great Newlight preacher," a slave who "pretends to be very religious," and, in a sarcastic aside, another who was "fond of singing hymns and exhorting his breathren of the Ethiopian tribe."[77] Of the seventeen converts, ten were preachers, only one of whom (a tradesman) was also listed as skilled. All the remaining of the nonpreaching religious were highly skilled and included two shoemakers, two blacksmiths, and two sawyers (one of whom was formerly a jockey and hostler). Four were also literate, two played musical instruments, and one was a dancer. Charles, a mulatto, for example, was an artful and cunning sawyer and shoemaker who read well, and as he is "a great Preacher. . . . I imagine he will pass for a Freeman." Adam, a light-complexioned cooper and sawyer, "pretends to be a Newlight, reads and writes a little (generally in a very small hand), and forges himself passes by examining which he may be easily discovered." Titus will attempt to pass for a free man, "being uncommon sensible for a negro." He is "fond of preaching and exhorting, being, as he says, of the Baptist persuasion." Two converts from Maryland included a mulatto who called himself John the Baptist, and Peter "but calls himself Johnston," who was thirty-five, "exceedingly well dressed," and "a very plausible, mannerly fellow who professes to be a Methodist."[78] In sum, more than any other group of runaways, these converts exhibited all of the main features of a later stage of assimilation — mobility, a supple manner when dealing with inquisitive whites, and, generally, a remarkable resourcefulness in coping with slavery.

Skills and demeanors of this type were shaped in urban environments. Lott Carey, an important black Baptist preacher, hired out in 1804 as a laborer in a large tobacco warehouse in Richmond. Teaching himself to read and write, Carey, promoted to warehouse superintendant, in 1813 bought his freedom and that of two children. As a member of the city's First Baptist Church, he also helped found the Richmond African Baptist Missionary Society and, with another black artisan, a harness maker, eventually led a group of black settlers in 1821 to Liberia.[79]

Other mainland black preachers and exhorters made an important departure earlier. They came to the Caribbean as part of the British defeat and evacuation of the South in the last years of the Revolutionary War. A closer view of what they accomplished in the islands uncovers further regional differences in the role of religion in slave resistance.

### Slave Evangelism in Jamaica: Methodists and Baptists

> The entire history of European relations with Africa, from slavery to imperialism, was popularly understood [by Bakongo] in the idiom of witchcraft.
>
> — Wyatt MacGaffey, 1983

> It now appears . . . that much of the religious practice during slavery was directed against the supposed sorcery of the white man.
>
> — Leonard Barrett, 1977[80]

Arriving at a time of radical changes in the way Jamaican slaves worshipped and reflected upon spiritual matters, the black preachers from mainland America shaped an evangelism that readily divided into town and country styles. While Baptists black and white dominated rural areas, Methodists were more successful in town, where dissenter chapels like the urban areas they served were comprised mostly of women, who usually were also the catechists who taught prospective converts. Meanwhile, in the tucks and folds of the countryside, "bush preachers" inspired by newcomers who preached in the new style wrought from their congregations visions, dreams, and possession—signs of the initial encounter between traditional and evangelical ritual.

Of middle- and working-class backgrounds, brave and dedicated, the white missionaries and their families while seasoning were leveled by appalling death rates. Naive (or playing a deep game) with regard to the subversive effects of such inspiring white folktales as Moses' deliverance of the Jews from Pharoah's Egypt, they were also an ambiguous lot. Missionaries went through the motions of cultivating official approval while teaching essentially one message—that all are equal in the eyes of God—and then wondering aloud why their slave members were increasingly restless. They also hungered for respectability, which in turn amplified the slaves' own embryonic status concerns stimulated by provision gardening and marketing. In Jamaica, Methodist missionaries generally supported the planters and in spite of themselves sometimes labored to earn their approval and respect. Several used black servants and horse and chaise while carrying on more ostentatiously than their colleagues did at home in England.[81]

In time, however, the Methodists realized that they had to extend their influence further afield, a reform that would obscure another link to the establishment—their Anglican origins. To do so they rode "circuits," one of which was drawn by a missionary for his bishop in London.[82]

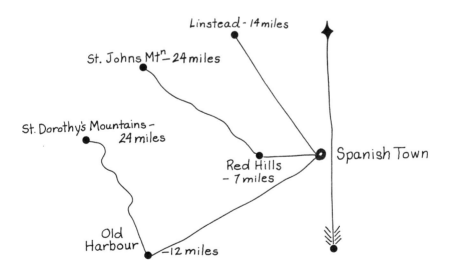

The familiar circuit rider image of the Methodist preacher is misleading in the islands, however, where in the countryside, particularly, they were not as effective as the Baptists. From the point of view of the more ambitious and able assimilateds, or head Negroes, the difference between the competing denominations was a matter of church polity. Baptists practiced congregational autonomy, which gave blacks a chance to be important locally, if not shape their own rites, whereas the Wesleyan approach to conversion— initiation, instruction, baptism—was to control all aspects of organization and worship rigorously through a "method" (the basis of the Wesleyan's name) that was more workable in a town rather than a rural setting.

Not satisfied with simply imposing a methodical approach to conversion and church organization, Methodists sought a new and morally repressive ethic. "It is not mere preaching," one claimed, it is *"entire Methodism* that will lastingly benefit the Slaves."[83] Hence, Methodists set out to combat "licentiousness" by attacking such basic West Indian institutions as the slaves' "plural mates," precious dancing, and play-full funerals. A conversation between a disbelieving governor and a preacher about dancing strikes the appropriate note: " 'His Excellancy must know that Negro dances were a system of prolificacy.' [The governor] said he did not mean those wicked dances, but a genteel, respectable dance he thought was perfectly innocent. 'I told his Excellency they were perfectly innocent, if they did not excite those passions which ought to be destroyed.' "[84]

At one level, "entire Methodism" meant education in classes run by the minister and his slave helpers. At another level, Methodist instruction was shaped by the sect's abiding suspicion of enraptured conversions. Methodists preferred a circumspect, drawn-out conversion that included the memorization of texts and rote recitations while effectively ensnaring the candidate in a web of procedures. Candidates at the Demerara (Guiana) station in the early 1820s, for instance, were first brought to the missionary John Smith, who then "presented" them to a deacon and directed the two to "go and discourse." After working on their own estate with an assigned teacher and later being reexamined by two deacons, candidates were returned to Smith, who interviewed them to see if they were "fit." If so, he recorded their names and considered them "engaged" to be baptized, usually six to twelve months later; they were then allowed to apply for full membership. When initiates did finally attend their first chapel, they sat "a little way off from the rest" before Smith introduced them: "will you receive this brother [or sister]? I find that he or she has good understanding," and "will any one speak about their faults?"[85]

Ambitious slaves who caught a minister's eye became the catechists who sought to inculcate the new learning and morality. Harry from Dutch St. Eustatius, for instance, "stirred up" slaves to "beg[i]n to have the Fear of God." The slave's sermons were seen as "all heart work" because Harry was illiterate but most effective. The governor visited and with other gentlemen soon made financial contributions to the black prayer group, while observing that if they had six more leaders like Harry stores could be left unlocked at night.[86]

Both slave and free colored women were conspicuous in Methodist chapels, and reports to general headquarters in London are filled with references to their enthusiasm for the new religion and its possibilities. Two-thirds of the members and twenty of the twenty-five class leaders of the Morant Bay congregation in 1831 were women; in the group's Sunday school, where girls outnumbered boys fifty-five to forty-eight, six of the ten school teachers were women.[87] From St. Ann's, further along the north coast, John Shipman, the missionary who described obeah in 1820, wrote in the same year that "I find the members of our Society are generally poor Free persons of Colour, principally Females and in a Town like this, where the community is divided into various classes those who have ranged themselves among the higher orders of Coloured persons feel very reluctant to come among the poor."[88] In 1804 a black woman convert struggling to make herself understood in English laid bare the sins and guilt that town women tried to relieve in emotionally tense Methodist services: "As for me pate, I have ocation to bless God, fo who he bin done fo me, befo time I used to be a high passion woman: curse, swear, fight, tell lie, theif, Quarrelsome, Adultry and many bad tings, I bin done. But now, dis time, since I put me foot a gospel; I cannot do so again being de Lod here done so much for me. O bless de Lod he done good for me poor mortal soul, he good to[o] much for me."[89]

In Roseau, the capital city of Dominica, a small revival in 1803 caught up a new missionary, Thomas Richardson, and several rapturously repentant young black women. At twenty-four, Richardson wrote conventionally about his conversion and subsequent temptations: "Read Bishop Newton's prophesies and met classes in the evening felt various very powerful Temptations this day 'Twas as tho' the Devil was let loose upon me, 'Lord save me.' " The following Sunday after preaching in a cane field, he wrote, the "Negroes seem'd to catch every word"; and later, several were so "deeply convicted that their whole frame was in agitation & they fell down crying loudly for mercy." On Sundays the missionary met the men's class of 113, the women's of 226, and baptized fourteen children. The congregation is large, he noted, it picked up country people coming to market.[90]

On this fertile ground a revival sprouted in late March led by women of color, a few of whom first came by for advice and prayer. Distressed, one lay on the floor "as tho' she was dying," but the Lord comforted her and she left "rejoicing what great things the Lord had done for her soul." And, "this Woman has like the Woman of Samaaria lived with one or more Men who were not her Husband, praise God he shall pardoneth the publicans & Harlots & giveth them a place among his people." A few days later another young mulatto woman arrived and displayed "very great anguish of Soul enquiring what she must do to be saved"; two others came by who had been saved the previous day, "Singing & praying . . . we rejoiced abundantly together." After dinner another woman came in "such distress, that I was afraid she would lose her sense . . . we met together in the evening & I explained the 2nd commandment"; another "began to weep & cry for mercy as tho her heart would break."[91]

Missionary reports of outbursts during "love feasts" described many who were deeply moved by the new preaching style even though they did not understand an English, which "went in one ear and out the de other, but after bit it det to my heart, and ah me it did so affect me dat it made me temble dust as if it was going to worry me up."[92] A head driver, his eyes upward and "with the Zeal of a Confessor," exclaimed "Before God Convert my Soul, me be like one Tigar, me Seize man-lick him, and den me be proud of this. But now, Massa Jesus, made me like one little lamb." And another: "Me be one poor Guinea Bird from Africa, all my friends be there in dat far Country. Me not have one friend in this country, but me Massa Jesus."[93] With this, the lonely woman sat down and wept. Then "what is called a filed teeth'd African" called out, "O Fader of haben heare me prayer, and send him 'pirit down on our dear Ministers, . . make them tongue like two edged sword that them may cut sinner on de right han and de lef!"[94]

The meaning of a few testimonials (which are rare in the voluminous collections) are not clear. Perhaps this is why they found their way into the report of a missionary who was still trying to figure out their real intent. An old woman "much affected . . . laid struggling on the floor till peace was imported to her." "Well Sisse what you are happy now?" The convert put her hand on her breast and exclaimed "Yes, O yes . . . happy now missa, me no let dis go, Massa, O no, no not let dis go."[95] A man with gapped teeth that "caused his words to have a hollow sound similar to that of water rushing into a cavern" and

> spoke so fast, and Negrofied that I could not understand all he said. From what little I gathered, from the response of the people, from his gestures, countenance, and eyes . . . he called the attention of the people repeatedly to these words, 'what we hear, put um to use.' 'Mind what I say, for if we no put um to use now when dat day (Judgment) come de will be no time den. De word do we no good in that day.' 'Mind what I saw, put de word to good use now.'[96]

In spite of their own moral inhibitions and ambiguity regarding social respectability and decorous services, Methodists were able to "get down off the horse"[97] and concern themselves directly with people's ordinary problems. The new familiarity between white and black in the worshipful setting of emotionally charged love feasts made for an intensity that was hardly recaptured in such reports home as "many spoke their experiences in a simple and affecting manner."[98] Occasionally, however, there are traces in a few accounts of power emanating.

> The whole scene was striking beyond anything of the kind I had ever seen. . . . the Singularity of a black audience seemingly lost in the deepest attention, but no sooner had our Children raised their voices and joined in the full Choir, than an effect was produced on them like that of Electricity [torn] . . . But what pleased me most was the effect of [the missionary] Clarke's preaching. He was exceedingly animated and energetic, and addressed himself . . . once or twice to the Children, in such a way as to rivet their attention, and to rowze their feelings. The grown people seemed to regard him as a being of a Superior order, and the children who were used either to Sleep, or to trifle away their time in church, gazed at him with open mouth, & Scarce turned their eyes from him during a long Sermon.[99]

And,

> the deepest attention and death-like silence pervaded . . . and while at prayer, tears and loud Amens attended every sentence. I thought surely the Lord is going to take possession of some of these souls tonight, and who can tell but he did.[100]

The reticence in the last sentence exposes the paradox of an early Methodism whose messengers persisted in exclaiming about "the spirit descending," while struggling to contain the slaves' profoundly excited reactions to an event blacks understood so well. Methodists did restore a dimension of the "old time religion" by bringing back singing and a provocative preaching style for services no longer restricted solely to churches ranged with lines of pews. Instead, movement and ceremony took place in the open spaces of chapels or out of doors. Nonetheless, conversion for this denomination meant ultimately mastering a text.

As for the planters, living as they did in an age of abolitionism, they were not easily put off by Methodist diffidence and attempts to fashion a genteel ritual. Believing that dissenter preachers of whatever denomination were abolitionist wolves in sheep's clothing, which in a fashion they were, planters passed tough licensing laws. For a time the new statutes effectively silenced dissenters but only in town, where the law and mobs could readily find them.

In the quickening pace of change in the late 1700s, religious developments in the countryside were much different than in the city. Arguing that the licensing that had kept all of them down in the early 1800s should be supported now that the Methodists had a foothold, Shipman pointed to the "many [who] think if they can only *Pray in public,* and have *a remarkable dream* they are called to preach the gospel." These shiftless "vagabonds," he charged "set themselves at the head of a small faction, and travel into the country." Shipman spoke of the Baptists black and white who sent their cultic followers on dream quests in the bush—"My head began to look quite big, as big as my body"—as a preparatory rite for a dramatic seaside baptism by full immersion, a magic death, and rebirth before a throng of blacks in full chorus.[101] For example, ninety-eight were "baptized in the sea, at Old Harbourt... when a great concourse of people assembled to witness the solemn scene."[102]

"The Ordenance of Baptism . . . Near Brown's Town, Jamaica in 1842" by John Baxter

The black preachers who left the South with the defeated British army after the Revolutionary War arrived in Jamaica at an auspicious moment. Dancing cults flourished, and in them slaves were experimenting vigorously with new forms of play based on the old ones that traditionally commemorated funerals. Whites who no longer took much note of play should have because slaves were busy redirecting its performances to question their condition and slavery itself. Out of the encounters of black émigré preachers and local cult leaders came a rich cross-fertilization of ideas and organization that prepared the ground, first for the white missionaries who followed a generation later and then for the largest rebellion ever.[103]

On the eve of anticolonial rebellion in Africa, the realm of the spiritual often gets out of hand[104] as authority is assailed or actually breaks down. This condition may characterize the religious setting in Jamaica as well, where from the late 1760s, from the ashes of the once exclusive and prestigious Coramantee rituals of war, healing cults sprang up to offer in rapid succession an array of syncratic religions — Myal, Convince, and bush Christianity. In a heartland of strident spirituality, St. Elizabeth Parish, for instance, the fissioning process stopped Moravian missionaries in their tracks. Having secured permission in the 1780s to proselytize next door to their old station at Barham's, the Moravians discovered that the opportunity was "useless"; the people of Lancaster Estate, troublesome to the point of rebellion, held to African "supersitition" with "a pertinacity that could never be overcome," the slaves had "formed a small [religious] colony for themselves," and on an estate near Montpellier (scene of the major battle in the 1831 war), the missionaries were asked in to check an "irregular" Christian bush preacher, probably George Lewis, who commanded a congregation of between three and four thousand.[105] Monica Schuler surmises that the slaves' idea of sin as a socially transmitted evil made the objective of their cults a narrow one: to find a workable ritual that promised to counteract whites conceived as malicious sorcerers, a view that complements research on religious expressions of anticolonialism in Africa.[106]

The argument is that Jamaica was the one Anglo-American plantation society in which, as the whites said obsessively, "a second St. Domingo War" was possible. Slaves were more likely in Jamaica than elsewhere to replicate the Haitian model of black liberation: a war led by an assimilated elite and powered by a ritual shaped by foot soldiers, the hitherto apparently acquiescent and cautious rural people. Obstacles to mass rebellion were formidable everywhere. Given such divisive features of plantation life as ethnicity, obeah, and the conservative aims of the family estate, only a profound change in outlook (as well as in ambitions) would ever move field people to armed resistance.

In Jamaica the pivotal decade was the 1760s. Before then obeah often was little more than a version of the potent but sorely tested Coramantee ritual that had steered a series of unsuccessful rebellions in the first half of the decade. From a cultural area of West Africa where secret associations were (and are) not prominent, the Coramantee were suddenly out of step when slave associationism became popular. Pragmatic reaction came at the end of the 1760s as blacks made concerted efforts to mix with their traditions new religious tools provided by various ethnic groups, including the whites.

In the 1769 Christmas celebrations, for instance, Ibo and Papaw (Dahomeans) asserted the authority of their ancestors by parading masks alongside those of the Coramantee, and twenty years later an important study of obeah by Edward Long and others noted that Papaw obeah had recently come to the fore.[107] At this juncture, with the breaking of the Coramantee's monopoly on the spiritual, slaves began experimenting seriously, first with Myal, an anti-witchcraft cult, and shortly thereafter with cultic versions of evangelical Christianity.

Erupting suddenly in the mid-1760s, Myal was persecuted with unusual vigor. "Hear Stompe, the Mial Man, was burnt alive this Evening," Thistlewood wrote, and his wife, a mulatto, "hang'd."[108] Later Phibbah told him that a Myal dance had been conducted twice in the house of Coobah (who had embroidered the assertive come-on into Silvia's smock). Myal, which Long said was "a kind of society," is seen now as a democratization of obeah. It promised a shared vision, as opposed to the obeahman's exclusive one. In his most feared and perhaps influential role, the obeahman was a solitary and malevolent poisoner. Comprising groups of dancers whose aim was to provide divine protection against witchcraft, however, Myal was a public statement. The Myal man was to obeah "what the antidote is to poison" is the way a late-nineteenth-century traveler put it. Myal men, who were called doctors, made toxins from natural substances that immobilized, then as the "proof of power," as Monk Lewis wrote, they miraculously raised from the dead the victims with whom they had danced.[109]

Eclectic and absorptive, Myal incorporated Christian elements, such as the resurrection of the "dead," that were compatible with old beliefs. It also included a millennial strain that is denied by those who wish to see slave religion as inherently passive.

> They went by the name of Myal people; they were also called angel men. They declared that the world was come to an end; Christ was coming, and God had sent them to pull all the Obeahs, and catch all the shadows that were spell-bound at the cotton trees. In preparation for these events they affected to be very strict in their conduct. . . . They accompanied their operations with violent animal excitement. . . . Sometimes one would bolt out of the ring and run into the bush and then the others would go after him declaring that the spirit had taken him away.[110]

Myal and the rural Baptist cults were closely connected—explicitly in one instance, an 1842 outbreak. Noting that Myal "is a strange delusion, Satan under the semblance of an Angel of light," an attorney reported its disappearance from Hampden Estate (in St. James Parish, a Myal center) while indicating surprise that it had prevailed there in the first place.

Hampden slaves had been catechised "for so long. . . . But the mystery is completely explained when it is known that many of the people were native Baptists."[111] "Native Baptist churches," with few exceptions, wrote the Anglican priest and historian William Gardner, "became associations of men and women who, in too many cases, mingled the belief and even practice of Mialism with religious observances, and who perverted and corrupted what they retained of these; among them sensuality was almost entirely unrestrained."[112]

With Africanized versions of evangelism in hand, cultists put forward their own "Christian" leaders, described by the contemporary Baptist preacher and linguist Richard Clarke as "some of them thought the old men were to dream dreams, and their young men were to see visions; that the disciples' feet were to be washed; and that fasting was necessary, with prayer, to overcome the daily temptations to which they were exposed."[113]

In the trenches and confronted by the lush array of indigenous ritual, missionaries complained wearily about the country peoples' "obstinate, headstrong prejudices," that made it so difficult to communicate in ways the slaves saw as spiritually intelligible. "Do you know God?, No, me say the word [God] but me no know God"; "line upon line, . . must be a thousand times repeated, before we get an inch"; or, it is like "talking to trees." To which a slave replied, "Buckra [white] man do not know preach from pray, that when they are praying Buckra man call it preaching."[114]

Slaves were also divided. Many coveted access to the Bible as a way to learn to read, yet realized that religious services based on written texts did not satisfy. In commenting on still another wilderness offshoot, "the John the Baptist religion,"[115] a missionary alluded to an implicit anti-intellectualism on the slaves' part (which was generally abandoned in the next generation as converts came to associate literacy with personal advancement and the abolitionist campaign). John the Baptist sectarians held "That the Book [the Bible] is for Backra, but God has given the dream to the negro, and it is a better guide than the Book for him. That John the Baptist is greater than Jesus Christ, for he baptized Christ. Hence, long after I came to Goshen, every such person whom I met; said that he belonged to John the Baptist's religion."[116]

The country people's fixation on John shaped the Presbyterian minister Hope Masterton Waddell's description of Moses Baker's deacons, who were attending Waddell's reading classes for children. "They took a very novel way to learn," the Presbyterian minister explained; they have their own Bibles that are always open to the same chapter, which is read with "great fluency and tolerable correctness." Otherwise, they could not read a word. What the catechists liked best was the story in the third chapter of Matthew about John baptizing people, including Jesus, in the River Jordan. These slaves, Waddell concluded, "knew more of John than of Christ."[117] Some believe that if converts are not immersed, they are not true Christians complained the Anglican rector Richard Panton. "If you no pass troo Jordan you don't hab no foundation" was the saying.[118]

Borrowing from the Methodists the policy of admission tickets, Baptist missionaries signed and distributed theirs in different colors representing grades of catechists. For their part, many slaves considered the tickets as talismans and placed them in coffins during burials, or they connected them somehow to John and the Jordan. Convinced that to lose her ticket was to lose her soul, a woman told Panton that her class leader had said that the ticket had been dipped in the Jordan and if she lost it, she herself was lost.[119]

John was more appealing than Jesus because John's medium was water, and slaves saw baptism, "the dip," as a rebirth. Water, which may also have been seen in Africa as a vehicle for reincarnation, was traditionally a medium in which spirits entered and exited from the world of the living. If Myal represented a democratization of the obeah figure's solitary possession dance, baptism promised an easier, more popular, way to communicate with the other side.

Convince, as another possession cult that sprang up and may have served inadvertently as another way station to bush Christianity, also was based on association rather than kinship. A shadowy figure in the sources, George Lewis, a founder of Convince, was an African who became a Baptist in Virginia before arriving in Jamaica and joining the Kingston congregation of the best known North American black émigré, George Liele.[120] Determined to "impart the knowledge of Christ" and to initiate among country people "a great inquiry after the truth," Lewis moved into the quintessential subversive job. He hired out as an itinerant peddler. Sending his owner a set sum monthly enabled him to travel into the traditional core area of both significant resistance and religious development: the western parishes of Cornwall including St. Elizabeth and Manchester (recently carved out of Vere), where he impressed the Moravian missionaries who raised money to set him free. The large numbers who gathered at night to hear Lewis came from neighborhoods where it was reported that every slave hut had its idol, and that slaves worshiped a cotton tree (traditional home of duppies) and lived quarrelsome lives that made poisonings common. But Lewis's preachings soon rendered these notions archaic. People came forward asking for instruction. They "coveted" the ideas of doing what whites would not have them do and knowing what others would not have them know, explains the Moravian missionary and historian J. H. Buchner. When white evangelicals did come out to Peru and other estates in the May Day Mountains, slaves who had heard Lewis's "home religion" asked "what must we do to be saved?"[121]

Convince constituted a movement, wrote Buchner, "a real and general awakening" in which some who joined were motivated by "their prevailing superstitions" and others by curiosity. "There was certainly much superstition intermingled with their religious exercises; many had wonderful dreams to tell, which they considered as prophetic visions; some excited themselves by fanatical notions, and fell into wild extravagancies, which they called 'The Convince', in which they had full faith as much as in a divine revelation."[122] Driven by music that induced ecstatic possession, dancers eventually swooned. This constituted the actual "convince," a state indicating that the Holy Spirit was moving within a candidate, who was therefore acceptable for baptism and full membership in the cult that was probably the unnamed group of three to four thousand.

White missionaries were threatened by and skeptical of visions as vehicles to conversion, however the Baptists among them kept open lines of communication to prominent bush preachers. When Moses Baker retired he turned his large congregation over to a regular missionary, Thomas Burchell of Montego Bay. Burchell's black class leaders organized the largest and most successful rebellion in the history of Anglo-American slavery.

Burchell's deacons, or "daddies," were among the approximately two hundred and fifty class leaders (counting Baptist catechists only) who emerged in the last years of slavery.[123] As artisans and drivers, most were from the top of the plantation hierarchy and concentrated in the western parishes, home of the Leeward Coramantee Maroons and the epicenter of major resistance. From the mid-1820s, Baptist missionaries began attracting great crowds of worshippers (whose number was said to be ten times that of the Methodists), and the thrust of their reports was that a movement was underway that excited them but made them unsure of its course and nature. Reports told of Burchell speaking to audiences of two thousand; of a rural station of five thousand who were "enquiring the Way to Zion"; and of dramatic 5 A.M. seaside baptisms to which people would walk all night before falling asleep under the trees.[124]

Into this auspicious situation came William Knibb, a Baptist missionary whom slaves regarded as his brother's double or spirit because of their close family resemblance. Knibb's excitement about the prospects of a major awakening breaks through the usual jargon of missionary reports. In 1830 he was called to the Falmouth station after a profoundly moving election — "I never saw such a scene . . . [they] burst into tears" — conducted by slaves, who rather suddenly had begun fixing on certain white as well as traditional religious figures. Falmouth, Knibb wrote, "is a pleasant and fashionable seaport," with a population of about 3,500 in a parish of twenty-seven

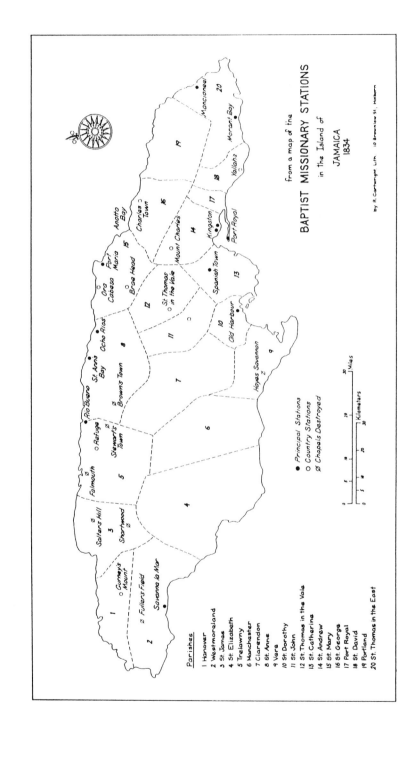

BAPTIST MISSIONARY STATIONS
in the Island of
JAMAICA
1834

from a map of the

by R. Cartwright Lith. 10 Brownlow St, Holborn

Parishes

1 Hanover
2 Westmoreland
3 St. James
4 St. Elizabeth
5 Trelawny
6 Manchester
7 Clarendon
8 St. Anne
9 Vere
10 St. Dorothy
11 St. John
12 St. Thomas in the Vale
13 St. Catharine
14 St. Andrew
15 St. Mary
16 St. George
17 Port Royal
18 St. David
19 Portland
20 St. Thomas in the East

● Principal Stations
○ Country Stations
Ø Chapels Destroyed

Miles
Kilometers

thousand, among whom he noted seven hundred members and two thousand enquirers, persons "professedly seeking after the one thing needful."[125] Of his reactions to another worship service, Knibb reported, "My Blood was thrilled through my Veins," and "Will not God Visit for these things?"[126]

Referring to the rural cults as "Christian Obeah," Mary Turner, in her study of missionaries and slaves in Jamaica, argues that their readiness to absorb and fission demonstrates the slaves' ability to put new ideas to their own uses, and that missionary Christianity could not be controlled by whites. The evidence is inconclusive on the matter of whether the cults represented a syncretism, an actual blending of old and new, as Turner's term implies, or if slaves, regarding both traditions as complementary, had recourse to one or the other as the occasion warranted. That is, was revivalistic Christianity simply superimposed on obeah, or did the two blend?[127] Accounts of religious developments from the 1760s suggest that the former was the case. Thus combinations of obeah and its immediate permutations of Myal, Convince, and early rural Christianity shared two preoccupations: healing and spirit possession. Moreover, an important ritual objective of rural religion in all its forms — African or Christian-oriented — was to somehow ensnare the power embodied in baptism and literacy while continuing to refine the most effective ways of keeping open lines of communication with recently deceased ancestor spirits. This development provides remarkable parallels with religious experimentation in Africa when anticolonial forces gathered. Led by their traditions, or because the political arena is closed to them, they seek "cultic answers to political problems." The pattern is for a leader's vision, often derived from dreams, to "take," like an inoculation. Adherents then learn the dance routines of the new spirit, which are how the new knowledge and power are transmitted.[128]

Play was the basic rite in both traditional and early evangelical ceremonies. Throughout the slavery era, its dances were convenient vehicles for promulgating — among people of oral cultures — radically new knowledge across the major social boundaries of work, workplace, and levels of acculturation. Traditionally, play was also the institution that bridged ethnicity among other divisive and demoralizing plantation conditions. Think about the effect on a new Negro, in a strange and hostile land, of hearing danceable music for the first time. On these occasions slaves customarily danced by "nations" (in their own language groups) wrote Charles Leslie in 1740, when most slaves were African. There were, nonetheless, times of "occasional Conformity," of intertribal mixing. Leslie implies that mixed dances took place at the slave community's central event — graveside ceremonies. "Their Notions of Religion are very inconsistent and vary according to the different Countries they come from: But they have a kind of occasional Conformity, and *join without Distinction* in their *Solemn Sacrifices* and Gambols" [my emphasis].[129]

Kumina and Jonkonnu, Cheryl Ryman explains, comprise the two "core" dances that in Jamaica have come down to the present from slave times.[130] Kumina, traditional and African in orientation, came originally from the mountains, while Jonkonnu, assimilated and urban, is the masquerade tradition commonly associated with the carnival-like pageants and parades — the Set Girls and Moko Jumbo stilt men — of Christmas holiday. Once all core dances as vehicles for communicating with the dead were features of ritual. Kumina, a healer's dance, is reminiscent of Cudjoe's "antick tricks" at the 1739 Treaty negotiations; it is violently acrobatic and so requires considerable space. The dance through time was Myal, then Convince, and continues; its traditional focus, contacting the dead, remains. In Thistle-wood's first neighborhood it is now referred to as St. Elizabeth Gumbay, a term that resonates with eighteenth-century descriptions of slaves who liked to "play" as Gombay drummers and Gombay men. The dance was also originally Maroon.

The reassertion of play as an experimental vehicle for making and broadcasting intelligible pivotal decisions in periods of basic change is described by Leann Martin. An anthropologist who lived among the Charles Town Maroons in the 1970s, Martin argues that after more than two hundred and fifty years, the Maroon way of life was at last threatened with extinction because of renewed missionary inroads and numbers of younger people moving away. At this juncture a Maroon leader, "Dancerman," a specialist said to have "science," performed a series of possession dances in order to ask the dead about the cause of the recent wrenching developments and prescriptions for solving them. Play, then, as in the revolutionary 1760s and afterwards, may be seen in part as a potent device for community cohesion and problem-solving.[131]

> A dog is a dog except when he is facing you.
> Then he is Mr. Dog.
> — Haitian farmer

Resistance by plantation slaves was day-to-day, low-key, and triggered by drought and hunger, a change of supervisors, or — most important — ground rules concerning work conditions: time off, provision grounds, and marketing. In such circumstances, Caribbean slaves acted as if the plantation was theirs as they organized collectively behind the leadership of a driver; Southern slaves reacted alone or with the support of family members in desperate and occasionally self-destructive ways.

In the Caribbean, a more significant level of rebelliousness was the work stoppage, which came to be a major tactic in the large preemancipation rebellions. Strikes were an old practice of two kinds. Either slaves withdrew into the woods for a few days while their leaders attempted to line up a local influential white person to intercede, or they occasionally traveled to town in order to put their case directly to the attorney. Thistlewood's last act before moving onto his own plantation nearby was to assemble the slaves in order to warn them not to expect him to intercede for them when they were in someone else's charge.[132]

Regionally, plantation resistance into the late eighteenth century remained typically sporadic and small in scale. In the Chesapeake Bay region, field people were kept in check by the custom of resident owners, who were their own managers as well as self-styled family patriarchs. Contact between slave and free was more intimate here than elsewhere. As planters pushed their ways into the corners of slave life while insisting that some slaves acquire the skills needed to maintain the diversification that distinguished tidewater plantations, assimilation was a one-way street: the abandonment of tradition and the acquisition of white customs.

In the Carolina lowcountry and the Caribbean, slaves were tied more intimately to the plantation than were the itinerant supervisors and generally kept the lid on in order to protect tangible interests. Along the Carolina rice coast, a malarial climate, a distinctive production system of black supervisors, tasking, and late-afternoon time off fortified the old belief that rice slaves did not transfer well to other crops. Thus in the postwar boom in cotton following the American Revolution and the introduction of Whitney's gin, the up-country piedmont was settled primarily by new Negroes. Remaining on the coast, the Gullah came to be the most immobile, entrenched, and culturally inbred of mainland slaves. Meanwhile in the Caribbean, slaves' interests were based on a clear stake in the estate — homes, property, markets, and graves — that until the last years of slavery kept rural people, especially Creoles, too enmeshed to see much beyond the plantation's horizons.

In plantation settings that were also demoralizing and sometimes incapacitating slaves were preoccupied with a malevolent kind of witchcraft, as described by Shipman and combated by Myal dancers. Meanwhile, on the ridges above, Maroons were part of a world more of their own making. While the "prophesies" of Maroon leaders had "orac[ular]" power, according to a contemporary, in the record obeah seems to be little more than a matter of figurines and amulets for predicting the future.[133] If Maroons were preoccupied with witchcraft only when fighting, and otherwise put their faith in their remote and naturally fortified sites, this distinction is reminescent of Bronislaw Malinowski's comparison of fishing by Trobriand Islanders either in lagoon or open sea: the latter was dangerous and so hedged about with ritual; the former, safe and secure, was free of ceremony.[134]

For most plantation slaves, life was like deep-sea fishing in flimsy boats amid unpredictable and potentially destructive rollers, winds, and currents. Throughout Anglo-America, plantation people experienced long periods of relative calm and oppressive boredom occasionally broken by squalls stirred by inexplicable illnesses and deaths (to say nothing of the intermidable beatings and sales or divisions of estates that split family and friends). Malinowski's functionalism may oversimplify the character of the dimly perceived phenomenon of witchcraft, but his insight is an effective reminder that plantation people, who were far more harassed than Maroons ever were, constructed a religious framework that helped explain what concerned their harassed lives most: illness and death, lovers' quarrels, and trespasses and thefts in valued provision grounds.

It is arguable that obeah figures represented a leadership of the slaves' own making and so were a feature of efforts to make a community while defying the humiliations of assimilative choices dominated by whites. However, the few surviving texts that are more than snippets are testimony to an often sad and randomly cruel plantation world wherein what once had been arguably a system of thought and ritual, the "cosmology" of the unseasoned, in time became a desiccated bundle of lore that no longer served its people well.

Slaves from the turbulent 1760s onward then struggled to create a new ritual that would help resolve the ordinary problems of living in a traditional manner while holding out the promise of finding ways out of slavery by acquiring that which seemed to animate white success. In a remarkable statement by a Jamaican rebel, rural slaves in the 1820s are overheard wrestling with a mélange of new and old lore and roles in a new kind of secular play that would distinguish the next round of artisanal resistance. "The head people at Balcarres went about getting preachers, and at the meeting of the chapel plotted the destruction of white people, and they had a court and jury just like the white people, and Montaignac read out the law to them, and a free woman [of color] named Sarah James sang numerous songs on the occasion; the governor came upon a jackass to the meeting, where about two hundred negroes were assembled . . . About two weeks before Christmas . . . they took the great swear."[135]

Yet in the Caribbean the outlook of rural people remained culturally conservative even as it developed from Myal and beyond. Its emotional core remained the pervasive fear of imminent victimization by inexplicable forces, and so by witches. Christian missionaries would see this fear as an opening to be exploited. As a tract that one such group carried to the Caribbean in the 1790s advised explicitly, "You will endeavour to conciliate as much as possible the good-will and affection of the Negro; . . . the most favorable opportunities of instilling principles of virtue and religion . . . [are]

the seasons of sickness and affliction, when their minds are most open to serious impressions."[136]

On river banks and in open fields evangelists unwittingly created a spiritually charged atmosphere that encouraged slaves to transform old rites by incorporating new lore inspired by missionary music, baptism by immersion, and an emphasis on literary.[137] Evangelicals preached simple parables laced with pungent references to God's blood, bowels, sacrifices, and purifying flames and swords; but what slaves appreciated even more — especially because few understood English readily — were sessions with songs, prayers, and intensely emotional conversion experiences that engaged worshippers totally as dancing had once done.

Slave Christianization as the actual moment of conversion differed from one region to another. In the American South slaves were more radically detribalized than elsewhere and accepted uncritically the main prize, the promise of an afterlife. Southern revivalistic conversions were exceptionally personal. At the height of the ceremony individuals stepped forward and declared their lives for Jesus. In the Caribbean, however, evangelical rebirth and salvation were muted by play, which carried the dancer/initiate/convert into a traditionally communal ritual focus — communication with spirits of the dead. Put somewhat differently, new converts' concepts of the afterlife and the dead differed regionally. Caribbean initiates saw themselves not so much joining the dead in the hereafter as controlling them here when they descended during the tumultuous dancing that was so readily and thoroughly stamped out by the morally inhibited Southern evangelicals. (There is an old and thoughtful argument that the shout and response is a form of possession.)[138]

Regional contrasts in the meanings slaves gave to the rites of conversion should not obscure understanding that Christianization everywhere shared one basic feature: the promise — and increasingly for many the actuality — of literacy, of learning to read the Bible, which evangelicals insisted was the word of God and the vehicle for conversion and salvation. Literacy also accelerated the acculturation process and changed the styles of resistance by slaves who, as mostly Creoles, eventually replaced Africans as the organizers of the major efforts to end slavery.

In the South the political effects of conversion followed slave demographic and acculturation patterns. In South Carolina, where new Negroes were numerous and slaves overall were not very assimilated, conversion for a while threatened to ignite serious resistance. In time, however, as the evangelicals assumed control of the slaves' leisure to the extent of stifling dancing and the rituals it generated, resistance was negligible until the Civil War. In the Chesapeake Bay region, a more mature slave society with a proportionately larger assimilated — and skilled — slave population, Christianization did not fuel significant resistance before Nat Turner's Rebellion in 1831. Earlier, Gabriel's conspiracy in 1800 took place in the midst of an extensive revival that was ignored by the rebellion's secular leadership. Yet from the rank-and-file, men rose to wonder aloud, in both African and Christian idioms, about the absence of charismatic leaders. One asked for the prophetic help of "outlandish wizards," and another cast doubt by claiming that he saw no "Moses" among them.[139]

The time when assimilated leaders would meet field people halfway religiously remained in the future. In the interim (while some rural blacks again contemplated maroonage) assimilateds organized a series of remarkably secular — and stillborn — conspiratorial associations. Upon this bitter and destructive legacy, however, a second generation of Creole assimilateds used a revivalistic Christianity impregnated with archaic knowledge to ignite mass uprisings by plantation Negroes.

PART III

# The Assimilateds

# 9

## Slave Resistance in an Era of War and Revolution, 1768–1805

> Attempts by our Slaves [are] not uncommon. But . . . those Born in the Island, have ever been unsuspected till now. . . . The topic of American Rebellion has been by the Dissaffected amongst us, dwelt upon and blandished off with strains of Virtuous Heroeism. . . . *Dear Liberty* has rang in the Heart of every House-bred Slave, in one form or another, for these ten years past . . . even the Creole Negroes, who were the savers of their Masters and Mistresses in the Rebellion of 1760 are now against them.
>
> — R. Lindsay, Jamaica, 1776

> The old English Islands still remain pretty quiet, but God knows how long that may be the case, or how soon the Contagion may spread among us. . . . The Bait which the French hold out of freedom is undoubtedly very tempting.
>
> — Robert Thomson, St. Kitts, 1795[1]

Erupting in the late 1700s and unfolding in two stages, a surge of revolutionary activity by slaves led to emancipation in the British Caribbean and repression and eventually Civil War in the South. In the first stage, major resistance was organized by assimilated artisans,[2] who in their new urban and conspiratorial associations spoke of revolution in secular and personal terms. The second stage, however, was defined by field hands whose outlook was more communal and spiritual. Given that the leaders of this stage were from the same group of mobile, non-field assimilateds who had led the first round, the question to ask is, Why in this instance were artisans able to establish a following among the hitherto conservative and divided plantation people? Or, to put the matter somewhat differently, Why were artisans able to inspire revolts that actually progressed beyond planning to action?[3]

In the first stage of rebellion members of conspiratorial associations performed variously depending on time and place. But generally they collected dues, made elaborate toasts, and distributed wood swords, cockades, and titles. Then, as kings, governors, and colonels, they danced, feasted, and marched ceremoniously. When artisans did talk about revolution, they did so ambivalently as an expression of how they felt about whites and the kinds of acculturative changes they had made in becoming adept in white society. To describe this dilemma, of being at once attracted to and repelled by whites and their ways — which was exhibited in all conspiracies, Southern and Caribbean, and makes them remarkably similar and comparable — is to begin to understand why planning did not generate action in the first stage, and beyond that to sense what assimilation as a slave was like.

Resourceful in both plantation and town, artisans in some societies, nonetheless, displayed the alienating effects of a rapid and thorough assimilation. Yet such symptoms of this alienation as anxiety when speaking, aphasia, and alcoholism were rarely exhibited by slave women or by male field hands. Hence, the apparently psychological nature of these afflictions, coupled with the artisans' ambiguous revolutionary objectives, argue for the need to consider the personal as well as the social dimensions of assimilation. To do so is also to think about why artisans and drivers in the early nineteenth century led slave revolts in the Caribbean but not in the United States.

## A Setting

> The Time in which we live will constitute
> an awful period in the history of the world;
> for a spirit of subversion is gone forth, which
> sets at nought the wisdom of our ancestors and
> the lessons of experience.
> — Bryan Edwards to the
> House of Commons, 1798[4]

The era between the American Revolution and the end of Napoleon's rule in France (1775–1815) was one of fundamental change in the Caribbean and the American South. In the new nation Southern planters joined Northern farmers and merchants to fight the British in a successful war of independence. The war also proved to be a major setback for the West Indians. Wartime embargoes, fierce storms and famines, and the collapse of the British mercantile system as far as trade with the United States was concerned affected the islands profoundly. Hereafter, the two regions diverged radically. In the Caribbean in the early nineteenth century, whites were staggered by a series of major slave rebellions followed by peaceful, compensated emancipation. In the South, whites had to contend with only one major revolt and a few conspiracies, followed a generation later by the Civil War and a tragically disillusioning emancipation.

For a time, Southerners did well. Sovereignty brought prosperity, optimism, and opportunities to expand westward. For West Indians, Jamaicans particularly, however, prospects were bleak and threatening. From the 1780s, with a brief respite in the 1790s, profits declined and bankruptcies increased. Lending to the atmosphere of crisis as well was the gathering momentum of abolitionism and the steady arrival of dissenting preachers, empire loyalists fleeing the American Revolution, and royalist émigrés from nearby French colonies torn by civil war and racial strife.

Behind these unnerving, kaleidoscopic, events loomed an even greater threat, the French Revolution, which for a while seemed remote.[5] But when its "Leveling *Influenza*" treatened to "spread [to] . . . This Side of the Western Ocean," whites reacted feverishly—and not unreasonably.[6] By the early 1790s, the revolution became a shattering reality when the urbane mulatto governor of Guadeloupe, Victor Hugues, aiming to create another Haiti by inciting slaves and Maroons, deployed mulatto brigands into various British islands. We are "preparing of the worse," a Jamaican governor reported home. All that our Slaves have to do, the Assembly added, is "to will it."[7]

In an atmosphere of acute anxiety, any form of slave entertainment that was secretive and sizeable was put down hard by whites obsessed with the notion that black associationism could lead to another Haiti, to "a second St. Domingo War" as they put it. "The slaves here are very inquisitive & intelligent & are immediately informed of every kind of news that arrives," the governor explained as he called attention to both the songs that blacks were busily "compos[ing]" on the Haitian Revolution, and to editions of Haitian newspapers circulating in Jamaica that carried mastheads from Voltaire's *Mohatmet*: "Chaque peuple, a son tour, a brille sur la terre" (each people in their turn shall light up the world).[8]

But the specter of black revolution in Haiti notwithstanding, whites reserved their most fear-ridden invective for a demonic combination of abolitionists, the missionaries they allegedly spawned, and the slave literacy that each group promoted. As early as 1788, the Assembly's agent informed Parliament that its historic investigations of the slave trade led slaves to "expect Emancipation" because Negroes "customarily . . . read English newspapers as constantly as the ships from England come in."[9] Our "slaves will be minutely acquainted with all the proceedings [in Parliament]," the agent wrote another British official, because "many of the domestic Slaves, born in that Island, & brought up in the dwelling house, read all the public prints, and instantly communicate any intelligence respecting themselves to their fellow slaves employed in the field."[10] To this reference of the blacks' urban information network, the governor's Council added, "perhaps nothing has contributed so much to the dissemination of these notions among our Negroes than the publication of the witnesses' examinations before the House of Commons, most industriously sent out by persons in England, and explained to our Slaves by free people of colour." In conveying this message to court, the agent was also to remind the king that the island would not be secure until the ministry silenced Parliament's discussion of the slave trade. This had to be done because the slaves refused to make a distinction between abolition of the trade and emancipation itself.[11]

Against this background, planters for the first time feared the collapse of authority and the mass disaffections of slaves from their estates. Subsequently, some ordered their managers in the most unusual terms to ease up on the field hands. Surveying the thousands of Virginia blacks who in 1775 ran off to fight with the British on the eve of the American Revolution, an owner said simply that if in the crisis slavery was not made less oppressive, "the natural consequence will be that we shall be left without [any slaves]."[12] Referring to the slave trade debate as a "great battle" that could have "dread[ful] consequences," a Jamaican absentee wrote, "I earnestly desire that all my Negroes may be used with the utmost tenderness & humanity." Steeped in the progressive sentiments of his age, this proprietor added, "salutary laws might have put an end to all cruel & inhuman treatment of the Negroes & make their Situation comfortable & pleasant to them."[13]

On the traditionally unstable Ceded Islands, harassed by French from without and maroons from within, plantation slaves came to be treated more circumspectly. While fighting a dangerous combination of slaves and maroons, the governor of Dominica in the late 1780s enclosed to officials in Britain a field commander's advice that to prevent "the Bomb [which] was ready to burst in every quarter," the slaves had to be placated, otherwise they would desert to the maroons in great numbers. When this threat eased, the slaves organized a work stoppage, the "immediate" causes of which the governor attributed to the "Idea of Liberty," a "general relaxation" in the enforcement of statutes concerning slave travel, passes, dances and assemblies, and—as "always"—the slaves' communication and dealings ("intercourse") with the little nearby French islands of Marigalante and the Saints.[14]

Meanwhile at the other end of the Anglo-American plantation world, South Carolinians, like Jamaicans, reacted aggressively to émigrés fleeing the Haitian Revolution (and to Caribbean ships and their black crewmen). "With the characteristic impetuosity of their nation," one planter warned, the French "had zealously declared Negro equality." The slaves responsible for disseminating this idea, he continued, were those "of superior advantages of improvement [who] can clearly conceive & readily explain to the more ignorant of their class the full force of this dangerous doctrine."[15] From Virginia, hitherto a remarkably stable slave society, a thoughtful writer pointed to the same slaves as instigators of the first major rebellion in 1800. This elite group comprised the acculturated and literate who worked in urban environments, and thereby had experienced a "prodigious change" in outlook between 1776 and 1800.[16] The preoccupation of many urbanizing slaves with the advantages of self-help and self-improvement was also exposed by a 1791 South Carolina legislative committee report that urged a prohibition of the Mason's practice of inviting black members, not because black Masons would then be on a level with whites, but rather that Masonry would provide "a bond of Union."[17]

In the last quarter of the eighteenth century assimilated blacks struggled persistently to form "bonds of Union" among themselves. To this end they created associations that in turning conspiratorial in an age of heightened anxiety about revolutionary change generated a mass of evidence gathered by white prosecutors. This quantity may be reduced to manageable proportions through of a brief narrative of the major plots, followed by a discussion of their organizers' motivation.[18]

An early and representative conspiracy by assimilateds was uncovered in 1768 in the small and sparsely settled island of Montserrat. Comprising twenty-six square miles of mountain, dry savannah, and lush alluvial fans, Montserrat is still only partially developed. The island's best year economically was 1772, when forty-two estates produced about 4,600 hogsheads of sugar and 537 bales of cotton. In the 1760s, the population of about 9,000 slaves and 1,300 whites (who by 1788 had dwindled to only 434) included a sizeable group of Irish, who lived chiefly in Plymouth, a port and "very pretty" village of a few hundred houses surrounded by coconut, tamarind, breadfruit, and orange trees.[19]

As the town prepared excitedly for the 1768 St. Patrick's Day celebration, officials discovered a major slave conspiracy. The presence of three Dutch vessels anchored offshore had inspired blacks to organize a mass escape by seizing a ship and sailing, perhaps, to Puerto Rico. The conspirators chose as their password a popular song, "Fire in the Mountains," which when played by the black fiddler at the whites' St. Patrick's dance was to signal the beginning of the revolt. To attack first at the dance, the conspirators reasoned, was to catch the white elite when it was concentrated, distracted, and could be taken in a rush. At the same time, house servants would secure their owners' swords, and slaves who were positioned outside would shoot the whites as they fled. News of the rising would run from the

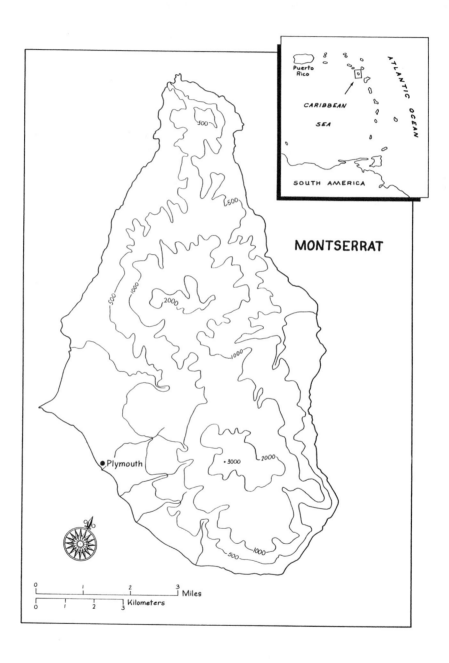

MONTSERRAT

Puerto Rico

ATLANTIC OCEAN

CARIBBEAN

SEA

SOUTH AMERICA

• Plymouth

Miles

Kilometers

ballroom to town then to the ridges above, where slaves would then light real fire in the mountains.

The plan unravelled disastrously as the slaves prepared for their own celebration. This party apparently revolved around a new dance that had been introduced by Antiguan blacks and was at the moment "the rage" in Montserrat. When a conspirator returned to a colored seamstress and was told his costume for the fete was unfinished, he reproached her angrily, "the thing I was going to do tonight, now I cannot do." For her turn, the seamstress went to the authorities, who matched her account with others they had heard and soon uncovered the whole.[20]

A farce? If so, a deadly one. As the plot broke the whites went berserk. They hacked, quartered, hanged, and starved in gibbets any suspects whose owners were foolish enough to send them to town for "trials." The belief is that the plot is part of a "general rebellion," wrote a Methodist missionary, who also described the arrival during the emergency of the commander of the Leeward Islands. In the atmosphere of murderous hysteria, the slaves received this officer as a deliverer. Streaming out to the beach and into the surf, pulling off their clothing so he would not have to touch cobblestones as he came into town, they cried: "Dadce God has come he an we! Dadce God has come he an we!" The commander also took the conspiracy seriously. Reporting that it was "deep laid" and "long projected," he posted when he left a detachment of fifty men and a man-of-war to intimidate and prevent further attempts. Yet his account leaves mixed impressions of the rebels' real objectives. After mentioning the uncovering of a "great Store of Arms and Ammunition" concealed in the mountains, he said the conspirators, "though Savages . . . were not insensible to the power of Beauty" for they had cast lots for the white "Ladies" they would take with them to Puerto Rico.[21]

Montserrat proved to be the first of a series of conspiracies formed by organizations of Creoles. As usual in the British Caribbean, black Jamaicans provided the main course, a bitter one for whites who in 1776 struggled to comprehend a novel change in the character of insurrectionary leadership. In that year it was not Africans who organized, an attorney wrote, but Creoles, who "were never known before to have been Concerned in anything of this sort."[22] This is the group, the governor reported, "in whose fidelity we had always most firmly relied."[23] Praised in the aftermath of the bloody Coramantee rebellion of 1760 as "the savers of their Mistresses and Masters," Creoles, the governor warned a few years later, were now those who "always" organized in the fall when defenses slipped as the fleet left to convoy the harvest to Britain.[24]

Conspiracies were also uncovered in Jamaica in 1791 and 1806. Depositions taken during the first one exhibit the whites' fears of Haiti and

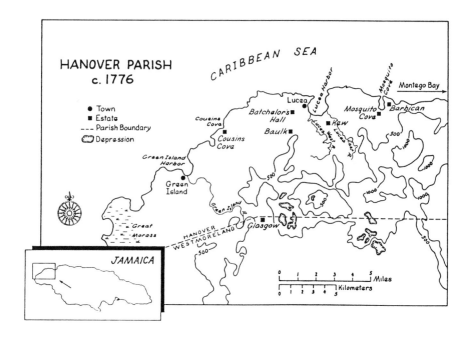

abolitionism, and a sudden change in the behavior of some slaves. In the affadavits, three hundred blacks were said to have gathered to celebrate Wilberforce's birthday. Also overheard were "head Negroes" talking "very unreservedly about St. Domingo," and other blacks saying "that Negroes at Hispaniola are now free and enjoyed the rights of white men and that the King of England wished Slaves in Jamaica to be on the same footing but that their owners were against it." When a millwright threatened his slaves "they literally laughed" at him. After a waiting girl was whipped, she said "you have about two more weeks," and another warned, "Slapp me again if you please, 'tis your time now, but we shall drink wine before Christmas."[25]

The exploits of Milburn's Jack provided more tangible evidence of trouble. A "principal" in the plot and a peddler of dry goods, Jack was the archetypal assimilated conspirator—unconnected to a plantation, mobile, and with considerable time of his own, which in this case the slave used to form an extensive network in the troublesome western parishes. Hired to a wharf operator for whom he refused to work, Jack feared he would be arrested and transported if he did not find another job. So he hired himself to a Jewish merchant, who sent him out selling, initially with a white clerk and then three times on his own. Insisting after his arrest that he was simply a peddler, the authorities charged Jack with trading for gunpowder provided by Spanish Negroes and Sephardic Jews.[26] When an Assembly committee later reported that "No character [was] so dangerous to this country" as slave itinerants, it pointed to the infamous Makandal, "long the terror of St. Domingo," who had helped raise rebellion by using peddlers "as agents."[27]

As revolution swept through Europe and the islands, and whites for the first time deployed black soldiers in the new West Indian Regiments, associations assumed a military appearance as they moved from riverbanks and barbeques to makeshift parade grounds. In the 1806 conspiracy, slaves who were hired-out formed "a Society" which, they insisted, was for purposes of mutual aid—to cooperatively cut thatch and build houses.[28] But a commander also reported that on Sunday afternoons the slaves mustered with wooden swords and guns, appointed officers "from Generals to Sergeants and Corporals," stuck spears of flowering cane into hat brims "to look like . . . feathers," and swore oaths "to Stand by one another."[29]

When in Trinidad a year earlier dancing societies assumed a military bearing and changed their names from "convoys" to "regiments," the authorities stepped in and uncovered the most significant conspiracy to date.[30] Its members included Africans, women, and free people of color as well as the usual Creole artisans, and its ceremonies synthesized major elements—Spanish, French, and English—of the island's diverse society and traditions.

As a neglected backwater of a Spanish New World empire that was dying on its feet, Trinidad was more than two hundred years old when in the 1780s officials sought to rejuvenate the colony by inviting French planters and their slaves to resettle the island. Basic change continued when the British arrived in 1797 and made Trinidad one of their empire's first Crown Colonies, ruled directly by the king in council.[31] Awash in a sea of Catholics black and white in an unusually open slave society where plantations had not yet taken root extensively, the new rulers imposed a divided administration that lurched along under the casually draconian, if not randomly sadistic, regime of General Thomas Picton, soon to be a hero of Wellington's Pennisular campaign against Napoleon.

Shortly after Picton's departure, nervous authorities in 1805 finally moved against town blacks, who seemed to conduct themselves even more brazenly than they did in the older British colonies.[32] As a "gentleman" reported to the military tribunal that tried the conspirators, "The Negroes are by no means diffident, particularly those who speak French." In Port of Spain, which the government had called a "Botany Bay," conspirators were accused of using the elaborate dancing fetes as a cover, to assign rank, swear oaths, and plan a rising at Christmas from their center, the *carenage* (king's

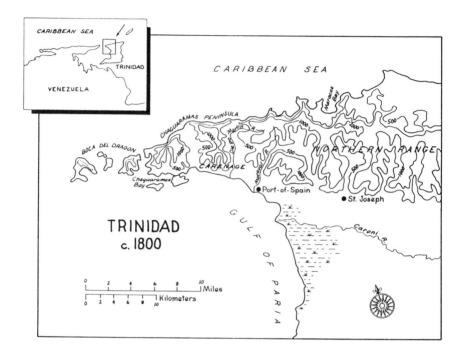

shipyard) in the Valley of Quez on the Chugaramous Peninsula. From here they would march south to the capital, Port of Spain, in order to perpetrate a "dreadful event," the governor concluded, that must be seen in light of "the diabolical scenes which led to . . . St. Domingo."[33]

Perhaps. But the convoys, of which there were several, also seemed as if they were preparing for carnival, when, it is argued, Trinidad's version of the annual Catholic pre-Lenten celebration had not yet emerged from the fancy aristocratic ballroom masques to be imitated and embellished in the streets and yards of black people. Nonetheless, like the modern bands of kings, queens, and their surrounding cast of dancers and musicians, the 1805 societies represented neighborhoods competitively by wearing distinctive garb, dancing their own kind of steps, and vying aggressively against one another for members who boasted of a king's uniform comprising a hat with black cockade, a black jacket with scarlet collar, and green ribbon over the shoulder. Others said the name of their convoy was Grenada because of their "mode of dancing." At their feasts and pageants, they also drank toasts and made oaths of mutual assistance—"to the King's health . . . to concern among [our]selves" — and to care for the sick and bury the dead. Some also collected money for members who were hired-outs and unable to come up with an owner's share of their wages. In calypso fashion they made a song, soon broadcast by market women, which played on elements in the Catholic communion service, "the flesh of white people is our bread, their blood our wine."[34]

The extensive trial proceedings also provide glimpses of the development and composition of the principal dancing societies. Sans Peur had branches in both the countryside and town, where members convened every two weeks near the market at the house of a free person of color. The convoy's king was Noel, a Creole from Grenada, who was owned by a former mistress of Picton; its queen, who had a court of princesses, was Madam Allou's Maria. Exalted titles, a mélange of those used by the three nations that had settled the island, for the men included aide-de-camp, treasurer, general, master of ceremonies, a grand judge who punished those who did not attend regularly, and an alquazil who served as sergeant-of-arms. In real life, this position, of Spanish origin and akin to an English constable, was by Picton's time filled by free people of color. Most conspirators had French names and spoke a French patois, and some of them had recently purchased their freedom, which was more easily accomplished in Catholic as opposed to Protestant plantation societies.

The military board met for several days before it reached one of the principal movers, Sampson, an elderly Ibo obeahman and king of Macque convoy. "Ill-treated" by the king of Sans Peur, Carenage branch, he formed his own society with the help of Baptiste, "a little active, shrewd and intelligent Negro, and confident" (according to the court clerk, who at the end of each statement characterized the defendant).[35]

Sampson formed his new society in three meetings, each of which carried through from Saturday night into Sunday. At the first, Baptiste and another leader with about nine others arrived at midnight for a supper of poultry, wine, and rum. A ceremony followed that, given the description of uniforms, titles, and numbers and kinds of musicians, was probably impressive. At Sampson's request Baptiste formed his regiment: two alquazils at the door announced visitors; then, to a drumroll, the grand judge moved to the front as officers presented arms at the head of soldiers. After this beginning, the new convoy grew to an "assembly" of twenty-five for the second meeting.[36]

Attempting to distinguish between subversion and entertainment, the military board dismissed charges against members of the Danish convoy. Denmark was considered to be a neutral nation, and the dancing society that derived its name from that country was known for conducting un-obtrusive ceremonies. As the trials wound down, the board ordered floggings, mutilations, exile, life imprisonments, and executions for scores of men,

*Africa in America*

while several women were whipped, and one, Adelaide Dixon, was condemned to work in chains for life.[37]

In the South, conspiracies were discovered in North Carolina in 1795 and Richmond, Virginia, in 1800. The first, concocted by slaves who wished to hold an election, was at first view similar to those Caribbean associations that on balance seemed to be more concerned with self-help and socializing than actual rebellion. But the second, with evidently no significant ceremonial dimension, was clearly insurrectionary.

In North Carolina the slave Quillo, from an inland county, decided in 1795 to make himself a candidate for a mock election that whites believed was conspiratorial. Quillo's election would include, as elections did then, a showy and popular "treat."[38] This was based on the custom of wealthy planters who displayed their rank, influence, and liberality at such competitive gatherings as horse races, cock fights, and elections. At the latter, candidates on courthouse greens dispensed liquor and familiarity to prospective voters. When asked about his treat of cider for "electors" at Cragg's Branch, Quillo said that his voters would elect officials who would "enable

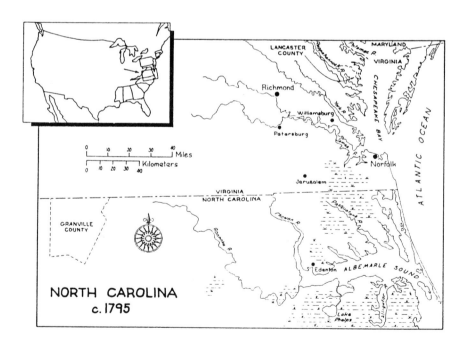

all the Negroes to have equal Justice in collecting the monies due to them in which case the weak persons might get their money as well as the Strong." This remark followed testimony that the conspirators first would arm themselves with clubs with nails driven through their ends, and "on the night of the attack they would go to every man's house, set fire to it, kill the men and boys over 6 or 7 years of age; the women over a certain age, both black and white were to share the same fate; the young and handsome of the whites they were to keep for themselves, and the young ones of their own Colour were to be spared for waiters." To this a slave added that he had already chosen his white wife, and a third mentioned that once all whites were killed, "the Black men were to take their places, [and] have their wives."[39]

Gabriel's plot, which unwound a few years later in and around the new state capital of Richmond, Virginia, was far larger, more plausible, and more tactically astute than most of the others in either region.[40] The conspirators' plan was based on an understanding that a small successful attack might generate a much greater one. They would begin at night by firing the state capital and the more combustible wood buildings of the warehouse district. In the confusion raiders would take the state arsenal, make the governor hostage, and wait for a general rising of rural slaves and an opportunity to negotiate.

Recruitment was extensive and revealing. A few Frenchmen and white Methodists were implicated as well as scores of mobile black artisans who seemed to have excessive time on their hands. Many were hired-outs — from probated estates of widows and orphans principally — to burgeoning new industries in the piedmont towns of Richmond and Petersburg. Their recruitment usually followed a pattern. Potential recruits were often approached in company and asked a version of "whether they would fight the white people for their freedom." They responded by declaring a hatred for whites and willingness to kill them without compassion, by sharing views of the insurrection's goals, and by requesting a command position. Patrick was asked, for instance, "if he was a Man." When told he "looked so poor and weakly that he could not kill a man," another replied "do not take me by my looks, I could kill a white man as free as eat." Another, Gilbert, who was young, eager, and unprepared, replied to a leader's vow "to turn and & fight with his stick" with "he was ready with his pistol, but it was in need of repair." Asked by Gabriel if he had a sword, he said he would use his master's and have a belt made for it. He would use his master's horse, too, but if it was gone on the day of the attack, he "would take the Bald."

But the recruits were never put to the test because a vicious rainstorm, which the whites referred to repeatedly as "Providential," struck the day revolution was to begin and washed out roads, bridges, and morale. How many conspirators would have rendezvoused then, or when the attack was rescheduled the following night, is a moot point. Few if any arrived at either meeting, by which time at least three slaves had informed.[41]

Why the conspiracy did not inspire much hope or commitment among rural slaves may have been accountable to their involvement in a religious revival that was sweeping the area. In *Black Thunder,* a novel about the rebellion, Arna Bontemps has Gabriel ignore an old conjurer woman's warn-ing that the rebels were inviting disaster by not seeking religious guidance (advice echoed in the actual record by a leader who observed at the climatic meeting "that he saw no Moses among them").[42]

By contrast, religion was part of the next and largest slave conspiracy in Southern history in 1822. Its leaders were city blacks and members of a splinter group of Methodists who used an obeahman, Gullah Jack, to recruit the rural Gullah.[43] Denmark Vesey's somewhat anomalous conspiracy com-pares most favorably to that of the dancing societies of Trinidad. Both took place in old and cosmopolitan port cities among large, active, and unintim-idated populations of slave and free colored who mixed more readily in work, churches, and leisure than was the case elsewhere in Anglo-America. There is reference in the records of both plots of collections among members to pay the owners of hired-outs, who would then have time to work for the conspiracy. Both also flirted with religion as a way of bridging the formidable barriers—ethnic, class, and acculturative—that generally thwarted the insurrectionary designs of artisanal associations.[44]

Officials defined the leadership of the Charleston plot in three ways: as "confined to" hired-outs or those who "worked out"—carters, draymen, sawyers, porters, laborers, stevedores, mechanics, and lumberyard workers who, "in short," had time at their "own disposal"; as having "secured. . . the unlimited confidence of their owners [and were] . . . indulged in every comfort"; and as members of "the African congregation."[45] This last referred to a few small black prayer groups that in 1817 split from the city's regular Methodist congregations; put *African* in their new organization's title, as the African Association; and whose founders traveled first to Philadelphia to be ordained by Richard Allen's (first ever) African Methodist Episcopal Church.[46]

Vesey's plot, which led to the arrest of about 130 and the conviction of 67, half of whom were executed and half were transported, lies between the two stages of the final revolutionary movement and shares characteristics of each. It began more than a decade after the suppression of the last artisanal association, and like them its tactics were muddled; its duration long and risky (it was four years in the planning which greatly increased the possibility of discovery); and its objectives unclear. The group would either take the city or find ships and sail to Santo Domingo. But the plot also looked to the future. As a talented, propertied, and literate freedman and church member, Vesey and the other leaders, who were slaves and many of them deacons, were typical of those who led the large preemancipation rebellions already underway in the Caribbean when the Charleston plot was discovered.[47]

Although at first view the religious dimension of the conspiracy seems prominent, it was not. As Margaret Creel argues, loss of nerve by the obeahman Gullah Jack (at his trial) was regarded as a failure of the power he commanded and "symbolized the African-Christian cultural limbo of the slaves."[48] This "cultural limbo" reflected the heavily evangelized, morally inhibited ethos of a slave conversion in the lowcountry that could not be transformed, as it was by converts elsewhere who led the final spate of rebellions. The loosely formed associations of city and country people who slipped in and out of the alleys and yards of Charleston to meet interminably at Vesey's various houses, or at Buckley's farm on the Neck, were little more than discussion groups whose proceedings—a lone reference to a dusk-to-dawn session of prayer and psalms notwithstanding—never displayed the costumed pomp and ritual dynamism of their counterparts in the Caribbean. The only record of an oath was a raising of the right hand, and of a rite, the mention of a chicken eaten half raw "as evidence of union" by members of the Gullah Society.[49]

The Gullah were one of several bands and groups that surfaced during the plot and reflected the archaic ethnic divisions of Carolina coastal society: Monday Gell's Ibo company, the French band (group), and Charles Drayton's country-born company. Potentially divisive ethnic strife was revealed by discussions of whether "country-borns" (Creoles) or domestic servants were trustworthy, and a recruit's claim that he was told, "If I did not join he [the recruiter] would turn all my country people against me."[50]

Nor was religion a dominant feature of Vesey's teaching and outlook. Called the "old man" whose touchstone was black pride, Vesey was determined to fight the battle where he lived, even though he was moved by the siren of separatism that his money, freedom, and milieu encouraged; more than once he said "he would not follow Craighton to Africa."[51] Vesey regarded religion as a tool and its places of worship as convenient for conducting his style of what is now termed consciousness-raising. Dynamic, well-read, and eclectic, he liked to position himself in gatherings, at either chapels or ordinaries, and push blacks to challenge their condition. He was as likely as not to use a fable, classical or biblical, to drive a lesson home: When his wagon stalled, the wagoner prayed. "You fool," said Hercules, "put your shoulder to the wheel [and] whip up your horses and your wagon will be pulled out."[52] Vesey also sought to inspire by disseminating a clutch of abolitionist pamphlets he had secured and by citing the Haitian Revolution and news of the intense debates in Congress that ended in the 1820 Missouri Compromise. The latter also inspired the belief — a primary spark for rebellion in the Caribbean — that emancipation had been granted but was mysteriously withheld.[53] As Vesey said to Rolla, "We are free, but the white people won't let us be so."[54]

The conspirators' other stated objectives mirrored the earlier fantasies of the power-starved associations. There was talk of the need to "keep on fighting till the English came to help them"; "that the Americans could do nothing against the English, and that the English would carry them off to St. Domingo"; and "that St. Domingo and Africa will assist us to get our liberty, if we will only make the motion first."[55] More personal statements included two by men whose unbelieving owners attended their trials. When Peter Poyas was asked how he could wish to see his master and mistress murdered "after they had treated him so kindly," he "only replied to the question by a smile." After a guilty verdict, the master of another conspirator said, "I still don't believe it 'til you tell me so — what were your intentions?" Answer: "To kill you rip open your belly and throw your guts in your face."[56]

Anger of this type — free-floating, ambivalent, and charged by a frustrating inability to do much about it — characterized many Southern assimilateds. Gilbert, the young recruit in Gabriel's rebellion who on the day of the attack would take possession of his owner's horse and sword, also asked that his "Master and Mistress be put to death, but by the men under him." He could not do it himself, "because they had raised him." Asking to be made a captain, Gilbert was told he "stuttered too much to give the word of Command."[57] Painfully conspicuous signs of emotional turmoil such as Gilbert's mark the descriptions of assimilated in those sources where such subjective matters as personality and motivation may be examined somewhat systematically.

Discussion of artisans, as pointed out in the case of Virginia in *Flight and Rebellion,* should begin with a paradox. Although they were slaves, many achieved a significant degree of satisfaction from their work.[58] Routines that were often challenging created opportunities to travel beyond plantation confines and to acquire and sustain the skills, including English and an "artful" demeanor, which in colonial Virginia were essential for those blacks who chose to cope with slavery by learning as much as they could about whites and their ways. Although this development may seem to be no real compensation while one remained a slave, assimilateds did not act in such a way. At work or while resisting as fugitives or conspirators, they displayed an ingenuity and resourcefulness that flowed from the social and psychological compensations of their tasks and rank. Artisans were less oppressed than other slaves, and they knew that they were.*

Not only self-image but also treatment by whites separated artisans from the other slaves. Afflicted by plantation people who ran off but only "lurked" nearby, Landon Carter identified Jamy as a special kind of fugitive, who while on his own actually "turn[ed] a free man," that is, attempted to pass as a free person of color. Being away a great deal, Carter continued, enhanced the slave's free outlook "for the people [who hire him] treat him so much like a gentleman that he can't fancy himself otherwise when he gets home."[59] The same dynamic was at work wherever talented slaves did their business off the plantation. In Jamaica a manager complained in 1770 in stark political and racial terms of a jobbing carpenter who had received at the estate attorney's insistance "a white man's allowance" of food and drink. Subsequently "spoilt" and insolent, Joe had also been openly defended by the attorney, "to the great triumph of the Slaves." These practices are "alwise Attended with the worst Consequences, inspiring them with a contempt of Authority & of the White Colour."[60] Occasionally a white's frustration about artisans perceived as too independent and willful spilled over into a newspaper notice, as in the case of a slave working out who "has the audacity to tell me, he will be free, that he will serve no Man, and that he will be conquered or governed by no Man."[61] Another lowcountry planter, Henry Laurens, summed up the situation with suburban slaves when he told his brother that his hired-outs, who were in Laurens's charge, "in some measure govern themselves."[62]

Confronted in this fashion as slaveholders rarely were by slaves of other occupational groups, some gave in and were grateful for what they could get. "I do hereby promise," wrote one advertiser for a runaway, "that ... Tom may have a ticket to look for another master & no notice taken of his past conduct" — and giving considerable leeway to the slave — "provided he returns within a month."[63] This message, evidently conveyed through networks that are now obscure, is representative and demonstrates how easily a clever and able slave could slip off, as many did if a wage cut, new working conditions, or a command to return more frequently to the plantation was not to their liking. In this situation, owners in the Carolina lowcountry and the Caribbean, but never in the Chesapeake Bay region, sometimes signed off on a notice with a direct plea or bargain: If she returns on her

---

* The approximately eight hundred artisans advertised as runaways in newspapers from the four societies under consideration worked in one of three ways: as builders, including such wood and stone workers as carpenters, coopers, masons, and bricklayers; as watermen, from local to overseas sailors; or as house servants, especially waitingmen (valets).

own she shall be "pardoned, or might be sold to any agreeable purchaser she pleases."[64] These messages are also important as a straightforward explanation of how it was possible for assimilateds to have so much unsupervised time and opportunity to plot the whites' destruction.

During this era Creoles came to be regarded as more threatening than Africans, and whites pointed to their extensive networks and notorious associational activity — dances, mock military displays, and clubs — as readily convertible to conspiracies or worse. The solution of the Jamaican Assembly was to keep slaves "constantly at home" and to "disarm them, prevent caballing, drumming, sounding Conches & Horns, securing the Rum & strong liquors, and also ammunition."[65] But as instances of too-little-too-late, statute law could not control slaves who worked on "the periphery" beyond the plantation's reach in the suburban dimension of slavery.

In one region, the Chesapeake Bay, however, assimilateds were described not so much by their milieu and collective ethic as by their physical and psychological characteristics. These more personal features included such nervous mannerisms as tics, uncontrollable movements of hands and face, and varieties of speech disturbances. The sources of these descriptions, fugitive slave advertisements, also indicate that the assimilateds' owners were far more inclined than those elsewhere to depict their slaves as physical specimens rather than as members of particular groups, ethnic or otherwise. Depictions of an assimilated's most conspicuous mannerisms varied regionally and by gender. In the Caribbean, a stronger and more traditional slave culture made for a greater distance between the two peoples, white and black, and made for descriptions that were more impersonal than in the South, where the sense of the notices is that assimilation could be alienating.

Slaves with named speech disorders were more assimilated than any others, and Southern slaves, men particularly, were more likely to be afflicted by aphasia than were Caribbean blacks. Stutterers in Virginia, for instance, were Creole, artful, spoke cogent English, worked in highly mobile and skilled occupations, and were exclusively men (among the group of forty-nine named in the runaway advertisements). Women comprised only 8 or 7 percent of stutterers in South Carolina, and 4 or 12 percent of the thirty-three runaways reported as stutterers in Jamaica.[66]

In a slave population that was more acculturated than elsewhere, assimilateds from the Chesapeake Bay region were more likely to be described by physical and psychological characteristics.[67] Their owners were more inclined than whites were in the other regions to depict them as individual physical specimens rather than as members of particular groups, ethnic or otherwise. While South Carolinians, for instance, would typically note a stutter and rarely say more — "stutters when surprised or angry" is a conspicuous exception — Virginians threw at their readers an array of symptoms that the assimilateds exhibited: "looks very queerly out of his eyes"; "when challenged with a fault, or surprised, an extraordinary motion with his hands, which he cannot avoid"; "a staring look when confused"; and "when spoken to, his eyes turn rather up . . . with a wildness in his look, and a tremor or shaking of his head."[68]

Heavy drinkers were also unusually acculturated, and more likely in the Chesapeake Bay region than elsewhere to be subjects of an uncommonly individualized portrait. When the same type was described in the Caribbean, however, only the surface of character was touched: for Guy, a waitingman, "very artful."[69] That alcoholics rarely appear in descriptions of South Carolina blacks at any level of cultural change is testimony to a Gullah community traditionally characterized as insular and cohesive. Those so described did not manifest the other visible afflictions carried by counterparts in the Chesapeake Bay region.[70] "Loves rum" was the sum of it for several: Jack, for instance, was plausible, sang psalms, and loved brandy.[71] Typical of the Chesapeake Bay region, on the other hand, was the more complex relationship between Thomas Jefferson and his mulatto shoemaker Sandy: "greatly addicted to drink, and when drunk is insolent and disorderly, in his conversation he swears much, and in his behavior is artful and knavish."[72]

Why were depictions of stressed and anxious assimilateds concentrated in the Chesapeake Bay region? and why were their owners so inclined to take up advertising space with more elaborate descriptions of afflictions, while slaveholders elsewhere were not? A social explanation for the concentration of such psychological portraits may lie in the fact that the region was laced with urban areas and dominated by the smallest average holdings of slaves anywhere. Both factors assured the interpenetration of the two communities: the relative absence of the large slave gangs and the cantonments in which they lived that afforded a degree of anonymity in numbers, and the numerous one-on-one encounters between slave and free that were clearly galling ordeals for some skilled and talented blacks. The more detailed descriptions of aphasia and drinking in this region may also be seen as symptoms of an assimilation that demeaned. Situation and affliction may have been reinforcing in this manner. Psychological quirks facilitated an owner's ability to ignore cultural for personal, that is physical and psychological detail, Jamaica, in rare instances, not excepted. What is certain is that during the African phase of resistance slaves in regions other than the Chesapeake were usually described as ethnic types. As slaves acculturated and Creoles moved to the fore, whites usually depicted them more individually and in doing so objectified them.

This line of inquiry should be pursued in light of the nomenclature used for fugitives in South Carolina and Barbados, which by the end of the eighteenth century were fairly comparable. Most slaves were Creole and part of naturally growing populations; and whites were no longer so inclined to see blacks as representatives of distinctive African societies, but rather as physical specimens—a view that is at the core of modern racism. Writing for a readership no longer capable of connecting a word or two to a West African language or pattern of ritual scarring in order to see a type, advertisers used increased physical detail. From Barbados: "[She is] seventeen inches over the Shoulders . . . drowsy countenance, large, thick lips, small fallen breasts & round belly, with country marks cut in diamonds on it, large buttocks, small legs, very small foot, a small hand but somewhat hard From working with the hoe."[73]

In the South, after a century of referring in notices to black men as "Fellows," they became "boys" in the gazettes of several states, and did so at the close of the War of 1812.[74] The year 1815 is everyone's starting date for major changes in the culture as the United States turned its back on Europe and became more than ever before self-consciously American. The musings of intellectuals complemented street talk. Regarding the racial attitudes of the French colonial Moreau Saint-Méry, the Jamaican Bryan Edwards, and Jefferson, David Brion Davis observes that West Indians were curious students of the culture of slaves, and of their music and dance especially. It seemed they "actually liked" Negroes, for whom Jefferson's dislike was "morbid."[75]

The characterization of assimilateds by the mannerisms they exhibited when trying to communicate with whites may be used to mark the point of greatest divergence between Creolization in the two regions. Outside the Chesapeake, advertisers maintained a distance between themselves and their human possession that also existed apart from the notice. And in this space— whether carved out by growing one's own food or building one's house, taking more than one wife, marketing, or replying to massa—Caribbean and to an extent rice coast slaves created a more autonomous life than did slaves in the region of tobacco, wheat, and general farming. In this light, the absenteeism in large slave holdings outside the Chesapeake Bay region should also be seen as the extent to which the slaves themselves carried out Creolization, or, by contrast, the extent to which it was shaped in the Chesapeake Bay region by the resident owner. As for that planter's style of ownership, no other source exposes so effectively the close and brutally personal, paternalistic nature of slavery in this region as do the advertisements that describe severely conflicted assimilateds in speaking situations. Of their verbal dexterity, one might ask to what extent (and to what effect) versions of "puttin' on ol' massa" were compensatory substitutes for the robust family and economic institutions of Caribbean slaves that fended off the worst psychological ravages of the slave condition.

Concerning Creolization and its diverse effects and legacies throughout

Anglo-America, then, a slave people's loss or abandonment of a traditional orientation, consciously or not, encouraged and sustained white racism, which in turn worsened the psychological afflictions of those slaves — those relatively assimilated — who from a vantage point of inequality had to deal with whites often and intimately. On any account, until the end of slavery Caribbean whites were more predisposed than Southerners to see Africans as a people and a culture rather than as a thing and a possession.

Given that Jamaican slaves were the least assimilated, those in the Chesapeake Bay the most, with lowcountry Gullah and Barbadian slaves ranging in between, the argument to this point may be summarized as a series of proposals. Creolization in the Caribbean should be seen as a relatively slow and uneven process that blunted the more destructive effects of slavery as it shaped and was shaped by the slaves' traditionally conservative strategies in matters of family, religion, and economics. In the South, however, it may be useful to revive an old sociological distinction and see cultural change as comparatively rapid, thorough, and as an assimilation, not acculturation, more in one direction (the whites') than in the Caribbean. One view of Southern slave artisans' painfully conspicuous quirks and collective resistance that never progressed from planning to action is that Creolization individualized, a possibility that seems more promising in light of the Caribbean, where the process did not come at the expense of slave culture and community.

> People know what they do; they frequently know why they do what they do; but what they don't know is what they do does.
> — Michel Foucault, 1979[76]

The question of the conspirators' real intentions was raised in their time as well as ours. Some owners opposed the trials of conspirators because the accused were valued artisans and difficult to replace. Or, believing that "the Negroes in my yard are trustworthy, but those down the road are not," others would not accept that "trusted servants" could be rebels. In this vein, a South Carolinan wrote skeptically in 1822 that "The folkes here are under a scare because some of their waiting men for want of better employment met together to drink grog and eat Homminy for which high offence, they are trying them for their lives." More commonly, whites were easily frightened when assimilateds began associating secretly and lashed out if officials seemed too cautious about rounding-up suspects. As a Trinidadian planter in 1805 put it for so many: "[the whites] will tamely submit to hav[ing] their Throats cut when the business will be to[o] far gone to be able to check it."[77]

In our time the motives of rebellious slaves in the era of democratic revolutions have been questioned in two ways: by arguments that the conspiracies simply did not exist, and that when they did, the rebel objectives were shaped mostly by outside influences. Of the first, it has been argued that conspiracies were exercises in white community solidarity; that confronted by acute economic readjustments, invasion fears, or religious revivals, whites lynched blacks in order to pull themselves together.[78] Assuming that the slaves' political outlook was based on the same philosophical underpinnings as the whites', another argument is that resistance developed progressively from the "archaic," pre-political reactions of slave outlaws to actual revolution — to overthrow the system — an idea of a "bourgeois-democratic character" imposed by "the liberal middle class."[79] But as in the earlier instance, of interpretations of maroonage, arguments that evaluate African Americans from the outside often obscure the people they seek to explain; they may mislead as well. A better approach to the conspiracies is exposed in an aside of A. J. R. Russell-Wood to the effect that the black religious brotherhoods of Brazil were the urban counterparts of maroonage; both were "places to feel at home."[80]

To see black associationism from the inside, while asking to what extent its thrust was ameliorationist or revolutionary, is to look more closely at the artisans' fascination with titles and hierarchies, their aggressive assertiveness toward women and mulattoes, and their own statements of intent. As among the least oppressed of non-field slaves, conspirators in a variety of sources were described as "the most valuable Negroes on the Estate" (Jamaica, 1776); coopers and boilers (St. Kitts, 1778); "Drivers and Head People" (Jamaica, 1807); and blacksmiths, waitingmen, and town Negroes (Virginia, 1800). Compared to the spartan existence of maroons, assimilateds, according to the characterizations of whites, aspired to or already lived the good life. Once the capital of Richmond was taken, "on the day it should be agreed to [Gabriel and his men] would dine and drink with the merchants of the City" (Virginia, 1800). The conspirators' tables were "covered with hogs, Guinea fowls, ducks and other poultry"; "they were not only in possession of the Comforts, but even the Luxuries of Life" (Tobago, 1801); and "they arrived about Midnight & found a supper of fowls, bread, wine & rum. . . . One day when there was a dinner at Baptiste's and [the deponent] saw a great Cake at the table of Kings and Generals. But he was not admitted [to] the Party" (Trinidad, 1805).[81]

Some joined, but only to fight ceremoniously by receiving a title and costume and thereby enjoy year around the role reversals previously restricted to the Christmas holiday, when "slaves appear an altered race of beings. They show themselves off to the greatest advantage, by fine clothes and a profusion of trinkets; they affect a more polished behaviour and mode of speech; they address the whites with greater familiarity; they come into their masters' houses, and drink with them; the distance between them appears to be annihilated for the moment." This nineteenth-century traveler went on to describe a slave military ball at which "one is General Campbell, another is Admiral Rowley, and a third is Colonel Russell; . . . and by these names they are generally addressed at their festive meetings."[82] On St. Kitts, Creoles assembled in 1770 and "affected to imitate their masters," that is, they held a council, an assembly, and then danced. Across in Trinidad, Scipio, founder and "prime minister" of a convoy, testified that his associates asked to call him "Lord Sir John" because he had accompanied his master to England, where the latter had known a "Nobleman of that Name."[83]

The militarism that pervaded the period also provided conspirators with a treasure chest of illusions. The well-known Southern fugitive Austin Steward in his published autobiography mentions his intoxication with the martial spirit of the Napoleonic era, when during the War of 1812 he longed "to be out on the line."[84] Steward's wish was echoed by a contemporary Caribbean rebel who claimed they were seeking "their rights" and that they "like Bonaparte were able and strong."[85]

At the artisans' feasts and pageants, there was much talk about the French, who were heroes to a great number of blacks throughout the Americas. "They wanted to follow the example of Guadeloupe and St. Domingo . . . in the Chief's house was a print representing the Execution of the King of France" (Tobago, 1801); "They would drive the white people into the Sea [and] give the Country to the French" (Jamaica, 1806); "Frenchmen were very good Masters for Negroes"; and "As soon as the French came they [would] fight for them against the English."[86] Much of this was focused by the Haitian Revolution, especially in Jamaica, where to this day, writes the linguist Frederic G. Cassidy, "French means Haiti."[87] The artisanal associations never generated revolution, however, if that was ever their real intention. Slaves no longer possessed the economic base, military leadership, athletic prowess, and ritual life of encampments of new Negro rebels and of the Maroon towns. "How should we think of such a thing," cried a conspirator under torture on Montserrat in 1768. "We have no arms! no powder! No camp, no any thing!"[88]

At one level, then, the plots, as Richard Cobb infers in another context, may be seen as compensatory, a kind of play acting by the dispossessed who, by creating arenas where participants could safely take on trappings of power and authority, sought to pump up powerless existences. Sooner or later, Cobb observes, the brotherhoods had to return to real life.[89] At another level, however, the proliferation of associations in small-scale societies may be seen as a reaction to political "emasculat[ion]." With no real power of their own, argues Peter J. Wilson in a study of Bermudian club life as a microcosm of the larger society, villagers construct organizations as alternatives to such authoritative institutions as courts and police. In them members dispense a profusion of offices, with high-sounding titles, that in effect satirize the external political apparatus that controls them.[90] Among other related phenomena, Wilson's study provides another way of looking at Quillos's courthouse election in North Carolina, which was repeated in Jamaica in the 1820s.

Yet once at the "courthouse," that is, on their own, assimilateds were put to the test and compelled to challenge the fine line between simply trying things out and perhaps flexing muscles a bit or actually fighting. Some were impaled on the dilemma. "The business is gone wrong [but when] you all thought it was fun [you] wanted to be in it," said a regiment's queen while cross-examining two men during her self-defense in the Trinidadian trials.[91]

In some ways the associations asserted an exclusiveness by marking as targets women and free people of color. Their members were to be "of one colour." "We shall kill coloured who are now fighting for buckra" was a reference to new policies in the Caribbean at the end of the century of employing brown and mulatto soldiers.[92] As for women, they could not be trusted to keep a secret. Shoving aside a young recruit in Trinidad in 1805, Old Michael said that this "business [is] . . . not a matter for Women or Boys."[93] Compared to women and people of color, artisans were newcomers to town. The free colored concentrated in towns; it was easier to get by there, and plantations were symbols of the degradations of dark-skinned people. Towns were also the chosen setting for black women, slave and free. Well established as higglers, washerwomen, mistresses, and dominant members in the new dissenter chapels, women made a world that, contrasted to the men's rule-bound and hierarchical associations, was relatively fluid and egalitarian.[94]

Yet, from another perspective, the associations were remarkably inclusive. This was their major achievement. They were meeting places for people from a variety of backgrounds. Harold, for instance, was a chief of a Trinidadian dancing society. He was also a carter and a freedman, a Christian convert born in Africa (of the Soso, a Windward Coast people) who had purchased his freedom and been a leader in the St. George convoy "since Spanish Times." Behind the pomp, ceremony, and vacillation there persisted in associations from Richmond, Virginia to Port of Spain, Trinidad, a design to bridge formidable ethnic and acculturative barriers among men like Harold, whose urban work had led them away from the old values and sanctions of the historically isolated plantation Negroes and Maroons.[95]

But was rebellion their aim? And, if so, rebellion of what kind? Were the assimilateds' objectives ameliorationist or truly revolutionary, against the institution or simply its abuses? The evidence is equivocal. Certainly, ameliorative objectives percolate in the rebels' own words: "They said they were not going to live in them small houses—they would have their Masters' [houses]." However, when it seems that assimilateds may be safely labeled impractical romantics who spun designs signifying more a matter of wish-fulfillment than actual revolt, feelings and principles such as the following are heard clearly: "if we don't get 'the Free' we'll take it." Another (for so many others) said he joined because "I can no longer bear what [I have] borne."[96]

In a few instances, whites looked back shrewdly at a conspiracy and struck the same chord. Following the 1791 Jamaican disturbance, absentee proprietors memorialized that the plot was not based on any "Pretense of Ill-treatment, as to Food, Clothing, or other Particulars," but accountable to "what they term their Rights."[97] St. George Tucker said the same when he examined the background of Gabriel's plot for the state legislature. Their motives, he argued, should be compared to those of the slaves, who in 1775, the first year of the American Revolution, joined the last royal governor and the British, who promised to free them if they did so. Then, Tucker argued, slaves merely saw freedom as "a good." Now they see it as "a right."[98]

The conspirators were slaves who had achieved openings; and it should never be forgotten how relatively easily members of this new class could run away and work out a better deal for themselves, as their predecessors, urban fugitives, had done for decades in all plantation societies. But in doing so, in simply finding another less restrictive "owner" or work situation, they still remained slaves, which they understood. In the era of democratic revolutions, maroonage and self-help associations represented two routes for those among the mass of field hands who chose to work for liberation. Each failed badly as revolutionary alternatives to plantation slavery. Following the Peace of 1739, Maroons pursued a policy of selective borrowing from white culture to the extent that by 1760 a royal governor spoke approvingly of "a spirit of Industry" among them.[99] Maroons, who occasionally asked physicians and clerics to visit, developed an array of enterprises, from an iron works to a flourishing local trade in tobacco and livestock. Nonetheless, they remained territorial and separate and so offered little that was new politically to plantation people, who also were territorial and sometimes divided ethnically.

On balance, the artisans' dancing and military societies may be seen as incipient forms of urban black associationism, a feature of African-American life ever since. Most were fraternal and antiwhite, but not necessarily antislavery. At some point members decided, sometimes explicitly, either to develop a following among plantation blacks in order to resist slavery or to continue to rebel symbolically by incorporating secular symbols of white power—expressed variously as the acquisition of guns, titles, horses, and white women—into their rituals and rhetoric.

Yet assimilateds came of age politically in an era of unparalleled religious fermentation when traditional knowledge and evangelical Christianity began feeding creatively from one another to produce sects — Myal, Convince, and other accretions of an Africanized evangelism — that captivated plantation people. Could leaders, as in Haiti, shape an ideology that made sense to plantation people, a vision that did not oppose the religious and the political? Could freedom and spiritual redemption be preached and danced as one and the same?

In confronting this challenge, artisans discovered that "failure" was only temporary in the era of democratic revolutions. Within a generation of the destruction of their associations, a new revolutionary style emerged shaped by an Africanized revivalism and such externals as missions, abolitionism, and the era's natural rights philosophy.

# 10

## Mission Christianity and Preemancipation Rebellion

> The end result was the typical native Christianity of West
> Indian society — mixing, so to speak, African spirit with Eu-
> ropean form.
> What all this meant, in ideological terms, has come to con-
> stitute one of the serious controversies of modern Caribbean
> scholarship. . . . Is it true — as scholars . . . have argued — that
> missionary Christianity simply served, by its socially quietist
> teachings, to buttress the slave-based social order . . . ? Or can
> it be argued that, ideologically, the doctrine of Christian political
> liberty ultimately worked, as it was applied to the slave person,
> to undermine that order? The enquiry is crucial, because it
> goes to the heart of the Caribbean condition, in which religious
> modes of thought have helped shape the basic communal psy-
> chology of the society.
> — Gordon K. Lewis, 1983[1]

First efforts to Christianize great numbers of slaves (and not simply favored
house servants) began in the South in the second half of the eighteenth
century. Fastening to a people who were already comparatively assimilated,
mass conversions created such exclusively black societies as the African
Methodist Episcopal Church. By the second quarter of the nineteenth century, as black congregations in the United States were preparing to send
missionaries to Africa, their counterparts in the Caribbean were plotting
how to get paid wages — as slaves — or how best to overthrow the system
entirely. In Jamaica some new black converts, influenced by the passivity

of the New Testament message "turn the other cheek," sought support for a general strike, a refinement of the old tactic of lying out as a gang in the bush while leaders negotiated. More radical church members, however, who were usually older and deacons, were convinced that work stoppages were risky and saw them instead as preludes to a war of liberation. These positions were hammered out in prayer and catechism groups that were part of mission stations, some of which were in place by the late 1700s. By the 1820s and 1830s a series of large rebellions swept through Anglo-America, all but one of which were organized either by members of mission stations or, like Nat Turner's, by leaders who were in part inspired by their understandings of biblical religion. By this time the dichotomy between urban and rural patterns of slave Christianization was breaking down in the Caribbean, especially in Jamaica, where members and leaders of an unusually large urban congregation in Montego Bay led the 1831 rebellion.

What slave converts did do with the new Christian lore differed sharply from one locale to another. But generally, the missionaries' Protestant preoccupation with disciplined self-improvement encountered some acceptance when it assumed the form of literacy and legalized marriages. When the new ethic attacked dancing and Sunday marketing, however, slaves were not as interested.

The degree to which the new learning was used to more effectively resist slavery itself depended on the tradition of resistance that slaves had achieved in their respective societies. While conversion made some converts assimilationist and accommodated, a perspective that has commanded interpretations of antebellum slave religion, others were only apparently that way. Instead they created cults that resembled African prototypes: they were autonomous and gathered around charismatic healing prophets steeped in play—the ancestral spirit dance tradition.

African in origin, play was an ideal assimilative tool for a people of oral traditions who were in some ways severely divided. Comprised of dance and music, which do not require words to communicate, play was amoebic: absorptive, constantly changing its steps, drum patterns, and singing to accommodate different locales and players. In its multiplicity of forms play continued to pop up in sects on the cutting edge of fundamental change. In the hands and minds of the stewards of the generation from the 1790s to the 1820s, the bush Baptists, it incorporated and disseminated such subversive Christian rites and texts as baptism and Exodus—Moses leading the Jews out of Pharoah's Egypt to the Promised Land. These combinations of Christian evangelicalism and traditional slave knowledge and spirituality stemmed from novel concepts of time and human nature, of a time reckoned as some Christians did—as millennial—and, of a humankind in which all made in the image of God were equal.

In order to refine answers to a familiar question—How and to what extent did conversion stifle or encourage slave resistance?—a series of studies is offered from along the spectrum of the diverse effects of slave Christianization: accommodated (Antigua), reformist (Demerara), revolutionary (Jamaica), and chiliastic (Virginia). The first three were products of neighborhood missionary stations that were, respectively, Moravian, Methodist, and Baptist; the last was a mixture of Christian and traditional beliefs and knowledge. The questions raised include: What were the conditions in which owners and missionaries were able to prevent organized attempts by the slaves to free themselves? What were some of the important regional differences in the ideology and leadership of major rebellions? And how may one account for uprisings in Barbados and Virginia, in which both assimilateds and Christianization so prominent in the other rebellions were negligble factors?

## Accommodated: The Moravians

The Moravians or United Brethren preceded other denominations in the islands by many years when they set up in Jamaica in 1754. Cautious and assiduously diffident toward both government and planters, Moravians were moderately successful; their converts were known as "good" slaves. Black Moravians of the Antigua station, the largest anywhere, were especially cooperative and assimilated, a tack that paid off in a fashion. When slavery was abolished throughout the empire in 1834, Antiguan slaves were emancipated outright, whereas blacks elsewhere were forced as "apprentices" to endure four more years before they were given freedom outright.[2]

The argument is that the acquiescent posture of Antiguan slaves was in part accountable to a fit or degree of congruence between facets of their culture and that of the Moravians. On the one hand, slave life as elsewhere was shaped by an African communalism tempered here by the grim realities of the island's geopolitics: minuscule gardens (or "bits") in a landscape that was drying out and had never been suitable for armed resistance. Whites were so confident in fact that they armed blacks during invasion scares. Against this uninspiring background, slaves developed few of the outlets— of maroonage, play, and artisanal associations—that prevailed elsewhere. On the other hand, Moravianism was shaped by German missionaries and the sanctuaries they established. In their reports home the missionaries exude an obeisant, patient, and artless air, and the chapel and yard stations they made were peaceful and enclosing. Operating in an institutional vacuum, the Moravian mission provided a place where slaves could meet and not feel slavish, while providing opportunities for talented and ambitious slaves— who were becoming so troublesome elsewhere—to use their skills and thereby enhance the modicum of mobility and respectability that their non-field tasks had afforded in the first place.

The missionary effort in the Caribbean, including the Moravian's, was rejuvenated by the liberal tide of abolitionism and philanthropy that swept the West in the late eighteenth century. In England, Jamaican absentees formed an association in order to inject new money and leadership into an old mission station at Barham's Island Estate. Their correspondence, which displayed the potent mix of mercenary and idealistic motives that propelled the missionary onslaught on slave quarters in the generation before emancipation, was filled with phrases reminiscent of the second generation of scientific agricultural reformers who sought to ameliorate slavery by modifying the slave's perception of it. "Let me tell you . . . every humane person [ought] to afford his Negroes everything which may promote their happiness and alleviate the inevitable hardships of their situation," wrote Peter Beckford, one of the mission's movers. Alluding to matters of security, another regarded the philanthropists' objective as "extremely urgent" because blacks were so numerous and "every means [ought to be made to] . . . get hold of [their] minds." The association decided to staff their mission with Moravians because, in the Danish West Indies, Antigua, and St. Kitts, as Barham wrote, that group had converted thousands of slaves "to the evident improvement of their manners."[3] In time the proprietors assessed themselves at the rate of 4 shillings per slave and provided each missionary passage and a salary of £100 per year. In return the Moravians promised explicitly not "to interfere in . . . [any way] with the external management of the Estate," code words for keeping their noses out of the abolition debates raging at the time.[4]

It is difficult to imagine initial encounters between blacks and a type of missionary that was not so overtly exploitive as whites usually were, and who sometimes made real efforts to understand the spiritual concerns that were so important to many slaves. But the available pictures couched in the evidence do convey a sense of the Moravians' style, and of the tight little communities the two made.

When they were able, the Brethren put their stations outside the plantations, which they slowly came to realize identified them with a symbol, for blacks, of degradation and oppression. A few years after the Jamaican subscription, they built a new Antiguan station at Grace Bay, sixteen miles south of St. Johns and at the foot of the Sheckerly Mountains. An architectural rendering of the station reveals that it was not a version of either the familiar Georgian Anglican church or of the less imposing, low-slung bungalow type of dissenter chapel.[5] Instead, the impression is of a smaller version of a frontier fort in the western United States, or of a Spanish hacienda. In either case, it consisted of two stories and four sides enclosing a small parade ground that provided a tactile and convenient reminder of the inward, sequestered, and "compound-like" character of the Moravian missionary style.

The new mission was set in a neighborhood of dilapidated rum stores, where about twenty people, chiefly mulattoes and a few aged watchmen guarding coconut trees, lived. The first missionary moved into an old ruin and made a chapel of one room and a store of another. Supplies were meager, the weather dry, and business slow. Most of the Negroes of the local big estate (the heirs of Clement Tudway) were Methodists, a missionary reported, "and you know we don't like to labour in another man's field." Nonetheless, within six months the missionaries were able to put up a sizeable building (25 by 40 feet). Otherwise, they proceeded cautiously and insisted that slaves who were prospective converts do the same. Regarding the evangelicals' methods of conversion as too quick and superficial, the Brethren stuck to their own slow and cautious way to what they called a "renewed heart."[6] There would be no imaginative leaps from biblical passages to old rites of dance and water because the Moravians' methods safeguarded against forms of play passed off as conversion experiences.

Thoughtful ideas about polygamy and slavery's impact on personality complemented the Moravian's careful approach to conversion. Slavery is a "slow, systematic murder of all intelligence and character," said J. H. Buchner, a Moravian church historian and Jamaican missionary whose writings reveal that even the most politically diffident missionary style could disguise abolitionist predispositions. While slaves are taught deception from childhood, "there is a shrewdness and sagacity" about them that a visitor and superficial observer may overlook "on account of the deference and respect which they pay to the white man. But they are not slow in forming a pretty correct estimate of the man they have to deal with, and shaping their course accordingly."[7]

The Moravians confronted slave polygamy, which other sects attacked with the zeal of crusaders, in a restrained and practical manner. Potential converts, a synod ruled, were not required to shed excess mates, that is, "to put away one," before undertaking the long and arduous period of religious instruction that led to baptism. Partners in polygynous unions could be members but not teachers. To acquire additional mates after membership was to risk expulsion from the society. In a similar situation, by contrast, Southern Baptists reacted more narrowly and punitively. Even when slave mates were separated by sale and distant moves over which, of course, they had no control, the mate left behind was usually expelled if he or she remarried. In the same situation, however, Moravians gave slaves room to maneuver. If a sale separated mates, members could remarry, acquire another "help-mate," and were encouraged to do so if children were involved. But

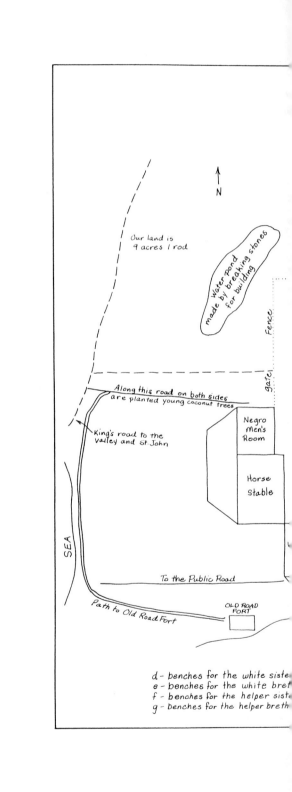

N

Our land is
9 acres 1 rod

Water pond
made by breaking stones
for building

Fence

gate

Along this road on both sides
are planted young coconut trees

Negro
Men's
Room

King's road to the
valley and St. John

Horse
Stable

SEA

To the Public Road

Path to Old Road Fort

OLD ROAD
FORT

d - benches for the white sister
e - benches for the white bref
f - benches for the helper siste
g - benches for the helper breth

# AN OF THE NEW MORAVIAN CHURCH
# GRACE BAY, ANTIGUA ~ 1812

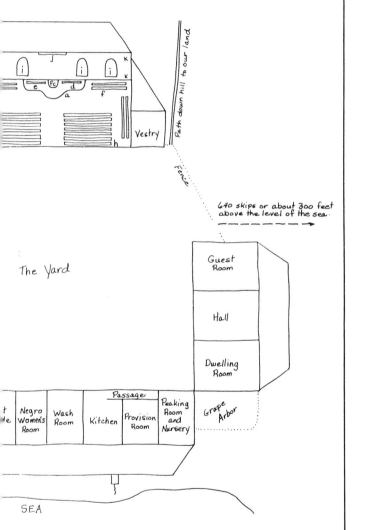

Path down hill to our land

Vestry

640 skips or about 300 feet above the level of the sea.

The Yard

Guest Room

Hall

Dwelling Room

Passage

| t | Negro Women's Room | Wash Room | Kitchen | Provision Room | Peaking Room and Nursery | Grape Arbor |

SEA

blackboard with the inscription over the pulpit,
To the Poor, the Gospel is preached" (in Golden Letters)
indows

as Christians, Moravians did promote monogamy, in part by instituting classes arranged by sex and age — the Single Sisters and the Single Brothers.[8]

In their own way, then, Moravians were as methodical as the Methodists when setting up the prayer and catechism groups that so readily got out of hand in Baptist Jamaica. Candidates were passed through a numbing hierarchy of meetings and officers. Slaves leaders in this denomination, who were expected to be influential, of sound judgment, and exemplary, were called "helpers" or "servants." Assigned districts, they were also given significant pastoral responsibilities that engaged the field people's basic concerns. They visited, attended the sick and infirm, held prayer meetings and tried to promote harmony by arbitrating quarrels. In 1774 an Antiguan missionary reported that all but one of the four men and six women helpers he employed were slaves with whom he met once a week.[9] Such groups constituted the bottom step in the hierarchy of meetings and examinations through which prospective converts were passed. Near the top, helpers and missionaries met monthly in "conference," where they reviewed lists of candidates in order to check the progress of their conduct and conversion. Eventually, at small local meetings, the catechists prepared for the "speaking" where — the men with the missionary and the women with the missionary's wife — they were asked about their lives and encouraged, admonished, and further instructed.[10]

In this way the Moravians "contract an intimacy" with the slave explained the antislavery Anglican priest James Ramsay. They "enter into [the slave's] little interest," and they listen patiently to the slave's doubts and complaints as they "lead them on slowly and gently [and] . . . exhort them affectionately," all the while avoiding "carefully magisterial threatenings and commands." Slave initiates are told first about the sufferings and crucifixion of Christ. When this takes hold, they "make them connect it with repentance and a good life, followed by Submission to masters as part of th[at] good life." This method, Ramsay assured his readers, produced slaves who were orderly, neat, diligent, humble, and honest. But this was the familiar public face of slave conversion. From the inside, the message the slaves received about their condition was more complex and ambivalent.[11] Sarah Wilson, one of the few Moravian converts implicated in the 1831 Jamaica rebellion, testified that she interpreted a missionary's teaching as "Suppose Buckra say some thing belongs to you, would you not take it; Mr Pfeiffer told me I was free and I took it."[12]

In the last quarter of the eighteenth century as evangelicals streamed into the Caribbean, they were regarded appreciatively by the Moravians, who had been in place for a long time. The newcomers, the Brethren reasoned, would spark revivals that would benefit all denominations. Reporting a surge in conversions in Antigua, a missionary counted 5,424 slave baptisms in the fifteen years between 1793 and 1808, or more than a third of the 13,278 converted during the Moravians' first fifty years in the island. The missionary also specified that this upswing had begun in 1773, when within two years a congregation of five hundred increased fourfold to two thousand. Here and throughout the Caribbean, however, success of this magnitude was suddenly checked by the repression of liberalism during the Napoleonic era (the early 1800s to 1815). But afterward in Jamaica, a Moravian missionary—as Knibb and Burchell did for the Baptists—reported on a second wave of conversions on the eve of the great 1831 rebellion. Whereas in 1827, he wrote, there were eight Moravian congregations of about 5,200 members, four years later there was three times that number of churches, twenty-four, with nearly eleven thousand members. Like his Antiguan counterpart, Buchner also placed the beginnings of the "general awakening" in the period of the American Revolution.[13]

Hence, the first mass conversion of slaves to Christianity may be characterized as a long, rolling ground swell that was temporarily flattened and divided by the Napoleonic era. When it finally broke, it did so massively and in the form of huge strikes. The first, which was violent around its edges, was organized by converts at a chapel in Demerara, British Guiana. The other, which quickly became a war, was led by Baptist teachers from the western parishes of Jamaica.

## Reformist: The Demerara Revolt, 1823

During the "awakening," an umbrella organization, the London Missionary Society, set up a station in a corner of the Caribbean at Demerara, the steamy, water-laced northeast tip of South America. Within a generation the colony had been passed back and forth between the Dutch and English and experienced a major uprising in late 1795. In his own defense during his trial, Jack Gladstone, a leader of the 1823 revolt, said that "had there been no methodists on the east coast, there would have been no revolt." Planters agreed. One called the rising "most peculiar," for nearly all of its leaders belonged to one station, Bethel Chapel, at a large coastal estate, Le Resouvenir. Another said the leaders were the principal artisans of their respective plantations, and "men in the Confidence and Favour of their Masters, who knew the hardships of Slavery only by name." Alluding to missionary educations and the new prestige of literacy, one rebel characterized another as a leader "although he does not read so well as Basson"; and another referred to the leaders simply as "those that understand books."[14]

The revolt, which peaked in a few days, eventually involved several thousand slaves, about 250 of whom (and three whites) lost their lives, either in battle or at the gallows. The rising consisted of a few small skirmishes, one large stand-off, and traces of the earlier artisanal plots. The rebels said they would kill every white in the capital of Georgetown, distribute ranks of emperor, king, and governor, and make the entire colony theirs.

Set in motion by the deacons of Bethel Chapel, the revolt was poorly organized; a sit-down for most, it was to be an insurrection for others. As one of a handful of massive statements that ranged between strikes and actual rebellions, the Demerara rising leaves one wondering what would have happened if, as in Haiti, momentum could have been sustained, and if leadership had been seen in an African-Catholic or bush Baptist way as sacred and concentrated in a few, rather than scattered among so many demystified, moralistic deacons and catechists. Acutely aware of the subversive nature of missions of any style, however, planters wished to see the revolt as the work of one person, a white man, the London Missionary Society's John Smith, "the Demerara Martyr." On the other hand, historians have argued that the rebellion was the slaves' from first to last.[15] In light of the slaves' own testimony and the ambivalent character of their tactics, objectives, and leadership (including that of the enigmatic Smith), both viewpoints are arguable.

In the sources, the rebels' uncertainty about objectives makes an impression similar to that of the artisans' preoccupation with planning in the conspiratorial associations. But tentativeness in the case of the deacons seemed a matter of Christian ambivalence regarding violence and bloodshed. This manifested itself in loose talk of help from the most unlikely sources, city blacks and maroons, and in an unusual concern for legality and its corollary, writing. While swarming around plantation yards as they tried to roust reluctant field laborers from their huts, the rebels hit on a tactic that provided both a quick payoff and a resolution whether the revolt was to be a war or a protest. Turning the tables, they shoved supervisors into the hated stocks and kept them there until paper and pen were marshalled and the whites had symbolically signed over the estates.

Once in command of the stocks it was easy to put whites in, out, and then back in as mood dictated. Usually, only supervisors were locked up. An owner—an old woman "of good physick" who spent much time in the hothouse among sick slaves—was hidden away. A physician who tried to talk his way out of trouble—he had sick people to attend to that morning—was told "who wants you for a doctor again?" One slave offered to get a pillow for his manager; another, who dragged his out of the house by the heels and down a flight of steps, later apologized and said he would work Monday. In reply the manager gave him and several others a drink. He was also slapped by Kate, who asked "how do you like it?" Another—alluding to the ubiquitous Exodus story—called his manager "a second

Pharoah." At the stocks the rebels also discussed the day after the revolution: "Quamina to be King, Jack governor, Mr. Hamilton [a manager, and a lover of Jack Gladstone's girl friend] was to have been a great man; . . . white ladies were to be allowed to leave the Colony, but the white men to work in the field, and anyone giving an insolent answer was to be killed. . . . Parson Smith head over us all when free."[16]

The rebel's fixation on written documents as proof of freedom, or that the estate was theirs, let off steam in the midst of an explosive situation. One rebel who freed some managers was given four bottles of wine. But as the tactic of signing official-looking papers caught on, the slave just as readily helped shove whites into the stocks until they agreed to sign. At Porter's Hope Plantation, Cudjoe said "they'd had their freedom since Governor Meerten's time, but the rascally buckras [whites] kept it from them," and that he had such command over the people that he was able to have a sickly manager released. Joe, a driver, asked "what was the good for them that was in the [news]papers?" and was told he was not understood. Joe responded, "You are like the rest of the white people, you won't tell any thing that's good for us."[17]

In the meantime, many refused to join. Duke tied up a head driver and then kicked in Thomas's door while yelling, "Thomas! Thomas! What do you mean by leaving us to fight your battles; we had you and the waterside just now, and you have run away from us, and come to your house again."[18] Thomas replied, "well, my wife has got supper for me." A house servant testified that Duke asked them all "to come out and fight," that they had been "fighting all the way from Chateau Margo and had put the Governor and Fiscal, and all the great people in the stocks." Duke struggled to get some to cut down a bridge before they again gave him the slip and returned home. That night he got "every" man out on the levee, broke down another door, beat Edwin, and, before being restrained, told the rest to come out or he would burn down their houses. At his trial Duke was characterized as a "very good workman" and a "parson."[19]

When the troops did arrive from Georgetown, the slaves, arrayed "in great force," negotiated twice. Hesitant the first time, they asked only for piecemeal reforms, two or three days off a week and Sundays for church; the second time they said simply, "they wanted their freedom." Stewart, a manager who had been defended by some and locked up by others, said that Monday the women's gang had worked very well but "talk[ed] very much about freedom." When the governor confronted the insurrectionists to ask what they wanted, he was told that they "were as good as white people . . . and they had no right to be slaves, nor would they be any longer, the king had sent out their freedom, and free they would be." Asking where they had heard that "God made all men [free] . . . and that they were as good as whites," the governor later "declared [that] the universal reply was, 'At Chapel, at Chapel.' "[20]

In order to build a case that John Smith organized his chapel for purposes of subverting slavery, the military court left one of the best records of the workings of a mission. The prosecution focused on religious texts and their explication, slave leadership, and the collection and disbursement of fees.[21] Sunday worship at Bethel Chapel began with prayer, songs, and a lesson from the Bible. Immediately before the revolt, a black teacher based his lesson on Luke 19:41–42: "When Jesus came near the city he wept over it."[22] But excerpts from printed sermons make it difficult to imagine the excitment they undoubtedly generated in the charged atmosphere of imminent revolt. Nor may one confidently infer intent from such ambiguous professions of faith as the following in which (in court proceedings) an insurrectionist in the same breath went from "blessings for massa" to "fire for massa": "at our prayer-meetings we prayed to God to help us and to bless us all, . . . that he would bless our masters, and the governor and fiscal; that we might be made good servants unto them, and they might be good masters unto us; and to give us health & strength to do what it might be our duty to do . . . we pray about our masters hearts, we pray to the Lord to bless, and change our hearts, and change our masters hearts likewise." But suddenly, "I have heard some of the boys who read the bible, speak about the Israelites and the Jews, about the fighting of the Israelites when they go to war; when the prisoner [Smith] read about the fighting of the Israelites, after[wards] they went home and read it again."[23] The deacon testified that he tried to explain Exodus uncontroversially, "but the people applied the story . . . and put it on themselves . . . they began to discourse about it; they said that this thing in the bible applied to us . . . as well as to the people of Israel." To this another said emphatically that church-goers "never" spoke of any other part of the Bible except Moses and the children of Israel.[24]

Hard-working and dedicated, Smith established a rapport with the slaves and delegated real responsibilities to the black deacons. The court record also includes a note that the slaves "always" chose their own teachers from among those who could read. When questioned about who Smith chose as catechists, Bristol, a deacon, replied, "I tell him."[25]

What slave deacons did before they became rebels included looking after the conduct of new members who lived on the same plantation as they did and reporting the initiate's spiritual progress to Smith. They also kept track of fees collected, maintained quiet during chapel service, and distributed communion bread and wine. Black church leaders included Quamina, the head deacon and a carpenter, who held the position before Smith took over in 1808. Of this leader, his brother-in-law Bristol noted that the missionary considered Quamina "more than white men."[26] A third deacon was an older freedman who lived with his slave granddaughter, and a fourth, Jack Gladstone, a cooper, was Quamina's popular son and an anomaly of sorts. Appointed by Jacob Wray, Smith's predecessor, and only occasionally in attendance, Gladstone was useful because he could read. One senses from the trial record that he enjoyed life too much to place himself resolutely under the mission's morally inhibited codes. In the bitter aftermath of this affair Quamina became a maroon before he was killed by Indian trackers; his son turned state's evidence and so was spared and transported.[27] At Smith's trial, both hostile and friendly witnesses agreed that the missionary never talked directly about slavery or slave treatment. However, in court, Smith admitted his "aversion" to the institution, while claiming that he had not read the Bible selectively but "right through." He then asked how it was possible to teach church history without an account of the Deliverance.[28] Of this testimony, a military officer concluded aptly that Smith, who soon died from an illness, certainly did expound on those parts of the Bible that were "entirely relative to the Oppressed State in which he considered them [the slaves] to be."[29] To this, a slave deacon added, "I always understood, as well as the rest of the Negroes, that although the parson preached in a way not directly telling us to take our freedom, yet [we] . . . understood he meant we could do so."[30]

The Bethel mission gathered an even greater diversity of slaves, African and Creole, skilled and field, than the earlier associations, and it did so while providing them with an Old Testament ideology that the congregation readily turned to its own revolutionary objectives. Yet conversion in Demerara never attained the emotional sweep that occurred in Jamaica, where the blend of old and new ignited a large and prolonged rebellion.

## Evanglical Revolutionaries: Jamaica, 1831

Altho it might be supposed that the Revolt had been subdued,
'The War had only begun'.
— A rebel leader at the place of execution: the "Argyle War," Jamaica, 1824

They [the rebels] said that I knew as well as themselves that Jamaica was now free, and half the estates from there to Montego-Bay were burnt down the night before; . . . that this was not the work of man alone, but they had assistance from God.
— Deposition of William Annand, overseer, 1832

Distant houses in flames appeared above the horizon . . . till, at length, the whole surrounding country was completely illuminated, and presented a terrible appearance, even at noon-day. When, however, the shades of night descended, and the buildings on the sides of those beautiful mountains . . . were burning, the spectacle was awfully grand.

— Theodore Faulks, 1833[31]

No slave rebellion in Anglo-America equaled the degree of preparation, duration, and spectacular destructiveness of the Jamaica rising from late December 1831 to early January 1832. Property losses to about 250 estates and smallholdings exceeded a million pounds, and more than 500 were killed, nearly all black. Not surprisingly, Parliament ceased procrastinating, gave up on slavery, and accelerated preparations for emancipation.[32]

The rebellion was preceded by a classic combination of preconditions: a stubborn epidemic of smallpox, a bitter drought that wrecked provision grounds, and the whites' blatantly provocative decision to change ground rules and shorten the Christmas holiday. A precipitant (reminiscent of the spark for the 1795 Maroon War) was the whipping of a driver's wife by a white whom the slaves hated more than any other, Colonel Grignon ("Little Britches"), who as head of the western militia would be forced to retreat ignominiously following his defeat in the major battle of the rebellion. Slicing through these events were rumors about the antislavery campaign in England, which had "creat[ed] an unprecedented level of hope and excitment" among a people, Mary Turner argues, who were dangerously provoked on the eve of the Christmas holidays when the whites held a series of public meetings about how best to keep slaves down, defy the crown, and perhaps seek an arrangement with a slave power to the north, the Southern United States. As chapel attendance rose dramatically, slaves decided not to work after the first of the year unless they were paid wages, or freed and paid wages.[33]

Armed conflict began in the Leeward parishes, the traditional center of major resistance in Jamaica. By 1831 assimilated leaders used Baptist prayer meetings rather than play to organize, but the oath, an old rite, was still a fulcrum. From his jail cell, a Baptist rebel warned in nearly the same words as those used by a Coramantee during Tackey's rising in 1760: "I tell you again, if the gentlemen do no keep a good look out, the negroes will begin this business in three or four years, for they think the Lord and the King have given them the gift [freedom], and because those who were joined in this business were all sworn."[34]

The following discussion complements the work of Turner, Michael Craton, and Edward Braithwaite and considers the recurring themes of leadership, religion, and the slaves' own expressions of motives and objectives. It is also best to approach the rebellion by way of the individual plantation.

To do so is to appreciate the range of reactions on the part of the slaves and their leaders, some of whom were drivers or teachers in the Baptists' rural chapels. The chapels in turn were linked to the mother church, the large Baptist congregation in Montego Bay, whose "daddy" or chief of them all was the black elder Samuel Sharpe.[35]

In an extensive region where most estates were heavily damaged or completely burned to the ground, some were spared, or suffered damage only to their tempting and very combustible trash houses. Confronted by armed insurgents, who were often "strangers" (a potent term in the islands), slaves reacted variously by continuing to work, leaving to join the rebels, remaining near their houses and garden plots to see how matters progressed, or fleeing into the woods before militia and insurgents alike. Riding through several estates when the war first broke out, the Presbyterian minister Hope Waddell described a variety of situations. Waddell's base, Barrett Hall, was "safe and quiet." Its people gathered around and said they were ready to return to work. At Crawle, the estate village was deserted: "doors open, fires burning, and dogs barking"; at Spring Estate, the slaves were "bold and independent, and ready to debate the question of their right to freedom." And at Spot Valley Estate, the people, "unruly" and plundering, replied to a proclamation ordering them back to the field: "We have worked enough already, and will work no more. The life we live is too bad; it is the life of a dog. We won't be slaves no more; we won't lift hoe no more; we won't take flog no more. We free now, we free now; no more slaves again." They shouted, laughed, and clapped their hands, Waddell continued, and "I could not help laughing with them, and my doing so increased their good humour."[36]

As revolution came, slaves riveted attention on their own plantation leaders, who played a primary role in determining which way their people turned. At Unity Hall, a driver, George Kerr, after a meeting of the chapel in the quarter ordered slaves "to make themselves easy and set down and eat their Christmas [meal], and not to meddle with no man, and they must let no man meddle with them." Quietly preoccupied in their houses during the holiday, when ordered out afterward the slaves again gathered before the driver's house as the white leadership caved in. The overseer, threatening to call in the Round Hill guard, armed himself and the bookkeeper and left. Returning home at this point to arm themselves for a brief symbolic exercise, the people fetched their hoes, brought them up, and threw them into the overseer's yard as a boy, at the command of a driver, set fire to the overseer's house. In the following week this group also burned down the great house, and killed one of the few whites to die in the rebellion, a man sent to collect the master's belongings.[37]

Elsewhere, John Dunbar, a driver, head cook, and Baptist, "not a ruler but a Follower," was further described by his owner as "always attentive to . . . duty." That is, until suddenly, about six weeks before Christmas, when Dunbar became "insolent, disobedient and would do nothing." Demoted to the field before the revolt, Dunbar ordered the plantation set ablaze when conflict broke out. Another driver, Alexander McIntosh, also identified as a "Doctor-Man," was "put in charge," he said, by his owner, who had left before Christmas. McIntosh also ordered the burning of the estate.[38]

At Kensington, the thirty-year-old Creole driver Blacque Lawrence put on his master's sash and rode on a horse to a neighboring plantation where he took a gun away from a Negro. "It's to shoot parrots eating my plantains," he said as he fired it around. He later said "that as he was the Driver, he was the Captain of the place." Returning from a trip, which may have been an alibi, and seeing that the great house had been torched, Lawrence ordered that nothing should be killed without his orders. He asked, "Why they burn it for?" and requested that the kitchen and stable not be fired, as he would live in them. To this, another witness added that Lawrence said that if he could get Mr. Morris, Joe Vernon, and Reid, "he would be satisfied." "The prisoner [Lawrence] said Mr. Ingram was the only person left whose head he wanted." A desire for personal revenge among other objectives thus mixed with the most unblemished principle. The man whose gun the driver took repeated Lawrence's remark that "free was sweet and he would fight hard for it."[39]

At the climatic meeting in Montego Bay after Christmas worship, two artisans were the principal speakers, George Taylor, a sadler, and the most prestigious teacher Sam Sharpe. Sometime after his arrival in 1824, Burchell made Sharpe a deacon (or in slave talk "ruler" or "daddy") for the Montego Bay congregation. The largest in the island, the congregation had nearly two thousand members and included in its circuit a station comprised of the congregation of Moses Baker, the "bush" Baptist who upon his retirement turned his large Convince society over to Burchell.[40]

Sharpe, sometimes called "Schoolmaster," regularly received extra newspapers from a nephew who worked in a print shop. These included the *Watchman* edited by Edward Jordan, a free man of color, whose newspaper was a conduit of information on the antislavery campaign in England. Informed, literate, and an eloquent speaker, Sharpe was of medium build, "fine sinewy frame," and "jet" black wrote Edward Bleby, a missionary who spent many hours among the condemned. Listening to Sharpe address his fellow prisoners "for a long time on various topics," Bleby was struck by the "power" and fluency of his delivery, which "kept all his hearers fascinated and spell-bound from the beginning to the end."[41]

Referring to the many evils and injustices of slavery, Sharpe asserted the natural equality of man and used biblical authority to argue that whites had no right to enslave blacks. He also spoke a great deal about the newspapers he had read, "showing that both the King and the English people wished the Negroes to be emancipated and expressed his belief that the 'freepaper' had already been sent out." Of Sharpe's last speech, "He said the thing is now determined upon — no time is to be lost. The King of England & the Parliament have given Jamaica freedom and as it is held back by the whites we must at once take it. . . . [He] kept on talking this way which roused us and made us nearly mad."[42]

There was a bluntness to the country people's articulation of motives that contrasts sharply with the bravado of the earlier conspirators. They would, one said, burn "the Blasted Estates and do away with all the sugar works; it was them that kept them from getting their freedom."[43] Some of the strongest statements of this kind were made by women and town people, hitherto not a significant part of major plots or rebellions in any region. In sight of militia closing in, one put down her washing and with a torch ran to fire a trash house, crying out before she was killed "I know I shall die for it, but my children shall be free!"[44] Ironically, although leaders and meetings centered in Montego Bay, country people by far did most of the fighting and dying.

Still, town blacks seemed to be unusually ready. At the trial of Elizabeth Butler, a free woman of color, a witness testified that they had looked down from a second-story window — "stillness" is the key to catching the sense of words as a power or force here — "and a great stillness" had come upon the market place. Below, a girl dressed in black stood beside a woman dressed in white whose husband had recently been arrested. The women "addressed" men who had been standing around: "My brothers what is this you about, you no see buckra and mulatto [because] they keep quard at Court-house because Mr. Grignon's woman take three pieces of Cane. Him beat the woman, most kill h[er]. Them no satisfy with that, but them call out militia."[45] Another, a witness to the same, said Elizabeth Butler was talking to the mountain people. She was telling them "free was done to them and they won't give it to them. She said why don't you fight the white People, the same as the Argyle people [did in 1824]. . . . take the Bill and Muschett and must fight them as fast as you catch them. You must chop . . . and cut them up."[46]

Intensity of this kind did not produce arms or a unified plan of action, the evidence (similar in this regard to the earlier conspiratorial associations) is filled with the likes of "we have no arms," "[well] come along with us, if it is only a knife it will do."[47] Still, the 1831 leaders were the most prepared to date. Plans included adopting an old and effective Maroon tactic. In Trelawny Parish they built twenty-one "houses ready for occupation" and stashed an "immense" quantity of powder and five hundred rounds of ammunition in a remote terrain characterized as "Master, you do not know what a wood there is up there," and "they can kill . . . easy without the white people seeing them."[48]

Outgunned, the rebels were most effective when, against the ropes, they broke into small hit-and-run bands as maroons did in the same predicament. They displayed a "surprising" degree of military science in avoiding "a regular engagement" according to one account.[49] They also used ambushes and briefly curtailed the cavalry's effectiveness by destroying bridges and building abatis. Many wore uniforms of sorts — blue jackets with black cross-belts — and, when challenged by a militia captain, "they hallooed war, war."[50]

Yet for others, at least initially, the conflict was only to be a work stoppage after Christmas. But "the word went out" to burn estate buildings ("so the guards who would be sent to compell them to work would have no place to live") and to lock whites in the stocks so they would not flee to Montego Bay and return as militia. One group insisted that an overseer trade his life for his "authority" on the estate, "which they demanded in writing," and that this paper with others would be presented at the hamlet of Black River. When a judge asked what he thought "their ultimate object" was, a black deacon replied, "there is no occasion for any one to ask that question; thinks it sufficiently shown by their destroying their masters' property and houses, and taking so much care of their own. What other object should they have but to take the country to themselves?"[51]

At the trial of the driver Blacque Lawrence, it was said that some wanted to "disturb" soldiers marching up on the road, but Lawrence stopped them, saying "They were the King's [on the slaves' side]." Others testified that had the slaves realized that the king's soldiers would fight against them, there would have been no revolt. Hence, there was "great rejoicing" with the news that a man-of-war had arrived in Montego Bay. "It was generally said it was the Black Man of War come with Plenty of Arms and Ammunition." After waking up to the truth, the response was much the same: "never mind, all people [who] come from England are our friends."[52] Hence, as earlier, this man and others believed that an outside power at a critical moment would mysteriously intervene on their side.

Traces of religion in the rebellion came from the entire rich spectrum of Jamaican knowledge, from permutations of obeah to denominational variants. Informed that the slaves were playing at the great house yard, Ann Gordon went to see "who were playing"; she wished to "dance with the Actors" and was told she could if she "did pay for it."[53] At Barham's Bogue Estate, slaves "assembled" and danced for two hours. Two implicated servants, one slave, one free, belonging to the governor were respectively Moravian and Methodist. When asked why people of leeward Westmoreland Parish did not join, a slave replied that not being Baptists they were "spoilt."

Moravian and Anglican (including Methodist) "tell their people to shed no blood; but that the Baptists tell them . . . they might shed blood in any day but Sunday."[54]

Additional references to the spiritual dimension of the rebellion are sparse. In some instances the venerated oath or "swear" was little more than a toast administered by a leader in his own way. Sharpe's men swore allegiance as they kissed the Bible, while others used more traditional mixtures.[55] George Kerr, a mason, provided gunpowder, saying that when his father was in Africa "when they wanted to fight they put powder in the Rum."[56] The sources are too fragmented to make much of this. But swearing allegiance, in the case of Sharpe's Bible, was followed by the deacon's admonition that his men must "set down," that is, refuse to work rather than take up arms. Elsewhere, the oath was accompanied with the aim "to exterminate all the white and free persons [of color] of this island."[57]

In another obscure ceremony, "throwing money," a "subscription" of 5 pence each taken to buy wine was held by Solomon, an older Creole head carpenter who had baptized several by immersion. Asked about the oath that accompanied this rite, one replied "we drink wine all around—drink Health . . . we say 'Bless Lord for give we free, we joy we see free come' . . . we praise the Lord that we get our free, we would take it." And, "Massa parson tell us we free, that massa King gib we free." A contemporary, Theodore Faulks, who recorded these words said they had "talismanic influence."[58] The traditional substrata of the slaves' new knowledge also poked through in these conceptions: "The Reverend Burchell [on leave in England] is to supply a ship of arms at Montego Bay"; or, ships had arrived off St. Elizabeth and unknown to whites were unloading boxes of black sand and gunpowder for the slaves' use. "The reason they [rebels] missed shooting the light infantry was because they did not pray daily to God Almighty for success," and "never mind . . . as long as the word of God is in you, balls [bullets] cannot hurt you."[59]

At Ginger Hill Plantation the overseer was taken gently and told he was a prisoner, to remain on the property and not interfere "and you will not be harmed," for "Jamaica was now free, . . . that they were obliged to assist their brethren in this work of the Lord; that this was not the work of man alone, but they has assistance from God." With the driver's help, the overseer escaped to the house of a free person of color. When he was retaken, the rebels waved cutlasses over his head and "made me swear that I would never stand between them and their rights." Sharpe was present and said much the same (as did many when trying to put words to questions about motivation): he "did not wish to take away the life of any person who did not stand between him and his rights."[60]

Sharpe's words reveal both the strengths and weaknesses of a rebellion of Christianzied slaves. By contrast, uprisings in both Barbados and Virginia, hitherto remarkably secure slave societies, were unusually free of missionary influence and guidance and not as divided as the Demerara and Jamaican examples between those who would make a work strike and bargain and those who would fight and destroy.

## Barbados and Virginia, 1816 and 1831

An Event [the Southampton, Va. insurrection] which produced
in the South something resembling a mass trauma, from which
the whites had not recovered three decades later.
— Kenneth Stampp, 1956[61]

Rebellions in Barbados and Virginia were, for the slaves' part, the most violently destructive — and improbable — of all nineteenth-century Anglo-America revolts. As predominantly Creole societies without a legacy of African rebellions of the spear, Barbados in 1816 and Virginia in 1831 witnessed uprisings that were sudden, rapidly executed, and readily crushed within a few days. Both struck in settler societies of whites who, contemptously indifferent to security, were caught napping. Both rebellions were tactically unique, which may explain the berserk reactions afterward as vigilantes and regulars alike hunted and killed scores of innocent blacks. Alone among the major Anglo-American insurrectionists through time, the 1816 rebels set fire to the cane fields. This potentially devastating action, which even Maroons at war did not adopt, was feared by whites more than any other. On the other hand, the Barbadian slaves, like all other nineteeth-century British West Indian rebels, did not systematically kill whites as Nat Turner's men did.

The Barbados rebellion during Easter week 1816 resulted in the deaths of more than four hundred slaves and the destruction of about sixty estates including Seawell's, the tight little ship Samson Wood had managed a few years earlier. In describing slavery at that time (in 1803), the governor mentioned the absence of a maroon tradition, for there were no woods and mountains "Capable of giving any large or permanent shelter to revolters," and slaves were "very quiet ... well disposed" and to his "astonishment (notwithstanding their unhappy situation)" more than once "patrioti[c]."[62] As there had been no organized resistance in Barbados since an archetypal Coramantee rebellion of the spear at the end of the seventeenth century, slaves by the 1760s as in Antigua were armed during invasion threats. Nonetheless, in 1816, the "quiet & well disposed" readily organized what was by far — given numbers and compactness of the flat terrain — the first, largest, and most destructive Creole insurrection anywhere in Anglo-America.

The revolt was also unusually secular, which was in keeping with the unique character of this slave community's development. By the early 1800s, Barbados slaves were assimilated in an obvious sense; they did not become maroons or form threatening associations. As their part of the bargain, the whites ignored the blacks' traditional dances, plays, and funerals, which had developed in their own way because missionaries were nowhere in sight. Anti-Quaker legislation had been on the books since the late 1600s, and evangelicals, so ubiquitous elsewhere, in the early 1800s were easily intimidated and routed by the unusually large proportion of middle-class and poor whites.[63] Even the unobtrusive Moravians chaffed ineffectually. They felt restricted, and they were—to five estates, according to a 1796 report that noted that the Brethren had managed to baptize only seven slaves in a population that spent Sundays "in dressing, dancing, eating, drinking..., [while] the noise of drums steadily sounds in our ears."[64]

Given the absence of a mass of recent black converts, the 1816 rebellion did not split ineffectually between advocates of Christian passive resistance on the one hand, and those who argued for the inevitability of violence on the other. Still, slaves' depositions bear traces of talk about how a new governor was "now off the Coast waiting for us to make a stand," the prince regent was on their side, and the royal troops would not fire upon them.[65]

There was, however, little of this. Instead, what comes through the snippets of voices that have survived is a starkly secular message. A driver waiting execution—as if to get a moment's relief from Anglican rectors trying to pry from the dying recognition of good treatment—put it simply for so many: "yes, I received food from my master's table," and that "to obtain [my] freedom had been the sole cause of ... joining in the Insurrection."[66] If a more encompassing ideology or ritual drove the 1816 rebellion, beyond the slaves' explicit desire to claim a legal freedom they understood was already theirs, it is not clear in the sources.

A more profitable approach is to look closely at the artisanal elite and its links to Bridgetown, the sole outlet for the adventuresome and able in a society lacking maroon settlements and mission stations. While the Virginia rebels of 1831 were corn-field slaves from an economic backwater, the black Barbadians, from the richest sugar region in the island (the south and east), were led by men—drivers, masons, rangers, carpenters, and coopers— who worked at the most responsible and demanding tasks. As "the richest and most comfortably situated," or simply the "opulent," according to the Assembly's report on the insurrection, many were also literate and so able to "gain ... an ascendancy" over the minds of other slaves.[67]

In town the assimilateds' hunger for news of the abolition debates drew them into the orbit of an aroused and harassed free colored population. Understanding that artisans were potentially inflammatory conduits to rural people, the free colored showered them with press accounts of the abolition movement. In turn, the artisans hammered "the news" into a potent symbol, "The Free." The "news" was that the talismanic Free (seen as adhering to certain official printed documents sent out from Britain) was rumored to be either on its way and just off-shore, or already ashore but hidden away. Accordingly, on the eve of revolt slaves reinterpreted the Registration Bill of 1816 (which authorized a census in order to curb the smuggling of new Negroes) as an emancipation proclamation that had been pocketed by the increasingly desperate and unpredictable planters.[68]

The slaves' reinterpretation was important. Although the artisans' move from planning to open resistance is explicable, what motivated the masses of rural people to act when they did is not so clear. But implicit in the evidence (beyond a determination to control their own fate), is the impression that great numbers, believing as they did about the treacherous reception of the Registration Bill/Emancipation Proclamation, had come to accept that the whites had broken a fundamental ground rule. Conservative rural people, products of an unusually secure slave society without nurturing mountains and a tradition of maroonage, had stoically suffered foreign oppression for centuries. That is, they endured until their leaders' reconstructions of "news" of the Free sparked a movement that risked many lives by reclaiming violently a land which — reminescent of the long-suffering peasants of northern Mexico in John Womack's study of Emiliano Zapata and the Mexican Revolution — they had never given up thinking of as their own.[69]

The Barbados Assembly's characterization of the 1816 rebels as rich and comfortably situated was a rationalization, but the charge does point to a major distinction between Southern and Caribbean slave leadership in the last years of slavery. Neither Denmark Vesey nor Nat Turner were artisans. Generally, acquiring responsibility and a bit of property worked differently in the two regions: politicizing assimilateds in the Caribbean, while co-opting them in the antebellum South. There is no scene at a Southern gallows comparable to that following 1816, when a leader, the Barbadian Sandy Waterman, who was probably aware of English legal precedence regarding treason and forfeiture of property, asked that his property of two houses and a crop of ginger be kept within his family once his debts were paid.[70] The profound attachment that Caribbean slaves, Barbadians included, manifested to their societies and home plantations was unmatched in the more mobile, rootless, and economically dynamic antebellum South where white supremacy reigned. The relentless killings by the field people who drove Turner's revolt may indicate black alienation as being the most pronounced in the Chesapeake Bay region — *the* settler society. Turner's men were poorly prepared field people who killed and destroyed as they went during a bloody rising that unfolded like an old rebellion of the spear.[71] In part, this course was accountable to Turner's milieu, the outlines of which are now familiar. His was a society shaped by masters who traditionally were residents not absentees, whose slaves were acculturated more readily and thoroughly than elsewhere and in return received hardly anything of worth and value from the white society that surrounded them. Of Turner's most recent owner (his third), the court said that Joseph Travis was "more humane and fatherly to his slaves than any man in the county." Turner agreed. Travis, he said, was "only too indulgent."[72]

Given the rebellion's slaughter and aimlessness, and so its idiosyncratic character, what was on Turner's mind? In the lengthy and powerful "Confession" created by Turner and the lawyer T. R. Gray from conversations held in Turner's jail cell, the insurrectionist implies that his chiliastic blend of archaic spirituality and biblical religion was meant chiefly as a message to whites and blacks—his contemporaries and later generations.

VIRGINIA

ROUTE OF NAT TURNER
AND HIS FORCES
1831

Mid-evening of the attack, Turner met with a few men in deep woods around a smouldering fire.[73] They moved out, and about 2 A.M. Sunday August 19, struck the first blow. As momentum gathered, a few became about seventy, many of whom were well armed and mounted. While killing about sixty, the rebels followed a circuitous route that in a day and a half covered only about twenty miles, which at first view seems to complement later opinions that they were soon so drunk and disorderly as not to know what they were about. But Turner's tactics were sound according to Henry Tragle, a former military officer who has studied the rebellion more closely than anyone while criss-crossing the terrain, searching out and photographing the remnants of the deadly march, and compiling the best documentary history of the event. Turner had the instincts of a good battle commander, Tragle argues; he stuck to the high ground and descended only to strike at relatively isolated farmsteads.[74]

After hours of exhausting fighting and killing, however, the attack quickly unravelled. Some may have been drunk. More were certainly disillusioned, because at Parker's field, scene of the final ignominious skirmish, they faced armed slaves who fought to protect whites. For his part, Turner said that his men, expecting to be joined by kin at Parker's, persuaded him to pull up.[75] This may have been a tactical mistake because the whites were initially stunned and probably closer to momentarily losing Jerusalem (the county seat) than we now realize. Still, once they rallied, their vastly superior weaponry, militia, and posse organization were decisive.[76]

Yet, this white victory could not conceal the galling fact that after nearly a century of no organized risings, Turner had marched, pillaged, and killed for nearly two days and then had simply disappeared. Worse yet, more than a week passed before the authorities were able to arrive at a reliable description of one who, after all, was the most notorious fugitive in Southern history. It is "remarkable," one reporter put it, "how little is known of Captain Nat. We could find no person who has seen him."[77] The runaway notice that eventually pursued Turner read:

> Nat is between 30 and 35 years old, 5 feet 6 or 8 inches high, weighs between 150 and 160 lbs, rather bright complexion, but not a mulatto — broad shouldered, large flat nose, large eyes, broad flat feet, rather knock-kneed, walks brisk and active, hair on the top of the head very thin, no beard except on the upper lip, and the top of the chin, a scar on one of his temples, also one on the back of his neck, a large knob on one of the bones of his right arm near the wrist produced by a blow.[78]

Turner was an intellectual, who near the end of the "Confession" confronts his formative years this way: "I must go back to the days of my

Infancy, and even before I was born."[79] His parents, sensing a special child, maintained a family tradition that one of the boy's dreams concerned events that had taken place before he was born. Coming to similar understandings later about his prowess, older slaves included Turner in forays on white peoples' property. But usually Turner was a loner, who in his teens preoccupied himself with experiments to make paper and gunpowder—convenient symbols of the Creole leadership's dilemma: strive peaceably for literacy and the knowledge it makes available, or prepare for armed struggle.

Experiments of another kind were like those of other acutely religious seekers of his era. Religion—conventional and esoteric—pervades the "Confession," which on a first reading, brings to mind such famous contemporary prophets as Joseph Smith and the Millerites. Like them, Turner had visions and received messages from God, angels, and "the Holy Ghost."[80]

Initially, and for long periods during his quest, Turner fasted, and prayed, and otherwise pursued conventional routes to redemption and saintliness. He wanted to be baptized, for instance, and to baptize others.

> About this time I told these things to a white man [Etheldred T. Brantley], on whom it had a wonderful effect—and he ceased from his wickedness, and was attacked immediately with a cutaneous eruption, and blood oozed from the pores of his skin, and after praying and fasting nine days, he was healed, and the Spirit appeared to me again, and said, as the Saviour had been baptized so should we be also—and when the white people would not let us be baptized by the church, we went down into the water together, in the sight of many who reviled us, and were baptized by the Spirit—After this I rejoiced greatly, and gave thanks to God.[81]

The "Confession" is rich with references to an ascetic regime, fasting, and watchings, to encounters with awesome spiritual powers and signs, and to such supernatural inclinations and feats as foresight and healing. Curious about the advice a particular spirit gave to Turner, Gray inserted in the "Confession" "I could not get him to explain in a manner at all satisfactory—nowithstanding I examined him closely upon this point, he alway[s] seemed to mystify."[82]

Nonetheless, Gray was either led to, or made shrewd guesses about, the real character of Turner's religious style. He says little about Turner as part of the familiar tradition of black Baptist exhorters, nor does that denomination provide keys to understanding this rebellion. Rather, Turner's orientation was archaic. "He became a dreamer of dreams." "Like a Roman Sybil" and "the character of a prophet" are phrases Gray used as he tried to grasp the nature of Turner's cultic orientation.[83] In the best newspaper account, he wrote:

He traced his divination in characters of blood, on leaves alone in the woods; he would arrange them in some conspicuous place, have a dream telling him of the circumstance; . . . I have in my possession, some papers given up by his wife, under the lash — they are filled with hieroglyphical characters, conveying no definite meaning. The characters on the oldest paper, apparently appear to have been traced with blood; and on each paper, a crucifix and a sun, is distinctly visible; with the figures 6,000, 30,000, 80,000 &c.[84]

At one point, Turner witnessed black spirits and white fighting in the sky, and "Then the Holy Ghost was with me, and said 'Behold me as I stand in the heavens.' " More hallucinogenic visions, which Turner interpreted as signs that he was God's chosen instrument, followed a regime of fasting and prayer. When the spirit came, Turner was alone (once at his plow), as opposed to its customary entrance in the Caribbean — publicly and ritually. Following these experiences, the slave saw himself as an agent with a mission. When Gray asked if he now considered himself mistaken, Turner replied, "Was not Christ crucified?"[85] In none of this, however, is there an indication that the insurrectionist's visions also inspired his men and thereby became a motor for rebellion.

Gray also got right Turner's simple and direct goal. From his time to ours, some have concocted elaborate objectives for the Southampton rebels: to break out of slavery completely and become maroons in the Dismal Swamp miles away from the only home base these insular people had known. Instead, as Gray put it, "His object was freedom and indiscriminate carnage his watchword. The seizure of Jerusalem, and the massacre of its inhabitants, was with him, a chief purpose, & seemed to be his *ultimatum.*"[86]

Gray is on the right track at this point. What Turner did after the revolt is probably most important to its meaning then and now. By remaining both alive and in the neighborhood, he kept himself available. By finding shelter until the lynch-mob hysteria had spent itself, it may be suggested that he gradually set up a safe and uneventful capture that would assure the transmission of a final statement about slavery as he knew it in Virginia, and his role in it.[87] This decision represented the most that a slave leader could expect to do given the police-state character of slavery in much of the antebellum South. A primary meaning of the revolt was that once Turner had focused attention, he had to keep himself alive and close at hand, and so able to deliver the "Confession" at the proper time and to the safekeeping of someone who would come his way.

That the revolt was a desperate act and doomed from its inception is a possibility Turner may have recognized. In this regard it is most comparable to the revolt in British southeast Africa of another Virginia-trained insurrectionist, George Chilembwe. Like Turner, Chilembwe, as he put it aptly for both, in a militarily hopeless situation desired to show the oppressed that black people could organize resistance and that whites, most assuredly, were vulnerable. A revolutionary's objectives in circumstances of this kind were "to Strike a Blow and Die."[88]

The colonial situation is an arena in which two ways of life, the colonized and the colonizers', are each transformed by persistent conflict and accommodation. In this equation, the colonized, usually dark-skinned people cast into a tribal or peasant way of life, often see their predicament in what we would call "religious" or "supernatural" terms. New World blacks, as slaves, customarily did the same, but by the early nineteenth century that habit of mind shifted significantly as slaves assimilated features of the whites' religion.

Evangelism appealed first to those slaves whose work took them beyond plantation boundaries. They were mobile, as were the wandering émigré preachers who arrived with the empire loyalists and immediately encountered obeah. Ritual experts of this tradition used capricious minor spirits to help resolve the local and ordinary problems that engaged the anxieties of rural people. As the tempo of wartime urbanization in the late eighteenth century picked up, however, this parochial outlook was at first challenged inadvertently by the comings and goings of artisans and market women and then breached, as slaves in the early 1800s became receptive to a religion of a single and more cosmopolitan outlook that also promised to deliver such useful tools for confronting whites and checking their power as baptism and literacy.

Regarding the political effects of Christianization, the extreme cases are Haiti and the antebellum South. In the first instance mass conversions produced vodun, which propelled the early stages of the Haitian Revolution; in the latter instance, conversion—Denmark Vesey and Nat Turner notwithstanding—may be seen as an important part of the slaves' incorporation into stifling plantation regimes. Vodun as a blend of European Catholicism and African animism was readily convertible to a successful ritual and ideology of national resistance. Nothing like this happened in Anglo-America, where the mix of Christianization and West African spirituality was not explosive. Nonetheless, in the British Caribbean the slaves, who were fascinated by things French, knew what the Haitians had achieved, and as best they could tried to emulate their success. Creoles in Jamaica made potent symbols by first recasting such evangelicals as Knibb and Burchell as emissaries of the Free and, second, the New Years' Day following publication of the Registration Bill of 1816—and several thereafter—as Emancipation Day.

# Epilogue:
# Africa in America

The brief pictures of three slave rebellions that opened this discussion of slave resistance and acculturation included Court's Coramantee *ikem* dance in Antigua in 1736 and about a century later in 1831 the risings of Baptists in Jamaica and Nat Turner in Virginia. Each one is a glimpse of a resistance that depending on time and place was shaped in varying degrees by African, or mixes of African and Christian, ritual and knowledge. The 1831 rebellions were led by slaves who as Creoles were more familiar with the Christian ideas and organization which, from the 1760s, gradually took precedence to the African ritual that prevailed earlier.

Slave religion and resistance in Anglo-America may be divided into three phases, none of which represent a correlation between acculturation and the rise or fall of incidences of significant resistance. Rather, the three phases highlight the importance of the relationship between acculturation and the form that rebellion assumed. The first, or African, phase from the 1730s to the 1760s may be characterized by the unseasoned, who were often Coramantee and Congolese whose resistance was characteristically sudden, violently destructive, and charged with African ritual. The second phase, by plantation slaves, from the late 1760s to the early 1800s concerned the usually limited reactions of a conservative and wary people who seldom undertook significant conspiracies or revolts. The third phase, from the late 1760s to the second quarter of the nineteenth century, was led by assimilateds, who in the first instance generally ignored the rural blacks' cultic experimentations with Myal, Convince, and their offshoots while creating their own conspiratorial and at first strikingly secular associations. Later, however, artisans used literacy, biblical imagery, and the class organization provided by Christian missionaries to lead major rebellions in both regions. Although Creole in source, these revolts represented a return to the charisma of the maroon camp and rebellion of the spear (eventually combined with the new inclusiveness of evangelical Christianity) that artisans in the first stage of the movement had struggled to create with mock court days, balls, and military clubs. The vehicle for this mix, a sect's catechism class, in effect may seem to our way of thinking unlikely and dull. Slaves, however, saw Bible instruction and literacy in part as they did such features of their traditional cosmology as play and the blood oath — as avenues to sources of spiritual power. Examining resistance at three stages of slave acculturation uncovers the importance between such seemingly unrelated issues as ancestralism and trance states in slave economic, family, and religious matters, or the links between marketing, gender relations, and such language problems as the acquisition of English and the incidence of aphasia.

The analysis presented here relates degree and content of acculturation to particular forms of resistance. That is, in the discussion that follows, it should be emphasized that the relationship is not between the degree of cultural change and amounts of overt rebelliousness, but between the varying types of acculturation and the form or shape that resistance in particular settings assumed.

The first, African, phase of resistance and acculturation may be depicted by unseasoned new Negroes fresh from the slaver, and by maroons who had rejected the plantation way of life. The important period between when the gangplank lowered and new Negroes arrived at the plantation is uncharted territory, which is a loss because the Africans' first experiences, and the whites' reaction to them, constitute nothing less than the clearest view we have of the beginnings of African-American institutions and values.

The recent literature concerning the problem is not encouraging. Statements by scholars (each of whom, ironically, is committed to the culture and community approach to slavery) characterize the very beginnings of the African phase of acculturation and resistance as one of disorganization. One influential statement, for instance, is based on the premise that the Africans "who reached the New World did not compose, at the outset, groups. In fact, in most cases, it might even be more accurate to view them as crowds, and very heterogeneous crowds at that."[1] A complementary view is that slave culture, in Jamaica, was "syncretic from the beginning," and that the "mingling" of new Negroes during the Middle Passage "determined that black culture was only generically African at most."[2] For the South, the argument for disorganization is even stronger: there the Africans "lost their social identity."[3] The question remains, however, why when the record is assumed to be blank, do explanations follow that usually underestimate the resiliancy of those raised in tribal societies and the worthiness of particular west and central African cultural elements they brought with them into slavery? As in the case of the new Negroes' plan to escape by returning to the point of their disembarkation, "mingling" is exactly what did not take place, if that implies Africans arrived disorganized.

Assuming that new Negroes communicated in only a crude patois or emergency language because their original speech communities were in disarray, scholars now stress syncretic combinations as lying at the base of Creolization. Assuming as well the absence of surviving evidence to the contrary, the prevailing argument is that ethnicity in slavery studies is beside the point; the real concern should be the mix of African ways and local "structures," demographic and otherwise. Reflecting the deconstructionist fashions of literary criticism in the 1980s, scholars like to discuss how readily "ethnics" reinvent themselves by putting culture on and off as if it were only a change of clothing. In part this research strategy is a reaction, and properly so, to an older image of acculturation as the pouring of liquid from one container into another, a plus and minus operation, a matter of losing elements of one culture while taking on those of another. Undeniably, this approach simplifies a daunting task. Given the vast reaches of the slaving area, how is one to pinpoint on a map where those new Negroes were actually from whom Jamaicans so confidently assigned to one ethnic group or another two centuries ago? Still, the contemporary record stands. For more than a century West Indians, Jamaicans particularly, said clearly that ethnicity counted. It did so when blacks first landed, when they resisted, and long after they were brought to the plantation. Accordingly, Thistlewood's early diaries are filled with African names and attributions for games, folklore, cures, beliefs, bits of technology ("a Congo bridge"), and local plants and animals.[4] Moreover, that such naming went on until the end of slavery is demonstrated by the fugitive slave notices and Monk Lewis's references to the Ibo faction at his estate—in a neighborhood where fifty years earlier Coramantee were the most conspicuous and remarkable of Africans.

In connection with the problem of the initial stages of acculturation in the New World, more needs to be done with the Coramantee. This may involve reasserting an earlier approach to the African dimension of American Negro slavery, the possibility of the cultural dominance of one people in a particular New World locale. The scheme once widely accepted was that the Moslem Hausa culture was dominant in northeastern Brazil (Bahia), the Yoruba (Nago) in Cuba and Trinidad, the Coramantee in Jamaica, the Dahomeans in Haiti, and the Angolan in South Carolina.[5] The Jamaican material certainly takes shape more coherently, usefully, and in agreement with contemporary understandings if the older approach to African-American acculturation is also kept in view. This may complicate matters considerably, but that is no reason to bury the possibility. Contemporaries such as Edward Long wrote that play, which became the acculturative vehicle for the reception and modification of new knowledge, was initially not syncretic, but the work of Coramantee. Their language was also unusually influential. That it was also, in Long's opinion, "more copious and regular than any other of the Negro dialects" was expanded by Jamaica's best nineteenth-century historian, the cleric William Gardner: "the influences of the Coromantyns seems to have modified, if not entirely obliterated whatever was introduced by the other tribes."[6]

Such scholarly observations were replicated by ordinary people, who advertised in the newspapers market women who, although African but not Coramantee, had nonetheless acquired at least a smattering of Akan as they learned English. Accordingly, as Sidney Mintz and Richard Price argue in an important essay, the truly "interesting" question concerns the cultural syncretisms of incoming Africans, not the characteristic peoples.[7] But the earlier emphasis on the dominance of one people in particular situations remains a promising approach to the whole question of slave acculturation. Moreover in this connection, the record of resistance by the unseasoned new Negroes and maroons, as fragmented as it may be, is especially valuable and warrants further examination. Even if it is demonstrated that particularly African peoples, say Coramantee in Jamaica and "Angolans" or Bantu in the Carolina lowcountry, did not lay down a kind of primary charter, at the very least once on the plantation Africans in the Caribbean did create kin-based communities that infused such basic activities and orientations as obeah and domesticity.

As for the second stage, that of plantation slaves, a basic distinction in their world, and in the differential rates of cultural change both within and between regions, was the degree to which slaves participated in their own maintenance. More generally, in the Caribbean and the South the processes of slave acculturation were essentially different because of the relationship between the internal economy and slave family and religious strategies.

Regional differences began immediately as new Negroes came ashore and, in the Caribbean, organized with shipmates and countrymen and later were placed as inmates on plantations. These moves set in motion an assimilation that remained African at its core. The pattern was sustained when new Negroes were given land for producing their own food, some of which was eventually sold in the dynamic internal markets dominated by slave women. No equivalent development occurred in the South, where shipmates, countrymen, and inmates were unheard of, and whites monopolized the marketing of food and most of its production.

At this point slave economic and cultural development became intertwined. Able to construct institutions to a degree on their own initiative from the beginning, Caribbean blacks refined African ways and values more at their own pace and choosing; whereas new Negroes shipped to the South had to begin from scratch. Although the situation in the South was not as drastic as some scholars would have it, incoming Africans began with little help from those who spoke their own language. Once on the plantation the African continued a relatively lonely seasoning—a process that meant, in the South, little more than the acclimation to a local climate and disease environment.

Regional contrasts in slave acculturation, and the many variables that colored the process, set in motion conditions that prevailed to the end of slavery and beyond. British reformist legislation to ameliorate slavery and prepare for emancipation, including savings banks and Sunday schools to promote literacy, were innovations understood to be grafted to existing slave institutions and values. Accordingly, indigenous Baptist congregations purchased wilderness crown land to be added to such liberated clusters as the free villages and provision grounds. Many freedmen were driven from their grounds, especially in the allowance islands where plots were not remote retreats but attached to the estates. Nonetheless, Caribbean blacks came out of slavery with a social base fortified by property arrangements from which they could bargain their labor with their former masters. If such schemes seem to be only a sop, keep in mind the tragedy that compounded emancipation in the United States, where Southern blacks, who got "nothing but freedom," slipped into share-cropping, tenantry, and peonage.[8] The key development was the West Indian slave's bit of land, which helped define identity as it provided a means of replanting ancestral ways of thinking. Lacking a base of this kind and the extensive and largely unsupervised marketing it engendered, Southern slaves were more susceptible to Christian views of life in the hereafter as an inspiring objective.

In the South, assimilation meant change (but not acceptance) in the direction of whites who persistently suppressed and demeaned things African. Whatever the measure—the whites' recognition and use of kin nomenclature, slave entrepreneurial activity, the assimilateds' symptoms of psychological stress, and the breakdown of traditional African notions of diffidence and reticence in speech and the concomitant rise of "artful" dissembling demeanors to portray the most assimilated—cultural change in the South was a more punishing and humiliating ordeal for blacks as individuals and a people than that experienced elsewhere.[9] More consistent and nutritious food, more impressive fertility rates, and height differentials (Creole to new Negro) notwithstanding, the notion of the comparatively benign character of Southern slavery should be reexamined.

Of course Caribbean whites dominated slaves, and often brutally, but they did so in a manner that was not nearly as thorough and systematic as was the case in the South, where antebellum planters eventually were able to regiment slave lives to a remarkable degree. We know a great deal about planter paternalism, but in light of the case studies, the allowance system of slave maintenance, and the thrust of "scientific" agricultural reform, more should be made of that surprisingly modern facet of an antebellum planter ideology that would enhance profits, efficiency, accountability, and systematic control by reducing slaves to ciphers. For a long while the novelist William Styron, among others, has sought recognition of the relationship between the distinctively modern, "bureaucratic," mentality manifested in the organizational structure of the Southern antebellum plantation and other, more sinister and parallel institutions of our own century such as the Nazis' use of slave labor.[10]

Ultimately, slaves acculturated more slowly and less thoroughly in the Caribbean than in the South because West Indian families were constituted differently—and thereby were stronger—than mainland slave families. There is a paradox here. The notorious vital statistics of West Indian slaves (of high death rates and low birth rates) obscure the remarkable success of those Caribbean families able to use the slave-oriented internal economy of provision grounds, surpluses, and markets to reconstitute families that were African in character, deeming property as collective and a basis of such ancestor rituals as play.

The third phase of slave acculturation and resistance may be divided into two stages. The first stage, organized by associations of conspirators, was secular in nature. But the second phase, also led by assimilated artisans, was cast in an evangelical mold.

In the first stage, the assimilation of artisans was accelerated by the endemic wars and revolutions in the late 1700s in North America, France, and Haiti. In the Caribbean, the ensuing crisis was felt more fiercely and for much longer than in the mainland South, as urbanizing slave artisans remained more conspicuously rebellious than their Southern counterparts. Nonetheless, in the first phases of rebellion neither assimilateds nor Maroons were able to inspire plantation slaves to a war of liberation as their counterparts had done in Haiti. Hence, in 1800, a prominent Jamaican politician wrote that after a season of fear, a turn of good weather and abundant provision crops had brought substantial prices for the produce of slaves, whom he deemed "happy and content."[11]

But Henry Shirley spoke prematurely. For whites soon had to contend with another spate of resistance in the form of the artisans' fraternal and increasingly martial associations. The dancing and military societies may not have been as subversive as they were regarded at the time. Still, as integrative vehicles for the rapid socialization of slaves of diverse backgrounds making the historic transition from rural to urban existences, the societies did represent dress rehearsals: initial efforts to establish more cosmopolitan allegiances among blacks than the traditional one of countrymen and ship-mate. This was a radical step forward, akin to a parallel development in African cities whereby migrants of diverse cultures establish group loyalties that replace or encompass the traditional allegiances based on kinship.[12]

Once urban slaves are compared as they should be to other groups of city migrants, it is possible to take on the important questions. In both Africa and in Brazilian slave society blacks who migrated to town, perhaps contrary to expectations, sometimes "retribalized." Roger Bastide sees the African cults of Bahia, for instance, as examples of a reverse acculturation, a process comparable to the reethnicization phenomenon in our own country of the third- and fourth-generation immigrants, who use dimly perceived ancestral ways to play "ethnic politics" for political and social gain.[13] The competitive and conspiratorial dancing societies of 1805 Trinidad comple-ment Bastide's argument. Erupting in a society in which the dominant culture was up for grabs — in contests pitting mixes of Spanish, French, English, and African — convoy members either made up "ghost nations," as did the members of the Danish convoy, who played at being neutral as they understood the essential character of the Danish state to be. Or, as members of other convoys, they boasted of the dance steps of their actual land of origin, as did the French Creoles from Guadeloupe and Martinique.

The assimilateds' associations as a form of immigrant aid have their equivalent in early twentieth-century black communities in the United States. Paradoxically, these agencies were both comprehensive and exclusive: as fraternal and benevolent associations they were not inclusive but exclu-sive — *landsmannschaften* — for immigrants from specific islands. In Har-lem, black migrants from the Danish West Indies kept pictures of the king of Denmark in their homes, former British subjects held coronation pageants and balls and flew the Union Jack, and black Frenchmen had annual Bastille Day dances.[14] So, like European immigrants when confronted with America's hard and competitive conditions, one response of West Indians in Harlem (much like their counterparts in post-conquest Port of Spain in the Picton era) was to develop an exaggerated sense of ethnic nationalism.

In the second stage of nineteenth-century revolution, recently converted blacks used the European missionary's classes to organize as they acquired the ritual and learning of evangelism that changed them. For slaves, the Free, a feature of all nineteenth-century conspiracies and rebellions, as the most potent symbol of that learning, was assumed to represent the written document as well as the actual act of freedom. Differences in the meanings slaves gave to conversion from one region to another should not obscure an understanding that Christianization everywhere shared one basic feature: the promise — and increasingly for many the actuality — of literacy, of learning to read the Bible, which evangelicals insisted was the word of God and so the vehicle for conversion and salvation. Slave parents found this feature most attractive, but for their children, not themselves. Many Africans and other older people were wary of conversion, at least until the early 1820s, because the missionaries' morbid Sabbatarianism was seen as an attack on the basis of their livelihoods and intellectualizing: Sunday marketing, polygyny, and drumming and dancing at funerals.

For slaves in an obeah sense, literacy was their door to sources of power and esoteric knowledge that whites commanded and protected selfishly. Then missionaries arrived who also had literacy but promised to share it, thus presenting an opportunity to reverse the outcome of an old Guyanese Maroon tale of God's offer of two gifts. Taking first choice, the black man chose the bigger one, which contained gold. The remaining, smaller package left for the white man held paper and pen.[15]

Literacy changed the slaves' outlook fundamentally. In this regard mass Christianization may be seen as a process in which black converts went from one information system to another: from a view of nature as indwelling and immanent and time as cyclical to a view of nature as objectively quantifiable and time as linear. The new reference point had important political implications. Nonliterate Africans were conservative in an obvious sense. From their verb tenses to ancestor rites they looked to the past, and this orientation — not time-future — concerned them most. Christianization introduced Africans to a sense of history moving lineally. In some areas the new idea of time also encouraged millennialism, which in western Jamaica, particularly in the chapels and stations of Knibb's ministry, was rechannelled as the expectation of a final judgment, or of a battle even, leading to emancipation.

The comparison of the four societies within the two regions in terms of the three phases of resistance and acculturation reveals important similarities in the first, African, phase between Barbados and Virginia, on the one hand, and Jamaica and South Carolina, on the other, that cut across the usual regional dichotomy. In this phase resistance seems to have been minimal in Barbados and Virginia, because in both societies by the time the surviving sources open up the slave trade was relatively unimportant and new Negroes no longer menacing, if they ever were. South Carolina and Jamaica, on the other hand, were insecure frontiers for much of the eighteenth century because of a sizeable slave trade in both colonies that led to the continual absorption of great numbers of new Negroes who heightened the anxiety of white settlers already nervously preoccupied with fears of the Cherokee in the lowcountry and the Maroons in Jamaica.

During the second phase of resistance by plantation slaves important comparisons, however, are regional—the South versus the Caribbean. Slaves who in the Caribbean were truly proto-peasants and in important ways African in their religious and economic practices shaped patterns of acculturation and resistance in Jamaica and Barbados that contrasted sharply with the experiences of the more rapidly acculturating slaves of the Chesapeake Bay region and the Carolina lowcountry.

With regard to the two-stage revolutionary movement of the third, or nineteenth-century Creole, phase of resistance, comparisons became more difficult. During the first stage of late-eighteenth-century wars and revolutions, differences between regions and societies break down. Artisans in all four societies created subversive associations whose membership, secular goals, and frustrated results were remarkably similar from one end of Anglo-America to another.

Nonetheless, the regional contrast reappeared in the second stage of revolutionary developments during the last years of slavery, although the picture is complex and in part ambiguous. Once again, rebel leaders used religious ritual and learning to inspire. In Jamaica, slaves organized a huge insurrection propelled by a potent mix of indigenous and Christian beliefs. In Barbados, on the other hand, a similar development was most unlikely because neither missions nor evangelism ever took hold in a slave culture that was remarkably African in some ways, assimilated in others, and quiet until the conflagration of 1815. In the South, developments were significantly different than in the Caribbean largely because slaves had been in the hands of evangelical missionaries for several generations. In the Carolina lowcountry, no resistance occurred after the 1731 Stono Rebellion, and in Virginia Nat Turner's revolt had little to do with either a local missionary station or with evangelical religion.

Thus, given the sharp regional contrasts in slave values and ways (particularly in family, economy, and religion) in the final analysis—and regardless of the familiar argument for the West Indian character of slavery in the lowcountry—the four societies of Virginia, South Carolina, Barbados, and Jamaica may be collapsed into two: the Caribbean and the South. This is the significant comparison, regardless of the useful similarities that may be drawn between Jamaica and South Carolina or Virginia and Barbados. From the perspective of Anglo-America as a whole rather than the more commonly narrow one that centers on the mainland plantation colonies, what stands out is that the Chesapeake and the Carolina lowcountry are a unit when compared to their counterparts in the British West Indies.

Finally, the ongoing comparison of slaves to colonial people elsewhere, and even to immigrants in our own society, promises release from the confines of an American Negro slavery usually construed as antebellum slavery and so as "the peculiar institution." Once our view is expanded outward to include the Caribbean and back to the colonial past, we are poised to pursue more accurately the problem of the uniqueness—or otherwise—of an American society and identity for which slavery, from our beginnings, was such an integral part.

# Appendixes

# I

# The Problem of the Provenance of African Slaves Brought to British America

There is a vast difference in the tempers and dispositions of the Negroes, according to the coasts they come from.
— J. B. Moreton, 1793

[A slave's nationality] forms only a presumptive evidence of quality, which may mislead, but is generally found so well supported by experience, as to occasion a variation in the prices of cargoes, of from eight to ten pounds a head.
— A Professional Planter, 1811[1]

My route to the issue of slave provenance was not the usual one, a demographic investigation of the slave trade. Instead, while I counted African runaways two unexpected patterns emerged that encouraged a closer look at the problem of the relationships between ethnic origins and patterns of slave resistance. There were significant differences in the percentages of women and of solitary runaways from one ethnic group to another. There were also marked regional contrasts (ranging from 3 to 99 percent) in the whites' use of ethnic distinctions.

As argued throughout, ordinary people identified Africans as members of particular societies more carefully than scholars have given them credit for doing. Using a new Negro's language to determine ethnicity, as the Jamaicans did, was particularly astute. Establishing the provenance of African slaves, P. E. H. Hair explains, is not, nor should it be, unnecessarily complicated. After observing that maps in existing ethnographic histories are criss-crossed with arrow-lines "hithering and thithering from focal points" as if indicating a freeway or railroad junction, he proposes "a different picture": not one of migration or of fundamental change, but rather "with very few exceptions" the ethnolinguistic units he uses "*stayed put,* topographically, over the centuries." To identify a vocabulary of a Guinea language appearing in a contemporary record "the rule is absolute, find where the vocabulary was collected and check first on the language spoken in that spot today."[2]

In the case of British America, the task of matching contemporary names with actual places in west and southwestern Africa was also made less demanding than elsewhere in the Caribbean as well because the English-speaking planters normally used far fewer ethnic labels than did their Spanish or French counterparts. Jamaicans (who were more discriminating about these matters than planters were in the other three societies) commonly talked about only seven societies: Mandingo (from the Senegambia), Coromantee (Gold Coast), Papaw–Nago (Bight of Benin), Ibo and Moco (Bight of Biafra), and Congo (Congo–Angola), and, to a lesser extent, about Chamba and Mungola (respectively, from the Gold Coast hinterland and Congo–Angola).

South Carolinians used the same catagories as the Jamaicans did, however, they refined "Mandingoes" from Senegambia considerably. Lowcountry public jailers who advertised fugitive new Negroes who had been recaptured distinguished the Senegambians to include, among others, Ballum, Jollof, Kissy, and Temne. As for Africans from further south and east along the coast, a case should be made that lowcountry whites through time also refined the generic "Guinea" to represent Coramantee. Of people from the Bight of Biafra, they recognized Ibo but not Moco, and because of the problems with Spanish St. Augustine, Florida, they paid particular attention to Gullah, that is, people from Angola. Major geographical divisions of West Africa that contemporaries used are shown on a map in Churchill's eighteenth-century compilation, *A Collection of Voyages and Travels* (Vol. 5 between pages 187–89), which lists the familiar coasts by their principal commodities and divides them by rivers: the Grain Coast: Cape St. Ann and the Sierre Leone River to the Isle of Palms; the Ivory Coast: Isle of Palms to Rio de Suerio; the Gold Coast: Rio de Suerio to the Volta River; and the Slave Coast: Volta River to the Formosa River.

## West African Peoples Identified as New Negroes

This section, which includes references not cited in the notes, is to help those who wish to continue to sort out terms contemporaries used to designate particular African people and then to establish their location, then and now, as precisely as possible.

Useful general works in this connection are Philip D. Curtin, *The Atlantic Slave Trade: A Census* (Madison, 1970); P. E. H. Hair, "Ethnolinguistic Continuity on the Guinea Coast," *Journal of African History* 8, no. 2 (1967): 247–68; David Pavy, "The Provenience of Columbia Negroes," *Journal of Negro History* 52 (Jan. 1967): 36–58; and Maurren Warner, "Africans in Nineteenth-Century Trinidad," *African Studies Association of the West Indies*, Bulletin 5 (Dec. 1972), 1: 27–29, 38–40.

Two promising and underused sources are newspaper for-sale notices for slaver cargoes and an administrative record, the War Office, and succession books for the West Indian regiments in the Public Record Office, Kew, which are filled with names of African recruits listed under such headings as name, rank, size, age, complexion, and "Where Born: Country, Town or Parish."[3]

The newspaper advertisements, which constitute the most useful source for estimating contemporary understandings of particular African ethnic groups and the degree of care with which identifications were applied, indicate that Jamaicans and South Carolinians were the most discriminating traders in the empire. If a slaver's cargo was comprised of mixed ethnic groups, Jamaicans would say as much: "Prime young Gold-coast, Papaw and Whydah Negroes." When they could not make an effective notice by pinpointing ethnicity, they proceeded somewhat like this: "lately, imported from Anamaboe on the Gold Coast."[4] South Carolinians preferred Senegambians first, and then Coramantee and Angolans. Like Jamaicans, they also used "Congo" and "Angola" interchangeably, as in "340 Congo Negroes from Angola": "JUST ARRIVED . . . from Angola, 280 young slaves Mostly of the MASSE-CONGO country, and are esteemed equal to the GOLD COAST and GAMBIA slaves."[5]

## Mundingo

*Present-day location:* Mende, as they are now commonly called, comprise speakers of the Manding language. After the collapse of the great medieval Mali empire, Mende settled in a heartland that roughly comprised an eight-hundred-mile arc from the mouth of the Gambia in the northwest to the interior of the Ivory Coast in the southeast.

*Contemporary understandings:* Mende are characterized by one expert as having a strong sense of cultural identity and pride, "especially in being able to maintain their identity across unnatural colonial and post-colonial boundaries."[6] It is, then, perhaps not accidental that Mende — many of whom (with the exception of Bumbara) are Islamic — once in the New World struggled to provide in one fashion or another a number of the existing "autobiographical" accounts even though proportionately they were relatively few in number. An antebellum planter recorded Salih Bilali's Recollections, another transmitted the account of Omar ibn Said.[7] There is also the extensive first-person material left by the *Amistad* captives, Mende who took over a slaver and were defended in court by the former president, John Quincy Adams.[8]

### Coramantee

*Present-day locations:* Coramantee speak Akan, are a subgroup of Twi, and are concentrated in the nations of Burkina Faso, Ghana, and Volta.[9]

*Contemporary understandings:* According to J. D. Fage, the Gold Coast until well into the nineteenth century meant "literally" a stretch of the shore of the Gulf of Guinea, from the mouth of the Tano River (west) to the mouth of the Volta River. Generally, then, Coramantee came from an area three hundred miles from Cape Appolonia to the mouth of the Volta River.

In South Carolina, Gold Coast slaves early on were called simply "Guiney Negroes."[10] But by the second quarter of the eighteenth century as Africans became more prominent in the slave population, conceptions of "Guiney" seem to have evolved. At first it meant a stretch of coast south and east of the Senegambia region and west of the Bights, and then the Gold Coast proper and areas to the immediate west and east — modern Burkina Faso and Benin. Subsequently, as the slave trade boomed in the late 1760s and early 1770s, advertisers tried to denote actual societies within the Gold Coast, and designations of slave cargoes from the same area became increasingly refined: from "the Factory at Sierra-Leon on the Windward-Coast of GUINEY"; "the Windward and Grain Coast of GUINEY"; "Coast of GUINEY . . . GOLD COAST SLAVES"; and, finally and most accurately, 150 healthy new Negroes "being chiefly of the CORAMANTEE and FANTEE Country, or what is commonly called GUINEA NEGROES."[11] The last, another sign of the lowcountry West Indian bias, should be compared to a Jamaican's discerning notice for the new Negro fugitive Belinda: "of a Gold Coast cargo, but not Coramantee, Fantee or Ashantee, subscriber does not know her country."[12]

### Chamba

*Present-day location:* Most scholars put this group roughly on the border between Niger delta peoples (Igbo, Ibidio, Moco) and the Cameroon highlands to the south and east.

*Contemporary understandings:* Jamaicans acted as if Chamba came from the Gold Coast hinterland. Roger Bastide, who is as close to a resolution of their provenance as anyone, identifies two branches of the people: the first one north of Asante (Coramantee), and the second on the Nigerian–Cameroon frontier.[13] Philip Curtin also accepts this positioning. To the English on the Gold Coast, he explains, "Chambas" simply meant any slaves brought down from the region north of Asante, or anyone speaking one of the Gur languages.[14] Using George Murdock's standard guide (with its useful maps), the area in question is the hinterland of the Bight of Benin—the Gurma cluster of people (which includes such people as Basari, Gurma, Konkomba, and Moba).[15] Finally, William Bascom defines Chamba linguistically as speakers of the Adamawa language of the Niger–Congo branch of the great Congo–Kordofanian language family, which includes most West African languages. Chamba belong to the Adamawa branch of Niger–Congo, whereas Yoruba belongs to the Kwa branch that also includes Igbo and Akan.[16]

Papaw–Nago

*Present-day location:* This composite comprises, respectively, Aja-Ewe of the Fon Kingdom, and later the powerful Kingdom of Dahomey, now from Volta roughly another fifty miles past Grand Popo. *Nago* was the term for Yoruba of southwestern Nigeria. Originally a subgroup of the northern Yoruba, it was extended to include any Yoruba-speaking group sent to the coast for sale at Oyo.[17]

*Contemporary understandings:* Southerners did not use this designation, and Jamaicans did so by lumping Fon and Yorubans together as Papaw–Nagoes. The hyphen was recognition that the two came from the same ports but spoke different langauges. These ports, midway on the Slave Coast between the mouth of the Volta and Lagos, were Great and Little Popo (hence "Papaw") and Ouidah (often written then as "Whidah").[18]

Patrick Manning explains that this area was more populous, compact, and intensively slaved than most others. That is, from an area of no more than 150 to 200 miles from the coast, a little less than a third of a million people were exported in the eighteenth century. Ninety percent were Aja peoples, Papaw, most of whom when shipped to British America came to Jamaica. Although Papaw is commonly Dahomean, the term was not used then; instead, people spoke of the "Fon" Kingdom, or generically of "Arada" (the specific origin Thistlewood assigned to one of his new Negro girl friends). On the other hand, Yorubans, who spoke a different langauge than Aja-Ewe, in the eighteenth century were Oyo Yoruba only.[19]

Papaw are characterized in a contemporary travel account (in Thomas Astley's large and popular collection) as very polite and civilized, most respectful of superiors before whom they immediately fell on their knees and kissed the earth while thrice clapping their hands. "The like deference is paid by the younger to the elder brother, the children to the father, and wives to their husbands." To this, a Yoruban scholar writes that religion is the keynote of their life, "As far as they are concerned, the full responsiblity of all the affairs of life belongs to the Deity; their own part of the matter is to do as they are ordered."[20] Complementing these stereotypes is Bryan Edwards's familiar characterization of fatalistic obeisance: "That punishment which excites the Koromantyn to rebel, and drives the Ebo Negro to suicide, is received by the Papaws as the chastisement of legal authority, to which it is their duty to submit patiently."[21]

Papaw–Nago are generally not heard of during the African phase of resistance that lasted into the 1760s. But they (and the Igbo), Edward Long observes, moved their ancestral masks to the fore in the 1769 Christmas holiday ceremonies.[22]

Ibo (Igbo)

*Present-day locations:* This group includes Ibo, Ibibio, and Efik and Cross River peoples who live mostly in southwestern Nigeria and the Cameroons.

*Contemporary understandings:* Most commonly, these people were referred to as "Eboe" or "Ibo" and, very rarely, as "Bonny" (the name of a port on the Bight of Biafra).

Although whites of the Chesapeake Bay region rarely mentioned an African's provenance, a larger percentage of Ibo among all new Negroes were imported there than anywhere else. Ibo may have comprised a sizeable percentage of those whose origin, although unlisted, were described as "knock-knee'd." This designation of a conspicuous physical condition appeared in runaway notices more than any other named affliction. That this symptom, presumably of a dietary deficiency, was common for slaves from the Bight of Biafra is suggested in Thistlewood's wish to purchase from a slaver an Ibo girl who did not have "bowed knees."[23]

Like Nago, Ibo were not prominent in the African phase of resistance. Still they were busy resisting in their own nonviolent way as revealed in Monk Lewis's journal, which pays tribute to their cagey resourcefulness and elan and to their music, including drum and song. Considered by some ethnographers as high achievers (or, in one instance, the Jews of West Africa), others characterize Ibo by such proverbs as "the Iboes know no king," and "one who is over cautious of his life is always killed by the fall of a dry leaf." Hence, S. N. Nwabara sees Ibo as competitive, individualistic, status-conscious, antiauthoritarian, pragmatic, and practical—a people with a strongly developed commercial sense.[24] In a Jamaican society where many Africans chose never to learn to be "sensible," that is to speak an English readily intelligible to whites—and those who became "sensible" took about three years to do so — Ibo-Mocoes were rapid learners.[25] Charles, a Moco, was imported eighteen months before and described as "talks English so as to be understood perfectly"; Toney was a stout and able "rather talkative and artful fellow, though not more than 2 years in the Country"; and a thirteen-year-old boy imported two years previously was described as speaking good English and artful. In Jamaican descriptions of all named peoples, Ibo were the most adroit in using language distinctively and in some instances deceptively. A young boy was advertised as adept in English "when he pleases," and another spoke English well but would also "affect to speak it very bad[ly]."[26]

### Moco

*Present-day location:* This group comprises Yako and Ekoi, that is, Cross River people living in Nigeria and the Cameroons. See W. B. Baikei, *Narrative of an Exploring Voyage up the River Kwora and Binue* (London, 1856); and Charles Kingsley Meek, *Law and Authority in a Nigerian Tribe; a Study in Indirect Rule* (London, 1937), 5. Both cite a 1688 description of Bonny by Dr. Dapper: that south of Moko, toward the sea, lies a fairly big market center in the district of Moko, where a certain kind of money is made of flat iron in the form of a fish.[27]

Were Moco Ibibio? Fugitive slave notices complement the tribal map in Murdock.[28] Yet on the basis of this map, contemporaries would put them further up the Cross River in the region of Yako and Ekio. For Curtin, Moco comprise a diverse range of peoples and cultures whom (in his reorganization of Knolle's language survey of liberated Africans to Sierra Leone in the 1830s) are said to speak languages that were nearly all Cameroon. In John R. Willis's annotated bibliography (1966) in G. T. Basden's *Among the Ibos of Nigeria,* Mocoes are one of five major divisions of Ibo; that is, Eastern or Cross River Igbo.[29]

*Contemporary understanding:* Ibo and Moco were seen as related or, at least, difficult to distinguish, as notices indicate: "Ebo or Mocco"; an Ibo with the "countrymarks" of Moco; and another Ibo who "speaks Moco and may pass as a Moco."[30] In sum, in the evidence the two are very similar, yet distinguished by Jamaicans while apparently lumped together by planters in all other regions.

### Congo-Angola

*Present-day location:* Daniel J. Crowley notes that there are 200 distinct tribal groups and about 150 languages belonging to either the Niger–Congo or Bantu family.[31] Accordingly, contemporaries were more unsure about which peoples comprised this vast area than they were about any other.

The two vast regions were usually seen as one. Exceptions from Jamaica, however, included "of Angola or Congo," and "Congo his country Kissy."[32] Simon Taylor, a rich and politically influential Jamaican planter and attorney (who discussed new Negroes in his private correspondence more than anyone), in the early 1780s said that the slaves of Carolina planters, who as empire loyalists emigrated to Jamaica after the American Revolution, were principally Senegambians ("Mandingoes") and Angolans.[33] These two people seem most prominent in the history of lowcountry slavery, whereas their counterparts in the Chesapeake Bay region and Jamaica were Ibo and Coramantee. Scholars from Lorenzo Turner to Joseph Holloway, Margaret Creel, and Robert F. Thompson have divided over the question of which African region to assign precedence to with regard to the origins and development of the lowcountry's "peculiar people," the Gullah.[34]

APPENDIX

# Runaways

I have tried to make the incomplete data as useful as possible by simply displaying the figures in columns to ease comparison and to indicate some of its possibilities.

Table 1. Numbers of Runaways, 1730s–1805

| | Total | New Negroes | Men | Women |
|---|---|---|---|---|
| Caribbean: | | | | |
| Jamaica | 2,612 | [525] | 1,981 | 631 |
| Barbados | 431 | [22] | 283 | 148 |
| South: | | | | |
| Chesapeake Bay Region | | | | |
| Virginia | 1,280 | [64] | 1,138 | 142 |
| Maryland | 1,031 | [18] | 901 | 130 |
| Carolina Lowcountry | | | | |
| South Carolina | 3,267 | [241] | 2,582 | 685 |
| Georgia | 998 | [116] | 816 | 182 |
| Total | 9,619 | 986 | 7,701 | 1,918 |

Table 2. Advertisers Designating Fugitive Africans by Nationality

|                          | Number      | Percent |
|--------------------------|-------------|---------|
| Chesapeake Bay Region:   |             |         |
| Virginia                 | 17 in 138   | 12      |
| Maryland                 | 3 in 62     | 4.8     |
| Carolina Lowcountry:     |             |         |
| South Carolina           | 175 in 506  | 35      |
| Georgia                  | 126 in 270  | 47      |
| Caribbean:               |             |         |
| Jamaica                  | 913 in 918  | 99.5    |
| Barbados                 | 2 in 61     | 3       |

Table 3. Women Runaways

|                          | Number   | Percent |
|--------------------------|----------|---------|
| Chesapeake Bay Region:   |          |         |
| Virginia                 | 1 in 9   | 11      |
| Maryland                 | 1 in 8   | 12.6    |
| (272 women in 2,311 runaways) | | |
| Carolina Lowcountry:     |          |         |
| South Carolina           | 1 in 5   | 21      |
| Georgia                  | 1 in 5   | 18      |
| (867 women in 4,265 runaways) | | |
| Caribbean:               |          |         |
| Jamaica                  | 1 in 4   | 24      |
| Barbados                 | 1 in 3   | 34      |
| (779 women in 3,034 runaways) | | |

Because in every plantation society women fugitives sought out a town as the best place to pursue diverse objectives for running away, a key issue is the relationship between the degree of urbanization in a particular society and a woman's perception of a successful flight. In the Chesapeake Bay region marginally more black women in Maryland than in Virginia ran off because by the late eighteenth century, it may be argued, Maryland was criss-crossed with hamlets and market towns. Barbados and South Carolina provided hospitable environments because of the presence of sizeable ports, Bridgetown and Charleston, which dominated hinterlands, where it is assumed those most likely to advertise anywhere were concentrated. (Appendix 4).

Africans, especially the unseasoned, saw enslavement as a problem to be solved collectively. Accordingly, three in four new Negro men in Jamaica and South Carolina run off in groups of two or more. Of those said to have ran off alone, the range is from one in seven of Coramantee (in Jamaica), who were the rebels of colonial Anglo-America and the most conspicuously co-operative of people, to two in five for the Nigerians, traditionally a people known as high achievers and willing to step forward, alone, if the opportunity seemed right to do so.

Table 4. New Negro Men Who Ran Off Alone

| | Jamaica | | South Carolina | |
|---|---|---|---|---|
| | Number | Percent | Number | Percent |
| Senegambians | 6 in 36 | 17 | 8 in 40 | 20 |
| Chamba | 7 in 22 | 32 | n.a. | |
| Bight of Benin | | | n.a.[a] | |
| Nago-Papaw | 7 in 23 | 30 | | |
| Coramantee | 18 in 47 | 38 | 5 in 34 | 15 |
| Bight of Biafra | | | | |
| Ibo | 24 in 42 | 57 | n.a.[a] | |
| Moco | 24 in 77 | 31 | | |
| Mungola | 5 in 21 | 24 | n.a. | |
| Congo/Angola | 33 in 126 | 26 | 10 in 37 | 27 |
| Unspecified | 24 in 54 | 44 | 28 in 105 | 27[b] |
| Total | 448 | | 216 | |

[a] 1 only, so not counted

[b] Higher than average because owners, beginning with their ethnicity, did not know them well and so were unclear about their motives as fugitives.

# Were Maroons the Whites' Clients?

## Maroon Demography and Relations
## with Plantation Slaves

Interpretations of a people who are a cultural minority should result from explorations of as many dimensions of their lives as the surviving evidence will allow. To do less than this is to risk seizing prematurely upon a feature or group within the subculture as representative of the whole. If a minority is unusually silent in the written record, it is especially vulnerable to interpretations that emphasize the surrounding culture's values as pervasive, or even as hegemonic, and those of the minority as derivative and dependent. Entire societies in fact have had to contend with such opprobrious and conventional characterizations of themselves as artificial, absentee, or client. Presumably, ethnocentric labels of this nature are to call attention to the real sources of oppression and control in plural and neocolonial settings. But the cost of such tough-minded social science is high. One loses sight of the inner workings of a marginalized people's values and ways which, at least initially, should be seen in their own terms and as fully as possible before they are put into the customary Euro-centric evolutionary scheme and thereby dubbed precapitalist or preindustrial and in other ways used implicitly to praise (or condemn) modern existences.

The Treaty Maroons of Jamaica who were and remain a separate people and a culture have been subjected to this kind of treatment. The historio-graphical tradition of Maroons as runaways who were essentially marauding males complements efforts to shove them into larger schemes of an American Negro slavery conceived as a powerful transforming phenomenon that left New World blacks with no real culture of their own. The strategy works this way: If Maroons can be studied against a backdrop of incessant wandering and warfare, then families as the vehicles for the orderly transmission of traditions may be conveniently ignored. After all, how could families be sustained in the war zone in which Maroons are said to have lived? Given this approach, structural explanations predominate at the expense of cultural ones. As the creatures of externals, rather than actors shaping a way of life, Maroons are seen before the peace treaties of 1739–40 as simply former slaves dependent upon the plantations from which they originated; and after the peace negotiations as the planters' janisaries. "Conceived as outlaw societies . . . central to their organization were procedures and practices adapted to societies at war." "Killing and being killed was common place" in societies that were "military to the core."[1] From such views as these it is only a rhetorical leap to arguments that maroon societies were "incomplete polities," "client states," whose members "ruthlessly" tracked plantation slave runaways and so cutoff escape to the wilderness for "future freedom-fighters."[2] The question remains why, when scholars assume the absence of surviving evidence to the contrary, do they argue as they do? They hold, in sum, that Maroons as the most African of New World blacks did not constitute a way of life, and certainly not one attractive to slaves.

A variety of types of sources support the recognition by contemporaries, officials, and ordinary people, that treaty provisions notwithstanding, Maroons were not reliable allies; that they were not the slaves' police; and most important, when the chips were down and war against the whites was raised, they were joined by significant numbers of plantation slaves. The evidence, from runaway advertisements and depositions of slaves who lived and fought with Maroons during the Second Maroon War (1795–96), also demonstrates how intricate and ambiguous the relations were among the three peoples.

During the Second Maroon War officials estimated that about two hundred plantation slaves joined and served the Maroons as either fighters or foragers. The latter, comprising the far greater number, lived with the Maroon women and children in a remote retreat. These foragers, who had to keep themselves and more than a hundred and fifty fighting men in food while on the run, literally worked around the clock. Two parties went out with armed escorts during a twenty-four-hour period, one leaving in the morning as the other returned.

The government, at war, asked locals to submit lists of the runaways. These accounts, some of which have survived in the Crawford Muniments in the National Library of Scotland, Edinburgh, help solidify the argument that for much of the eighteenth-century Maroons lived in families, some of which by the 1790s were of three generations. Plantation women who joined the Maroons, in one such account, included Bessy Bowen's slave woman. Described as "very successful in treating wounds," she joined after the Maroons burned her house. Six others taken at one time included another doctor, Olympia, but called by the slaves Aquashiba, a Coramantee day-name; Twist, an Ibo woman with filed teeth; Claretta, a Creole and yellow-complexioned "tacky looking wench"; Peggy, rather black; and Emma, a Congolese with very small features and ritual markings resembling those of a Chamba.

Whether these women were also Maroon plantation wives (of which there were a considerable number) is uncertain. But families headed by slave women and described as "connected" to Trelawny were included in a surrender list that reads in part:

> Lilly, black mother of
> 　　Nancy McLaughlin　　mulattoes, children
> 　　John Mostyn　　　　　of Lilly
> 　　Ja[me]s Allen　　　　son of Lilly
> Betsy Borthwick
> 　　*Mary Sharpe
> 　　John Quick
> 　　John Anglin Earl　　children of
> 　　Betsy Quick　　　　　Rosanna Scarlett
> 　　William Scarlett Earl

The list continues and contains thirty-six names of sixteen adults, thirteen of whom were women, including eight mothers of seventeen children. Eleven children were under ten (and marked with an asterisk). Three mothers and eleven of their children were mulattoes, and three were sisters. Shortly after the Maroons were exiled to Canada (and then to Sierra Leone before returning to Jamaica in 1841), another group of mulatto women and children petitioned a local court, on the basis of a recent law, to change their status from Maroon to free people of color. Assuming these women were the grown daughters of Maroon parents, exogamy may have been an old practice. White men did marry Maroon women,[3] and Maroon men did take wives from among slave women through whom they had access to provision grounds, including those at Chatsworth Estate, said to be the best on the island, and an invaluable source of food for the Maroons when they went to war. In sum, no knowledgeable contemporary pretended that Maroons and plantation slaves were natural enemies, or that plantation slaves would not become Maroons if they were inclined to do so. Citing his field commander, Governor Balcarres reported home that even if you reduce the Maroons to five only, those five would be a "rallying point for more runaways to resort to."[4]

In the 1820s, an Accompong Maroon captain estimated that there were about six thousand fugitives out: a third in Kingston and its hinterland, a third in the country parishes, and a third secreted in grounds and woods. The nineteenth-century Jamaican cleric and historian William Gardner noted that the captain's source was unknown, but emancipation "proved" that this was an underestimate. On any account, Gardner explained, "few" runaways were actually caught and returned because the Maroons took bribes.[5] Bribes were not inconsiderable, and presumably it was the runaways themselves and their families who were making the payoffs, further testimony to the wherewithall commanded by some slaves and their families. There is a 1785 account of a payment of £2.7.6 for taking up the runaway Cudjoe (compared to 2 shillings, 1 pence cost to hire a field hand for a day).[6]

## The Evidence

Maroon Censuses

1. "1738/9":
"Jamaica, Negroes in the Several Negroe towns formerly Rebels that surrender'd in 1738/9"

| | | | | |
|---|---|---|---|---|
| Trelawny | 276 (men: 112 | women: 85 | boys: 40 | girls: 39) |
| Accompong | 85 | 31 | 25 | 13 | 16 |
| Crawford Town | 233 | 102 | 80 | 26 | 25 |
| Nanny Town | 70 | 28 | 21 | 9 | 12 |
| | 664 | | | | |

Source: British Library, Addit. MSS, 12, 435, p. 19

2. 1776. August:
A note that the Maroons have increased "at least a third" since Edward Long's "very full and authentic account" (taken in the early 1770s).
Source: Lt. Gov. Keith to Lord Germaine, Jamaica, Aug. 6, 1776, C.O.
    137/71, f. 230.

3. 1788. November 20:

| | |
|---|---|
| Trelawny Town | 594 |
| Accompong | 159 |
| Scotts Hall | 95 |
| Charles Town | 250 |
| Moore Town | 228 |
| | 1,326 |

Source: Enclosed in Lt. Gov. Clarke's of Nov. 20, 1788 (which also noted: 226,432 slaves, 18,347 whites, and 9,405 free people of color), C.O.

137/87. In an Assembly report of the slave trade (p. 13) is the note, "last returns of Maroons (about 1787): 1300." Enclosed in Clarke's, Oct. 19, 1788, C.O. 137/87.

4. 1795. July 1:
Return of "Maroons bearing Arms" [Trelawny Town]

| | |
|---|---|
| Old Town | 78 |
| New d[itt]o | 43 |
| nonresidenters | 17* |
| Boys (12–15 years) | 27 |
| Men who have joined the Maroons: | 5 |
| | 170 |

(2 from Accompong, 2 free mulattoes, and a slave of Capt. Forbes)

Source: File 23/11/223, Crawford Muniments, National Library of Scotland, Edinburgh.
* Living out was forbidden by the treaties.

5. 1795. August 14:

| | |
|---|---|
| Charles Town | |
| Effective men (5 officers) | 60 |
| Young men without arms | 21 |
| Superannuated [old] men | 5 |
| Boys 7–14 | 18 |
| Male children | 33 |
| Women | 81 |
| Girls 11–15 | 22 |
| 7–13 | 13 |
| Children | 35 |
| Increase d[itt]o | 4 |
| | 292 |

Source: John Ingram to Simon Taylor, St. George, Charles Town, Aug. 14, 1795, in Taylor to Lt. Gov. Balcarres, Head Quarters, Kingston, Aug. 17, 1795, 23/11/91, Crawford Muniments.

6. 1796. February 22:

| | |
|---|---|
| Moore Town | |
| Number of officers | 6 |
| Able men | 39 |
| Men boys | 10* |

Numbers of women:  70
Girls                      14
Children:              <u>102</u>
                              241

Source: Charles Douglas (superintendant) to Balcarres, Feb. 22, 1796, file 23/
    11/15, Crawford Muniments.
* "Nine of the Boys are good Shot."

7. 1796.  July 1: A Return of the Charles Town Maroons, by James Anderson,
    superintendant:

Officers      5
Men shot   72
Women      73
Boys          51
Girls          54
Children    33
Invalids     <u>2</u>
                 290

decrease since March 18, 1796      men    3
                                              women  2
                                              children  <u>3</u>
                                                          8

Source: File 23/11/221, Crawford Muniments.

8. 1797. October 21:
    A "moderate calculation" is that the Maroons [those exiled to Nova
Scotia] will increase by forty-five children each year; as to how many die
yearly, he doubts a third of forty-five, or fifteen.
Source: Balcarres to Portland, Oct. 21, 1797, C.O. 137/100.

## Officials' Lists of Plantation Slaves
## Who Joined the Maroons during the
## Second Maroon War

1. From Trelawny Parish (Feb. 28, 1796): an account of eighty-six plantation runaways (nine of whom were women) from twenty-nine different
properties (including eighteen, twelve, and seven runaways, respectively,
from Weston Flavel, Retreat, and Silver Grove estates). Source: 23/11/226,
Crawford Muniments.

2. From Clarendon Parish (Feb. 15, 1796): still out fifty-nine runaways
(eight of whom were women) from twenty-six plantations and settlements

(including six from Mr. Dawkin's old plantation and five each from Hall's, Ramble, and Four Paths). Source: 23/11/244, Crawford Muniments.

3. From Westmoreland Parish (March 1, 1796): A list of about sixty runaways, nine of whom were women, from about forty properties. The writer observed that an estimate of about one thousand runaways from all twenty parishes "isn't an exaggerated calculation." Source: T. Barker to Hon. George Murry, Savannah la Mar, March 1, 1796, 23/11/174, Crawford Muniments.

4. A list taken aboard a prison ship (May 11, 1796): forty-eight men, nine women, and five children from estates other than those indicated in the preceding lists. Source: 23/11/246 (also 247), Crawford Muniments.

## In Their Own Words: Depositions of Slaves Who Had Spent Time with the Maroons

1. A slave who who spent four weeks with the Maroons said that they received intelligence daily from plantation slaves, sometimes by three or four slaves at a time and, with the exception of an Ibo, all who joined were Coramantee (corroborated by evidence indicating administration of the blood oath to prospective slave fighters). Source: Examination of Jacob Graham's Neptune, Oct. 10, 1795, 21/11/232, Crawford Muniments, 21/11/232.

2. On an estate where six Coramantee slaves joined, slave said that he thinks that it was part of a preconcerted plan to do so, driver blew his horn as a warning, and when told to stop and did not, he was "instantly" shot and his house burned down. Source: Examination of John Reid's Jamaica reprinted in *Jamaica Royal Gazette* [Nov. 27], 1795.

3. Testimony that there were two hundred runaways capable of bearing arms, and that the Maroons had been hard-pressed but had made up numbers of fighting men by recruiting Coramantee slaves. A month later several families came in, and it was noted that about 150 runaways were still out. Source: Examination of Jumbo, *Jamaica Royal Gazette,* Dec. 27, 1795.

4. During the war, seventy-five slaves were executed, which represented more than three-fourths of all those executed (ninety-six) in the 1790s; sixty-one were also transported, which represented a third (of 185) of all those exiled in that decade. Source: Committee of the Gov.'s Council to the Board of Trade, March 23, 1800, C.O. 137/104.

## Runaways and Maroons: Evidence from the Fugitive Slave Notices

1. *Women:* Ruth, advertised as middle-aged and well known, likely to be in a Maroon town where she has a husband, a tailor named Martin;

Janetta, a Papaw (Dahomean), thirty, and assimilated — she spoke "very good English" — was also listed as probably in either Accompong or Trelawny "Negro towns." Source: *Cornwall Chronicle and Jamaican General Gazette,* Aug. 7, 1784-S., Ann Clark, Feb. 19, 1785-S., Thomas Leigh.

2. *Artisans:* Bob, a Congolese, who spoke good English and worked aboard the king's ships on the wharf: *Jamaica Royal Gazette,* Feb. 2, 1782-S., Richard Donohue; Joe, a waitingman but recently a carpenter, who took his tools with him: May 7, 1796-S., a news clipping in 23/11/261, Crawford Muniments; and Richmond, a Cormanatee carpenter, very well known in Trelawny Town: *Cornwall Chron.,* Oct. 11, 1788-S., Elizabeth Allan; *Jamaica Royal Gazette,* April 21, 1792-S., Jan. 5, 1793–P.S., Solomon Elkins; *Jamaican Gazette,* July 4, 1812-P.S., Netham Tory [advertising for a runaway who had once spent nearly two years with the Maroons]; and for "seen among the Maroons," *Jamaica Mercury and Kingston Weekly Advertiser,* Dec. 11, 1780, Alex. Campbell.

3. For the other side of the picture, Maroons as the pursuers of runaways, there are advertisements with the heading, "To the maroons," followed by a description of the fugitive, in *Jamaica Mercury and Kingston Weekly Advertiser,* March 29, 1794-P.S., William Rugless; Sept. 27, 1794-P.S. William Gardner warned explicitly that if his runaways did not return, the Maroons would be asked to pursue them; see June 9, 1781–S., E. B. Lousada. Milly was taken up as a runaway (out of Colches Estate Negro houses) by the Maroons. *Cornwall Chron.,* April 22, 1786-S., William Mills.

4. *From plantation documents:* a runaway from Balcarres' troubled coffee plantation, Dick was out for thirteen to fourteen years with the Charles Town Maroons. The estate attorney suggested the slave's sale to the Spaniards because if the fugitive was returned to the property he would be a "bad example." Source: Matthew Atkinson to Balcarres, April 20, 1802, 23/8/18, Crawford Muniments.

# Provision Grounds, Pens, and Market Women

The object here is to describe more closely the average size of West Indian slave provision grounds, the suburban character of pens (specialized provision farms), and how both helped market women (and some artisans) test the system profitably.

For whites, grounds fed slaves, and pens that were managed properly did make money. But if pens were not managed well, they could be "pick pockets," said a Jamaican planter who, among others, also associated the farms with an environment—suburban and commerical—that dampened slave fertility and made artisans and market women more difficult to control.[1] For blacks, grounds and pens provided opportunities for self-improvement and a kind of resistance that was beneficial and relatively free of risk.

The initial advantage at emancipation that West Indian (but not Southern) slaves possessed in the form of a modicum of property and entrepreneurial sense came slowly and incrementally. Nonetheless, by the end of the slavery era, the grounds of some were in a high state of development that complemented the ambitions of those officials who wished to encourage slave self-sufficiency. In December 1829, for instance, the Grenada Agricultural Society presented awards to slave contestants whose properties in land, produce, and stock were described.[2]

1. to Rufine, head superintendant of Field Work
   of Lower Latante Estate:
   Extent of grounds, as nearly as can be ascertained
   about                                                        4 acres
   Full-grown Plantain Trees............................... 955

| | |
|---|---|
| Of which are Bearing | ...158 |
| Yam Roots of different kinds | ...524 |
| Manioc, of different ages, estimated as | |
| equal to bushels of Cassada Flour | ...32 |

In addition to the above, there is a considerable extent of white yams and Tannias. . . Corn, Ockroes, and Sweet Potatoes.

Live Stock

| | |
|---|---|
| One goat, with two kind, worth | ...7 |
| Two smaller goats | ...6 |
| One hog | ...2 |
| Two Smaller Hogs | |
| Ten Fowls, at a quarter dollar ea. | ...2 1/2 |
| 2. to Rudagone, a female field labourer... | |
| Extent of Grounds, as far as can be | |
| ascertained | ...1 1/2 |
| full-grown Plantain Trees | 74 |
| Yam roots of different kinds | 550 |

Manioc, of different ages, equal to 33 bushels of Cassada flour. Also corn, white yams [and a] remarkably fine field of Tannias.

Introduced to the society's president, the successful candidates assured the official that the grounds were their own work. In turn, the judges noted that the woman, Rudagone, was a field laborer in the great gang whose garden and provisions were hers entirely, "the fruits of her individual labour and industry." The woman's reward was £4.10, double that given to Rufine, who was a driver, and like artisans "tradesmen had more opportunities and greater facilities in cultivating their provisions."[3]

The money that market gardeners could make in the bountiful tropical clime of Jamaica is revealed in this account by Thomas Thistlewood, who at the end of 1776, added up his sales for the year (which are rearranged by amount of income).[4]

| | | | |
|---|---|---|---|
| asparagus | 308 bitts | fish | 33 |
| wax candles | 216 | okra | 25 |
| turkies | 185 | lima beans | 25 |
| wild ducks, teall | 165 | eggs | 18 |
| honey | 139 | pork | 16 |
| kidney beans | 85 | cocoa nuts | 14 |
| mutto | 70 | turnips | 6 |
| veal | 67 | watermellon | 5 |
| Indian kale | 63 | dunghill fowls | 4 |
| Muscovy ducks | 48 | mush mellon | 2 |

| Guinea fowl | 48 | radishes | 2 |
|---|---|---|---|
| pears | 43 | | |
| cassada | 41 | | 1626 bitts |
| | | | or £50.16.3 |

Allotments of provision ground in Jamaica were given to women as well as to men, as a distribution by Thistlewood indicates:[5]

> PM. I went to [Top]hill (William with me) Ambo, Phibbah, and the Mountain Negroes, gave them grounds as follows—
> George's to Benjamin_____Belinda's to Punch
> Cudjoe's to Lucy_____old Moll's to Beck_____Wills to Pero
> Plimouth's to Bathsheba_____Dover's to Susannah
> Little Member's to Bess, Roger's to Cynthia
> Nero's to Hanah, Prue's to Princess, Quacco's to Rose
> Hazat's to Ellin & Sharper_____old Sybbill's to Congo Sam
> Quasheba's to Nago Jenny_____Lydde & Mazarine . . . with Phib-bah in Quashe's grounds

Allotments varied considerably in size and quality. In 1825, at Montpelier (an estate at the center of the 1831 rebellion), for instance, plots ranged from only ten yards square to thirteen acres. The latter is sizeable, but the evidence upon which this notation and those that follow is based rarely indicates the quality of the land, how much of it was tilled, nor the size of the family (if any) that it supported. On average, each Montpelier slave worked between three-quarters to an acre and a third. They also owned two or three chickens, a hog, and a third to half a share in a goat or cow. At Lord Seaford's three properties, 589 acres of provision grounds supported 864 slaves, or .67 an acre each; at another estate that average jumped considerably to 1,200 acres for 421 slaves, or just under three acres each.[6]

The following is a schematic rendering of four notations, representing first, an estate's acreage; second, its total acres in sugarcane (or other major crop); third, acreage in provision grounds; and fourth an estate's complement of slaves. The acreage of grounds is divided by 60 percent of the total number of slaves (which assumes that two in five were younger than fifteen and so not holders of allotments). The evidence comprises mostly newspaper for-sale advertisements and, in a few instances, plantation records. Scarce but preferable, the plantation accounts sometimes indicate acreage probably set aside only in part for the use of slaves: pasture for house provisions, the land on which the slave houses and house garden plots were situated, and ruinate (the estate's margins). Given the slaves' African slash-and-burn methods for preparing grounds, ruinate is an important and indeterminate variable because it was intermittently in and out of production (and as in the case of Perrin's large Blue Mountain sugar estate was used to feed the whites and slaves who could or would not support themselves).

Coffee Plantations and Pens[7]
1. 1,040/800/100 acres of grounds for 89 slaves, or 1.9 acres for each adult
2. 400/60/40 for 75, or .89
3. 401/50/13/40 for 40, or .54

Sugar Estates[8]
1. 200/n.a./30/18, or 1.64
2. 550/160/40 for 40, or 1.64
3. 840/270/150 for 231, or 1.08
4. 950/238/150/170, or 1.47
5. 250/n.a./20 for 45, or 1.67
6. Duckenfield Hall, St. Thomas in the East:[9]
   1764: 2,180/n.a./358 for 375 or, 1.59 each
   1784: 2,075/519/250 for 353, or 1.18
   1797: 2,095/262/220 for 270, or 1.67

Perrin's Estates
8. Grange and Perrin's
   a. 1,743/270/40 for 255, or .26
   b. 1,225/250/150 for 208, or 1.2 (includes general provisions)
9. Blue Mountain
   a. 1,044/400/50 for 397, or .21 acre each
   b. 1,000/400/50 for 400, or .21. (The manager also noted that on 264 acres of ruinate and mountain lands, two miles distant from Blue Mountain, they grew provisions for "the sick, weakly, young children and the [estate's] whites.")[10]

Finally, some idea of the relative value of types of crops, including provisions, is seen in this August 1797 appraisal of a pen (Ardock) in St. Anns:[11]

| | |
|---|---|
| plantain walk: | 40 £ per acre |
| pasture: | |
|     Guinea grass | 10 |
|     common | 5 |
| Negro provision grounds | 8 per acre |

Pens were common throughout the island, from the coast to the interior ridges, where they were called "mountains" or "polinks."[12] They were also concentrated in the two most urban parishes (St. Andrews and St. Catherines that surrounded the major towns), where they served as rural retreats for wealthy townspeople and as headquarters and food sources for jobbing gangs of Negroes. Chiefly, however, pens produced the fuel, fodder, meat, and vegetables that provisioned Kingston, Spanish Town, and the thriving naval yards at Port Royal.

The three Jamaica towns were situated in a great amphitheater formed by the Blue Mountains that jut suddenly from the upland expanses of Liguanea Plain in the Kingston hinterland. A spur of this great range curves east and, as Long Mountain, reaches nearly to the sea above the shipyards. Dotting the suburban flanks of the range were settlements of free people of color, some of whom owned slaves, a few who were comfortably situated, and many who made a habit of concealing the runaways that continually and in considerable number passed through the area. Here fugitives heading for town easily obtained the produce that provided a means of support and an excuse, if one was needed, for being on the road in the first place.

By the late 1700s, suburban neighborhoods of this type were seen as responsible for a far more disturbing problem than that of sheltering runaways. Slaves who lived close to a market and spent much of their time selling either their own or a pen's produce had too many opportunities, planters reasoned, to pursue the sexual relationships that encouraged them to remain childless or, if infected with a veneral disease, to become infertile. Appraisers of a large windward estate in 1810 typified the estate's slaves as "None are richer." The slaves had "fine Lands to cultivate," great quantities of provisions, and ready access to "the Provision Boats that Call at Manchioneal on their way to the Kingston Market." But this enterprise had been destructive. The gang was weak and afflicted with sores from the promiscuous "connection[s]" with the slaves of the shipping at Manchioneal Harbor and Plantain Garden River, the effects of which "has got into the blood of every Family, and few of them sound." Concerning infertility and a plantation's suburban location, one planter put the matter directly. "Younger" slave women, "more especially [from] those Estates situated near any large Town," he wrote, "indulge themselves" in "promiscuous intercourse . . . by which means they either begin to breed late in life, or become entirely barren for the remainder of their lives," and nothing can be done to prevent this, he concluded.[13]

It was also assumed that pen slaves did not work as hard as slaves did in sugar estate gangs. Instead, their tasks entailed a considerable degree of independent action and skill and provided more opportunities for shirking than did routines on a sugar estate.[14] Suburban slaves cannot be pushed, wrote an attorney in 1776 to his new employer (a governor's widow), and they generally show "a strong inclination to be in Town."[15]

With gold earrings and necklaces and a swagger to their walk, black town women are "the proudest mortals I have ever seen," wrote an early-nineteenth-century traveler. They are of erect and stately carriage, mentioned another, and are barefoot, in short petticoats and short white jackets, and enter freely into conversations "in a sad, drawling accent." In the Caribbean — but not the South — black women, as they had in Africa, dominated marketing, where they were called "huxsters" in Barbados and "higglers" in Jamaica.[16]

In town some were seamstresses and house servants, and many more took in washing, but predominately they higgled — sold fruit, vegetables, and fodder. While it has been argued that this development did not take place until after emancipation, the sources indicate otherwise.[17] Nearly every issue of a Jamaican, and to a lesser extent Barbados, newspaper contains notices for women fugitives who were in town selling, whereas only a handful of male runaways over the entire period of this study were advertised as doing the same.*

Provision marketing encouraged resistance by women. Their weekends were largely their own, selling allowed them to travel lengthy routes unchallenged, and their owners were mostly concerned with regularly catching up with them in order to assure that they received a cut of a higgler's earnings. But the networks, which permeate descriptions of women fugitives, frustrated an owner's control. Mimba, a pregnant washerwoman, usually higgled through St. Andrews Parish, Wag Water, and Above Rocks. Chloe, a seamstress and cook, "now goes a-higgling" to Fort Augusta, Rock Fort, Spanish Town, and Withywood; and Bella, as many others, was described as "well known in the three towns" but also at Fort Augusta, The Farm, Hunt's Bay, Caymanas, Pieriera's Pen, The Walks, St. Andrews, and "intimate" at Dr. Hunter's and adjoining "mountains" (farms).[18]

These routes, touching nearly all of the low-land bases used by women, comprised three neighborhoods principally. There was first the heavily traveled corridor that ran from Spanish Town through Dawkin's Caymana to Kingston–Port Royal. Second — for ready access to additional food to sell and for quick cover or protection — women went into the foothills at Above Rocks or Red Hills. Located above the plain between Spanish Town and Kingston, this area was filled with pens and small settlements (and, Edward Long noted, had more runaways per square mile than any other area in

---

* Fourteen fugitives were listed as selling in town. Their commodities were limited to wood fuel (three), fodder (one), and fish (three). Two others were also on the docks higgling, one was a dry goods peddler, and what four were selling (or where) was not indicated. That three of the fugitives were also skilled suggests that selling was only a stratagem — Glocester "sculks around during the day" then cuts wood and brings "it to sell in town in the Evening."[19]

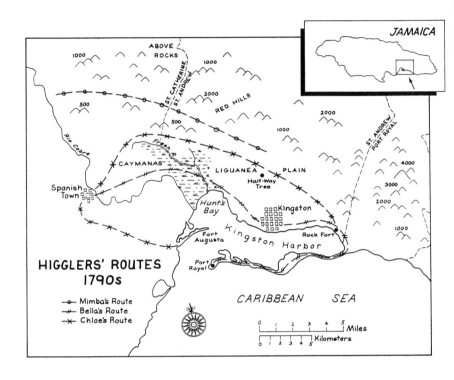

HIGGLERS' ROUTES 1790s

●— Mimba's Route
—✗— Bella's Route
—✕— Chloe's Route

the empire). Third, women plyed the shipping in Port Royal, one of the major ports in the islands and home of the fleet.

Owners could know to the very street, gate, or yard where "their" women were and still not be able to put their hands on them. "Jenny frequents Busgan's Yard near the River in Spanish Town where she higgles"; Cuba sells cake at the corner of Harbour and West streets; and Celia, "well known in Kingston, was seen about Mrs. Dixon's gate in North Street and between there and Sarah Sollas' house in upper King Street." Alcy was described in part as "much about a wherry wharf and the bottom of Orange Street selling spruce beer."[20]

Networks also characterized women in the South Carolina lowcountry, where owners knew where their Charleston women were but could not retake them. Molly, the property of Thomas Smith of Liberty Street, was "supposed to be harboured in that street or by her husband." Jenny, fourteen months a runaway in British-occupied Charleston during the American Revolution, was harbored in King Street. Her owner lived on Queen Street. Like Bridgetown, Charleston was a tight little face-to-face society; Amy, another woman identifed by the street in which she worked, was also known cozily as "this is the same wench that dealt formerly with a certain Jew."[21]

By contrast, networks were rarely used to describe slave women in the Chesapeake Bay region, the ultimate patriarchal society, where, in fact, relatively few women were listed as fugitives. Or, to put the matter more precisely, the ratio of women to men advertised as runaways in the four societies is a fair measure of the extent to which women were active at all in the urban environments in their respective regions. That is, in the Chesapeake Bay region women in any condition or color were seen as most unusual if unattended on the road, let alone in cities. Hence, in Virginia only one fugitive in nine was a woman (and slightly more in Maryland). In South Carolina, Jamaica, and Barbados, however, one in every three to five runaways was a woman, including pregnant women and those nursing infants. Further, if, as I assume future research will show, the percentage of women as runaways and urban sellers is an important and substantial indication of the extent to which slaves dominated the internal markets of their respective societies, a scale may be offered that is very close to that which measures relative degrees of acculturation. One end is the Chesapeake Bay region, where slaves were typically the most assimilated and where women normally did not sell in town; on the other end is Jamaica, where women did market and slaves were comparatively the least assimilated; in the center are South Carolina and Barbados.

# Abbreviations Used in the Notes

*Barb. Merc. and B-T. Gaz.*: *Barbados Mercury & Bridge-Town Gazette*

*Barb. Gaz., and Genl. Intel.*: *Barbados Gazette and General Intelligencer*

*Brit. Parl. Papers*: Irish University Press volumes of the Parliamentary Papers/Slave Trade hearings

*Cornwall Chron.*: *The Cornwall Chronicle and Jamaica General Gazette* [Montego Bay]

*Jam. Merc.*: *Jamaica Mercury and Kingston Weekly Advertizer*

*Jam. Royal Gaz.*: *Jamaica Royal Gazette*

*Md. Gaz.*: *Maryland Gazette.*

P.R.O.: Public Record Office, London (Kew)

Thistlewood's Journal: Manuscript diary of Thomas Thistlewood, Monson 31, Lincolnshire Record Office, Lincoln

*S. C. Gaz.*: *South Carolina Gazette*

*S. C. and Amer. Genl Gaz.*: *South Carolina and American General Gazette*

*S. C. Gaz. and Ct. J.*: *South Carolina Gazette and Country Journal*

*S. C. Royal Gaz.*: *South Carolina Royal Gazette*

S.P.G.: Society for the Propagation of Gospel in Foreign Parts Archives, London

*Va. Gaz.*: *Virginia Gazette*

# Notes

## Introduction

1. I worked on the problem of time and space in comparative views of slavery in the 1970s in a series of conference papers for meetings of the American Historical Association in 1972, the Southern Historical Association in 1974, and the Organization of American Historians in 1975. These concerned, respectively, religion, the internal economy, and resistance to 1807. Parts were published as "Slave Obeahmen and Slaveowning Patriarchs in an Era of War and Revolution (1776–1807)," in *Comparative Perspectives on Slavery in New World Plantation Societies*, ed. Vera Rubin and Arthur Tuden, *Annals of the New York Academy of Science* 292 (June 1977): 481–90; and "British Caribbean and North American Slaves in an Era of War and Revolution, 1775–1807," in *Southern Experiences in the American Revolution*, ed. Jeffrey J. Crow and Larry E. Tise (Chapel Hill, 1978), 235–67. In the 1980s, I extended my research into the nineteenth century and focused on maroons, missions, and gender, see "Women and the Comparative Study of Slavery," *Slavery and Abolition* 6 (May 1985): 23–40.

2. Michael Craton, *Testing the Chains: Resistance to Slavery in the British West Indies* (Ithaca, 1982).

3. Stanley M. Elkins, "The Slavery Debate," *Commentary* 60 (Dec. 1975): 40–1, repr. in Elkins, *Slavery: A Problem in American Intellectual and Institutional Life,* 3d ed. (1959, Chicago, 1968). For a more recent and refined restatement, see August Meier and Elliott Rudwick, *Black History and the Historical Profession, 1815–1980* (Urbana, 1986), 249ff, 267.

4. For the resistance or community and culture approach, see John Blassingame, *The Slave Community: Plantation Life in the Antebellum South* (1972, rev. ed., New York, 1979); John F. Szwed, "An American Anthropological Dilemma: The Politics of Afro-American Culture," in *Reinventing Anthropology,* ed. Dell Hymes (1969, New York, 1972), 153–81, esp. 162f on the social pathology or "deficient

culture" approach. The most thoughtful statement to date remains Sidney W. Mintz and Richard Price, *An Anthropological Approach to the Afro-American Past: A Caribbean Perspective* (Philadelphia, 1976).

5. Roger Bastide, *African Civilizations in the New World* (1967, repr. New York, 1971); and, Bastide, *The African Religions of Brazil: Toward a Sociology of the Interpenetration of Civilizations* (1960, repr. Baltimore, 1978).

6. Willie Lee Rose, ed., *Slavery and Freedom*, exp. ed. by William H. Freehling (New York, 1982), 31; cf. Seymour Dresher's review of Craton, *Testing the Chains, Journal of Social History* 18 (Fall 1984): 149–51.

7. Gerald W. Mullin, *Flight and Rebellion: Slave Resistance in Eighteenth-Century Virginia* (New York, 1972).

8. Earl of Balcarres to the Duke of Portland, Jamaica, March 23, 1800, C.O. 137/104.

9. The phrase is T. C. McCaskie's from "Anti-witchcraft Cults in Asante: An Essay in the Social History of an African People," *History in Africa* 8 (1981): 146.

## Chapter One. Naming Africans

1. *Jamaica Royal Gazettte [Jam. Royal Gaz.]*, July 25, 1795-Supplement, Mary Bees, advertiser. Hereafter for Jamaican newspapers *S.* or *P.S.* will stand for the supplement or postscript of the particular edition cited. Occasionally two newspapers with the same title will be distinguished by their respective editors, whose names appear in parenthesis, for example, *Virginia Gazette* (Purdie and Dixon).

2. *Jam. Royal Gaz.*, June 29, 1799-P.S., Elizabeth Burton.

3. I first explored the terms that whites applied to incoming Africans in Gerald W. Mullin, *Flight and Rebellion: Slave Resistance in Eighteenth-Century Virginia* (New York, 1972), 17f.

4. *Jam. Royal Gaz.*, Jan. 3, 1801-P.S., William Robertson.

5. For background, begin with J. H. Parry, *Trade and Dominion: The European Oversea Empires in the Eighteenth Century* (1971, repr. London, 1974); Parry, *The Spanish Seaborne Empire* (New York, 1966); and C. R. Boxer, *Four Centuries of Portuguese Expansion, 1415–1825* (1961, repr. Berkeley, 1969).

6. See Peter H. Wood, " 'More Like a Negro Country': Demographic Patterns in Colonial South Carolina, 1700–1740," in *Race and Slavery in the Western Hemisphere: Quantitative Studies*, ed. Stanley L. Engerman and Eugene D. Genovese (Princeton, 1975), 131–71.

7. Richard Sheridan, *Sugar and Slavery: An Economic History of the British West Indies, 1623–1775* (Baltimore, 1973), 124ff.

8. Michael Craton, *Testing the Chains: Resistance to Slavery in the British West Indies* (Ithaca, 1982), 254.

9. Landon Carter, cited in Jack P. Greene, *Landon Carter: An Inquiry into the Personal Values and Social Imperatives of the Eighteenth-Century Gentry* (Charlottesville, 1965), 26. For background, see Mullin, *Flight and Rebellion*, ch. 1; Rhys Isaac, *The Transformation of Virginia, 1740–1790* (Chapel Hill, 1982), chs. 1–2; and Allan Kulikoff, *Tobacco and Slaves, the Development of Southern Cultures in the Chesapeake, 1680–1800* (Chapel Hill, 1986), chs. 1–2.

10. Mullin, *Flight and Rebellion,* 23ff.

11. Ibid., ch. 2.

12. This section is based on Sheridan, *Sugar and Slavery;* and Barry W. Higman, *Slave Population and Economy in Jamaica, 1807–1834* (Cambridge, 1976).

13. For the demography of eighteenth-century South Carolina, see Peter H. Wood, *Black Majority: Negroes in Colonial South Carolina from 1670 through the Stono Rebellion* (New York, 1974), 142–66, 218–20; and Wood, " 'More Like a Negro Country.' "

14. C. Vann Woodward, *Thinking Back: The Perils of Writing History* (Baton Rouge, 1986), 127–28. The estimates of ratios stem from the work of Marvin L. Michael Kay and Lorin Lee Cury, " 'They Are Indeed the Constant Plague of Their Tyrants': Slave Defense of a Moral Economy in Colonial North Carolina, 1748–1772," *Slavery and Abolition* 6 (Dec. 1985): 45; and Philip D. Morgan, "Colonial South Carolina Runaways: Their Significance for Slave Culture," *Slavery and Abolition* 6 (Dec. 1985): Table 2, p. 61.

15. *Jam. Royal Gaz.,* April 8, May 6, 1780-S., Daniel Singer; Simon Taylor to Chalonder Archdeckne, Mullet Hall, St. Thomas in the East, Sept. 3, 1787, box 2, bundle 13, Vanneck MS, Manuscripts Room, Cambridge University Library.

16. Henry Laurens to James Grant, April 26, 1765, bundle 659, John Graham to Grant [Savannah, Ga.], Jan. 25, 1769, bundle 401, Grant-MacPherson Papers, Ballindalloch Castle, Scotland. Cf. Daniel Littlefield, *Rice and Slaves: Ethnicity and the Slave Trade in Colonial South Carolina* (Baton Rouge, 1981), ch. 1.

17. *The Papers of Henry Laurens,* 9 vols., ed. Philip M. Hamer and George Rogers, Jr., et al. (Columbia, S.C., 1968–79), 1:252, 270, 333, 334; 2:348, 358.

18. *South Carolina Gazette* [*S. C. Gaz.*], Aug. 13, 1737, plantation of Isaac Porcher; see also *South Carolina Gazette and Country Journal* [*S. C. Gaz. and Ct. J.*], workhouse inmate notices Oct. 11, Nov. 15, 1774, Jan. 31, 1775.

19. Will of Thomas Waring in *Virginia Colonial Records,* 5 vols., ed. Beverley Fleet (Richmond, 1931–38), 14:23–24; [May?] 1724 entry, Robert Carter Diary, 1722–24, Carter Papers, Alderman Library, University of Virginia; Carter to John Pemberton, July 23, 1728, Carter Letterbook, 1728–29, Virginia Historical Society, Richmond; John Carter to Richard Gilbart, Shirley, August 1, 1738, no. 4996, Carter-Wellford Papers, Alderman Library, University of Virignia.

20. Caroline County Order Book, July 9, Aug. 13, 1752, microfilm reel no. 16; Aug. 21, Nov. 20, 1759, Fairfax County Minute Book 1756–63, Virginia State Library, Richmond.

21. James Wedderburn to William Vassal, Oct. 11, 1771; William Vassal Letterbooks, 1769–96, Archives Department, Central Library, Sheffield.

22. Daniel Warner to Benjamin Spencer and Co., Antigua, March 14, 1756, no. 60549/246, Spencer-Stanhope Cannon Hall Muniments, Archives Department, Central Library, Sheffield.

23. Malcolm Laing to William Philip Perrin [Kingston, Jamaica], Jan. 10, 1773, E16753–54, Fitzherbert-Perrin Papers, Derbyshire Record Office, Matlock.

24. John Jacques to Perrin, Feb. 8, 1794, E17141, Fitzherbert-Perrin Papers.

25. John Ferguson to Hugh Hamilton, Feb. 25, 1786, Hugh of Penmore Muniments, GD142/2/1, no. 32, Scottish Record Office, Edinburgh.

26. Taylor to Archedeckne, Mullet Hall, St. Thomas in the East, Sept. 3, 1787, box 2, item 13, Vanneck MS; Journals of Thomas Thistlewood [Thistlewood's Journal], Oct. 13, 1763, March 17, 1761, Monson 31, Lincolnshire Record Office, Lincoln.

27. James Pinnock Plantation Journal, 1756–93, Oct. 22, 1781 entry, British Library, Addit. MSS, 33,316.

28. James Wedderburn to Samuel Vassall, April 15, Sept. 13, 1774, William Vassall Letterbooks; William Beckford, Jr., *Remarks upon the Situation of the Negroes in Jamaica* (London, 1788), 23–24; see also, Laing to Perrin, Jan. 10, 1773, E16753–54, Fitzherbert-Perrin Papers.

29. "Negro and Stock Accts For York Estate, 1778 and 1782," 3/c/1–2i, Gale-Morant Papers, Roborough Library, University of Exeter; see also, Inventory of Good Hope Estate Slaves, 1804, 55/7/132.2, Tharp Papers, Cambridge Record Office.

30. *Jam. Royal Gaz.*, Aug. 26, 1797-P.S., David Owens.

31. "List of Negroes on Kings Valley Estate taken 1 Jan[uar]y 1807," no. 1455, Penrhyn Papers, Department of Manuscripts, University College of North Wales Library, Bangor; Deposition of William Stevenson, Esqr., C.O. 140/84, p. 39; attorney's report, letterbook fragment (1801–5) of Scarlett (no first name) minor and owner of Peru Estate, Langsdale MS, University of Hull Archives.

32. "[Ac]count of the Number of Slaves exported from [Cape Coast Castle] Gold Coast of Africa to his Maj[esty's] Plantations . . . in America Since 1757," no. 41, bundle 471, Dickinson Papers, 1.1, Somerset Record Office, Taunton. The Tobago census is in Lt. Gov. William Young to the Sec. of State, April 29, 1772, C.O. 101/16, f. 126ff; see also, "State of the Island of Tobago from the 24th June 1771 to 1st of May 1773," in Gov. Leyborne to Dartmouth, Grenada, July 17, 1773, C.O. 101/17, f. 181.

33. From a pocketbook, "Barbados Memorandums, Prices &c" [1772–82], E23918, Fitzherbert-Perrin Papers.

34. Bryan Edwards, *The History, Civil and Commercial, of the British Colonies in the West Indies*, 2 vols. (Dublin, 1793), 2:65. To the familiar contemporary reference that Coramantee were "all born heroes," may be added the following from a planter's manual: They are "habituated to war from infancy" and consequently are athletic, independent-minded, and dangerous. In the Windward Islands whites will buy them only if they are infant, except in Tobago which has been plagued with insurrections. *A Professional Planter; Practical Rules for the Management and Medical Treatment of Negro Slaves, in the Sugar Colonies* (London, 1811), 35–36.

35. *Jam. Royal Gaz.*, June 29, 1799-P.S., Elizabeth Burton; Oct. 21, 1797-P.S., John Kelly.

36. For South Carolina, *South Carolina Gazette* [*S.C. Gaz.*], Sept. 6, 1773, John Champneys; and for Virginia, *Virginia Gazette* [*Va. Gaz.*], Nov. 5, 1726, Benjamin Neddler; March 1, 1737, Philip Lightfoot.

37. [Kingston] *Daily Advertiser*, July 16, 1790, J. Stokes; *Jam. Royal Gaz.*, May 23, 1801-S., S. Waddington and Co.

38. *Jam. Royal Gaz.,* Feb. 22, 1794-P.S., W. Weir; Jan. 3, 1801, Francis Ashir; July 4, 1801-S., Richard Brooks. See also, Thistlewood's Journal, June 19, 1765, for the new Negro Damsel. Maureen Warner's Trinidadian informants remember Chamba as having three marks on either cheek, "Africans in Nineteenth Century Trinidad," *African Studies Association of the West Indies Bulletin* 5 (Dec. 1972):

39. For evidence that some slaves used ritual scarring into the second generation, see notices for scars or filed teeth on Creoles in *Jam. Royal Gaz.,* Jan. 19, 1782-S., George McCormack; Aug. 26, 1780, Joseph Gaskarth; and *Cornwall Chronicle and Jamaica General Gazette* [*Cornwall Chron.*], Oct. 3, 1789-S., James Findlater.

39. Public Record Office, War Office/25/644, p. 118, Feb. 18, 1820 entry.

40. *Va. Gaz.* (Purdie and Dixon), Dec. 12, 1771, Peter Pelham; *Maryland Gazette* [*Md. Gaz.*], Sept. 13, 1745, Anne Greenfield; Aug. 20, 1761, George Washington; *S.C. Gaz.,* Nov. 27, 1755; see also, ibid., Feb. 12, 1737, Richard Wright; Feb. 16, 1768, workhouse notice for a Yallunka new Negro; July 5, 1768; Nov. 27, 1755, Oct. 18, 1769 (for Molly); Jan. 7, 1764, John Guerard; *S.C. Gaz. and Ct. J.,* March 3, 1767 (for Peter). For a good series of descriptions, see those of the public jailer Michael Kateisen, ibid., Sept. 27, 1774-S.; *Va. Gaz.,* Oct. 10, 1745, Margaret Arbuthnott; Sept. 16, 1773, P. Pelham; (Rind), July 12, 1770, William Dudley; (Dixon and Nixon), Dec. 18, 1779, S. Calland.

41. *Jam. Royal Gaz.,* Jan. 18, 1794-P.S., I. Pearkins; Aug. 17, 1782-S., Dr. R. Davies; April 6, 1793-P.S.; Overseer at Dry River Course [Kingston] *Daily Advertiser,* Jan. 9, 1790, James Lawrence.

42. Cf. Sidney W. Mintz and Richard Price, *An Anthropological Approach to the Afro-American Past: A Caribbean Perspective* (Philadelphia, 1976), 7, 9–11; and Laura Tanna, "African Retentions: Yoruba and KiKongo Songs in Jamaica," *Jamaica Journal* 16 (Aug. 1983): 47–52.

43. *Cornwall Chron.,* Nov. 10, 1792-S., Thomas Deane; *Jam. Royal Gaz.,* July 25, 1795-S., Mary Bees; Nov. 17, 1781-S., Richard Saunders; Jan. 3, 1801-P.S., Sam Wolinwood; see also, Fanny an Ibo who "says she is Mundingo . . . and speaks Eboe, Mundingo and English very well": May 11, 1782-S., James Watson.

How discriminating were the advertisers concerning the real linguistic abilities of their runaways? A 1768 inventory, "Description of House Negroes," from multilingual Dominica, listed the following: (1) an Antiguan Creole who spoke English "well" and "understands" French; (2) another as simply "speaks" English and French; (3) a Barbadian Creole who speaks "tolerable" English and "understands French a little"; and (4) a Creole from Guadeloupe as "speaks Negroe French and English": box 3/1, Balfour-Melville Muniments, Scottish Record Office.

44. *Jam. Royal Gaz.,* June 29, 1799-P.S., Elizabeth Burton; March 1, 1794-P.S., Richard Saunders; [Kingston] *Daily Advertiser,* Sept. 1, 1790, Jacob Pereira and Co.

45. Ibid., Nov. 28, 1801-S., Cleland and Bull; Oct. 20, 1781-S, John Cosens; see also, "Socco Country, talks Coramantee," *Jam. Merc.,* Dec. 4, 1779-S., Mathew Hinegan.

46. *Jam. Royal Gaz.,* April 11, 1801-P.S., William Christie; May 25, 1805-S., John Deans; Oct. 21, 1797-P.S., John Kelly (cf. *Cornwall Chron.,* Dec. 21, 1776-

S., M. Hunt). For a new Negro boy who did not speak English and who was advertised as either Coramantee or Chamba, see [Kingston] *Daily Advertiser,* July 13, 1790 (Apply to the printer).

47. *Va. Gaz.* (Purdie and Dixon), Jan 28, 1773; ibid. (Purdie), Oct. 20, 1775, M. Wills or James Moore; June 27, 1777, Peter Many; see also (Purdie), Nov. 21, 1777, Mary Wills; (Rind), Sept. 5, 1777, Ed Hurst; *Jam. Royal Gaz.,* July 18, 1795-S., David Cumming.

48. *S.C. Gaz.,* June 22, 1734, Roger Saunders; *South Carolina and American General Gazette,* June 3, 1774, John Savage.

49. *Barbados Mercury and Bridge-Town Gazette,* Dec. 20, 1788, Jonathan Perkins; Nov. 19, 1805, Francis Greenridge.

50. *Va. Gaz.* (Rind), Sept. 22, 1768, John Daniel; *S.C. Gaz.,* Aug. 31, 1765; *S.C. Gaz. and Ct. J.* (Clinch), Sept. 6, 1768; *Va. Gaz.* (Purdie), Oct. 16, 1778, Hampshire County jailer; *S.C. Gaz. and Ct. J.,* Feb. 7, 1767, Jan 3, 1769; see also, March 22, 1774, John Hutchins Jr.; *S.C. Gaz.,* Dec. 3, 1768, workhouse notice for Toby; and the discussion in Mullin, *Flight and Rebellion,* 41–42, 45–46. For reckoning time by phases of the moon in West Africa, see John Beecham, *Ashantee and the Gold Coast* (London, 1841), 185; and John Duncan, *Travels in Western Africa in 1845 and 1846, comprising a Journey from Whydah . . . ,* 2 vols. (London, 1847), 1:219.

51. C.O. 152/22, f. 313; Gersham Ely to the President of the Council, St. Ann, April 9, 1734, C.O. 137/55, f. 209v; [Anon.], *A Short Journey in the West Indies in which Are Interspersed Curious Anecdotes and Characters* (London, 1790), 72 (British Library pressmark 10480 aa. 12); *Brit. Parl. Papers, Slave Trade* (1823–24), 66/108. When a Jamaican conspirator was asked in 1791 when they would rise, he replied "when the corn was ready to eat at a state called Mutton Corn," C.O. 137/90, f. 53. For the lowcountry Gullah, who "have no knowledge at all of numbers," see Dec. 26, 1863, Arthur Sumner letters (typescript), vol. 4, Penn School Records, Southern Historical Collection, Chapel Hill, N.C.

52. Orlando Patterson, *The Sociology of Slavery: An Analysis of the Origins, Development and Structure of Negro Slave Society in Jamaica* (1967, repr. Rutherford, 1969), 150; Mintz and Price, *An Anthropological Perspective,* 22–23.

53. *Cornwall Chron.,* Jan. 2, 30, Feb. 6, June 5, 1790.

54. *S.C. Gaz.,* Sept. 1, 1759 (for Betty); *Cornwall Chron.,* Aug. 22, 1789-S., William Campbell; see also *S.C. Gaz. and Ct. J.,* Oct. 11, 1774, George Parker.

55. *Jam. Royal Gaz.,* Nov. 30, 1799-P.S., Alexander McInnis; April 13, 1793-P.S., A. Fitzgerald.

56. Ibid., July 29, 1809-P.S., p. 28, Francis Asher.

57. *Va. Gaz.,* Sept. 26, 1745, Aaron Trueheart.

58. Ibid., June 23, 1768, Gibson and Granbe.


## Chapter Two. Africans Name Themselves

1. Edward Long, *The History of Jamaica,* 3 vols. (1774, repr. London, 1970), 2:310.

2. The literature is vast, but for a good sense of the story's possibilities, see

Daniel P. Mannix with Malcolm Cowley, *Black Cargoes: A History of the Atlantic Slave Trade, 1518–1865* (New York, 1962); Philip D. Curtin, *The Atlantic Slave Trade: A Census* (Madison, 1969); James A. Rawley, *The Transatlantic Slave Trade: A History* (New York, 1981); and the work of Herbert S. Klein and Joseph Miller.

3. Olaudah Equiano, *Equiano's Travels; His Autobiography: The Interesting Narrative of Olaudah Equiano, or Gustavus Vassa, the African. Written by Himself . . .*, abridged and ed. Paul Edwards (1789, repr. London, 1967), 25–26, 30–31.

4. Long, *History of Jamaica,* 2:397; Elizabeth Donnan, ed., *Documents Illustrative of the History of the Slave Trade to America,* 4 vols. (Washington, D.C., 1930), 2:460; House of Commons, Sessional Papers (1790), 29/189; "Captain Shirley's Account, 1693–1694," in John Churchill, *A Collection of Voyages and Travels,* 6 vols. (London, 1750–58), 6:235ff; *Georgia Gazette* [*Ga. Gaz.*], Dec. 29, 1797. Cf. [Mrs. Flannigan], *Antigua and the Antiguans,* 2 vols. (London, 1844), 2:37.

5. *Jamaica Royal Gazette* [*Jam. Royal Gaz.*], Sept. 29, 1781-S., William Butler.

6. Ibid. July 27, 1805-S., George Spering; April 28, 1792-P.S., Wallens Plantation; Feb. 18, 1792-P.S., Cabbage Valley Estate overseer; see also, April 13, 1793-P.S., John Ingrahm; May 11, 1793-P.S., Alex. Kiffock; March 1, 1794-P.S., Thomas Fox; July 1, 1797-S., Dunsinnane. For men and women who were countrymen and shipmates, see, four Gold Coast slaves: *Jam. Royal Gaz.,* June 9, 1792-P. S., Thomas Raffington; five Moco: June 2, 1792-P.S., George Rodon; four "Portuguese Congo" to St. Thomas in the Vale where they have "countrymen and shipmates": May 30, 1795-S., Thomas Fox; three Mandingo: *Cornwall Chronicle and Jamaica General Gazette* [*Cornwall Chron.*], Jan. 12, 1782-S., William Melvin.

7. [Kingston] *Daily Advertiser,* Dec. 7, 1790, Samuel Stone; *Jam. Royal Gaz.,* March 28, 1801-S., Lawrence Cashin; April 13, 1793-P.S., A. Fitzgerald; March 1, 1794-P.S., Richard Saunders.

8. *Jam. Royal Gaz.,* Sept. 6, 1794-P.S., Robert Loosely; [Kingston] *Daily Advertiser,* Jan. 23, 1790, Richard Jones. "They [the runaways] are so expert with their Bows that they will shoot the Swiftest flying Bird upon [the] wing," "Journal of a Voyage to Jamaica, 1823–24," Jan. 1824 entry, p. 37, MS 17956, National Library of Scotland, Edinburgh.

9. See the *Cornwall Chron.* issues for Jan. and Feb. 1790, esp. Jan. 2-S., Isaac Woofe; June 5-S., Charles Loughnan; Feb. 6, 1790, John Stokes; and Jan. 30, 1790-S., J. L. Watt. [Kingston] *Daily Advertiser,* Oct. 18, 1790, John Wheeler. The last two notices, for groups of seven and eight, were among the largest reported.

10. *Jam. Royal Gaz.,* July 21, 1792-S., William Hudson; June 30, 1801-S., T. S. Kuckahn; Journals of Thomas Thistlewood [Thistlewood's Journal], Jan. 28, 1756, Monson 31, Lincolnshire Record Office, Lincoln; see also, *Jam. Royal Gaz.,* Jan. 17, 1801-S., William D. Hall.

11. Ibid., May 25, 1782-S., Alex Fraser; Aug. 24, 1782-S., Simon Taylor; *Cornwall Chron.,* June 19, 1784-S., Benjamin Davis; *Jam. Royal Gaz.,* May 18, 1793-P.S., P. Churnside. See also, two Coramantee, two Angolans: March 9, 1799-P.S., Duckinfield; three Mandingo, one Foulah: Aug. 15, 1801-S., Morse; two Ibo men and four Congolese (two men and two women): Jan. 24, 1801-S., Lewis Lubin; an

Ibo and two Moco: Jan. 8, 1794-S., Jonathan Ludford; two Nago and a Chamba: Feb. 22, 1794-P.S., N. Weir.

12. *Barbardos Mercury and Bridge-Town Gazette [Barb. Merc. and B-T. Gaz.]*, June 23, 1807, John Griffith; Nov. 12, 1805, John Heyes; Nov. 19, 1805, William B. Baker; also, Oct. 9, 1784, John Agard; Jan. 24, 1807, Pickering's estate.

13. *South Carolina and Country Journal [S.C. Gaz. and Ct. J.]*, (Clinch), Nov. 21, 1769, David Williams; see also, Feb. 25, 1772, Daniel Revenal.

14. *South Carolina Gazette [S.C. Gaz.]*, Feb. 9, 1734, Mr. Paine's plantation; Oct. 2, 1758, William Smith.

15. Ibid., July 28, 1766, George Smith; Feb. 1, 1759, William Smith; Feb. 9, 1767, White Outebridge; see also, *S.C. Gaz. and Ct. J.* (Clinch), Dec. 4, 1770, William Webb; *South Carolina and American General Gazette,* Nov. 18, 1774, John Strothar; *S.C. Gaz.,* Feb. 24, 1767, Robert Croft.

16. *Maryland Gazette and Baltimore Advertiser* (Dunlop's), Dec. 2, 1777, William Johnson; *Virginia Gazette [Va. Gaz.]*, June 23, 1768, Gibson and Granbe.

17. *Va. Gaz.* (Purdie and Dixon), Oct. 28, 1773, John Burnley; Oct. 20, 1768, Jordan Anderson; see also, Nov. 2, 1739, John Shelton; May 16, 1745, William Hunter; (Purdie and Dixon), Sept. 12, 1771, George Robertson.

18. See breast and belly burnt "pretty much [from] sleeping near a fire," had on a shirt only: *S.C. Gaz. and Ct. J.* (Clinch), Jan. 16, 1770, taken up at Lucas' Old Field — Wappo; "nothing on but a blanket": Jan. 9, 1762; gunshot wounds, frostbite, fire burns: Sept. 7, 1734 for London; *S.C. Gaz. and Ct. J.,* March 1, 1774, for Sarah; Feb. 11, 1766-S., taken up on Elias Ball's plantation; "entirely naked, and their Feet and Legs are swelled very much by lying in the Cold": *S.C. Gaz.,* Jan. 3, 1771, William Heatly.

19. Monica Schuler, "Akan Slave Rebellions in the British Caribbean," *Savacou* 1 (1970): 8–31.

20. Thistlewood's Journal, May 26, 1760. The unfolding of the rebellion may be followed in entries between May and Dec. For the St. Mary's origins of the rising, see Long, *History of Jamaica,* 2: 447ff; Bryan Edwards, *The History, Civil and Commercial, of the British Colonies in the West Indies,* 2 vols. (Dublin, 1793), 2:59–63; and William J. Gardner, *A History of Jamaica from Its Discovery by Christopher Columbus to the Year 1872* (London, 1873, repr. 1971), 132ff. For another vivid eyewitness account, see Simon Taylor to Chalonder Archedeckne, Kingston, Dec. 9, 1765, box 2, bundle 1, Vanneck MS, Manuscripts Room, Cambridge University Library.

21. Thistlewood's Journal, May 26, 29, June 2, Sept. 30, Oct. 3, 1760.

22. Ibid., May 29, 30, June 20, July 27, Sept. 30, 1760.

23. Ibid., Sept. 27, Oct. 19, 26, Nov. 9, 1760; see J. Omosade Awolalu and P. Adelumo Dopamu, *West African Traditional Religion* (Ibadan, 1979), 269.

24. Thistlewood's Journal, May 28, 31, June 7, July 29, 1760.

25. Ibid., June 4, 19, July 17, Aug. 1, 27, Sept. 2, 1760.

26. Ibid., Oct. 24, 1760.

27. Oct. 5, 1766 entry, Pinnock Plantation Journal, 1756–93, British Library, Addit. MSS, 33,316; Roger Hope Elletson to Brig. Gen. Lewis, Hope Estate (Jamaica),

Oct. 18, 1766, Elletson Letterbook, Institute of Jamaica, Kingston; Thistlewood's Journal, Oct. 6, 1766.

28. C.O. 9/9, f. 66; C.O. 9/10; David Barry Gaspar, *Bondmen and Rebels: A Study of Master-Slave Relations in Antigua* (Baltimore, 1985), 253: "the *ikem* dance was above all a formal declaration of war."

29. *Great Newes from the Barbadoes, or a True and Faithful Account of the Grand Conspiracy of the Negroes against the English, & the Happy Discovery of the Same with the Number of those that were burned alive, Beheaded, and Otherwise Executed for their Horrid Crimes....* (London, 1676), 9–10 (British Library pressmark 1197g5).

30. Thistlewood's Journal, Dec. 4, 1760. The west coast contact of the Coramantee rebel Wager was also the father of Thistlewood's employer. See the Royal African Company records: John Roberts to Captain Thomas Hill, Dec. 1, 1749, Royal African Company Letterbook (Oct. 1748-Jan. 1750), f. 37, Public Record Office, Treasury 70/1746, wherein the senior Cope is mentioned as "primal manager of the Company's Affairs, on the Gold Coast [and later] Chief of Commenda [Castle]."

31. See John J. Te Paske, "The Fugitive Slave: Intercolonial Rivalry and Spanish Slave Policy, 1687–1764," in *Eighteenth-Century Florida and Its Borderlands*, ed. Samuel Proctor (Gainesville, 1975), 1–12; Lt. Gov. William Bull to the Duke of Newcastle, May 9, 1739, C.O. 5/388 (1), f. 159. For archaeological excavations at Fort Mose, the black refugee settlement at the North River on the outskirts of St. Augustine, see *New York Times*, Feb. 26, 1987, p. 1; and Jane Landers, "Garcia Real de Santa Teresa de Mose: A Free Black Town in Spanish Colonial Florida," *American Historial Review* 95 (Feb. 1990): 9–30.

32. Lt. Gov. William Bull to Newcastle, Oct. 5, 1739, C.O. 5/388 (1), ff. 164–65v; Allan D. Chandler, ed., *The Colonial Records of the State of Georgia* (New York [1904–16], repr. 1970), 22: 233–35; Michael Mullin, ed., *American Negro Slavery: A Documentary History* (New York, 1976), 84–88; see also, the Report to the Council, Jan. 19, 1739, Upper House Journal no. 7, South Carolina Department of Archives and History, Columbia; James H. Easterby, ed., *Colonial Records of South Carolina, Journal of the Council House of Assembly* (Columbia, 1951), 595–96.

33. Eugene Sirman's argument that Stono was "less an insurrection than an attempt by slaves to fight their way to St. Augustine" is correct, see *Colonial South Carolina: A Political History, 1663–1763* (Chapel Hill, 1966), 208. For another point of view — that Stono was a climax — see Peter H. Wood, *Black Majority: Negroes in Colonial South Carolina from 1670 through the Stono Rebellion* (New York, 1974), ch. 12. For the important international context, see Darold D. Wax, " 'The Great Risque We Run': The Aftermath of Slave Rebellion at Stono, South Carolina, 1739–1745," *Journal of Negro History* 67 (Summer 1982): 136–47.

34. *S.C. Gaz.*, Dec. 7, 1739, James Bullock.

35. "Extract of a Letter from S. Carolina dated Oct. 2" [1739], *The Gentleman's Magazine*, new ser. 10 (1740): 128; see also, Report to the Council, Jan. 19, 1739, Upper House Journal no. 7, South Carolina Department of Archives and History,

Columbia; and Wax, " 'The Great Risque We Run,' " 136–37. Stono was not a climax. The 1740s were more troublesome for whites with regard to rebellious slaves; during the era of the American Revolution and into the 1780s, runaways set up in camps on the lower reaches of the Savannah River. See Thomas R. Statom, "Negro Slavery in Eighteenth-Century Georgia," Ph.D. diss., University of Georgia, 1982, 208f, 210–12.

36. Prince George County, St. Paul's Parish, Court Record Liber X, 1738–40, 573ff; Somerset County Court Levy Accounts for Nov. 1747, 1751, and 1759, Hall of Records, Annapolis, Md.

37. Sir William Gooch to the Board of Trade, Williamsburg, June 29, 1729, C.O. 5/1322, 19 Virginia Colonial Records Project, Colonial Williamsburg Research Center.

38. Byrd to Mr. [Johann Rudolph] Ochs, n.d. [summer 1729], *Virginia Magazine of History and Biography* 9 (Jan. 1902): 225.

39. The seed for this discussion was the discovery in a 1795 issue of the *Jam. Royal Gaz.* (Nov. 14, 1795-S.) of excerpts of a soldier's diary that provided another meaning for Cudjoe's notorious gesture when, during the negotiations that led to the treaty between the whites and Maroons, he apparently embraced the boots of the commander of the whites' forces. My revisions were in "Jamaican Maroon Women and the Cultural Dimension of American Negro Slavery," which concerns Maroon population growth and family, presented to the Richmond American History Seminar, Virginia Commonwealth University, Nov. 1979, and to the Twelfth Annual Conference of Caribbean Historians at The University of the West Indies, St. Augustine, Trinidad, March-April 1980. Cf. Kenneth Bilby and Filomina Chioma Steady, "Black Women and Survival: A Maroon Case," in *The Black Woman Cross-Culturally*, ed. Filomina Chioma Steady (Cambridge, Mass., 1981), 451–67.

40. Gov. Edward Trelawny to the Duke of Newcastle, Dec. 4, 1738, C.O. 137/56, ff. 158. Cf. John Gregory to the Sec. of State, Oct. 9, 1735, C.O. 135/55, f. 209v; and Lt. Gov. Balcarres to the Duke of Portland, Headquarters, Dromilley, near Wills (Jamaica), Nov. 16, 1795, C.O. 137/96.

41. In addition to Richard Price's useful *Maroon Societies: Rebel Slave Communities in the Americas* (1973, repr. Baltimore, 1979), see Philip Wright, "War and Peace with the Maroons, 1730-1739," *Caribbean Quarterly* 16 (1970): 5–27, the best interpretation of its kind, and Kenneth Bilby, "Jamaica's Maroons at the Cross Roads, Losing Touch with Tradition," *Caribbean Review* 9 (Fall 1980): 18ff. For a Maroon view, see Johannes King, "Guerrilla Warfare: A Bush Negro View," in *Maroon Societies*, ed. Price, 298–311.

42. For a sense of the long and often sharp exchanges in the historiography see, for the eighteenth century, Philip Thicknesse, *Memoirs and Anecdotes* (Dublin, 1790), 77; Robert C. Dallas, *The History of the Maroons, From their Origin to the Establishment of Their Chief Tribe at Sierra Leone. . . .*, 2 vols. (London, 1803, repr. 1968), 1: 26ff, 78ff. For the present, see Barbara Klamon Kopytoff, "Jamaican Maroon Political Organization: The Effects of the Treaties," *Social and Economic Studies* 25 (June 1976): 87–105; Eugene D. Genovese, *From Rebellion*

to Revolution: *Afro-American Slave Revolts in the Making of the Modern World* (Baton Rouge, 1979), 36, 118; Orlando Patterson, "Slavery and Slave Revolts: A Socio-Historical Analysis of the First Maroon War, Jamaica, 1655–1740," *Social and Economic Studies* 19 (Sept. 1970): 289–325; and Orlando Patterson, "Slavery, Acculturation and Social Change: The Jamaica Case," *British Journal of Sociology* 17 (June 1966): 155ff.

43. Thistlewood's Journal, March 5, 1751, July 7, Aug. 1, 1760; "Examination of Charles of Bluehole . . . Monday July 29th, 1776," in C.O. 137/71, f. 288; "Examination of Negro Jamaica," *Jam. Royal Gaz.*, Sept. 19–26, 1795-S., from newspaper clippings forwarded to Balcarres in file 23/11/255, Crawford Muniments, National Library of Scotland. This collection, which was first consulted at the John Rylands University Library of Manchester, includes three boxes of documents concerning Balcarres and the Second Maroon War: incoming letters to the governor, arranged alphabetically in file 23/11/1ff; letters forwarded to Balcarres in file 23/11/91ff; and examinations of slaves, Maroon censuses, memorials, and plans in file 12/11/221ff (23/8 comprise accounts for Balcarres' own Jamaican properties). Items therein are hereafter cited by the box and item numbers. "Examination of Mr. Reid's Jumbo," Lucea, Dec. 27, 1795, in Balcarres to Portland, Dec. 30, 1795, C.O. 137/96. See also, Long, *History of Jamaica*, 2:338f.

44. Thistlewood's Journal, Oct. 23, 1750; Dallas, *History of the Maroons*, 2:251–52. When taken up, a runaway woman said that she had been raised by the Maroons and apparently given ritual scars, which were identified as "Coramantee," *Jam. Royal Gaz.*, Aug. 26, 1780, Joseph Gaskarth. When Asante from the Gold Coast (taken from a foreign slaver by the Royal navy after the British prohibited the trade) were resettled in Sierra Leone, Maroons there (who had once lived in Trelawny Town, Jamaica) welcomed them as countrymen: Christopher Fyfe, *A History of Sierra Leone* (London, 1962), 115.

45. Cited in Patterson, "Slavery and Slave Revolts," 263n.

46. Long, *History of Jamaica*, 2:445.

47. Balcarres to Portland (Jamaica), March 26, 1796, C.O. 137/96; Bryan Edwards, "Introduction," *The Proceedings of the Governor and Assembly of Jamaica in Regard to the Maroon Negroes. . . .* (London, 1796), 318.

48. Concerning the Maroons' military prowess, see Memorandum from Trelawny to Newcastle, Dec. 4, 1738, C.O. 137/56, ff. 158ff; cf. the same from Lt. Gov. Robert Hunter, the Council and Assembly, Feb. 21, 1733, C.O. 140/25.

49. Lt. Gov. Keith to Lord Germaine, Jamaica, Aug. 6, 1776, C.O. 137/71, ff. 230–30v. Cf. Robert Hunter to Germaine, Knightsbridge [London], Dec. 27, 1779, C.O. 137/73, f. 250; and Jamaican agent Stephen Fuller, Southampton Street [London], June 6, 1775, Memorial to the Board of Trade, C.O. 137/71, f. 106v.

50. Lt. Gov. Keith to Lord Germaine, Assembly Memorial to the Government, Dec. 24, 1778, C.O. 137/73, ff. 246v–47. In light of the following, the burden of proof may be on those who argue that officials assumed that the Maroons were reliable allies (Appendix 3). For white mistrust of Maroons in the conspiracy of 1776, see C.O. 137/71, 269v, 274–74v, 288–88v. After an incident at Old Harbour, some feared a combination of new Negroes and Maroons, see John Shickle to John

Pennant, April 16, 1774, no. 1210, Penrhyn Papers, Department of Manuscripts, University College of North Wales Library, Bangor. As late as 1824, during a small uprising on a remote plantation (the "Argyle War"), a local commander of the western interior regiment wrote that the Accompong Maroons were the "instigators," and that the slaves were "acting only a secondary part." A. Campbell to [the Gov.], Argyle, June 14, 1824, half-past 12 o'clock P.M., C.O. 137/156.

51. Keith to Germaine, Dec. 24, 1778, C.O. 137/73,ff. 246v.

52. "Examination of Charles belonging to Bluehole . . . Monday 29th July 1776," enclosed in the Lucea Magistrates to Gov. Keith, July 31, 1776, C.O. 137/71, ff. 288–88v.

53. "Extract of Ebenez[er] Lamb's Journal who commanded a Party to Leeward," Sept. 22, 1732, C.O. 137/54, ff. 116–17.

54. "A Journal of the proceedings of the Parties commanded by Edward Creswell and Ebenezer Lambe, Kept by Ebenezer Lambe" [Feb.-March 1733], C.O. 137/54ff. 162v, 163v; Thicknesse, *Memoirs,* 56ff, 72; Journal of William Lamport and Thomas Williams [Feb.23-March 8, 1735], C.O. 137/55, f. 165. This dimension of Maroon warfare — the horn blowing, shouted insults, and dismembering of foe — ought to be seen in a ritual context as well, cf. David C. Dorward, "Ritual Warfare and the Colonial Conquest of the Eggon," *History in Africa* 11 (1784): 83–98.

55. Patterson, "Slavery and Slave Revolts," 275ff.

56. Lt. Sadler's Journal, extracts for Feb. 13–21, 1739, were reprinted during the 1795 War in the *Jam. Royal Gaz.,* Nov. 7, 1795-S., and reported as enclosed in his Feb. 17, 1738 report to Gov. Trelawny, C.O. 137/56, f. 185. Cudjoe's dance should be compared to Long's description, *History of Jamaica,* 2.:348–49. Also, see Minutes of the Governor's Council, vol. 24, 163ff, Jamaica Archives, Spanish Town; and Commander Guthrie's account, Feb. 17–18, 1738, C.O. 137/56, f. 183.

57. Ebenezer Lamb's Journal, C.O. 137/54, f. 118; for additional inventories of the Maroons' material culture, see C.O. 137/55, f. 58.

58. "Examination of an Ebo Lad Named Cupid" [Jan. 30, 1735], enclosed in John Ayschough to the Duke of Newcastle, Feb. 27, 1735, C.O. 137/55, f. 156, 158.

59. *Jam. Royal Gaz.,* Oct. 24, 1795-S.; "Examination of Robert Montgomery," in Henry Shirley to Balcarres, Falmouth, Nov. 28, 1795, 23/11/74 Crawford Muniments.

60. Eleanor Leacock, "Women's Status in Egalitarian Society," *Current Anthropology* 19 (June 1978): 247–75; Richard B. Lee, "Population Growth and the Beginnings of Sedentary Life Among the !Kung Bushmen," in *Population Growth: Anthropological Implications,* ed. Brian Spooner (Cambridge, Mass., 1972), 329–42; Richard J. Perry, "The Fur Trade and the Status of Women in the Western Subarctic," *Ethnohistory* 26 (Fall 1979): 372–73.

61. "Parasitic" is used by Stuart B. Schwartz, "The Macambo: Slave Resistance in Colonial Bahia," *Journal of Social History* 3 (Summer 1970): 322. Cf. Thomas Flory, "Fugitive Slaves and Free Society: The Case of Brazil," *Journal of Negro History* 64 (Spring 1979): 118f.

62. John Hearne, "The Fugitives in the Forest: Four Novels by Wilson Harris,"

in *The Island in Between: Essays in West Indian Literature,* ed. Louis James (London, 1968), 151.

63. See Appendix 3 and for Maroon population in 1749, British Library, Addit. MSS., 12,435, p. 19; the 1793 census is enclosed in Lt. Gov. Adam Williamson to Henry Dundas, Jan. 23, 1793, C.O. 137/91.

64. James Knight, "The Natural, Moral and Political History of Jamaica . . . to the Year 1742," C. E. Long MS, British Library, Addit. MSS, 12,419, f93, hereafter cited as Knight, *History of Jamaica to 1742.* Important background is provided by Rhett S. Jones, "White Settlers, Black Rebels: Jamaica in the Era of the First Maroon War, 1655–1738," Ph.D. diss., Brown University, 1976, ch. 4.

65. For the transition from runaway bands to settlements, see Richard Price, *'First-Time': The Historical Vision of an Afro-American People* (Baltimore, 1983).

66. In *History of Jamaica to 1742,* Knight says that Cudjoe was the son of a rebel who participated in the major 1690 Coramantee uprising at Sutton's Plantation in Clarendon Parish.

67. For Maroon receptiveness to doctors and clerics (Anglican and Moravian), see a April 29, 1774 letter from Trelawny Town Superintendant John James read at the Governor's Council May 30, 1774, C.O. 140/55; and Samuel Vaughan to Lewis Cathbert, Montego Bay, July 26, 1795, Minutes of Council (May 1, 1792–May 14, 1799), Central Government, Jamaica Archives, Spanish Town; [Anon.], *United Brethren in Jamaica* (London, 1854), 9; Edward Braithwaite, *The Development of Creole Society in Jamaica, 1770–1820* (Oxford, 1971), 249; Balcarres to Portland, Oct. 27, esp. Nov. 16, 1795, C.O. 137/96.

68. Dallas, *History of the Maroons,* 1:112, 114, 2:183n. On the political conflict generated by the decision to exile the Maroons, see Dallas's appendixes; Portland to Balcarres, March 3, 1796, and Balcarres to Portland, Jan. 30, 1796, C.O. 137/96.

69. Dallas, *History of the Maroons,* 1:110–14.

70. Ibid., 1:110–12.

71. Balcarres to Portland, Aug. 14, Oct. 27, 1795, Head Quarters, Vaughan's Field, C.O. 137/96: "They must take the horrid step of murdering all their women . . . I suspect the Children already sacrificed."

72. Dallas, *History of the Maroons,* 1:112–13, 2:222ff; Appendix to C.O. 137/101.

73. Dallas, *History of the Maroons,* 1:93–4.

74. Ibid., 1:105.

75. "Examination of Abraham of Bog Estate," Minutes of Council for Sept. 21, 1795 (May 1, 1792–May 14, 1799), Central Government file, 1B/5/3, Jamaica Archives.

76. "They should be settled near Spanish Town, or some other of the large Towns in the Low Lands. The access to spirits will soon decrease their numbers, & destroy that hardy constitution which is nourished by an healthy, mountainous situation." Walpole to Balcarres, Old Maroon Town, Dec. 24, 1795, C.O. 137/96.

77. Extract of a letter to Mr. William Green, Good Hope, Trelawny, May 15, 1798, C.O. 140/84. James McGhie in Trelawny Parish returns, 1799, is listed with

two other McGhies, Robert and Jonathan, at Greenside. He owned 202 slaves; at another unspecified estate, perhaps Hampstead, he owned 833. Census dated March 28, 1799, C.O. 137/104.

78. "Deposition of Peter of Peru Estate," C.O. 140/84; "Patty's Examination," in Balcarres to Portland, July 28, 1798, C.O. 137/100. This small war is well documented in C.O. 137/99–100, and 140/84; see also, Simon Taylor to Chalonder Archedeckne, Kingston, May 9, 1798, item 22, box 2, Vanneck MS, Manuscripts Room, Cambridge University Library; and Mrs. E. V. Scarlett to her father J. Scarlett, Oct. 22 [1798], Letterbook 1798–1806, Langdale MS, Hull University Archives.

79. For Congo Town, see "Examination of Mr. Reid's Jumbo," Lucea, Dec. 27, 1795, in Balcarres to Portland, Dec. 30, 1795, C.O. 137/96; Dallas, *History of the Maroons,* 1:101; "Jumbo's Examination," Montego Bay, Dec. 30, 1795, in W. D. Quarrell to Balcarres, Montego Bay, Dec. 30, 1795, 2.3/11/51, Crawford Muniments. For Highwindward, see Balcarres to Portland, July 28, 1798, C.O. 137/100. For Me No Sen, see *Cornwall Chron.,* Nov. 13, 1724, p. 785.

80. Balcarres to Portland, July 28, 1798, C.O. 137/100.

81. Juba's examination is enclosed in ibid.

82. Balcarres to Portland, July 28, 1798, C.O. 137/100. The implication is that some towns — self-contained and relatively unobtrusive — were ignored by officials. Even the strenuous Balcarres recognized this policy. In the midst of the 1798 troubles he described a maroon group in the mountains of St. Elizabeth as "the antient occupiers of these fastnesses." They were a "kind" of "Runaways" that was "Impossible" to remove without costs that were "boundless." Balcarres to Portland, April 30, 1798, C.O. 137/99.

83. *Cornwall Chron.,* Nov. 13, 1824, p. 785.

84. Robin Horton, "African Traditional Thought and Western Science," *Africa* 37 (Jan., April 1967): 50–71, 155–88.

85. Interview with Colonel Rowe of Accompong, in Joseph J. Williams, *The Maroons of Jamaica* (Chesnut Hill, 1938), 387f.

86. M. I. Finley, *Aspects of Antiquity; Discoveries and Controversies* (1968, repr. London, 1977), 14.

87. *Cornwall Chron.,* Nov. 13, 1824, p. 785. For a contemporary's precise location of Me No Sen: "from Schroeter's ingenius plan, in the Police Office at the Court-house . . . [Me No Sen] is 7 miles directly S. S. by E. of *Dromilly,* 7 1/2 S of *Pantrepant,* 6 S.W. from *Windsor,* 3 1/2 from *Mount Ridgeway,* & 8 N. of *Accompong Town.*" [Alfred], "Account of a Shooting Excursion on the Mountains near Dromilly Estate, in the Parish of Trelawny . . . October, 1824!!!" (London, 1825) in a "Album of anti-slavery pamphlets" (1820s–30s), Baptist Missionary Society, London. (This collection has been moved to Augus Library, Regent's Park College, Oxford.)

## Chapter Three. The Blood Oath, Play, and Ancestors

1. Charles Leslie, *A New and Exact Account of Jamaica . . . ,* 3d ed. (Edinburgh, 1740), 325.

2. For Akan, the most insightful writings are by T. C. McCaskie, esp. "Anti-Witchcraft Cults in Asante: An Essay in the Social History of an African People," *History in Africa* 8 (1981): 125–54; and "State and Society, Marriage and Adultery: Some Considerations towards a Social History of Pre-Colonial Asante," *Journal of African History* 22 (1981), esp. 484–85.

3. Edward Long, *The History of Jamaica,* 3 vols. (1774, repr. London, 1970), 2:473.

4. Long, *History of Jamaica,* 2:475.

5. See, for example, Melville J. Herskovits, *The Myth of the Negro Past* (Chicago, 1939); and Margaret Washington Creel, '*A Peculiar People*': *Slave Religion and Community-Culture Among the Gullah* (New York, 1988).

6. Journals of Thomas Thistlewood [Thistlewood's Journal], Monson 31, Lincolnshire Record Office, Lincoln, July 21, 1752, Aug. 7, 1767, Oct. 2, 1750, Feb. 5, April 1, 1756; A. B. Ellis, *The Yoruba-Speaking Peoples of the Slave Coast of West Africa. . . .* (London, 1894), 253.

7. "They bury each other promiscuously in the fields, and their near and dear relations at the back of their huts, and sometimes under their beds": J. B. Morton, *West India Customs and Manners* (London, 1793), 162.

8. Thistlewood's Journal, Sept. 18, 1760, July 5, 1767.

9. Ibid., Sept. 7, 1780; cf. Long, *History of Jamaica,* 2:420–21: The slaves' burials are "the very reverse of our English ceremony. . . . [it] is a kind of festival." Missionary reports contrasting the two peoples' funeral styles included a cleric who said that while at a Catholic burial he had heard for the first time crying in the streets at a funeral in the West Indies; another characterized black burials as conveying "almost [a] total absence of . . . Solemnity . . . a feast rather than any thing else"; and another said simply that a proper Christian funeral meant no drumming, dancing, and offerings, and a service read at the grave. J. Crofts, Spanish Town (Jamaica) May 28, 1824, 29/121, Methodist Missionary Society Archives, School of Oriental and African Studies Library, University of London. Hereafter the location of all documents in this collection will be indicated by item and box number, for instance the foregoing is item 29 in box 121; Journal Extracts of T. Hyde, Monteserrat, Feb. 19, June 30, 1824, 12, 29/51; and John Shipman, Montego Bay, May 13, 1820, 1/588.

10. Thistlewood's Journal, March 21, 1758.

11. Leslie, *A New and Exact Account of Jamaica,* 325–26.

12. George Pinckard, *Notes on the West Indies including observations relative to the Creoles and Slaves of the Western Colonies . . . ,* 2 vols. (London, 1816), 1:131–34.

13. Ibid., 132–33.

14. Thistlewood's Journal, July 20, 1754, July 25, 1756.

15. Arthur Holt to Bishop Gibson, Christ Church Parish [Barbados], March 7, 1729, West Indies: vol. 15 (Barbados), f. 266v, Fulham Papers, Lambeth Palace Library, London.

16. Bryan Edwards, *The History, Civil and Commercial, of the British Colonies in the West Indies,* 2 vols. (Dublin, 1793), 2:80.

17. Roger Abrahams defines "play" in *Folklore Studies in the Twentieth Century: Proceedings of the Centenary Conference of the Folklore Society* (1980), ed. Venetia J. Newall, 119–22; cf. Sally Price and Richard Price, *Afro-American Arts of the Suriname Rain Forest* (Berkeley, 1980), 169.

18. S. Allen Counter and David L. Evans, *I Sought My Brother: An Afro-American Reunion* (Cambridge, Mass., 1981), 147–48.

19. "Examinations of Sundry Slaves in the Parish of Trelawny — Jamaica respecting an intention to revolt," see especially examinations of Robert William Linton's Duke, Jan. 5 and 11, 1792. Enclosed in Lt. Gov. Adam Williamson to the Sec. of State, Feb. 12, 1792, C.O. 137/90; plays, dances, and rebellion intertwined in 1823 disturbances: "Copy of all Judicial Procedings relative to the Trial and Punishment of Rebels, or alleged Rebels, in the Island of *Jamaica,* since the 1st of January 1823 . . . ," *Brit. Parl. Papers, Slave Trade* (1825), 67/41, 43, 48, 50, 51–52, 69, 70, 72, 73, 78; and *Cornwall Chronicle and Jamaica General Gazette* [*Cornwall Chron.*], June 4, 1794-S., Henry Thornbill Gibbes; May 10, 1777-S., W. H. Ricketts; *Jamaica Royal Gazette* [*Jam. Royal Gaz.*], March 4, 1797-P.S., Thomas Anderson; Frederic G. Cassidy, *Jamaica Talk: Three Hundred Years of the English Language in Jamaica* (London, 1961), 181. Captain John Stedman, who left a remarkable journal of his experiences among the Maroons and other Coramantee in Dutch Guiana also used the term *banja* in a context of Congo-Angolan slaves' "the Loango Dance." The editor notes that the Loango people are Ba-Wili from the area south of the mouth of the River Kwilu, that is "Congo." Captain John Gabriel Stedman, *Narrative of a Five Years' Expedition against the Revolted Negroes of Surinam in Guiana on the Wild Coast of South America from the Years 1772–1777. . . .* (1796, repr. Amherst, 1971), 197, 458n. See also, Thistlewood's Journal, Nov. 28, 1762, May 5, 1764. "Much afraid of the Spanish," he stopped a play at a driver's house, and later wrote, "hear there is an Inform[atio]n against Samuel Say of Cabretta Estate for permitting a Negroe play (for Venus' Mother, who is lately dead), last Sunday afternoon."

20. Leslie, *A True and Exact Account of Jamaica,* 324–25; For an example of an oath, Maroon to slave, see the "Examination of William" (Aug. 17, 1795) read at the Governor's Council, Sept. 21, 1795, Minutes of Council, 1 May 1792–14 May 1799, Central Government, 1B/5/3, Jamaica Archives, Spanish Town.

21. "Letters of Philo-xylon," *Barbados Gazette and General Intelligencer* [*Barb. Gaz. and Genl. Intell.*], Nov. 21, 1787, p. 13 bound as "B. Tracts 491" in the British Library copy of James Ramsay, *An Essay on the Treatment and Conversion of African Slaves. . . .* (London, 1784).

22. Anglican Reverend Bridge cited in W. J. Gardner, *A History of Jamaica: From Its Discovery by Christopher Columbus to the Year 1872* (1873, repr. London, 1971), 262; Thistlewood's Journal, Sept. 15, 1750; cf. Oct. 21, 1782: Achilles' death is attributed to "drinking grave dirt."

23. Letter of Trelawny Town Superintendant John James, April 29, 1774 read at the May 30, 1774 Council, C.O. 140/55; see Samuel Vaughan to Lewis Cathbert, Montego Bay, July 26, 1795, Minutes of Council (May 1, 1792–May 14, 1799), Central Government, Jamaica Archives, Spanish Town. By conspirators: "Exam-

ination of Luckey," Rio Bueno, Jamaica, Dec. 31, 1791, enclosed in Lt. Gov. Adam Williamson to Sec. of State, Feb. 12, 1792, C.O. 137/90. Cf. Sarah Gilbert to the Secretary, English Harbour, Antigua, June 1, 1804, box 4/9, Methodist Missionary Society Archives.

24. K. A. Busia, "The Ashanti of the Gold Coast," in *African Worlds: Studies in the Cosmological Ideas and Social Values of African Peoples*, ed. Daryll Forde (London, 1954), 201; Joshua N. Kudadjie, "Aspects of Religion and Morality in Ghanaian Traditional Society with Particular Reference to the Ga-Adangme," in *Traditional Life, Culture and Literature in Ghana*, ed. J. M. Assimeng (Owerri, 1976), 20; R. S. Rattray, *Ashanti Law and Constitution* (Oxford, 1929, 1969), 2, 8, 10–12, 15, 219; I. Chukwukere, "Agnatic and Uterine Relations Among the Fante: Male/Female Dualism," *Africa* 52, no. 1 (1982): 61–68. For oaths among Africans generally, see John C. Messenger, Jr., "Religious Acculturation Among the Anang Ibidio," in *Continuity and Change in African Cultures*, ed. William R. Bascom and Melville J. Herskovits (1959, repr. Chicago, 1962), 284.

25. House of Commons Sessional Papers (1790), 30/332–33.

26. James Moxon cited by Clifford D. May in a *New York Times* article about custom-made coffins in Teshi, Ghana, reprinted in the *San Franciso Chronicle-Examiner* (*Sunday Punch* magazine), Nov. 25, 1984, p. 7; Robert Farris Thompson, *African Art in Motion: Icon and Act* (Berkeley, 1974), 28. That ancestor veneration presupposes a people with a strong communal life who assume that ancestors are the custodians of traditions upon which corporate existence is based is the argument of Marion Kilson, *Kpele Lala: Ga Religious Songs and Symbols* (Cambridge, Mass., 1971), 98; and William Howells, *The Heathens, Primitive Man and His Religions* (Garden City, 1948), 172f.

27. Willy de Craemer, Jan Vansina, and Renée C. Fox, "Religious Movements in Central Africa: A Theoretical Study," *Comparative Studies in Society and History* 18 (Oct. 1976): 462.

28. Douglas Fraser, ed., *African Art as Philosophy: A Photographic Exhibition* (New York, 1974), 3.

29. McCaskie, "Anti-Witchcraft Cults in Asante," 129.

30. Alan P. Merriam, *An African World: The Basongye Village of Lupupa Ngye* (Bloomington, 1974), 111ff; Meyer Fortes, *Religion, Morality and the Person: Essays on Tallensi Religion* (Cambridge, England, 1987), 71–72. See also, Ian Stevenson, "The Belief in Reincarnation Among the Igbo of Nigeria," *Journal of Asian and African Studies* 20 (Jan.–April 1985): 15ff, 20. For an account of the transmission of the concepts of dual souls by Congolese in Jamaica, see Monica Schuler, *"Alas, Alas, Kongo": A Social History of Indentured African Immigration into Jamaica, 1841–1865* (Baltimore, 1980), esp. ch. 5, and 151 n24 for a comparison of Akan and central African ideas concerning blood and spirit as respectively representing female and male descent.

The meaning of African suicide in slavery deserves more attention. That the element of fate may have predisposed West Africans as slaves to suicide is a point of comparison between religion in West Africa and religion elsewhere in Africa in Meyer Fortes, *Oedipus and Job in West African Religion* (Cambridge, England,

1959), ch. 3. For an Anglican missionary in Jamaica who used suicide to distinguish among the beliefs of African and Creole slaves, see G. Duquesne to Henry Newman, Jamaica, May 15, 1728, West Indies, vol. 17, f. 153, Fulham Papers, Lambeth Palace Library.

31. John Beattie, "Review Article: Representations of the Self in Traditional Africa," *Africa* 50, no. 3 (1980): 313–20; Dominique Zahan, *The Religion, Spirituality, and Thought of Traditional Africa* (1970, repr. Chicago, 1979), 81.

32. Proverb cited by Kofi Asare Opoku, "Aspects of Akan Worship," in *The Black Experience in Religion*, ed. C. Eric Lincoln (Garden City, 1974), 298.

33. Robin Horton, "Types of Spirit Possession in the Kalabari Religion," in *Spirit Mediumship and Society in Africa*, ed. John Beattie and John Middleton (London, 1969), 15. The classic statement remains Henri Frankfort et al., *The Intellectual Adventure of Ancient Man: An Essay on Speculative Thought in the Ancient Near East* (1946, repr. Chicago, 1977), ch. 1. See also, Wyatt MacGaffrey, "Fetishism Revisited: Kongo *nkisi* in Sociological Perspective," *Africa* 47, no. 2 (1977): esp. 176–80; Helaine K. Minkus, "The Concept of Spirit in Akwapim Akan Philosophy," *Africa* 50, no. 2 (1980): 182–92.

34. Thistlewood's Journal, July 6, 1751.

35. Long, *History of Jamaica*, 2:424–25. For useful discussions of Canoe, see Orlando Patterson, *The Sociology of Slavery: An Analysis of the Origins, Development and Structure of Negro Slave Society in Jamaica* (1967, repr. Rutherford, 1969), 238–39, 243–44; and Judith Bettelheim, "Jamaican Jonkonnu and Related Caribbean Festivals," in *Africa and the Caribbean: The Legacies of a Link*, ed. Margaret E. Crahan and Franklin W. Knight (Baltimore, 1979), 80–100.

36. William Knibb to Sarah Griffiths, Kingston, March 29, 1828; also Knibb to A. G. Fuller, Kingston, Feb. 19, 1825, box WI/3, Baptist Missionary Society Archives, London (now located in the Angus Library, Regent's Park College, Oxford).

37. Knibb to Mr. S. Nicholas, Kingston, March [?] 1826, box WI/3, Baptist Missionary Society Archives.

38. Blake Touchstone, "Planters and Slave Religion in the Deep South," in *Masters and Slaves in the House of the Lord: Race and Religion in the American South, 1740–1870*, ed. John B. Boles (Lexington, Ky., 1988), 125.

39. Anita Pitchford, "The Material Culture of the Traditional East Texas Graveyard," *Southern Folklore Quarterly* 43 (1979): 277–79, 284–85; Robert Farris Thompson, *Flash of the Spirit: African and Afro-American Art and Philosophy* (New York, 1983), 132–42; Georgia Writers' Project, *Drums and Shadows: Survival Studies Among the Georgia Coastal Negroes* (New York, 1972), 128; Albert J. Raboteau, *Slave Religion: The "Invisible Institution" in the Antebellum South* (New York, 1978), 44; and the important bibliographical note in Sterling Stuckey, *Slave Culture: Nationalist Theory and the Foundations of Black America* (New York, 1987), 367–68, n99.

40. Prints of the statue are now reproduced in many U.S. history survey texts, as well as in John Michael Vlach, "Arrival and Survival: The Maintenance of an Afro-American Tradition in Folk Art and Craft," in *Perspectives on American Folk*

*Art*, ed. Ian M. G. Quimby and Scott T. Swank (New York, 1980), 177–271. Vlach (189) argues that the statue resembles the work of Bambara (Mende-speaking) blacksmiths.

41. Testimony of Ben Woolfolk at the trial of George Smith, in the folder "Negro Insurrection 1800," Executive Papers (Sept.–Dec. 1800), Virginia State Library, Richmond.

42. T. C. McCaskie, "Time and the Calendar in Nineteenth-Century Asante: An Exploratory Essay," *History in Africa* 7 (1980): 179–200. See also, Donald G. Mathews, *Religion in the Old South* (Chicago, 1977), 195, 210, 222–23; Earl McKenzie, "Time in European and African Philosophy: A Comparison," *Caribbean Quarterly* 19 (Sept. 1973): 77–85; and Gerald W. Mullin, *Flight and Rebellion: Slave Resistance in Eighteenth-Century Virginia* (New York, 1972), 41–42.

43. The South Carolina examples are from a 122-page court record in the Council Journal (1748–49), no. 17 (beginning Jan. 24, 1748–49), pp. 49, 51, 60, 70, 72–73, 78, 79, 83, South Carolina Department of Archives and History, Columbia. For parallels among Jamaican slaves (mostly Coramantee), "four Moons ago" and "when the corn was ready to eat at a State called Mutton Corn," see "Examinations of Slave Conspirators in 1791," enclosed in Lt. Gov. Adam Williamson to Sec. of State, Feb. 12, 1792, C.O. 137/90, f. 53.

44. Jack Goody, *The Domestication of the Savage Mind* (Cambridge, England, 1977), 13, 24ff, especially ch. 3. The most engaging statement remains Claude Lévi-Strauss, *Tristes Tropiques: An Anthropological Study of Primitive Societies in Brazil* (1955, repr. New York, 1964), ch. 25.

45. John S. Mbiti, *African Religions and Philosophy* (New York, 1969), 17.

46. Mullin, *Flight and Rebellion*, 174n; Lawrence W. Levine, *Black Culture and Black Consciousness: Afro-American Folk Thought from Slavery to Freedom* (New York, 1977), 58f.

47. Mary Kingsley, cited in Levine, *Black Culture and Black Consciousness*, 58.

48. Igor Kopytoff, "Knowledge and Belief in Suku Thought," *Africa* 51, no. 3 (1981): 712.

49. Erika Bourguignon, "Spirit Possession and Altered States of Consciousness: The Evolution of an Inquiry," in *The Making of Psychological Anthropology*, ed. George D. Spindler (Berkeley, 1978), 479–515.

50. Fortes, *Religion, Morality and the Person*, 67.

51. J. Omosade Awolalu and P. Adelumo Dopamu, *West African Traditional Religions* (Ibadan, 1979), 111.

52. Horton's "Ritual Man" used by Wyatt MacGaffey in *Modern Kongo Prophets: Religion in a Plural Society* (Bloomington, 1983), 14ff; see also, MacGaffey, "The West in Congolese Experience," in *Africa and the West: Intellectual Responses to European Culture*, ed. Philip D. Curtin (Madison, 1972), 49–74; and Michael Lambek, *Human Spirits: A Cultural Account of Trance in Mayotte* (Cambridge, England, 1981), 5, ch. 5, esp. 75ff.

53. For an answer to the argument that peasant resistance is "pre-political," see Audrey Wipper, *Rural Rebels: A Study of Two Protest Movements in Kenya* (Nairobi, 1977), 2–3, ch. 13.

54. Sidney W. Mintz and Richard Price, *An Anthropological Approach to the Afro-American Past: A Caribbean Perspective* (Philadelphia, 1976), 9–10.

55. Peter L. Berger, *The Sacred Canopy: Elements of a Sociological Theory of Religion* (1967, repr. New York, 1969), 22.

## Chapter Four. Plantations: Case Studies

1. On the important questions of the degree of familiarity — of "intimacy" — between owner and slave on the large plantations where most slaves lived, see for opposing points of view, Eugene D. Genovese, *Roll, Jordan, Roll: The World the Slaves Made* (New York, 1974), 91, 255, 437–39, 445–46, 587; and Paul D. Escott, *Slavery Remembered: A Record of Twentieth-Century Slave Narratives* (Chapel Hill, 1979), ch. 2, esp. 19–22.

2. William Byrd to Charles Boyle, Earl of Orrery, Westover, Va., July 5, 1726, in *The Correspondence of the Three William Byrds of Westover, Virginia, 1684–1776*, ed. Marion Tinling, 2 vols. (Charlottesville, 1977), 1:35.

3. Journals of Thomas Thistlewood [Thistlewood's Journal], Monson 31, Lincolnshire Record Office, Lincoln, March 15, 1752, April 11, 1768.

4. Ibid., April 14, 29, 30, 1750. The first case study concerns the assimilation of an immigrant planter as well as that of his slaves. In a diary lasting a quarter of a century, only a a few pages record what Thistlewood's life was like before immigration. Still, his jottings highlight the continuity of his basic passions and pastimes in the Old World and the New. At home in Lincolnshire (and while sight-seeing in London) he took long walks, noting with care plants, animals, and women. In London he hiked from Blackwell Dock to Islington, examined an apple tree that bore year round, and had "a whore." In Lincolnshire (he lived near Bardney, characterized in 1979 by a Lincoln bed-and-breakfast proprietoress as "it's wild out there"), he fished in the pool with his brother, exchanged books, and displayed his fascination with language and dialects this way: "In Lincolnshire, many Say *huz* instead of us."

5. Ibid., May 10, 26, July 1–2, 1750.

6. Ibid., July 9, 1750.

7. Ibid., March 31, April 20, 1756. On Nov. 24, 1763 Thistlewood noted that a neighbor, Daniel Hughes (once secretary to the Earl of Orrery), loaned him Orrery's *Remarks on the Life and Writing of Dr. Jonathan Swift* and two editions of *The North Britain*. Given the extensive circulation of key Enlightenment texts in Thistlewood's backwater, it does not make much sense to continue to characterize Jamaica as an absentee or client culture. See April 1, 8, 12, July 5, 11, 25, 1755, May 29, 1756, Dec. 14, 1763, May 1, 1774; for the book account, see July 10, Sept. 25, 1782 (172–73).

8. Ibid., Oct. 25, 29, Nov. 24, 1750, April 17, 1751.

9. Ibid., Jan. 28, Feb. 24, 1751.

10. Ibid., March 8, 1758.

11. Ibid., Jan. 8, 1751.

12. Ibid., Dec. 25, 1750; cf. April 29, 1750.

13. Ibid. May 12, 1751.

14. Ibid., July 6, 1751. Other leisure activities attributed to particular African peoples included: "to Night our Coromantee Negroes had a Trick which they call Tabraboah, a Rope 7 or 8 yards long, one end tied to a post Close to the ground, a person swings the other, whilst one danced in the Middle above and beneath it" — calypso dancing, in other words (Dec. 26, 1750); and "The Congo Negroe Men put a Stick about 9 Inches long, between their Feet, and throw it over the head backwards" (Jan. 26, 1751).

15. Ibid., Jan. 28, 1751, Feb. 27, 1751, May 10, 1751, Nov. 5, 1750.

16. Ibid., April 17, 1751; Jan 31, 1767; also April 21, May 11, 23, 1751; July 27, 29, Aug. 12, 1755.

17. Ibid., Aug. 21, 1750, July 20, Aug. 30, 1752, July 6–7, Aug. 22, Oct. 1, 7, 1755, July 4, 1757, Aug. 17, 19, 1759, July 25, 1754. See also, Jenny "not come over too Stubborn," Oct. 22, 1752; Phibbah "too saucy" in the hammock in the hall way and would not come to bed, Jan. 4, 1755; "took her things out of my house while I was away," July 6, 1755.

18. Ibid., May 22, Oct. 18, 1752, July 14, 1754. Of a report that Henry McCormich was killed by a tree felled by slaves who then ran away, Thistlewood wrote, "said to have been murdered for medling with their Women." April 9, 1768.

19. Ibid., May 10, 1751, July 28, Aug. 5, 7, 1755. The picture here is the norm — a mid-range between a few instances of kinky sex by Thistlewood and his trying to force some kind of monogamous relations upon slave couples: Feb. 16, 1752, Aug. 11, 1756, Jan. 6, 1760, March 30, 1761, Nov. 17, 1774.

20. Ibid., March 17, June 29, Dec. 3–4, 27, 1752, July 6, 7, 1755, Feb. 22, 26, 27, March 2, 17, 22, 1752, Sept. 27, 1751, and entries for early Feb. 1755.

21. Ibid., Dec. 27, 1752.

22. Ibid., Feb. 5, 1768.

23. Ibid., July 12, 13, 1754; for another good series, see Jan.-Feb. 1756.

24. Ibid., July 17–20, 31, Aug. 1, 1750; for similar reactions by the new Negro George: Oct. 8, 9, 11, 12, 24, Nov. 6, 22, 23, 1750.

25. Ibid., May 25, June 13–14, 28, 1754.

26. Ibid., Jan. 26, 1756.

27. Ibid., Jan. 28, 1756.

28. Ibid., Jan. 13, 16, 19, 20, 27, 28, Feb. 2, 4, March 1, 13, 16, May 26, July 23, 24, Aug. 3, 13, 18, 1756. During the harvest four years later Derby was still breaking [eating] cane (Nov. 13, 1760).

29. Ibid., Aug. 28, 1756.

30. Ibid., Aug. 8, 1754.

31. Ibid., Aug. 29, 1754.

32. Ibid., Jan. 4, Aug. 14, 1758, Feb. 5, 6, 1774; *Jam. Royal Gaz.,* May 9, 1795-S., P. Clajon.

33. Thistlewood's Journal, July 3, 1784. Michael Craton has estimated that one in ten new Negroes imported to Jamaica died in passage, another third died within their first three years in the island. Survivors, who were as "durable" as Creoles, in the eighteenth century lived an average of thirty years, and an average

of forty years by 1830: "Jamaican Slave Mortality; Fresh Light from Worthy Park, Longville and the Tharp Estates," *Journal of Caribbean History* 3 (Nov. 1971): 26.

34. In *Roll, Jordan, Roll* (425, 428f), Eugene Genovese characterizes the South as Victorian in this way. Many of its men were "prudes," and women had not been raised to share, nor would they tolerate sharing, their husbands. In an antebellum society that did not justify sexual aggression, white men too often directed that impetus "toward sadism which accompanies self-contempt and self-hatred."

35. *The Diary of Colonel Landon Carter of Sabine Hall, 1752–1778,* ed. Jack P. Greene (Charlottesville, 1965), Sept. 18, 1775, 944. Folder 3 of the Carter Papers, William and Mary College Library Archives, contains a photocopy of the inventory of Carter's estate (Feb. 1779) listing 401 slaves on quarters in six counties, including 181 at Sabine Hall in Richmond County. In his lifetime Carter saw his slaves double in number from those he inherited, and did so without purchase — unheard of in the West Indies. See Richard S. Dunn, "A Tale of Two Plantations: Slave Life at Mesopotamia in Jamaica and Mount Airy in Virginia, 1799 to 1828," *William and Mary Quarterly,* 3d ser., 34 (Jan. 1977): 32–65.

36. Edmund S. Morgan, *Virginians at Home: Family Life in the Eighteenth Century* (Charlottesville, 1963), 53–54.

37. Gerald W. Mullin, *Flight and Rebellion: Slave Resistance in Eighteenth-Century Virginia* (New York, 1972), 7ff.

38. Louis Morton, *Robert Carter of Nomini Hall: A Virginia Tobacco Planter of the Eighteenth Century* (Charlottesville, 1941), 205f.

39. *Diary of Colonel Landon Carter,* ed. Greene, Oct. 3, 1772, 736, Oct. 6, 1774, 867, Oct. 24, 1757, 185, Feb. 18, 1770, 360, Aug. 8, 1777, 1122, March 8, 1776, 996.

40. Mullin, *Flight and Rebellion,* 23f.

41. Ibid., 24f.

42. Byrd to Charles Boyle, Earl of Orrery, Westover, Virginia, July 5, 1726, in *Correspondence of the Three William Byrds,* ed. Tinling, 1: 355.

43. *Diary of Colonel Landon Carter,* ed. Greene, July 18, 1777, 1114, June 25, 1770, 428, June 19, 1770, 422.

44. Ibid., May 8, 1772, 677–78, Dec. 12, 1774, 894–95, Sept. 6, 1757, 174–75, Dec. 9, 1763, 244.

45. Ibid., Dec. 9, 1763, 244, July 2, 1766, 312, April 30, 1770, 400.

46. Ibid., Sept. 16, 1757, 177, Sept. 6, 1757, 174–75.

47. Ibid., Aug. 7, 10, 1771, 604f, 609, Jan. 21, 1757, 138. See also for inspections and counts in the henhouse, plow rows, tea cannisters in a locked desk, corn and wheat stores, hills per acre, and turkeys (296, 299, 304, 307, 318, 319–20, 329, 338–39, 444–45, 553, 678).

48. Ibid., Sept. 24, 1770, 502.

49. Ibid., April 7, 17, 1771, 556, 557, April 13, 1770, 388, June 5, 1773, 755; acts of sabotage on 362, 367–68, 376, 396–97, 504.

50. Ibid., May 9, 1772, 678.

51. Ibid., Feb. 11, 1770, 355.

52. Mullin, *Flight and Rebellion*, 70ff.

53. Jack P. Greene, *Landon Carter: An Inquiry into the Personal Values and Social Imperatives of the Eighteenth-Century Virginia Gentry* (Charlottesville, 1965, 1967), 10.

54. Mullin, *Flight and Rebellion*, 27ff.

55. *Diary of Colonel Landon Carter*, ed. Greene, Sept. 19, 1771, 636, Nov. 6, 1771, 639, April 7, 1771, 556, Oct. 14, 1772, 740.

56. Samson Wood to Thomas Lane, Oct. 19, 1798, no. 381(1), cf. 343, Newton Estate Papers, Paleography Room, University of London Library. All of the following references concerning Wood and the Lanes unless indicated otherwise are contained in this collection of estate papers.

57. Wood to Lane, July 18, 1798, no. 352(1), Newton Estate Papers. This is one of the best surviving plantation collections in Britain. In addition to Wood's plentiful and informative letters, there are a few from his widow; reports from the proprietors' brother, a naval officer in the Caribbean; and extensive ledgers and account books. The written record is enhanced by a fine archaeological one, Jerome S. Handler and Frederick W. Lange, *Plantation Slavery in Barbados: An Archaeological and Historical Investigation* (Cambridge, Mass., 1978).

58. John Burke, Philip Lovell, and Thomas Burton, freeholders of Christ Church Parish (a copy), May 11, 1803, no. 279, Newton Estate Papers.

59. Wood to Thomas Lane, Nov. 2, 1797, no. 324, March 31, 1798, no. 334, April 21, 1802, no. 474(1), May 3, 1797, no. 303; Wood to [John Lane], Nov. 18, 1801, no. 458; Richard Lane to Thomas Lane, Port Royal, Jamaica, Feb. 25, 1797, no. 332. Of the Woods, the brother reported, the wife "is a neat [and] good humor'd woman, but upon my word their want of common comforts shocked us much." See, too, Wood to Thomas Lane, June 20, 1797, no. 306(2).

60. See the clear and sizeable fold-out map in Richard S. Dunn, "The Barbados Census, 1680: Profile of the Richest Colony in English America," *William and Mary Quarterly*, 3d ser., 26 (Jan. 1969): 3–30.

61.

Profits and Losses for Newton Estate, 1793–1801

| Year | Expenses (£) | Gains (£) | Loss (£) |
|------|--------------|-----------|----------|
| 1793 | 1,339.9.10 | 1,539.5 | |
| 1794 | 1,237.9.10 | 491.6.7 | |
| 1795 | 960.4 .8 | 901.5.5 | |
| 1796 | 2,088.5 .5 | 1,909.4.7 | |
| 1797 | 1,955.1 .8 | — | 282.6 |
| 1798 | 2,438.9 .9 | 6,052.2.1 | |
| 1799 | 4,841.4 .2 | 6,163.5.8 | |
| 1800 | 2,189 | 939.7.5 | 734.3.4 |
| 1801 | 1,987.19.11 | | 1,016.6 |
| | 19,037.12.3 | | |
| − | 16 | | |
| Total | 36,016.19.6 | 17,995.16.9 | |

1,016. 9.6

16,979.7.3

---

(For Seawell Estate from 1793 to 1801 the total produced was £23,975.3.10.) Source: July 1796 reports, nos. 261, 289, 290.

62.

Slave Populations, 1776–1803

|          | 1776 | 1782 | 1784 | 1796 | 1803 |
|----------|------|------|------|------|------|
| Newton   | 242  | 240  | 242  | 253  | 264  |
| Seawell  |      |      | 188  | 182  | 177  |

Source: July 1796 Report on the Negroes, no. 288.

Wood reported being "overstocked" in one report, and a few months later said that in the year the slaves had increased naturally from 255 to 268 and several women were pregnant. He called the increases "severe," a rather different outlook than that of Jamaican planters of the same period. See Wood to Lane, May 16, Oct. 19, 1798, nos. 343 and 381(2). For an overview and a useful three-stage explanation of planters' strategies regarding slave treatment and vital statistics, see Richard Sheridan, "Mortality and the Medical Treatment of Slaves in the British West Indies," in *Race and Slavery in the Western Hemisphere: Quantitative Studies*, ed. Stanley L. Engerman and Eugene D. Genovese (New York, 1969), 287–88.

63. Daybooks nos. 110, 111 (1796), Newton Estate Papers.

64. Wood to John Lane, Sept. 8, 1797, no. 321, Nov. 2, 1797, no. 324, Newton Estate Papers.

65. Wood to Thomas Lane, May 3, 1797, no. 303(1); Wood to John Lane, Nov. 18, 1801, no. 458, Feb. 13, 1801, no. 434; July 1796 Report on the Negroes.

66. Wood to Thomas Lane, Oct. 19, 1798, no. 381(1), July 18, 1798, no. 352(1), May 7, 1798, no. 340(1); July 1796 Report on the Negroes, no. 973.

67. July 1796 Report on the Negroes, no. 288.

68. Wood to Thomas Lane, May 7, 1798, no. 340(1), June 22, 1798, no. 345, Oct. 21, 1800, no. 423.

69. Ibid., cf. Wood to Thomas Lane, Oct 21, 1800, no. 423. In the July 1796 Report on the Negroes, Wood requested white linen shirts "for the officers [and] those who behave well." Further, if the "rewards" were blue or red common pocket handkerchiefs, which slave women put on their heads, they would stir up a great spirit "of pride and emulation." George Saur's reward, a Christian burial, was described in part as "handsome . . . and an encouragement to others," and "what they esteem the best reward of services after death." July 18, Oct. 19, 1798, nos. 352(1), 381(1); also see Handler and Lange, *Plantation Slavery in Barbados*, 79–80, 203.

70. Wood to Thomas Lane, July 21, 1798, no. 353.

71. Wood to Thomas Lane, July 20, Sept. 8, Oct. 15, 1797, nos. 315, 321, 322.

72. Daybook, May 5–September 28, 1796, no. 110; Wood to Thomas Lane, Oct. 19, 1798, no. 381(1).

73. July 1796 Report on the Negroes no. 288; Wood to Lane, Sept. 22, 1802, no. 503; Nov. 13, 1802, from the St. Joseph parsonage; no. 507(1), Dec. 15, 1802, from Portsmouth, England; Oct. 3, no. 550. On the back of Wood's last, Oct. 21, 1803, Thomas Lane scrawled to his brother (Dec. 8, 1803) that he mistrusted Wood, that the manager may have run out on his debts in Tunbridge Wells, and that Lane "won't be made a Cat's Paw" to pay them off.

74. [Margaret Baron-Wilson], *The Life and Correspondence of M. G. Lewis . . . with Many Pieces in Prose and Verse, Never Before Published,* 2 vols. (London, 1839), 1:362; M. G. Lewis, *Journal of a West India Proprietor, 1815–17,* ed. Mona Wilson (London, 1929), 171.

75. Lewis, *Journal,* 52–53; see also 54, 55, 56, 57; Cynric Williams, *Tour of the Island of Jamaica . . . [in] 1823* (London, 1826), 63.

76. Ibid., 128. In a printed MS, "A Roll of land, slaves, stock, wheels and persons saving deficiency for the parish of Westmoreland March 28, 1814," Cornwall Estate was rated at 3,632 acres, 4 white men, 293 slaves, and 281 stock. Miscellaneous Mesopotamia Accounts, Clarendon Deposit, b. 34, Bodleian Library, Oxford University.

77. Lewis, *Journal,* 110, 195; see also 101–4, 130–31, 162.

78. Ibid., 291.

79. Ibid., 112, 156, 186; see also 109, 114, 158, and 160–61.

80. Ibid., 111, 155, 194, 196.

81. Leslie A. Marchand, ed., *Byron's Letters and Journals,* 12 vols. (London, 1973–82), 9:18, 3:227; Baron-Wilson, *Life of M. G. Lewis,* 1:212, 224–25; 2:62; Lewis, *Journal,* 91.

82. Baron-Wilson, *Life of M. G. Lewis,* 1:128, 133; *Coleridge's Miscellaneous Criticism,* ed. Thomas Middleton Raysor (London, 1936), 374; Mario Praz, *The Romantic Agony* (London, 1933, 2d ed., 1951), 60f.

83. Lewis, *Journal,* 104.

84. Ibid., 60.

85. Frances Anne Kemble, *Journal of a Residence on a Georgian Plantation in 1838–1839* (1863, repr. New York, 1971), 50.

86. Lewis, *Journal,* 82.

87. Ibid., 90, 97, 98, 101–4.

88. Ibid., 194–96, 283–84, 333.

89. Ibid., 181–82, 185, 189–90.

90. Ibid., 182, 190.

91. Ibid., 130–31, 272–73.

92. Ibid., 189.

93. Ibid., 303, 331–32.

94. Ibid., 206, 254; Baron-Wilson, *Life of M. G. Lewis,* 2:271–86, 371.

95. Lewis Manigault [L. M.] to Charles Manigault [C. M.], Nov. 24, 1861, *Life and Labor on Argyle Island: Letters and Documents of a Savannah River Rice Plantation, 1833–1867,* ed. James M. Clifton (Savannah, 1978), 328. This portrait is based principally on the letters and business records compiled by Clifton, whose introduction was also most helpful.

96. C. M. to Alfred Huger, Paris, April 1, 1847, 52; and Clifton, ed., *Life and Labor,* xix–xxi. See James M. Clifton, "A Half-Century of a Georgia Rice Plantation," *North Carolina Historical Review* 47 (Oct. 1970): 388–415. The following advertisement appeared in the *South Carolina Gazette,* Dec. 3, 1770, half a century earlier for the first Gowrie: "To be Sold (or exchanged for Negroes) A Trace of Tide-Swamp, on the Island of ARGYLE seven Miles above the Town, Savannah, containing (as imagined) near 700 acres; near 250 cleared and completely banded in, with buildings of every kind suitable for a plantation, equal at least to any in the province, a machine that beats six large b[arre]ls of rice per day, maybe bought with the place if agreeable to the buyer; near 20 head cattle. . . . The situation of the plantation admits of receiving the Tides from two rivers at once, so that there is no Doubt of watering your Field every fortnight, if required. [signed] WILLIAM WILLIAMSON."

97. C. M. to James Haynes, Paris, Nov. 1, 1846, April 1, 1847; *Life and Labor,* ed. Clifton, 41, 52. How extensive was absenteeism in the lowcountry? Of 111 rice plantations fewer than half had resident owners, most of whom were absent during the harvest. Ibid., xxviii note.

98. Ibid., xi-xvi; Michael Mullin, ed., *American Negro Slavery: A Documentary History* (New York, 1975), 137ff.

99. C. M. to L. M., Charleston, Oct. 18, 1856, 230; C. M. to Haynes, Paris, Aug. 15, 1846, March 1, 1847, in *Life and Labor,* ed. Clifton, 37, 50.

100. C. M. to Robert Habersham and Son, Paris, Feb. 1, 1847, ibid., 48.

101. Haynes to C. M., Gowrie, Jan. 6, 1847, ibid., 46.

102. C. M. to Haynes, Paris, Jan. 1, 1847, ibid., 45.

103. Haynes to C. M., Argyle, Dec. 7, 1846, ibid., 43; C. M. to Jesse T. Cooper, Paris, July 12, 1848, ibid., 63.

104. L. M. to C. M., Gowrie, March 10, 1854, ibid., 181; cf. same to same, March 6, 1853, 143–45.

105. L. M. to C. M., Gowrie, March 10, 12, 1854, ibid., 180, 182; C. M. to L. M., Charleston, March 6, 1854, 177; Plantation Journal no. 4, April 1850. I used the originals in the Southern Historical Collection, University of North Carolina Library, Chapel Hill (reproduced in *Life and Labor,* 75).

106. C. M. to L. M., Charleston, Jan. 20, 1857, ibid., 244; L. M. to C. M., Gowrie, Feb. 27, 1854, 173.

107. Jesse T. Cooper to C. M., Encampment [Ga.], Aug. 8, 14, 1849, ibid., 70, 71–72; L. M. to C. M., Pulaski House [Savannah], Dec. 25, 26, 28, 1854, 188–93; "List of Negroes at Gowrie and East Hermitage, the 23rd April 1854," Plantation Book 1833, vol. 2, Manigault Papers, Southern Historical Collection; L. M. to C. M., Savannah, Nov. 22, 1852, 127–28. There is a nice sketch of seven tents in a forest at the cholera retreat in L. M.'s Daybook for 1852: Nov. 24, 1852 entry, no. 2347, Manuscript Division, Duke University Library, Durham, N.C.

108. For a view of a lowcountry white's time reckoning (and representative absenteeism and itineracy), see L. M.'s Daybook for 1852 (Duke University Library):

21 Nov. 1852 left Charleston for Savannah and the cholera camps.

25 Nov.  "  returned to Charleston

21 Dec. 1852 left Charleston for Gowrie
31 Jan. 1853 returned to Charleston
13 Feb. *"* left Charleston for Gowrie [where he remained until 1 May].
Manigault saw this chunk of time as the winter season, as in "Thus has passed the Winter."

109. C. M. to Jesse T. Cooper, Paris, July 12, 1848, C. M. to Haynes, Paris, Nov. 1, 1846, C. M. to Cooper, Naples, Jan. 10, 1848, all in *Life and Labor,* 64, 41, 61–62. William Scarborough estimates that overseers on the rice coast remained on a job on average about three and a half years: *The Overseer: Plantation Management in the Old South* (Baton Rouge, 1966), 39.

110. C. M. to L. M., Charleston, March 10, 1854, and C. M. to Haynes, Paris, March 1, 1847, *Life and Labor,* ed. Clifton, 178–79, 50.

111. C. M. to L. M., Marshlands, April 7, 1859, ibid., 286; C. M. to Haynes, Paris, March 1, 1847, 49–50; see also, C. M. to L. M., Charleston, Jan. 20, 1862, 337; C. M. to William Capers, Sr., Charleston, Jan. 20, 1862, 339.

112. K. Washington Skinner to C. M., Hermitage, Jan. 21, 24, 1852, ibid., 88, 89; see also, C. M. to L. M., Marshlands, Dec. 6, 1855, 201.

113. Gowrie Plantation Book, vol. 3, Manuscript Division, Duke University Library; L. M. to C. M., Gowrie, Dec. 5, 1861, in *Life and Labor,* ed. Clifton, 331; C. M. to William Capers, Sr., Charleston, Jan. 26, 1862, 339; C. M. to L. M., Charleston, Jan. 17, 1860, Jan. 20, 1862, 291, 337.

114. L. M. to C. M., Gowrie, Dec. 5, 1861, ibid., 330, 331.

115. Plantation Journal, in *Life and Labor,* ed. Clifton 340–44, 347–48; C. M. to L. M., April 30, 1865, ibid., 353. On Savage, see L. M. to C. M., Gowrie, Nov. 24, Dec. 5, 1861, 328, 331; William Capers, Sr., to C. M., Sept. 15, 21, 28, 1863, 345; C. M. to Capers, Charleston, Jan. 26, 1862, 339: "After this War is over I hear many Planters say that a new Code of management, of the strictest nature will have to be established for the Government of our Negroes." Cf. Albert House, "Deterioration of a Georgia Rice Plantation During Four Years of Civil War," *Journal of Southern History* 9 (Feb. 1943): 98–117.

116. Plantation Journal, March 22, 1867, 355.

117. Ibid., 356–57, 359, 361.

118. Ibid., 357ff, 359, 361. For a matching comment on a reaction of Jamaica slave women to emancipation, see Lord Sligo, Oct. 12, 1834, C.O. 137/193, f. 65: "In justice to masters [I] must say the Negroes are more insolent especially the women."

## Chapter Five. "Scientific" Planters

1. John Kenyon review of William Doyle, *The Old European Order, 1660–1800, Observor* (London), Sunday, Feb. 4, 1979, 37; David Brion Davis, *The Problem of Slavery in the Age of Revolution, 1770–1823* (Ithaca, 1975), 460.

2. Shorter versions of this chapter appeared earlier in *Southern Studies* 12 (Summer, 1973): 398–422, and as the Introduction to Michael Mullin, ed., *American Negro Slavery: A Documentary History* (New York, 1976). Cf. James Oakes,

*The Ruling Race: A History of American Slaveholders* (New York, 1982), 127ff, and chs. 6–7; and Oakes, *Slavery and Freedom: An Interpretation of the Old South* (New York, 1990), 144ff; see also, John Hebron Moore, *The Emergence of the Cotton Kingdom in the Old Southwest: Mississippi, 1770–1860* (Baton Rouge, 1988), ch. 5, esp. 82–85.

3. See Eugene D. Genovese's comments on Barrington Moore, Jr., *The Social Origins of Dictatorship and Democracy* in *Towards A New Past: Dissenting Essays in American History*, ed. Barton J. Bernstein (New York, 1968), 117.

4. Concerning the first-generation agricultural reformers, see Louis C. Gray, *History of Agriculture in the Southern United States to 1860*, 2 vols. (New York, 1941), 2:611ff.

5. For references to late-summer rural markets, see Journals of Thomas Thistlewood [Thistlewood's Journal], Monson 31, Lincolnshire Record Office, Lincoln, weekend entries Aug.–Sept. 1755 and 1756. See also, *Jamaica Royal Gazette [Jam. Royal Gaz.]*, June 15, 1793-S., and, for complaints of a market attended by more than a thousand slaves, *Cornwall Chronicle and Jamaica General Gazette [Cornwall Chron.]*, Feb. 1, 1783, Lemon Law. Lawrence.

6. See James C. Bonner, "Genesis of Agricultural Reform in the Cotton Belt," *Journal of Southern History* 9 (Nov. 1943): 475–500; and Chester M. Destler, "David Dickson's 'System of Farming' and the Agricultural Revolution in the Deep South, 1850-1885," *Agricultural History* 31 (July 1957): 32.

7. Frederick Law Olmsted, *A Journey in the Back Country* (New York, 1860, 1863), 64–65. By contrast, the mobility of the large antebellum planters has been likened to "musical chairs" by Gavin Wright in *Old South, New South: Revolutions in the Southern Economy Since the Civil War* (New York, 1986), vii. How well could planters know slaves individually under such circumstances? See, for instance, Bobby Frank Jones, "A Cultural Middle Passage: Slave Marriage and Family in the Antebellum South," Ph.D. diss., University of North Carolina, 1965, 9–11, for a good discussion of why an owner could not "practically" be a "pater familia" because of his basic responsibilities to the plantation concerning its management and efficiency.

8. Olmsted, *Journey in the Back Country*, 64.

9. Ibid.

10. *Southern Cultivator* 4 (March 1846): 44; "Management of Slaves," *De Bow's Review* 18 (June 1855): 716, 718.

11. Olmsted, *Journey in the Back Country*, 81–82. Cf. "On the great estates something like a military organization was effected," in Charles S. Sydnor, *Slavery in Mississippi* (Baton Rouge, 1966), 76.

12. Sidney W. Mintz, *Caribbean Transformations* (Chicago, 1974), 47–48.

13. "Account of an Agricultural Excursion made into the South of Georgia in the winter of 1832," *Southern Agriculturalist* 6 (Nov. 1833): 571; "Management of Slaves," *The Southern Cultivator* 4 (March 1846): 44; and Frederick Douglass, *Narrative of the Life of Frederick Douglass: An American Slave* (1845, repr. New York, 1963), 14.

14. "Notions on the Management of Negroes &c," *Farmers' Register* 4 (Dec. 1836): 494.

15. "Management of Slaves," *Southern Cultivator* 4 (March 1846): 44.

16. "On the Management of Negroes," *Farmer's Register* 1 (Feb. 1834): 565.

17. Record Book, 1859–66 (p. 25 entries for Feb. 25–March 2 1861), Le Blanc Family Papers, Louisiana State University Archives, Baton Rouge.

18. James A. Tait, Memorandum Book, 1831–40, Alabama State Archives, Montgomery.

19. Robert Williams, "Thomas Affleck: Missionary to the Planter, the Farmer, and the Gardener," *Agricultural History* 31 (July 1957): 46.

20. *De Bow's Review* 8 (Jan. 1850): 98.

21. William Fitzherbert Diary [1771]–72, 54–55, Fitzherbert-Perrin Papers, no. 20772A, Derbyshire Record Office, Matlock.

22. Ibid., 55.

23. James Ramsay, *An Essay on the Treatment and Conversion of African Slaves in the British Sugar Colonies* (London, 1784), 100–101, 113–14.

24. Ibid., 96–7, emphasis added.

25. Ibid., 100–101.

26. On Steele, useful sketches include the *Dictionary of National Biography;* Jill Sheppard, *The 'Red Legs' of Barbados* (Millwood, 1977), 45–46; the comments of a royal governor's secretary in the *Journal of the Barbados Museum and Historical Society* 10 (Feb. 1943); and an anonymous article, probably by Steele, in the *Barbados Gazette and General Intelligencer,* March 5, April 9, Oct. 11, 1788.

27. [Joshua Steele], "Letters and Papers of the Late Hon. Joshua Steele" (bound with William Dickson's "Letters to Thomas Clarkson") in *The Mitigation of Slavery* (London, 1814) (British Library pressmark 8156 df2).

28. Ibid., 7, 10. Cf. Lafayette's proposal to George Washington in the 1780s that they buy a West Indian plantation in order to experiment with slaves as tenants. John C. Fitzpatrick, ed., *The Writings of George Washington, from the Original Manuscript Sources, 1745–1799,* 39 vols. (Washington, 1931–44), 26: 300n. See also, George Frederickson's review of Janet Sharp Hermann, *The Pursuit of a Dream* in *New York Review of Books,* May 28, 1981, 9.

29. Steele, *Letters and Papers,* 12ff.

30. Rowland Fearon to Penrhyn, Jan. 26, 1805, no. 1355 (cf. no. 1361), Penrhyn Papers, Department of Archives, University College of North Wales Library, Bangor. Various absentees also sent orders to attornies and managers that slave children were to be fed hot dinners at the overseers' doors. Fearon to Penrhyn, July 14, 1804, no. 1328; Edward East to Roger Hope Elletson, Aug. 19, 1772, "Letters from Jamaica, 1769–1773," vol. 1., ST 14, Stowe MS, Henry E. Huntington Library, San Marino, Calif.

31. "The Copy of a Letter from a Gentleman [George Davidson] in the Island of *St. Vincent* to the Reverend Mr Clarke, One of the Reverend Mr. Wesley's Missionaries in the *West Indies,* Containing a Short History of the *Caribbs*." (dated Byera, St. Vincent, July 24, 1787), p. 18 of a small pamphlet *"The Case &c.,"* C.O. 260/8.

32. William Young, *A Tour through the Several Islands of Barbados, St. Vincent, Antigua, Tobago, and Grenada, in the Years 1791 and 1792* (London, 1801), 300n.

33. Robert Renny, *An History of Jamaica with Observations . . . to which is Added, An Illustration of the Advantages, which are likely to Result, from the Abolition of the Slave Trade* (London, 1807), 185.

## Chapter Six. Slaves' Economic Strategies

1. Sidney W. Mintz, "The Caribbean Region," *Daedalus* 103, no. 2 (1974): 62.

2. Sidney W. Mintz and Douglas Hall, "The Origins of the Jamaican Internal Marketing System," in *Papers in Caribbean Anthropology*, ed. Mintz, Yale University Publications in Anthropology no. 57 (New Haven, 1960).

3. See Appendix 4. The 1781 Jamaican Consolidated Slave Act required owners to allot provision grounds to each slave, along with time to work them. In addition, one acre per four Negroes was required for plantain walks and ground provisions "exclusive" of the slaves' own holdings. Slaves were also to be given a day off every two weeks (Sundays and crop times excepted) to grow their own food. The act was revised in 1787, and included a penalty of £50 and a clause that required an oath to be taken before the parish vestry accompanying an account of the quantity of land (over and above the slaves' regular allotments) that had been set aside for "the Use of their slaves, & when land was not available an account of how they proposed maintaining them." See Committee Report, Henry Shirley, Nov. 12, 1788, *Votes of Assembly,* 80, 88, C.O. 140/73.

4. Barbara J. Fields, "The Nineteenth-century American South: History and Theory," *Plantation Society in the Americas* 2 (April 1983): 9, 9n (emphasis added). Cf. Roderick A. McDonald, " 'Goods and Chattels': The Economy of Slaves on Sugar Plantations in Jamaica and Louisiana," Ph. D. diss., University of Kansas, 1981, 148. There was little selling by slaves off the plantation. The planter instead was their intermediary, and the plantation replaced the town as the slaves' retailing and purchasing outlet. For the Carolina lowcountry, the most persuasive case for a modicum of slave selling, based on the claims of freedmen to the Southern Claims Commission, is Philip Morgan's in "Work and Culture: The Task System and the World of Lowcountry Blacks, 1700 to 1880," *William and Mary Quarterly* 3d ser., 39 (Oct. 1982): 587ff.

Increasingly, the existence of provision grounds in the Caribbean and the absence of them in the South are points of departure — as they should be — for comparisons of emancipation in the two regions. One of the most important essays is Jean Besson, "Land Tenure in the Free Villages of Trelawny, Jamaica: A Case Study in the Caribbean Peasant Response to Emancipation," *Slavery and Abolition* 5 (May 1984): 3–23. See also, Sidney W. Mintz, "Slavery and the Rise of Peasantries," in *Roots and Branches: Current Directions in Slave Studies,* ed. Michael Craton (Toronto, 1979), 213–42, and "From Plantations to Peasantries in the Caribbean," in *Caribbean Contours,* ed. Sidney W. Mintz and Sally Price (Baltimore, 1985), 127–53; Stanley L. Engerman, "Economic Adjustments to Emancipation in the United States and the British West Indies," *Journal of Interdisciplinary History* 13 (Autumn 1982): 191–220; Douglas Hall, "The Flight from the Estates Reconsidered: The British West Indies, 1838–42," *Journal of Caribbean History* 10–11

(1978): 643–66; B. Marshall et al., "The Establishment of a Peasantry in Barbados," in *Social Groups and Institutions in the History of the Caribbean* (San Juan, 1975), 85–104; and a special issue of *Slavery and Abolition* 12 (May 1991): "The Slaves' Economy: Independent Production by Slaves in the Americas," ed. Ira Berlin and Philip D. Morgan.

5. Edward Long, *The History of Jamaica,* 3 vols. (1774, repr. London, 1870), 2:413; W. J. Gardner, *A History of Jamaica from Its Discovery by Christopher Columbus to the Year 1872* (1873, repr. London, 1971), 182.

6. Barry W. Higman, "African and Creole Slave Family Patterns in Trinidad," in *Africa and the Caribbean: Legacies of a Link,* ed. Margaret E. Crahan and Franklin W. Knight (Baltimore, 1979), 45.

7. House of Commons Sessional Papers (1790), 29/218 also, 29/144, 189; Gordon Turnbull, *An Apology for Negro Slavery,* 2d ed. (London, 1786), 21ff, 25; "Extracts from Minutes of Evidence taken by the Committee of Council for Inquiring into the Negro Character as Exhibited in this Colony [Trinidad]," *British Parliamentary Papers, Slave Trade* 73 (1826–27), 21.

8. Journals of Thomas Thistlewood [Thistlewood's Journal], Monson 31, Lincolnshire Record Office, Lincoln, May 25, 1754, July 6, Dec. 10, 1761, and a note that some new Negroes take an "ugly name," one which they think will deter death (June 23, 1750).

9. William Young, *A Tour Through the Several Islands of Barbados, St. Vincent, Antigua, Tobago, and Grenada, In the Years 1791 and 1792 . . .* (London, 1801), 289–90.

10. Young, *A Tour,* 289; Simon Taylor to Chalonder Archedeckne, Kingston, June 11, 1782, box 2, bundle 11, Vanneck MS, Manuscripts Room, Cambridge University Library. Sir Christopher Codrington, a Barbados proprietor, directed his attornies to assign new Negroes as inmates, to give every slave Friday afternoons to work their grounds, and to provide new Negroes with their own grounds rather than placing them in those of older residents. Codrington to Thomas Jones and John Lightfoot, June 27, 1715, C-2, microfilm 347(1), Codrington Papers, Gloucestershire Record Office, Gloucester.

11. Thistlewood's Journal, July 16, 1763.

12. Ibid., Feb. 22, 1761 (a Sunday when nearly all such activities took place).

13. Ibid., March 20–21, 1754; see also, March 28, 29, 1754.

14. Ibid., May 18, 25, June 7, 15, mid-July 1754.

15. Ibid., June 15, 1754, Sept. 10, 1758.

16. Ibid., Aug. 6, 1754.

17. Ibid., July 16, 19, 1754.

18. The same nerves-on-edge behavior took place during the summer of 1756.

19. Ibid., June 25, 28, 29, 1754.

20. Ibid., May 1, 3, 4, 13, 17, 1751, April 8, 1754, Aug. 4, 1750, April 12, 1759.

21. Ibid., Sept. 10, 1758, Nov. 30, 1767, July 3, 1759; see also, Aug. 1, 1752, April 18, 1756, May 30, 1762, Oct. 27, 1763, June 25, July 30, 1758, March 18, 1764.

22. Ibid., March 19, 1764.

23. Ibid., March 24, 25, 1764, Feb. 1, Sept. 7, 1761.

24. Ibid., May 4, 1755.

25. Ibid., Sept. 30, 1767; see also, Oct. 1, 1786, and Sept. 6, 1761: "Egypt Lucy sold 15/ worth of my Salt Beef to day in the Road, rec'd the money & gave her some Salt Beef."

26. Ibid., end sheets of the 1776 journal; cf. entry following Dec. 30, 1774 and Oct. 1, 1786.

27. Ibid., June 23, 1750, Sept. 22, 27, 1751.

28. Ibid., Sept. 24, 1752, April 1, 1756; see also, June 29, 1754, Aug. 14, 1755.

29. Ibid., May 27, 1758, Jan. 27, April 5, Sept. 28, 1760.

30. Ibid., July 21, 1755, April 13, 1779, Oct. 23, 1750, Nov. 26, 1752, Aug. 25, 1754; see also, April 22, 1758, July 16, 1761, Jan. 17, July 28, 1764, March 14, 1776, Dec. 26, 1784.

31. Ibid., Sept. 4, 8, 17, 25, Oct. 7, 9, 18, Nov. 19, 1767.

32. Ibid., Oct. 2, 3, 8, Nov. 8, Dec. 2, 1780; see also, Aug. 3, 1785. The inhabitants of Westmoreland Parish wrote the council president (Aug. 11, 1781) that "the dread of famine absorbs all other Considerations," C.O. 137/81, f. 12v. Robert LeVine notes that a feature of being African is an emphasis on material transactions (of food, particularly) in interpersonal relations. See "Patterns of Personality in Africa," in *Responses to Change: Society, Culture, and Personality*, ed. George A. DeVos (New York, 1976), 121ff. For another side of gifting, as displaced aggression and marking territory, see Bruce Chatwin, *Songlines* (New York, 1987), 113.

33. M. G. Lewis, *Journal of a West India Proprietor, 1815–17*, ed. Mona Wilson (London, 1929), 120–21.

34. Lewis, *Journal*, 166–67.

35. Ibid., 333–34.

36. Wood to [John Lane], Nov. 18, 1801, no. 458, Newton Estate Papers, Paleography Room, University of London Library.

37. Wood to Thomas Lane, Oct. 28, 1801, no. 457(1), Newton Estate Papers.

38. Wood to Thomas Lane, Aug. 24, 1802, no. 496(1), May 18, 1797, no. 304(1), Nov. 18, 1801, no. 458, Newton Estate Papers.

39. Wood to John Lane, Oct. 19, 1798, no. 381(1), Newton Estate Papers.

40. Ibid.; Wood to Thomas Lane, May 16, 1798, no. 343, Newton Estate Papers.

41. "Report on Negroes," July 1796, no. 288, Newton Estate Papers.

42. Wood to Thomas Lane, Feb. 10/13, 1801, no. 434, Newton Estate Papers.

43. Jerome S. Handler and Frederick W. Lange, *Plantation Slavery in Barbados: An Archaeological and Historical Investigation* (Cambridge, Mass., 1978), 141ff.

44. John Taylor, "Arator: being a Series of Agricultural Essays Practical and Political," *Farmers' Register* 8 (Dec. 31, 1840): 703ff; the citation is on 730–31.

45. Robert Ascher and Charles H. Fairbanks, "Excavation of a Slave Cabin: Georgia, U.S.A.," *Historical Archaeology* 5 (1971): 14; see also, John S. Otto, "A New Look at Slave Life," *Natural History* 88 (Jan. 1979): 8ff.

46. Paul Leland Haworth, *George Washington: Farmer* (Indianapolis, 1915), 210–11.

47. Landon Carter, *The Diary of Colonel Landon Carter of Sabine Hall, 1752–1778,* 2 vols., ed. Jack P. Greene (Charlottesville, 1965), Sept. 8, 1770, 484; also, April 19, 26, 1770, 390, 396.

48. Ibid., April 20, 1777, 1095–96.

49. Baylor Ledger, 1719–21, M–62–5, Colonial Williamsburg Research Center, microfilm of the original at the Alderman Library, University of Virginia; Feb. 11, 1760, Robert Bristow Letterbook, AO 13/84, M494; Benjamin Harrrison to Miles King, Feb. 3, 1788, Harrison Letterbook, 1787–89, M–1208–2, Colonial Williamsburg Research Center, microfilm of the original at the New York Historical Society; Mount Vernon Storebook, Jan. 1–Dec. 31, 1787, Rum Account, transcript of the original in the Mount Vernon Museum, Mount Vernon, Virginia.

50. Lloyd Papers, Legal Papers, roll 40, shelf no. 1244, white servants' depositions [James Hollard's], Aug. 17, 1793, Maryland Historical Society, Baltimore.

51. Charles Manigault [C. M.] to Louis Manigault [L. M.], Jan. 10; 1859, in *Life and Labor on Argyle Island: Letters and Documents of a Savannah River Rice Plantation 1833–1867,* ed. James M. Clifton (Savannah, 1978), 270–71.

52. C. M. to James Haynes, March 1, 1847, ibid., 49.

53. C. M. to L. M., Charleston, March 6, 1853, ibid., 142.

54. C. M. to Jesse T. Cooper, Naples, Jan. 10, 1848, ibid., 62. See also, Instructions for Overseer Agreement, enclosed in C. M. to L. M., Charleston, Feb. 20, 1859, ibid., 280–81.

55. C. M. to Jesse T. Cooper, Naples, Jan. 10, 1848, ibid., 62.

56. C. M. to L. M., March 29, 1857, ibid., 246; C. M. to James Haynes, Paris, Aug. 15, 1846, ibid., 38.

57. Lt. Gov. Balcarres to the Duke of Portland, Dromilley near Wills (Jamaica), Nov. 16, 1795, C.O. 137/96.

58. House of Commons Sessional Papers (1790), 29/101–3.

59. From a meeting of ministers in Charleston, March 4, 1721, reel 2, 427f, microfilm copy of Society for the Propagation of the Gospel transcripts in the New York Public Library.

60. Oct. 26, 1779 entry in a small daybook, 1776–79, Alexander Johnston Books, 1792–87, box 29B, Powell Family Collection, Historical Society of Pennsylvania, Philadelphia.

61. Thistlewood's Journal, Sept. 26, 1750; see also, May 16, 25, and June 28, 1754 for actual allotment lists, including distributions to women.

62. Denbigh Estate plans, no. 2790 (1781), Coates's and Denbigh's Outbounds, Penrhyn Papers, Department of Archives, University College of North Wales Library, Bangor.

63. William Sutherland to William Philip Perrin, Greenwall, St. Davids, Dec. 20, 1795, no. 17814, Fitzherbert-Perrin Papers, Derbyshire Record Office.

64. Ibid. A good description of cultivating plantain trees appears in the House of Commons Sessional Papers (1790), 29/143.

65. [Joshua Steele],"Queries from His Excell[enc]y Governor Parry in Barbados" [April 26, 1788], C.O. 28/61. Cf. a newspaper account of agent John Braithwaite's testimony to the Lords of Council, *Barbardos Mercury and Bridge-Town Gazette* [*Barb. Merc. and B-T. Gaz.*], July 26, 1788.

66. Braithwaite's testimony is reprinted in ibid. Cf. the important letter "Mr F——of Society," which mentions that the present annual support per slave — food, clothing, tools, medicines, and sick care — was £5 per head, and that three hundred acres of food crops would support three hundred slaves "in families." ibid., Nov. 12, 1788. Mainsweet Walrond to Clement Tudway, April 24, 1781, bundle 4, box 11, Tudway MS, Somerset Record Office, Taunton.

67. July 7, 1783 account of attorney, Edward East, Hope Estate Plantation Accounts, 1777–83, Stowe MS, uncataloged Henry E. Huntington Library, San Marino, Calif.

68. John Tharp to the Trustees, Sept. 12, 1785, June 17, 1786, Account Book, 1786, 8v, 3/e/2; 1790, 9v, 3/e/4, Gale-Morant Papers, Roborough Library, University of Exeter.

69. Deposition of John Whitaker, Montego Bay, Jan. 11, 1792, C.O. 137–90, ff. 35–36.

70. Account Book, 1791, 3/e/5, Gale-Morant Papers; cf. Thistlewood's Journal, Jan. 27, 1760.

71. "Account Increase and Decrease of Stock . . . ,"Jan. 1, 1779, Account Book, 1775–81, Accounts and Plan for Hampden Estate, T-SK 22, Sterling Family of Keir and Cawder, Strathclyde Regional Archives, Glasgow.

72. From a printed plantation journal for Vere Estate, 1798, box 2 (old indexing), Fitzherbert-Perrin Papers. Concerning buying the slaves' yearlings to replenish the estate's herds, see David Ewart to Penrhyn, Oct. 26, 1807, no. 1479, Penrhyn Papers.

73. Testimony of Thomas Nurse, chief overseer, River Plantation, in *The Report from a Select Committee of the House of Assembly Appointed to Inquire into . . . the late Insurrection* (Barbados [1816]), 49, Department of Archives, Black Rock, Barbados.

74. Wood to Thomas Lane, July 2, 1796, Report no. 288, Newton Estate Papers.

75. Account Book, 1756–57 for settling the estate of William Fitzherbert, pp. 14, 17 (old indexing), bundle marked "West Indian Plantation Account, 23 Ledgers, 1756–92," Fitzherbert-Perrin Papers. See note to the effect that Robin had put for safe-keeping £25 into the hands of the estate attorney, Benjamin Alleyne, to be paid to his children after his death.

76. "Quarterly Report of the Belle Plantation conducted by Thomas Marshall, Ending the 30th June 1836," Harewood Manuscripts, Archives Division, Leeds Central Library. For big estates forced to buy provisions locally from slaves, see Nov. 20, 1790 entry for £4.5 paid Watson's Negroes, Ballard's Valley Accounts, 1790, box 1766–1827, Ballard Valley Papers, Manuscript Department, Duke University Library, Durham, N.C.

77. John Luffman, *A Brief Account of the Island of Antigua. . . . In Letters to a Friend Written in the Years 1786, 1787, 1788,* 2d ed. (London, 1784), 94; [Mrs. Flannigan], *Antigua and the Antiguans,* 2 vols. (London, 1844), 2:101–2. Cf. James Ramsay, *An Essay on the Treatment and Conversion of African Slaves in the British Sugar Colonies* (London, 1784), 126–28n, concerning the numerous black tradesmen of Barbados whose wages supported impoverished white families.

78. Edward Turner to the Secretary, "Accounts, Antigua, 1805–1806," May 15, 1806, no. 25, box 111, Methodist Missionary Society Archives, School of Oriental and African Studies Library, University of London; *Barb. Merc. and B-T. Gaz.*, Dec 17, 1805, William Hill; Aug. 29, 1807, Nathaniel Weekes.

79. W. Stanford to Bishop Porteus, Westmoreland [Jamaica], July 22, 1788, West Indies, vol. 18, 67v, Fulham Papers, Lambeth Palace Library.

80. House of Commons Sessional Papers (1790), 29/262–64.

81. Sir P[hillip] Gibbes to Sir William Fitzherbert, June 9, 1788, bundle marked "Sir p[hillip] Gibbes — Negro Houses," Turner's Hall, Barbados, pre–1821 box (now as a separate document E20555), Fitzherbert-Perrin Papers. Also see clothing distribution lists indicating larger allotments to "Principle Negroes": Mr. Concannon to R. H. Elletson, Hope Estate (Jamaica), May 6, 1779, MS29a, Institute of Jamaica, Kingston; Barry W. Higman, *Slave Population and Economy in Jamaica, 1807–1834* (Cambridge, 1976), 169; Higman, "Household Structure and Fertility on Jamaican Slave Plantations: A Nineteeth-century Example," *Population Studies* 27 (1973): 537, 541; and Douglas V. Armstrong, *The Old Village and the Great House: An Archaeological and Historical Examination of Drax Hall Plantation St. Ann's Bay, Jamaica* (Urbana, 1990), ch. 4, esp. 93ff.

82. [Anon.], *A Short Journey in the West Indies in which are Interspersed Curious Anecodotes and Characters* (London, 1790), 115–16 (British Library pressmark 10480 aa. 12).

83. William Sutherland to William Philip Perrin, April 9, 1787, E17803, Fitzherbert-Perrin Papers. See also, a Jamaican manager's note concerning provisions for new Negroes and "thin people," 775/948/2, p. 16 (1799), Dukenfield Hall Papers, Middlesex Record Office, London; and an attorney's request for woolens, especially for "the poorer sort of Negroes," who have "only what is given to them," Mainsweet Walrond to Clement Tudway, Aug. 25, 1774, bundle 4, box 11, Tudway MS.

84. John Whitaker, "Affidavits of white People and confessions of Negroes," enclosed in J. L. Winn, chairman of the St. James Parish Committee of Security and Safety, Jan. 13, 1792, pp. 35–36 in Lt. Gov. Adam Williamson to Sec. of State, Feb. 12, 1792, C.O. 137/90, ff. 1–2.

85. Ibid., f. 40.

86. Orders-in-Council "for Improving the Condition of Slaves in Trinidad," in Bathurst, Downing Street, May 11, 1826, C.O. 137/163.

87. Douglas Hall, *Free Jamaica, 1838–1865; An Economic History* (1959, repr. London, 1969), 158.

88. "Memorandum of Money . . . ," Charles Dabney Account Book, 1767, vol. 6, Dabney Papers, Colonial Williamsburg Research Center microfilm of the original in the Southern Historical Collection.

89. Guardian Accounts, Oct. 28, 1793, Talbot County, 1790–97, no. 11292, p. 230, Hall of Records, Annapolis, Md.; William Randolph Farm Account and Daybook, 1783–1829, new acquisition file folder (no. 1811), Colonial Williamsburg Research Center.

90. Thomas Jefferson, Account Book, trans. James A. Baer, Jr., Alderman Library, University of Virginia.

91. A study based on late antebellum census returns uncovers instances of slave property — in crops and cattle, principally — that although widely scattered and unrepresentative of the whole, were substantial. See Loren Schweninger, *Black Property Owners in the South, 1790–1915* (Urbana, 1990), chs. 1–2.

92. Daybook of Henry Ravenal of Hanover, South Carolina Historical Society, Charleston.

93. Nov. 29, 1798, Aug. 1795, Jan. 6, 1797, item no. 336, box 17, John Gibbons Memorandum Book, Savannah, 1791–1800, Georgia Historical Society, Savannah; cash payments to Negroes of Thomas Gibbons, March-June 1787, £12.10 to Peter for hogs; Dec. 1771, William Gibbons Account Book, 1765–82, items no. 433, 455, box 26; Jan. 1792 entry for payment for potato slips, Richard Leake Account Book, 1786–1800, Georgia Historical Society. See also payments of slaves for fence repair and as a crew, June 20, 1796, July 24, 1810, John Ball, Sr., Papers, 1773-1823, South Caroliniana Library, University of South Carolina, Columbia.

94. Caleb Coker Plantation Book, 1856–61, South Caroliniana Library; see also Foner, *Nothing but Freedom*, 55.

95. Gabriel E. Manigault's Memorandum Book for Silk Hope, 1861–73, box 11-277, South Carolina Historical Society.

96. Duncan Clinch Heyward, *Seed from Madagascar* (Chapel Hill, 1937), 180–81; Theodore Rosengarten, *Tombee: Portrait of a Cotton Planter, with the Journal of Thomas B. Chaplin (1822–1890)* (New York, 1986), 160; also 69, 118, 158. The sea island St. Helena planters, Rosengarten concludes, condoned theft and the black market in order to promote tranquillity and open discussion of "the human wants of their slaves." For a North Carolina view of slaves selling turned inward to the plantation, see Bennett H. Wall, "The Founding of the Pettigrew Plantations," in *Plantation, Town and County: Essays on the Local History of American Slave Society*, ed. Elinor Miller and Eugene D. Genovese (Urbana, 1974), 181. Two issues should be emphasized: the precarious nature of the bits of garden patches and stock of antebellum slaves, and the fact that buyers of the produce of slaves were rarely anyone other than their owners. See "The Narratives of James Curry," in *Slave Testimony: Two Centuries of Letters, Speeches, Interviews, and Autobiographies*, ed. John W. Blassingame (Baton Rouge, 1977), 136; and Charles Joyner, *Down by the Riverside: A South Carolina Slave Community* (Urbana, 1984), 129f. Edward Countryman summarizes Joyner on the internal economy in part as "a theatrical acting out of the links of power and dependency." Review in *Slavery and Abolition* 6 (Sept. 1985): 164. On the other hand, the best argument for slaves participating in an actual market comes from Charleston, when during the Vesey conspiracy in 1822, reference was made to "several hundred" blacks in canoes who brought down produce to the city. Lionel H. Kennedy and Thomas Parker, *An Official Report of the Trials of Sundry Negroes, Charged with an attempt to raise An Insurrection in the State of South-Carolina. . . .* (Charleston, 1822), 39f. See also, Schweninger, *Black Property Owners in the South*, ch. 2.

97. [John] Hook Account Book, 1788–1805, pp. 10, 34, 34f, Manuscripts Division, Duke University Library.

98. Ibid., 10, 71ff.

99. Ibid., 12, 12f, 30, 30f. There is another slave shopping list, at a plantation company store, in no. 3240, box 1, A. H. Arrington Papers, Southern Historical Collection, University of North Carolina Library, Chapel Hill.

100. Cf. Michael Mullin, "Women, and the Comparative Study of American Negro Slavery," *Slavery and Abolition* 6 (May 1985): 25–40.

101. *Virginia Gazette* [*Va. Gaz.*] (Rind), March 17, 1768, March 29, 1770; Gerald W. Mullin, *Flight and Rebellion: Slave Resistance in Eighteenth-century Virginia* (New York, 1972), 61.

102. *Diary of Colonial Landon Carter,* ed. Greene, Feb. 3, 1772, 649; *Va. Gaz.* (Rind), March 17, 1768, Nov. 16, 1769, March 19, 1770.

103. Washington to William Pierce, Philadelphia, June 8, 1794, in *George Washington and Mount Vernon,* ed. M. D. Conway, vol. 4 of *Memoirs of the Long Island Historical Society* (Brooklyn, 1889), 81; Haworth, *George Washington: Farmer,* 142–43.

104. [March 20, 1735], Records in the P.R.O. Relating to South Carolina ["Sainsbury Transcripts"], 36 vols. (1663–1782), 18:304, South Carolina Department of Archives and History.

105. *Cape-Fear Mercury,* Sept. 22, 1773, William Hooper.

106. J. P. Kennedy and H. R. McIlwaine, eds., *Journal of the House of Burgesses, 1619–1776,* 13 vols. (Richmond, 1905–15), 1752–58:20.

107. Kent County Circuit Count Papers, 1774–94: sheriff's fine list for Nov. 1, 1790–Nov. 1, 1791, folder "Criminal Papers" (1794); March terms 1793 and 1794, Colonial Williamsburg Research Center microfilm of a Virginia State Library holding.

108. Mullin, *Flight and Rebellion,* 118–19.

109. Feb. 1790 entry, Tussekiah Church, Lunenberg County (Corcord Association) Minutes, 1784–1826, Virginia Baptist Historical Society, University of Richmond.

110. Mullin, *Flight and Rebellion,* 60.

111. Thomas Pinckney to Harriet Horry Fairchild, June 25, 1789, red box, no. 8, Pinckney Family Papers, Library of Congress.

112. Cited in Ulrich B. Phillips, *The Slave Economy of the Old South: Selected Essays in Economic and Social History,* ed. Eugene D. Genovese (Baton Rouge, 1968), 31.

113. Daniel McKinnon, *A Tour through the British West Indies in the Years 1802 and 1803, Giving a Particular Account of the Bahama Islands* (London 1804), 68–69; [Janet Schaw], *Journal of a Lady of Quality: Being the Narrative of a Journey from Scotland to the West Indies, North Carolina, and Portugal, in the Years 1774 to 1776,* ed. Evangeline Walker Andrews and Charles M. Andrews (New Haven, 1922), 88, 107f.

114. James White to Bishop Gibson, Vere, April 23, 1724, West Indies Series, vol. 17, f. 185, Fulham Papers, Lambeth Palace Library; Long, *History of Jamaica,* 2: 105.

115. Thomas Atwood, *History of the Island of Dominica* (London, 1791), 178–80.

116. Edward Locksley Cox, "The Shadow of Freedom in the Slave Societies of Grenada and St. Kitts, 1763–1833," Ph.D. diss., Johns Hopkins University, 1977, 166ff.

117. *Santiago de la Vega Gazette* [Jamaica], Feb. 12, 1803; Gov. Ralph Woodford Proclamation, Trinidad, Dec. 18, 1813 in Trinidad Duplicate Dispatches, vol. 2, part 1, 1815–16, National Archives, Port of Spain, Trinidad.

118. Luffman, *A Brief Account of the Island of Antigua,* 138ff.

119. Philip Thicknesse, *Memoirs and Anecdotes* (Dublin, 1790), 46.

120. R. R. Madden, *A Twelve Month's Residence in the West Indies,* 2 vols. (Philadelphia, 1835), 1:42–43.

121. Robert Renny, *A History of Jamaica* (London, 1807), 138.

122. *Barb. Merc. and B-T. Gaz.,* Feb. 14, 1784.

123. "John Poyer's Letter to Lord Seaforth," *Journal of the Barbados Museum and Historical Society* 8 (May 1941): 163ff, 150, 157; Jerome S. Handler, *The Unappropriated People: Freedmen in the Slave Society of Barbados* (Baltimore, 1974), 125ff.

124. Conversation with William M. Kelso, state archaeologist, Williamsburg, Va., June 24, 1976.

125. Cited in Haworth, *George Washington: Farmer,* 196f. The Polish poet was Niemcewitz, who spent twelve days and left the most detailed description of a slave quarter according to "Specific Purpose Intramural Document: Housing and Family Life of the Mt. Vernon Negro" (Oct. 1954), in-house report, Mount Vernon Research Room.

126. "Subjects Particular Respecting the Negroes in reply to Mr. J. Sinclair," bundle 2, C381, Miscellaneous Political, Barham Papers, Clarendon Deposit, Bodleian Library, Oxford University.

## Chapter Seven. Family

1. Elizabeth Fox-Genovese and Eugene D. Genovese, *Fruits of Merchant Capital: Slavery and Bourgeois Property in the Rise and Expansion of Capitalism* (New York, 1983), 168; Orlando Patterson, "From Endo-deme to Matri-deme: An Interpretation of the Development of Kinship and Social Organization among the Slaves of Jamaica, 1655–1830," in *Eighteenth-century Florida and the Caribbean,* ed. Samuel Proctor (Gainesville, 1976), 51.

2. Journals of Thomas Thistlewood [Thistlewood's Journal], March 21, 1758, Monson 31, Lincolnshire Record Office, Lincoln.

3. William Sells, *Remarks on the Condition of the Slaves in the Island of Jamaica* (London, 1823), 28–29, Bryan Edwards, *History of the British West Indies,* 2 vols. (Dublin, 1794), 2:73; Sidney W. Mintz and Richard Price, *An Anthropological Approach to the Afro-American Past: A Caribbean Perspective* (Philadelphia, 1976), 22–23.

4. Barry W. Higman, *Slave Population and Economy in Jamaica, 1807–1834* (Cambridge, 1976); Higman, *Slave Populations of the British Caribbean, 1807–1834* (Baltimore, 1983); Higman, "Household Structure and Fertility on Jamaican

Slave Plantations: A Nineteenth-century Example," *Population Studies* 27 (1973): 527–50; Higman, "African and Creole Slave Family Patterns in Trinidad," in *Africa and the Caribbean: The Legacies of a Link,* ed. Margaret E. Crahan and Franklin W. Knight (Baltimore, 1979), 41–64; Michael Craton, "Changing Patterns of Slave Families in the British West Indies," *Journal of Interdisciplinary History* 10 (Summer 1979): 1–35; Craton, "Hobbesian or Panglossian? The Two Extremes of Slave Conditions in the British Caribbean, 1783 to 1834," *William and Mary Quarterly,* 3d ser., 35 (April 1978): 324–56; Craton, "Jamaican Slave Mortality: Fresh Light from Worthy Park, Longville and the Tharp Estates," *Journal of Caribbean History* 3 (Nov. 1971): 1–27; Craton, *Searching for the Invisibile Man: Slaves and Plantation Life in Jamaica* (Cambridge, Mass., 1978), esp. pt. 1 and appendixes; Richard S. Dunn, "A Tale of Two Plantations: Slave Life at Mesopotamia in Jamaica and Mount Airy in Virginia, 1799 to 1828," *William and Mary Quarterly,* 3d ser., 34 (Jan. 1977): 32–65.

5. Christopher Codrington to his uncle, Betty's Hope, Antigua, May 12, 1790, D1610/C 19, Codrington Family Papers, Gloucestershire Record Office, Gloucester.

6. Sidney W. Mintz, "History and Anthropology: A Brief Reprise," in *Race and Slavery in the Western Hemisphere: Quantitative Studies,* ed. Stanley L. Engerman and Eugene D. Genovese (New York, 1975), 493–94. Cf. Barbara Bush, *Slave Women in Caribbean Society, 1650–1838* (Bloomington, 1990), 84–91.

7. Thistlewood's Journal, March 25, 1756.

8. Jamaica: kin terms in the *Jamaica Royal Gazette* [*Jam. Royal Gaz.*], for uncle: Oct. 17, 1780, George Bannett; Aug. 16, 1794-P.S., Moses de Campos; May 30, 1795-S., Thomas Priddie; Oct. 17, 1795-S., R. Craighton; for aunt, Oct. 25, 1794-P.S., John Christopherz; May 23, 1801-S., James Wilson; grandfather: Oct. 14, 1797-P.S., Colin M'Larty. Barbados: kin terms in the *Barbados Mercury and Bridge-Town Gazette* [*Barb. Merc. and B-T. Gaz.*], for aunt: Nov. 30, 1805, H. W. Straghan; grandmother: Feb. 12, 1788 for-sale notice; for father-in-law: Oct. 4, 1806, Jacob Blozada; Oct. 17, 1807, Gabriel B. Byer.

9. *Maryland Gazette* [*Md. Gaz.*], March 25, 1790, Sarah Blake's Estate; August 29, 1799, John Francis Mercer; also for a woman and boy for sale and "they may be had low for ready money, but will not be sold separate." *Virginia Herald and Fredericksburg Advertiser,* Nov. 14, 1793; July 25, 1793, Burges Ball: "I would prefer selling in families, if convenient to purchasers." Same wording in ibid., Oct. 11, 1792, James Lewis; Dec. 11, 1794, Richard Hackley; and in the *Virginia Gazette* [*Va. Gaz.*], Oct.11, 1776, Richard Kidder Meade. Probate records: Will of Short Young, Sept. 4, 1795, Chesterfield County, Hawkins and McGehee Family Papers, 1769–1800, Alderman Library, University of Virginia; plantation correspondence: James Mercer to Battaile Muse, July 10, 1777, Muse Papers, Manuscript Division, Duke University Library, Durham, N.C.

A profitable question is whether the Upper South, especially the old tidewater region, set the tone for the entire South in the antebellum era. Was it the case "that 'the father of a slave is unknown in our law' was the universal understanding of Southern jurists"? From an 1811 case cited by Stanley Elkins, *Slavery: A Problem in American Institutional and Intellectual Life,* 2d ed. (1959, repr. Chicago, 1968), 55.

10. *South Carolina Gazette* [*S.C. Gaz.*], March 26, 1750, George Gabriel Powell; July 9, 1750, William Duke. July 19, 1760, James Reid; April 24, 1762, Francis Pelot; Dec. 4, 1752, Joseph Gibbon; *Gazette of the State of South Carolina*, Dec. 1, 1779, Thomas Pinckney. For the same in probate records: Judith Villepontoux's estate distinguishes children as either "hers" (mother's) or "theirs" (both parents); Anthony Toomer's does the same for grandchildren as well in the Charleston Will Book C, 1798–1800, 731–58; see also, estate of Mrs. Mary Philip, Aug. 28, 1785, Charleston District Inventories, Book B, 1787–93, 11, and Arthur Middleton's Cedar Grove and Middleton Place, Feb. 25–26, 1793, 502ff, South Carolina Department of Archives and History. In plantation records, see "Valuation of Property Settlement by McCartan Campbell on his Wife Sarah in conformity to his marriage Bond," Aug. 23, 1792, blue box no. 3, Pinckney Family Papers, Library of Congress; Francis Wilkinson Pickens Plantation Book, 1839–68, 3, Manuscript Division, Duke University Library. The Butler Family Papers, box 5, f. 6, Historical Society of Pennsylvania, Philadelphia, contains a remarkable inventory listing slaves through four generations, that is following "parents," "children," "Grand Children," and "Great grand Children": "A list of Negroes (who belonged to Mrs Blake) and their Children . . . June 29th, 1817."

11. *Brit. Parl. Papers, Slave Trade* (1831–32), 2/162; cf. James Henry to Government House, Barbados, Aug. 16, 1838, C.O. 28/125.

12. Balcarres to Sec. of State, Duke of Portland, July 4, 1797, C.O. 137/96, f. 258v.

13. Kenneth F. Kiple, *The Caribbean Slave: A Biological History* (Cambridge, England, 1981), 106ff (on fertility), 113ff (infant mortality).

14. Richard Beissett, John Sharp, William Barnett, assessors for Rooke Clarke, Feb. 10, 1775, Tweedie Estate Records, Institute of Jamaica, Kingston.

15. Malcolm Laing to William Philps Perrin, Jan. 25, 1774, E16779; Laing to Perrin, Dec. 17, 1770, May 14, 1771, E16720, E16724. "It is a very difficult matter to prevail upon Negroes to change the[ir] situation of their houses from a spot they have been long habituated however sensible they may be to its unhealtheness": John Jacques and Ralph Fisher to Perrin, June 21, 1791, E17126. All in Fitzherbert-Perrin Papers, Derbyshire Record Office, Matlock.

16. Balcarres to Messrs. Atkinson, Bogle and Company, London, Feb. 8, 1811, Letterbook 1807–18, vol. 8, manuscript volumes, 23/14–116, Crawford Muniments, National Library of Scotland, Edinburgh.

17. William Philip Perrin's Daybook, 1783–84, 22 (old ref. box 101, item i), and Jacques and Fisher to Perrin, Jan. 18, 1785, Fitzherbert-Perrin Papers. A good series of comments appears in the Penhyrn Papers, see June 24, July 6, Aug. 3, 1805, nos. 1384, 1378 and 1380, Department of Manuscripts, University of North Wales Library, Bangor.

18. Joseph Manesty and John Mosley, Portland Parish, Jan. 10, 1754 enclosed in Chapone and Yeates, Kingston, Feb. 9, 1754; also John Davis to Mosley, Dec. 20, 1754, Bill Book, (1747–) for the Estate of Sarah Smith, MS 230. Both in the Institute of Jamaica, Kingston.

19. Thistlewood's Journal, March 17, 1754, Oct. 21, 1782.

20. William Beckford, Jr., *Remarks Upon the Situation of the Negroes in Jamaica* (London, 1788), 91.

21. *Brit. Parl. Papers, Slave Trade* (1826–27), 73/27; Cynric R. Williams, *A Tour through the Island of Jamaica, . . . in the Year 1823* (London, 1826), 12f.

22. "Instructions from the Council and Assembly of the Island of Antigua to . . . [the] Agents of the said Island [1788]," Query 35, D/1610/E34, Codrington Family Papers, Gloucestershire Record Office, Gloucester.

23. M. G. Lewis, *Journal of a West India Proprietor, 1815–17,* ed. Mona Wilson (London, 1929), 405f.

24. John Blyth to Joseph Foster Barham, Jamaica, Sept. 4, 1809, Sept. 4, 1809, bundle 1, 1809–16, c. 358, Barham Family Papers, Clarendon Deposit, Bodleian Library, Oxford University. Emphasis added.

25. House of Commons Sessional Papers (1790), 29/187.

26. Beckford cited in Edward Braithwaite, *The Development of Creole Society in Jamaica, 1770–1820* (Oxford, 1971), 215. From the Jamaican Assembly's *Enquiry into the Moral and Religious Improvement of the Slave Population Since 1823 . . .* (Kingston, 1833) came the following replies taken from a copy of the pamphlet in the Fitzherbert-Perrin Papers. An attorney noted, "[The slaves] will it [their property] away, and their will is considered as sacred as my own; they often leave the master their executor. I am executor of one or two" (45); A Baptist minister (at Brown's Town, Dry Harbour in St. Ann's), when asked if a slave could will property, replied, "As fully as any free person" (52, see also 73). A plantation physician testified that "They make verbal bequests of their property, which the proprietor generally sees carried into effect" (72ff).

27. Edward Long, *The History of Jamaica,* 3 vols. (1774, London, 1970), 2:410.

28. [A West Indian], *Notes in Defense of the Colonies; on the Increase and Decrease of the Slave Population of the West Indies* (London, 1826), 25, 26, 28–30.

29. Robert F. Gray, *The Family Estate in Africa: Studies in the Role of Property in Family Structure and Lineage Continuity,* ed. Robert F. Gray and P. H. Gulliver (Boston, 1964), 4ff.

30. "1826 Barbados — Codrington College Remarks in Codrington Estate and Treatment of Slaves," series C/WI, box 8, Society for the Propagation of the Gospel Archives, London.

31. [A West Indian], *Notes in Defense of the Colonies,* 29, 34.

32. Jonathan R. Webb to Barham, St. Elizabeth, June 16, 1809, bundle 1, 1809–16, c. 358, Barham Family Papers; cf. Craton, "Changing Patterns of Slave Families," 12.

33. *Barb. Merc. and B-T. Gaz.,* Dec. 2, 1786, George White's Ned Boy, enclosed in C.O. 7/1 (71); Aug. 3, 1805, J. Malloney, Sen., Oct. 6, 1807, Isaac Agard; see also, Oct. 8, 1788, E. G. Thomas; Nov. 2, 1805-S., Jacob Goodrige; Aug. 30, 1783, Richard Redwar; Jan. 11, 1806, J. C. Roach; and Aug. 16, 1788, Abel Hinds. A plantation record notes that slaves with two wives are "very common." Gill Slater to Lady Fitzherbert, June 3, 1793, E20565, Fitzherbert-Perrin Papers.

34. *Jam. Royal Gaz.,* Feb. 25, 1797-S., William Ramsay; Jan. 14, 1792-P.S., John

James Vidal; see also, Dec. 22, 1792-P.S., Hector McKay; Feb. 2, 1782-S., Elizabeth Cargill; April 4, 1795-S., Thomas Chisholm; May 18, 1805-P.S., Charles Keene; cf. Higman, "Household Structure," 539.

35. *Md. Gaz.*, Jan. 20, 1803; *Va. Gaz.* (Dixon and Hunter), Oct. 31, 1771, James French; *Va. Gaz.* (Purdie and Dixon), April 21, 1768, John Holladay.

36. *The Aristocratic Journey: Being the Outspoken Letters of Mrs. Basil Hall Written during a Fourteen Months' Sojourn in America, 1827–1828*, ed. Una Pope-Hennesy (New York, 1931), 223.

37. For contemporaries' awareness of demographic factors (which are sometimes overlooked in recent interpretations), see Votes of Assembly for 12 Nov. 1788, 94–95, C.O. 140/73. There are traces of real understanding in House of Commons Sessional Papers (1789), 29/112, for example, of testimony implying an understanding of the relationship of breast feeding to birth intervals; see also, 89, 157, 215, 260–62, 300, 207ff, 321ff, 30/351–52, for the testimony of two plantation physicians and a minister (John Castles of Grenada, Samuel Athill, and Robert Boucher Nicholls). See also, E. Pool to Eliza Elletson, Sept. 10, 1778, Elletson Letterbooks, MS 29a, Institute of Jamaica.

38. Lewis, *Journal*, 334; also, 86–87, 273, 314–15, 320–21.

39. Ibid., 277, 320, 76. In order to balance my argument about the degree of choice, the more familiar external factors that pushed women into unhappy, often unsafe, and tragic pregnancies were well known by the early 1800s. See Rowland William Fearon to Lord Penhryn, June 9, Oct. 30, 1804, Jan. 26, 1805, nos. 1327, 1349, 1355 (1361 for a clearer copy). All in the Penhryn Papers. Cf. Samson Wood to Thomas Lane, May 16, Oct. 19, 1798, nos. 343, 381(1), Newton Estate Papers, Paleography Room, University of London Library.

40. *The Diary of Colonel Landon Carter of Sabine Hall, 1752–1778*, ed. Jack P. Greene (Charlottesville, 1965), Sept. 21, 1770, 496, July 5, 1775, 919. For slave women using difficult pregnancies to keep out of field work for up to a hundred days, see Theodore Rosengarten, *Tombee: Portrait of a Cotton Planter: with the Journal of Thomas B. Chapin (1822–1890)* (New York, 1986), 157.

41. Thistlewood's Journal, March 18, 1754, Feb. 9, Dec. 16, 1768. For a mother who maimed herself in order to be with her sick child, see April 2, 1769.

42. Ibid., Oct. 1, 1768. For further glimpses of Coobah's love life, see Aug. 24, 1761, May 4, 1767, Aug. 28, 1768.

43. The citation ends: "This stopped any further Conversation." Alexander Orr to Lt. Gov. John Orde, Thursday A.M., Jan. 27, 1791, Rosaly Estate (Dominica), C.O. 71/19.

44. John Shipman, "Thoughts on the Present State of Religion among the Negroes of Jamaica," Montego Bay, May 13, 1820, p. 17, box 1 no. 588, West Indies, Biographical no. 1, Methodist Missionary Society Archives, School of Oriental and African Studies Library, University of London.

45. Margin note to an inventory for the estate of Edmund Jenings, Esqr., Dec. 16, 1712 by John Hawkins, Francis Porteus Corbin Papers, Colonial Williamsburg Research Center, microfilm of the original at the Manuscript Division, Duke University Library.

46. Edward Kimber, *The History of the Life and Adventures of Mr. Anderson, Containing His Strange Varieties of Fortune in Europe and America* (Dublin, 1754), 129ff (pagination scrambled, follows 216), Maryland Historical Society, Baltimore.

47. Examinations taken by the St. Ann's militia (before J. J. and W. S. Sharker), Jan. 13, 16, 1832, James Johnson box, letters, 1770–1838/1877, folder: "Letters 1832," Powell Collection, Historical Society of Pennsylvania.

48. Melville J. Herskovits, *Life in a Haitian Valley* (1937, repr. New York, 1971), 106ff. See George E. Simpson's comment on Price-Mars, "Le Processus d'une culture," in *Acculturation in the Americas: Proceedings and Selected Papers of the XXIXth International Congress of Americanists,* ed. Sol Tax (1952, repr. New York, 1967), 149f.

49. Ali A. Mazrui, *The African Condition: A Political Diagnosis* (New York, 1980), 57. See also, John E. Eberegbulam Njoku, *The World of the African Woman* (Metuchen, 1980), 14; cf. Eugene D. Genovese, *Roll, Jordan, Roll: The World the Slaves Made* (New York, 1974), 450–75.

50. Caroline H. Bledsoe, *Women and Marriage in Kpelle Society* (Palo Alto, 1980), 48, esp. ch. 3; cf. T. C. McCaskie, "State and Society, Marriage and Adultery: Some Considerations towards a Social History of Pre-Colonial Asante," *Journal of African History* 22 (1981): 484f, 488; Ronald Cohen and John Middleton, eds., "Introduction," in *From Tribe to Nation in Africa: Studies in Incorporation Processes* (London, 1970).

51. B. E. Harrell-Bond, review of Caroline Bledsoe, *Women and Marriage in Kpelle Society, Times Literary Supplement,* Dec. 12, 1980. See also, Niara Sudarkasa, "The 'Status of Women' in Indigenous African Societies," in *Women in Africa and the African Diaspora,* ed. Rosalyn Terborg-Penn, Sharon Harley, and Audrea Benton Rushing (Washington, D.C., 1987), 25–41.

52. Dominique Zahan, *The Religion, Spirituality, and Thought of Traditional Africa* (Paris, 1970, repr. Chicago, 1978), 31; Edmund Leach, *Lévi-Strauss* (New York, 1970), 57.

53. Wilhemina J. Kalu, "Modern Ga Family Life Patterns: A Look at Changing Marriage Structure in Africa," *Journal of Black Studies* 11 (March 1981): 349–60: "The family place is defined as where most or all of the children live." Also see Eugene Hillman, *Polygamy Reconsidered: African Plural Marriage and the Christian Churches* (Maryknoll, 1975), 116ff.

54. R. T. Smith citing Meyer Fortes in "The Matrifocal Family," in *The Character of Kinship,* ed. Jack Goody (London, 1973), 123; R. Radcliffe-Brown and Daryll Forde, eds., *African Systems of Kinship and Marriage* (London, 1950); Arthur Phillips, ed., *Survey of African Marriage and Family Life* (Oxford, 1953). Madeline Manoukian, *Akan and Ga-Adangme Peoples* (London 1950), 26–31, argues that marriage is a partnership, not an organic union, in polygynous relationships that are also less stressful emotionally and tend to avoid conflict more than is the case with monogamous ones, for a traditional element is "the pursuit of separate identities." See also, M. D. McLeod, *The Asante* (London, 1981), 30–31. Among the Bakongo, "the family has never been a clearly defined unit, nor

is it identified by a particular word in the language"; Wyatt MacGaffrey, "Lineage Structure, Marriage and the Family Amongst the Central Bantu," *Journal of African History* 24 (1983): 174. For a different slant, see Sudarkasa, "The 'Status of Women' in Indigenous African Societies," 25–41, 31–35.

55. Mary Beth Norton, Herbert G. Gutman, and Ira Berlin, "The Afro-American Family in the Age of Revolution," in *Slavery and Freedom in the Age of the American Revolution*, ed. Ira Berlin and Ronald Hoffman (Charlottesville, 1983), 175–91. Cf. Herbert G. Gutman, *The Black Family in Slavery and Freedom, 1750–1925* (New York, 1976), 61ff; and Jack Goody and Joan Buckley, "Inheritance and Women's Labour in Africa," *Africa* 43, no. 2 (1973): 108–21.

## Chapter Eight. Plantation Religion and Resistance

1. Alberto Moravia, *Which Tribe Do You Belong To?* (1972; London, 1974), 34.

2. Cf. Albert J. Raboteau, *Slave Religion: The "Invisible Institution" in the Antebellum South* (New York, 1978); Donald G. Mathews, *Religion in the Old South* (Chicago, 1977), 198ff.

3. Eugene D. Genovese, *Roll, Jordan, Roll: The World the Slaves Made* (New York, 1974), 185, 592–94; Robert I. Rotberg and Ali A. Mazrui, eds., *Protest and Power in Black Africa* (New York, 1970), xxiii; cf. Vincent Harding, "Religion and Resistance among Antebellum Negroes, 1800–1860," in *The Making of Black America*, ed. August Meier and Elliott Rudwick, 2 vols. (New York, 1969), 1:179–97; and Sterling Stuckey, *Slave Culture: Nationalist Theory and the Foundations of Black America* (New York, 1987), 43ff.

4. Mary Douglas cited in "Purity and Danger Revisited," *Times Literary Supplement*, Sept. 19, 1980, 1045.

5. "Answers returned the 12th of April 1788 by Messrs. Fuller, Long & Chisholme to the Questions put to them by their Lordships respecting the practice of Obeah in the Island of Jamaica," Public Record Office [P.R.O.], Board of Trade 6/10, pp. 171ff. Hereafter, "The Practice of Obeah, 1788." Bryan Edwards, *The History, Civil and Commerical, of the British Colonies in the West Indies*, 2 vols. (Dublin, 1793), 2:84, 90, 95ff.

6. Journals of Thomas Thistlewood [Thistlewood's Journal] [June 25?] 1751, Monson 31, Lincolnshire Record Office, Lincoln, 131f; cf. Thomas Astley, *A New General Collection of Voyages and Travels*, 4 vols. (London, 1745–47), 2:655 (for the cure of "Head-Ach" on the Gold Coast); and M. G. Lewis, *Journal of a West India Proprietor, 1815–17*, ed. Mona Wilson (London, 1929), 145.

7. Thistlewood's Journal, Nov. 11, 1760.

8. The failure of Christianity to meet African cosmology more on its own ground has produced hundreds of separatist movements — "the independent churches" — organized by healing prophets. See Robin Horton, "Ritual Man in Africa," *Africa* 34, no. 2 (April 1964): 95ff; D. B. Barrett, *Schism and Renewal in Africa; An Analysis of Six Thousand Contemporary Religious Movements* (Nairobi, 1968), 18ff; Sydney George Williamson, *Akan Religion and the Christian*

Faith; A Comparative Study of the Impact of Two Religions (Accra, 1965), 162–63; Steven Feierman, "Struggles for Control: The Social Roots of Health and Healing in Modern Africa," African Studies Review 28 (June–Sept. 1985): 73–147.

9. John S. Mbiti, African Religions and Philosophy (New York, 1969), 169.

10. Cited in Edward Brathwaite, The Development of Creole Society in Jamaica, 1770–1820 (Oxford, 1971), 162. For a good discussion of women sorcerers, see Dominique Zahan, The Religion, Spirituality, and Thought of Traditional Africa (Paris, 1970, repr. Chicago, 1979), ch. 7, esp. 94–97.

11. Lewis, Journal, 89–90, 286–87, also 85–86.

12. Ibid., 115, 118, 124–25, 127; on poisons: 183–84, 275–76: the whangra plant, cassava root, arsenic beans "in almost every negro garden," liver, and the gall bladder of an alligator. For an account of the sophisticated use of poisons in Haitian vodun to produce a Myal-like death trance, see Wade Davis, The Serpent and the Rainbow (New York, 1985); and Davis, Passage of Darkness: the Ethnobotany of the Haitian Zombie (Chapel Hill, 1988).

13. The manuscript, dated Montego Bay, May 13, 1820, is in West Indian Biographical, no. 1, box 588. Shipman rehearsed some of his ideas in an earlier report on June 12, 1819, no. 64, box 114, Methodist Missionary Society Archives, School of Oriental and African Studies Library, University of London.

14. Ibid.

15. [A West Indian], Notes in Defense of the Colonies; on the Increase and Decrease of the Slave Population of the West Indies (London, 1826), 29; cf. Lewis, Journal, 390, where an obeahman, the protege of Adam, put magic on a sister-in-law to miscarry in order to restrict the number of heirs.

16. Cited in Max Gluckman, Custom and Conflict in Africa (1956, repr. New York, 1969), 86, ch. 4.

17. "The Practice of Obeah, 1788," 176–77.

18. Thomas Dancer, The Medical Assistant; or Jamaica Practice of Physic: Designed Chiefly for the Use of Families and Plantations (Kingston, 1801), 175. The literature on dirt eating is considerable. For clinical data that belief in witchcraft does literally frighten some to death, see Barbara W. Lex, "Voodoo Death: New Thought on an Old Explanation," American Anthropologist 76 (Dec. 1974): 818–23; Emersen Douyon, "Research Model on Trance and Possession States in the Haitian Voodoo," in Papers on the Conference on Research and Sources of Haiti, ed. Richard P. Schaedel (New York: Research Institution for the Study of Man, 1969), 415–27; Jacob Elder, "Folk Beliefs, Superstitions and Ancestor Cult Activities in Relationship to Mental Health Problems," typescript of a lecture to the Nurses' Training School, Jan. 15, 1970, St. Ann's Hospital, Trinidad, BL2490 E37, F6/A, West Indies Collection, University of the West Indies, St. Augustine Campus, Trinidad.

19. Mainsweet Walrond to [Clement Tudway], Antigua, Oct. 4, 1765, Letterbook 1759–83, "Letters from Antigua," box 15, Tudway MS, Somerset Record Office, Taunton. Cf. Daniel Barnjum to J. F. Barham, July 15, 1768, c. 367, bundle 1, Barham Family Papers, Clarendon Deposit, Bodleian Library, Oxford University.

20. "The Practice of Obeah, 1788," 187.

21. Cited in Mary Douglas, "Primitive Thought-Worlds," in *Sociology of Religion: Selected Readings*, ed. Roland Robertson (London, 1969), 94–95; and E. E. Evans-Pritchard, *Witchcraft, Oracles and Magic among the Azande* (1937, abridged ed., Oxford, 1976), 25ff. For witch detecting, see Edward Long, *The History of Jamaica*, 3 vols. (London, 1774, repr. 1970), 2:420–21.

22. Lewis, *Journal*, 117, 124ff, 291–93.

23. Ibid., 87, 293.

24. Ibid., 126, 293–96.

25. A version of this ceremony still survives in Haitian vodun; Wade Davis has investigated the making of "zombies" through ingestion of toxins of puffer fish and the dutra plant. See, *The Serpent and the Drum*, a story about Haiti's "living dead" which broke sensationally in U.S. newpapers (and Garry Trudeau's *Doonesbury*) in early February 1986. For several articles regarding zombification, including one by Davis, see *Caribbean Review* 12, no. 3 (1983).

26. Lewis, *Journal*, 294–95.

27. On the "convulsive drunkenness and electrifying results" of Congolese Petro dancers in Haiti, see John M. Janzen, *Lemba, 1650–1930: A Drum of Affliction in Africa and the New World* (New York, 1982), 277ff. For a sense of the excitment and movement of the witch-finding "water-mamma" dance, see *British Parliamentary Papers, Slave Trade* (1825), "Further Papers Relating to Slaves in the West Indies," 67/28–30.

28. "Trial of a Slave in Berbice, for the Crime of Obeah and Murder, . . . Proceedings" (July 29, 1822), *Brit. Parl. Papers, Slave Trade* (1823), 65/25.

29. Ibid., 15, 23, 24, 25, 26, 27.

30. Ibid.; Fiscal's Report, Sept. 18, 1821, 16; also, 15, 20, 21–22, 33. Cf. 28, 29–30, 32–33.

31. The insurrection is in *Brit. Parl. Papers, Slave Trade* (1825), 67/102ff.

32. Ibid., 103, 105, 106, 107, 109, esp. 103–4: "Jack prepar[ed] the great swear with rum, blood and gunpowder. Henry cut his hand and pour[ed] blood into the mixture." Oaths included "By God, you must all stand to the battle . . . to rise and murder the white people"; and "that they must all have one heart, one tongue, and one desire." In another version they put into the mix "a little dirt from a place showing the print of a white man's foot."

33. "Confession of Jack . . . this 8th day of April 1824," ibid., 108f.

34. From a *Jamaica Royal Gazette* [*Jam. Royal Gaz.*], Aug. 5, 1781-S. in *Percy's Anecdotes* and found reprinted in the *Royal Gazette and Sierra Leone Advertiser*, Feb. 22, 1823, C.O. 271/2, ff. 229–29v. For a "body" of twenty Coramantee who got an overseer fired, see Charles Hiern to Caleb Dickinson, St. Elizabeth, Nov. 12, 1765, bundle 474, no. 221, Dickinson MS, Somerset Record Office, Taunton.

35. "The Examination of a Negro man named Peter belonging to Peru Estate. . . ," May 24, 1798, C.O. 137/100; "The Deposition of Henry Paulett and Alexander Steel, planters of Trelawny on 18 April, 4 P.M. [1798]," C.O. 140/84; Deposition of John Young, Trelawny [1798], C.O. 140/84.

36. Council Meeting, Scarborough [Tobago], Nov. 27, 1770, C.O. 288/1; Robert Steward (President of the Council) to Gov. Gen. Melville, Tobago, Nov. 30, 1770,

enclosed in Melville to Sec. of State Hillsborough, Grenada, Dec. 3, 1770, C.O. 101/15, no. 24, ff. 58–59. See also, "An Account of the Insurrection among the Coramantee Slaves at Tobago," enclosed in George Gibb to Francis Reynolds, Tobago, Dec. 21, 1770, Captain Francis Reynolds Papers, D340a x/16, Gloucestershire Record Office, Gloucester.

37. Michael Craton, *Testing the Chains: Resistance to Slavery in the British West Indies* (Ithaca, 1982), 180ff; Gordon Turnbull, *A Narrative of the Revolt and Insurrection in the Island of Grenada,* 2d ed. (London, 1796), 11–12.

38. Cited in Robert Jackson to Balcarres, Canaan [Estate], Jan., 6, 1796, 23/11/33, Crawford Muniments, National Library of Scotland, Edinburgh.

39. Balcarres to the Duke of Portland, Nov. 16, 1795, Dromilley near Wills, C.O. 137/96.

40. "Examinations of Sundry Slaves in the Parish of Trelawny — Jamaica, respecting an intention to revolt" (esp. of Robert Linton's Duke, Jan. 5, 1792) enclosed in Lt. Gov. Adam Williamson to Sec. of State, Feb. 12, 1792, C.O. 137/98; copy of "Frank's Examination before William Bullock, Esq.," St. Catherine, March 8 [1807], C.O. 137/118; also an extract of Council Minutes, March 9, 1807, C.O. 140/92.

41. Sarah Gilbert to the Secretary of the Society, English Harbour, Antigua, June 1, 1804, Correspondence In-Coming, West Indies, box 588, 1803–1813, Methodist Missionary Society Archives; W. Stanford to Bishop Porteus, Jamaica, July 22, 1788, West Indies, vol. 18, ff. 66–66v, Fulham Papers, Lambeth Palace Library, London. In the last portion of "The Practice of Obeah (1788)," 531, 533, Antiguans described obeah figures as fading — "a few do yet exist" — and obeah as having become only a matter of "juggling tricks" because Creoles were far more numerous than new Negroes. But these are only impressions of a complex problem: the decline, if that is the proper term, of obeah. More profitably, does witchcraft wane or wax with cultural contact? See T. C. McCaskie, "Anti-witchcraft Cults in Asante: An Essay in the Social History of an African People," *History in Africa* 8 (1981): 126ff; and M. J. Field, *Search For Security: An Ethno-psychiatric Study of Rural Ghana* (Evanston, 1960), 35ff, for an argument that witchcraft is the "fragmentary and garbled tradition of a widespread pre-agricultural religion."

42. Olli Alho, *The Religion of Slaves: A Study of the Religious Tradition and Behaviour of Plantation Slaves in the United States, 1830–1865* (Helsinki, 1976).

43. Alho, *The Religion of Slaves,* 201f.

44. Ibid., 204, 209. For instances of obeah in the lowcountry, see notice for slave "Doctor Hercules," *Gazette of the State of Georgia,* Oct. 19, 1788; Welsh Neck Baptist Church Minutes, May 21, June 3, 1826, Works Progress Administration typescript, 110ff, South Caroliniana Library, University of South Carolina, Columbia, for an account of one slave killing another who was allegedly a witch.

45. Alho, *The Religion of Slaves,* 204; see also, 203–11.

46. Cited in Betsy Fancher, *The Lost Legacy of Georgia's Golden Isles* (Garden City, 1971), 50.

47. Fancher, *The Lost Legacy,* 49–50.

48. See Notitia for St. Paul's Parish in Orr to the Secretary, March 30, 1744;

and Lewis Jones to the Secretary, May 1, 1739, St. Helena, reel 5 of the Society of the Propagation of the Gospel Records of local Anglican missionaries to the Secretary of the Society in London, South Carolina Department of Archives and History, Columbia, microfilm of transcripts in the New York Public Library. Unless indicated otherwise all references to Anglican missionaries in South Carolina are to reels in this microfilmed collection.

49. Rev. A. Garden to the Secretary, Charleston, May 6, 1740, reel 5.

50. Joseph Senhouse, "Observations of Barbados" [1779], p. 65, Lonsdale MS, Cambria Record Office, Carlisle.

51. Stephen J. Stein, "George Whitefield on Slavery: Some New Evidence," *Church History* 42 (June 1973): 243–56; Clarence ver Steeg, *Origins of a Southern Mosaic: Studies of Early Carolina and Georgia* (Baton Rouge, 1977), ch. 4, esp. 109ff; Allan Gallay, "Planters and Slaves in the Great Awakening," in *Masters and Slaves in the House of the Lord: Race and Religion in the American South, 1740–1870,* ed. John B. Boles (Lexington, Ky., 1988), 19–36; Charles Joyner, *Down by the Riverside: A South Carolina Slave Community* (Urbana, 1984); Margaret Washington Creel, *"A Peculiar People": Slave Religion and Community-Culture Among the Gullahs* (New York, 1988), ch. 4.

52. Louis Morton, *Robert Carter of Nomini Hall* (1941, repr. Charlottesville, 1945), 251–52.

53. Harriott Horry Ravenal, *Eliza Pinckney* (1896, repr. Spartanburg, 1967). 32–33.

54. See George Howe, *History of the Presbyterian Church in South Carolina,* 2 vols. (Columbia, 1870), 1:239–40, 244–46; J. H. Redding, *The Life and Times of Jonathan Bryan, 1708–1788* (Savannah, 1901), 9, 30–32; Alan Gallay, "The Origins of Slaveholders' Paternalism: George Whitefield, the Bryan Family, and the Great Awakening in the South," *Journal of Southern History* 53 (Aug. 1987): 369–94; also, *South Carolina Gazette* [*S.C. Gaz.*], March 27, 1742; Edward McCrady, *The History of South Carolina Under the Royal Government, 1719–77* (1899, repr. Columbia, 1969), 238–39.

55. Ravenal, *Eliza Pinckney,* 33.

56. The Grand Jury presentment against Bryan is reprinted in *S. C. Gaz.,* March 27, 1742. As a member of a powerful sea island family, Bryan was able to get himself (and the government) off the hook when he recanted "with shame and joy," saying that he had been duped by Satan, "the father of lies."

57. Lewis Jones to the Secretary, St. Helena's, Dec. 27, 1743, reel 2.

58. Le Jau to the Secretary, St. James, Goose Creek, Feb. 1, 1710, reel 1.

59. Gov. William Henry Lyttleton to the Board of Trade, Charleston, Sept. 1, 1759, Records in the P.R.O Relating to South Carolina [the "Sainsbury Transcripts"] 36 vols. (1663-1782), 28:213–14, South Carolina Department of Archives and History, Columbia.

60. Council Journal no. 28 (June 6, 1750–April 1, 1760), July 9, 1759; Commons House of Assembly Journal (1759), 9, 11, D 235, C.O. 5/473, British Manuscript Project microfilm, South Carolina Department of Archives and History; *S.C. Gaz.,* Sept. 1, 1759. In the Sept. 29, 1759 edition is a prediction that a severe drought would reduce the colony's rice production by about 25 percent.

61. Willie Lee Rose, *Rehearsal for Reconstruction: The Port Royal Experiment* (1964, repr. New York, 1967), 73ff.

62. Lydia Parrish, *Slave Songs of the Georgia Sea Islands* (New York, 1942), 17–18.

63. Anthony F. C. Wallace, "Revitalization Movements," *American Anthropology* 58 (1956): 264–81; see also, Weston La Barre's useful "Materials for a History of Studies of Crisis Cults: A Bibliographical Essay," *Current Anthropology* 12 (Feb. 1971): 6ff.

64. The phrase is R. J. Zwi Werblowsky's in " 'A New Heaven and a New Earth': Considering Primitive Messianisms," *History of Religions* 5 (Summer 1965): 170.

65. Ibid.

66. Raboteau, *Slave Religion*, 120.

67. For background, begin with Wesley F. Gewehr, *The Great Awakening in Virginia, 1740–1790* (1930, repr. Gloucester, Mass., 1965); and Rhys Isaac, *The Transformation of Virginia, 1740–1790* (Chapel Hill, 1982).

68. On the settlers' original goals and their relationship to labor needs, see Edmund S. Morgan, *American Slavery, American Freedom: The Ordeal of Colonial Virginia* (New York, 1975), esp. Book 1.

69. Most helpful were George W. Pilcher, *Samuel Davies; Apostle of Dissent in Colonial Virginia* (Knoxville, 1971), and Pilcher, "Samuel Davies and the Instruction of Negroes in Virginia," *Virginia Magazine of History and Biography* 74 (July 1966): 293-300; George H. Bost, "Samuel Davies: Colonial Revivalist and Champion of Religious Toleration," D.D. diss., University of Chicago, 1942, Colonial Williamsburg Research Center microfilm.

70. Bost, "Samuel Davies," 55, citing a July 4, 1751 letter.

71. *Letters from the Rev. Samuel Davies etc., Showing the State of Religion in Virginia* (Castle-Yard, Holborn, 1757), 19. The relative success of Anglican missionary effort in Virginia is revealed in a parochial survey ordered by the Bishop of London in 1724. Directed to each parish rector, the questionnaire asked in part "are there any infidels, bond or free, within your parish; and what means are used for their education?" The number of black converts in South Carolina was minuscule, whereas in Virginia about eighteen in twenty-eight responding parishes reported that some slaves were receiving instruction leading to baptism: William S. Perry, *Historical Collections Relating to the American Colonial Church,* 3 vols. (Hartford, 1870–78), 1:257–318. See also, Jerome W. Jones, "The Established Virginia Church and the Conversion of Negroes and Indians, 1620–1760," *Journal of Negro History* 46 (Jan. 1961): 12–30.

72. Pilcher, *Samuel Davies*, 110, 113–14, and "Samuel Davies and the Instruction of Negroes," 295–96.

73. Davies to Philip Doddridge, n.d., Literary Manuscripts, New College [London], Colonial Williamsburg Research Center Survey Report L61/3/1, 45f; and extracts from Fulham Papers, Lambeth Palace Library, Colonial Williamsburg Research Center microfilm M-987.

74. Pilcher, *Samuel Davies*, 113–14; Albert Barnes, *Sermons on Important Subjects by the Revd Samuel Davies....*, 3 vols. (New York, 1854), 3:228-29.

75. Ibid.; see also, Pilcher, "Samuel Davies and the Instruction of Negroes," 297.

76. Raboteau, *Slave Religion,* 134ff.

77. *Virginia Gazette* (Purdie), May 1, 1778, Turner Bynam; May 29, 1778, John Gordon.

78. Ibid. (Purdie and Dixon), April 18, 1771, Sarah Floyd; (Purdie), May 9, 1777; April 23, 1772, John Fox; *Virginia Herald and Fredericksburg Advertiser,* June 18, 1793, Thomas McGee; *Maryland Journal and Baltimore Advertiser,* Dec. 4, 1792, Luke Raven; June 16, 1778, James Young; July 21, 1778, George Fitzhugh.

79. Raboteau, *Slave Religion,* 179

80. Wyatt MacGaffey, *Modern Kongo Prophets: Religion in a Plural Society* (Bloomington, 1983), 5; Leonard Barrett, "African Religion in the Americas: The 'Islands in Between,'" in *African Religions: A Symposium,* ed. Newell S. Booth, Jr. (New York, 1977), 190.

81. For background, including insights into the selection of missionaries, see Elizabeth K. Nottingham, *Methodism and the Frontier: Indiana Proving Ground* (1941, repr. New York, 1966), ch. 3, esp. 43–45; and Donald G. Mathews, "North Carolina Methodists in Nineteenth-century Church and Society," in *Methodism Alive in North Carolina,* ed. O. Kelly Ingram (Durham, 1976), 62ff.

82. The drawing is in William Ritchie, Spanish Town, Feb. 23, 1843, 18/197. Unless indicated otherwise, the following Methodist missionary reports were sent to the secretary of the society, whose records, first consulted at the Methodist Missionary Society (Marylebone, London), have since been moved to the School of Oriental and African Studies Library at the University of London. The form of citation is, first, the missionary's name, then the date and place from which the report was written, followed by the item's document and box number: T. Jones, Jamaica, Jan. 4, 1823, 12/122.

It is not intended to imply that the Methodists' West Indian urban orientation prevailed as well in the South, where as early as the 1790s an Anglican cleric who appreciated the Methodists' rural itinerancy wrote that "The Methodists have abundantly more success in the woods, the swamps, the pine barrens, all new & dispersed settlements than in populous cities." The writer, the Anglican cleric James Ramsay (*History of South Carolina: from its first settlement in 1670 to the year 1806,* 2 vols. [1858, repr. Spartanburg, 1958], 2:19n), acknowledged the Methodists' superior organization in his count of the sect's twelve districts, twenty-six itinerant preachers preaching 156 sermons weekly in about two hundred churches or stations.

83. William J. Shrewsbury, Barbados, Aug. 25, 1823, 134/119. For instance, see the Adultery Account for Antigua, 1818–23, by years and station enclosed in A. Whitehouse, St. Johns, Sept. 9, 1823, 3/120.

84. Patrick French, St. Bartholomew [exchange with Gov. Sir John Norderling], July 30, 1823, 112/119.

85. *Brit. Parl Papers, Slave Trade* (1823–24), 66/63; also 59, 65, 108. This record (of the court martial of the missionary John Smith following the Demerara rebellion of 1823) is important because it throws an unusual amount of light upon the

routines of slave deacons, many of whom were instigators of the great preemancipation rebellions.

86. "Some Account of Harry the Black mentioned in Dr. Coke's History, taken from a recital of a Black woman in St. Bartholomew" [Jan. 1819], 1/114, Methodist Missionary Society Archives.

87. Daniel Barr, Morant Bay, July 7, 1831, box 130.

88. John Shipman, Belmont, St. Anns, Jamaica, July 10, 1823, 103/119; Thomas Isham, Nevis, Aug. 12, 1807 and George Johnston, Montego Bay, Feb. 10, 1811, box 111; John Crofts, July 10, 1823, 119/104, who said of his Spanish Town congregation, "[Members] are generally poor Free Persons of Colour, principally Females."

89. John Taylor to Joseph Benson, April 7, 1804, box 1, West Indies In-Coming, 1803–13.

90. Thomas Richardson's Journal, Roseau, Dominica, Feb. 7–Aug. 30, 1803, entries for Feb. 8, March 7, 23–29. On the disruptive and desireable character of black women in city congregations in Jamaica, see Mary Smith, a class leader, to the Secretary, Kingston, Aug. 15, 1807, 32/111. Item no. 29 [summer 1807], from nine congregants is also suggestive.

91. Ibid.

92. W. Binning, Grateful Hill, Jamaica, Jan. 26, 1819, 20/114.

93. William Gilgrass, Basseterre, St. Kitts, Jan. 30, 1819, 26/114.

94. Extracts from the Journal of Mr. Ratcliffe, Wesley Chapel House, Kingston, June 15, 1819, 62/114.

95. W. Binning, Grateful Hill, Jamaica, Jan. 26, 1819, 20/114.

96. William Gilgrass, Basseterre, St. Kitts, Jan. 30, 1819, 26/114.

97. Edward Kamau Braithwaite, "The Slave Rebellion in the Great River Valley of St. James, 1831–1832," *Jamaica Historical Review* 13 (1982): 14.

98. The remarks of John Brownell in his journal and reports are typical: Journal, 1800–1804, 41; and Brownell, Old Road, Sandy Point, St. Kitts, May 11, 1803, both in box 1, West Indies In-Coming 1803–13; see also, May 4, 1823 entry, Journal of Charles Janion, Parham, Antigua, July 1, 1823, 91/119.

99. Macaulay Journal [Sierra Leone], March–Nov. 1796 [mid-March 1796], Macaulay MS, Journals 1–3, My 418(9), Henry E. Huntington Library, San Marino, Calif.

100. J. Mortier, City Road Chapel, Nevis, Dec. 30, 1816, 32/113. Cf. Slaves "treasure up select sentences in their minds, on which they *feed* during the week . . . many hundreds appear to be deeply acquainted with things of the Spirit": William Ratcliffe, Kingston, Oct. 20, 1817, 12/113

101. John Shipman, Spanish Town, July 18, 1817, 26/113; Alexander Robb, *The Gospel to the Africans; a Narrative of the Life and Labours of the Reverend William Jameson in Jamaica and Old Calabar,* 2d ed. (London, 1862), 34.

102. *The New Baptist Miscellany Conducted by Members of the Baptist Society* (London, 1831), 5:80; for a good description, see William and Mary Knibb to Margaret Williams, Kingston, May 28, 1827, box WI/3, Baptist Missionary Society Archives, London (now at Angus Library, Regent's Park College, Oxford).

103. Cf. Leonard Barrett, "African Religions in the Americas," in *African Religions,* ed. Booth, 189ff.

104. Aidan Southall cited in *The Historical Study of African Religion,* ed. T. O. Ranger and I. N. Kimambo (Berkeley, 1972), 13. On the character of conversion, see Robin Horton, "African Conversion," *Africa,* 41, no. 2 (1971): 85–108; for an opposing view, that conversion is a syncretism and not a movement from outside the main religion, see Humphrey J. Fisher, "Conversion Reconsidered: Some Historical Aspects of Religious Conversion in Black Africa," *Africa* 43, no. 1 (1973): 38n. See also, T. C. McCaskie, "Anti-Witchcraft Cults in Asante," *History in Africa* 8 (1981), 125–54, esp. 133ff.

105. J. H. Buchner, *The Moravians in Jamaica: History of the Mission of the United Brethren's Church to the Negroes in the Island of Jamaica from the Year 1754 to 1854* (London, 1854), 33; manuscript volume, "S.F.G. [Society for the Furtherance of the Gospel] 1803–13," Feb. 20, 1803, 14, Moravian Archives, Muswell Hill, London. Another émigré preacher, Moses Baker, is also alluded to as early as Sept. 1789 as the "teacher of an unknown sect" in St. James. See "A State of the Rectories and Rectors in the Island of Jamaica . . . ," Jamaica, Sept. 28, 1789, C.O. 137/88.

106. Monica Schuler, *"Alas, Alas, Kongo": A Social History of Indentured African Immigration into Jamaica, 1841–1865* (Baltimore, 1980), 134, n74, 136 n8.

107. Long, *History of Jamaica,* 2:424–25; and "The Practice of Obeah, 1788" describes the execution of a Coramantee obeahman during the 1760 rebellion in "all his Feathers and Trumperies about him." The execution struck the rebels with a "general panic" from which "they never recovered" (181). More fundamentally, the Coramantee's unshakable attachment to ancestralism made them impervious to assimilation. Even now, an African scholar argues, the thrust of much research is that the effects of "Christian and western teaching [on Ghanaians] . . . ha[ve] not been profound." If a Ghanaian wants to be "modern," especially Western and Christian, he or she is "bound to live at two levels." See Joshua N. Kudadjie, "Aspects of Religion and Morality in Ghanaian Traditional Society with Particular Reference to the Ga-Adangme," in *Traditional Life, Culture and Literature in Ghana,* ed. J. M. Assimeng (Owerri, 1976), 29, 51 n4. For the view that no secret societies existed among Fante and Asante, see Melville J. Herskovits, *The Myth of the Negro Past* (1941, repr. New York, 1958), 82.

108. Thistlewood's Journal, July 2, 1768.

109. C. Rampini, cited in Orlando Patterson, *The Sociology of Slavery: An Analysis of the Origins, Development and Structure of Negro Slave Society in Jamaica* (1967, repr. Rutherford, 1969), 188n; Long, *History of Jamaica,* 2:416–17; Monica Schuler, "Myalism and the African Religious Tradition in Jamaica," in *Africa and the Caribbean: The Legacies of a Link,* ed. Margaret E. Crahan and Franklin W. Knight, (Baltimore, 1979), 65–79; Anthony J. Williams, "The Role of the Prophet in Millennial Cults: Politico-Religious Movements in Jamaica, 1800–1970," B.A. thesis, Exeter College, Oxford, 1974, copy deposited in the West Indies Collection, University of the West Indies, St. Augustine Campus, Trinidad, esp.

95ff; Simon Barrington-Ward, " 'The Centre Cannot Hold . . .' Spirit Possession as Redefintion," in *Christianity in Independent Africa,* ed. Edward Fasholé-Luke et al. (Bloomington, 1978), 457ff; W. J. Gardner, *A History of Jamaica: From Its Discovery by Christopher Columbus to the Year 1872* (1873, repr. London, 1971), 191; Martha Beckwith, *Black Roadways; a Study of Jamaican Folk Life* (1929, repr. New York, 1969), ch. 9. Beckwith links Myal to John Canoe (149).

110. R. T. Branbury cited in Patterson, *The Sociology of Slavery,* 187–88.

111. George Blyth to A. Stirling, Hampden, Oct. 9, 1743, T-SK, 13/21, no. 6, Sterling Family of Keir and Cawder, Strathclyde Regional Archives, Glasgow.

112. Gardner, *History of Jamaica,* 357.

113. John Clarke, *Memorials of Baptist Missionaries in Jamaica . . .* (London, 1869), 9–10. On early leaders, see "Letter from Jamaica" (Thomas Nicholas Swingle, late 1790s) in *Baptist Annual Register to 1798, 1799, 1800 and part of 1801,* ed. J. Rippon (London, 1802), 212–14.

114. J. Shrewsbury, Bridgetown, Barbados, July 3, 1823, 95/119; I. Purkis, Tobago, Aug. 7, 1809, Tobago box 1 (1807–13); Jacob Wray to the Directors of the London Missionary Soceity, Le Resouvenir, Demerara, Oct. 9, 1812, box 1, British Guiana-Demerara (1807–14); "Testimony of Planters in the West Indies, 1818," box 1, West Indian Biographical, Methodist Missionary Society Archives.

115. Cf. Mrs. Coultart to her brother, Kingston, Aug. 6, 1817, in "Memoir of Mrs. Coultart, Wife of Reverend James Coultart, Missionary at Jamaica," *Periodical Accounts Relative to the Baptist Missionary Society* (Bristol, 1817), 6:417, Baptist Missionary Society Archives.

116. Cited in Robb, *The Gospel to the Africans,* 35. Reference to leaders of two distinct religions, that is, adherents of John or Jesus, are in William Fitzer Burchell, *Memoir of Thomas Burchell, Twenty-two Years a Missionary in Jamaica* (London, 1849), 78.

117. Hope Masterton Waddell, *Twenty-nine Years in the West Indies and Central Africa. . . .* (London, 1863), 35–36. John Rowe, the first regular Baptist missionary to Jamaica in the spring of 1815, was instructed to "unite" with Moses Baker for purposes of "instructing the Negroes." Arriving at Montego Bay, Rowe was warned by his sponsor, the powerful west country politician the Hon. Samuel Vaughan, that people disliked Baptists more than any other sect; another member of the white elite advised Rowe to first conceal his position and real intentions and instead advertise himself as a teacher. See B. W. O. Amey, "John Rowe, First BMS Missionary to the West Indies," *Missionary Harold* (Jan. 1963): 70–71.

118. Philip Wright, *Knibb "The Notorious": Slaves' Missionary, 1803–1845* (London, 1973), 204.

119. Ibid.

120. Buchner, *Moravians in Jamaica,* 47ff. Donald Hogg, "The Convince Cult in Jamaica," Yale University Publications in Anthropology 58 (New Haven, 1960): 3–24 makes a strong argument (19–20) that its origins were African and then Maroon (as its members insisted). On Liele, see Raboteau, *Slave Religion,* 140–41, 267–68; Rippon, *Baptist Annual Register, 1790–1793,* 332–35 (a Dec. 1791 autobiographical letter from Leile); and gleanings from Jamaican newspapers: har-

assed by nervous officials, *Jam. Royal Gaz.*, April 5, 1794-P.S.; advertises for a runaway slave, ibid., Jan. 5, 1793-P.S.; runaways identified as Liele converts, ibid., Sept. 6, 1794-P.S., Robert Loosely, and [Kingston] *Daily Advertiser*, Dec. 18, 1790, William Thomas.

121. Buchner, *Moravians in Jamaica*, 48f.

122. Ibid., 50.

123. "Table of Stations Connected with the Baptist Missionary Society," in *The New Baptist Miscellany*, 5:127. The Methodists, on the other hand, published a circular warning missionaries about using black catechists, who were to be selected only with "great caution and prudence." Enclosed in W. Gilgrass, Antigua, Feb. 10, 1825, 175/121. An invaluable glimpse of the inroads of conversion into a plantation slave hierarchy appears in Dickinson's Appleton Estate, list for Jan. 1, 1828. Of 187 slaves, almost equally divided between men and women, converts are listed by both their "old" names and "Christian" names. Of the eighty-seven women, two in five (thirty-three) were Christian, whereas nearly half that number, one in five (eighteen) of the men were converts, of whom drivers and artisans predominated. The first four on the list, for instance, were Christian (the head driver, the blacksmith, head carpenter, and head pen keeper); a cooper, masons, the second driver, and an apprentice carpenter followed, all Christians, surrounded by nineteen field workers of whom only one was a convert as opposed to ten of the seventeen artisans on the estate. Half of the women were field workers (forty-eight) of whom not quite a third (fourteen) were Christians; more than half (eleven of nineteen) of the non-field workers were converts and included cooks, domestics, clothes washers, the midwife, two nurses, a woman who worked in the poultry house, and one who hired-out. See bundle 479, slave list for Jan. 1, 1828, Dickinson MS, Somerset Record Office. Even though drivers were important leaders and organizers of West Indian rebellions, Michael Craton follows Genovese and characterizes them as intermediaries and buffers between owners and slaves; cf. *Sinews of Empire: A Short History of British Slavery* (Garden City, 1974), 221–22; and Genovese, *Roll, Jordan, Roll*, 388.

124. William Knibb to Mary Knibb (his mother), Savannah la Mar, Sept. 7, 1830; cf. Knibb to Mary Knibb (his sister) Dec. 20, and 30 [1828], box WI/3, Baptist Missionary Society Archives.

125. Ibid.; Burchell, *Memoir of Thomas Burchell*, 151; *The New Baptist Miscellany*, 5:81f.

126. Knibb to Sister, Dec. 30, 1828, WI/3, Baptist Missionary Society.

127. Mary Turner's *Slaves and Missionaries: The Disintegration of Jamaican Slave Society, 1787–1834* (Urbana, 1982), esp. chs. 3 and 4, has been most helpful. For a contemporary's use of the term *Christian obea*, see W. Stanford to Bishop Porteus, Westmoreland [Jamaica], July 22, 1788, West Indies, vol. 18, f. 66v, Fulham Papers, Lambeth Palace Library, to the effect that blacks respected obeah figures because they charged fees while "Christian obea" (baptism) can be worth little, "since obtained at no expence, nay some proprietors have threatened baptism as a punishment, but their reasons are too gross to explain to your Lordship."

128. The argument leans on Willy de Craemer, Jan Vansina, and Renée C.

Fox, "Religious Movements in Central Africa: A Theoretical Study," *Comparative Studies in Society and History* 18 (Oct. 1976): 458–75.

129. Charles Leslie, *A New and Exact Account of Jamaica . . .*, 3d ed. (Edinburgh, 1740), 323. Emphasis added. For links among song, dance, and language retention, see Laura Tanna, "African Retentions: Yoruba and Kikongo Songs in Jamaica," *Jamaica Journal* 16 (Aug. 1983): 47–52, esp. the remark of Rachel Albert Fenton (48).

130. Adapted from Cheryl Ryman's two essays, "Jonkonnu: A Neo-African Form, Part 1," and "The Jamaican Heritage in Dance," *Jamaica Journal* 17 (Feb. and May, 1984): 13, 61, 3–14.

131. See Leann Thomas Martin, "Maroon Identity: Processes of Persistence in Moore Town," Ph.D. diss., University of California, Riverside, 1973, 40ff; and Kenneth Bilby, "Jamaica's Maroons at the Cross Roads, Losing Touch with Tradition," *Caribbean Review* 9 (Fall 1980): 18ff. The Kromanti dance focuses Maroon identity; ancestors possess dancers, especially during a crisis, and a ritual specialist (the fete-man) emerges to take over. Many are healers and herbalists as well. For the current situation, see Jay D. Dobbin, "The Jombee Dancer: Friendship and Ritual in Monserrat," *Caribbean Review* 10 (Fall 1981): 29f. Cf. Michael Lambek, *Human Spirits: A Cultural Account of Trance in Mayotte* (Cambridge, England, 1981), ch. 5.

132. For example, John Vaughton to the Secretary of the Society, July 15, 1738 [Barbados], box 4, Codrington MS, Society for the Propagation of the Gospel Archives, London; Thistlewood's Journal, Sept. 3, 1767; cf. Aug. 14, 1755, Oct. 3, 1760, July 16, 1765; Lewis, *Journal*, 144, 236, 328.

133. James Knight, "The Natural, Moral and Political History of Jamaica . . . to the Year 1742," British Library, Addit. MSS., 12419, f. 93.

134. Branislow Malinowski, *Magic, Science and Religion* (1927, repr. New York, 1955), 25–35, 30–31; and Paula Brown, "Patterns of Authority in West Africa," *Africa* 51 (Oct. 1951): 261–76 concern the flourishing of witchcraft in an atmosphere of fear and repression.

135. *Brit. Parl. Papers, Slave Trade* (1825), 67/131, trials of Joe and of Chance.

136. *Instructions for Missionaries to the West Indian Islands*, printed at the Philanthropic Reform, St. George Fields [London], 1795, 6 (British Library pressmark 4193.cc.49).

137. Cf. Isaac, *Transformation of Virginia*, 171–72, 171n.

138. An old and thoughtful view is that the shout and response is a form of possession. I like the way the argument is made in Morton Marks, " 'You Can't Sing Unless You're Saved': Reliving the Call in Gospel Music," in *African Religious Groups and Beliefs: Papers in Honor of William R. Bascom*, ed. S. Ottenburg (Sahar, India, 1982), 305–31; Paul Radin, Foreword to Clifton H. Johnson, ed., *God Struck Me Dead; Religious Conversion Experiences and Autobiographies of Ex-Slaves* (Philadelphia, 1969), ixff; and Sterling Stuckey, *Slave Culture, Nationalist theory and the Foundations of Black America* (New York, 1987), ch. 11, esp. 95–97 (even though Stuckey may exaggerate the African content of Virginia slave culture).

139. Testimony of Ben Woolfolk at the trial of Smith's George; "Confessions

of Ben alias Ben Woolfolk, Sept. 17th 1800 Nos. 4," Executive Papers (Sept.–Dec. 1800), Virginia State Library, Richmond.

## Chapter Nine. Slave Resistance

1. R. Lindsay to the Reverend Dr. William Robertson, Aug. 6, 1776, McDonald-Robertson, MS3942, ff. 260–61, National Library of Scotland; Robert Thomson to Ellis Yonge, April 6, 1795, Addit. MSS, 3232, Bedrhyddan, Department of Archives, University College of North Wales Library.

2. This group was first discussed in Gerald W. Mullin, *Flight and Rebellion: Slave Resistance in Eighteenth-Century Virginia* (New York, 1972), chs. 3–5. Elsa Goveia also found that as slaves acculturated their resistance as runaways changed perceptibly, see *Slave Society in the British Leeward Islands at the End of the Eighteenth Century* (New Haven, 1965), 158ff.

3. For a somewhat different approach to slave resistance in the era, see Michael Mullin "Slave Obeahmen and Slaveowning Patriarchs in an Era of War and Revolution," in *Comparative Perspectives on Slavery in New World Plantation Societies,* ed. Vera Rubin and Arthur Tuden, Annals of the New York Academy of Sciences (New York, 1977), 292:481–90, and Mullin, "British Caribbean and North American Slaves in an Era of War and Revolution, 1775–1807," in *The Southern Experience in the American Revolution,* ed. Jeffery J. Crow and Larry E. Tise (Chapel Hill, 1978), 235–67.

4. Edwards cited in J. H. Perry and P. M. Sherlock, *A Short History of the West Indies* (1956, repr. London, 1960), 160.

5. For a provocative argument of the era as a watershed in Western culture, see George Steiner, *In Bluebeard's Castle: Some Notes Towards the Redefinition of Culture* (London, 1971). For background, see Adolphe Roberts, *The French in the West Indies* (1942, repr. New York, 1971); on Victor Hugues, see C. L. R. James, *The Black Jacobins: Toussiant L'Ouverture and the San Domingo Revolution,* 2d ed. rev. (New York, 1964), 143, 161. For Jamaica, the most important treatment of the era is in the concluding chapters of Edward Braithwaite's *The Development of Creole Society in Jamaica, 1770–1820* (Oxford, 1971). For an opposite view, that the 1790s was not a time of profound crisis, see David Geggus, "The Enigma of Jamaica in the 1790s: New Light on the Causes of Slave Rebellions," *William and Mary Quarterly,* 3d ser., 44 (April 1987): 274–99.

6. Council's Address enclosed in Lt. Gov. Adam Williamson to the Sec. of State [Jamaica], Nov. 30, 1791, C.O. 137/91. For an overview of the colony during "this momentous crisis" (p. 13), see an Assembly Committee's "Report . . . [on] the State of the Colony as to Trade, Navigation and Culture . . . 23d of November, 1792" enclosed in Balcarres to Sec. of State, May 25, 1800, C.O. 137/104.

7. Extract of a letter from Jamaica dated Kingston 18th Novr. 1791, C.O. 137/89; Assembly Committee of Correspondence (which included Bryan Edwards, John Palmer, and Samuel Vaughan, Jr.) to the Agent, Stephen Fuller, Spanish Town, May 23, 1792, C.O. 137/90.

8. Maj. Gen. Adam Williamson to Henry Dundas, Sec. of State, Jamaica, Sept.

18, 1791, C.O. 137/87. The phrase "second St. Domingo War" is from an extract of a anonymous letter, Spanish Town, Dec. 4, 1798, enclosed in "John Bayleys of 21 Jan. 1799," in the "misc[ellanous]" section of C.O. 137/102; "Numero 1," *Gazette Officielle de L'Etat D'Hayti du Jeudi 7 Mai 1807 . . .*, in Edmund P. Lyon to Viscount Castleraegh, Devonshire Place, Aug. 4, 1807, C.O. 137/120.

9. "Papers relating to the Slave Trade 1787–1823," vol. 22, ff. 6–6v, Liverpool Papers, British Library, Addit. MSS 38,416. From a wealthy attorney came a comment that news of the slave trade hearings "spread like wild fire amongst our Negroes": Robert Hibbert to the Dutchess of Chandos, May 20, 1788, Letterbook, 1779–89, Stowe 626, Henry E. Huntington Library, San Marino, Calif.

10. Governor's Council to Fuller, Nov. 5, 1792, C.O. 137/90.

11. Ibid. The Negroes are "elated by the Abolition of the Slave Trade, which few of them rightly understand": Lt. Gov. Coote to Viscount Castlereagh, King's House, Jamaica, Dec. 4, 1807, C.O. 137/120.

12. John Mercer to Battaile Muse, Aug. 9, 1782, Muse Papers, Manuscript Division, Duke University Library, Durham, N.C.

13. William Vassal to his manager, Clapham Common [London] Feb. 6, 1788, William Vassall Letterbook, 1769–96, Archives Department, Central Library, Sheffield. Such reactions were shaped by traditions of resistance in particular societies. From Barbados, officials reported "a perfect State of tranquility" (1781); slaves of a "mild, Tractible, & obedient disposition" (1791); and Gov. Seaforth reminded Whitehall in 1802 that his island was "safe and secure": Lt. Gov. Cunningham to Sec. of State, Jan. 22, 1781, C.O. 28/58 f. 64; Gov. D. Perry to Dundas, Barbados, Dec. 26, 1791, C.O. 28/63 (sec. 2); and Seaforth to [Sec. of State] Hobart, Pilgrim [Barbados], June 6, 1802, Seaforth Letterbooks, Scottish Record Office, Edinburgh. On Antigua, like Barbados an unusually quiet slave society, slaves by the 1760s were armed when invasions were expected. See David Barry Gaspar, *Bondmen and Rebels: A Study of Master-Slave Relations in Antigua, with Implications for Colonial British America* (Baltimore, 1985), 139.

14. Bruce to Lt. Gov. Sir John Orde, 1 A.M., Jan. 15, 24, 1791, enclosed in Orde to Lord Grenville, (Dominica), Feb. 3 [1791], C.O. 71/19. See also, Orde to Sec. of State, Dec. 15, 1785, C.O. 71/9.

15. Committee Report to the House of Assembly, Feb. 4, 1791, concerning a 1791 Grand Jury Presentment for the Charleston District, old filing system: "Slavery before 1800," South Carolina Department of Archives and History, Columbia.

16. [St. George Tucker], *Letter to a Member of the General Assembly of Virginia on the Subject of the Late Conspiracy of the Slaves. . . .* (Richmond, 1801).

17. Rusticus [probably Alexander Garden], July 14, 1794 (see also letters of June 20, and Aug. 7, 1794) to Committee of Public Safety, St. Andrews Parish, file 235, South Carolina Historical Society, Charleston.

18. For important parallels between the following plots and associations and those elsewhere, see Neville Hall, "Slaves' Use of Their 'Free' Time in the Danish Virgin Islands in the Later Eighteenth and Early Nineteenth Century," *Journal of Caribbean History* 13 (1980): 21–43; and Joseph P. Reidy, "Negro Election Day and Black Community Life in New England, 1750–1860," *Marxist Perspectives* (Fall 1978): 102–17.

19. Yolanda Theresa Moses, "Female Status and Male Dominance in Monteserrat, the West Indies," Ph.D. diss., University of California, Riverside, 1976, 13. The following is based on a missionary's manuscript, "A Natural, Civil, and Religious History of Monteserrat in the West-Indies, Including a Particular Account of the Struggles of the Free Coloured Inhabitants . . . by a Wesleyan Missionary who Resided Five Years in the Island" ["History of Montserrat"], West Indies/ Biographical, box 588, Methodist Missionary Society Archives, School of Oriental and African Studies Library, University of London; and on an extract of a letter from Montserrat, March 21, 1768 in the *Virginia Gazette* [*Va. Gaz.*], May 5, 1768; St. John's, Antigua, March 30, 1768, reprinted in the *Georgia Gazette* [*Ga. Gaz.*], May 18, 1768.

20. "History of Montserrat," 46–47.

21. Ibid., 28–29. Two military reports following the end of proceedings provide an overview and summary. Gov. William Woodley to Sec. of State, Antigua, June 21, 1768, C.O. 152/30, states that he left a detachment of fifty men and a man-of-war "to prevent further attempts." On April 22, 1768, Woodley reported (C.O. 152/48, ff. 7–8) that the plot was "deep laid & long projected"; the conspirators had concealed arms and ammunition in the mountains. It was initiated by house servants, and their goal was to sail with the white women to Puerto Rico. On the general problem of Montserrat runaways using Puerto Rico as a refuge, see Gov. George Thomas to the Board of Trade, Antigua, Feb. 6, 1754, C.O. 152/28.

22. Edward East to Anna Eliza Elletson, July 31, Sept. 3, 1776, Hope Estate Letterbook (1770–83), MS/29a, Institute of Jamaica, Kingston.

23. Sir Basil Keith to Lord Germaine, Aug. 6, 1776, C.O. 137/71, ff. 229; see also ff. 236–37, 248, 250–51.

24. Lt. Gov. Sir Adam Williamson to Sec. of State, Feb. 12, 1792, C.O. 137/90; Keith to Germaine, July 1, 1776, C.O. 137/71, ff. 201–4.

25. Extract of a letter from Kingston Nov. 18, 1791, and Extract of a letter from Spanish Town, Nov. 6, 1791, C.O. 137/89; C.O. 137/90, ff. 37–38, 44, 45, 47, 49; see also ff. 23–24, 55–56.

26. Ibid., 15ff, for Jack's insurrectionary career: "The Result of the examinations &c. of Philip, A Spanish Negro, Jack, a slave, Mr. Milburn, his Master . . . upon a suspicion that the Spanish were purchasing Powder for the purpose of selling it to the Negroes."

27. L. Winn, Chairman of the Committee of Security and Safety, St. James, 13th January 1792, C.O. 137/90, 23–24.

28. C.O. 137/90, ff. 60–61; see C.O. 137/118, 120, and 140/92, especially the "Miscellany" section at the end of 120.

29. Simon Taylor to Thomas Haughan, Kingston, Jan. 7, 1807, enclosed in Gov. Coote to Windham, King's House, Jamaica, Jan. 9, 1807, C.O. 137/118.

30. The trials, as Council proceedings, are in C.O. 298/2, 97ff. The first meeting dealing with the plot was Dec. 10, 1805, and interpreters of the conspirators' French patois were used throughout. As late as 1823, a distinguishing feature of some runaways was that they spoke "English only." *Trinidad Gazette,* Feb. 22, 1823, Jean Liquier's Rouk; June 14, 1823, Cipriani and Cipriana. Typical of the

truly multicultural character of Trinidad was a runaway notice for Soussigne, which was placed by an English-speaking Scot, who carried a hybrid Spanish-English title while advertising in French for a slave woman with a classical (Roman) name and a French patois nickname. *Trinidad Gazette,* Jan. 23, 1822, Herbert Mackworth, Alquacil Mayor, West Indian Reference Division, Trinidad, Public Library Reference, Port of Spain.

The existence of the slaves' dancing associations requires another examination of the traditional view — from Errol Hill to Bridget Brereton — that what became Carnival stemmed first from the whites' entertainments. Errol Hill, *The Trinidad Carnival, Mandate for a National Theatre* (Austin, 1972), esp. 10ff; and Bridget Brereton, "The Trinidad Carnival, 1870–1900," *Savacou* 11/12 (Sept. 1975): 50; cf. Edward Braithwaite, *Daedalus* 103 (Spring 1974): 76n.

31. According to William A. Green, the advent of crown colony government at the end of the eighteenth century "reflected an important change in the character of the British Empire." See *British Slave Emancipation: The Sugar Colonies and the Great Experiment 1830–1865* (Oxford, 1976), 76

32. Trinidad, "Puerto d'Espana, 23 May 1802," Cumberland Papers, vol. 9, British Library, Addit. MSS, 36,499ff. 98–98v.

33. For the first warnings, see Brig. Gen. and Lt. Gov. Hislop to Castlereagh, Trinidad, Dec. 8 and 17, 1805, C.O. 295/11, f. 227 and 198/2, 97v–100; for free people of color, C.O. 318/76, 244–45. Population more than doubled between 1795 and 1805, from 10,422 to 25,245. C.O. 325/3, ff. 84v–85v; see also "the Reform of the Population of Trinidad. 18th August 1804," C.O. 295/8, f.265.

34. C.O. 198/2, 102–4, 117, 117v.

35. Ibid., 134v.

36. Ibid., see also 111–13v.

37. Ibid., 144, 147–48v, 135.

38. The following is based on the Trial of Quillo, April 1794, and "The Examination of Peter a negro Slave the property of William Bullock . . . 19th day of April 1794, Granville County," Records of Slaves and Free Persons of Color, 1755–1859, North Carolina Division of Archives and History, Raleigh. Cf. Jeffrey J. Crow, "Slave Rebelliousness and Social Conflict in North Carolina, 1775 to 1802," *William and Mary Quarterly,* 3d ser., 37 (Jan. 1980): 79–102; and Alan D. Watson, "Impulse Toward Independence: Resistance and Rebellion Among North Carolina Slaves, 1750–1775," *Journal of Negro History* 63 (Fall 1978): 317–28.

39. Ibid., "The Examination of Peter . . . 1794."

40. The testimony of William Young's Gilbert at the trial of William Galt's Armstead. This testimony and the following are in two boxes of file folders marked "Negro Insurrection 1800" in the Executive Papers (Sept.–Dec. 1800), Virginia State Library, Richmond. Cf. Philip J. Schwarz, "Gabriel's Challenge, Slaves and Crime in Late Eighteenth-Century Virginia," *Virginia Magazine of History and Biography* 90 (July 1982): 283–309; and Douglas R. Egerton, "Gabriel's Conspiracy and the Elections of 1800," *Journal of Southern History* 56 (May 1990): 191–214.

41. For a more detailed account, see Mullin, *Flight and Rebellion,* 142.

42. Arna Bontemps, *Black Thunder* (1935, repr. Boston, 1968), 166–67; cf. 45–47, 53 f., 85 f., 103.

43. For background and a good collection of primary sources as well as interpretations, see Robert S. Starobin, ed., *Denmark Vesey: The Slave Conspiracy of 1822* (Englewood Cliffs, 1970); and Margaret Washington Creel, *"A Peculiar People": Slave Religion and Community-Culture Among the Gullahs* (New York, 1988), 148–66.

44. "Confession of Bacchus, the Slave of Mr. Hammet," William and Benjamin F. Hammet Papers, Manuscript Division, Duke University Library.

45. Lionel H. Kennedy and Thomas Parker, *An Official Report of the Trials of Sundry Negroes, Charged with an attempt to raise An Insurrection in the State of South-Carolina.* . . . (Charleston, 1822), 22–23, 26, 41, 44; cf. 172–73. I used the Houghton Library (Harvard University) copy which does have the same pagination of the more accessible John Oliver Killens, *The Trial Records of Denmark Vesey.* . . . (Boston, 1970).

46. Creel, *"A Peculiar People,"* 148ff, 22–23, 44, 72, 75–76. Cf. [James Hamilton, Jr.], *Negro Plot. An Account of the Late Intended Insurrection Among a Portion of the Blacks in the City of Charleston, South Carolina* (Boston, 1822); M. Richardson to Dr. James P. Screven, Savannah, July 6, Sept. 18, 1822, Arnold-Screven Papers, Southern Historical Collection, University of North Carolina Library, Chapel Hill.

47. Hamilton, *Negro Plot,* 45–46; Kennedy and Parker, *Official Report,* 41, 120. In a 1969 conversation, Beth Cole of the Charleston Records (Auditor's) Office said that in Vesey's time whites sometimes held property for blacks in their names.

48. Creel, *"A Peculiar People,"* 157.

49. "Confession of Bacchus"; Kennedy and Parker, *Official Report,* 170–71, 103–4, 106, 106n.

50. Ibid., 91, 100, 114, 116, 120; Hamilton, *Negro Plot,* 38, 39, 41.

51. Ibid., 38.

52. Kennedy and Parker, *Official Report,* 19–20, 89.

53. Ibid., 19, 30–31, 61, 125.

54. Hamilton, *Negro Plot,* 36.

55. "Examinations of Mr. La Roche's Joe" in "Examinations" of several, House of Representatives, enclosed in Governor's Message no. 2 [July 18, 1822], South Carolina Department of Archives and History; Kennedy and Parker, *Official Report,* 67–68; Hamilton, *Negro Plot,* 40, 46.

56. Kennedy and Parker, *Official Report,* 46; M. Richardson to Screven, Savannah, Aug. 7, 1822, Arnold-Screven Papers, Southern Historical Collection.

57. Testimony of William Young's Gilbert at the trial of William Galt's Armstead, Executive Papers (Sept.–Dec. 1800), Virginia State Library.

58. Mullin, *Flight and Rebellion,* ch. 3, esp. 83, 89ff.

59. Landon Carter, *The Diary of Colonel Landon Carter of Sabine Hall, 1752–1778,* ed. Jack P. Greene (Charlottesville, 1965), June 4, 1773, 754.

60. Malcolm Laing to William Philip Perrin, Kingston [Sept. 1770], no. 11770; see also Laing to David Munro, Kingston, Sept. 11, 1770, Fitzherbert-Perrin Papers, Derbyshire Record Office, Matlock.

61. *Gazette of the State of South Carolina,* Nov. 14, 1775, Joshua Eden.

62. Henry Laurens to James Laurens, Charleston, Jan. [?], 1776, Laurens Papers, Roll 13, South Carolina Department of Archives and History microfilm. Cf. Hall, "Slaves Use of Their 'Free' Time."

63. *South Carolina and American General Gazette* [*S.C. and Amer. Genl. Gaz.*], July 30, 1778, Isaac McPherson.

64. *Barbados Mercury and Bridge-Town Gazette* [*Barb. Merc. and B-T. Gaz.*], Aug. 21, 1787, John Fayerman; *Jamaica Royal Gazette* [*Jam. Royal Gaz.*], March 9, 1799-S., Thomas Goulburn (cf. April 13, 1799-S., Susanna Goulburn); May 2, 1795-S., Andrew Rhodes; *South Carolina Royal Gazette* [*S.C. Royal Gaz.*], June 18, 1780, Charles Atkins.

65. Stephen Fuller to Dundas, Southampton, Oct. 30, 1791, C.O. 137/90.

66. See Oliver Bloodstein, *A Handbook on Stuttering,* 3d ed. (Chicago, 1969, 1980); Mullin, *Flight and Rebellion,* 98ff, 185–86. Stutterers comprised 3.8 percent of the runaways in Virginia, 2.2 percent in South Carolina, and 1.6 percent in Jamaica.

67. On the psychosocial aspects of acculturation in traditional societies, see R. J. Zwi Werblowsky, " 'A New Heaven and a New Earth': Considering Primitive Messianisms," *History of Religions* 5 (Summer 1965): 165–67; and Rolf Wirsing, "The Health of Traditional Societies and the Effects of Acculturation," *Current Anthropology* 26 (June 1985): 303–22 (see esp. the commentary of David Nyamwaya, 317).

68. *South Carolina Gazette and Country Journal,* Aug. 12, 1766, William De Brahm; also July 29, 1766, Josiah Smith, Jr., Oct. 13, 1767, William Coachman; *Va. Gaz.* (Purdie and Dixon), Jan. 22, 1772, John Stratton; *Virginia Independent Chronicle,* Jan. 21, 1789, Arthur Branch; *Maryland Gazette,* Jan. 17, 1792, Nicholas Worthington, March 13, 1794, William Hall; Mullin, *Flight and Rebellion,* 99.

69. [Kingston] *Daily Advertiser,* April 15, 1790, L. French; April 7, 1790, Robert Sewell; *Jam. Royal Gaz.,* March 16, 1793-P.S., A. Aikman.

70. Mullin, *Flight and Rebellion,* 77–78, 98.

71. *S.C. Royal Gaz.,* July 4, 1781, John M'Culloch; *S.C. and Amer. Genl. Gaz.,* Sept. 10, 1779, formerly the Reverend Dr. Purcel's.

72. *Va. Gaz.* (Purdie and Dixon), Sept. 14, 1769, Thomas Jefferson. For Maryland, *Maryland Herald and Eastern Shore Intelligencer,* Jan. 20, 1793, Thomas Ozment; June 27, 1797, Robert Goldsboro; April 11, 1797, James Clayland; June 4, 1802, Matts Bordley.

73. *Barb. Merc. and B-T. Gaz.,* Dec. 30, 1788, Philip Hackett; April 12, 1788, Henry Fowke; May 17, 1806, J. Jones.

74. *Port Gibson Correspondent* (Mississippi), Feb. 12, 1841, Thomas H. Wade; *The Mississippian* (Jackson), March 26, 1845, C. W. Judd; *Daily Picayune* (New Orleans), March 20, 1840, D. H. Bleasoe & Co. Nathan Huggins comes closest to the milieu outlined here when he discusses the "feebleness" of American community and its "destructive individualism." See *Black Odyssey: The Afro-American Ordeal in Slavery* (New York, 1977), ch. 6, esp. 155, 159–60.

75. David Brion Davis, *The Problem of Slavery in the Age of Revolution, 1770–1823* (New York, 1975), 194–95.

76. Cited in Sherry B. Ortner, "Theory in Anthropology since the Sixties," *Comparative Studies in Society and History* 26 (Jan. 1984): 157n.

77. Benjamin S. Screven to Major John Screven, Beaufort, S.C., Sept. 18, 1822, Arnold-Screven Papers, Vesey file, Southern Historical Collection; James Metiver, Garrison surgeon to Hislop, Trinidad, Dec. 8, 1805, C.O. 298/2, f. 100.

78. Bertram Wyatt-Brown, *Southern Honor: Ethics and Behavior in the Old South* (New York, 1982), ch. 15, esp. 405ff; Christopher Morris, "An Event in Community Organization: The Mississippi Slave Insurrection Scare of 1835," *Journal of Social History* 22 (Fall 1988): 93–111.

79. Eugene D. Genovese, *From Rebellion to Revolution: Afro-American Slave Revolts in the Making of the Modern World* (Baton Rouge, 1979), passim.

80. A. J. R. Russell-Wood, *Fidalgos and Philanthropists: The Santa Casa da Misericórdia of Bahia, 1550–1755* (Berkeley, 1968), 142. The phrase is taken from F. B. Welbourn and B. A. Ogot, *A Place to Feel at Home: A Study of Two Independent Churches in Western Kenya* (Oxford, 1966). Concerning the continual splintering of African Protestantism into healing sects, see D. B. Barrett, *Schism and Renewal in Africa: An Analysis of Six Thousand Contemporary Religious Movements* (Nairobi, 1968).

81. Mullin, "British Caribbean and North American Slaves in an Era of War and Revolution, 1775–1807," 244.

82. J. Stewart, *A View of the Past and Present State of the Island of Jamaica, with Remarks on the Moral and Physical Condition of the Slaves, and on the Abolition of Slavery in the Colonies* (Edinburgh, 1823), 270–71. A good description of "entertainment" by Creoles in Charleston, S.C., is Peter H. Wood, *Black Majority: Negroes in Colonial South Carolina from 1670 Through the Stono Rebellion* (New York, 1974), 342–43.

83. Gov. William Woodley to the Lords of Trade and Plantations, St. Kitts, April 20, 1770, C.O. 152/31; also C.O. 152/50, f. 29; and C.O. 299/2, f. 139, testimony of Mr. Rochard's Scipio.

84. Austin Steward, *Twenty-two Years a Slave and Forty Years a Freeman* (1857, repr. Reading, 1968), 77.

85. "Copy of all Judicial Proceedings relative to the Trial and Punishment of Rebels, or Alleged Rebels, in the Island of Jamaica, since the 1st of January 1823; . . . ," *Brit. Parl. Papers, Slave Trade* (1823), 67/48.

86. Mullin, *Flight and Rebellion*, 152; "Confession of Will, Examined by Brig. Gen. Carmichael," Tobago, Dec. 23, 1801, in Carmichael's report "on the General Massacre of the White and Coloured People . . . to have taken place at Eight o clock p.m. on the 25th Dec. 1801," C.O. 258/8; St. Kitts, "Examinations of Negroes," April 24, 1788, enclosed in Gov. Burt to Germaine, April 28, 1778, C.O. 152/58, f. 32v; for Jamaica, "Examination of Frank," March 8, 1807 in Gov. Coote to William Windham, King's House, Jamaica, C.O. 137/118.

87. Frederic G. Cassidy, *Jamaica Talk: Three Hundred Years of the English Language in Jamaica* (London, 1961), 231.

88. "A History of Monserrat," 46–47.

89. Richard Cobb, "A Mentality Shaped by Circumstance," in *The French*

Revolution: Conflicting Interpretations, ed. Frank A. Kafker and James M. Laux (New York, 1968), 246, 247–49. Testimony of Lt. Whitson, 37th Regiment, C.O. 298/2, f. 117; cf. Eric Hobsbawn, Primitive Rebels: Studies in Archaic Forms of Social Movement in the Nineteenth and Twentieth Centuries (New York, 1959), 153.

90. Peter J. Wilson, Crab Antics: The Social Anthropology of English-speaking Negro Societies of the Caribbean (New Haven, 1973), 209.

91. Testimony of Adelaide Dixon, C.O. 292/2, f. 135. This division between participants viewing Carnival as a cultural event versus those who see it as a political demonstration telescopes to the present. See Abner Cohen, "Drama and Politics in the Development of a London Carnival," Man 15 (March 1980): 65–87.

92. Deposition of Alice Carroll, April 10, 1778, in Gov. Burt to Lord Germaine, April 28, 1778, C.O. 152/58; Testimony of Little Tom of Friendsfield at trial of Anthony of Mesopotamia [Dec. 1801], C.O. 285/8; Testimony of George Knox's Zabette, C.O. 298/2, 104v; Testimony of Adelaide Dixon, f. 108v; James Metiver to the Gov., Dec. 8, 1805, f. 99v.

93. Testimony of the attending priest (who alluded hypocritically to his confessional vow of secrecy before telling the judges a great deal about what the condemned had confessed to him), C.O. 298/2, f. 125v, 126; Testimony of Adelaide Dixon, f. 113. On West African associations for controlling women, see "Travels into the Inland Parts of Africa by Francis Moore," in A New General Collection of Voyages and Travels, ed. Thomas Astley (London, 1745–47), 4:327–28; and Francis Moore, Travels, concerning the Mumbo Jombo stilt men and the subjection of women; Roy L. Austin, "Understanding Calpyso Content," Caribbean Quarterly 22 (June–Sept. 1976): 74–83.

94. Cutting down to size women who were long-distance traders is a function of some African antiwitchcraft rites argues S. F. Nadal in "Witchcraft in Four African Societies: An Essay in Comparison," American Anthropologist 54 (1952): 18–29.

95. Testimonies of Noel, Marie Catherine, and Harold, C.O. 298/2, ff. 102v, 103, 106. In the most cosmopolitan slave society in Anglo-America, however, the old divisiveness exhibited itself, nonetheless, in comments about the San Peur convoy as "comprised wholly of Creoles, without any Africans" (f. 102). The Trinidadian dancing societies should be compared to their African counterparts, see T. O. Ranger, Dance and Society in Eastern Africa, 1890–1970: The Beni Ngoma (Los Angeles, 1975), 10, 15, 18. Ranger's point is that through urban dances performers adopt symbols of progress toward a new life.

96. Brit. Parl. Papers, Slave Trade (1825), 67/47; Mullin, Flight and Rebellion, 161.

97. Memorial to Grenville, March 1791, C.O. 318/2, 265–65v.

98. [St. George Tucker], On the Subject of the Late Conspiracy of Slaves, 157–58, 203.

99. Gov. Knowles, speech to the Council and Assembly [undated, probably April 1753], copy received at Whitehall, Sept. 20, 1753, C.O. 137/26.

## Chapter Ten. Missionary Christianity
## and Preemancipation Rebellion

1. Gordon K. Lewis, *Main Currents in Caribbean Thought: The Historical Evolution of Caribbean Society in Its Ideological Aspects, 1492–1900* (Baltimore, 1983), 199.

2. For background, see G. G. Oliver Maynard, *A History of the Moravian Church, Eastern West Indies Province* (Port of Spain, 1968); Oliver W. Furley, "Moravian Missionaries and Slaves in the West Indies," *Caribbean Studies* 5 (July 1965): 3–16; and Fred Linyard, "The Moravians in Jamaica from the Beginning to Emancipation 1754 to 1838," *Jamaica Journal* 3 (March 1969): 7–11. A manager for a big Jamaican estate requested Antiguan slaves in 1774 because "in general [they] are the best disposed." William Monroe to Jacques and Fisher, March 15, 1774, E17749, Fitzherbert-Perrin Papers, Derbyshire Record Office, Matlock.

3. "La Trobe Letters," and "Principles on which the Mission of the Unitas Fratrum in the Island of Jamaica is to be Conducted," in a file of drafts, accounts, and undated letters 1799–1804 [1808], bundle 1, c. 378, Clarendon Deposit, Bodleian Library, Oxford University. For a manager's view of a Moravian minister as "he knows his place perfectly well," and of his congregation as one of "order & Decorum," see William Smalling to Barham, July 16, 1770, c. 367(1).

4. "Diary of a Negro Congregation in Jamaica, 1 May to the end of Year 1784" [Barham's Mesopotamia Estate], in "Jamaica, Letters and Papers 1768–1818," Moravian Missionary Society Archives, Muswell Hill, London; *Retrospect of the History of the Mission of the Brethren's Church in Jamaica, for the Past Hundred Years* (London, 1854), 7f (British Library pressmark 4745 C34).

5. "Plan of the New Church at Grace Bay, Antigua, 1812," in bundle labeled "Letters from Antigua, 1787–99," Letters and Papers, 1777–1823, Moravian Missionary Society Archives (unless otherwise indicated references that follow are to manuscripts from this collection).

6. John Frederick Reiclal to La Trobe, Grace Bay [Antigua], Oct. 9, 1797; Samuel Watson to La Trobe, St. Johns, Antigua, June 5, 1792 ibid.; J. H. Buchner, *The Moravians in Jamaica: History of the Mission of the United Brethren's Church to the Negroes in the Island of Jamaica from the Year 1754 to 1854* (London, 1854), 27, 31.

7. Buchner, *Moravians in Jamaica,* 20, 127. What may have been a major attraction to slaves was the fact that although Antiguan cemeteries were segregated and blacks were buried out at "The Point," Moravian slaves were buried in a large field close to their church: Sarah Moore to the Secretary, London, Nov. 16, 1814, box 96/item 114, Methodist Missionary Society Archives. Moore also noted that 410 slave children attended Sunday schools at two Moravian stations, an unheard of number for any other congregation anywhere in the islands.

8. Buchner, *Moravians in Jamaica,* 44–45. For the disciplining of slaves by Southern Baptists, see the church minutes of Feb. 18, 1820, and Jan. 18, 1829 for Welsh Neck, South Caroliniana Library, University of South Carolina, Columbia; July 4, 1791, and July 1793 monthly meeting Antioch (Dover); July 3, 1801, Lyles (Albemarle); Oct. 8, 1780, Morattico; May 18, 1777, Albemarle, Virginia Baptist

Historical Society, University of Richmond. See also, Randy J. Sparks, "Religion in Amite County, Mississippi, 1800–1861," in *Masters and Slaves in the House of the Lord: Race and Religion in the American South, 1740–1870,* ed. John B. Boles (Lexington, Ky., 1988), 72–76.

9. Maynard, *A History of the Moravian Church,* 30ff.

10. Buchner, *Moravians in Jamaica,* 41.

11. James Ramsay, *An Essay on the Treatment and Conversion of African Slaves in the British Sugar Colonies* (London, 1784), 164.

12. *British Parliamentary Papers, Slave Trade* (1831–34), 80/249.

13. Buchner, *Moravians in Jamaica,* 50; "S.F.G. [Society for the Furtherance of the Gospel] 1776–1794," Sept. 6, 1776, 13, May 13, 1777, 28; "Report of Brother Tschirpe," in "S.F.G. 1803-1813," Aug. 15, 1803, 32–33; W. J. Gardner, *A History of Jamaica from Its Discovery by Christopher Columbus to the Year 1872* (1873, repr. London, 1971), 360.

14. *Brit. Parl. Papers, Slave Trade* (1823–24), 66/101, 175, 215, 220. Gladstone, thirty and six feet two, was characterized by one witness as he "keeps all white peoples' wives" (215). Resistance was somewhat unfocused until he was taken up, after which "everyone rose together" (72). After Gladstone's trial, the longest on record (208–21), his death sentence was commuted to transportation. See also, C.O. 111/42, ff. 32–33, 490; Mortier to the Secretary, Sept. 8, 1823, Georgetown [Guiana], 143/144, Methodist Missionary Society Archives.

15. The revolt is described by Michael Craton, *Testing the Chains: Resistance to Slavery in the British West Indies* (Ithaca, 1982), ch. 21.

16. *Brit. Parl. Papers, Slave Trade* (1823–24), 66/166, 227, 239; also 169, 200–201, 232. Concerning the actual outbreak and few skirmishes, see the military commander's descriptions, 68ff, 202. See also 166; cf. 119. On a key but shadowy figure, the manager John Hamilton, whose mistress, Susan, was also Gladstone's woman, see 99ff, 218–19.

17. Ibid., 177, 187, 229.

18. Ibid., 225; cf. 231.

19. Ibid., 225

20. Ibid., 101–2 (cf. 232); C.O. 111/42, 457; J. Mortier to the Secretary, Georgetown, Sept. 8, 1823, 143/144, Methodist Missionary Society Archives.

21. Ibid., 81ff, 59, 200, and C.O. 111/42, ff. 7; 10ff for Smith's Journal "containing Various Occurences at Le Resouvenir . . . March 1817," London Missionary Society, *Quarterly Chronicle,* Dec. 9, 1816, London Missionary Society Papers [included in the Methodist Missionary Archives].

22. *Brit. Parl. Papers, Slave Trade* (1825), 59; cf. 61, 109, and C.O. 111/42, f. 450: "The Negroes had been told . . . that the Enemy the Jews fought against and conquered meant the Men did not believe in or fear God — that Jerusalem was to be destroyed because the Men of that City did not believe in God."

23. Ibid., 65. The prosecutor claimed that Smith's official instructions from the society were to stick to the New Testament "and [to] never glance at, or allude even most distantly to the Old Testament." C.O. 111/42, f. 430; cf. 463.

24. Ibid., 65, 67; cf. 61.

25. Ibid., 63, 66. An account by Smith's wife Jane is also useful for views of relations between the missionary family and the revolt's leaders: *Supplement to the Quarterly Chronicle of the Transactions of the London Missionary Society* (London, 1825), box, West Indies, Odds 4; *Quarterly Chronicle,* Dec. 4, 1823; and Jane Smith, Affadavit, Nov. 13, 1812; all Methodist Missionary Society Archives.

26. *Brit. Parl. Papers, Slave Trade* (1823–24), 66/166.

27. Wray's letters are in box 1 "B. Guiana-Demerara, 1807-1814," Methodist Missionary Society Archives.

28. *Brit. Parl. Papers, Slave Trade* (1823–24), 66/83ff, 106; C.O. 111/42, f. 436, cf. 469ff.

29. C.O. 111/42, f. 7.

30. *Brit. Parl. Papers, Slave Trade* (1823–24), 66/166; cf. 109.

31. Duke of Manchester to Bathurst, King's House, Jamaica, July 31, 1824; C.O. 137/156; Deposition of William Annand, Overseer of Ginger Hill Plantation, St. Elizabeth, Jan. 2, 1832, C.O. 111/142, 1831–34, 80/293; Theodore Faulks, *Eighteen Months in Jamaica; with Recollections of the Late Rebellion* (London, 1833), 76.

32. The Assembly estimated property damage at £1,154,589.2.1, C.O. 137/182, f. 286. Cf. Barry W. Higman, *Slave Population and Economy in Jamaica, 1807– 1834* (Cambridge, 1976), 227. There is an official map of the extent of destruction: "A Plan of the Parish of St. James together with a part of the Parishes of Hanover, Westmoreland and St. Elizabeth Situated in the County of Corn- wall. . . . Constructed from Recent Survey by Orders From the Authorities in March 1832" (London, Sept. 1832). The map bears an "explanation": "The places underlined, in red were those Destroyed during the Rebellion in 1832." About 280 properties are underlined, and the very few on which trash houses only were burned, such as Roaring River and Deans Valley estates in Westmoreland, are so indicated, as are the locations of the killing of whites at Marchmont and Rock Pleasant. Tharp Papers, R63/20, Cambridge Record Office.

33. Mary [Turner] Reckord, "The Jamaican Slave Rebellion of 1831," *Past and Present* 40 (July 1968): 108–25; Edward Kamau Braithwaite, "The Slave Rebellion in the Great River Valley of St. James, 1831-1832," *Jamaica Historical Review* 13 (1982): 11–30; Craton, *Testing the Chains,* ch. 22; and, for an official overview, Gov. Belmore to Viscount Goderich, Jan. 6, 1832, C.O. 137/181, 1ff.

34. *Brit. Parl. Papers, Slave Trade* (1831–34), 80/217–18. Volume 80 is essentially the Jamaica House of Assembly's "Report of a Committee to enquire into recent Rebellion — Retn'd to England — 22 June 1832."

35. Edward Kamau Braithwaite, "Caliban, Ariel, and Unprospero in the Con- flict of Creolization: A Study of the Slave Revolt in Jamaica in 1831-32," in *Comparative Perspectives on Slavery in New World Plantation Societies,* ed. Vera Rubin and Arthur Tuden, Annals of the New York Academy of Sciences (June 1977), 292:41–62.

36. Hope Masterton Waddell, *Twenty-nine Years in the West Indies and Cen- tral Africa: A Review of Missionary Work and Adventure, 1829–1858* (London, 1863), 59, 63ff. From the perspective of the individual estate and its slave leadership,

viewing the 1831 rising as "the Baptist War" (most recently in Craton's *Testing the Chains*) may miss the mark somewhat. See William Knibb's heated and explicit denials of Baptist complicity among converts on "70 estates" where no arson was reported, and of only three of 983 members of his own congregation in Falmouth. Knibb and P. Borthwick, *Defence of Baptist Missionaries from the Charge of Inciting the Late Rebellion in Jamaica . . .*, 2d ed. (London, 1833), 5ff. Cf. Thomas Burchell, *Memoir of Thomas Burchell* (London, 1845), 230, citing Cox's *History of Baptist Missionaries* that a third of the slaves (twenty-five of seventy-four) that the Assembly rewarded after the revolt were Baptist.

A contemporary observed that "elders" among the slaves initiated the rebellion, then "as a matter of course" young people followed their parents: Richard R. Madden, *A Twelvemonths Residence in the West Indies*, 2 vols. (London, 1835), 2: 168–69. Barry Higman argues similarly in *Slave Population and Economy in Jamaica, 1807–1834*, 228. A preliminary view of the hundreds tried for rebellion indicates that a clear majority were non-field slaves (artisans and drivers, principally) and in their thirties or older.

37. C.O. 137/185, 246–46v, 357–58.

38. Ibid., 210v–11v, 314ff.

39. Ibid., ff. 240, 373–75v.

40. Ibid., ff. 308v–13, 324. Concerning who "owned" Sharpe, there seems to be two views: he either belonged to a Montego Bay soldier or to Croydon Estate. In either case, he lived and worked in Montego Bay. Two whites said he belonged to Croydon. *Brit. Parl. Papers Slave Trade* (1831–34), 80/200, 222–23, 225, 226, 294, 295.

41. Henry Bleby, *Death Struggles of Slavery: Being a Narrative of Facts and Incidences, which occurred in a British Colony, During the two years Immediately Preceding Negro Emancipation* (London, 1853), 111–12; John Clarke, *Memorials of Baptist Missionaries in Jamaica* (London, 1869), 92ff; *Brit. Parl. Papers, Slave Trade* (1831–34), 80/222–25 for the confessions of two leaders, Dove and Gardner.

42. Bleby, *Death Struggles*, 111–12, 115.

43. C.O. 137/185, f. 553.

44. Clarke, *Memorials of Baptist Missionaries*, 103; cf. C.O. 137/185, f.220f.

45. C.O. 137/185, 115v–16. Another reference to the small and relatively unknown insurrection at Argyle Pen is in *Brit. Parl. Papers, Slave Trade* (1831–34), 80/217–18.

46. C.O. 137/185, 116v.

47. *Brit. Parl. Papers, Slave Trade* (1831–34), 80/219, 220.

48. Ibid., 221; cf. 317.

49. Ibid., 224–25; Foulks, *Eighteen Months in Jamaica*, 80–82.

50. *Brit. Parl. Papers, Slave Trade* (1831–34), 80/218, 301.

51. Ibid., 294, 227.

52. Ibid., 209, 217, 218, 226; C.O. 137/182, 308v, 373ff; cf. 319, 325.

53. C.O. 137/185, f. 424.

54. Ibid. 137/182, f. 321–22; *Brit. Parl. Papers, Slave Trade* (1831–34), 80/220.

55. Ibid., f. 318, 514, 742; C.O. 137/182, 307v, 308v, 310v, 311–11v; *Brit. Parl.*

*Papers, Slave Trade* (1831–34), 80/217, 219, 225, 309; see also, Bleby, *Death Struggles,* 112.

56. C.O. 117/185, f. 742.

57. *Brit. Parl. Papers, Slave Trade* (1831–34), 80/199; cf. 200–201, 217.

58. C.O. 137/185, pt. 4, f. 730; Foulks, *Eighteen Months in Jamaica,* 78. There is explicit evidence that the old Coramantee blood oath the "Swear," and the new legal kissing of the Bible in court, were in the minds of some slaves one and the same: *Brit. Parl. Papers, Slave Trade* (1825), in "Papers Relating to Slaves in the West Indies," 67/129.

59. *Brit. Parl. Papers, Slave Trade* (1831–34), 80/219, 220, 249, 294.

60. Ibid., 293–94.

61. Kenneth Stampp, *The Peculiar Institution: Slavery in the Ante-Bellum South* (New York, 1956), 134.

62. Seaforth to Hobart, Pilgrim, June 6, 1802, C.O. 28/68, ff. 55–60v. Cf. "I have never perceived the least Discontent, or Dissatisfaction among them [the slaves]": Gov. D. Parry to Lord Grenville, May 23, 1791, C.O., 28/63. A contemporary churchman considered briefly why more slave rebellions occurred in Jamaica than Barbados, see O. F. Christie, ed., *The Diary of Revd. William Jones, 1777–1778* (London, 1929), 30ff.

63. The argument that dissenters got nowhere in Barbados is based on the following: Methodist leader Thomas Coke cited in Joshua Steele, "Letters and Papers of the Late Hon. Joshua Steele," in *The Mitigation of Slavery* (London, 1814), xii (British Library pressmark 8156 df2): "The Negroes in Barbados, for some reason which he cannot explain, are much less prepared for the reception of genuine religion [evangelism] than those of any other island." Steele himself reported no missionaries in the late 1780s. C.O. 28/61, f. 246. At the same time the Anglican church reported one dissenter chapel. Henry Frere to Sec. of State, Aug. 24, 1789, C.O. 28/62. After the 1816 rising a planter and councilor from St. Kitts reported that "There was not a missionary on the island [of Barbados]." MS vol. "Testimonials of planters of the West Indies — 1818," William Thomson, St. Kitts, p. 61, box 1, West Indian Biographical, Methodist Missionary Society Archives. A comparison of congregations a year after the rebellion reported three thousand black Methodists in St. Vincents but only fifty-four in neighboring Barbados. "Extract from Mr. Morgan to the Committee," St. Vincents, July 17, 1817, box 113/24. The Barbados contribution to Parliament's major inquiries of 1788 read in part "Their [the Negroes'] Superstitions [also] . . . seem to be almost insurmountable. . . . Even the better sort amongst them almost universally believe in Witchcraft." Enclosed in Gov. Parry's of May 13, 1788, C.O. 28/61, f. 182v.

64. Benjamin Bracksham, Barbados, to Mr. John Wollin [Barbados], June 1, 1796 in bundle marked "letters from Barbados, 1768–1813," Moravian Missionary Society Archives.

65. *The Report from a Select Committee of the House of Assembly, appointed to Inquire the Origins, Causes, and Progress of the late Insurrection* (Barbados, n.d.) 35, 45. Hereafter *Assembly Report on the Insurrection.*

66. Ibid., 37.

67. Ibid., 6, 32, 49, cf. 26, 36–37, 42–43, 46.

68. Ibid., 6–7, 26, 29, 33–34, 36, 37–38, 40, 42–43, 45. See also, Seaforth to Lord Hobart, Pilgrim, June 6, 1802, C.O. 28/68, ff.55; and Jerome S. Handler, *The Unappropriated People: Freedmen in the Slave Society of Barbados* (Baltimore, 1974), 85ff.

69. John Womack, Jr., *Zapata, and the Mexican Revolution* (New York, 1969). The field commander reported that the rebels' said the country belonged to them. Col. Edward Codd to Gov. James Leith, St. Ann's [Bridgetown], April 25, 1816, C.O. 28/85.

70. *Assembly Report on the Insurrection,* 37; cf. Dainty's request, 35.

71. The state reimbursed owners whose slaves were executed as insurrectionists. Valuations, in increments of $50, ranged between $300 and $450, with Turner, a corn-field Negro, in the middle and worth less than one woman and such artisans as Hark at $450. From the commissioner of revenue's tax lists, it is immediately apparent that owners and victims were very small slaveholders. Turner's owner Joseph Travis had about twelve to fifteen slaves older than twelve, four horses, and mules. Southampton County tax lists for 1830 and 1831, Virginia State Archives microfilm.

72. Thomas W. Higginson's (1862) account in *The Southampton Slave Revolt of 1831: A Compilation of Source Material,* ed. Henry I. Tragle (Amherst, 1971), 330. Cf. T. R. Gray's account of Nat Turner's Confessions, ibid., 310 (hereafter, "Nat Turner's Confession").

73. For accounts of the actual march, see the newspaper accounts in *The Southhampton Revolt,* ed. Tragle, 67–70, 95–97.

74. Conversations with Henry Tragle, Northampton Mass., 1969–70.

75. "Nat Turner's Confession," 313–14.

76. For a report that a "large number of the effective" male population was away at a camp meeting, see *Easton [Md.] Gazette,* Aug. 27, 1831, Maryland Historical Society, Baltimore.

77. *Richmond Whig,* Sept. 7, 1831. This and the other newspapers cited are from the Virginia Historical Society, Richmond; see also, Gov. John Floyd to Brig. Gen. Richard Eppes, Executive Dept. [Richmond], Sept. 13, 1831 in *The Southampton Revolt,* ed. Tragle, 274.

78. Ibid., 423. In an Oct. 21, 1831 issue of the *Enquirer,* it was noted, in reaction to charges of ill-treatment made by William Lloyd Garrison, that Turner was scarred on the temple from the kick of a mule, and on his neck and elbow from fights. When he was taken, the *Enquirer* wrote (Nov. 8), "he answers exactly the description annexed to the Governor's Proclamation except that he is of a darker hue, and his eyes, tho large, are not prominent — they are very long, deeply seated in his head, and have rather a sinister expression."

79. "Nat Turner's Confession," 306ff, 316–17.

80. Ibid., 309.

81. Ibid., 309–10.

82. [T. R. Gray], *Richmond Enquirer,* Nov. 8, 1831; cf. "Nat Turner's Confession," 307–9.

83. *Richmond Enquirer,* Sept. 30, 1831, *Richmond Whig,* Sept. 26, 1831, both in "Nat Turner's Confession," 92. For reactions to allegations that Turner was a Baptist, see *Richmond Enquirer,* Aug. 29, Sept. 7, 1831.

84. *Constitutional Whig,* Richmond, Sept 26, 1831, in *The Southampton Revolt,* ed. Tragle, 92.

85. "Nat Turner's Confession," 310.

86. *Richmond Whig,* Sept. 26, 1831, in *The Southampton Revolt,* ed. Tragle, 95.

87. A useful newspaper account of the capture is *Norfolk and Portsmouth Herald,* Nov. 4, 1831, Beinecke Rare Book and Manuscript Library, Yale University. We are not sure what Turner looked like, but the Nov. 14 issue mentions Gray's promise that his transcription of the confession would include "an accurate likeness" of Turner by John Crawley "to be lythographed by *Endicott & Swett,* of Baltimore."

88. Robert I. Rotberg, "Psychological Stress and the Question of Identity: Chilembwe's Revolt Reconsidered," in *Protest and Power in Black Africa,* ed. Robert I. Rotberg and Ali A. Mazrui (New York, 1970), 337–73; cf. George Simeon Mwase, *Strike a Blow and Die; A Narrative of Race Relations in Colonial Africa,* ed. Robert I. Rotberg (Cambridge, Mass., 1967).

## Epilogue. Africa in America

1. Sidney W. Mintz and Richard Price, *An Anthropological Approach to the Afro-American Past: A Caribbean Perspective* (Philadelphia, 1976), 9.

2. Michael Craton, "Jamaican Slavery," in *Race and Slavery in the Western Hemisphere: Quantitative Studies,* ed. Stanley L. Engerman and Eugene D. Genovese (Princeton, 1975), 265.

3. Allan Kulikoff, "Uprooted Peoples: Black Migrants in the Age of the American Revolution, 1790–1820," in *Slavery and Freedom in the Age of the American Revolution,* ed. Ira Berlin and Ronald Hoffman (Charlottesville, 1983), 153. The argument remains unresolved in our generation. See Herbert G. Gutman, "The Middle Passage . . . Failed to Obliterate Social Memory," in *The Black Family in Slavery and Freedom, 1750–1925* (New York, 1976), 222. Consequently, the observation that the two sides continue to talk by one another is most apt. See Roger D. Abrahams and John F. Szwed, eds. *After Africa: Extracts from British Travel Accounts and Journals . . . Concerning the Slaves, Their Manners, and Customs in the British West Indies* (New Haven, 1983), 5–6.

4. Journals of Thomas Thistlewood [Thistlewood's Journal], July 15, 1761, Monson 31, Lincolnshire, Record Office, Lincoln. Consider, too, "We have a good Many Tagge Nutts, produced from a few our Negroes brought from Guinea" (May 20, 1755).

5. Edward Long, *The History of Jamaica,* 3 vols. (1774, repr. London, 1970), 2:474; W. J. Gardner, *A History of Jamaica: From Its Discovery by Christopher Columbus to the Year 1872* (1783, repr. London, 1971), 184. Cf. R. B. La Page and D. DeCamp, *"Jamaican Creole": Creole Language Studies* (New York, 1960), 75–

77, who view Akan-speakers (that is, Coramantee) as "centers of linguistic and cultural conservatism for a large part of the island"; Mavis Campbell, "The Maroons of Jamaica: Imperium in Imperio?" *Pan-African Journal* 6 (Spring 1973): 52f; Edward Braithwaite, review of Patterson's *Sociology of Slavery* in *Race* 9 (1968): 338ff. The treatment of an Asante dialect of Akan as a prestige language in the Brong region of West Africa is discussed in Florence Abena Dolphyne, "Akan Language Patterns and Development," *Tarikh* 26, no. 2 (1982): 35–45 (issue on Akan history and culture, ed. J. K. Fynn). For non-Coramantee Africans of Jamaica who spoke Coramantee, see *Jamaica Royal Gazette,* Nov. 17, 1781-S., Richard Saunders; April 14, 1792-S., William Anderson Sr.; April 11, 1801-S., William Christie; May 25, 1805-S., John Deans.

6. See, for example, Melville J. Herskovits, *The Myth of the Negro Past* (Boston, 1941), ch. 2; Roger Bastide, *The African Religions of Brazil: Toward a Sociology of the Interpenetration of Civilizations* (1960, repr. Baltimore, 1978), esp. ch. 9; cf. Mervyn Alleyne, *Roots of Jamaican Culture* (1988, repr. London, 1989), ch. 2. My argument for the primacy of Akan-speaking slaves in Jamaica adds to the work of J. J. Williams, Orlando Patterson, and Leonard Barrett. See the latter's *The Sun and the Drum: African Roots in Jamaican Folk Tradition* (Kingston, 1976), 16.

7. Mintz and Price, *An Anthropological Approach to the Afro-American Past,* 7f, 9–11.

8. Eric Foner, *Nothing but Freedom: Emancipation and Its Legacy* (Baton Rouge, 1983).

9. Cf. Dominique Zahan, *The Religion, Spirituality, and Thought of Traditional Africa* (1970, repr. Chicago, 1979), ch 8, esp. 112–14.

10. William Styron, "Introduction" to Richard L. Rubenstein, *The Cunning of History: The Holocaust and the American Future* (1975 New York, 1978), ix-xiv. Donald G. Mathews refers to the antebellum South as a "totalitarian regime" in a discussion of separate black churches in *Religion in the Old South* (Chicago 1977), 189.

11. Henry Shirley to Edward Shirley, Kingston, May 21, 1800, C.O. 137/104.

12. James O'Toole characterizes friendship networks of urban black men as transitory and as substitutes for real organization in *Watts and Woodstock: Identity and Culture in the United States and South Africa* (New York, 1973), 79; see also, Bruce T. Grindal, *Growing Up in Two Worlds: Education and Transition among the Sisala of Northern Ghana* (New York, 1972).

13. Bastide, *The African Religions of Brazil,* 66, 71, 89, 95–96. Cf. The argument of Emmanuel Wallerstein and Clyde Mitchell that "tribalism is a phenomenon arising out of cultural contact," in *Ethnicity in Modern African,* ed. Brian M. du Toit (Boulder, 1978), 7; and Kenneth Little, *West African Urbanization: A Study of Voluntary Associations in Social Change* (Cambridge, England, 1965), 24–29.

14. Gilbert Osofsky, *Harlem: The Making of a Ghetto* (1963, repr. New York, 1966), 132.

15. Cf. Edward Long's version (*History of Jamaica,* 2:379) and the discussion in Henry Louis Gates, Jr., *The Signifying Monkey: A Theory of African-American Literary Criticism* (New York, 1988), ch. 4.

## Appendix 1. The Problem of Provenance

1. J. B. Moreton, *West India Customs and Manners: . . . with the Methods of Establishing and Conducting a Sugar Plantation. . . .* (London, 1793), 145; [Anon.], *A Professional Planter, Practical Rules for the Management and Medical Treatment of Negro Slaves, in the Sugar Colonies* (London, 1811), 38.

2. P. E. H. Hair, "Ethnolinguistic Continuity on the Guinea Coast," *Journal of African History* 8 no. 2 (1967): 266, 268.

3. I was led to this source by Roger Norman Buckley's *Slaves in Red Coats: The British India Regiments, 1795–1815* (New Haven, 1979).

4. *Jamaica Royal Gazette* [*Jam. Royal Gaz.*], Jan. 4, 1794; *Cornwall Chronicle and Jamaica General Gazette* [*Cornwall Chron.*], May 3, 1777; also, Dec. 1, 1781-S., Jan. 5, 1782, Dec. 20, 1783.

5. *Jam. Royal Gaz.*, Sept. 6, 1794; *South Carolina Gazette* [*S.C. Gaz.*], June 6, 1771, Miles Brewton.

6. David Dalby, "Distribution and Nomenclature of the Manding People and Their Language," in *Papers on the Manding*, ed. Carleton T. Hodge (Bloomington, 1971), 1–13.

7. Philip D. Curtin, ed., *Africa Remembered: Narratives by West Africans from the Era of the Slave Trade* (Madison, 1967), 17–59; George M. Callcott, "Omar Ibn Seid, a Slave Who Wrote an Autobiography in Arabic," *Journal of Negro History* 39 (Jan. 1954): 58–62.

8. John W. Blassingame, ed., *Slave Testimony: Two Centuries of Letters, Speeches, Interviews and Autobiographies* (Baton Rouge, 1977), 30–46.

9. D. Kiyaga-Mulindwa, "The 'Akan' Problem," *Current Anthropology* 21 (Aug. 1980): 503–6.

10. Daniel C. Littlefield, *Rice and Slaves: Ethnicity and the Slave Trade in Colonial South Carolina* (Baton Rouge, 1981), ch. 1; Margaret Washington Creel, *"A Peculiar People": Slave Religion and Community-Culture Among the Gullahs* (New York, 1988).

11. *South Carolina Royal Gazette*, Aug. 29, 1781, B. Cape; *S. C. Gaz.*, June 30, 1759, Snow Betsey, Robert Deas, master; Sept. 1, 1759, Austin, Laurens and Appleby; Aug. 24, 1765, Brewton and Smith; (Clinch), April 9, 1771, Elias Vanderhorst.

12. *Cornwall Chron.*, Nov. 19, 1785-S., John Willox.

13. Roger Bastide, *The African Religions of Brazil: Toward a Sociology of the Interpenetration of Civilizations* (1960, repr. Baltimore, 1978), 445, n57.

14. Philip L. Curtin, *The Atlantic Slave Trade: A Census* (Madison, 1969), 187.

15. George Peter Murdock, *Africa: Its Peoples and Their Culture History* (New York, 1959), 93 (12. 30–33; cf. 13.52).

16. William Bascom, *The Yoruba of Southwestern Nigeria* (New York, 1969), 8.

17. Curtin, *The Atlantic Slave Trade*, 186–87.

18. [Kingston] *Daily Advertiser*, Dec. 7, 1790, S. Tone; *Jam. Royal Gaz.*, Jan.

26, 1793-P.S., Hugh Gillespie; and, for a rare instance when the two people were seen as distinct: June 15, 1793-P.S., Downes Coveo.

19. Patrick Manning, "The Slave Trade in the Bight of Benin, 1640–1890," in *The Uncommon Market: Essays in the Economic History of the Atlantic Slave Trade,* ed. Henry A. Gamery and Jan S. Hogendorn (New York, 1979), 107–41.

20. Thomas Astley, *A New General Collection of Voyages and Travels. . . ,* 4 vols. (London, 1745–47, repr. 1968), 3:18; E. Bolaji-Idowu, *Olódùmarè: God in Yoruba Belief* (London, 1962), 5f.

21. Bryan Edwards, *The History, Civil and Commercial, of the British Colonies in the West Indies,* 2 vols. (Dublin, 1793), 2:68.

22. Edward Long, *The History of Jamaica,* 3 vols. (1774, repr. London, 1970), 2:425.

23. Journals of Thomas Thistlewood, Aug. 10, 1776, Monson 31, Lincolnshire Record Office, Lincoln.

24. *Iboland: A Century of contact with Britain, 1860–1960* (London, 1977), 16; V. C. Uchendu, *The Igbo of Southeast Nigeria* (New York, 1965), 19; A. E. Afigbo, "Prolegomena to the Study of the Culture History of the Igbo-speaking Peoples of Nigeria," in *West African Culture Dynamics: Archaeological and Historical Perspectives,* ed. B. K. Swartz, Jr., and Raymond E. Dumett (The Hague, 1980), 308.

Concerning the high-achievers argument, see Phoebe Ottenberg, "The Afikpo Ibo of Eastern Nigeria," in *Peoples of Africa,* ed. James Gibbs (New York, 1965), 6; Paul Merceir, "The Meaning of Tribalism in Black Africa," in *Race and Ethnicity in Africa,* ed. Pierre L. van den Berghe (Nairobi, 1975), 23–26; Austin Metumara Ahanoto, "The Economics and Politics of Religion: A Study in the Development of the Igbo Spirit of Enterprise, 1800–1955," Ph.D. diss., UCLA, 1971, esp. 32ff on Igbo individualism; and J. Omosade Awolalu and P. Adelumo Dopamu, *West African Traditional Religion* (Ibadan, 1979), 3.

25. Three years is an estimate only. Alone among planters in their concern (and expectation) about blacks learning to speak white English, Virginians left traces in their fugitive slave notices that indicate that new Negroes became "sensible" in about two years.

26. *Jam. Royal Gaz.,* Dec. 21, 1801-P.S., James McGill's Bellvere; Toney: April 25, 1795-S., James Hunt; Charles: July 4, 1795-S., Andrew Sutherland; April 26, 1794-S., M. Meecham.

27. G. I. Jones, *The Trading States of the Oil Rivers: A Study of Political Development in Eastern Nigeria* (London, 1963), 36, 39

28. See Murdock's map 31.4, "Bantoid cluster," in *Africa,* 243.

29. John R. Willis, annotated bibliography (1966) to G. T. Basden, *Among the Iboes of Nigeria: An Account of the Curious and Interesting Habits, Customs, and Beliefs. . . .* (1921, repr. London, 1966), 307–12.

30. *Jam. Royal Gaz.,* April 25, 1795, James Hunt; *Cornwall Chron.,* Nov. 10, 1792-S., Thomas Deane. For a how-to manual reference to Eboes as "commonly called Mocos," see *A Professional Planter,* 37.

31. Daniel J. Crowley, "Folklore Research in the Congo," in *Folklore Research*

*Around the World: A North American Point of View,* ed. Richard M. Dorson (Port Washington, 1961), 173–74.

32. *Jam. Royal Gaz.,* June 22, 1793-P.S., Thomas Nelson; April 5, 1794-P.S., Richard Poore.

33. Simon Taylor to Chalonder Archedeckne, Mullet Hall, St. Thomas in the East [Jamaica], Sept. 3, 1787, box 2, item 13, Vanneck MS, Manuscripts Room, Cambridge University Library.

34. Lorenzo Turner, *Africanisms in the Gullah Dialect* (New York, 1944). For a discussion of both the Senegambian and Angolan roots of important lowcountry slave traditions, see Creel, *"A Peculiar People"*; Joseph Holloway, "The Origins of African-American Culture," in *Africanisms in American Culture,* ed. Holloway (Bloomington, 1990), ch. 1; and Robert Farris Thompson, *Flash of the Spirit: African and Afro-American Art and Philosophy* (New York, 1983), ch. 2.

## Appendix 3. Were Maroons the Whites' Clients?

1. Barbara Klamon Kopytoff, "Jamaican Maroon Political Organization: The Effect of the Treaties," *Social and Economic Studies* 25 (June 1976): 99, 102.

2. Eugene D. Genovese, *From Rebellion to Revolution: Afro-American Slave Revolts in the Making of the Modern World* (Baton Rouge, 1979), 36, 118; Orlando Patterson, "Slavery and Slave Revolts: A Socio-Historical Analysis of the First Maroon War, 1655–1740," *Social and Economic Studies* 19 (Sept. 1970): 312, 317.

3. Enclosed in Gen. John Palmer to Balcarres, Montego Bay, Sept. 22, 1795, 23/11/46, Crawford Muniments, National Library of Scotland, Edinburgh; Thistlewood's Journal, April 4, 1751.

4. Cited in Edward Braithwaite, *The Development of Creole Society in Jamaica, 1770–1820* (Oxford, 1971), 247.

5. Both estimates are cited in W. J. Gardner, *A History of Jamaica: From Its Discovery by Christopher Columbus to the Year 1784* (1873, repr. London, 1971), 254, 266–67, 267n.

6. Account, 3/e/i, p. 8, Gale-Morant Papers, Roborough Library, University of Exeter.

## Appendix 4. Provision Grounds, Pens, and Market Women

1. Edward East to Anna Eliza Elletson, Sept. 10, 1780, Stowe MS 26, Henry E. Huntington Library, San Marino, Calif.

2. *The Barbados Globe and Demerara Advocate,* Dec. 14, 1829, C.O. 33/1.

3. Ibid.

4. Thistlewood's Journal: end sheets of the 1776 journal; cf. entry following Dec. 30, 1774.

5. Ibid., May 16, 1754.

6. Orlando Patterson, *The Sociology of Slavery: An Analysis of the Origins, Development and Structure of Negro Slave Society in Jamaica* (1967, repr. Rutherford, 1969), 218–19; Mary Turner, *Slaves and Missionaries: The Disintegration of Jamaican Slave Society, 1787–1834* (Urbana, 1982), 43.

7. Alexander McLeod to William Sterling, Spanish Town, Aug. 18, 1797, Abercairny Muniments, GD21/1/461, Scottish Record Office, Edinburgh; *Jamaica Royal Gazette* [*Jam. Royal Gaz.*], Oct. 3, 1801-S., for Sun Flower and New Garden plantations (St. Thomas in the East).

8. *Jam. Royal Gaz.*, April 22, 28, and May 12, 1781-S. (Invermay Estate, James Henry, David Jones); July 4, 1795 (Moor Park and Canewood estates); Oct. 24, 1795 (Golden Grove).

9. "Valuation of Moses and Aaron Franks Duckenfield . . . June 19 [1784]," Duckenfield Hall Records, Acc. 775/932, Middlesex Record Office, London.

10. "A Sketch" is an 1810 inventory of three Perrin properties, old filing system box 108/8, Fitzherbert-Perrin Papers, Derbyshire Record Office, Matlock.

11. McLeod to Sterling, Aug. 18, 1797, Abercairny Muniments, National Library of Scotland, Edinburgh.

12. For background, see Richard Sheridan, "The Wealth of Jamaica in the Eighteenth Century," *Economic History Review*, 2d ser., 18 (Aug. 1965): 299–301; Edward Long, *The History of Jamaica*, 3 vols. (1774, repr. London, 1970) 2:59, 105–6, 123ff; for a good contemporary discussion, see Simon Taylor to Chalonder Archedeckne, Kingston [Jamaica], Oct. 29, 1782, box 2, item 10, Vanneck MS, Manuscripts Room, Cambridge University Library.

13. "A Sketch," box 108/8, Fitzherbert-Perrin Papers; Robert Thompson to Ellis Yonge, March 7, 1797, St. Kitts, no. 3233, Bodrhyddan (Langford) Addit. MS, Department of Archives, University College of North Wales Library, Bangor.

14. Barry Higman, "Household Structure and Fertility on Jamaican Slave Plantations: A Nineteenth-century Example," *Population Studies* 27 (1973): 534.

15. Edward East to Anna Eliza Elletson, May 16, 1776, Letterbook, Stowe MS.

16. George Pinckard, *Notes on the West Indies. . . .*, 2d ed., 2 vols. (London, 1816), 1:113–14; Sir William Young, *A Tour Through the Several Islands of Barbados, St. Vincents, Antigua, Tobago, and Grenada, In the Years 1791 and 1792. . . .* (London, 1801), 261–62.

17. The overwhelming number of women to men sellers does not support Sidney Mintz's claim that women higglers only appeared after emancipation, an argument based on the assumption that slave men dominated provision grounds. See "Men, Women, and Trade," *Comparative Studies in Society and History* 13 (July 1971): 256; Mintz, "Economic Role and Cultural Tradition," in *The Black Woman Cross-Culturally*, ed. Filomina Chioma Steady (Cambridge, Mass., 1981), 519–20, 528. Cf. Mintz and Richard Price, *An Anthropological Approach to the Afro-American Past: A Caribbean Perspective* (Philadelphia, 1976), 41. With emancipation, men "took over" agricultural production from women, which may have represented adaptation to sex role expectations of the broader European society.

18. *Jam. Royal Gaz.*, May 2, 1795-S., Archibald McLachlan; Jan. 4, 1794-P.S., Francis Love; July 25, 1795-S., E. B. Davidson; and Sept. 28, 1782-S., Richard Miles.

19. *South Carolina Gazette* [*S.C. Gaz.*], June 11, 1744, Thomas Wah; July 1, 1745, Richard Hill; Feb. 26, 1753, Richard Powers; Sept. 6, 1770, Wood Furman. See also, Aug. 16, 1770 advertisement to see "A young Negro Fellow, who is a good Boatman, Marketman and Butcher"; Jack, "good market man, butcher, plow-

man and mower," Sept. 17, 1763, John Ernest Poyas. *South Carolina Gazette and Country Journal* [*S.C. Gaz. and Ct. J.*], Oct. 6, Nov. 24, 1772. There is a good record of the activities of the poultry sellers Pompey and Amey in the 1760s, in the Daybook of Henry Ravenal, South Carolina Historical Society, Charleston.

20. *Jam. Royal Gaz.*, Oct. 26, 1782, Mary Crawford; May 2, 1801-S., Rosanna Gregory; March 29, 1794-P.S., William Young; see also, June 9, 1781-S., Mary Roberts.

21. *South Carolina Royal Gazette*, Sept. 10, 1781, John Wigfall; *Carolina State Gazette and Country Journal*, March 7, 1769, H. Gray for Amy; *S.C. Gaz.*, Oct. 18, 1773, Elizabeth Timothy; *Charleston Gazette*, Jan. 11, 1780, Benjamin King; *S.C. Gaz.*, Dec. 6, 1751, Elizabeth Bullock; *South Carolina and American General Gazette*, May 22, 1767, Humphrey Sommers; *S.C. Gaz. and Ct. J.*, June 3, 1766, John Mitchell.

# Bibliography

This study is based, principally, on four types of sources: official (governmental) records, plantation records, missionary papers, and newspapers.

## Plantation Records

West Indian plantation societies were dominated by absentees, and the best sources for studying slavery in that colonial region are located in Britain, where proprietors often lived. Helpful in locating and gaining access to plantation records (especially if held privately) were the National Registry in Quality Court (The City, London), George P. MacKenzie of the National Register of Archives, Scotland, and Peter Walne's indispensable *A Guide to Manuscript Sources for the History of Latin America and the Caribbean in the British Isles* (Oxford, 1973).

The best plantation papers (not counting those used for the case studies) include the Vanneck Manuscripts at the Cambridge University Library, and the Fitzherbert-Perrin and Penrhyn Papers at, respectively, the Derbyshire Record Office, Matlock, and the Library of the University of North Wales in Bangor. The Vanneck Manuscripts contain the letters of Simon Taylor, a shrewd and very rich Jamaican planter and politician, who as attorney for several other planters had more to say about the actual process of incorporating new Negroes than anyone else. The latter collections, of Fitzherbert and Penrhyn, are also extensive, underused, and comprehensive: they include reports through time of some unusually conscientious managers and attorneys. Complementing these are numerous yearly "accounts produce" — inventories of profits, expenses, numbers of slaves, and stock. Also largely untapped are three sizeable plantation collections in the west of England, the Penney Papers at the University of Bristol (last used systematically by Richard Pares) and the Dickinson and Tudway papers in the Somerset Record Office.

For the South, the Colonial Williamsburg Research Center has an extensive collection of microfilms, among which are numerous plantation records. The Manigault material compiled by James Clifton was supplemented by material in the Division of Manuscripts at the Duke University Library and the Southern Historical Collection at the University of North Carolina, Chapel Hill. The Department of Archives at Louisiana State University, Baton Rouge, has a number of plantation records that were kept in printed account books (featured in chapter 5).

Collections in the United Kingdom

*Ballindalloch Castle, Scotland:* Grant-MacPherson Papers, bundles 249–50, 295, 303, 305, 344, 359, 370, 401–2, 412–13, 474, 491, 514, 522, 534, 552, 626, 628–29, 639, 659.

*Bangor, Wales, Department of Manuscripts, University College of North Wales:* The Penrhyn Castle manuscripts (Pennant family's Jamaican holdings); the Bodrhyddan manuscripts: Stapleton West Indian estates.

*Cambridge, The University Library, Manuscripts Room:* Vanneck manuscripts (for the Archedeckne family of Jamaica), boxes 1 and 2. *Cambridgeshire Record Office:* Tharp Family Papers: 7.128 letters (1775–1820); R. 55.7.22 (a) bundle 11; (c) bundle 19, 132.2; Inventory of Good Hope, 1804.

*Cumberland Record Office, The Castle, Carlisle:* Senhouse manuscripts: William Senhouse "Recollections"; Joseph Senhouse, "Observations" of his brother.

*Derbyshire Record Office, Matlock:* Fitzherbert-Perrin Papers.

*Edinburgh, The National Library of Scotland:* Journal of a Voyage to Jamaica, 1823–24, no. 3240; Robertson/MacDonald Muniments, MS 3942, ff. 216–18, 259–63; Sterling (Ardock Pen, St. Ann's, Jamaica), MS 10924. The Crawford Muniments, originally consulted at the John Ryland's Library, University of Manchester, and the collection for the study of the culture of Treaty Maroons, contain censuses of town superintendents and, during the 1795 War, correspondence from the principals — Walpole, Shirley, Taylor, Palmer, and Vaughan. *Scottish Record Office:* Balfour-Melville, boxes 3/1 and 20; Seaforth Letterbooks: 46/17/10, 24, 25; 46/7/5, 7, 11–12; Abercairny (Charles Sterling's letters from St. Ann's Jamaica).

*Exeter, Roborough Library, the University:* Gale Morant Papers: 7/e/1–17; 3/b–f.

*Glasgow, Strathclyde Regional Archives:* Inter Boreale and Haywood Hall estates (Jamaica); Stirling Family of Keir and Cawder: Hampden Estate accounts and plans, 1764–78, 1775–81, and TS-K 11, vol. 2, nos. 68, 81; vol. 13, folder 11, 57–58; folder 21, nos. 3–9; 15/13, Letterbooks (1780s); Blyth Letters on Myal (13/21/3).

*Gloucestershire Record Office:* Codrington Papers (vast, now owned privately, and available only on microfilm) microfilm no. 347/1; Papers of Captain Francis Reynolds (D340a X16).

*Hull, The University Archives:* Letterbook for Peru Estate (Jamaica), Langsdale manuscripts.

*Leeds Central Library, Archives Department:* Harewood manuscripts (letterbooks and papers, 1795–1873 — remnants only of a large collection destroyed during World War II).

*Lincolnshire Archives, The Castle, Lincoln:* Journals of Thomas Thistlewood

(1749–86) in Monson 31; examined 1748–64, 1767–68, 1775–76, 1779–80, 1782, and 1785–86.

*London: British Library:* Pinnock Plantation Journal (1760s-90) Addit. MSS 33,316; Samuel Martin, Jr., Letterbooks (1750–62) Addit. MSS 41,346–49, 41,351, and 41,363; Liverpool Papers, vol. 227 Addit. MSS 38,416; Sir James Lowther's plantation accounts (Christ Church Parish, Barbados, 1756,1825), Addit. MS 43,507. *University of London Library, Paleography Room:* Newton Estate Papers.

*Middlesex Record Office:* Duckinfield Hall Papers.

*Oxford, The Bodleian Library:* The Barham Papers, Clarendon Deposit: b. 34 Misc. Mesopotamian Accounts, c. 357 bundle 1 (1760–89; 358), bundle 1, 1809–16, c. 366 bundle 2, c. 367 "Jamaica Correspondence" (1760–89), c. 378 bundle 1, La Trobe (Moravian) letters, c. 381.

*Sheffield Central Library, Archives Division:* Spencer-Stanhope, Cannon Hall Muniments; William Vassal Letterbooks (1769–96).

*Somerset Record Office, Taunton:* Dickinson (of Kingston) manuscripts, boxes 221, 468, 471, 473–74, 479; Tudway manuscripts, boxes 8 (ledgers for 1720s), 9 (slave lists), 11 (bundles 1 and 4), 15 (Letterbook, 1759–84).

*University of Exeter, Roborough Library:* Gale/Morant Papers: 1/e/7–17, 3/a/1, 3/b/1–38, 3/c, 4/a, 6/d/3.

Collections in the United States

*Alabama, Department of Archives and History, Montgomery:* Charles Crommelin Papers; James A. Tait Memorandum Book (1831–40).

*California, Henry E. Huntington Library, San Marino:* Macaulay Papers, boxes 1–3; Stowe MSS: Elletson/Chandos Letterbooks for Hope Estate, Jamaica.

*Georgia, Historical Society, Savannah:* John Gibbons Memorandum Book (1791–20); William Gibbons Account Book (1765–82); Richard Leake Account Book (1786–1800); Telfair Family Papers.

*Louisiana, Department of Archives, Baton Rouge:* Cabell (Eli J.), Amite County, Mississippi, Pleasant Hill Plantation Book, 1850; Duncan (Stephen and Stephen, Jr.), Journal (1856–65); Evan (Nathaniel and Family), Plantation Record Book (1853–65); Kilbourne (J. G. and Family) Papers, Comite County, Mississippi, Plantation Record Book for 1857; Le Blanc Family Papers, Record Book (1859–66); William J. Minor: Stewart's Diary for 1851, or Daily Register.

*Maryland Historical Society, Baltimore:* Lloyd Papers, microfilms: 39–40.

*North Carolina, Southern Historical Collection, University of North Carolina Library, Chapel Hill:* Arnold-Screven Papers: Plantation Journal vol. 4 (1851–56); A. R. Arrington, box 1; Elliott-Gonzales Papers: PonPon Plantation Book, vol. 3; John Edwin Fripp: Plantation Account Books, vols. 1 and 2; Alexander J. Lawton Plantation Book (1816–31); Manigault Plantation Book nos. 2 and 4; Penn School Records, Arthur Sumner Letters, vol. 4 (typescripts). *Manuscript Division, Duke University Library, Durham:* Ballard's Valley Estate Records (St. Mary's, Jamaica); William Gibbons Jr., Papers; [John] Hook Account Book (1788–1805); Stephen Fuller Papers; Louis Manigault Letterbook, 1852 (no. 2347); Manigault Plantation, vols. 1–4; Edward Telfair Letterbook (1769–70); Daybooks (1774–75, 1775–81); Francis Wilkinson Pickens Plantation Book (1839–68).

*Historical Society of Pennsylvania, Philadelphia:* Butler Family Papers; Powell Family Papers, Alexander Johnson Books, box 29B (1762–87).

*South Carolina, South Caroliniana Library, University of South Carolina, Columbia:* John Ball, Sr., Papers, 1773–1823; John Stapleton Papers, 1818 slave list for Frogmore Plantation. *The South Carolina Historical Society, Charleston:* Daybook of Henry Ravenal; Gabriel E. Manigault Memorandum Book for Silk Hope, (1861–73), box 11–277; Thomas Procher Ravenal Collection, boxes 1 and 2; Hering-Middleton Papers, 24–63.

*Virginia, The University (Alderman) Library, Charlottesville:* Carter Letterbook (1732–81), no. 4996; Carter-Wellford Papers; Hawkins and McGehee Family Papers. *Mount Vernon Research Room:* Intermural papers: "Mount Vernon during the American Revolution" by Charles Wall; "Housing and Family Life of the Mount Vernon Negro," by Frank Morse. *The Virginia Historical Society, Richmond:* Carter Letterbook (1728–29). *The Colonial Williamsburg Research Center:* Inventories of Negroes, Edmund Jenings Estate (1712–13), Francis Porteus Corbin Papers (originals at Duke) microfilm (M–36–3).

*Washington, D.C., Library of Congress:* Pinckney Papers, red box; Lloyd Papers (Turner's Rebellion).

Collections in the West Indies

*Jamaica, Institute of Jamaica, Kingston:* Roger Hope Elletson Letterbook; East, Elletson, Pool Letterbook, 1770–83 (MS 29a); Harmony Hall, Somerset Plantation Journal, 1782–96; Somerset Plantation Journal, 1782–96 (Hinton East's); Tweedie Estate Records (Queenhithe Estate, St. Ann's, 1790s); Braco Estate, Trelawny Account Book (1781–89); Estate of Sarah Smith (1740s–50s); Somerset Plantation Journal, 1782–96; Hope Estate records (MS 29, 29a, 1760s).

## Government

Special mention should be made of the proceedings of Parliamentary investigations of the slave trade (beginning in the late 1780s) published handsomely in facsimile volumes by the Irish University Press. Even the apologists are useful (and there were many); expert witnesses included slaver captains, plantation managers, and attorneys. More importantly, by the early 1800s, the volumes contain court records and correspondence concerning the major slave rebellions.

In Britain, one should start with the colonial records at the Public Record Office (at Lincoln Inns Fields when I began my research), now at Kew. Most of the volumes of general correspondence for Barbados and Jamaica from the 1730s to the early 1800s were read. I also looked at the same for the late 1700s and early 1800s for Antigua, Dominica, Trinidad, and for the general series for the Leewards. For each colony, types of documents are bound in separate series — statutes, the royal governor's correspondence, and legislative sessional papers (occasionally invaluable for the inclusion of testimony in major slave rebellions, but often disappointing because notes of meetings are so brief and sparse). In addition to detailed overviews of the colony's economic, demographic, and religious condition, the governors occasionally enclosed with their reports newspapers, private letters from concerned citizens, slave depositions, intelligence (during Maroon wars), newspaper clippings, and censuses. The following notations list the colony, series, and volume number.

Antigua: 7/1, 9/4-7, 30.

Barbados: 28/14, 16, 21, 30-35, 42, 49-77, 81, 85-86, 125; 31/47.

Demerara: 111/42.

Dominica: 71/1, 9, 11-12, 14, 19, 30, 32, 50, 61.

Grenada: 101/288.

Jamaica: 137/25-30, 32-78, 87-91, 96-102, 104, 111, 118, 120, 121, 154, 156, 179, 181-82, 185; 138/7, 30; 140/5, 55, 84; 141/6, 27.

Leeward Islands: C.O. 101/1-2, 8-9, 11, 14-18, 45, 51, 53, 61; 152/15-21, 27, 31, 49, 50, 57, 59-91; 155/6-7; 260/9; 285/2.

Montserrat: 177/6, 9, 11.

St. Vincents: 260/4-6, 7-9, 16.

Tobago: 285/8, 13, 21; 288/1, 5.

Trinidad: 198/2; 295/2, 5-6, 8, 11-13, 21, 14, 32.

Board of Trade: BT 6/10.

Treasury 70/1746: Royal African Company Letterbook (Oct. 1748-Jan. 1750).

War Office: 25/644.

House of Lords, Record Office: Manuscript minutes of slave trade testimony "Copy Evidence of Mr Franklyn 13th March 1794."

In the United States I used government records in the following archives: Georgia, State Archives, Atlanta: probate: microfilm 187/24.

Maryland, Hall of Records, Annapolis: Prince George County, St. Paul's Parish, Court Record, Liber X (1738-40); Somerset County Court Levy Accounts for Nov. 1747, 1751, 1752, 1759.

North Carolina, Department of Archives, Raleigh: Granville County Records of Slaves and Free Persons of Color, 1755-1859.

South Carolina, Department of Archives and History, Columbia: "Sainsbury Transcripts" of colonial records of South Carolina (at Public Record Office, Kew): vols. 28, 35; Council Journal, vol. 28; probate records (estate inventories): BB 1776-84, CC 1776-78, T 1758-61; Charleston County A 1783-87 (film 4380), AA 1774-85; Charleston District, B 1787-93; Port Royal, vols. X, T, Will Book, vol. 7; House of Representatives: Governor's Message no. 2 [18 July 1822] and approximately eighty pages of enclosures — trial transcripts and slave examinations concerning Vesey's plot.

Virginia, The State Archives, Richmond: Local court records on microfilm: Carolina County Court Order Book (1752); Fairfax County Minute Book, 1756-63; Southampton County (Court) Minute Book (1831); Executive Papers: Sept.-Dec. 1800, Executive Papers, Sept.-Oct. 1831.

For the British West Indies almost all available governmental records are in the archives of two countries. At the National Archives, Spanish Town, Jamaica, I used the Central Government Records of the Council (minute books) 23 and 25 (1771-84, 1792-99), and at the National Archives, Black Rock, Barbados, the Assembly Report on the 1816 Insurrection.

## Missionary

This class of evidence was surprisingly useful, particularly the very large Methodist Missionary Society archives (and a scattering of London Missionary Society papers) at the School of Oriental and African Studies Library of the University of London. The missionaries' reports are tedious, filled with dross and conventional rhetoric about conversions (the circuit riding journals, while promising, seldom deliver), but occasionally something of real value surfaces, particularly when a missionary cannot explain well a slave's reaction to a sermon or service. The Baptist records are thin (although there may be others in Bristol), and the Moravian are not well indexed. The Baptist archives, consulted in London, have since been moved to Angus Library, Regent's Park College, Oxford.

*Anglican: Society of the Propagation of the Gospel Archives, London:* series C, West Indies, Boxes 6, 8, and Codrington 4/; *Lambeth Palace Library:* Fulham Papers, West Indies series: vols. 15, 17–20. *South Carolina, The Department of Archives and History:* Society of the Propagation of the Gospel Archives: Reports from South Carolina copies of transcripts in the New York Public Library of originals at Lambeth Palace, microfilm reels 1–7 (early 1700s-late 1760s).

*Baptist: Baptist Missionary Society Archives, London:* [J. Rippon], *The Baptist Annual Register for 1790, 1791, 1792 and Part of 1793;* Letters, box 3 (Knibb's letters) Memoir of Mrs. Coultart, wife of Rev. James Coultart, Missionary at Jamaica. *Virginia Baptist Historical Society, University of Richmond:* Church minutes for Albemarle, Antioch (and Antioch, Dover), Broad Run, Morattico, Llyle's (Albemarle), South Quay, and Wecommocomnin. *South Caroliniana Library, University of South Carolina:* Welsh Neck minutes.

*Methodist: Methodist Missionary Society Archives, University of London:* School of Oriental and African Studies Library Biographical/West Indies: box 588 (old no. 1); In-coming correspondence: North America, box 1 (1801–18); West Indies (general): box 111 (1803–13, old no. 1), 113 (1816–18), 114 (1819), 119 (1823), 120 (1823 contains queries on slave marriages), 122 (1824), 121 (1824–25), 123 (1823–24 contains adultry accounts), 124–26, 127 (1818–29), 130 (1831), 197 (1843–47). Antigua: box 208 (1833–40); British Guiana/Demerara: box 1 (1807–14); Berbice: box A (1813–22 contains John Wray's reports); Jamaica: boxes 195 (1833–39) and 197 (1833–39).

*Moravian: Church Archives, Muswell Hill, London:* MS vol. "Conclusions of the General Synod at Barby, July 1–Oct. 9, 1775"; Minutes of the Society for the Furtherance of the Gospel: 1794–1802, 1776–94, 1768–72, 1803–13; Letters and Papers, 1777–1823; bundles: "Letters from Barbados 1768–1813," "Letters from Antigua 1787–99," "Jamaica, Letters and Papers, 1768–1818."

## Newspapers

For the runaway advertisements I used the extensive collection of Jamaican newspapers at the Institute of Jamaica Library, of which major series included the

Royal Gazette of which I read alternate years from 1790 through 1805, all the extant issues of the Cornwall Chronicle and Jamaica General Advertiser (the 1780s and 1790s), and the odd surviving issues of the St. Jago de la Vega Gazette, the Jamaica Mercury and Kingston General Advertiser, and the Weekly Jamaica Courant from the early 1700s. Issues from the 1820s as background to the 1831 rebellion were consulted on microfilm at the British Library Newspaper Room at Colindale (North London). I also used issues of the Trinidad Gazette from the early 1820s (for runaway notices and comments on early Carnival) at the West India Reference Division, Public Library Reference, Port of Spain. What remains of the Barbados Mercury and Bridge-Town Gazette and Barbados Gazette and General Intelligencer are in the Public Library, Bridgetown; and the eighteenth-century newspapers of South Carolina and Virginia comprised the usual micro-filmed collections of extant issues (consulted at the University of California, Berkeley). For Georgia, I used the compilation in Lathan A. Windley, Runaway Slave Advertisements: A Documentary History from the 1730s to 1790, 4 vols. (Westport, 1983), vol. 4; and for Maryland I used microfilm provided by the Beinecke Rare Book and Manuscript Library, Yale University. For Nat Turner's rebellion, the documentary compilation by Henry Tragle samples generously from the contemporary press; I also used originals of the Constitutional Whig and Enquirer at the Virginia Historical Society, Richmond, and of the Norfolk and Portsmouth Herald in the Beinecke.

## Printed Primary Sources:
## Official Documents

British Parliamentary Papers. Slave Trade Hearings, 1788–1833 (Irish University Press). Vols. 65–67, 80 (1831–34). Jamaican Assembly Committee Report on the 1831 Rebellion.

Examinations taken Before a Committee of the House of Assembly of Jamaica to Inquire into the Moral and Religious Improvement of the Slave Population Since 1823 . . . to Report What obstacles, If Any, Have been opposed Thereto. Kingston, 1833.

House of Commons, Accounts and Papers (1790). Vols. 29–30. Microcard, University of California Berkeley Library.

[Jamaica] House of Assembly Committee Report on the Religious Conduct of the Slaves. Kingston, 1833. In Fitzherbert-Perrin Papers, Derbyshire Record Office, Matlock.

Proceedings on the Maroons (1796). Committee Report, Jamaica Assembly. British Library pressmark 179.h.14.

The Report from A Select Committee of the House of Assembly, appointed to inquire into the Origin, Causes, and Progress, of the late Insurrection (Barbados, n.d.). National Archives, Black Rock, Barbados.

## Printed Primary Sources: Travelers' and Other Eye-Witness Accounts

Astley, Thomas, ed. *A New General Collection of Voyages and Travels*. 4 vols. London, 1745–47.

[A West Indian]. *Notes in Defense of the Colonies; on the Increase and Decrease of the Slave Population of the West Indies*. London, 1826.

Beckford, William, Jr. *Remarks upon the Situation of Negroes in Jamaica*. London, 1788.

Blassingame, John W. *Slave Testimony: Two Centuries of Letters, Speeches, Interviews, and Autobiographies*. Baton Rouge, 1977.

Bleby, Henry. *Death Struggles of Slavery; being a narrative of Facts and Incidences, which occured in a British Colony, during the Two Years Immediately Preceding Negro Emancipation*. London, 1853.

Buchner, J. H. *The Moravians in Jamaica: History of the Mission of the United Brethren's Church to the Negroes in the Island of Jamaica from the Year 1754 to 1854*. London, 1854.

Burchell, Willlam Fitzer. *Memoir of Thomas Burchell, Twenty-two Years a Missionary in Jamaica*. London, 1849.

[Carter, Landon]. *The Diary of Colonel Landon Carter of Sabine Hall, 1752–1778*. Edited by Jack P. Greene. 2 vols. Charlottesville, 1965.

Chapin, Thomas B. *Plantation Journal*. Ed. Theodore Rosengarten as, *Tombee: Portrait of a Cotton Planter*. New York, 1986.

Clarke, John. *Memorials of Baptist Missionaries in Jamaica*. London, 1869.

Dallas, Robert C. *History of the Maroons, from their Origin to the Establishment of their Chief Tribe at Sierra Leone*. . . . 2 vols. London, 1803. Reprint 1968.

Dancer, Thomas. *The Medical Assistant; or Jamaica Practice of Physic; designed Chiefly for the Use of Families and Plantations*. Kingston, 1801.

Douglass, Frederick. *Narrative of the Life of Frederick Douglass: An American Slave*. 1845. Reprint New York, 1963.

Edwards, Bryan. *The History, Civil and Commercial, of the British Colonies in the West Indies*. 2 vols. Dublin, 1793.

Foulks, Theodore. *Eighteen Months in Jamaica; with Recollections of the Late Rebellion*. London and Bristol, 1833.

Francklyn, G. *Observations, Occasioned by the Attempts Made, in England to Effect the Abolition of the Slave Trade; Shewing, The Manner in which Negroes are Treated in the West Indies*. . . . London, 1789.

Gardner, W. J. *A History of Jamaica from Its Discovery by Christopher Columbus to the Year 1872*. London, 1873. Reprint 1971.

Grainger, James. *Essay on the More Common West Indian Diseases* . . . *Some hints on Management of Negroes*. 2d ed. Edinburgh, 1802.

*Great Newes from the Barbados, or a True and Faithful Account of the Grand Conspiracy of the Negroes against the English, & the Happy Discovery of the Same with the Number of those that were burned alive, Beheaded, and Otherwise Executed for their Horrid Crimes*. . . . London, 1676. British Library pressmark 1197g5.

Hamilton, James Jr. *Negro Plot: An Account of the late Intended Insurrection Among a Portion of the Blacks of the City of Charleston, South Carolina.* Boston, 1822.

Kennedy, Lionel H., and Thomas Parker. *An Official Report of the Trials of Sundry Negroes, charged with an attempt to raise An Insurrection in the State of South-Carolina....* Charleston, 1822. Houghton Library, Harvard University copy.

Knibb, William, and P. Borthwick. *Defence of Baptist Missionaries from the Charge of Inciting the Late Rebellion in Jamaica....* 2d ed. London, 1833.

Laurens, Henry. *The Papers of Henry Laurens.* Edited by Philip M. Hamer, George Rogers, Jr., et al. Vols. 1–2. Columbia, 1968–79.

Leslie, Charles. *A New and Exact Account of Jamaica....* 3d ed. Edinburgh, 1740.

Lewis, M. G. *Journal of a West India Proprietor, 1815–17.* Edited by Mona Wilson. London, 1929.

Long, Edward. *The History of Jamaica.* 3 vols. London 1774. Reprint 1970.

Luffman, John. *A Brief Account of the Island of Antigua, together with the Customs and Manners of its Inhabitants, as well white as black . . . In Letters to a Friend, Written in the Years, 1786, 1787, 1788.* 3d ed. London, 1788.

Madden, R. R. *A Twelve Month's Residence in the West Indies.* 2 vols. Philadlephia, 1835.

Manigault, Charles, and Lewis Manigault. *Life and Labor on Argyle Island: Letters and Documents of a Savannah River Rice Plantation, 1833–1857.* Edited by James M. Clifton, Savannah, 1978.

Moreton, J. B. *West India Customs and Manners: . . . with the Method of Establishing and Conducting a Sugar Plantation . . .* New ed. London, 1793.

Olmsted, Frederick Law. *A Journey in the Back Country.* New York, 1860. Reprint 1963.

Pinckard, George. *Notes on the West Indies....* 2d ed. 2 vols. London, 1816.

Ramsay, James. *An Essay on the Treatment and Conversion of African Slaves in the British Sugar Colonies.* London, 1784.

Renny, Robert. *An History of Jamaica with Observations . . . to which is Added, An Illustration of the Advantages, which are likely to Result, from the Abolition of the Slave Trade.* London, 1807.

Robb, Alexander. *The Gospel to the Africans; a Narrative of the Life and Labours of the Reverend William Jameson in Jamaica and Old Calabar.* 2d ed. London, 1862.

Sells, William. *Remarks on the Condition of the Slaves in the Island of Jamaica.* London, 1823.

Stedman, John Gabriel. *Narrative of a Five Years' Expedition against the Revolted Negroes of Surinam in Guaina on the Wild Coast of South America from the Years 1772–1777....* 1796. Reprint Amherst, 1971.

Steele, Joshua. *Letters and Papers.* London, 1814.

Stewart, J. *A View of the Past and Present State of the Island of Jamaica, with Remarks on the Moral and Physical Condition of the Slaves, and on the Abolition of Slavery in the Colonies.* Edinburgh, 1823.

Taylor, John. *Arator: being a Series of Agricultural Essays Practical and Political.* In *The Farmer's Register,* Dec. 8, 31, 1840.

Thicknesse, Phillip. *Memoirs and Anecdotes.* Dublin, 1790.

Tinling, Marion, ed. *The Correspondence of the Three William Byrds of Westover, Virginia, 1684–1776.* 2 vols. Charlottesville, 1977.

Tragle, Henry I. ed. *The Southampton Slave Revolt of 1831: A Compilation of South Material.* Amherst, 1971.

Tucker, St. George. *Letter of a Member of the General Assembly of Virginia on the Subject of the Late Conspiracy of the Slaves. . . .* Richmond, 1801.

Turnbull, Gordon. *Letters to a young planter; or observations on the management of a sugar plantation, to which is added the planter's calendar. Written in the island of Grenada* (1785).

————. *A Narrative of the Revolt and Insurrection in the Island of Grenada.* 2d ed. London, 1796.

Waddell, Hope Masterton. *Twenty-nine years in the West Indies and Central Africa: A Review of Missionary Work and Adventure, 1829–1858.* London, 1863.

Young, William. *A Tour Through the Several Islands of Barbados, St. Vincents, Antigua, Tobago, and Grenada, In the Years 1791 and 1792. . . .* London, 1801.

## Dissertations and Theses

Bost, George H. Samuel Davies: "Colonial Revivalist and Champion of Religious Toleration." D.D. diss., University of Chicago, 1942.

Cox, Edward Locksley Cox. "The Shadow of Freedom in the Slave Societies of Grenada and St. Kitts, 1763–1833." Ph.D. diss., Johns Hopkins University, 1977.

Green, Edward Crocker. "The Matawai Maroons: An Acculturating Afro-American Society." Ph.D. diss., Catholic University of America, 1974.

Higman, Barry W. "Slave Population and Economy in Jamaica at the Time of Emancipation." Ph.D. diss., University of the West Indies, 1970.

Jones, Bobby Frank. "A Cultural Middle Passage: Slave Marriage and Family in the Antebellum South." Ph.D. diss., University of North Carolina, 1965.

Jones, Rhett S. "White Settlers, Black Rebels: Jamaica in the Era of the First Maroon War, 1655–1738." Ph.D. diss., Brown University, 1976.

Kopytoff, Barbara Kamen. "The Maroons of Jamaica: An Ethnohistorical Study of Incomplete Polities, 1655–1905." Ph.D. diss. University of Pennsylvania, 1973.

Lenoir, J. D. "The Paramanca Maroons: A Study in Religious Acculturation." Ph.D. diss., New School of Social Research, 1973.

McDonald, Roderick A. "Goods and Chattels: The Economy of Slaves and Sugar Plantations in Jamaica and Louisiana." Ph.D. diss., University of Kansas, 1981.

Mallard, Annie H. "Religious Work of the South Carolina Baptists Among the Slaves from 1781 to 1830." M.A. thesis, University of South Carolina, 1946.

Martin, Leann Thomas. "Maroon Identity: Processes of Persistence in Mooretown." Ph.D. diss., University of California, Riverside, 1973.

Moses, Yolanda Theresa. "Female Status and Male Dominance in Montserrat, the West Indies." Ph.D. diss., University of California, Riverside, 1976.

Staton, Thomas R. "Negro Slavery in Eighteenth-Century Georgia." Ph.D. diss., University of Georgia, 1982.

Van der Elst, D. H. "The Bush Negroes of Suriname, a Synthesis." Ph.D. diss., Northwestern University, 1970.

Williams, Anthony J. "The Role of the Prophet in Millennial Cults: Politico-Religious Movements in Jamaica 1800–1970." B.A. thesis, Exeter College, Oxford University, 1974. University of the West Indies, St. Augustine Campus Library West Indies Collection copy.

## Selected Secondary Sources: Books

Abrahams, Roger D., and John F. Szwed, eds. *After Africa, Extracts from British Travel Accounts and Journals . . . Concerning the Slaves, Their Manners, and Customs in the British West Indies.* New Haven, 1983.

Alho, Olli. *The Religion of the Slaves: A Study of the Religious Tradition and Behaviour of Plantation Slaves in the United States, 1830–1865.* Helsinki, 1976.

Alleyne, Mervyn. *Roots of Jamaican Culture.* 1988. London, 1989.

Armstrong, Douglas V. *The Old Village and the Great House: An Archaeological and Historical Examination of Drax Hall Plantation St. Ann's Bay, Jamaica.* Urbana, 1990.

Awolalu, J. Omosade, and P. Adelumo Dopamu. *West African Traditional Religions.* Ibadan, 1979.

Bannerman-Richter, Gabriel. *The Practice of Witchcraft in Ghana.* Winona, 1982.

Barrett, D. B. *Schism and Renewal in Africa: An Analysis of Six Thousand Contemporary Religious Movements.* Nairobi, 1968.

Barrett, Leonard. *The Sun and the Drum: African Roots in Jamaican Folk Tradition.* Kingston, 1976.

Bastide, Roger. *African Civilizations in the New World.* 1967. Reprint New York, 1971.

————. *The African Religions of Brazil: Toward a Sociology of the Interpenetration of Civilizations.* 1960. Reprint Baltimore, 1978.

Beckwith, Martha. *Black Roadways; A Study of Jamaican Folk Life.* 1929. Reprint New York, 1969.

Berger, Peter L. *The Sacred Canopy: Elements of a Sociological Theory of Religion.* 1967. Reprint New York, 1969.

Bledsoe, Caroline H. *Women and Marriage in Kpelle Society.* Palo Alto, 1980.

Boles, John B. ed. *Masters and Slaves in the House of the Lord: Race and Religion in the American South, 1740–1870.* Lexington, Ky., 1988.

Booth, Newell, S., Jr., ed. *African Religions: A Symposium.* New York, 1977.

Braithwaite, Edward. *The Development of Creole Society in Jamaica, 1770–1820.* Oxford, 1971.

Buckley, Roger Norman. *Slaves in Red Coats: The British West India Regiments, 1795–1815.* New Haven, 1979.

Bush, Barbara. *Slave Women in Caribbean Society, 1650–1838.* Bloomington, 1990.

Cassidy, Frederic G. *Jamaica Talk: Three Hundred Years of the English Language in Jamaica.* London, 1961.

Counter, S. Allen, and David L. Evans. *I Sought My Brother: An Afro-American Reunion.* Cambridge, Mass., 1981.

Craton, Michael. *Searching for the Invisible Man: Slaves and Plantation Life in Jamaica.* Cambridge, Mass. 1978.

————. *Sinews of Empire: A Short History of British Slavery.* Garden City, 1974.

————. *Testing the Chains: Resistance to Slavery in the British West Indies.* Ithaca, 1982.

Creel, Margaret Washington. *"A Peculiar People": Slave Religion and Community-Culture Among the Gullahs.* New York, 1988.

Curtain, Philip D. *The Atlantic Slave Trade: A Census.* Madison, 1969.

Davis, David Brion. *The Problem of Slavery in Western Culture.* Ithaca, 1966.

Davis, Wade. *The Serpent and the Rainbow.* New York, 1985.

Elkins, Stanley. *Slavery: A Problem in American Institutional and Intellectual Life.* 1959. Reprint Chicago, 1968.

Engerman, Stanley L., and Eugene D. Genovese, eds. *Race and Slavery in the Western Hemisphere: Quantitative Studies.* Princeton, 1975.

Escott, Paul D. *Slavery Remembered: A Record of Twentieth-Century Slave Narratives.* Chapel Hill, 1979.

Fancher, Betsy. *The Lost Legacy of Georgia's Golden Isles.* Garden City, 1971.

Fasholé-Luke, Edward, Richard Gray, Adrian Hastings, and Godwin Tasie. *Christianity in Independent Africa.* Bloomington, 1978.

Foner, Eric. *Nothing but Freedom: Emancipation and Its Legacy.* Baton Rouge, 1983.

Fox-Genovese, Elizabeth, and Eugene D. Genovese, *Fruits of Merchant Capital: Slavery and Bourgeois Property in the Rise and Expansion of Capitalism.* New York, 1983.

Gaspar, David Barry. *Bondmen and Rebels: A Study of Master-Slave Relations in Antigua.* Baltimore, 1985.

Gemery, Henry A., and Jan S. Hogendorn, eds. *The Uncommon Market: Essays in the Economic History of the Atlantic Slave Trade.* New York, 1979.

Genovese, Eugene D. *From Rebellion to Revolution: Afro-American Slave Revolts in the Making of the Modern World.* Baton Rouge, 1979.

————. *Roll, Jordan, Roll: The World the Slaves Made.* New York, 1974.

Gluckman, Max. *Custom and Conflict in Africa.* 1956. Reprint New York, 1969.

Goody, Jack. *The Domestication of the Savage Mind.* Cambridge, England, 1977.

Gray, Lewis C. *History of Agriculture in the Southern United States to 1860.* 2 vols. New York, 1941.

Gray, Robert F., and P. H. Gulliver, eds. *The Family Estate in Africa: Studies in the Role of Property in Family Structure and Lineage Continuity.* Boston, 1964.

Green, William A. *British Slave Emancipation: The Sugar Colonies and the Great Experiment, 1830–1865.* Oxford, 1976.

Gutman, Herbert G. *The Black Family in Slavery and Freedom, 1750–1925.* New York, 1976.

Hall, Douglas. *Free Jamaica; 1838–1865: An Economic History.* 1959. Reprint London, 1969.

Handler, Jerome S., and Frederick W. Lange. *Plantation Slavery in Barbados: An Archaeological and Historical Investigation.* Cambridge, Mass., 1978.

Herskovits, Melville J. *Life in a Haitian Valley.* 1937. Reprint New York, 1971.

————. *The Myth of the Negro Past.* 1941. Reprint Boston, 1958.

Higman, Barry W. *Slave Population and Economy in Jamaica, 1807–1834.* Cambridge, England, 1976.

Hogg, Donald. *The Convince Cult in Jamaica.* New Haven, 1960.

Holloway, Joseph E., ed., *Africanisms in American Culture.* Bloomington, 1990.

Huggins, Nathan Irvin. *Black Odyssey: The Afro-American Ordeal in Slavery.* New York, 1977.

Janzen, John M. *Lemba, 1650–1930: A Drum of Affliction in Africa and the New World.* New York, 1982.

Jones, Norrece T., Jr. *Born a Child of Freedom, Yet a Slave: Mechanisms of Control and Strategies of Resistance in Antebellum South Carolina.* Hanover, 1990.

Joyner, Charles. *Down by the Riverside: A South Carolina Slave Community.* Urbana, 1984.

Kemble, Frances Anne. *Journal of a Residence on a Georgian Plantation in 1838–1839.* 1863. Reprint New York, 1971.

Kilson, Marion. *Kpele Lala: Ga Religious Songs and Symbols.* Cambridge, Mass., 1971.

Kiple, Kenneth F. *The Caribbean Slaves: A Biological History.* Cambridge, England, 1981.

Kiple, Kenneth F., and Virginia Himmelsteib King. *Another Dimension to the Black Diaspora: Diet, Disease, and Racism.* Cambridge, England, 1981.

Lambek, Michael. *Human Spirits: A Cultural Account of Trance in Mayotte.* Cambridge, England, 1981.

Levine, Lawrence W. *Black Culture and Black Consciousness; Afro-American Folk Thought from Slavery to Freedom.* New York, 1977.

Lewis, Gordon K. *Main Currents in Caribbean Thought: The Historical Evolution of Caribbean Society in Its Ideological Aspects, 1492–1900.* Baltimore, 1983.

Littlefield, Daniel C. *Rice and Slaves: Ethnicity and the Slave Trade in Colonial South Carolina.* Baton Rouge, 1981.

MacGaffey, Wyatt. *Custom and Government in the Lower Congo.* Berkeley, 1970.

————. *Modern Kongo Prophets: Religion in a Plural Society.* Bloomington, 1983.

————. *Religion and Society in Central Africa: The BaKongo of Lower Zaire.* Chicago, 1986.

McLeod, M. D. *The Asante.* London, 1981.

Malinowski, Branislow. *Magic, Science and Religion.* 1927. Reprint New York, 1955.

Mathews, Donald G. *Religion in the Old South.* Chicago, 1977.

Mazrui, Ali A. *The African Condition: A Political Diagnosis.* New York, 1980.

Mbiti, John S. *African Religions and Philosophy.* New York, 1969.

Meier, August, and Elliott Rudwick. *Black History and the Historical Profession, 1915–1980.* Urbana, 1986.

Merriam, Alan P. *An African World: The Basongye Village of Lupupa Ngye*. Bloomington, 1974.

Miers, Suzanne, and Igor Kopytoff, eds. *Slavery in Africa: Historical and Anthropological Perspectives*. Madison, 1977.

Mintz, Sidney W. *Caribbean Transformations*. Chicago, 1974.

Mintz, Sidney W., and Richard Price. *An Anthropological Approach to the Afro-American Past: A Caribbean Perspective*. Philadelphia, 1976.

Mullin, Gerald W. [Michael]. *Flight and Rebellion: Slave Resistance in Eighteenth-century Virginia*. New York, 1972.

Mullin, Michael, ed., *American Negro Slavery: A Documentary History*. New York, 1976.

Oakes, James. *The Ruling Race: A History of American Slaveholders*. New York, 1982.

————. *Slavery and Freedom: An Interpretation of the Old South*. New York, 1990.

Patterson, Orlando. *The Sociology of Slavery: An Analysis of the Origins, Development and Structure of Negro Slave Society in Jamaica*. 1967. Reprint Rutherford, 1969.

Pilcher, George William. *Samuel Davies, Apostle of Dissent in Colonial Virginia*. Knoxville, 1971.

Price, Richard. *First Time: The Historical Vision of an Afro-American People*. Baltimore, 1983.

————. *The Guiana Maroons: A Historical and Bibliographical Introduction*. Baltimore, 1976.

————, ed. *Maroon Societies: Rebel Slave Communities in the Americas*. 2d ed. Baltimore, 1979.

Raboteau, Albert J. *Slave Religion: The "Invisible Institution" in the Antebellum South*. New York, 1978.

Ranger, T. O. *Dance and Society in Eastern Africa, 1890–1970: The Beni Ngoma*. Berkeley, 1975.

Ranger, T. O., and I. N. Kimambo, eds. *The Historical Study of African Religion*. Berkeley, 1972.

Rattray, R. S. *Ashanti Law and Constitution*. Oxford, 1929. Reprint 1969.

Russell-Wood, A. J. R. *Fidalgos and Philanthropists: The Santa Casa da Misericórdia of Bahia, 1550–1755*. Berkeley, 1968.

Scarborough, William. *The Overseer: Plantation Management in the Old South*. Baton Rouge, 1966.

Schuler, Monica. *"Alas, Alas Kongo": A Social History of Indentured African Immigration into Jamaica, 1841–1865*. Baltimore, 1980.

Schweninger, Loren. *Black Property Owners in the South, 1790–1915*. Urbana, 1990.

Sheridan, Richard B. *Sugar and Slavery: An Economic History of the British West Indies, 1623–1775*. Baltimore, 1973.

Sirmans, Eugene. *Colonial South Carolina: A Political History, 1663–1763*. Chapel Hill, 1966.

Stampp, Kenneth. *The Peculiar Institution: Slavery in the Ante-Bellum South.* New York, 1956.

Steiner, George. *In Bluebeard's Castle: Some Notes Towards the Re-definition of Culture.* London, 1971.

Stuckey, Sterling. *Slave Culture, Nationalist Theory and the Foundations of Black America.* New York, 1987.

Thompson, Robert Farris. *African Art in Motion: Icon and Art in the Collection of Katherine Coryton White.* Los Angeles, 1974.

————. *Flash of the Spirit: African and Afro-American Art and Philosophy.* New York, 1983.

Turner, Mary. *Slaves and Missionaries: The Disintegration of Jamaican Slave Society, 1787–1834.* Urbana, 1982.

Wilson, Peter J. *Crab Antics: The Social Anthropology of English-speaking Negro Societies of the Caribbean.* New Haven, 1973.

Wood, Peter H. *Black Majority: Negroes in Colonial South Carolina from 1760 through the Stono Rebellion.* New York, 1974.

Wright, Philip. *Knibb "The Notorious": Slaves' Missionary, 1803–1845.* London, 1973.

Zahan, Dominique. *The Religion, Spirituality, and Thought of Traditional Africa.* 1970. Reprint Chicago, 1979.

## Articles and Chapters in Edited Works

Abrahams, Roger. "Play." In *Folklore Studies in the Twentieth Century: Proceedings of the Centenary Conference of the Folklore Society,* edited by Venetia J. Newall, 119–22. Suffolk, England, 1978, 1980.

Barrett, Leonard. "African Religion in the Americas: The 'Islands in Between.' " In *African Religions: A Symposium,* edited by Nowell S. Booth, Jr., 183–215. New York, 1977.

Beattie, John. "Representations of the Self in Traditional Africa" (a review article). *Africa* 50, no. 3 (1980): 313–20.

Besson, Jean. "Land Tenure in the Free Villages of Trelawny: A Case Study in the Caribbean Peasant Response to Emancipation." *Slavery and Abolition* 5 (May 1984): 3–23.

Bettelheim, Judith. "Jamaican Jonkonnu and Related Caribbean Festivals." In *Africa and the Caribbean: The Legacies of a Link,* edited by Margaret E. Crahan and Franklin W. Knight, 80–100. Baltimore, 1979.

Bilby, Kenneth, and Filomina Chioma Steady. "Black Women and Survival: A Maroon Case." In *The Black Woman Cross-Culturally,* edited by Filomina Chioma Steady, 457–67. Cambridge, Mass., 1981.

Bilby, Kenneth. "Jamaica's Maroons at the Cross Roads, Losing Touch with Tradition." *Caribbean Review* 9 (Fall 1980): 18ff.

Bourguignon, Erika. "Spirit Possession and Altered States of Consciousness: The Evolution of an Inquiry." In *The Making of Psychological Anthropology,* edited by George D. Spindler, 479–515. Berkeley, 1978.

Braithwaite, Edward Kamau. "The African Presence in Caribbean Literature." *Daedalus* 103 (Spring 1974): 73–109.

———. "Caliban, Ariel, and Unprospero in the Conflict of Creolization: A Study of the Slave Revolt in Jamaica in 1831–32." In *Comparative Perspectives on Slavery in New World Plantation Societies,* edited by Vera Rubin and Arthur Tuden, 41–62. Annals of the New York Academy of Sciences 292 (June 27, 1977).

———. "The Slave Rebellion in the Great River Valley of St. James, 1831–1832." *Jamaica Historical Review* 13 (1982): 11–30.

Brereton, Bridget. "The Trinidad Carnival, 1870–1900." *Savacou* 11/12 (Sept. 1975): 50–57.

Busia, K. A. "The Ashanti of the Gold Coast." In *African Worlds: Studies in the Cosmological Ideas and Social Values of African Peoples,* edited by Daryll Forde, 190–209. London, 1954.

Campbell, Mavis. "The Maroons of Jamaica: Imperium in Imperio?" *Pan-African Journal* 6 (Spring 1973): 45–55.

Chesnutt, David R. "South Carolina's Penetration of Georgia in the 1760s": Henry Laurens as a Case Study." *South Carolina Historical Magazine* 73 (Oct. 1972): 194–208.

Chukwukere, I. "Agnatic and Uterine Relations Among the Fante: Male/Female Dualism." *Africa* 52, no. 1 (1982): 61–68.

Clifton, James M. "A Half-Century of a Georgia Rice Plantation." *North Carolina Historical Review* 47 (Oct. 1970): 388–415.

Cohen, Abner. "Drama and Politics in the Development of a London Carnival." *Man* 15 (March 1980): 65–87.

Crow, Jeffrey J. "Slave Rebelliousness and Social Conflict in North Carolina, 1775–1802." *William and Mary Quarterly,* 3d ser., 37 (Jan. 1980): 79–102.

Crowley, Daniel T. "Folklore Research in the Congo." In *Folklore Research Around the World: A North American Point of View,* edited by Richard M. Dorson, 173–74. Bloomington, 1961.

De Craemer, Willy, Jan Vansina, and Renée C. Fox. "Religious Movements in Central Africa: A Theoretical Study." *Comparative Studies in Society and History* 18 (Oct. 1976): 458–75.

Dobbin, Jay D. "The Jombee Dance: Friendship and Ritual in Montserrat." *Caribbean Review* 10 (Fall 1981): 29f.

Dunn, Richard S. "A Tale of Two Plantations: Slave Life at Mesopotamia in Jamaica and Mount Airy in Virginia, 1799–1828." *William and Mary Quarterly,* 3d ser., 34 (Jan. 1977): 32–65.

Fields, Barbara Jeanne. "The Nineteenth-Century American South: History and Theory." *Plantation Society* 2 (April 1983): 7–27.

Gallay, Alan. "Planters and Slaves in the Great Awakening." In *Masters and Slaves in the House of the Lord: Race and Religion in the American South, 1740–1870,* edited by John B. Boles, 19–36. Lexington, Ky., 1988.

Geggus, David. "The Enigma of Jamaica in the 1790s: New Light on the Causes of Slave Rebellions." *William and Mary Quarterly,* 3d ser., 44 (April 1987): 274–99.

Hair, P. E. H. "Ethnolinguistic Continuity on the Guinea Coast." *Journal of African History* 8, no. 2 (1967): 247–68.

Hall, Neville. "Slaves' Use of Their 'Free' Time in the Danish Virgin Islands in the Later Eighteenth Century and Early Nineteenth Century." *Journal of Caribbean History* 13 (1980): 21–43.

Higman, Barry W. "African and Creole Family Patterns in Trinidad." In *Africa and the Caribbean: Legacies of a Link*, edited by Margaret E. Crahan and Franklin W. Knight. 42–60. Baltimore, 1979.

Horton, Robin. "Types of Spirit Possession in Kalabari Religion." In *Spirit Mediumship and Society in Africa*, edited by John Beattie and John Middleton, 14–49. New York, 1969.

Kopytoff, Barbara Klamon. "Jamaican Maroon Political Organization: The Effects of the Treaties." *Social and Economic Studies* 25 (June 1976): 87–105.

La Barre, Weston. "Materials for a History of Studies of Crisis Cults: A Bibliographical Essay." *Current Anthropology* 12 (Feb. 1971): 3–44.

Landers, Jane. "Garcia Real de Santa Teresa de Mose: A Free Black Town in Spanish Colonial Florida." *American Historical Review* 95 (Feb. 1990): 9–30.

Leacock, Eleanor. "Women's Status in Egalitarian Society." *Current Anthropology* 19 (June 1978): 247–75.

Levine, Robert. "Patterns of Personality in Africa." In *Responses to Change: Society, Culture, and Personality*, edited by George A. DeVos, 112–36. New York, 1976.

McCaskie, T. C. "Accumulation, Wealth and Belief in Asante History." *Africa* 53, no. 1 (1983): 23–43.

—————. "Anti-Witchcraft Cults in Asante: An Essay in the Social History of an African People." *History in Africa* 8 (1981): 125–54.

—————. "Time and the Calendar in Nineteenth-Century Asante: An Exploratory Essay." *History in Africa* 7 (1980): 179–200.

MacGaffey, Wyatt. "Fetishism Revisited: Kongo *nkisi*, in Sociological Perspective." *Africa* 7, no. 2 (1977): 140–52. 47, no. 2 (1977): 172–84.

—————. "The West in Congolese Experience." In *Africa and the West: Intellectual Responses to European Culture*, edited by Philip D. Curtin, 49–74. Madison, 1972.

Marks, Morton. " 'You Can't Sing Unless You're Saved': Reliving the Call in Gospel Music." In *African Religious Groups and Beliefs*, edited by S. Ottenberg, 305–31. Sahar, India, 1982.

Martin, Leanan Thomas. "Why Maroons?" *Current Anthropology* 13 (Feb. 1972): 143–44.

Mintz, Sidney W. "History and Anthropology: A Brief Reprise." In *Race and Slavery in the Western Hemisphere: Quantitative Studies*, edited by Stanley L. Engerman and Eugene D. Genovese, 477–94. New York, 1975.

—————. "Men, Women, and Trade." *Comparative Studies in Society and History* 13 (July 1971): 247–69.

Mintz, Sidney W., and Douglas Hall, "The Origins of the Jamaica Internal Marketing System." In *Papers in Caribbean Anthropology*, edited by Mintz. New Haven, 1960.

Morgan, Philip D. "Colonial South Carolina Runaways: Their Significance for Slave Culture." *Slavery and Abolition* 6 (Dec. 1985): 57–78.

————. "Work and Culture: The Task System and the World of Lowcountry Blacks, 1700 to 1880." *William and Mary Quarterly,* 3d ser., 39 (Oct. 1982): 563–99.

Mullin, Michael. "British Caribbean and North American Slaves in an Era of War and Revolution, 1775–1807." In Jeffrey J. *The Southern Experience in the American Revolution,* edited by Jeffrey J. Crow and Larry E. Tise, 235–67. Chapel Hill, 1978.

————. "Slave Obeahmen and Slaveowning Patriarchs in an Era of War and Revolution." In *Comparative Perspectives on Slavery in New World Plantation Societies,* edited by Vera Rubin and Arthur Tuden. Annals of the New York Academy of Sciences, 292:481–90. New York, 1977.

————. "Women, and the Comparative Study of American Negro Slavery." *Slavery and Abolition* 6 (May 1985): 25–40.

Norton, Mary Beth, Herbert G. Gutman, and Ira Berlin. "The Afro-American Family in the Age of Revolution." In *Slavery and Freedom in the Age of the American Revolution,* edited by Ira Berlin and Ronald Hoffman, 175–92. Charlottesville, 1983.

Ortner, Sherry B. "Theory in Anthropology since the Sixties." *Comparative Studies in Society and History* 26 (Jan. 1984): 126–66.

Patterson, Orlando. "Slavery and Slave Revolts: A Socio-Historical Analysis of the First Maroon War, Jamaica, 1655–1740." *Social and Economic Studies* 19 (1970): 289–325.

Pilcher, George W. "Samuel Davies and the Instruction of Negroes in Virginia." *Virginia Magazine of History and Biography* 74 (July 1966): 293–300.

Reidy, Joseph P. "Negro Election Day and Black Community Life in New England, 1750–1860." *Marxist Perspectives* (Fall 1978): 107–17.

Rotberg, Robert I. "Psychological Stress and the Question of Identity: Chilembwe's Revolt Reconsidered." In *Protest and Power in Black Africa,* edited by Robert I. Rotberg and Ali A. Mazrui, 337–73. New York, 1970.

Ryman, Cheryl. "Jonkonnu: A Neo-African Form, Part 1," and "The Jamaica Heritage in Dance." *Jamaica Journal* 17 (Feb. and May 1984): 13ff, 3–14.

Schuler, Monica. "Akan Slave Rebellions in the British Caribbean." *Savacou* 1 (1970): 8–31.

————. "Myalism and the African Religious Tradition in Jamaica." In *Africa and the Caribbean: The Legacies of a Link,* edited by Margaret E. Crahan and Franklin W. Knight. Baltimore, 1979, 65–79.

Schwartz, Stuart B. "The Macambo: Slave Resistance in Colonial Bahia." *Journal of Social History* 3 (Summer 1970): 313–33.

Schwarz, Philip J. "Gabriel's Challenge, Slaves and Crime in Late Eighteenth-Century Virginia." *Virginia Magazine of History and Biography* 90 (July 1982): 283–309.

Sheridan, Richard B. "The Jamaican Slave Insurrection Scare of 1776 and the American Revolution." *Journal of Negro History* 61 (July 1776): 290–308.

Stevenson, Ian. "The Belief in Reincarnation Among the Igbo of Nigeria." *Journal of Asian and African Studies,* 20 (Jan.–April 1985): 13–30.

Szwed, John F. "An American Anthropological Dilemma: The Politics of Afro-American Culture." In *Reinventing Anthropology,* edited by Dell Hymes, 153–81. New York, 1972.

Touchstone, Blake. "Planters and Slave Religion in the Deep South." In *Masters and Slaves in the House of the Lord: Race and Religion in the American South, 1740–1840,* edited by John B. Boles, 99–126. Lexington, Ky., 1988.

Vlach, John Michael. "Arrival and Survival: The Maintenance of an Afro-American Tradition in Folk Art and Craft." In *Perspectives on American Folk Art,* ed. Ian M.G. Quimby and Scott T. Swank. 177–271. New York, 1980.

Wade, Richard. "The Vesey Plot: A Reconsideration." *Journal of Southern History* 30 (1964): 143–61.

Wallace, F. C. Wallace. "Revitalization Movements." *American Anthropology* 58 (1956): 264–81.

Warner, Maureen. "Africans in Nineteenth-Century Trinidad." *African Studies Association of the West Indies Bulletin* 5 (Dec. 1972): 1:27–29, 38–40.

Watson, Alan D. "Impulse Toward Independence: Resistance and Rebellion Among North Carolina Slaves, 1750–1775." *Journal of Negro History* 63 (Fall 1978): 317–28.

Wax, Darold D. " 'The Great Risque We Run': The Aftermath of Slave Rebellion at Stono, South Carolina, 1737–1745." *Journal of Negro History* 67 (July 1982): 136–47.

Werblowsky, R. J. Zwi. " 'A New Heaven and A New Earth': Considering Primitive Messianisms." *History of Religions* 5 (Summer 1965): 164–72.

Williams, Robert. "Thomas Affleck: Missionary to the Planter, the Farmer, and the Gardener," *Agricultural History* 31 (July 1957): 40–48.

Wright, Philip. "War and Peace with the Maroons, 1730–39." *Caribbean Quarterly* 16, no. 1 (1970): 5–27.

# Index

# About the Author

Michael Mullin, a native Californian, received his Ph.D. from the University of California at Berkeley and teaches history at California State University, Sacramento. He has also taught at the City College of San Francisco, Smith College, the University of Hull, and Rutgers, Newark. He is the author of *American Negro Slavery: A Documentary History* and *Flight and Rebellion: Slave Resistance in Eighteenth-century Virginia,* which was nominated for a Pulitzer Prize.

Books in the Series

BLACKS IN THE NEW WORLD

Slavery and Freedom in the Age
of the American Revolution
*Edited by Ira Berlin and Ronald Hoffman*
Diary of a Sit-In, Second Edition
*Merrill Proudfoot, with an introduction by Michael S. Mayer*
They Who Would Be Free:
Blacks' Search for Freedom, 1830–61
*Jane H. Pease and William H. Pease*
The Reshaping of Plantation Society:
The Natchez District, 1860–1880
*Michael Wayne*
Rice and Slaves: Ethnicity and the
Slave Trade in Colonial South Carolina
*Daniel C. Littlefield*
The Creation of Jazz: Music, Race,
and Culture in Urban America
*Burton W. Peretti*